RĀJA-ÇEKHARA'S
KARPŪRA-MAÑJARĪ

HARVARD ORIENTAL SERIES

Edited with
the Cooperation of Various Scholars
by
CHARLES ROCKWELL LANMAN
Professor of Sanskrit in Harvard University

VOLUME IV

RĀJA-ÇEKHARA'S

KARPŪRA-MAÑJARĪ

A Drama by the Indian Poet Rājaçekhara
(About 900 A.D.)

Critically Edited in the Original Prākrit, with a Glossarial Index, and an Essay on the Life and Writings of the Poet

by

STEN KONOW
University of Christiania, Norway

and

Translated into English with Notes

by

CHARLES ROCKWELL LANMAN
Honorary Member of the Asiatic Society of Bengal (Calcutta)
Foreign Member of the Royal Bohemian Society of Sciences (Prague)

MOTILAL BANARSIDASS PUBLISHERS
PRIVATE LIMITED • DELHI

*Reprint: Delhi, 1963, **2007***
(First Published: Cambridge, USA, 1901)

ISBN: 978-81-208-1148-5

MOTILAL BANARSIDASS
41 U.A. Bungalow Road, Jawahar Nagar, Delhi 110 007
8 Mahalaxmi Chamber, 22 Bhulabhai Desai Road, Mumbai 400 026
203 Royapettah High Road, Mylapore, Chennai 600 004
236, 9th Main III Block, Jayanagar, Bangalore 560 011
Sanas Plaza, 1302 Baji Rao Road, Pune 411 002
8 Camac Street, Kolkata 700 017
Ashok Rajpath, Patna 800 004
Chowk, Varanasi 221 001

Printed in India
BY JAINENDRA PRAKASH JAIN AT SHRI JAINENDRA PRESS,
A-45 NARAINA, PHASE-I, NEW DELHI 110 028
AND PUBLISHED BY NARENDRA PRAKASH JAIN FOR
MOTILAL BANARSIDASS PUBLISHERS PRIVATE LIMITED,
BUNGALOW ROAD, DELHI 110 007

To

PROFESSOR RICHARD PISCHEL

of the University of Halle

and

PROFESSOR SYLVAIN LEVI

of the College De France

In Recognition of their Contributions to the History of the Hindu Theater

This Volume is Dedicated by the Collaborators

CONTENTS

PART IV.

PREFACE OF THE GENERAL EDITOR AND TRANSLATOR

HARVARD UNIVERSITY has undertaken the publication of a HARVARD ORIENTAL SERIES. The primary object of this Series, as conceived by the two friends most concerned in its establishment, is an historical one, — the elucidation of the history of religions, more especially, of those of India.

The central point of interest in the history of India is the long development of the religious thought and life of the Hindus, — a race akin, by ties of blood and language, to our own Anglo-Saxon stock. The value of the study of religions is coming to be recognized more and more every day. The study tends to broaden and strengthen and universalize the bases of religion, — a result of practical and immediate benefit. Works which promote this study stand first in the plans of the Oriental Series; and they are especially timely now, when so much of the widespread interest in Buddhism and other Oriental systems is misdirected by half-knowledge, or by downright error concerning them. We may add that such works supply the material for the helpful constructive criticism of the foundations of religious belief, to offset the all too abounding destructive criticism of the day.

But to any one acquainted with the ways of the progress of science, it will be evident that the purposes of this Series are not to be achieved wholly by the direct means of publishing books upon the religions of India. The indirect means to its end must be the publication also of works concerning Indian literature and history and antiquities in their manifold diversities of time and of system (Vedic, Brahmanical, Jaina, and Buddhist), and in their considerable diversities of language (Vedic, Sanskrit, Prākrit. and Pāli).

The work now presented to the world of scholars is the first critical edition of the only Prākrit drama extant, the Karpūra-mañjarī of Rājaçekhara, who flourished about 900 A.D. The sacred scriptures of the Jaina religion are written in Prākrit. And, considering the extreme dearth of books for students of that tongue, it is hoped that this volume, in connection with Jacobi's Handbook, may prove highly serviceable as an introduction to the language of that very ancient religion.[1]

"A critical edition of the Karpūra-mañjarī is an urgent necessity for the advancement of Prākrit studies." Thus wrote Pischel in 1876, in the preface to his Hemachandra, p. xii. For the realization of his long-deferred hope, we have at last to thank one of his own pupils, Dr. Konow, whose work, as I trust, will clearly show the training in rigorous philological method which he has received at the hands of his eminent master.

The interest of this play is largely philological;[2] but, as is elsewhere shown,[3] it is not without its importance for the history of the Indian drama. It abounds in material which may well engage the attention of the student of antiquities[4] and of folk-lore.[5] And its allusions to matters of geography or of the calendar, to facts of natural history or to popular beliefs concerning those facts,[6] challenge the widest erudition of the expositor. It presents questions of broader literary interest, such, for example, as concern the degree to which Rājaçekhara is indebted for motifs or for modes of expression to his predecessors,[7] Kālidāsa, Bhavabhūti, Daṇḍin, Bāṇa, and Bhartṛhari. Its literary merit is, on the whole, meagre. The plot is scanty. And the playwright knows little or nothing of the development or depiction of character. Much of its fun is such as is proper to the cheapest vaudeville; so, for example, the parrot incident that is lugged in at iv. 2^4. The long-drawn discussion of love at iii. 10–19 is invested with a singular negative interest by reason of its sad lack of all nobility of conception.

[1] Pischel's Prākrit Grammar is now soon to appear. It will mark the beginning of a new epoch in these studies.

[2] See pp. xxi, 201–3.

[3] See p. 196.

[4] For example, the merry-makings at the Banyan festival, iv. 10–18; palace-life, i. 36; iv. 9^6 ff.; the Magician's homage to the Dreadful Goddess, iv. 19.

[5] E.g., rain-drops transformed into pearls, iii. 3^{14}, note; mirage, ii. 40^5.

[6] Cp. i. 18^{15}, 20^a, ii. 50^c, ii. 50^a, iv. 18^{36}. Botanical allusions — passim.

[7] See p. 204, and, e.g., ii. 10^b, iii. 2^d.

The entrance of the Magician (at i. 21[8]) is signalized by several ribald stanzas which throw a good deal of light on certain pathological phases in the evolution of religion, such as have repeated themselves over and over again in the history of the most varied peoples. To study these phases from a point of widest scope is an essential condition for an intelligent diagnosis of all such vagaries, whether exhibited in the fervors of an American camp-meeting or of a Hindu temple-precinct.

The literary merit of a piece like this, however, is not, in my opinion, to be summed up in any brief and disparaging dictum.[1] The play is surely redeemed from sweeping condemnation by the swing scene (ii. 30–40). Here, specifically in stanzas 30–32, the author shows himself a consummate master, not only of imitative language, but also of metrical forms. And the Sanskrit student must be dull indeed who is not charmed by the liquid music and smoothly swinging rhythm of stanza 30; while the stanzas 33–40, although contravening some of the canons of Occidental taste, are really remarkable for the ingenuity and beauty of their conceits. The King's verses of admiration upon the bursting into blossom of the açoka tree (ii. 47) need no apologist. And the descriptive stanzas (as of sunset, evening, or moonrise, ii. 50, i. 35–36, iii. 25) deserve high praise for their vividness and genuinely poetic sense of the fairest aspects of nature. And some of the "enamored verses"[2] will bear the test of Occidental criticism, — their tenderness and beauty and dignity unimpeached. The contrasts between the love-lorn solemnity of the King and the mocking badinage of his Jester[3] show a command of the shadings of expression that is by no means contemptible.

The Text and the Critical Apparatus. — I need add little to what is said by Dr. Konow, pages xxiii–xxvi, about this part of the work. I am confident that students will appreciate the pains I have taken to have the typography convenient, especially that of the various readings. I regret that these last are so copious; but the exceptional nature of the text must excuse their fulness.

Method of Citation. — The verse-portions are cited by act and stanza and line, the line being indicated by *a*, *b*, *c*, or *d*. The prose clauses

[1] Such as Apte's, in his Rājaçekhara, p. 24.

[2] Cp. i. 32, ii. 5, 9, 10.

[3] For example, at ii. 40^{1-6}, ii. 50^{1-2}, iii. 29.

between any two stanzas are numbered consecutively with Arabic numerals, and are cited by the number of the act with that of the preceding stanza and that of the clause. Thus iv. 19^{67} is the last clause between iv. 19 and iv. 20. Similarly ii. 0^{5} is used to indicate the fifth of the prose clauses preceding stanza 1 of act ii. It is thus apparent at a glance whether any given citation refers to a passage of prose or of verse.

A simple and sufficient means of citation is absolutely indispensable for any text of mingled verse and prose that is of consequence enough to be studied and cited at all. The editor who fails to provide such means is guilty of flagrant neglect of plain duty and of gross disregard for the time and convenience of students and of his colleagues. By way of punishment he may count upon the seriously circumscribed usefulness of his book and the silent maledictions of those who are forced to use it. Let me here call renewed attention to Ernst Leumann's "Request to the future editors of dramas and post-Vedic prose texts of the Indian literature,"[1] commending it to most thoughtful consideration.

The Glossarial Index. — To the Prākrit forms of this text I believe that the Index will prove a very accurate and complete concordance. The words of the stage-directions are in Sanskrit and are not included. The English definitions may, I fear, seem inadequate by reason of brevity. It is therefore well to mention that the reader must supplement the definition of any given Prākrit word by a study of the senses of its Sanskrit counterpart, or by reference to Pischel's edition of Hemachandra's Prākrit Grammar and Dictionary,[2] where these are cited. Failing these books, it is hoped that the Translation will serve as an entirely adequate complement to the Index.

The arrangement of the Index demands a word of explanation. Verbal forms are assembled under the Sanskrit form of the root to which they belong when this can be given; otherwise, they are put under the heading of the third singular present indicative of the Prākrit form. Thus *pa-aḍei* stands under *kaṭ;* while *khuṭṭai* is given under *khuṭṭai.*[3] Similarly, *jantia* is put under *yantra-*, while *janta* comes in alphabetic place. Again, *vi-iṇṇa* is given under *tṛ;* but *vi-tthiṇṇa* and *uṇ-ṇaa* (as

[1] Zeitschrift der deutschen morgenländischen Gesellschaft, xlii. 161.

[2] Cited by the initials "H." and "HD."

[3] For other examples, see my note to ii. 4.

quasi adjectives) and *milāna* (on account of the splitting of the ***ml***-group) are set in their alphabetic places and not under ***stṛ*** and ***nam*** and *mlā*. I trust that the occasional hints in my notes will reduce to a minimum any practical inconveniences resulting from the arrangement of the Index.

The Translation. — It is a part of the fundamental plans of this Series that none of the texts published in it shall be without a translation. The Series does not aim to consult the interests of Sanskrit students exclusively. For better, for worse, this part of the plan is at all events in accord with the dictates of absolute frankness. The wisdom of the Wise Men of the East is to be estimated by Occidental readers with entire fairness — nothing less, nothing more. And for this reason we may neither withhold its excellencies nor cloak its defects. I am, moreover, strongly persuaded that Indian studies would have exerted much larger influence upon the intellectual life of our day, and would even have made more rapid progress, if the masters of Indology had devoted more of their time to the work of translation and popular exposition. The new recruits for this field must be drawn from the circle of those interested. To enlarge that circle is therefore indispensable. Moreover, the comparative study of literature is now a recognized discipline with clear aims and zealous votaries. And to such students also this translation makes its appeal.

After the Text and Index were completed, I requested Dr. Konow to make a translation; and to my request he acceded with the utmost kindness and promptness. But upon this matter, his own remarks, p. xxii, may be consulted. The play is very difficult to translate. The metaphors, be it for their boldness or their accumulation, are at times most intractable. And often the point of a stanza or phrase requires for its reproduction in English such a command of delicate nuances of expression as cannot be expected of one to whom English is not vernacular. The revising of Dr. Konow's rendering proved to be not feasible. And therefore, after trying and failing to find an American who was both willing and able to translate the piece, I set myself most reluctantly to the delightful and interesting work of making a new version.

Most reluctantly, — because it involved a delay of weeks in the progress of the labor of issuing the works of my two departed friends, the Atharva-Veda of Professor Whitney and the Visuddhi-Magga of Henry Clarke Warren. This delay has been a sore grief to me, although tempered by the feeling that these Prākrit studies would at any rate inure to the benefit of my equipment for the completion of Mr. Warren's work.

The translation here presented is accordingly an essentially independent one, of my own making. A good many of the best stanzas I have rendered in metrical form. That I have not so rendered the rest may be set down in part to their intrinsic inferiority, and in part to the extreme pressure under which the keen sense of the above-mentioned delay caused me to do the work. The marked diversities of tone and style[1] I have endeavored faithfully to reproduce in the tone and style of my English.[2] The translator must be able *to feel* the atmosphere of each of the varying scenes and to adapt his version to their subtile changes.

Almost at the outset it appeared that the translation, unless provided with a running comment, would necessarily be obscure in many points even to the Sanskritist. I hope that no one will find these notes unacceptable. That this portion of the volume is intended in part for non-Indianists, is the reason for writing the *ch*-sound in proper names with *ch* (instead of the usual *c*) and for giving such notes as that on the Asuras at ii. 31^b^.

Scant as the action or stage-business of this play may be, it is the interpreter's duty to make it intelligible to the otherwise unaided student. In the introductory paragraphs, therefore, pages 213–222, I have done my best to make clear the sequence of the inferential as well as of the explicit parts of the action, and likewise the place and time of each element thereof.

One little detail perhaps needs a word from the prefacer, to wit, the version of *piya-vaassa* as 'old man.'[3] The German *hoch* = 'high,' and *Abend-zeit* = 'even-tide.' So Prākrit *piya* = 'dear,' and *vaassa* = 'friend.'

[1] Well illustrated at ii. 40^2 ff. Or compare i. 16^1 ff. with i. 18^1 ff.

[2] For this reason, readers whose native tongue is not English may find occasional colloquialisms for the explanation of which no dictionary less complete than the Century Dictionary, for example, will suffice.

[3] See note to i. 18^{17}.

But it is hardly less grotesquely incongruous to render *piya-vaassa* by 'dear friend' than to render *Hochzeit* by 'high tide.' The connotation of the colloquial "old man," as used even by very young men to one another, with all its suggestions of jovial good-fellowship, shows for itself how fatally misleading a wooden literalness may be.[1] We all know that a *green black*-berry is *red*.

There are some things in this play which are repellent to a mind that is bred to the large variety of wholesome interests[2] that characterize our best modern life. Instead of making the offensive ideas conspicuous by the thin veil of an occasional Latin phrase, I have judged it better to give them in English, simply toning down their more drastic features.

Wer den Dichter will verstehen
Muss in Dichters Lande gehen.

Never was the truth of this couplet brought home to me with more force than in the making of this translation. My own sojourn in India was, alas, too short to absolve me from dependence upon books. I was therefore glad to have the help of the native scholiast, Vāsudeva. No other scholia were accessible to me. And I gratefully record my indebtedness to Roxburgh's Flora Indica; and to several of the systematic Sanskrit treatises on plants and minerals, mentioned below, p. 177; and, last, not least, to my venerable friend, Böhtlingk. I am glad to bear the shame of not having realized earlier the profit to be had from his Hemachandra as an aid to the study of Sanskrit synonymy, if by this confession any are led to take to heart the excellent words of three and fifty years ago with which he closes his preface:

Ich bin überzeugt, dass mit dieser neuen Ausgabe Vielen gedient sein wird; nur Einer, der es sich zum festen Vorsatz gemacht zu haben scheint, bei seinen Sanskrit-Studien nie an die reinere Quelle zu gehen, wird zu seinem eigenen Nachtheil und zu aller derer, die seine Werke

[1] COROLLARY. — Taking due account of the diversities of tone, I have rendered *vaassa* by 'my man' at ii. 6^2; by a slightly impatient 'man' at iii. 2^1; and by a dignified and stately 'O friend' at iv. 5^d.

[2] We must remember that these were often utterly lacking to the Indian villager. The Sanskrit student may make this point clear to himself by consulting in the lexicons the articles upon *grāma* and its derivatives.

benutzen, nach wie vor Alles bei Seite liegen lassen, was auf diesem Gebiete erscheint.

It is fitting, in this fourth volume of the Series (the first to contain a preface from the General Editor), to acknowledge the twofold indebtedness of Harvard University to an alumnus, Dr. Fitzedward Hall, of the class of 1846. He has, on the one hand, honored his Alma Mater by his achievements in Oriental[1] as well as in English philology; and, on the other, he has made to the Library of the University a gift which is unique. With pride of nativity[2] and with loyalty to his college unimpaired by years of absence, he has given to it his rare and early Indian printed books, and — what is more — his precious collection of Sanskrit manuscripts.[3] These manuscripts, with some five hundred purchased by me in Western India, constitute the largest and most valuable collection of the kind in America. It is my fervent hope that they may be of much service in realizing the plans of this Series, not only directly, but also by way of stimulus to Oriental research.

C. R. LANMAN.

HARVARD UNIVERSITY,
March 31, 1900.

Postscript. — July 8, 1900. In the meantime, I have submitted the proof-sheets of the entire translation to Dr. Konow, and he has returned them all with many useful suggestions of improvement or correction. For these it gives me great pleasure to make public acknowledgment of my sincere thanks.

[1] Students of English, considering the part he has borne in the production of the great "Oxford English Dictionary," and the marvellous learning thereby attested, might well enough be excused for not knowing that he had, long before, attained distinction as an Indianist. The first Sanskrit texts ever published by an American were his editions of Ātmabodh and Tattvabodh (Mirzapore, 1852). And his early writings on Indian philosophy, dramaturgy, epigraphy, etc., are still cited with deference by the best authorities of to-day.

[2] His ancestor, John Hall, immigrated just 270 years ago from England to Charlestown, about three miles from the seat of Harvard College.

[3] Acquired during long official residence in India, as Professor at Benares and as Inspector of Public Instruction.

PREFACE BY THE EDITOR OF THIS TEXT.

TWENTY-FOUR years have passed since Professor Pischel, in the preface to his edition of Hemacandra's Prākrit grammar, declared a critical edition of the Karpūramañjarī to be a necessity for the advancement of Prākrit studies. Rājaçekhara has been highly esteemed for his proficiency in the Prākrits, and it was to be hoped that a careful edition of his only Prākrit play might throw some light upon the linguistic history of India. But unfortunately, the materials then available proved to be insufficient. Since that time new manuscripts have been found, and some years ago Professor Pischel proposed to me to undertake the work, and at the same time he kindly put at my disposal the collations which he had formerly made with the view of editing the play himself. Though regretting that the edition should not proceed from his master's hand, I thankfully accepted his proposal, as he declared it impossible to find the leisure necessary for the work himself.

I have myself collated only the manuscripts NRSTUW. For ABCP, I used the collations made by Professor Pischel; and Dr. Lüders kindly collated O for me.

In the notes I have quoted all truly various readings. I leave unmentioned the ya-çruti and the dental n in the Jaina mss.; whereas, in the readings of STU, I have always transcribed the dot + consonant as double consonant. I also pass by all evident blunders in silence. The anunāsika is generally indicated by the same sign as the anusvāra; and this fact must be remembered in using the critical notes.

The chief aim of this edition then is a linguistic one. But besides, I have also been guided by another consideration. I often had to regret that no chrestomathy of the Prākrits of the plays exists, and it was my hope that the Karpūramañjarī might be used as such one. This consideration has also, to some extent, influenced my work. Thus I have, in some places, introduced the peculiar forms of the two dialects, even against the reading of all manuscripts. Further, the vocabulary is composed with the aim to serve students learning Prākrit. To study those dialects it is, naturally, necessary to know Sanskrit, and I therefore always refer to the corresponding Sanskrit form, where this is possible. I have not made any attempt to give an etymological index, nor have I intended to furnish a vocabulary which might be sufficient without knowledge of Sanskrit.

From the same point of view I did not think it convenient to add a translation. And I was also convinced that it should be impossible to me to translate such an intricate text satisfactorily, as long as English was not more familiar to me. On the other hand the general editor, from quite another point of view, thought it necessary to add a translation. Upon his request I therefore made an attempt to render the text in English. But I soon felt how unsatisfactory my work must be, and what I sent Professor Lanman can hardly be called more than a rude paraphrase. I was therefore very glad to hear that he would work out a translation himself.

My best thanks are due to those who have, in various ways, aided me in the work, to Professor H. Jacobi, Dr. H. Lüders, and Dr. A. Stein; to the government of Madras for the courtesy and kindness with which it forwarded new materials to me; but above all to Professors Pischel and Lanman. To the rich knowledge and kind benevolence of the former I never appealed in vain, and though overloaded with other works, he has kindly read the proofs of text and vocabulary. And the kind interest which Professor Lanman has taken in my work, and the unselfish assistance which he has rendered me, cannot, in any respect, be measured from his prefatory remarks.

STEN KONOW.

University of Kristiania,
June 29, 1900.

CRITICAL ACCOUNT OF THE MANUSCRIPTS.

The Text. — This edition of the text of the Karpūra-mañjarī is based upon the following manuscripts:

A. Jaina ms., 8 leaves, with 9–13 lines on each page; 9½ inches by 4¼ inches. Contains javanikāntara i. See Bhandarkar, Report on the search for Sanskrit mss. in the Bombay Presidency during 1882–83, Bombay, 1884, p. 156, no. 418. The colophon reads: iti çrīkharatāṇavabhogaṇadinamaṇiçrījīvasāgarasūriçiṣyavācanācāryaviracitāyāṁ karpūramaṁjarīmahānāṭikāyāṁ prathamaṁ javanikāṁtaraṁ vivṛttam idaṁ ‖ çrī ‖ çrī ‖ rājanpure likhitaṁ ‖ rājanpure likhitaṁ ‖. Vācanācārya must be the author of a commentary on the Karpūramañjarī. Of this commentary a few traces are left. An incorrect ms. Aspirates are doubled; nd is often substituted for nt. Codex A is therefore possibly copied from a South Indian original. Cp. Pischel, Nachrichten, Göttingen, 1873, 206 ff.

B. Jaina ms., 8 leaves, with 15 lines on each side; 10½ inches by 4½ inches. Prākrit text, Sanskrit translation, and some glosses. Contains javanikāntara i., the beginning of ii., as far as hidaāvajjaṁ (ii. 1^{3}), and the end from sā rayaṇamayī (iv. 19^{65}). See Kielhorn, Report on the search for Sanskrit mss. in the Bombay Presidency during 1880–81, Bombay, 1881, p. 83, no. 22. The colophon reads: iti çrīkarpūramaṁjarīnāṭikā kasya [!] samāptā. saṁ. 1600 varṣe çrīmahimanagare.

C. Jaina ms., 11 leaves, with 8 lines on each page; 9¾ inches by 4½ inches. Fol. 3 is wanting. Contains javanikāntara ii. See Bhandarkar, l.c., p. 156, no. 419. The colophon reads: iti çrīkhugatāṇanabhogaṇaçrījinasāgarasūriçiṣyavācanācāryaviracitāyāṁ karppūramaṁjaryyāṁ dvitīyaṁ javanikāṁtaraṁ vṛttaṁ ‖ çrī ‖ ciṭhṭhadu edaṁ likhidaṁ ḍāva diṇeso diyo mahio | ehi payaṭṭadu saṁto saccaṁ saccaṁ kuṇaṁto vva ‖ 1 ‖ rāyapuraṭhṭhideṇa udīyajādisirorattasirinarasiṁhasūṇujādeṇa likhidaṁ jjeva | Kappūramaṁjarīṇāḍaaṁ. Codex C has the same peculiarities as A, and seems to be a continuation of that ms.

N. A modern Nāgarī ms., 16 leaves text, 13 leaves translation, with 15 lines on each page; 13 inches by 8¼ inches. The water-mark has the date 1859. Several lacunas. Conclusion of the text wanting. See

Weber, Verzeichniss der Sanskrit- und Prākrit-handschriften der Königlichen Bibliothek in Berlin, Berlin, 1886, no. 1558. The doubling of the aspirates and the occasional writing of nd for nt point to a South Indian origin; and forms such as ḍiṁṇṇa for ḍiṁbha and a few instances of ya-çruti (or writing of an intervocalic y in cases of secondary hiatus, as in *rayaṇa* for *raaṇa*) show influence from Jaina mss.

O. A modern Nāgarī ms., 21 leaves, with 18 lines on each page; 10¼ inches by 9½ inches. Prākrit text with some glosses. Sometimes corrections in the margin. In a few places defective. The ms. was copied after the year 1830. See Aufrecht, Catalogue of the Bodleian mss., p. 146[b], no. 313.

P. Copy from a Jaina ms., 46 leaves, with 15 lines on each page, 11¾ inches by 5¾ inches. Complete text and translation. Modern and very incorrect. See Kielhorn, l.c., p. 83, no. 23. After each javanikāntara is the following colophon: iti çrīmatsūryavaṁçodbhavasahigilakulāvataṁsaçrīmatprayāga (i. and ii., prayoga) dāsāṁgajaçrīpremarājaviracite karpūrakusumanāmni karpūramaṁjarībhāṣye . . . yavanikāṁtaraṁ samāptaṁ. Ends: çubhaṁ bhavatu || saṁvat 1931 prathamaāṣāḍhaçuklapakṣe tithāu ṣaṣṭyāṁ çanīvāre likhitam idaṁ vyāsagopīdāsātmajena || malākhyanāmnā || çrījayaçīlanagare ||.

R. Copy of the ms. no. 417 of the Raghunatha temple library. See Stein, Catalogue of the Sanskrit manuscripts in the Raghunatha temple library of His Highness the Maharaja of Jammu and Kashmir, Bombay, 1894, p. 77. I owe the possession of the transcript to the kindness of Dr. Stein, who had his assistant, pandit Sahajabhaṭṭa, make it for me. Incorrect; some lacunas; conclusion wanting. Text, with the commentary of Vāsudeva.

S. Copy of the Tanjore ms., no. 10634, prepared for me through the liberality of the government of Madras. Text with some lacunas. See Burnell, Classified index to the Sanskrit mss. in the palace at Tanjore, London, 1880, p. 168[a]. Grantha letters.

T. Copy of the Tanjore ms., no. 5253, made for Professor Pischel at the request of the late Dr. Burnell. Complete text, with some lacunas. Very incorrect. See Burnell, l.c.

U. Copy of the Tanjore ms., no. 10633[a], Grantha, prepared for my use. Text with Sanskrit version. Some lacunas. See Burnell, l.c.

W. Jaina ms., 21 leaves, with 13–14 lines on each page, 10½ inches by 4½ inches. Complete text, with marginal paraphrase. See Weber, no. 1557. The colophon reads: samattā kappūramaṁjarī ṇāma ṇāḍikā mahākaiṇo sirirāyasehassa kadā . . . saṁvat 1520 varṣe çāke. The groups ṭṭh and ddh are, as a rule, not to be distinguished in this ms.

Commentaries.—Furthermore, I have used the following commentaries: Vāsudeva's gloss in the Raghunatha temple ms. and in the edition of our play in the Kāvyamālā.

K. The commentary of Kṛṣṇasūnu in a transcript of the Tanjore ms., no. 10633^{b}, belonging to Professor Pischel (see Burnell, l.c.). A new copy was given me by the government of Madras together with S and U.

J. Pītāmbara's Jalpatiratnamañjarī (Kielhorn, l.c., p. 65, no. 242), collated by Professor Pischel. This is a different work from that contained in the corrupt mss. described by Weber, l.c., nos. 1559, 1560.

Among these mss. we can distinguish two distinct groups: a South Indian group, comprising STU; and a Jaina-group, to which belong ABCPW.

STU agree in most particulars and must be traced back to a common source. The doubling of a consonant is indicated by a dot before the consonant; lingual ḻ is substituted for dental l; etc. Moreover, where the discrepancies between the manuscripts are very considerable, STU have, generally speaking, the same reading. Thus e.g. i. 6, 7, 8^{3}, 9, 10, 14^{2}, 18^{13}, $20^{1,2}$, 22^{a}, 32^{1}; ii. 29^{c}, 34^{a}, 41^{5}; iii. $4^{1,5}$, 5^{2}, 8^{*}, 20^{3}, 22^{8}; iv. 1^{b}, $9^{5\text{ ff.}}$, $18^{29\text{ ff.}}$, 20^{9}, etc. And in the South Indian group, STU, the conclusion (which is entirely missing in the Jaina group) is different from that in NO (R is incomplete).

Burnell was of opinion that T was copied from S. But in iv. 24, T and U agree, as against S. See also i. 20^{30}, 21^{b}, 30^{a}, 33^{d}; ii. 41^{9}, 42^{3}; iii. 1^{d}, $3^{8,9}$, $4^{a,5,8,9}$, etc. It must therefore be concluded that T is copied from U, perhaps with corrections from S (cp. ii. 11^{1}, 16^{b}, $41^{9\text{ f.}}$; iii. 22^{9}, etc.). The commentary of Kṛṣṇasūnu agrees with this group; and in the final stanza, with S.

The Jaina mss. are characterized by some common blunders and omissions. Cp. rīdīāu, i. 1^{d}; further, i. 7, 19^{7}, 20^{11}; iii. 4^{1}, etc. Moreover, the complete absence of the conclusion in all these mss. is too extraordinary to be a mere accident. In many readings also, this group differs from the other mss. Cp. i. $9^{a,b}$, 15^{d}; ii. 11^{b}; 48^{b}; iii. 1^{b}, iv. 2^{10}, 6^{d}, etc.

Among the Jaina mss., B and W are relatively old. B is very corrupt; W is much better. Both are North Indian mss. B was copied in Mahim (in the Rohtak District) and bought for government in Bikaner. The origin of W is not known.

A and C are attributed in their colophons (which mention the lost commentary) to Vācanācārya, the pupil of Jinasāgara, "the sun in the sky of Kharatāṇa." "Jinasāgara was the first high-priest of a new branch of the Kharatara sect, which was established in 1630 A.D.," says Bhandarkar, l.c., p. 44. Cp. Klatt, Indian Antiquary, xi. 250, and Specimen of a literary-bibliographical Jaina-onomasticon, Leipzig, 1882, p. 39. A and C were copied in Rājanpur, Punjab, perhaps from a South Indian original. See above; cp. also the reading gauttāṇā in A, i. 19[5].

P is a modern transcript, copied and bought in Jesalmir, from a Jaina ms. It is perhaps in some places influenced by the South Indian group (cp. i. 12[8]; ii. 45[b], etc.); but it is clearly shown to belong to the Jaina group by the agreements mentioned above, p. xxv.

The remaining mss., NOR, are all quite modern. They generally agree with the Jaina group, as against STU; cp. i. 18[8, 9, 13], 20[1, 2], 22[a], etc., and consider, above all, the blunder which they have in common at ii. 28[c]. They therefore seem to be derived from the same source as the Jaina mss. On the other hand they have so many common blunders and various readings that they must be classed apart; cp. i. 8[b], 9[b], 10[b], 15[b], 18[10, 19], 20[7], 34[8]; ii. 1[3], 6[19], 29[a], etc. In the first act, N shows a nearer connection with R, as at i. 7, 8, 12[8], 13[1], 15[a], 16[1, 3], 20[34], 32[2], 34[b, 25], 35[c], etc. Both N and R have the aspirates doubled in the South Indian way.

O and R are much more closely connected; cp. the critical notes to i. 4[1]. Some common blunders, which are not mentioned in the critical notes, point in the same direction: such are joehaṁ instead of joṇhaṁ, i. 1[d]; ṇihittagā- instead of -gga- , i. 4[c]; esya instead of ettha, i. 12[b]; lagohiṁ instead of laggehiṁ, i. 16[d]; the very frequent writing of d instead of ṭṭ, etc. Many other readings are common characteristics of O and R: see i. 4[10], 5[5], 9[b]; ii. 0[5], 12[b], 25[b], 29[9], 31[d], 42[23, 27]; iii. 1[b], 22[5, 6]; iv. 9[5 ff.], etc.

NOR also sometimes differ from each other. Especially we find not seldom that N agrees with the South Indian group (cp. i. 4[d, 2, 17]; ii. 31[d]; iii. 20[11]; iv. 20[11], etc.) and OR with W (e.g., ii. 45[b]; iii. 16[c]; iv. 9[b, 8], 17[a], 18[38], 20[4], etc.). But still NOR must be classed together.

The manuscripts of the Karpūramañjarī must therefore be classed according to the following diagram:

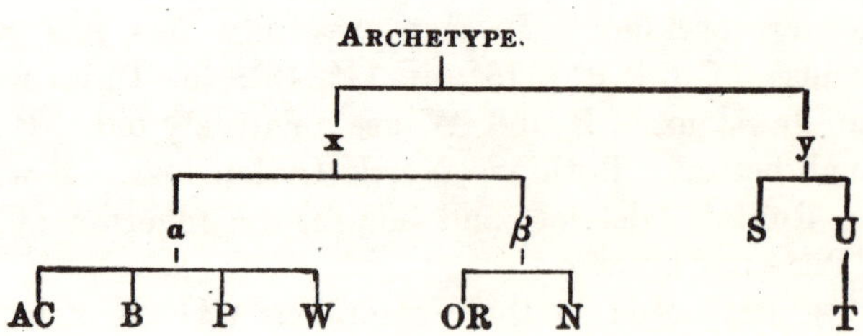

PART I

TEXT AND CRITICAL APPARATUS

OF THE

KARPŪRA-MAÑJARĪ

EDITED BY

STEN KONOW

ABBREVIATIONS

For explanations of abbreviated forms of titles under which certain books have been cited, see the Chronological List of Books, etc., pages 175 to 177.

भद्दं होउ सरस्सईअ कइणो णन्दन्तु वासाइणो
अण्णाणं पि परं पअट्टउ वरा वाणी छइल्लप्पिआ ।
वच्छोमी तह माअही फुरउ णो सा किं च पञ्चालिआ
रीईओ विलिहन्तु कव्वकुसला जोण्हं चओरा विअ ॥ १ ॥

अवि अ[1] ।

अकलिअपरिरम्भविब्भमाइं अजणिअचुम्बणडम्बराइँ दूरं ।
अघडिअघणताडणाइँ णिच्चं णमह अणङ्गरईण मोहणाइं ॥ २ ॥

नान्द्यन्ते[1]

स्थापकः ।

ससिहण्डमण्डणाणं छम्मुहणासाणँ सुरअणपिआणं ।

1a ABPWNORT भोदु. SU होदु. — AB सरस्सई, W °ईए. — A कइयणो, B क इणो. — TU णंदंदु.

1b STU वि. — ABWNR पअट्टदु, P पेयट्टदु, O यअदट्टदु, STU पवट्टदु. — ASTU परा. — T घउल्लंपिआ.

1c W वत्थोमी, N वत्सोमी. — ABPWSTU मागही. O माअधी. — ABPWR फुरदु. N प्फुरदु. T पुणउ. — B णा. — WO किं पि. — N पंचाडिआ.

1d ABPW रीदीआउ. NORT रीदीओ. — A लिहंदु, B विलहंत्, W लिहंतु, S °हंदु. — BW चउरा इव.

1[1] BWST omit. — T transposes verses 2 and 4.

2a AT °विब्भमाई. — O अअणिअ°. — B °चुंबणाइ. — A °डंबराई, P °डंडंबराई, STU °राइ.

2b AN अघणिअ° - ABPWORS °घण°, N °द्धण°. — A °ताडणांई. BSTU °णाइ. — ANT मोहणाई.

2[1] AN नां° सूत्रधारः, B नाट्यंते सूत्रधारः, W नाट्यंते सूत्रहारः. OS omit ना° स्था°; RT अवि अ.

3a T °खंड°. — P °मंडणायाण. — AB समोहणासाणं, BWO समोहणासाण. P

गिरिसगिरिन्दसुआणं संघाडी वो सुहं देउ ॥ ३ ॥

अवि अ[1]।

ईसारोसप्पसाअप्पणइसु बहुसो सग्गगङ्गाजलेहिं
आमूलं पूरिआए तुहिणकरकलारुप्पसिप्पीअ रुद्दो।
जोण्हामुत्ताहलिल्लं णअमउलिणिहित्तग्गहत्थेहिँ दोहिं
अग्घं सिग्घं व देन्तो जअइ गिरिसुआपाअपङ्केरुहाणं ॥ ४ ॥

परिक्रम्य नेपथ्याभिमुखमवलोक्य[1]। किं उण णट्टप्पउत्तो विअ दीसदि अम्हाणं कुसीलवाणं जणो[2]। जदो एक्का पत्तोइदाइं सिअआइं उच्चिणेदि[3]। इदरा कुसुमावलीओ गुम्फेदि[4]। अण्णा पडिसीसआइं पडिसारेदि[5]।

संमोहणासाण. N संमोहणासाणं, SU संमुहणासाण, T छम्मुहणासाण.

3b B सिरिसिगिरिंद°, P गिरिसि°. — A °सुदाणं, B °सूयाणं. — NU संघाटी, R संछली, T संघाटि. — NSTU भो. — P दिसउ, NO देदु.

3[1] BT omit.

4a ABPWNOSTU °प्पसाद°.—ABPWNOR °प्पणदिसु, T °पणदिसु. — O सयागंगा°. — BW °जलेणं, P °अलेण.

4b APWNORT पूरिदाए, R परिदाए. — ORTU तुहिणअर°. — R °अला°. — A °सुप्पोई, BW °सिप्पोए, P °सिप्पोइ, SU °सुत्तोए, T °सुत्तोअ.

4c T दुद्ध° instead of जोण्हा°. — BR °मोत्ता°, O °मेत्ता°. — P °हल्लिल्लं. — mss. णद°. — T °मुउड°. — AP °णिहत्त°. — A °हक्केहि, BPSTU °हत्थेहि.

4d A व्व, NSTU omit. — AB दंतो, N दक्षंतो, STU ददंतो. — ABWNR जअदि, P जयति, T जरअइ. — ABP गिरिसुदा°.

4[1] A omits. — B सूत्रधारा परि°, P सूत्रधार नेपथ्याः इतिमुखमवलोक्य. WN सूत्रधारः परि°, OR नांद्यंते सूत्रधारः परि°, T नाद्यंते स्थापकः परि°.

4[2] ABPWN पुण. — A °पयदो, BWNOR °पअट्टो, P °पयट्टा, SU °प्पअट्टो, T °पउट्टो. — O दिसइ, N दीसति, STU अ° कु° जणो दीसइ. — BPW अम्ह. — BP कुशीलवाण, W °वाण, T कुसी°. — ABWR पवंचो, P पचंचो, O वग्गो.

4[3] A पत्तोच्चियाई, B यतोच्चियाई, PO पत्तोचिआंइ, W पत्तोच्चिआइं, N पत्तोचिआइं, R यत्तोच्चिआइँ, SU पत्तोइआइ, T पत्तोचिआइ. — A सिचयाई, B सिचियाइं सियं, P सिचयांइ, W सिचि°, N सिह°, O सिचआंइ, STU °आइ. — AP उच्चिणोदि, B उच्चेणोदि, SU °णोइ, T उच्चिणोदि का वि लहुवक्खिआओ पट्टए घट्टइ.

4[4] A अयरा, BPWNORSU इअरा, T ईअरा. — SU °वली. — B गुंफदि, STU गुंफेइ.

4[5] N पडिसाइँ, T °आइ. — A पडिसारयदि, P परि°, W पसारेदि, SU उवणेइ.

का वि हु वखिआओ पट्टए घट्टेदि[6] । एसो वंसो ठाविदो ठाणे[7] । इअं वीणा पडिसारीअदि[8] । इमे तिण्णि वि मिअङ्गा सज्जीअन्ति[9] । एस पक्खाउज्जाणं हलबोलो सुणीअदि[10] । एदं धुवागीदं आलवीअदि[11] । ता किं पि कुडुम्बं हक्कारिअ पुच्छिस्सं[12] । नेपथ्याभिमुखमवलोक्य संज्ञापयति[13] ।

प्रविश्य[14]

पारिपार्श्विकः । आणवेदु भावो[15] ।

स्थापकः । किं उण णट्टप्पउत्ता विअ दीसध[16] ।

4[6] T see above, at i. 4[3]. — B वि, P पि. — B हुए, PNR omit; O खु, SU बहु. — A पट्टए वखियाउ, B पट्टए वखिआउ, P मुहवणियाउ प°, W प° वणिआउ, N वणिआयट्ठिओ प°, O प° वणिआओ, SU वखिआ वट्टए. — AP वट्ठदि, BWNORT वट्टेदि, SU घट्टेइ.

4[7] ABWNORT एस. — A वंस, B वंसे. — A ठ्ठविदि, B वविदो, PW ठविदो, N ठिदो, O ठाविदो, SU ओट्टट्ठाविअट्ठाणो, T वोट्टट्ठाविदट्ठाणो. — A ठाणोदं, BWR ठाणो, O ढाणे.

4[8] N वीणं. — A परिसरियदि, B पडिसंसारी। आदि, N °सारेदि, O °सारिअदि.

4[9] W एमे, SU इमे वि. — BSU ति, P तिण, N तीणि. — BPNRT omit वि. — WO मुअंगा. — A सज्जियंदि, B मज्जांयंति, P सज्जीयंते, W सज्जिज्जंति, STU °अंदि.

4[10] After एस A inserts कंसालताल, BW कंसतालाण, P कंसातालाणु, NORSTU कंसतालाणं. — B पक्काउज्जाण, P पखवाउजाणं, W पक्खाउजाण. N पक्खावुज्जाणं, OR पक्खालयुज्जालण, STU भप्फालोप्फालण. — A कोलाहलो, B हलवालो, P हलउलो, W हलवोलो, NORSTU हलहलो. — ABPWNOR omit सुणीअदि.

4[11] P एवं पदं, W एवं, STU इदं. — OR धुआगोदमा°, STU °गोदअं; A adds त्ति. — P आलवोदि, S omits; U विजप्पेइ.

4[12] P किं संदेहेण, O कं वि, SU किं ति, T अहं वि. — A कुटंबं, BP कुडंबं, W कुडवं, N कुटुंबं, O कुडुंबादो. — P हकारिय, T हंकरिअ.

4[13] A omits; BWNOR °मुखं संज्ञापयति, P °मुखमवलोकयति.

4[14] A ततः प्रविशति पारिपार्श्वकः प्रविश्य सूत्रधारमाह, BN ततः प्रविशति, P प्रविस्यति, WR ततः प्रविशति पारिपार्श्विकः

4[15] B अणुवेदु, W अणवेदु. — PW भाउ.

4[16] APWOSTU सूत्रधारः, B omits; NR सूत्रधारः विचिंत्य. — ABPW पुण. A °प्रयदा, B °पयत्ता, PWORT °पअट्टा, N °घअट्टा, SU °प्पउट्टा. — A दोसधं, B दोस्सधा, P दोसध्धं. STU दीसह.

पारिपार्श्विकः । अध इं[17] । सट्टअं णच्चिदव्वं[18] ।

स्थापकः । को उण तस्स कई[19] ।

पारिपार्श्विकः ।

भाव कहिज्जउ एअं को भणइ रअणिवल्लहसिहण्डो ।
रहुउलचूडामणिणो महिन्दवालस्स को अ गुरू ॥ ५ ॥

स्थापकः । विचिन्त्य[1] । अए पणहोत्तरं खु एदं[2] । प्रकाशम[3] । राअसेहरो[4] ।

पारिपार्श्विकः । सो एदस्स कई[5] ।

स्थापकः । स्मृत्वा[6] । कधिदं जेव छइल्लेहिं[7] ।

सो सट्टओ त्ति भणइ दूरं जो णाडिआइ अणुहरइ ।
किं उण पवेसविक्खम्भङ्काइं केवलं ण दीसन्ति ॥ ६ ॥

4[17] A पारि° प्राह. — ABPWO omit अध इं; N पारि । अध इं । सूत्र । किं उण णच्चिदव्वं । पारि भाव etc.; R भाव instead of अध इं; SU अह इं, T पारी । अह इ । सूत्र । किं पुण एदं । पारि. भाव etc.

4[18] A सट्टकेण in the margin corrected to °कं. N सटअं. — P णट्टिदव्वं.

4[19] Mss. सूत्रधारः. — AOT कइ.

5ᵃ P अज्ज instead of भाव. — ABPWOR कहिज्जदु, N कइज्जदु, SU कहीअदु, T कहि ॥ अइ. — APWNORSTU एदं, B एवं. — BSTU किं. — B भस्सइ, P भणाय. N भणिज्जदि. T भणिज्जइ. — P रयणाध्व°, N रजणी°, T रअणी°. — B °सिहिंडो. N °णिहंडो.

5ᵇ ABW रहुकुल°, P रहकूला°. — BSU महिंदपाल्लस्स, W महिंदबाल्लस्स. NRT महेंदपाल्लस्स. — P को इ, N क ओ, SU को ण. T को ण.

5[1] Mss. सूत्रधारः. — SU स्व°, T आत्मगतं.

5[2] PNRT omit अए. — P पणहत्तरं, O पसहुतरं. SU पणहुत्तरं. — ABPWSU omit खु; NR क्खु. — N सएदं.

5[3, 4] A omits. — PO राज°, STU अविराअ°.

5[5] A पारि° आह. — SU तस्स. After कई OR add सूत्र° किं सट्टअं.

5[6] AO omit स्थापकः; BWNSTU सूत्रधारः, PR पारिपार्श्विकः. — A omits स्मृत्वा; N सात्वा.

5[7] P कथिदं, STU कहिदं. — A ज्जेव, B ज्येव, P येव, W ठेव, NO जेव्व, R ज्जेव्व, SU एव्व, T जव्व. — P थलेहिं. — A adds जहा, SU जह.

6ᵃ PSU omit त्ति. — B भस्स, N भणादि, STU भणिज्जइ. — A जो दूरं. — A नाडियाई, BWSTU °आए, P °यांइ, O °आओ, R °आइँ. — WOT अणुहरदि.

6ᵇ ABPW पुण. R उण एत्थ. — OR पवेसअ°. — A °पिक्खंभयाई, B °विक्कंभा-

विचिन्त्य[1]। ता किं ति सक्कदं परिहरिअ पाउदबन्धे पउत्तो कई[2]।

पारिपार्श्विकः।

परुसा सक्कअबन्धा पाउअबन्धो वि होइ सुउमारो।
पुरिसमहिलाणँ जेत्तिअमिहन्तरं तेत्तिअमिमाणं ॥ ७ ॥

सव्वभासाचदुरेण तेण भणिदं जेव। जधा[2]।

अत्थविसेसा ते च्चिअ सद्दा ते चेअ परिणमन्ता वि।
उत्तिविसेसो कव्वं भासा जा होइ सा होउ ॥ ८ ॥

स्थापकः। ता अप्पा किं ण वण्णिदो तेण[1]।

यांइं, P °विक्खंभयाइं, W °विक्खंभयाइ. NT °विक्खंभांआइं. OR °विक्कंभआइं. — ABPWO इह केवलं णत्थि, N इह केवलं ण, R ण केवलं होंति, SU होसंदि.

6[1] AP सूत्रधारः instead of विचि°, R सूत्र° वि°.

6[2] STU omit ता. — BR किंत्ति, APSTU omit ति; W हि. — A सक्कियं, BPWNORSTU सक्कअं. — A पायियबंधे, B पाईयबंधे, P पाईयबांध. W पाईअबंधे, NOR पाउअ°, SU पाउड°, T परिहरिआउअ°. — A पइट्टो, BPWNOR पअट्टो, SU पउट्टो. — A सो कई, P त्ति, N omits; SU सखो.

7 ABPW omit; in NR verse 7 stands after verse 8, in O after 7[2]. NOR insert अवि अ between the two verses.

7[a] SU पाउड°, T याटअ°. — N इ, O अ, STU खु. — T भोइ. — N सोमारो, STU °मालो.

7[b] NRST पुरुस°, O पुरीस°. — N °मोहिलाण, O °लाण. — O जेत्तिअमहं°, T जत्तिअ°, SU °लाणमेत्तिअ°. — N तेत्तिअं च्चेअ, STU तत्तिअ°.

7[1] B °चदुष, PNRSU °चउरेण, W °चतुरेण, T °चचउरेण. — A भणिदं ज्जेव तेण. — B य्येव, P य्ये, W ठेव, NO जेव्व, R ज्जेव्व, STU श्च्व.

7[2] B यथा, WNOR जहा, STU जह.

8[a] P अत्थे, R अस्था°, T अद्ध°. — AOT °णिवेसा, P णिविसेसा, N °विएसा, R °णिएसा. — APW त, N तें. — ABPWRSTU च्चिअ, N विअ; O च्चिअ. — B च्चेव, P सद्धविसेसेसु, W त्ति च्वेव, N ते च्चिअ सद्दा, O सद्दा ते च्चिअ, STU च्चिअ. — AP परिणमंते, N अत्थपरिणमंतो. — A omits वि; P च, N इ. R इँ.

8[b] NOR कव्वो. — PW होउ, N होइ. — N होहि. STU होदु.

8[1] Mss. सूत्रधारः, A सू° प्राह. — PSTU omit ता. — P वण्णिदा, N विण्णिदो, O वत्थिदो. — SU देण.

पारिपार्श्विकः । सुणसु[2] । वण्णिदो ज्जेव तक्कालकईणं मज्झम्मि मिअङ्कलेहाकधाकारेण अवराइदेण[3] । जधा[4] ।

बालकई कइराओ णिब्भरराअस्स तह उवज्झाओ ।
इअ जस्स पएहिँ परम्पराइ माहप्पमारूढं ॥ ९ ॥
सो अस्स कई सिरिराअसेहरो तिहुवणं पि धवलेन्ति ।
हरिणङ्कपाडिसिद्धीअ णिक्कलङ्का गुणा जस्स ॥ १० ॥

स्थापकः । ता केण समादिट्ठा पउञ्जध[1] ।

पारिपार्श्विकः ।

चाहुआणकुलमोलिमालिआ राअसेहरकइन्दगेहिणी ।

8[2] A पारि॰ प्राह. — ANO सुणु, B सुणो, P सुखां, W सुणादु, SU सुणुसु. .

8[3] P सुवण्णद. — PW ढोव, NOT जेव्व, R ज्जोव्व, SU एव्व. — BW ॰कईण, O ॰कइण, SU ॰कइ. — AW मयंक॰, T मृगांकलेखा॰. — A ॰कहाकारणेण, B ॰लेहाकारेण, P ॰लहाकहा॰, W ॰कहाकारणेणावराइएण, N ॰कहाहारेण, O ॰कधाआधारेण. R ॰कहारेआण. SU ॰कहा॰, T ॰कथा॰. — A अवराईएण तेण. B अवराईण, P कइराण, NOR अवराइएण, S बोब्बरराएण अ॰. T बबराएण अपरा॰, U बब्बरराएण अ॰.

8[4] W omits; N जहा, STU जह.

9[a] N कइराअ. O कराओ. — APW णिब्भय॰. B णाब्भअ॰. O णिभर॰, R विब्भम॰. STU णिब्भरदेवस्स. — B उवज्जाय. P वि उझ्झउ, N उज्झाओ. O उवज्जोओ.

9[b] A पएहि. B एएहिं. — ABW परंपराए. — N इअँ इ ज:स परंपराए अप्पा. OR इअ जस्स परंपरए अप्पा, SU इअ (S इइ) तस्स गुणाण परंपराए, T इण तस्स जणाणं परंपरंपराए. — A महाप्प॰, B माहत्म्य॰. — NOR ॰रूढो.

10[a] A एदस्स, BW एअस्स. STU एव्व. — U कविराअ॰. — ABWOR तिहुअणं, N तिहुणं. — STU वि. — A धवलयंति, B धवलयति, P धवलंसाति, STU धवलेदि.

10[b] APSU ॰पाडिसिद्धीए, B ॰पाडसिद्धीए, W ॰पडिसिद्धीए, NO ॰पाडिसिद्धिए, R ॰पालिसिद्धिए, T ॰पाडिपहीए णक्कलंका. — N गुण. — B यस्य.

10[1] A सूत्र॰ पारि॰ प्रति; BPWNORTU सूत्रधारः. — B समादइज्ज, W समाइठा. — A पउजधं, P पयुंदिट्ठु, N पाऊजस्स, O पडंजधि, STU अणुचिट्ठह.

11[a] A पारि॰ सू॰ प्रति. — P चाहुवाण॰, R चाउहाण॰. TU बाहुआण॰. — ABPNOR STU ॰मौलि॰, W ॰मउलि॰.

भत्तुणो किइमवन्तिसुन्दरी सा पउञ्जइउमेअमिच्छइ ॥ ११ ॥

किं च[1]।

चण्डवालधरणीहरिणङ्को चक्कवट्टिपअलाहणिमित्तं।

एत्थ सट्टअवरे रससोत्ते कुन्तलाहिवसुअं परिणेइ ॥ १२ ॥

स्थापकः। ता एहि[1]। अणन्तरकरणिज्जं संपादेम्ह[2]। जदो महाराअदेवीणं भूमिअं घेत्तूण अज्जो अज्जभारिआ अ जवणिअन्तरे वट्टन्ति[3]।

इति परिक्रम्य निष्क्रान्तौ[4]।

प्रस्तावना[5]।

ततः प्रविशति राजा देवी विदूषको विभवतश्च परिवारः[6]। सर्वे परिक्रम्य यथोचितमुपविशन्ति[7]।

11[b] Mss. किदि°. — A °भवंदि°, B °मावंति°, U °मवंदि°. — P एतां नाडि सा. — A पओजयिदु°, BWNO पउंजइदु°, P पउंजइवु°, R पउंतदु°, STU पओजइदु°. — ABPWNORSU °मेदमि°, T °मेतमि°. — ABR °च्छदि, P °त्यति, W °छति, N °च्छब्दि.

11[1] A किं च ग्रंथाभिधेयत्वं सूचयति पारि; B omits.

12[a] B चंडपाध°, P वडवाल°, NOR चंद°, T चंडपाल°. — A °हरिणो°, PO °धरिणो°. — O चक्कवत्ति°. — A °पद°, B °ययलाभ°. — W °णमित्तं, N °णिमिच्चं, O °णिमित्ते.

12[b] B अत्त, P एतु सट्टक°. — B °सोत्त. — AN कुंदला°, O कुंदना°. — ABWNOR °सुदं, P °सुत्तं. — APWNORT परिणेदि, B °णेद.

12[1] ABPWNOR omit स्थापकः; TU सूत्र°. — ABPWNOR भाव एहि; A एहि दाव.

12[2] BW °करिणिज्जं, N °कज्जं. — A संपादयम्ह, B संपाडिम्ह, P संपाडियम्ह, W संपाडम्ह, U संपादम्ह.

12[3] BP यदो. — N महाराअस्स देईए भूमिं. — B पित्तण, N घेलण, STU घेत्तूण (S घत्तूण) भू°. — B अप्पा, P आज्जा. — A अजभरिया, BP अज्जा°, N अज्जघरिणो, R °घडिणिआ. — P omits अ. — B जवणिअंर, P जवणिंतरे. — AU वट्टंदि, PN वट्टदि, W चिट्ठंति, R ददि, T कट्टइ.

12[4] B प्रक्रम्य, SU omit. — B यथोचितं निःक्रांतो. — A adds सूत्रधारपारिपार्श्वकौ.

12[5] A adds नाटकावसरः.

12[6, 7] AU only ततः प्रविशति राजा. — P विदूषको विचक्षणा दासी त्रिभवतश्च प्रतीहारादिपरिकरः, T विदूषकेण विचक्षणा च. — P यथोचितासनेपूप°.

राजा । देवि दक्खिणाहिवणरिन्दणन्दिणि वड्ढावीअसि इमिणा वसन्तारम्भेण[8]। जदो[9]।

बिम्बोट्ठे बहलं ण देन्ति मअणं णो गन्धतेल्लाविला
वेणीओ विरअन्ति लेन्ति ण तहा अङ्गम्मि कुप्पासअं।
जं बाला मुहकुङ्कुमम्मि वि घणे वट्टन्ति ढिल्लाअरा
तं मण्णे सिसिरं विणिज्जिअ बला पत्तो वसन्तूसवो ॥ १३ ॥

देवी । अहं पि पडिवड्ढाविआ भविस्सं[1]। जधा[2]

छोल्लन्ति दन्तरअणाइ गए तुसारे
ईसीस चन्दणरसम्मि मणं कुणन्ति।
एण्हिं सुवन्ति घरमज्झिमसालिआसु

12[8, 9] U omits राजा देवि. — B दक्षिणा°, N दक्षिणापहणरिंद°, R दक्खिणावहणरिंध°, S देक्खिणा°. — TU °णरिंद°. — B °निंदने, OW °णंदणे. — APW वद्धावीअसि, B वद्धावियासि, O वट्ठावीहसि, R वड्ढावीअसि. — ABW omit इमिणा. — A omits वस°; B वियंतारंभेण यदो.

13[a] AP बहुलं, B विहल. — BS दंति, P दिति. — SU म° ण दे° बहुलं. — B णो दिंति तित्ताविला, W °तिल्लाइरा, N °तैला°.

13[b] B वाणीओ, O वेणाओ. — B वियरंति, OS विरएंति. — P लंति, OSU णेंति, T लेति. — P अंगं. — A कुप्पासकं, P किमप्पासयं.

13[c] SU कुअकुं°, T कुचकुं°, N °कुंकुम्मि. — W व. — N omits घणे. — A वट्टंदि. — ANRSU ठिल्ला°, B ढिल्लाक्षयरो, T टिल्ला°

13[d] STU ता. — B विणज्जिय. — P वसंतोच्छवो, W वसंतो°, OR °तूसओ, T °तुसओ.

13[1] B देव वि°, P विभ्रमलेखा, WO देवी वि°. — NR देव अहं पि तुज्झ, STU वि. — AW °वद्धाविआ, B °बद्धा°, P °व्वढाबिया, N °विदा, O पदिवठ्ठाविअदे, R °वव्वाविआ, SU °वड्ढावइस्सं, T °वाड्ढावट्टिसं.

13[2] BP यथा, O जहा. SU जह, T जधा.

14[a] P त्यालंति, W त्योल्लंति, T छोलहंति. — W दंति°. — B °रइणाइ, POR °रअणाइं, N °रअणाणि — ABPWNOR गदे, T दे.

14[b] A इसीस, BWNORSTU ईसीसि.

14[c] BP इयाहं. — ANR सुअंति, B सुहंति. — AB °मज्जिम°, NSTU °मज्झम°, O °मज्जम°. — BP °मालियासु, STU °पालिआसु (S °सुं).

पाअन्तपुञ्जिअपडं मिहुणाइ पेच्छ ॥ १४ ॥

नेपथ्ये[1]

वैतालिकयोरेकः[2] । जअ जअ पुव्वदिसङ्गणाभुअङ्ग चम्पाचम्पअकण्णऊर राढाणिज्जिदराढाचङ्गत्तण विक्कमक्कन्तकामरूव हरिकेलीकेलिआर अवमण्णिदजच्चसुवण्णवण्ण सव्वङ्गसुन्दरत्तणरमणिज्ज सुहाअ दे भोदु सुरहिसमारम्भो[2] । इध हि[3] ।

पण्डीणं गण्डवालीपुलअणचवला कण्णवालावलाणं
माणं दोखण्डअन्ता रइरहसअरा चोलसीमन्तिणीणं ।

14[d] AB पायंद°, P पायंति°. — ABO °पुंजिद°, W °त°, N °युंजोअ°. — AP WNR मिहुणाइं, B महुणाइ. — P पित्य.

14[1] A वैतालिकौ नेपथ्ये.

14[2] A द्वयोर्मध्ये एकः प्राह. PNR वैतालिकः, STU वैतालिकौ, S adds विजयतां देवः । प्रथमः ।. — ABWOR जअ once only. — APWN °दिगंगणा°, B °दिसाभु°, ORT °दिअंगणा°. — APO जअ चंपा°. — O चंपंगणाचंपअ°. — B °कस्सकुर, T °कण्णपूर. — APO जअ रा°. — A राठजणियराठ, B °जणियराढ, PW °जणिदराढ, N लोलाणिज्जोअराढदेस, O राढाजणिआयांद, R रौठाणिज्जिअराठदेस, SU °णिज्जिअ°. — A जय विक्कमक्कंतकामरूय जय चंगत्तणविणिज्जियकामरूव, B चंगत्तणविणिज्जियकामरूय, P विगित्तणविक्खिज्जियकामरूवा, W चंगत्तणणिज्जिदकामरूव, N चंगत्तणविणिज्जिअकामरूअ, O जअ चगत्तणविणिज्जिअकामरूअ, R °कामरूअ. — A जय कदलिहरकेलिकार, B °कारय, P °कलियारक, N हरिकेलिकारअ, O जअ हरिकेलीकेलिआरअ, R °कारअ, T हरिकेलि°, U भरि°. — A जय अठगणिद°, BPW NORSTU अवमण्णिअ°. — N °पच्चगयुवण्ण°, ST °कण्णसुवण्णदाणा, U °अण्णसुवण्णदाणा. — A जय स°. B °त्तणमणिज्ज, P °सुरत्तणरम°, S °सुंदररमणिज्ज, U सव्वंगरमणिज्ज. — BPWO देवस्स. — W सुरहिसमयसमारंभो, STU सुरभिसमारंभो होदु.

14[3] A जदो, BPWNORSTU इह हि.

15[a] STU गंडपालो°. — T °पुणअण°. — P °चवल, S °चउरा. — P °चालाबालाणं, NR °वालावलीणं, S चोलबालाबलाणं.

15[b] AOR °हंडअंता, P °हंडयंतो, N °अंतो. — BW रदि°, P रेदृहरस°, NSTU °रभस°. — ANR °कला, BP °करा. — A लोलचूलालयाणं, B लोलचालंगणाणं. P चोलवालंगणाणं, W चोडचोडालयाणं, NOR लोलचोलप्पिआणं, S कंचिसोमंतिणीणं.

कप्पाडीणं कुणन्ता कुरलतरलणं कुन्तलीणं पिएसुं
गुम्फन्ता णेहगण्ठिं मलअसिहरिणो सीअला एन्ति वाआ ॥ १५ ॥

अत्रैव[1]

द्वितीयः ।

जाअं कुङ्कुमपङ्कलीढमरढीगण्डप्पहं चम्पअं
थोआवट्टिअदुद्धमुद्धकुसुमा पप्फुल्लिआ मल्लिआ ।
मूले सामलमग्गलग्गभसलं लक्खिज्जए किंसुअं
पिज्जन्तं भसलेहि दोसु वि दिसाभाएसु लग्गेहि व ॥ १६ ॥

राजा । पिए विब्भमलेहे को अहं वड्ढावओ तुज्झ का तुमं पि वड्ढाविआ मज्झ[1] । किं उण दुवे वि अम्हे वड्ढाविदा कञ्चणचण्डरदणचण्डेहिं बन्दीहिं[2] । ता विब्भमप्पअट्टावअं तरट्टीणं णट्टावअं मलअमारुदन्दोलिदलदाणञ्चणीणं चारुप्पवञ्चिदपञ्चमं कलकण्ठ-

15c N कुणंतो. — B कुरुलाकुरुल°, N चिकुल°, O कुरुल°, R चिउर°. — P पियसु, T पियेसं.

15d A गुंफुंता, N गुंफंतो, S फंता, T गुंपुंता, U गुंभंता. — B राणगंठी, T °गंथिं मलह°. — B °सिह्वरणो. -- AP सिंहला, B संहला, W सिंघला. — BT यंति, P इति, N वांदि, R वंति. — N वादा, T वासा.

15[1] ASTU omit; B अत्रोव, P अत्र.

16a A द्वितीयवैतालि°, P द्वितीयो वैतालिक पठति, N omits द्वि°; S अस्सं च, U अवि अ instead of द्वि°; T द्वि° अस्सं. — ABPWNORSTU जादं. — P °लोद°, STU °पिंग°. — A °रयणीगंड°, B °चमठोगंड°, PWO °रमणीगंड°.

16b AB थोवा°, P थाआ°, NR धोआ°. — ABPWOR °वट्टिद°, N °वढ़ठिद°, S °वंठिअ°. — P °सुद्धकुसमा, W °कुसमा, NOR °कलिआ. — BPORSTU पप्फुल्लिआ, N प्पफुलिआ.

16c N °लगाब्भमलं, O °भसले. — B शालज्जए, N लक्विवज्ज. — B जिंसुयं, P omits.

16d A महुवेहि, B महएहिं, P महुएहि, W भमरेहिं, N भमलेहिं, OR भसलेहिं. — B हाहि वि, P दोसु चि, W दोहि वि, N दोंहि सु, O दोहिं वि, R दोहिँ धि, T दोहिस. — B सदिसा°. — N लग्गोंहि, OR लग्गेहिं, T लेगेहि. — A omits व; S अ.

16[1] NR एक्को, O का. — AB हं, P omits. — B बद्धावओ, PW वद्धावउ, N वढ़ढाविदो. — P को, NR एक्का. — AOT वि, NRSU omit. — B वद्धाविय, P वद्धाय, W वद्धाविआ, N वढ़ढाविदा, S °पआ.

16[2] ABPW पुण. — W दो, N दुवो, O

कण्ठेसुं कन्दलिदकन्दप्पकोअण्डदण्डाखण्डिदकण्डचण्डिमं सिणिद्धबन्धवं वसुंधरापुरंधीए पसारिदप्पसदिप्पमाणेहिं अच्छीहिं महूसवं जधिच्छं पेक्खदु देवी[3]।

देवी। जधा णिवेदिदं बन्दीहिं पउत्ता जेव मलआणिला[4]। तधा हि[5]।

दुए. — U अम्ह, O transposes वड्ढा° अम्हे. — ABORSTU वड्ढाविआ, PW वद्धाविआ. — O इमेहिं कं°. — B कंचरणचंड°. — Mss. °रअण°. — B °दंडेहिं. — BWRSTU वंदीहिं.

16[3] AWR त्रिब्भममरट्ठ°. — APWOT °पअट्टावअं, B °परिवत्तयं, N °पअट्टा·अं, R °पअदाविअं, SU °प्पवट्टावअं. — A तरुणीणं, W तरुहीणं, T तरट्टिणो, U तरलच्छीणं. — B °मारुयंदोलिदलता°, P °मारुददोलियफणिलदाणच्चिरणीणं, W °दोलिदचंदणलदाणच्चईणीणं, SU मलआणिलंदोलिअललिदलदाणच्चईणं, T मलआणिलंदोलिअजदाणच्चईणं.—AWNOR °पवंचि°, B °पवंचित°, P चोरुपिवंविदयंपंचमं, S °पवंचिअ°, T °प्पपंचिअ°, U °प्पवंचिअपंचम. — A कलकंठीकंठकंदलोसु, B कलकंठीकंठकंदलो, P कलयठीकंठेषु, W कलअंठिकंठेसु, N कलकंठिकंठकंदलेसुं, O कलकंठीकंठेसु, R कलकंटिकंठकंदलेसु, S कलकंठकंदलोसुं, T कलअंटकंदलोसु, U कलकंठकंठकंदलोसु. — A किदकंदप्पकोदंडदंडाखंडिदकडचंडमत्त, B कंदलिदकंदप्पकोदंडाखंडिदकंडचंडिमं, P कंदलितकंदप्पकोदंडमंडितं, W कंदलिदकंदप्पकोदंडदंडचंडिमं, N कंदलोदकंदय्यकोअंडदंडखंडिदचंडिमं, O कंदलिदकंदप्पकोअंडदंडचंडिमं, R कंदप्पकोअंडदंडखंडिदचंडिमं, SU कंदप्पकोअंडदंडाखंडिआकंडचंडिमं, T कंदप्पकोअंडाखंडिआखंडचंडिमं. — ABW णिद्ध°. — NR °बंधुं. — A वसुधा°, O वसुहा°. — B °पुरंदीए, T °पुरंधिए. — BWO ता वि°. — A विछरिय हत्थसुप्पसारिय पसइसरिछेहिं अछोहिं, B वित्थारिय पसइपमाणछिणो, P पसारिसइप्पमाणलोयणो, W वित्थारिदपसइपमाणछिणो, N विस्सारिअपस्सइप्पमाणे अच्छणो, O वित्थारिअपसइ°, R विसारिअ पसइप्पमाणे अच्छिणो, SU पसारिअपसरिसरिच्छेहिं, T पसारिअपसारिसरिच्छेहिं. — BPW महोछवं, N महूस्सवं, STU वसंतमहूसवं. — AP जहित्थं, BWOR STU जहिच्छं, N जहिछूं. — ABPWOS पेच्छ, RTU पेच्छदु. — ABPWNOSU omit देवी.

16[4] A देवी राजानमाह. — AWO जहा, PSTU जह; PNR add किल. — B णिदेविदं, STU °दिअं. — BWRS वंदीहिं, T वंदहिं; A transposes बं° णि°. — A तहा प°. — APWOR पअट्टा, B पयज्ज, N प्पअट्टो, S तह पवट्टदित, TU तह पवट्टंत. — AW ज्जेव, B ध्वेव, P यिव, N जेव्व, O ज्जेघ, R ज्जेव्व, STU एव्व. — NS °लो.

16[5] APNR तथा हि, BWO तहा अ, ST तह हि, U omits.

लङ्कातोरणमालिआतरलिणो कुम्भुब्भवस्सासमे
मन्दन्दोलिअचन्दणदुमवणा कप्पूरसंपक्किणो ।
कङ्केल्लीकुलकम्पिणो फणिलआणिप्पट्टणट्टावआ
चण्डं चुम्बिअतम्बवण्णिसलिला वाअन्ति चेत्ताणिला ॥ १७ ॥

अवि अ[1] ।

माणं मुञ्चह देह वल्लहजणे दिट्ठिं तरङ्गुत्तरं
तारुण्णं दिअहाइ पञ्च दह वा पीणत्थणुत्थम्भणं ।
इत्थं कोइलमञ्जुसिञ्जिअमिसा देवस्स पञ्चेसुणो
दिण्णा चेत्तमहूसवेण सहसा आणा व्व सव्वंकसा ॥ १८ ॥

विदूषकः । भो तुम्हाणं सव्वाणं मज्झे अहं एक्को कालक्खरिओ[1] । जस्स मे ससुरस्ससुरो परघरे पोत्थअभारं वहन्तो आसि[2] ।

17ª U °माणिआ°. — BPSTU °तरलणा. — A कुंभभभवस्सासमं, B कुंभब्भ°, W कुंभोभ°, SU कुंभब्भवस्सस्समे, T कुंब्भुब्भु°.

17ᵇ ABPWOR °दोलिद°, N °दोलित°. — A °चंदल°. — WNOR °लदा. — P °संचम्मिणो.

17ᶜ A कंकेल्ली°, BPNR कंकोल्ली°. W कंकोल्लो°, S तंकोलिफलअंपणा. T कोल्लीफल°, U तक्कोलिफल°. — ABPWNOR °लदा. — P °णिपट्ट°, N °विप्पट्ट°, O °विप्फट्ट°, STU °णिव्विग्घ°. — T °णाट्टाविआ.

17ᵈ B चुंदु. — ABPWOR चुंबिद°. — B °तंवपचि°, PT °तंबपणि°, SU तंबपण्णि°. — STU आअंति.

18ª APW मुंचद, BNOR मुंचध. — A धेह्रि. — B दिट्ठी, W दिट्ठुं, N दिठ्ठी. — A तरंगोत्तरा, O तरंगाडलं.

18ᵇ B दिव°, APWNOR °हाइं. — BP पीणु°. — ABNORT °त्थणा°, P °त्सवं°. — B °कुंभणां.

18ᶜ W इत्थो. — BP °मुंज°. — ART °सिंजण°, B °संजणा°, P °सजिण°, N °सिंऊण°, O °सिंजिद°. — N मिसाद्देअस्स, R देअस्स.

18ᵈ P °महूसावणा, N चेत्महूस्स°. — R भुअणो instead of सहसा. — N आणां, SU आणो, T अक्खे क. — B कव्वंकसा:.

18¹ A ततो विदूषकः भो भो, T omits भो; U अहो. — W सव्वेसिं. — A अहं ज्जेव, STU अहं किल. — A omits एक्को; BPW एको, SU एक्को एव्व. — A कालाक्खरिदो, T कालक्खरिवो पंडिवो.

18² A जदो ममावि य, O मम, SU मह. — A सुस्सरस्स सुस्सरो, B ससुरस्स ससरओ, P ससुरयस्स ससुरउ, W ससुरउ, O ससुरस्स ससुरो, R ससुरसुरो; SU add वि. A पंडिआघरें, BPWO परघरेसु, NR

चेटी । विहस्य[3] । तदो आगदं दे पण्डिच्चं परंपराए[4] ।

विदूषकः । सक्रोधम[5] । आ दासीए धूदे भविस्सकुट्टिणि णिल्लक्खणे विअक्खणे ईद्दिसो अहं मुक्खो जेण तए वि उवहसीआमि[6] । अक्खं च[7] । रे परपुत्तविट्टालिणि भमरटेण्टे टेण्टाकराले तुडिदसंघडिदे परंपरा पण्डिच्चस्स मह किं दूसणं आसि[8] । पेक्ख अकालजलदवंससंभूदाणं परंपराए पण्डिच्चं[9] । अध वा हत्थे कङ्कणं किं दप्पणेण[10] ।

पंडिअघरे, S परके घरंमि, T पंडिअघर, U परघर. — A पोत्थियाई, B पुत्थइयाइ, P पोथआंइ व, W पोत्थाइ, N पोत्थिआइं, O पोत्थाई, R पुत्थिआइँ, S पोत्थभारं, T पुत्थिअभारं, U पोत्थिअभारं. — BWO वहंतओ.

18[3] SU विचक्खणा. — A विहस्य प्राह.

18[4] A कमागदं टे पंडित्तणं. B यत् कमागदं ते पं°, PWO कमागदं दे पं°, NR आगदं दे अक्खरणा पंडितत्तणं (R °अत्तणं), T दे पंडिअत्तणं परंपराए आअदं अकालजलदवसभूदाणं परंपराए पंडिच्चं अह वा हत्थत्थम्मि कंकणे किं दप्पणेण see i. 18[9, 10].

18[5] A सकोपं प्राह.

18[6] APNORSU आः, T आम. — A दासीसुदे, B धूए, P पुत्ति, N पुत्तीए. ORU धीए, T धुत्ते. — A भवस्ससिकु°, OR °कुट्टणि; SU add रच्छालोट्टिणि. — A omits णिल्ल°; P णिलक्खवयक्खणे. — B omits विअक्खणे; WR अविअक्खणे. — B ईदिसो. NRSTU ईरिसो, O एदिसो. — BPWNORSU हं. — P मुवा. — BWO जं, N omits; R जो. — N तुण, ORSTU तुए. — WT omit वि. — A °हासियामि, B °हसियदि, PRSTU °हसिज्जामि, N °हसिज्जइ.

18[7] A अक्खं च पुनर्विदूषकः, OT अक्खं अ.

18[8] STU omit रे; NOR हे. — B पुरपुत्तविट्टालणि, O °विदालणि, S °विद्दाविणि. — After पर° P adds कोससत्थचट्टणि, R adds रच्छालोदणि, STU add कोसवट्टिणि. — A भमणटिंटे, N भमणझोले, OT भमर, SU °टंटे. — N द्यूतप्पिए टेंटाकराले, O टेटा°, T ठेंठा°. — After टेंटा° N adds कोससव्वस्सापहारिणि, R adds कोससआपहारिणि, T adds रेच्छालोट्टिणि. — A °घट्टिदे, B तुट्टिअं°, P तुट्टसंघडेदो, W तुट्टसं°, NR दुट्टसं°, O दुधुत्तट्टसं°. — ABPWNOR omit परं°-आसि; T omits मह.

18[9] ABPWNORT omit. — S पेच्छ. — SU °जलदस°. — U °व्वस्स°.

18[10] T omits, see i. 18[4]. — B अहा, PWNORSU अह. — S व. — After वा U adds रत्थारोहिणि मेहुज्जोविणि. — B इत्थंमि, R हत्थ, S हत्थंमि, U हत्थत्थंमि. — ABRSU कंकणे. — A ता किं. — N दपणेण पेक्खीअदि, O द° लक्खिज्जदि. R द° पेक्खिअदि.

विचक्खणा । विभाव्य[11] । एवं णेदं[12] । धावन्तस्स तुरंगमस्स सिग्घत्तणे किं सक्खिणो पुच्छीअन्ति[13] । ता वक्खअ वसन्तं[14] ।

विदूषकः । कधं पञ्जरगदा सारिआ विअ कुरुकुराअन्ती चिट्ठसि[15] । ण किं पि जाणासि[16] । ता पिअवअस्सदेवीणं पुरदो पढिस्सं[17] । जदो ण कत्थूरिआ कुग्गामे वणे वा विक्किणीअदि ण सुवण्णं कसवट्टिअं विणा कसीअदि[18] । इति पठति[19] ।

फुल्लुक्करं कलमकूरसमं वहन्ति
जे सिन्दुवारविडवा मह वल्लहा ते ।

18[11] ASTU omit.

18[12] ABNORSU एव्वं, T पेच्छ एव्वं. — ABN णेदं, STU एदं.

18[13] ABPWNOR omit धावंतस्स. — ABPWOR तुरंगस्स. — A सिग्घत्तणा. — A पुछिज्जंति, B पुछिज्जमि, P पुत्थियंति, WOSU पुच्छिज्जंति, N पुछिअंति, R पुच्छिअन्ति, T पुच्छिजंदि.

18[14] A तथा त्वं यदि पंडितो सि ता वक्खय वसंदं, T वसंदअं.

18[15] ASTU omit कधं; P तुमं, NR तुमं उण, O कधे. — W पंजरि°. — P °गद, WSTU °गआ. — BPNOR सारिअ व्वय, W सारि व्व, STU विअ सारिआ. — W कुरुकुरुयंती, STU चिरं घुरुघुरा° (T खुरुखुरायंति). — A पुरो चिठ्ठसि.

18[16] BW omit. — SU ण हु किं पि तुमं, T ण कि वि तुमं. — NR जाणेसि.

18[17] B पियवस्स°, NRSU पिअवअस्सस्स देवीए (S adds अ), T °देवीए पुदो. — A पठ्ठिस्सं, P पढिस्सं, SU पठिस्सं, T पट्टिसं.

18[18] A जदो कछूया गामे ण, S कत्थूरी, T कंथूरिआ ण, U कत्थूरी ण. — BW गामे, P गामावणे omit वा; ASTU omit वणे वा. — A विक्किणियदि, W विक्कणीयदि, T विक्किअदि. — W णेदं, STU ण अ. — W सुवण्णं जं. — A कस्सटणा, B कंजसवट्टियं, P कसवट्टयं, S वट्टअं, T कसणावट्टिअं, U कसणावट्टअं. — N सिलापट्टए क°, R पट्टए क°. — O त सुवण्णं जं कसवट्टे णिव्वहइ सा घरिणी जा पदिं रंजेदि तं पठिअं जं सभासु पठीअदि instead of ण सु°-कसीअदि, see i. 19[7].

18[19] A ततः पठदि विदूषकः, P ततः पठति, NOR राजा पिअवअस्स ता (N omits ता) पढ (O भाभणा) सुणीअदु (N °दि) विदूषकः पठति.

19[a] A फुल्लक्कुरं, BN फुल्लक्करं, P फुल्लकरं, SU पुप्फुक्करं. — TU कमल°. — STU °णिाहं.

19[b] N सिंधु°. — RSU टे.

जे गालिअस्स महिसीदहिणो सरिच्छा
ते किं च मुद्धविअइल्लपसूणपुञ्जा ॥ १९ ॥

विचक्खणा । विहस्य[1] । णिअकन्तारत्तणजोग्गं दे वअणं[2] ।

विदूषकः । ता उआरवअणे तुमं पढ[3] ।

देवी । किंचित्स्मित्वा[4] । सहि विअक्खणे अम्हाणं पुरदो तुमं गाढकइत्तणेण गव्वुत्ताणा होसि[5] । ता पढ संपदं अज्जउत्तस्स पुरदो सअंकिदं किं पि कव्वं[6] । जदो तं कव्वं जं सहासुं पढीअदि तं सुवण्णं जं कसवट्टिआए णिव्वडदि सा घरिणी जा पदिं रञ्जेदि सो पुत्तो जो कुलं उज्जलेदि[7] ।

विचक्खणा । जं देवी आणवेदि[8] । इति पठति[9] ।

19c AO गालिदस्स, P गालिडस्स. — B महसो°. — R °हहिनो. — T सरिक्खा.

19d T विअकोल्ल.

19[1] A विहस्य प्राह, NR omit.

19[2] APOR °कंतारंजखा°, B °कंतारत्तूण°, N णिाजकज्जारंभणा°, U °कंदार°. — O °जोमां.

19[3] BW किं पि, O किं चि instead of ता. — ABPWOSTU उदार°. — BSTU °वअणा. — W तुमं पि, U omits. — APORSTU पठ.

19[4] A अथ देवी विहस्य किंचित्रामाह, B किं च स्मित्वा, S omits किंचित्.

19[5] STU omit सहि; P अह. — A अम्ह, STU अह्म. — A पुर. — P तुवं, NR तुअं. — ANOR गाढं. — A °कइत्तणे, P °कइत्तेण. — A गउत्ताणा, B उत्तणा, P उत्ताणा, W उत्ताणो, N उत्तिखा, O उत्ताणोल्ला, R उत्तिणा, S ग.उत्ताणा. — W भोसि.

19[6] W omits ता. — A पठसु, ORSU पठ. — BWNOR °कदं. — BWO omit किं पि. — STU किं वि सअं° कव्वबंधं.

19[7] ANRSTU omit जदो; B यतः. — N omits तं कव्वं. — APOSTU सहासु, BW सभाए, NR सहाए. — AOR पठी°, BN पढि°, STU पट्ठी°. — O omits तं सु°-रंजेदि, see i. 18[18]. — A कसट्टे, N कसवट्टिणं, R कसवदे, ST कसणावट्टए, U कसणपट्टए. — A णिवडदि, BW णिव्वहदि, P णिवडेदि, NR णिवट्टेदि, STU कसीअदि. — AB घरणी. — NR पिअं, STU पइं रंजेइ — ABPW omit सो-उज्जलेदि. — N उत्तो, T पुत्तओ. — STU उज्जलेइ.

19[8] S आणवेइ.

19[9] APNR omit इति; BWOSTU त्ति. — A पठदि विचक्खणा.

जे लङ्कागिरिमेहलाहि खलिआ संभोअखिण्णोरई-
फारुप्फुल्लफणावलीकवलणे पत्ता दरिद्दत्तणं।
ते एण्हिं मलआणिला विरहिणीणीसाससंपक्किणो
जाआ झत्ति सिसुत्तणे वि बहला तारुण्णपुण्णा विअ ॥ २० ॥

राजा। सच्चं विअक्खणा विअक्खणा चदुरत्तणेण उत्तीणं विचित्तदाए रीदीणं[1]। ता किं अण्णं कइचूडामणित्तणे ठिदा एसा[2]।

विदूषकः। सक्रोधम्[3]। ता उज्जुअं जेव किं ण भणीअदि अच्चुत्तमा विअक्खणा कव्वम्मि अच्चहमो कविञ्जलो बम्हणो त्ति[4]।

20ᵃ A °मेखलाहि, WR °हिं, O °लिहिं. — ABWNOR खलिदा, P खलदा, SU चलिआ. — N °विंणोरई.

20ᵇ APWR फार°. — APWNRT °फुल्ल°. — B °कणावलीकमलणे, P °कवलिदा, S °कबलणे. — B दलिदत्तणं.

20ᶜ B विरहणी°. — N °णीस्सास°, O °णिसास°, SU °णिस्सास°.

20ᵈ APWNORT जादा, B जाद ज्जत्ति, O दसत्ति. — N पि. — AP बहुला.

20¹ A राजानंतरोक्तं निशम्य, STU राजा विहस्य. — A सच्चं २, STU सव्वहा. — A वियक्खणा। तथा वियक्खणा, PN वि° once only, STU वि° वि° एव्व. — B चदुरत्तणा, P अहो चदुरत्तरणं भत्यस्स, W चउरत्तणे, N चदुरत्तणे. S विच। उरत्तणेण, TU चउर°. — A सत्तीणं, W चदुरत्तीणं, N उत्तिणं, R उत्तिणा. — A वयणविचित्तदाए य, B ता किं पि अण्णं विचित्तादाए, P विचित्तदा ता अचं विचित्तदाए, W ता अ किमणं चदुरवयणविचित्तदाए, NR omit वि°; O ता किं अणं वि°, T विइत्तदाए. — ABPWNOR omit रीदीणं; T रीईणं. Here A inserts सुकइणं पि सुकई वियक्खणा, B कईणं सुचइ त्ति, P कईण सुकइ त्ति, W सुकईणं पि सुकइ त्ति, NR कईणं पि कई, O कसेणं वि कइ त्ति.

20² BPO omit. — A ता भणइ, W किं भणइ omits ता. — A सुकइ°, W सुकइचूडामणे, S कइंदचू°. — ST णिट्ठिदा, W ठिदाए. — NR omit एसा. — Here A inserts देवी श्रुत्वाह। जं देवेण निदिठ्ठं तत्तथैव, BNOR देवी विहस्य कवि(NR °इ°)चूडामणित्तणे (B °णेण) ठिदा एसा, P देवी विहस्य कइचूडामणित्वे स्थिता एषा देवी विहस्य महीयलंसरस्सई एसा, W देवी अज्ज किं एदं महीयलसरस्सई एसा वियक्खणा एव देवी विहस्य कविचूडामणित्तणेण ठिदा एसा.

20³ A सक्रोधमाह.

20⁴ A ज्जेव, B ठोव, P येव, W व्वेव, N ज्जेव्व, O जेव्व, R लच्च. STU एव्व. — APWT भणइ. B भिणइ. NR भ° देवीए. OS भणइ. — A अच्चंताधमो,

विचक्खणा। अज्ज मा कुप्प[5]। कव्वं जेव दे कइत्तणं पिसुणेदि[6]। जदो कन्तारत्तणणिन्दणिज्जे वि अत्थे सुउमारा दे वाणी लम्बत्थणीए विअ एक्कावली तुन्दिलाए विअ कञ्चुलिआ काणाए विअ कज्जलसलाआ ण सुट्ठदरं रमणिज्जा[7]।

विदूषकः। तुज्झ उण रमणिज्जे वि अत्थे ण सुन्दरा सद्दावली[8]। कणअकडिसुत्तए विअ लोहकिङ्किणीमाला पडिवट्टए विअ तसरविरअणा गोरङ्गीए विअ चन्दणचच्चा ण चङ्गत्तणं अवलम्बेदि[9]। तधा वि तुमं वक्खीअसि[10]।

B अच्चाधमो, P अच्चंताधम्मो, W अच्चाधम्मे, N अच्चाहमो, O अच्चधमो. — BNR कविंजल, STU कइंजलो. — AW बंभणो. — A adds देवी। अध कि। एदं महीवल्लस्स हरस्सद वियक्खणा compare PW i. 20[2].

20[6] A जदो कव्वं, B कधिदं, T कःपकःवं. — ABWN ज्जेव, P य्येव, O जेव्व. R ज्जेव्व, SU एव्व, T एव्वं एव्व. PNRSTU omit दे. — BW कवि°. — B पिसुणोदि, STU पिसुणेइ

20[7] A कंतारंजणाजोग्गे णिजे, B णियक्कंतारत्तणणिंदिलिज्जे, P निकयंतारजतणे णिंदणिय्ये, W णिअकंता°, N णिअकज्जारंभणजोग्गे णिंदणिज्जे, O णिअकंतारंजणजुग्गे णिंद°, R णिअकत्तारंजनजोग्गणिंद°. — ATU omit वि; BP व, S अत्थे वि. — AP सुकुमारा, B कुसमारा, W सुकमारा, NR सोमारा, STU सुउमाला omit दे. — A जहा। लंबत्थनीए विय एकाउली। तथा। तुंदि°. — BW तुंडिलाए, N तुंदिलाआए, R तुंदिलिआए. O कड्ढिअकेसाए विअ मालएकुसुममाला तुंदिलाए, U omits तुं° विअ. — B कुंचलियाए, NR कंचुलिआ कढिद (N कड्ढिद°) केसाए (R °स-आए) विअ मालदीकुसुममाला, O कंचुलिआ ठेराए विअ कउक्खविब्भमो. — A तथा कणाए, N कंणाए, STU काणीए. — B वि. — A अंजणसिलाया, B °सिलाया, T °सलाहा. — A omits ण-रमणिज्जा. — P omits ण; BWO सु° ण. — B सुद्धत्तरे, P सट्ठदरं, W सुट्ठअरं, N सुठ्ठदरं, O सुठुदरं, RU सुट्ठुतरं T सुठुअरा. — Before र° BWNOR add भादि. — S रमणिज्जालंबिआ.

20[8] AB तुज्ज, W तुब्भ. — A पुण. — A ज्जेव, P विय instead of वि. — A STU omit ण. — STU असुंदरा.

20[9] A °सुत्ते. — WN किंकणी°. — BWO °मालिआ. — A पडसूत्तपट्टए, B पडियट्टि, P पट्टवत्थे, W पडिपट्टे, N पट्टवट्टाण, O पट्टपडे. R पदपदए, T पडिवट्टवट्टए. — N इत. — AWO टसरि°, B तसरि°, P सरि°, T तिसर°, U टसंसरस°. — T गोरीए. — W विंव. — B चंदसरुच्चा. — ABPWNORT चारुत्तणं. — STU अवलंबेइ.

20[10] A तथा, NR तहा, STU तह. — A

विचक्षणा । अज्ज मा कुप्प[11] । का तुम्हेहिं समं पाडिसिद्धी[12] । जदो तुमं णाराओ विअ णिरक्खरो वि रदणतुलाए णिउज्जीअसि[13] । अहं उण तुला विअ लद्धक्खरा वि ण सुवण्णतुलणे णिउज्जीआमि[14] ।

विदूषकः । एवं मं हसन्तीए तुह वामं दक्खिणं च जुहिट्ठिरजेट्ठभादरणामहेअं अङ्गं तडत्ति उप्पाडइस्सं[15] ।

विचक्षणा । अहं पि उत्तरफग्गुणीपुरस्सरणक्खत्तणामहेअं अङ्गं तुह तडत्ति खण्डिस्सं[16] ।

राजा । वअस्स मा एवं भण[17] । कइत्तणे ठिदा एसा[18] ।

---

omits वि. — B तुवं, NR तुअं, STU इत्थं. — N वक्खिअसि, U वाणो आसो.

20[11] ABPWSU omit मा कुप्प.

20[12] B तुम्हे, PW तुम्हेहि, SU तुम्ह, T तुम्हहिं. — NR सह, STU omit; APW समं अम्हाणं. — A पडिसिद्धा, P पडि°, N °सिद्धिआ, T पडिपहा.

20[13] A यदो. — BW तुवं, NR तुअं. — R omits णा° विअ. — NSTU omit वि. — ABPWNRSTU रअण°, O रण°. — W °तुल्लाए, SU °तुलणे. — P णिजुंजीयसि, S णिउज्जीआसि, U णिउज्जी°.

20[14] S omits. — ABW पुण, R दुण. — BPWNOR तुल व्व, U omits. — B लद्धअक्खरा, T लद्धबहलक्खरा तुला विअ. — N omits ण. — A सुवण्णलवेणावि, B सुवण्णतया । तोलणेण नउंजो (illegible), PWOR सुवण्णलवे, N कप्पासतुलणे; PWR add वि. — A युंजामि, B see above, P णिकुविज्जियामि, N णिउंजिआम्हि, TU णिउज्जी°.

20[15] W वि° सक्रोधं. — BRSU एव्वं. — BPWNOR मह भणंतीए, T उवहसंतीए omits तुह. — A व, P वा, OU अ, NR omit च. — A जुहिढ्ठल°, B जुहिट्ठर°, WO जुहिट्ठिल°, NSU जुहुट्ठिर°, R जुहिट्ठिल°. — ABWR °भाअर°, P °भादुणो, N °भाउ°, STU °भादु°. — ABPWNR °धेअं. — ANOR अंगजुअलं. — A झडत्ति, B तडित्त, POR STU omit; N झत्ति. — A तोडिस्सं P खंडिस्सं, W उप्पाडयस्सं, STU खंडइस्सं.

20[16] P omits विच°. — ABPSU omit अहं पि; P inserts तह; W तुज्झ पुणो हं omits पि; N ता अहं पि, O वि — A उत्तय°, P °पुरस्सरां omits णक्खत्त°; O °पुरत्थिम°. — ABWNOR °धेअं. — A अंगुयुगलं, N अंगजुअलं. — ABPW omit तुह; O ते. — APO तडित्ति, B तडित्त, NR झत्ति, STU omit. — S पाडइस्सं, TU छेदइस्सं.

20[17] B वदस्स. — ABPWOSU omit मा भण, NR omit एवं; T जेव्वं.

20[18] P अपुव्वकइत्तणे. W कयत्तणे, SU कइं-

विदूषकः । सक्रोधम्[19] । ता उज्जुअं जेव किं ण भणीअदि अम्हाणं चेडिआ हरिउड्ढणन्दिउड्ढपोट्टिसहालप्पहुदीणं पि पुरदो सुकइ त्ति[20] । इति परिक्रामति[21] ।

विचक्खणा । विहस्य[22] । तहिं गच्छ जहिं मे पढमसाहुलिआ गदा[23] ।

विदूषकः । वलितग्रीवम्[24] । तुमं उण तहिं गच्छ जहिं मे मादाए पढमा दन्तावली गदा[25] । ईदिसस्स राअउलस्स भद्दं भोदु जहिं चेडिआ बम्हणेण समसीसिआए दीसदि मइरा पञ्चगव्वं च एक्कस्सिं भण्डए करीअदि कच्चं माणिक्कं च समं आहरणे पउञ्जीअदि[26] ।

दच्चूडामणित्तणे, T कइच्चूडामणित्तणे. — B णोविदा, WN णिठिवा, O परिणिट्ठिदा, T णिट्टिविदा.

20[19] A स° प्राह.

20[20] NR omit ता. — AP उज्जयं. — A ज्जेव, B चेव, P य्येव, W व्वेव, NR ता, O जेव्व, STU एव्व. — A भणाई, BNOR भणाइ, PS भक्खइ, W भक्खेइ राजा, T भणासि. — SU चेडी. — A हरयट्ठनंपियट्ठपाहिसयपुभ्भुदीणां पि वृद्धपाराशर्यप्रभतीनामपि कवीनां, B हरिउट्टनंदियट्टपोट्टिसहालपहुदीणां, PW हरियट्ठ (W °ट्ट°) णंदियट्टपुट्टिसहलप्पहुदीणं, N हरिआटपदिअंदपोट्टीलसाहासलप्पहुदीणं. O हरिउड्ढणंदिउड्ढ° R हरिअंदनंदिअंदयोदासहाल°, STU हरिबम्हसिद्धि (S °द्धो°) ओड्डीस- (T °अंटिस°) पालित्तअचंपअराअमल्लसेहराणं (T °मलअसिंहाणं) omit पि. — A मध्ये, BW पुरउ. STU मज्झे.

20[21] A राजा एव्वं णेदं विदूषकः रुष्ट इवोत्थाय परिक्रामति, P राजा एवं णेदं विदूषकः परि°, W परि° राजा एवं नेदं विदूषकः रुष्ट इव सक्रोधमुत्थाय परि°, R राजा एव्वं णेदं विदूषकः सक्रोधं परि°, U omits; ST omit इति.

20[22] B omits विच°. — A विहस्याह, B NOR omit.

20[23] N एवं णेदं तहिं. — P गच्छ लंबंकुअ. — W मे मादाए, STU दे. — NO पठमा, R पठमा, S पुढम°, T पुट्टमा, U पुढमं. — A °साहल्लिया, B °साहुल्लीया, P °साहुल्लिआ, W °साहोलिया. NOR साहिआ, S °स्साहु°, T समुलिआ.

20[24] A °ग्रीवमाह, P विहस्य वलित°.

20[25] W तुवं, NR तुअं. — AW पुण, B मणु, P पि. — STU दे. — B मदो, P पढमे मादाए, O माराए. — A पढम°, BP पढम°, STU omit. — T गलिदा, U गआ. — After गदा A adds भणां च, W adds अचं च.

20[26] P ता ई°, O एरिसस्स, STU ईरिसस्स. — A रयउ°, BPWOR राउ°. — SU होदु. — A बंभणेहिं. WR बंभणेण. O मह्मणेण. — A समं पाडिसिद्धिं करेदि. P समं समसमसीसियाय, N समं सोसिआए. R ममं समीसिआए, SU सम-

विचक्खणा । इध राअउले तं दे भोदु कण्ठट्ठिदं जं भअवं तिलोअणो सीसे समुव्वहदि तेण अ दे मुहं चूरीअदु जेण असोअतरू दोहलं लहदि[27] ।

विदूषकः । आ दासीए पुत्ति टेण्टाकराले कोससदचट्टिणि रच्छालोट्टिणि एवं मं भणासि[28] । ता मह महाबम्हणस्स वअणेण तं तुमं लह जं फग्गुणसमए सोहञ्जणो दोहलं लहदि जं च पामराहिंतो गलिबइल्लो लहदि[29] ।

सोत्तआ, T समसोत्ता. — STU वोसइ. — O मदिरा. — OU अ. — B एकरिसं, W एगस्सिं, N एकस्सि, O एअस्सिं. — A भांडे, W भंडे, N भंडण. — A करदि, BWR कोरदि, N किजइ, S करीअइ, T करइ. — B कव्वंधं, STU काअं. — OS अ. — A आहरणेहि, B आहारणे, SU आभनणे. — A निउंजेदि, N पउंजीअदि, S पउज्जीअइ, T पउंजीअइ, U णिउज्जीअदि. — P omits-कच्चं-प°.

20[27] A चेटी विहस्याह, BPNR चेटी. — A इध हि, BWNORSTU इह, P एत्थ. — A राजकुले, BPWNOR राउले. — AN ते, B भो दे instead of दे भोदु; W omits दे; P तं हाव, U एव्वं एदं दे. — P देउ, O भोदु दे, STU होदु. — After भोदु A runs जं असोयतरु दोहलं लहदि । भणं च । जं भयवं तिलोयणो सीसे वहदि तं ते कंठे व लगिदं भोदु. — P omits कंठ°; SU °ट्ठिअं, T °तिअं. — P यत्. N omits. — B तिलोयणा भभवं, P भगवान् त्रिलोचनो महेश्वरः, WO ति° भ°, STU भ° तिणअणो. — SU सीसए. — OSTU °हइ. — B तेणं. — BOSTU omit अ; NR व. — P ते, O दे मुहे, S मुहं ते, T मुहं दे. — B चूरयदु, P चूरिज्जदु, N चुरिअदु, O चूरिअदु, S फूरीअदु, T पूरइज्जइ, U फूरिज्जइ. — P असोयरु, S वउलतरु. — B दोहलयं, P दोहयलं, W तरुणीणं दोहलअं. — ABO लहेदि, P लहेहि, N लहेति, SU लहइ, T लहेइ.

20[28] ANRS आः, T आम. — A दासीपुत्ति भमरटिंटे टिंटाकराले, S पुत्ति लच्छालोट्टिणि एव्वं भणासि मं and omits the rest. — B टंटा°, U लच्छालोट्टिणि टेंटा°. — ABOR कोससअ°, P कोसासय°, W कोससयअ°, N कोससअल°, T कोसवट्टिणि, U omits. — BNR °चट्टिणि, P °वट्टिणि, WO °चट्टिणि. — A °तुट्टिणि, P omits रच्छा°; O °लेट्टिणि, T रच्छालोट्टिणि कोसलुंटिणि, U रच्छालोट्टिणि. — A जं एवं, NORSTU एव्वं. — AN omit मं; O मे, STU भ° मं. — Mss. भणासि (N भणिासि).

20[29] O omits ता. — WNSTU मह°. —

विचक्षणा । अहं उण तुह एवं भणन्तस्स णोउरस्स विअ पाअलग्गस्स पाएण मुहं चूरइस्सं[30] । अण्णं च उत्तरासाढापुरस्सरणक्खत्तणामहेअं अङ्गजुअलं उप्पाडिअ घल्लिस्सं[31] ।

विदूषकः । सक्रोधं परिक्रामति जवनिकान्तरे किंचिदुच्चैः[32] । ईदिसं राअउलं दूरे वन्दीअदि जहिं दासी बम्हणेण समं पाडिसिद्धिं करेदि[33] । ता अज्ज-

---

AWOR °ढंभणस्स, B °बब्भणस्स, P °बंभस्स, SU °ब्बह्मणस्स. — BPWNOR भणिदेण. — SU दाणिं तं. — P तुमं पि, NR तुअं. T तुमं दाणिं and omits तं. — A लहि, W लहइ, NR लहसु, S लहेहि. — B फग्गणा°, R फुगिन°, T फग्गुणी°. — A सोहिंजणो, BPO सोहंजणओ, STU °जणा. — A जणाओ instead of दोहलं; BPO omit; WRT जणादो, N जदो, S दो. — PON लहेदि, W लहइ, STU लहंति. — BPRT omit च; NO अ, SU वा. — B पामरहिंतो, S पामरादो, U पामराहिं. — A गालियव°, B गलवियल्लो. PR गलो°, W गलोयवयलो, N गलिल्ल°, O गलद°, SU वुड्ढ°, T गट्ठि°. — S °बेहिल्लो, T °वहिल्लो, U °अलिल्लो. — W लहहि, NO लहेदि, STU लहइ

20[30] A विचक्षणा विहस्य वक्ति. — AB पुण, N पि उण. — P तह, W तुअ, U omits. — ASTU omit एवं भणंतस्स; BO have ए° भ° after पाअ°. — NR एव्वं. — W णेवरस्स. — B वि, T व्व instead of विअ, U omits. — A पायग्गलग्गस्स adds पायेण-चूरिस्सं in the margin. — N पएण, S पादेण, TU पाअवोहिं. — U तुह मुहं. — A चूरिस्सं, PW चूरिइस्सं, SU फूरिस्सं. — A adds तथा । उत्तरफग्गुणीपुरस्सरणक्खत्तणामधेयं अंगं तडित्ति खंडिस्सं.

20[31] S omits च; TU अ. — A उत्तराखाढनक्खत्तपुरस्सरणामधेयं, B °साढपुरस्सरस्स°, P °साढ°, WN °साढ°, R °साठ°. — O °परट्ठिद°, R °पुरणक्खत्त°. — BP WNR °धेअं. — A अंगजुगलं, S अं° दे, T अंग दे, U दे अंग°. — STU उप्पाडइस्सं omit घल्लिस्सं; A खिप्पिस्सं, P ल्लिस्सं, N घालि:सं.

20[32] PWO विदूषकः अहं च ते (O तुह) पअणा (P पअक्ख°) णिक्कमणो (O °मु°)-क्कमणविवरट्ठाणमंगं खंडिअ घल्लिस्समिति सक्रोधं. — ST परिक्रामन. — A किंचिदुच्चैर्वक्ति च.

20[33] A इदिसं, PNRSTU ईरिसं, W इदिस्सं. — ABPWNR राउलं, O लाउलं. — W दूरेण, O दूले. — A वंदीयदु. B वंद्दीयदि, SU वंदिज्जइ, T वंजीअदि. — A जह्नी, B यहि. — BO वम्ह° समं दा°. — W बंभणेण. — A पलपदि, B पडिसिद्धी, PWT पडि°. — STU करेइ.

प्पहुदि णिअवसुंधराबम्हणीए चलणसुस्सूसओ भविअ घरे ज्जेव चिट्ठिस्सं[34]।

सर्वे हसन्ति[35]

देवी। कीदिसी अज्जकविञ्जलेण विणा गोट्ठी कीदिसी णअणञ्जणेण विणा पसाहणलच्छी[36]।

नेपथ्ये[37]

विदूषकः। ण हु ण हु आगमिस्सं[38]। अखो को वि पिअवअस्सो अखेसीअदु[39]। एसा वा दुट्ठदासी लम्बकुच्चं टप्परकण्णं पडिसीसअं दइअ मह ठाणे करीअदु[40]। अहं एक्को मुदो तुम्हाणं मज्झे तुम्हे उण वरिससदं जीवध[41]।

20[34] A omits ता. — ABORTU °पहुदि. — A णियवसुंधराए बंभणो। ए. B णियवसुंधरवम्हणीए, P णीयवसुंहरानामबंभणीए, W णियवसुंधराणामबंभणीए, NR णिअगेहिणीए वसुंधराणामधेआए बम्हणीए, O णिअवसुंधरावंभणीए, S णिअवसुंधराबह्मणी, T णिअघरं गदुअ घरणिए वसुंधराणामहेआए बह्मणीए, U घरअं गदुअ णिअवसुंधराबह्मणी. — A चलणन्हूराओ, B °सुसूओ, PW °सुस्सूसगो, N °सुसतुओ, T °सुस्सूओ. — A णियगेहे, BPWO गेहे, NR omit; TU घरए. — NRU omit ज्जेव; O ज्जेव्व, S एव्व, T एव. — A विकटिस्सं.

20[35] A इति श्रुत्वा सर्वे, BNR इति सर्वे, O ति सर्वे.

20[36] A विभ्रमलेखा, N omits देवी. — A अज्ज की°, NR अज्जउत्त की°, SU कीरिसी, T देव कीरीसी. — A कपिंजलेण, N कइजएण कइणा, R कविंजलेण, STU °कइंजलेण. — B कीदिसं, PW की° उण, STU कीरिसी. — A णयणाणं कज्जलेण, N णणा-णमंजणेण, SU अंजणेण, T अंजणेणाअणाणं omits विणा. — A पसाह°, PW पसाहणा°. — S adds अच्छीणं.

20[37] NR आकाशे, U ने° सगर्वः.

20[38] ABPWNRU omit विदू°; ST विदू° आकर्ण्य सबहुमानं. — OT ण हु once only. — S आअमिस्सं.

20[39] B अखे and omits को वि; A पि. — P पियवस्सो पियवयस्सेण, W पि° वयस्सेण, O वअस्सो, T पिअवस्सस्सस्स, U °वअंसस्सं. — A अणेसियदु, U अक्खेसणीअदु.

20[40] BO इअं, NR अहवा एसा. — AWNR omit वा; SU वो. — A बढकुच्चं, N °कुचा, SU °कुच्चअं, T °हुचं. — A टब्भकण्णं, P ट° पडिल्लसीसं चा, W ट° कडिल्लसीसं पडिल्लसीसं, N °कण्णा, T टप्पकण्णं, U अप्परकण्णं. — AB दईय, PW दाविय, N देपिअ, R देइअ, S रइअ corrected to कदुअ, T धरीअ, U कदुअ. — P मह थाणे, ST अह्मट्ठाणे, U अम्हठाणे, APWNR कीरदु, BO पहमणं कीरदु, ST क्रिदु, U करिज्जउ.

20[41] A अह्मेको, B अह्ममेको. — A मुदो

विचक्षणा । मा अणुसंधेध[42] । अणुणअकक्कसो क्खु कविञ्जलो बम्हणो सलिलसित्तो विअ सणगुणग्गण्ठी गाढदरो भोदि[43] ।

देवी । समन्तादवलोक्य[44] ।

गाअन्तगोवअवहूपअपेङ्खिआसु
दोलासु विब्भमवईसु णिविट्ठदिट्ठी ।
जं जाइ खञ्जिअतुरङ्गरहो दिणेसो
तेण च्च होन्ति दिअहा अइदीहदीहा ॥ २१ ॥

प्रविश्य पटाक्षेपेण[1]

विदूषकः । आसणं आसणं[2] ।

---

after मज्झे; STU मुओ. — BWO तुम्हाणं सव्वाणं. — A मज्जे, B ज्जेव, PW मज्झंमि, O जेव्व मज्झे, STU omit. — N तुझे. — A व instead of उण; U omits. — N विरसि°. — BPW NRSTU °सभं. — B जौवधं, NOR जोअध, SU जोविस्सह, T जवोस्सह. — APWO add राजा कविं(AW °ञ्जं°)-जलेण विणा कुदो सिअअस्स णिव्वुदो.

20[42] A हे देवि मा, SU मा णं. — AN अणुसंधेहि, BO °धेह, P अणुसुंधह, R omits; STU अणुणेह.

20[43] A जेण अणुणयिदुकक्कसो, B अणुणेयक°, O °कक्कसो. — APW खु, BOSTU omit. — A एसो कइंजलो, PW कविंजलओ, OSTU कइंजलो. — A दिओ instead of बम्हणो, BPWO omit. — A विभमलेखा । सलोलसित्ता, P °सत्तो. — AO omit विअ. — BO °गंठि व्व, P °गंठी य, AWNRT °गंठो. — PW add दिढं, NR add चिरं. — A in the text only यरो भोदि and adds विय गाढयरो भोदि in the upper margin. — BWOSTU गाढअरो, P गाढरो, N गाढतरो, R गाठअरो. — PW NO होदि, SU होइ, T होहि. — NOR add णं दंसणाोअं दोसदु.

20[44] A देवी पुनः, PW विभमलेखा, NR omit देवी. — BON समस्तमव°, W °लोक्य.

21[a] B गायंति°, N गाअनगोवअबहू°, O °गोवहू°, STU °तगअवहू°. — A °पंखिदासु, B °पंकदेसु, PWO °दासु, N °पेक्खिआसु, T °पेखिआसु.

21[b] STU डोलासु. — APWR °वदोसु, B विब्भमसदेसु, N °वदिसु, O °जुदासु, S °वतोसु, TU °पएसु. — B णिविट्ठिदिट्ठी, N णिसह°, R णिसण°.

21[c] ABPWNOR जादि, AW खंचिद°, BP ORU खंजिद°, N खंडिदतुरंअ°. — B °सरंगरहो.

21[d] N तेणे, RT तेणेव. SU तेणे. — ABP WNOSU व्व, A होंदि. — P दिवहा, N दिअसा. — P दृह दीह°. OT अदिदो°.

21[1] A अथ प्रवीश्य. — O नटोक्षेपेण.

21[2] A विदू° वक्ति. — N आसणामासणं दुवारे चिळ्ळादि भेरवाणंदो.

राजा । किं तेण[3] ।

विदूषकः । भेरवाणन्दो दुवारे चिट्ठदि[4] ।

देवी । किं सो जो जणवअणादो अच्चब्भुदसिद्धी सुणीअदि[5] ।

विदूषकः । अध इं[6] ।

राजा । पवेसअ[7] ।

विदूषको निष्क्रम्य तेनैव सह प्रविशति[8]

भैरवानन्दः । किंचिन्मदमभिनीय[9] ।

मन्ताण तन्ताण ण किं पि जाणे झाणं च णो किं पि गुरुप्पसाआ।
मज्जं पिआमो महिलं रमामो मोक्खं च जामो कुलमग्गलग्गा ॥ २२ ॥

अवि अ[1] ।

रण्डा चण्डा दिक्खिआ धम्मदारा
मज्जं मंसं पिज्जए खज्जए अ ।

21[3] A राज्ञाह. — N राजा । संपत्तो भेरवाणंदो. — T ते, U देण.

21[4] N omits. — Only O and occasionally SU have भइरवाणंदो; the others read here and in the following भेर°. — A उपवेस्सदि, B उपविस्सदि, P उपविसदि, W उवविसदि, R आअच्छदि, STU दवारे वट्टइ.

21[5] N omits. — W राजा. — A भो जो and omits किं; BPW जो सो — A °वयणाओ, P °वअणादो. — A अच्चुब्भुदा°, B अच्चुब्भुद°, P अच्चब्भुय°, W अच्चुब्भुअ°. — P सुणीयदि

21[6] A omits विदू°. — STU अह. — APW किं, BO ई.

21[7] NSU पवेसअ पवेसअ.

21[8] B निसृत्य, T तहेति निष्क्रम्य. — STU तेन सह. — A विशति

21[9] B °मंदमभि°, N °मंदाचमभि°. — NR add पठति.

22[a] ABPWO मंतो ण तंतो ण, N मंतं ण तंतं ण, R मत्तो ण त्वत्तो ण. — AN हु किं, BPWO अ किं, R च किं. — STU वि. — ABPR झाणं, W झ्राणं. N जाण, O ण्हाणं. — A धाणं, W झाणं. — B पि णा, O अ णो किं तु, STU वि. — PWRS °सादा, N गुरुप्पसादो, OTU °सादो.

22[b] BW पिवामो, PNSU पिबामो. — N मिहिलं. — T रमामोक्खं. — PN अ-जामो, O अ जामो.

22[1] A अयं च.

23[a] P चंडा रंडा, O चंडो. APNR दिक्खिदा, B सिक्खिदा, W दिक्खदा. — O धम्मादिरा.

23[b] A मांसं मज्जं, B मद्यं मंसं, T मज्जं

भिक्खा भोज्जं चम्मखण्डं च सेज्जा
कोलो धम्मो कस्स णो भाइ रम्मो ॥ २३ ॥

किं च[1]।

मुत्तिं भणन्ति हरिबम्हमुहा वि देवा
झाणेण वेअपढणेण कउक्किआहिं।
एक्केण केवलमुमादइएण दिट्ठो
मोक्खो समं सुरअकेलिसुरारसेहिं ॥ २४ ॥

राजा। इदं आसणं[1]। उववसिदु भेरवाणन्दो[2]।

भैरवानन्दः। उपविश्य[3]। किं कादव्वं[4]।

राजा। कहिं पि विसए अच्छरिअं दट्ठुं इच्छामि[5]।

भैरवानन्दः।

दंसेमि तं पि ससिणं वसुहावइण्णं
थम्भेमि तस्स वि रइस्स रहं णहद्धे।

समं. — ABPR स्व॰ पि॰. — ABPW वा, T अ.

23c B भिक्ता. — N भोक्जा. — O अ. — T भ्रेजा.

23d N कालो. — ABPWOR भादि, N भटिद. S होव. U हाद.

23[1] T अवि अ.

24a APO ॰बंभमुहा, B ॰मुहादि, PU इ, NOR हि, ST अ. — NRT देआ, O देव्वा.

24b A ज्झाणेण, O झाणेण. — STU वेद॰. — ARSU ॰पठणेण, T ॰पटणेण. — AWORS कदु॰, BPU कदु॰. — B ॰किअयाहिं, P ॰कियाहिं. NRT ॰क्किआए.

24c B इक्केव, P एकेण. — A ॰दयिएण. NRT ॰दइढेण. — B दिट्ठे.

24d N मोक्को. — B सुरद॰. — W ॰सुहारसेण.

24[2] ABNRSTU उव॰. — A omits भइ॰; B ॰णंद.

24[3] A उपवीश्य भै॰, B omits भै॰.

24[4] AWSU काअव्वं, B कत्तव्वं.

24[5] STU वि. — T विअसे. — P अत्थरियं, SU अच्छेरं, T अच्चरिअं.

25a OSTU वि. — T ससयं. — B वसुधा॰. — W ॰इवचं, N ॰वतिष्ठं.

25b B छंभेमि. O पंभेमि, T थंवेमि. — ABPNR रविस्स, T रहं रइणो. — B रथं. SU गहं. — B णभद्दे, P णभद्दे, ST णहोद्धे.

आणेमि जक्खसुरसिद्धगणङ्गणाओ
तं णत्थि भूमिवलए मह जं ण सज्झं ॥ २५ ॥

ता भण किं करीअदु[1]।

राजा । विदूषकं विलोक्य[2] । वअस्स भण[3] । कहिं पि अपुव्वं दिट्ठं महिलारदणं[4] ।

विदूषकः । अत्थि एत्थ दक्खिणावधे वच्छोमं णाम णअरं[5] । तहिं मए एक्कं कण्णारदणं दिट्ठं[6] । तं इध आणीअदु[7] ।

भैरवानन्दः । आणीअदि[8] ।

राजा । अवदारीअदु पुण्णिमाहरिणङ्को धरणीदले[9] ।

भैरवानन्दो ध्यानं नाटयति[10]

ततः प्रविशति पटाक्षेपेण नायिका[11] । सर्वे ऽवलोकयन्ति[12]

राजा । अहह अच्छरिअं अच्छरिअं[13] ।

25ᶜ W जक्खु°, STU सव्वसुर°. — P °गणा-गणाओ.

25ᵈ S णंतिभुवणे, TU एत्थ भुवणे. — ABR सज्जं, NOSTU सक्कं.

25¹ B भणाए, S भणादु. — A करदु, BW कोरदु, P कोरवो, NT करिअदु.

25² ABPWNOR omit.

25³ AS omit वअस्स. — N तुअ, R तए, SU कहेहि, T तुए instead of भण.

25⁴ S अ कहिं, B किमपि, PWO किं पि, STU वि. — B अउव्व, PW अउव्वं. — STU दि° अ°. — A कणा°. — Mss. °रअणं. — N म° दि°. — O (and R in the translation) adds विदू दिट्ठं दावं राजा कहेहि.

25⁵ N omits. — RT omit एत्थ. — AB PWNOR °वहे. ST °पहे, U °पथे. — A वत्साम, W वत्थोवमं, STU वच्छोमो.

25⁶ N omits. — AO अपुव्वं, B अउव्वं instead of एक्कं. — W कण्णाया°, STU कण्णआ°. — Mss. °रअणं.

25⁷ A राजा त. — Mss. इह. — ST आणेदु भैरवाणंदो, U भइर° आणेदु.

25⁸ O आणिअदि. SU omit; T आणिज्जइ.

25⁹ SU omit राजा. — A अवदारियज्जदु, B अवियारिज्जदु, PW °रिज्जदु, NU °तारीअदु, O °आरिज्जदु, T °अरिदु. — BPO धरणि°, SU महो°, T omits. — APW °यलंमि, BNR °अले. SU °अलं.

25¹⁰ BPSU omit भै°. — STU निमीलिताक्षो ध्यानं ना°.

25¹¹, ¹² A कटाक्षक्षेपेण, U °शत्यपटा°. — A सर्वे चित्रमव°, BR आलो°, O सर्वेप्यव°, STU सर्वे साश्चर्यं पश्यंति.

25¹³ A अएह. — P अत्थरियं अत्थरियं, O अच्चरिअं once only, R अ° once only, SU omit; T अच्चरिअ २.

जं धोअञ्जणसोणलोअणजुअं लग्गालअग्गं मुहं
हत्थालम्बिअकेसपल्लवचए दोलन्ति जं बिन्दुणो।
जं एक्कं सिअअञ्चलं णिवसिअं तं ण्हाणकेलिट्ठिआ
आणीआ इअमब्भुएक्कजणणी जोईसरेणामुणा ॥ २६ ॥

अवि अ[1]।

एक्केण पाणिणलिणेण णिवेसअन्ती
पोत्तञ्चलं घणथणत्थलसंसमाणं।
चित्ते लिहिज्जइ ण कस्स वि संजमन्ती
अण्णेण चङ्कमणओ चलिअं कडिल्लं ॥ २७ ॥

विदूषकः।

ण्हाणावमुक्काहरणुच्चआए तरङ्गभङ्गक्खअमण्डणाए।
ओल्लंसुओल्लासितणुल्लआए सुन्देरसव्वस्समिमीअ दिट्ठी ॥ २८ ॥

26ª N °सोणु°. — A °जुगं. B °युजं, P °जुवं. — A लग्गायलग्गं. B भग्गा°, R लंबा°, STU लंबाल°. — T °कम्मं.

26ᵇ S अत्था°. — ABPWNORU °लंबिद°, S °लंबिय°. — N °पल्लअ°. — NR दोल्लंति, S बोल्लंति, U बोलंति.

26ᶜ ABPWNOR सिच°. — ABPWO °वसिदं, N °असिदं, R °वसिदा. — B तम्हाणकेलिट्ठिदो. — APWNORSU °ट्ठिदा.

26ᵈ ABPWRSTU आणीदा, NO आणिदा. — ABNORTU °ब्भुदेक्क°, P °ब्भदिक्क°, W °ब्भुदिक्क°, S °ब्भुदक्क°.

27ª N एक्कोण. — A निवेसिऊण.

27ᵇ A पोत्तिंचलं, PWOSTU वत्थंचलं, N पोत्तंचलअपि. — B घणघणक्कल°, N घणत्थणसंस°, S घणथणंथणसं°.

27ᶜ APWOR लिहिज्जदि, B लिहंज्जदि, N लिहज्जदि. — O व.

27ᵈ ANORSTU चंकमणादो, B चंकमणचल्लददो, P °णादे, W °णिदो. — AWNR चलिदं. B omits; P चडिदं, O वलिदं, S सिढिलं, T सिट्ठिलं, U सिढिलं. — B चडिल्लं, ST कठिल्लं, U णिअंबं.

28ª P तथा instead of विदू°. — B होणाविमुक्का°, N ह्लाणमुक्का, S °वमुक्का°. — ST °भरणु°, U °भलणु°. — STU °णुज्जलाए. — NR तरंगसंग°. — ABWNORSTU °क्खद°, P °क्खिद°.

28ᵇ APWOR उल्लंसुउल्लासि°, B दुल्लंसुउ°, N उल्लंग्नु°, SU °उल्लासि°. — A °तणुल्लदाए. B °घणुल्लणाए, P °घणुल्लआए, W °थणुल्लदाए, N °अगुक्कआए, OS °थणुक्लदाए, R °थणूलआए, TU °तणूलदाए. — AW °मिमोड, BR °मिमीए, ST °ममीए, U °मिमाए. — STU दिटं.

नायिका । सर्वानवलोक्य स्वगतम[1] । एसो महाराओ को वि इमिणा गम्भीरमहुरेण सोहासमुदएण जाणीअदि[2] । एसा वि एदस्स महादेवी तक्कीअदि[3] । अद्धणारीसरस्स वामद्धे अकधिदा वि गोरी मुणीअदि[4] । एसो वि जोईसरो[5] । एस उण परिअणो[6] । विचिन्त्य[7] । ता किं त्ति एदस्स दइदासहिदस्स वि दिट्ठी मं बहु मक्खेदि[8] । इति त्र्यस्रं वीक्षते[9] ।

राजा । विदूषकमपवार्य[10] ।

जं मुक्का सवणन्तरेण सहसा तिक्खा कडक्खच्छडा
भिङ्गाअड्ढिअकेअअग्गिमदलद्दोणीसरिच्छच्छवी ।

28[1] A स्वगतं चिंतयति.

28[2] APWSTU एस. — B °राय. — B इ-मया. — A गंभीरसाणेण, B रभीरमहुरसरस्स, O °महुर. — B मोह°. — PNORS °समुदाएण. — APNR जाणिज्जदि, B लक्खियदि, O लक्खीअदि, SU णिक्खिज्जइ. T मुणिज्जइ.

28[3–5] T omits. — B एसा य, R omits वि. — A एदस्स महारायस्स, B एतस्स. — O °देई, S °देवि त्ति, U देवि त्ति. — AS तक्केमि, P लक्खीयदि, W लच्छीयदि, N तक्खिअदि. — SU °णारीसरीरस्स; U adds हरस्स, ANOR add विअ after अद्ध°. — B विअमदेसु, O वामअद्धे. NR omit. — AB कहिया, PSU अकहिदा, WNOR अकहिआ. — W इ. — A गोरि व्वेव, SU देवी गोरी. — A जाणीज्जदि, PW मुणिज्जदि. NR मुणीअदि, O मुणिज्जदि, SU °ज्जइ. — A एसो को वि.

28[6] N सो एसो. — A omits उण. — B परि° एस एव परियणो.

28[7] A विचिंत्य नायिका, W omits.

28[8] AON त्ति, B च, WT omit. — B स-स्स. — PWNR महिला°, OSU दइआ°. — A °सचिहिदस्स, SU °सहिअस्स, T सहि-अस्स. — N omits वि. — A दिट्ठिणो, P दिट्ठा. — AB omit मं. — SU मक्खेइ. T मयोइ.

28[9] U omits. — A त्र्यस्तं, B त्र्यास्यं, P त्र्यंशं कटाक्षसहितं, NO तृत्यक्षं, R अक्षं, T त्र्यस्रं.

28[10] A विदू° प्रति, B °मवकार्यं. — BO add एदाए.

29[a] STU सवणंतरंमि. — A तरसा, NR तरला. — S कडच्छ°.

29[b] A भिंगाहिंठिद°, B भिंगाअड्डिद°, P भिंगाहिट्ठिद°, W भिंगाहिट्ठेद°, NR भिंगाअट्ठिद°, O भिंगाकड्ठिद°, S भिंगाअड्डिअ°, T भिंगावड्डिअ°, — ABPWSTU °केदअ°, N °केअग°. — B °सकच्छवी, W °सरिस्स°, NRS °कई, T °गलद्दोणीसरसकई.

तं कप्पूररसेण णं धवलिओ जोण्हाइ णं ण्हाविओ
मुत्ताणं घणरेणुण व्व छुरिओ जाओ म्हि एत्थन्तरे ॥ २९ ॥

तधेव[1]। अहो से रूवसोहा[2]।

मज्झे मज्झं तिवलिवलिअं डिम्भमुट्ठीअ गेज्झं
णो बाहूहिं रमणफलअं वेढिउं जाइ दोहिं।
णेत्तच्छेत्तं तरुणपसईदिज्जमाणोवमाणं
ता पच्चक्खं मह विलिहिउं जाइ एसा ण चित्ते ॥ ३० ॥

विदूषकः। कधं ण्हाणधोदविलेवणा वि समुत्तारिदभूसणा वि रमणिज्जा[1]। अध वा[2]।
रूवेण मुक्का वि विहूसअन्ति ताणं अलंकारवसेण सोहा।

29c STU ता. — NSTU °रएण. — ST णु. — ABPWOR धवलिदो, N धवलीदो. — W जुण्हावि, RTU जोण्हाअ, S जोण्हाए. — STU णु. — ABPWORT ण्हाविदो, N ह्णादो णादु आह्णए.

29d A °रेणुणि, B °रेणुय व्व, NSTU °रेणुणो. — ABPWNOR छुरिदो. — Mss. जादो. — A सि.

29[1] AU omit. — BR विदू° तधेव, PW विदूषकः तधेव राजा, N विदू°, O विद° तधेव्व. S तह अ. T तहेव्व.

29[2] A omits. — T omits अहो. — B उमोए, O इमोए, T एदाए. — WNOR रूअ°. — TU add पेक्ख.

30a AO मज्जं, B उज्जं. — A °वलिदं. B °वलयं. — A हिंभ°. — AW °मुट्ठीद, BNRU °मुट्ठीए. — A गिह्णं, B गिज्जं, O गेज्जं. S गज्झं, TU गेयहं.

30b A बाहाहिं, T वाहहिं. — U जहण°. — AT वेढ्ढिं. BNU वेढ्ढिदुं, PWO वेढिदुं. R वेठिदुं, S वेड्ढिउं दोहि जाइ, ABP WNR जादि.

30c N °क्खेत्तं, U °च्छत्तं. — BR तरुणि°. — T °पसदि°. — ABW °किज्जमा°, P °खिज्जमा°, N °दिज्जमाणावमाणं, O °दीअमाणोप°.

30d N पच्चक्खं. — ABPOS मम, W महि. — AORSTU विलिहिदुं, B °लिखिदुं, PN °लहिदुं, W सिहिदुं. — ABPW NOR जादि.

30[1] BPNOR omit विदू°. — P कथं, STU कहं. — P ण्हाणा°, T ण्हाअ°. — P °धाद°, N °धाविद°, OSTU °धोअ°, R धोविद°. — ANRSTU omit वि. — SU समवदारिअ°, T समोसारिअ°. — B °त्रिभूसणा, P °विभूसणा, NOR °विहूसणा.

30[2] BPWNORSTU अह. — SU व.

31a B मुक्का उविभूसिअरूवेयंति. — A रूवेण मुत्ताउ, PO णा रूवमुक्का, NR जे (R ते)

णिसग्गचङ्गस्स वि माणुसस्स सोहा समुम्मीलइ भूसणेहिं ॥ ३१ ॥

राजा । एदाए दाव एदं[1] । जदो[2] ।

लावण्णं णवजच्चकञ्चणणिहं णेत्ताण दीहत्तणं
कण्णेहिं खलिअं कवोलफलआ दोखण्डचन्दोवमा ।
एसा पञ्चसरेण कड्ढिअधणुद्दण्डेण रक्खिज्जए
जेणं सोसणमोहणप्पहुइणो विन्धन्ति मं मग्गणा ॥ ३२ ॥

विदूषकः । विहस्य[1] । जाणादि रच्छावादो लुम्बीसोडीरत्तणं[2] ।

राजा । विहस्य[3] । पिअवअस्स कधेमि दे[4] ।

रूअमुक्का. — A omits वि; N ण, STU हि. — PRSTU विभू°, W विहूसियंति, O वहूस°.

31b B °चंसग्गस्स. — STU ण instead of वि. — Mss. °मीलदि. — N भूसणाहिं, O भूसणेसुं.

31¹ B एयाए तत्तवेत्, P एदाए एदं रूवं दाव, W एदाए एव दाव, N एदए दाव एव्वं, O एदाए एदं दाव, STU एव्वं एदं एदाए दाव.

31² B यतः, STU omit.

32a N लाअंणं. — A °कंकणा°.

32b BW खलिदं, P थलिदं, O क्खुडिदं, N खडिदं, R खडिदं. — N कुओल°, RSU कओल°. — AU °फलिआ, NT °फलए. — AWO दोहंड°. — APWNR °चंडो°. — NST °पमा, O °प्पमा.

32c AW संधिद°, B कट्टिय°, PN सज्जिद°, O कड्ढिद°, R सज्जिद°, SU कस्सिअ°, — T रचअ°. — B °धणु°, PN °धणुदं°, ORT °धणूदं°. — NT रक्खिज्जई.

32d A तेणं, P जणं, T जाणं. — A सोसह°. — Mss. °प्पहुदिणो. — A विंधींद, B बंधंति, W विंधिंति, NRSU विन्धंति, O विज्जंति, T भिंदंति. — B मग्गणो.

32¹ A तथा एवं विहस्य, B एवं विहस्य, P तदा ततः एवं विहस्य, W एवं तदो विहस्य, N एषु एवं विहस्य, T omits.

32² A जाणेमि रथ्यासु लुंठदि तुह सोंडीरत्तणं, B जाणाइ रत्थाउलंबलुबीसोडीरत्तणं, P जाणादि य्येव रत्थासु तुह लुट्ठदि सोंडारत्तणं, W जाणेदि ज्जेव रक्कावाकाए (वा is cancelled) से लुट्ठिज्जइ सोंडीरत्तणं, N जाणे रक्कावादे तुह सोडिरत्तणं, O एव्वं जाणे रत्थाए पलोट्टदि ये सुंदेरत्तणं, R जाणे रक्कावादे तुह सोडीरत्तणं, SU जाणे रच्छावाएण तुह सुंदरं वक्खिदं सोंडीरत्तणं, T जाणे रच्छाव्वक्कअणेण वक्खिदं तुह सोंडीरत्तणं.

32³ AN omit.

32⁴ ABPNSTU कहेमि, O कहामि. — A से and adds सुणु, BO add सुण.

अङ्गं चङ्गं णिअगुणगणालंकिअं कामिणीणं
पच्छाअन्ती उण तणुसिरिं भाइ णेवच्छलच्छी।
इत्थं जाणं अवअवगआ का वि सुन्देरमुद्दा
मण्णे ताणं वलइअधणू णिच्चभिच्चो अणङ्गो ॥ ३३ ॥

अवि अ[1]। एदाए[2]।

तहा रमणवित्थरो जह ण ठाइ कञ्चीलआ
तहा सिहिणतुङ्गिमा जह णिएइ णाहिं ण हु।
तहा णअणवड्ढिमा जह ण किं पि कण्णुप्पलं
तहा अ मुहमुज्जलं दुससिणी जहा पुण्णिमा ॥ ३४ ॥

देवी। अज्ज कविञ्जल पुच्छिअ जाण का एस त्ति[1]।

विदूषकः। तां प्रति[2]। एहि मुद्धमुहि उववि सिअ णिवेदेहि का तुमं ति[3]।

देवी। आसणं इमाए[4]।

33a N °गुणागुणालं°. — ABPWNORSU °किदं, T °किंअं.

33b P संत्थायंदी, W सछायंती, SU गुच्छाअंती, T पच्चाअंती. — APWO omit उण; BN पुण. — APWO तणुगुण°. — AB ठादि, PWNOR भादि, SU ठाइ.

33c B इछं. — N अवजव°, T णावयन°. — Mss. °गदा. — N कापि. — T दुंदेर°.

33d ANR वलइद°, BW वलइव°, T वलयि°, U वलइय°. — O °मिच्छो, T °भुच्चो.

33[1] W अचं च, B omits अ.

33[2] N omits.

34a N रमहारमणा°. — AB °विछरो. — BW ठादि, O ठाइ, SU माइ. — BPWOR °लदा, N °लंदा, T कंचालआ.

34b BW सिहण°, R सिणिह°, STU अ थण°. — ABPRSU ण एइ, N ण एद, O णिरेइ. — A लहु, NRSU मुहं.

34c B णायणिवड्टिनीं जह णं, T जह ज ण. — STU वि.

34d B तह. — A दुससिणी, N दुसोतणी.

34[1] A देवी कपिंजलमाह अज्ज कविंजण, STU कइंजल. — T पुछिवु. — S जाणक्न, T जावणाम, U जाक्स. — T एसे.

34[2] BNR अथ वा, O अह वा instead of विदूषकः. — A तामाह, W अथ तां प्रति, S वि° होदु तां प्रति, T वि° होदु २ अहं जंव्व पुच्छिस्सं तां प्रति, U वि° होदु २ तां प्रति.

34[3] WU उप°. — STU °विस. — A णिवेदोहि, B णिविदेहि.

34[4] A विभ्रमलेखा, P वि°, BT omit देवी;

विदूषकः । एदं मे उत्तरीअं[5]।

विदूषकनायिके वस्त्रदानोपवेशने नाटयतः[6]

विदूषकः । संपदं कधीअदु[7]।

नायिका । अत्थि एत्थ दक्खिणावधे कुन्तलेसुं सअलजणवल्लहो वल्लहराओ णाम राआ[8]।

देवी । स्वगतम्[9]। जो मह मादुच्छओ भोदि[10]।

नायिका । तस्स घरिणी ससिप्पहा णाम[11]।

देवी । स्वगतम्[12]। सा वि मे मादुच्छिआ[13]।

नायिका । विहस्य[14]। तेहिं अहं खलखण्डेहिं किणिदा दुहिद त्ति वुच्चामि[15]।

देवी । स्वगतम्[16]। ण हु ससिप्पहागब्भुप्पत्तिं अन्तरेण ईदिसी रूवसो-

---

NR राआ, O विच°. — ABWORS इमोह, P इमोय, U अमोए.

34[5] T omits विदू°. — A एतत् ममोपरिधानवस्त्रमेव, B एवं मे उ°, W ता पुच्छिय जाणिस्सं एदं मे उ°, U इदं. — NR add आसणं.

34[6] A ततः विदूषकनायिकौ, B नायका, P विदूषको नायिकाया, T देवीविदू°. — B °वेशनं, P वस्त्रदानं, S °वेशं. — BP नाटयति. — W adds नायका उपविशति.

34[7] AP विभ°, SU राजा instead of विदू°. — B संपयं. — APWNR कहिज्जदु, BO कहीअदु, S कहिज्जइ, T कहिज्जइ, U कहिज्जउ. — W adds का तुमं ति.

34[8] B अत्था इह. — AP omit ए° द°; B दक्खिणापहे, W °वहे, N वत्सोमणामणअरं, OR वच्छोमं णाम णअरं instead of दक्खि°; SU omit द°; T °पहे. — ANSU °लेसु, B °लेशो, P °लेषुसु, O तहिं कुंतलेसो, T ज्वेंदलेसरो. — N omits वल्लहराओ.

34[9] A ततो राज्ञी, P राज्ञी, T omits. — A स्वगतं चिंतयति.

34[10] AWO माउ°, B भाउछंउ, P माउत्थउ, N माउसिओ, R माउस्सिओ, T मे मातुओ. — A होई, B होउ, PWNOR होइ, STU omit.

34[11] BW घरणी, N गहिणी. — A ससिप्पिहा, N ससिपहा णाम देई.

34[12] AP विभ°, B omits; N राज्ञी. — P omits स्व°.

34[13] W वि हु, T पि. — A मम मच्छिया होई, BWOS माउ°, P माउट्ठआ, NR माउस्सिआ, T माउसीआ, U माउसिच्छिआ.

34[14] A विहस्याह, T omits.

34[15] STU omit अहं. — B °खंडेहि, W °ऋखंडेण, O खलि°, NR खडि°, SU केलि°, T कलकंटेहिं. — A किदा, BP WOR कीदा, N omits, T कीडाविदा. — A दुहि, NRSTU दुहिदे, O दुहिदु. — A मुच्चामि, N वुझ्झामि, SU उच्चामि, T omits.

हा[17]। ण हु विडूरभूमिं अन्तरेण वेरुलिअमणिसलाआ णिप्पज्जदि[18]।

प्रकाशम[19]। णं तुमं कप्पूरमञ्जरी[20]।

नायिका अधोमुखी तिष्ठति[21]

देवी। एहि बहिणिए आलिङ्गसु मं[22]। इति परिष्वजते[23]।

नायिका। अम्महे कप्पूरमञ्जरीए एसो पढमो पणामो[24]।

देवी। अज्ज मए भेरवाणन्द तुज्झ पसाएण अपुव्वं संविहाणअं अणुभविदं बहिणिआए दंसणेण[25]। ता चिट्ठदु दाव पञ्चदस दिवसाइं[26]। पच्छा झाणविमाणेण पुणो णइस्सध[27]।

34[17] BW हि, P खु, O ह, T omits. — B सिस°, T °प्पभा. — A °गब्भोप्प°, B °एप्पुप्प°, P °गब्भुउप्प°, W °गब्भमंतरेण. — B omits ईदिसा- °भूमिं अन्तरेण. — A इदिसा, STU ईरिसी. — A रूपरेहा, P रूअरेहा, WNOR रूअ°, SU सोहा. — NR add भोदि.

34[18] W णो. — P हु खु, W वा, O ह. STU हि. — A विदुर°, PO विदूर°, W विडूरभूमिगब्भुप्पत्तिमंतरेण, NR वेरु- (R °डु°)लिअभूमिगब्भुप्पत्तिमंतरेण. — B वेरुहिय°, P विडूरयिलाया, O. वेदूरिअ°, R वेडुलिअ°, SU वेडूरिआ°, T वेडूरीआ°, — AO °मणिसिला. — PW णिप्पज्जंति, SU उप्पज्जइ, T णिप्पज्जइ.

34[20] BO omit णं; P न, T ण ह, U ण हु. — B तुवं, P तु, NR तुअं. — A °ञरित्ति.

34[21] W अहोमुही चिट्ठदि, NR लज्जते अधो°, T अधोमुखं.

34[22] AP विभ्रमलेखा, V SU omit देवी. — B एहि २. — APO बहिणि, B बहिणिया, S भगिणि, T भद्दणि, U भद्दणी. — N आलिंगःस, R °गेसु, S °गेमि omits मं; TU °ग.

34[23] AP इत्युत्थाय. — W परिष्वजेते, U परिष्वजति.

34[24] A omits. — BN अम्मो, P अंब, W अम्ह, O अम्महे. R अज्जे, S अंके, TU omit. — W एस कप्पू°. — B सो. S एस. — BP पढम, R पठमो, S पुढमो, T पुटमो, U पुढमो.

34[25] A omits देवी-संविहाणअं. — P विभ्र°, U omits. — T अम्मए instead of अज्ज मए. — O अद्द° मए, S मे भेर°, B भेरवाणंदा, N °णंदप्पसाएण, R °णंदप्पसादेण. — O तुज्झ, S तुम्ह, U तुह. — B पसाए, S प्पसादेण, T पसादेण तुह. U omits. — PW अउव्वं. — P विहाणं, STU °हाणं. — A अनुभूतं, O अणुहूदे. — AP बहिणी, B बहिणआए, NR कप्पूरमंजरी, SU भइणिआ, T भइणीए.

34[26] BNR omit ता; O ता एवा. — S चिट्ठउ. — B चवि, O दाव. — ABPWO पंचसत्त, S पंचहाइ, TU °दहाइ. — AP दियहा. B दिवहा, WO दिवहाइं, NR दिअहाइं. SU दिअहाइ, T दीअमाइं.

34[27] B ज्जाणविवाखे. P झाणविमाणेण, O माण°. SU झाणेण. — P उणो. N पु-

भेरवानन्दः । जं भणादि देवी[28] ।

विदूषकः । राजानमुद्दिश्य[29] । भो अम्हे परं दुवे वि बाहिरा तुमं अहं च[30] । जदो एदाणं मिलिदं कुडुम्बं वट्टदि[31] । जदो इमाओ दुवे वि बहिणिआओ[32] । भेरवाणन्दो उण एदाणं संजोअअरो अग्घिदो महग्घिदो अ[33] । एसा वि महीदलसरस्सदी कुट्टिणी देहन्तरेण देवी जेव[34] ।

देवी । विअक्खणे णिअजेट्ठबहिणिअं सुलक्खणं भणिअ भेरवाणन्दस्स हिअइच्छिदा सवज्जा कादव्वा[35] ।

णो वि, R omits. — A णायस्सध. B बहस्स, N णोःसध, SU °स्सह, T णाइः-सदि.

34[28] A भे° वददि जा जेण यह्नणादि, P भणा, WT भणदि, S भणाइ. — TU दे°भ°.

34[29] B omits विदू°. — A °नमुद्दिश्याह.

34[30] WTU omit भो, NR भो वअस्स, T व-अस्स. — A अह्म, S अह्मे खु. — P पुरं, W परं इत्थ. — A दुवे corrected to दुवो; B दुए, P दवे व. — A बाहि. N बहिए, S वाहिआओ, T वाहिआ राजा, U बाहि । रा ।. — S omits तुमं अहं च. — BW तुवं, O तुअं. — OTU अ. — NR एत्थ instead of तुमं अहं च.

34[31] AW कुडंबं, B कुटंबं, P कुटं, N कुदुंबं, T कुठुंबंअं, U कुडुंबअं. — STU वट्टइ.

34[32] B यदो, W omits. — AWNORSU इमोओ. P अमोतुं, T एदो. — AWO दो वि, B दा वि, P दो व, T दुवे दुवे, U omits वि. — A बहिणी, B वहणीया, P वेहिणीतु, O वहिणीओ, SU भइणीओ, T बहिणीओ.

34[33] A omits उण; P पुनः एतयो, N एदाए, TU ताणं. — A संजोग°, B संजोयरो. — ABPWSU अग्घिदो. — A महाअग्घिदो, BPW महग्घिदो, N माणिदो, O मग्घिदो, R मणिदो, S महाविदो. TU omit. — T omits अ.

34[34] T विदू° एसा. — A omits वि; W वियखणा, U पि. — A महियल°, BWNOR STU °अल°, P °तल°. — Mss. °सरस्सई; NR add अ. — A कुट्टिणि, R कुदणी, T संभली अ. — B omits देहन्त°-जेव; W transposes देवी ज्जेव देहंतरेण. — A कुट्टिणी instead of देवी. — A ज्जेव, P य्येव, NR जेव्व, O ज्जाव्व, STU एव्व. — W adds वट्टदि.

34[35] A विभ°विचक्षणामाह, P विभ°. — A °हिणीं, B °बहिणिअए, P °हिणीयं, W °वहिणिय, N °हिणीअ, O °बहिणिआए, S °हिणिं, T °भअणिं, U °भइणिं. — B सुलक्खणाए, P सुल्लक्खणं, O सुलक्खणाए. — B भणियं, P भणिया, W भणीय. — N भेरवाणंद. — A हिययट्ठिदा, B °इच्छिया, POR हिअअट्ठिआ, N हिअट्ठिदा, SU हिअअच्छिआ, T omits. — A पुज्जा, P सपुज्जा, WNR सपज्जा, S पूआ, T अभज्जा. — ASU काअव्वा, B कदेव्वा.

विचक्षणा । जं देवी आणवेदि[36] ।

देवी । राजानं प्रति[37] । अज्जउत्त पेसेहि मं जेण अहं बहिणिआए एदावत्थाए णेवच्छलच्छीलीलाणिमित्तं अन्तेउरं गमिस्सं[38] ।

राजा । जुज्जदि चम्पअलदाए कत्थूरिआकप्पूरेहिं आलवालपूरणं[39] ।

नेपथ्ये[40]

वैतालिकयोरेकः । सुहाअ संझा भोदु देवस्स[41] ।

एअं वासरजीवपिण्डसरिसं चण्डंसुणो मण्डलं
　को जाणाइ कहिं पि संपइ गअं पत्तम्मि कालन्तरे ।
जाआ किं च इअं पि दीहविरहं सोऊण णाहे गए
　मुच्छामुद्दिअलोअणा व्व णलिणी मीलन्तपङ्केरुहा ॥ ३५ ॥

34[36] BSTU omit. — A देवि. O आ° दे°. — A adds त्ति भैरवानंदेन सह निष्क्रांता विचक्षणा, P adds इति निःक्रांता भैरवानंदेन सह, W adds तं कुणेमि, O adds तं कुणामि.

34[37] AP राज्ञो, BWSTU omit. — A राजानमाह.

34[38] A त्त अज्ज°. — B पडिउंजसु, NR पेसिहि, O पडिणोउंजसु. — U omits मं. — ABP जेणाहं, W omits अहं, STU omit जेण अहं. — AP बहिणीए, W वहिणीए, O बहिणीआ, S भइणिआए. T भअणिआए, U बहिणिएआ. — B यदावत्थाए, N °वच्छाए. — NT °लच्छि°, O omits °लच्छी°. — A अंगेउरं गमिस्सि.

34[39] B तुज्झइ, O जुज्जइ एवं, STU जुज्जइ. — B चंपइ°, OT पंचअ°, U चंपइअ°, N चंपलादाए, ST °लआए. — A कक्कूरिया°, W °कप्पूररसेहिं, NU कत्थूरीआ°, T कत्थूरीकप्पूरेहि. — PNR °परिपूरणं.

34[41] A °रेकः प्राह, P वैतालिको. — A सुह संझा, B °संज्झा, P only सुन्झा, WS सुहसंझा, O सुहा संझा, U सुसंझा. — OSTU होदु. — O adds जदो.

35[a] Mss. एदं. — BNORT °जोअ°. — A चंदंसुणो.

35[b] ABPWNORT जाणादि. — S कहिं षु, TU वि. — ABPWNOR संपदि गदं. T संपडि. — O पत्तेम्मि.

35[c] Mss. जादा. — A इसं. — ST वि. — B °विरहे, NR °विरहा. — B सोऊण, W सोउण, NR सोएण, O णाऊण, T सोहेण. — B णाधे. — ABPWNOR गदे.

35[d] BWNOR णिद्दा°. — BNR °मुद्दिद°. — NSTU °लोअणो. — B त्य ण° मीलंति°, NU मीलत्त°.

द्वितीय ।

उग्घाडिज्जन्ति लीलामणिमअवलहीचित्तभित्तीणिवेसा
पल्लङ्का किंकरीहिं उडुसमअसुहा पत्थरिज्जन्ति झत्ति ।
सेरन्धीलोलहत्थङ्गुलिचलणवसा पट्टसद्दो पअट्टो
हुंकारो मण्डवेसुं विलसइ महुरो रुट्ठतुट्ठङ्गणाणं ॥ ३६ ॥

राजा । अम्हे वि संझं वन्दिदुं गमिस्सामो[1] ।

इति निष्क्रान्ताः सर्वे[2] ।

प्रथमं जवनिकान्तरम्[3] ।

36a A द्वि° वैतालिकः, P omits द्वि°; W द्वि° पठति. — B उग्घाडं । जंति, N उग्घाडिअंति, R उग्घाडीअंति, TU उग्घाटि°. — O °वडही°. — B चित्तभित्तीणवेशा, W °चित्ति°, N °भित्ति°.

36b SU किंकरेहिं. — BW उड°, ORSU उदु°, N रअसमअ°, T टदु°. — P °सुहा. — A पक्खरिअंति, B पंकुरिज्जंति, N पक्खरिज्जंति, T पत्थरिज्झंति, U पत्त°. — A झत्ति.

36c A छेलंधोगंधहत्थ°, T सेलंधोलोहत्थांगुली°. — S °चलस°. — BO पट्टवादो, W पट्टसदो, N पट्टनादो, R पदवादो, SU वट्टआदो, T वट्टअदो. — STU पवट्टो.

36d S टंकारो, T झुंकारो, U संकारो. — B मंडएसुं. P मंडपेसुं, NR मंडलेसुं, O मंदिरेसुं, STU मंडणेसुं. — Mss. विलसदि. — A मधुरो, SU मुहलो, T मुहरो. — R तुट्ठरुट्ठं°, S रुट्ठतुट्ठं.

36[1] O ता अम्हे. — B सज्झां, O सं. — TU पविसामो.

36[2] ABOS इति परिक्रम्य नि°.

36[3] N इति प्र°. — PWSTU यवनिकांतरं.

ततः प्रविशति राजा प्रतिहारी च[1]

प्रतिहारी । परिक्रामितकेन[2]। इदो इदो एदु महाराओ[3]।

राजा । कतिचित्पदानि गत्वा तामनुसंधाय[4]। तहिं खु अवसरे[5]

ण ट्ठाणाहि तिलन्तरं पि चलिआ सुत्था णिअबत्थली
थोउव्वेल्लवलीतरङ्गमुअरं कण्ठो तिरिच्छि ट्ठिओ।
वेणीए उण आणणेन्दुभमणे लद्धं घणालिङ्गणं
जाआ तीअ चउव्विहा तणुलआ तंसं पुलन्तीअ मं॥ १ ॥

प्रतिहारी । स्वगतम्[1]। कधं अज्ज वि सो ज्जेव सिरितालीपत्तसंचओ ताओ ज्जेव अक्खरपंतीओ[2]। ता वसन्तवण्णणेण सिढिलआमि से त-

---

0[1] C श्री ॥ ततः. — BWRSU प्रतीहारी.

0[2] BO omit प्रति°. — PWOST परि° प्रति°. — C परिक्रम्य, NU omit.

0[3] NOR इदो once only. — BCS omit एदु; T एत्थ, U एव्व.

0[4] BN omit राजा. — N कानिचित्पदानि. — BW दत्वा. — B तामनुसध्याय । तां स्मत्वा, U तामनुध्याय.

0[5] B तहिं खलु, OR जं तस्सिं क्खु, N क्खु

1[a] C अठ्ठाणाहि, W णो ठाणाहिं. — B लंतरं, C तलंतरं. — BSU चि, T omits. — BCPWNOR चलिदा. — P सथा, SU वुड्ढा, T उट्टा.

1[b] B धोउन्विल्लवलतरंगमुदिरं, CT थोओवेल्ल°, W थोउव्विल°. — CPWOR °मुदरं. — B तिरिछ्कु, C तिरित्थ, P तिरत्थो W तिरित्थो. NOR तिरिच्छ SU तिरच्छि. T चिरच्छि. — B ट्ठिदो, CPNOR ट्ठिदो, W ठिदो.

1[c] B णाणणांदुघडणो, W °भमणे, N °घलणो. — C लभ्भत्थणा°, N लद्धत्थणालिं°.

1[d] BCPWNOR जादा. — BN तीए, C तीइ, W तीइं. — B सतरंगमुदरंधउविहा, N चउव्विध, R चउव्विआ, T चउ त्थणविहा. — BCPWNORT °लदा. — B तिस्सं. C नंसं, R तस. STU तिंस. — BCPWOR चलंतो, N चलन्तो, SU पुलंतीए, T पुलत्य. — B मयो, CPW मयि, N समं. OR मए, T मई.

1[1] N omits; S आ, U आत्मगतं.

1[2] BO कथं. STU कहं. — B चेत, CP चेव, W च्चेच, N जेव्व, OSU च्चेअ, R च्चेअ,

ग्गदं आवेसं[3]। प्रकाशम[4]। दिट्ठिं देदु महाराओ ईसीसिजरढाअमाखे कुसुमाअरे[5]।

मूलाहिंतो परहुअवहूकण्ठमुद्दं दलन्ता
देन्ता दीहं महुरिमगुणं जम्पिए छप्पआणं।
संचारेन्ता विरहिसु णवं पञ्चमं राअराअं
राउम्मत्ता रइकुलघरा वासरा वित्थरन्ति ॥ २ ॥

राजा। तदनाकर्ण्य सानुरागम[1]।

अत्थाणीजणलोअणाण बहला लावण्णकल्लोलिणी
णाणाविब्भमहासवासणअरी सोहग्गपालित्तिआ।
णेत्तेन्दीवरदीहिआ मह पुणो सिङ्गारसंजीविणी
जं जाआ अह वम्महेण धणुहे तिक्खो सरो पुङ्खिओ ॥ ३ ॥

T असो च्चिअ. — B ताडिस्संचतु, C ताडिस्सचउ, P सिरताडसंचउ, W सिरिताडीसंचउ, N सिरित्तालिसंचअ, OR ताहिसंचओ, S सिरिंताल°, TU °तालि°. — N ता. — BN च्चिअ, COR व्विअ, P चेव, W च्चेव, S च्चेअ, T विअ, U चेअ.

1[3] B ता त्रि धसंतयस्सणेण, O °वम्हणेण. — B सिढिलयाइम्मि, C सिठल°, P सित्थिल°, N सिल°, SU सिढिलेम्मि, T सि:ढिलेम्मि. — NT omit से. — B तदग्ग. STU तग्गअं. — B reads हिदआग्रज्जं and omits all that follows as far as सा रयणामयी iv. 19[65]; C हिययखेवं, P हिययदुक्खं, WSTU माणसं, N तग्गदमावेसं, OR हिअआवेसं.

1[5] CWNORS देउ. — C ईसीस, T ईसिस. — CPORU जरठा°, N जरठ्ठा°, T जरग्गअ°. — C कुसुमायुरंम्मि, PWNSU °माअरंम्मि.

2[a] W परहुद°. — P °बहु°. — T °कंटमुहदलंतो.

2[b] C दिंतो, NS दंता. — CP दीहिं. — S महिरिम°. — SU जप्पिए, T जप्पये. — N छप्पिआणं.

2[c] C सिंचरिंता, PRS °रंता. — CW सिंचिरायं, NOR किंचराअं.

2[d] C राउमत्ता, P राओमत्ता. — CP °हरं, WO °हरा, R °हए, U °घरं. — N वस्सारा. — C विछरंति, N वित्थरति.

2[1] CP omit राजा. — COR तदाकर्ण्य, P तदेतदाक°, N तदेवाक°. — W पुनस्तामनुसंधाय सा°, S omits सा°.

3[a] C अछाणी°, N अत्थाणा°. — PTU बहुला. — PNU लाअण्ण°.

3[b] CWOR लीलाविब्भ°, SU °विब्भमभंगि°. — C °णयरा. — S सोभग्ग°. — C °पालट्ठिया, P °पालिध्धया, W °पालिट्ठिया, N°पारिछिआ, OR°पालंकिआ, SU °लित्तआ.

3[c] PS णेत्तं°, NU णत्तें°, T णेंतिं°. — PSTU पुरो, N उणो. — P °संजीवणी, N सिंगासंजीअणी.

3[d] CPWNORT जादा. — P हअ, N तह.

सोन्मादमिव[1]। दंसणक्खणादो पहुदि कुरङ्गच्छी[2]

चित्ते पहुट्टइ ण खुट्टइ सा गुणेसुं
सेज्जाइ लोट्टइ विसट्टइ दिंमुहेसुं।
बोलम्मि वट्टइ पअट्टइ कव्वबन्धे
झाणे ण तुट्टइ चिरं तरुणी तरट्टी ॥ ४ ॥

अवि अ[1]।

जे तीअ तिक्खचलचक्खुतिहाअदिट्ठा
ते कामचन्दमहुपञ्चममारणिज्जा।
जेसुं पुणो णिवडिआ सअला वि दिट्ठी
वट्टन्ति ते तिलजलञ्जलिदाणजोग्गा ॥ ५ ॥

सस्मरणमिव[1]। अवि अ[2]।

— CWNORU मम्महेण. — STU धणुए. — CWN संधिदो, POR पुंखिदो.

3[2] C दंसणलक्खणादो, W °क्खणादो कुरंगच्छीए, S सा कु°.

4[a] C वदुट्टदि, P वहुट्टदि, W वहुट्टदि, N विलुट्टदि, O विहुट्टदि, R चिहुदादि. — CNOR खुट्टदि, P घुट्टिदि, W हुट्ठदि, SU तुट्टइ, T दुट्टइ. — CNU गुणेसु.

4[b] P सज्जइ, NSTU सेज्जासु. — CPW लुट्टदि, NOR लोट्टदि. — CWNO विसट्टदि, P विसप्पद्धि, R विसदाट्टि, T विसप्पइ. — CNORTU °मुहेसु.

4[c] CPWNO वट्टदि, R वददि. — CPWNOR पअट्टदि, SU एव°, T विवट्टइ.

4[d] CR जाणे, S झाणेसु, U जाणेनु. — SU omit ण. — CWOS तुट्टदि, P तुटदि, N तट्टदि, R ठोदादि, T दुट्टइ, U तिट्टइ. — OR तलुणी. — W तरुणी.

4[1] CW omit. — SU अवि अ पोणात्थणीए, T पणात्थणाए.

5[a] W तोइ, SU तीए, T तअ. — T °तिभाअदिग्ग, U °तिआअ°.

5[b] O °चंदमहुपुंचम°. — STU °वाहणिज्जा.

5[c] The line in P twice. — C जेसं, P जेसुं and जेसि, W जेसिं, N जिसु. — C णिपडिया, PWNOR °दा. — P सुपुणो and सयला. — N ं च, S अ instead of वि.

5[d] C वट्टंदि. — W °दाणु°.

5[1, 2] U omits. — C संस्मरं। अवि य, P अपि च। सस्मरणं. WN संस्म°. — PORST omit इव. — OR omit अवि अ.

अग्गम्मि भिङ्गसरणी णअणाण तीए
 मज्झे पुणो कढिअदुद्धतरङ्गमाला ।
पच्छा अ से सरइ तंसणिरिक्खिएसुं
 आअण्णकुण्डलिअचावहरो अणङ्गो ॥ ६ ॥

विचिन्त्य[1] । चिराअदि वअस्सो[2] ।

प्रविश्य विदूषको विचक्षणा च परिक्रामतः[3]

विदूषकः । अइ विअक्खणे सव्वं सच्चं एदं[4] ।

विचक्षणा । सव्वं सच्चदरं[5] ।

विदूषकः । णाहं पत्तिआमि जदो परिहाससीला खु तुमं[6] ।

विचक्षणा । अज्ज मा एवं भण[7] । अण्णो बब्बरकालो अण्णो कज्जविआरकालो[8] ।

विदूषकः । पुरो ऽवलोक्य[9] । एसो पिअवअस्सो हंसो विअ मुक्कमाणसो करी

6[a] U omits verse 6. — C मग्गम्मि. — N भिंग°. — C णअणाण.

6[b] ST उणो. — C कचिद°, P गेढिद°, WO कढिद°, NR कठिद°, S घटिटदुस्सरंग°, T घटोअ°. — N °तरंअ°.

6[c] C पच्छा इ दे. — ST omit से. — CPW NOR सरदि, ST संचरइ तिंस°. — C °निरीक्खिदेसुं, PWNORS °देसुं, T °देसु.

6[d] CPWN °मंडलिद°, OR °कुंडलिद°. — NOR °धरो.

6[1] C omits, W वि° विदूषकं प्रति.

6[2] C omits. — P चिरयदि, WOR चिरअदि, N कधं चिरअअदि प्पिअवअःस्सो.

6[3] C विदूषकः प्रविश्य विदूषको, OR वि° प्र°, STU ततः प्रविशति. — PSTU omit परि°.

6[4] W अय, TU अवि. — NO सच्चं सच्चं, STU omit सच्चं. — PW add कप्पूरमंजरीए महाराय (P °जे°) संनिहं (W °हिदा) पेसिदा (P °या) तुमं त्ति (W omits त्ति).

6[5] N सच्चं. — CP सच्चतरं, WORSTU °अरं.

6[6] C अहो वियक्खणे नाहं, P णो हं. — C पदिज्जामि, P पत्यिज्जामि, W पत्तिज्जामि, N पडिवज्जेमि, OR पत्तिज्जामि, SU पच्चेमि, T पतिअमि अदो. — W °लीला. — N क्खु, OR सि, CSTU omit. — C omits तुमं; W तुवं.

6[7] PSTU ए° मा. — W एवं, NORSTU एव्वं.

6[8] C चक्कोराकालो, and omits the rest; PWRS वब्बर°, N वब्बरत्तिकालो, O व-ब्बर°, TU वब्बकालो. — P कज्जावदार°, W कज्जावयार°, N कज्जकालो, SU क-ज्जालाव°, T कज्जलाह°.

6[9] OR पुरतो. — WOR विलोक्य.

विअ मअक्खामो मुणालदण्डो विअ घणघम्ममिलाणो दिणदि-
सदीवो विअ विअलिदच्छाओ पभादपुण्णिमाचन्दो विअ पण्डुर-
परिक्खीणो चिट्ठदि[10] ।

उभौ । परिक्रम्य[11] । जअदु जअदु महाराओ[12] ।

राजा । वअस्स कधं पुणो वि विअक्खणाए मिलिदो सि[13] ।

विदूषकः । अज्ज विअक्खणा मए सह संधिं कादुं आअदा[14] । किदसं-
धीए ताए सह मन्तअन्तस्स एत्तिआ वेला लग्गा[15] ।

राजा । संधिकरणस्स किं फलं[16] ।

विदूषकः । एसा अहिमदजणप्पेसिदलेहहत्था जं विअक्खणा आअदा[17] ।

राजा । गन्धं सूचयित्वा[18] । केदईकुसुमगन्धो विअ[19] ।

6[10] P सस. — T omits हंसो, P विअ. — CSTU मद°, W मयजल°. — C मुणा-ण°, P मुणालिया°, T विणाल:. — W व्व, T वि. — N °मलिणो, S घम्ममिलाअमाणो. — COR °दीओ, P °दीवउ, N नदिणादिओ, T °दिओ. — S omits विअ. — C विअलित°, PWNOR विअलिअ°, SU विलुलिअ°, T लुलिअछावो. — C पभाय°, P पहाय°, N प्पहाद°, SU पहादसमअपु°, T पभादसमअपु°. — C अपंडुरपरिक्खाणो, S परिक्खामो, TU °परिक्खामो. — STU चिट्ठइ.

6[11] C तत उभे, PNOR उभे. — C परिक्रामत:, PW परि° उपसृत्य च.

6[12] O जअदु once only. R जअ once only, SU जेदु once only, T जेदु २.

6[13] C राजा । को सि instead of this sentence. — P omits राजा. — U भो वअस्स. — PSU कहं, WN कहिं, T कह. — PN पुणा, S उणा, U पुरा. — PWNSTU omit वि. — N अोलदो.

6[14] CORSTU omit अज्ज. — STU omit सह. — N कादुकामा. — CW °गदा.

6[15] OR किअ°. — CO समं तोए, PN इमोए, W एदाए, R तोए समं मंतंस्स. — C मं° मम. — W एदा. — ST गआ, U गदा.

6[16] C राजा तं पत्तीसि. — W °कारणस्स, N °कलाणस्स, T °कलणस्स.

6[17] N omits. — CSTU अभि°. — CW °पेसिदा°, OR °पेसिआ°, ST °पेसिअ°. — R omits जं वि°. — C वियक्ख. Here ends fol. 2; fol. 3 is wanting; fol. 4 begins विओए see ii. 9[c]. — W वियक्खणागदा.

6[18] N omits, STU omit गं° सू°.

6[19] POSU केअई°, N केअइ°, T केअर°. — N adds आअछदि, OR आआदि.

विचक्खणा । केदईदललेहो एसो मह हत्थे[20] ।

राजा । महुसमए कधं केदईकुसुमं[21] ।

विचक्खणा । भेरवाणन्ददिस्समन्तप्पहावेण देवीए भवणुज्जाणे केदईलट्ठीए एक्को दाव पसवो दंसिदो[22] । तस्स दलसंपुडेहिं अज्ज हिन्दोलअप्पभञ्जणीए चदुत्थीए हरवल्लहा देवी देवीए अच्चिदा[23] । अण्णं च दलसंपुडजुअलं उण कण्णिट्ठबहिणिआए कप्पूरमञ्जरीए पसादीकिदं[24] । ताए वि एक्केण दलसंपुडेण भअवदी गोरी जेव अच्चिदा[25] । अण्णं च[26]

केअईकुसुमपत्तसंपुडं पाहुडं तुह सहीअ पेसिअं ।
एणणाहिमसिवण्णसोहिणा जं सिलोअजुअलेण लञ्छिअं ॥ ७ ॥

6[20] P only Sanskrit. — N केअइ॰, OR केद(O ॰अ॰)ईकुसुमदललेहो ज्जेव्व, STU केअईकुसुमलेहो. — NSTU omit एसो. — W adds चिट्ठदि.

6[21] P म॰ व हु कहिं, WOR म॰ किं. N म॰ कुदो, STU कहं म॰. — ST add वि. — PORSU केअई॰, N केअइ॰, T केअर॰. — PW ॰कुसमं, N ॰माईं

6[22] W ॰विस्सस्स॰ instead of ॰दिस्स॰, STU omit. — P ॰तंतप्पभावेण, W ॰तंतप्पहाएण. OR ॰प्पहाएण. — NO देवी, R देई. — O भमणुज्जाणे. — PNOR SU केअई॰, W केअइ॰, T केअर॰. — P क्को. — STU omit दाव. — P एसवो. OR पसओ. — SU दंसिओ.

6[23] N तस्स वि, OR ताए; PN add तीए. — PW दोहिं दल॰. — N अज्जुतए, ST omit. — P हिंदोलण॰, W हिंडोलयपभंजणी, N ॰लप्पवचणीए, O हिंदोलण, R हिंडोलण, S हिंदोलांअंपअट्टमाणाए, T हिं...अंपउट्टमाणाए, U अंदोलिअम्मि पअट्टमाणाए. — PWORT चउत्थीए, N चउत्थिए, SU चउद्दहीए. — W ॰वल्लहाए. — STU omit देवी. — W देवीए देवी. — POR omit देवीए.

6[24] TU अ. — ORS ॰जुअं, SU केअईकुसुमसंपुड॰, T केअरकुसुमदलसंपुट॰. — PW पुण, STU omit. — N कणिठ्ठाए बहिणीआए, ST ॰भइणीए, U ॰बहिणीए. — S पदसादी॰. — PW ॰कदं.

6[25] PWNOR तीए, TU तए. — N omits वि-खरपवण see ii. 14[b]. — U omits वि. — O भवअदी, SU ॰वई. — OR गोरि. — P य्येव, W च्चेव, OR ज्जेव्व, STU omit.

7[a] PWR केदई॰, O केदद्री॰, T केअर॰. — WR ॰कुसम॰, ST ॰कुसुमसंपुडं, S adds ताए, TU तए. — P पाहडं, OR पाहुअं तुअ. — P सहीइ, W सहीए, STU समीवे. — P जं कदं, WORSTU पेसिदं.

7[b] P तं, T णं. — STU सुलोअ॰. — PW OR लंछिदं, T लंभिअं.

इति लेखमर्पयति[1]

राजा । प्रसार्य वाचयति[2] ।

हंसिं कुङ्कुमपङ्कपिञ्जरतणुं काऊण जं वञ्चिओ
तब्भत्ता किल चक्कवाअघरिणी एस त्ति मण्णन्तओ ।
एअं तं मह दुक्कअं परिणअं दुक्खाण सिक्खावणं
एक्कत्थो वि ण जासि जेण विसअं दिट्ठित्तिहाअस्स वि ॥ ८ ॥

द्विस्त्रिर्वाचयित्वा[1] । एदाइं ताइं सवणरसाअणाइं अक्खराइं[2] ।

विचक्षणा । दुदिओ उण मए पिअसहीए अवत्थाणिवेदओ कदुअ सिलोओ लिहिदो एत्थ[3] ।

राजा । वाचयति[4] ।

सह दिअहणिसाहिं दीहरा सासदण्डा
सह मणिवलएहिं बाहधारा गलन्ति ।
तुह सुहअ विओए तीअ उब्बिग्गिरीए
सह अ तणुलआए दुब्बला जीविआसा ॥ ९ ॥

विचक्षणा । एत्थ ज्जेव एदाए अवत्थाए मह महल्लबहिणिआए सुल-

7[1] W लेखं समर्पयति.

7[2] STU राजा गृहीत्वोद्वेष्ट्य वाचयति.

8[a] P हंसी. — P °तणं. — PWOR वंचिदो.

8[b] SU °भट्टा, T लब्भटा. — W °घरणी, R चक्कवालचरिणि. — S एसे.

8[c] Mss. एदं, S तं एदं. — T मम. — PW OR दुक्किदं, S दुक्किअं. — PORSTU °णादं, W °णिदं. — S °वअं, TU °पअं.

8[d] OR विसए. — PW दिट्ठी°. — P °महायस्स but below °तिहागस्स, W °तहायस्स, OR °तिहाआण (R °णं), S °त्तिआअस्स, T °भागस्स, U °भाअस्स.

8[1] W राजा द्विस्त्रि वाचयता विदूषकः, O राजा द्वि°, STU इति द्वि° वाचयति.

8[2] T एताइं. — STU omit ताइं. — PW OR मअणरसाअणक्खराइं.

8[3] POR दुदीओ, W दुविउ, T उदीवो. — SU मए उण. — P कडुय. — W सिलउ, SU सुलोओ. — W लिहिदा.

9[a] S एसह. — W दिवस्स°. — T दिहणीसास°, O °दंडो, S सा.

9[b] OS °वलएहि, T मणीवलयेहिं.

9[c] ORSU सुहअ तुह. — PW विउए. — C तोइ, WSU तीए, T तिए. — C उब्बंबरीए, P व्विंबरीए, W उव्विंविरीए, O उच्चिंविरीए corrected to उच्चेइंरीए, R उव्विवरीए, SU उत्तम्भिरीए, T उत्तमलीए.

9[d] CPWORTU °ल्दाए. — CPWORT जीविदासा.

क्खणाए ओलग्गाविआए भविअ सिलोओ किदो तं महाराओ सुणादु[1]।

णीसासा हारलट्ठीसरिसपसरणा चन्दणुच्छोडकारी
चण्डो देहस्स दाहो सुमरणसरणा हाससोहा मुहम्मि।
अङ्गाणं पण्डुभावो दिअहससिकलाकोमलो किं च तीए
णिच्चं बाहप्पवाहा तुह सुहअ कए होन्ति कुल्लाहि तुल्ला॥ १०॥

राजा । निश्वस्य[1]। किं भणीअदि कइत्तणेण तुह जेट्ठबहिणिआ खु एसा[2]।

विदूषकः । एसा विअक्खणा महीदलसरस्सदी[3]। एदाए वि जेट्ठबहिणिआ तिहुवणसरस्सदी[4]। ता एदाहिं समं पाडिसिद्धिं ण करिस्सं[5]।

9[1] C वि° पुनराह, POR वि° विहस्य. — WOR इह. — P य्येव, OR ज्जेव्व, STU एव्व. — CPSTU omit एदाए. — C वल्लहबहिणीयाए, P जिट्ठबहिणी-याए, OR जेट्ठवहि°, STU वसंतरबहि-णीआए (T °भडअणीए, U °बहिणीए). — C ओलग्गविया, P ओलग्गवियाए, W उलग्गभवीया, O उल°, R उग्गाविआए, S ओलग्गिआए, T आदेसंकरणीए. — OR हुविअ. — CW सिलोगो, STU सु°. — C कुदो, PWO कदो, SU कओ. — C सुणोदु. P सुणादु, W सुणेदु. — STU सु°म°. — OR add पठति.

10[a] S णीस्सासा. — C हारवल्लीसरसियसरणा, W °जट्ठीसरिसपसवणा, O °ससरिस°, SU हारवल्ली°. — C चंदणोच्चाट°, P चंद-णुघोड°, ORSTU चंदणुव्वेअ°. — STU °आरी.

10[b] PO चंदो. — C सुमरणासरसा, W समर°, U सुमरविसरणा.

10[c] W °भाउ. — CP दिवस°. — S °करा°. — WSU °कोमला. — W किं चि.

10[d] C निभच्चा, P निदि च्चा, T णीव. — C बाहवाहा, P वाहचाहा. — R तअ. — STU सु° तुह. — CPWO कदे, ST किए. — O हिंहोति. — W कु-ल्लाइ, OR कुल्लाअ.

10[1] C निःश्वस्याह, PW निःश्वस्य.

10[2] CRT भणइ, PWOSU भणइ. — CP कवित्तणे, W सुकयत्तणेण, OR सुकइत्तणेण, T कइत्तणेणावि; SU add वि. — OR तुअ. — C °बहिणीया, W °विहिणिया, S °भइणी, TU जेट्ठा बहिणी. — COR omit खु. — CPSTU सा.

10[3] STU omit एसा. — COR महिअल°, PWSTU महीअल°. — Mss. here and in the following line °सरस्सई.

10[4] S दाए, T एव्व एव्व एदाए. — CSTU omit वि; W उण. — C °बहिणीया, PW °बहिणी, STU °भइणी सुलक्खणा. — CPWR तिहुअण°, O तिहूअणसर-स्सइ adds त्ति, R adds त्ति.

10[5] OR एआहिं. STU एदाए समं. — T प-डि°. — P °सिट्ठि.

किं उण पिअवअस्सस्स पुरदो मअणाअल्लअं अत्तणो उड्डेहिं अक्खरेहिं णिवेदेमि[6]।

विचक्खणा। पढ[7]। एदं सुणीअदि[8]।

विदूषकः।

परं जोण्हा उण्हा गरलसरिसो चन्दणरसो
खअक्खारो हारो रअणिपवणा देहतवणा।
मुणाली बाणाली जलइ अ जलद्दा तणुलआ
वरिट्ठा जं दिट्ठा कमलवअणा सा सुणअणा ॥ ११ ॥

राजा। वअस्स तुमं पि थोएण चन्दणरसेण समालम्भणीओ सि[1]। ता कधेहि तग्गदं कं पि वुत्तन्तं[2]। अध अन्तेउरं णइअ देवीए किं किदं तिस्सा[3]।

विदूषकः। विअक्खणे किं किदं[4]।

10[6] CPW पुण. — C वयस्सस्स, P °वस्सस्स, WR °वअस्स. — CSU omit पुरदो. — C मयणालसस्स अवत्थं, P मयणालसस्स, WOR मअणावत्थं (O °त्थअं), SU म° उद्दिसिअ. — C अप्पणो. — CORT उच्चिदेहिं, P उच्चिदेहि, W उच्चिदेहं. — C अक्खरपंतीहिं णिवेदेहि, P अक्खरेहिं अवत्थं किं पि णिवेदयेमि.

10[7, 8] U omits, C राजा. — PW पढइ, RS पढ. — P एद, ST एव्वं संपदं.

11[a] ST वि° पठति, U विच° पठति. — T धरं. — W omits उण्हा.

11[b] CPW खरं खारो, ORST खद°, U मद°.

11[c] C मुलाणा. — OR जलदि. — CP व. — CPWORT °लदा.

11[d] C मदा दिठ्ठिठ्ठाखं सरसममहोजअलतणुए. — STU तणिट्ठा जं दिट्ठा क° दीहणअणा.

11[1] C राजा तमाह. — OR णं instead of वअस्स. — PW ता तुमं, OR तुअं. — ST वि. — C य त्थोवेण, W थोवेण, TU थोयेण, S omits. — WOR °रसेण य. — CW समालिहिज्जसि, P °लहिज्जसि, OR °लहिस्ससि, S °लंभणिज्जो सि, T समलंभणीओ सि, U °लिसो सि.

11[2] CW कहसु, P काधसि, O कहेहि. RSTU कहेहि. — C तग्गतं, O तगादे, STU तग्गअं. — CPWORSU किं. — STU वि. — C वित्तं, PW वत्तं. T उत्तंतं.

11[3] P अज्ज, SU अह, T अह अ. — CW अंतेउरे. — C तीए देवीए. — CPR कदं, O कदे. — C सुंदरीए, SU तिस्स.

11[4] PU omit. — C विदू° विचक्खणामाह। वि° कधहि किं. — COR कदं. —

विचक्खणा । देव मज्जिदा टिक्किदा भूसिदा तोसिदा अ[5]।

राजा । कधं विअ[6]।

विचक्खणा ।

घणमुव्वट्टिअमङ्गं कुङ्कुमरसपङ्कपिञ्जरं तिस्सा ।

राजा ।

रोसाणिअं फुडं ता कञ्चणपञ्चालिआरूवं ॥ १२ ॥

विचक्खणा ।

मरगअमञ्जीरजुअं चलणा से लम्भिआ वअंसीहिं ।

राजा ।

भमिअमहोमुहपङ्कअजुअलं ता भमरमालाहिं ॥ १३ ॥

विचक्खणा ।

राअसुअपिच्छणीलं पट्टंसुअजुअलअं णिअत्था सा ।

राजा ।

कअलीअ कन्दली ता दरपवणपणोल्लिअदलग्गा ॥ १४ ॥

OR add कहेहि, T adds त्ति देव्वो विचारेदि.

11[5] C विचक्खणा राजानमाह. — WS omit देव; OR देव्व, T देअ. — CPWOR मंडिदा, T मंजिदा टक्किदा भूमिदा. — P omits तोसिदा; S दो, U दोसिदा. — C omits अ.

11[6] C राजा तामाह. — CP कथं, STU कहं. — P omits विअ; W वियक्खणो.

12[a] W omits विच°. — P °व्वट्टिद°, W °व्वट्ठिद°, O °च्चदिद°, R °व्वदिद°, S खणमुव्वत्तिअ°, U °व्वत्तिद°. — CSU omit °पंक°. — S °पंकिलंकिदं, T °पिंअले, U °पिंगिदंकिदं. — CS तिस्स.

12[b] C अथेति श्रुत्वा राजाह. — T उज्जलंकिदं. — C कुडं, P फुटं, OR परं, T पुडं. — U दा. — C कंचणमियबालियारूपं, PW कंचणमयबालियारूवं, OR °मअवालिआएतंरूवं, U °रुव्वं. — Read कञ्चणबाउल्लिआरूवं?

13[a] C5 °युयं, T मरंगअरंजोरेहिं. — WORSTU चरणा. — PT लंभिअ. — CSTU वअस्सीहिं, P वेयंसीहि, OR वअस्साहिं.

13[b] SU °पंकज°. — C भमलमालाहिं, WOR °मालाए.

14[a] C पुनर्विचक्षणा । रायसूय°. — WS °पिंछ°. — P °जयलक. — C णियछा, PSTU पिणद्धा, OR णिवसिआ.

14[b] CPWOR कअलीए, S ता राजकेलि, T कदलीए, U राअकेलि. — W कंदलया, SU कदली, T कंदलि. — SU omit ता. — CPWOR खरपवण°. — OR °पलोल्लिअ°, N begins here again ल्लोलिअग्गिमदला. — U adds सा.

विचक्षणा ।

तीए णिअम्बफलए णिवेसिआ पोम्मराअमणिकञ्ची ।

राजा ।

कञ्चणसेलसिलाए ता बरिही कारिओ णट्टं ॥ १५ ॥

विचक्षणा ।

दिण्णा वलआवलीउ करकमलपओट्ठणालजुअलम्मि ।

राजा ।

ता भणह किं ण रेहइ विवरीअं मअणतोणीरं ॥ १६ ॥

विचक्षणा ।

कण्ठम्मि तीअ ठविओ छम्मासिअमोत्तिआण वरहारो ।

राजा ।

सेवइ ता पंतीहिं मुहअन्दं तारआणिअरो ॥ १७ ॥

विचक्षणा ।

उहएसुँ वि सवणेसुं णिवेसिअं रअणकुण्डलजुअं से ।

राजा ।

ता वअणवम्महरहो दोहि वि चक्केहि चङ्कमिओ ॥ १८ ॥

15ª C पुनर्विचक्षणा. — P ताए. — N णिअंबलफ°. — C °फलहे. — N णिएसिआ. — CN पम्म°, PORSTU पंम्र°, W पोम°.

15ᵇ CW ब° ता, PWN बरहो, STU बहिणो. — NRS णच्चं, O णच्चे.

16ª C पुनर्विचक्षणा. — P दिण्णायो रयणावलयावलीओ तिस्सा पउट्ठदंडेसु. — CW वलयालीओ (W °लिउ), NOR °आवलिओ, S °आवरओ, T वलिआवलीवो, U °लीओ. — COR °पउट्ठ°, W °पउठ°.

16ᵇ C भरियं तूणीरजुयलं सरेहिं ता मणयदेवस्स ॥ १६ ॥ त भभणह . . . , P ता भामियमयणसरा दिट्ठा सुतोणीरुबंधजुया, ST ता भाविअमअणसराहिंडिअतूणीरवद्धभुआ, U ता भाविअमअणसरापूरिअतूणीरवद्धभुजा. — WN भण. — W किं न हि, N किं णु हु. — C सोहइ, N रेहद विपरीअं, O तिवरीअं. — NR °तूणीरं, O °तूणिरं.

17ª CWNORST तीए, U ए. — W ठविदो, N ठ़ठविदा, T टाविओ. — C सम्मासिय°, W छम्मासय°, N छमासिअं°.

17ᵇ STU ता से°. — C मुहइंदुं, W °चंदं. — C तारिया°.

18ª N विदू. — C उभयेसुं, P उभएसु, W उहएस, N उहए, OR °सु, S अह दोसुं, T विहवेसुं, U अवहेसुं. — CSTU omit वि. — N कंणेसु, T सवणेसु. — C णिवेसिदं रयणाकुंडलं तीए. — W °कुंडलु°. — T °जुअलं से.

18ᵇ W तो — WNRU °मम्मह°. — CNORS

विअक्खणा ।

अच्छञ्जणजणिअपसाहणाइँ तीए कआइँ णअणाइं ।

राजा ।

ता उप्पिउ णवकुवलअसिलीमुहो पञ्चबाणस्स ॥ १९ ॥

विअक्खणा ।

कुडिलालआण माला णिडाललेहग्गसङ्गिणी रइआ ।

राजा ।

ता ससिबिम्बस्सोवरि वट्टइ मज्झाउ सारङ्गो ॥ २० ॥

विअक्खणा ।

घणसारतारणअणाइ गूढकुसुमुच्चओ चिहुरभारो ।

राजा ।

ससिराहुमल्लजुज्झं ता दंसिअमेणणअणाए ॥ २१ ॥

विअक्खणा ।

इअ देवीअ जहिच्छं पसाहणेहिं पसाहिआ कुमरी ।

TU दोहिं. — N विअ, STU omit वि. — CWNORT चक्केहिं. — CW °मिदो. N °मिल. T चकलीओ.

19ª C अछंजणपसाहणाइं P जच्चजणाणियपसहणाइं. N अंऊणाजणिदप्पसाहणानि, OR °जणिद°, SU अच्छंजणाजणिअपसाहणमणहारिणी. T अच्छंजणिअपसाहणमणहारिणी. — C जायाइं तीए, P जायाइं तीय, N आअंइ तीए. — STU omit क°.

19ᵇ NOR omit ता. — C उप्पिय, P उप्पंत्ति, WO उप्पणो, N उप्पुंखिआ, R उप्पंणो, STU कुप्पइ. — C णवकुलयसिलीमुहमुह, P णच्चकुवलयसिलीमुहे, W णयकुवलयसिलिम्मुहे, NOR °मुहे, U णवकुलअ°.

20 U omits.

20ª C कुंडिला°, P कुटिला°, T कुडिलाअलआण. — C णिहाल°, PW णलाड°, T णिललेंहग्गसंगीणी. — WOR °लोलग्ग°, N °फलअग्ग°. — W रईया.

20ᵇ C तं. — O वट्टइ, ST चिट्ठइ. — CO मज्जाउ, P वज्झाइ, N omits; S मज्झाइ, T मज्झहिणो. — NOR कसणसारंगो.

21ª N omits विच°. — CORTU °णअणाए, W घणसारमंजरीए, N °णआअणाए, S °तारअणा. — C फुल्लेहिं रंविओ, P °सुमुच्चईउ, W रुठकुसुमुच्चउ, N °कुसुमुक्करो, OR णिगूढकुसुमोच्चओ, S गुंभिअकुसुमंचिदो, TU गम्भकुसुमंचिदो. — P विउर°, O चिठुर°, NSTU चिउर°.

21ᵇ CN °जुज्जं, O °जुजुं SU °जुद्धं. — C विय, P व, W वं, NOR omit; T तं. — CPN दंसिअं ए°, W दंसिदं ए°, OR पदंसिअं ए°, TU दंसिद°.

22 T omits.

22ª PS इय. — CPNORSU देवीए, W

राजा ।

ता केलिकाणणमही विहूसिआ सुरहिलच्छीए ॥ २२ ॥

विदूषकः । देव इदं परमत्थं णिवेदीअदि[1] ।

जिस्सा दिट्ठी सरलधवला कज्जलं तीअ जोग्गं
जा वित्थिण्णत्थणकलसिणी रेहए तीअ हारो ।
चक्काआरे रमणफलए को वि कञ्चीभरट्टो
जिस्सा तिस्सा पुणु अ भणिमो भूसणं दूसणं च ॥ २३ ॥

राजा । पुनस्तामनुसंधाय[1] ।

तिवलिवलिअणाहीबाहुमूलेसु लग्गं
थणकलसणिअम्बाडम्बरेसूससन्तं ।
जलणिविडमिमीए लग्गहअं ण्हाणपोत्तं
पिसुणइ तणुलट्ठीलच्छिमं चङ्गिमं च ॥ २४ ॥

देवीए. — C अहित्थं, P अहित्थिय, W अहिछिय, N अहित्थकप्पसा°, R प-साअणेहिं, SU पसाहणपसाहिआ. — C NOSU कुमारी. — SU add सा.

22b S विभूसिआ, U विभूसिदा. — C °लच्छी-णं. S सुरभि°, U कुसुमलच्छीए.

22[1] C विदूषको राजानमाह, WS विचक्षणा. — SU omit देव. — COR एदं, U इमं. — C परत्थ. — P खिवेदियदि, WOR विण्णवीअदि, N विंणविअदि, STU णिवेदेमि.

23a C जासा, OR जेस्सा, S जाए, U जस्सा. — COR सअलधवला, P सरवा°, WTU तरल°. — CW तीए, STU तीए.

23b C कठठिचायणाकलसिणी, W विछिय°, N विच्छिण्णाथणअलससिरी, SU °अलसिणी. — C सोहए, N सोअए, T रोहए. — CW तीए, SU तीए, T तिए हारो.

23c STU °री. — POR °फलके, N अमण-फलए, STU °फलओ. — W °रमट्टो, O कंचीरठो.

23d CNSU जस्सा. — U तस्सा. — CPOR पुण, NSU उण. — CW पभणिमो, P पत्तणिमो, N पि भणिमो. — C व्व, PN अ, SU वा.

23[1] C राजा कर्पूरमंजरीमनुसंधायाह. — NS omit पुनस्.

24a N °ललिअ°, ORS °वलअ°, U °वणअ°. — W °मूलंमि.

24b C घण°. — NST °अलस°. — T °णि-अंबाढुंबरे. — W °रेसूससंभं, N °रेसूसव-सत्तं, OR °रेसूस्स°, S °संति, T ऊससंतं.

24c P °णिवड°, TU °णिबिड°. — STU °ममीए. — W णायहयं, OR लग्गहअं, SU लग्गअं, T सीदसव्वालं. — ORSTU °वत्थं.

24d CPWNOR पिसुणादि. — WORT °स-

विदूषकः । सक्रोधमिव[1] । भो मए सव्वालंकारालंकिदा वण्णिदा[2] । तुमं उण जलविलुत्तप्पसाहणं जेव सुमरसि[3] । ता किं ण सुदं देवेण[4] ।
णिसग्गचङ्गस्स वि माणुसस्स सोहा समुम्मीलइ भूसणेहिं ।
मणीण जच्चाण वि हीरएहिं विहूसणे लग्गइ का वि लच्छी ॥ २५ ॥
राजा ।

मुद्धाण णाम हिअआइ हरन्ति हन्त
णेवच्छकम्मणगुणेण णिअम्बिणीओ ।
छेआ पुणो पअइचङ्गिमभावणिज्जा
दक्खारसो ण महुरिज्जइ सक्कराए ॥ २६ ॥

विचक्खणा । जधा देवेण आदिट्ठं[1] ।

थोराणं थणआणँ कसकलिआलङ्घीणँ अच्छीणँ वा

छो°, U °जट्ठो°. — COR °चंगिमं लंगिमं च, P °चंगीमत्तं लहुत्तं, N °लग्गिमं चंगिमं च, SU °लग्गिमं तुग्गिमं च, T °लंगिमं तुंगिमं च.

24[1] T omits विदू°. — C सक्रोधमाह.

24[2] T भो वअस्स. — STU मए सा तरट्ठी. — C सब्बालंकिदा, P सव्वालंकिदा, W सव्वालंकिदा, N सव्वालंकारसहिदा, OR सव्वाभरणालंकिदा. — W विण्णिदा.

24[3] N तुअं. — CPW पुण. — C °लुत्तसोहणा. P गहाणविलुत्तपसाहियं S °लुलिअप°, T जललुलिअपसाणा, U °लुलिआ°. — CW ज्जेव. P य्येव, NR जेव्व. O ज्जेव्व. S omits; TU गव्व. — W समरिसि. N लुमरसि; P adds से.

24[4] T सुणिदं.

25[a] N रिगमग्गचंगस्स हि. — Mss. °मीलदि.

25[b] N मणीण मुत्ताण. — P °एहि. W वि कंचणेण, N विहूमणेहिं, OR वहो°, STU वि हीरएहिं. — CWSU विभूसणे, R विदूसस्से. T विदूसणे. — CN लग्गदि, W लब्भदि, OR सज्जदि, T लंभइ. — N लल्ली.

26[a] C राजाह, U omits राजा. — P मुद्धाण. — CPWOR °आइं, N हिंअआंइ. — N णिहंति, STU हरंतु.

26[b] C नेत्रत्थ°. — PWN °कप्पण°. — T °उणेण.

26[c] T छेल्ला. — STU उणो. — N पकिइ°, STU पकिदि°. — CU °चंगम°, — N °हारणिज्जा. S °हावणिज्जा.

26[d] CNOR °रिज्जदि, PW °रज्जदि. — T सक्खरेहिं.

26[1] STU जह. — C निद्दिट्ठं, PNOR देवेणादि°, W दिट्ठं.

27[a] CW थोयाणं. — Mss. °आण. — Mss. °लंघोण (P °लंघोण). — Mss. अच्छीण. — N व. O च R अं.

भूचन्दस्स मुहस्स कन्तिसरिआसोत्तस्स गत्तस्स अ।
को णेवच्छकलाइ किज्जइ गुणो जं तं पि सव्वं पिअं
सुव्वन्तं सुण तत्थ कारणमिणं रूढीअ का खण्डणा॥ २७॥

राजा। अवि अ सुप्पञ्जल कविञ्जल एस सिक्खावीअसि[1]।
किं कज्जं कित्तिमेणं विरअणविहिणा सो णाडीणं विडब्बो
तं चङ्गं जं णिअङ्गं जणमणहरणं तेण सीमन्तिणीओ।
जस्सिं सव्वङ्गसङ्गो सअलगुणगणो सो अ संभोअलम्भो
तस्सिं णेच्छन्ति काले परमसुहअरे किं पि णेवच्छलच्छिं॥ २८॥

विचक्षणा। देव इदं विसवीअदि[1]। ण केवलं देवीए णिओएण ताए

27[b] SU किंति°. — O °ओत्तस्स. — CW गत्तस्स वि, S आ.

27[c] C णेवत्थकलाहि, NORSU °लाए, T °ला-स. — C किज्जदि, P किज्जद्, WOR कीरदि, N करिआदि, T कज्जइ. — ST वि. — O सच्च पिअं.

27[d] CN सच्चंतं, P सव्वंतं, W सुत्तव्वं, OR संजुत्तं, SU णेवच्छं, T वोचंतं. — COR पुण, NST सुणु, U किल. — C तस्स. — P कारणमिद, WSTU °णमिमं, N °णमिमा, STU काल°. — C रुठ्ठीइ, PW रुढीइ, SU रुढीए. — C खंडला.

27[1] CPSTU omit राजा. — WN omit अवि अ. — CP सुपंजल. WOR सुपिंजल. N सुप्पजल. STU सुप्पज्ज. — C STU कइंजल, OR कपिंजल. — STU omit एस. — C तक्खवीयसे. P सिक्खवीअसि, WOR सिक्खवी°, N सिक्खावि°, S सुसि°.

28[a] CS कत्तिमेणं. NOT °मेण. U °माणं. — P विरयिण°. — N विलंबो.

28[b] CPW जं चंगं तं, O जं चंगं तं जं. — WNOR णिसम्मं. - R omits °मण°. — CT सीमंतणीओ, W तेणीउ.

28[c] T स जस्सिं. — W सव्वंगचंगो. — C °गणा, STU वसइ गुणगणो (T °अणो). — CPWNOR दंभीअलंभो, T °लंवो.

28[d] P नेत्थंति. S णेवच्छकाले. — C °सुहपरे. — S का. — ST वि. — N णेपछ°. — T °लछो.

28[1] CPSTU omit विचक्षणा. — C किं चि देव. P किं च देव, W omits देव; STU अखं च देव. — C अेदं परमत्थं. P इदं च. N एदं च. O एदं, R एव्वं. — C निवेदीयदि. O विणविअदि.

अणुगद म्हि[2]। तारामेत्तीए वि सहित्तणं पत्ता कप्पूरमञ्जरीए[3]। तेण तक्कज्जसज्जा अहं पुणो ओलग्गाविआ भविस्सं[4]।

तिस्सा तावपरिक्खणाअ णिहिओ हत्थो थणुच्छङ्गओ
दाहुड्डामरिओ सहीहि बहुसो हेलाइ वाड्डिज्जइ।
किं तेणावि इमं णिसामअ गिरं संतोसिणिं तासिणिं
हत्थच्छत्तणिवारिएन्दुकिरणा बोलेइ सा जामिणिं॥ २९॥

कज्जसेसं कविञ्जलो णिवेदइस्सदि[1]। तं च तधा कादव्वं[2]।

इति परिक्रम्य निष्क्रामति[3]

राजा। वअस्स किं उण तं कज्जसेसं[4]।

28[2] C देवोनोएसेण, PW देवोणियमेण, OR देव्रोए वअणेण णिअमेण, S देवोए णिवोएण, T देवोअक्खाए, U देवोए विओएण. — CWNOR तिस्सा, P तस्सा.

28[3] P तारामेलाए, W तारयमित्तोए, N °मोत्तिए. — P तोए वि, N उण वि, OR उण, TU omit वि. — C हसित्तणं, TU पिंअसहि°. — W उवगदा. — OR omit कप्पूर°.

28[4] C omits तेण; U देण अ. — CT °सज्जाहं. — PN पुणो वि, SU omit; T उण. — C ओलगविया, PW उलग्गा°, S ओलंगआ. — P हविस्सं पुणो सुणोदु, N भविअ णिवेदइस्सं, OR भविअ भणिस्सं, S भणिस्सं.

29[a] N त:सा. — NOR दाव°, STU दाह°. — CT °परिक्खिणाअ, P °णाइ, O °णास्य, R °णत्थ. — C णिहिओ, P तिहिदो, WNORSTU णिहिदो. — C त्थणु°, SU तणु°. — CPWT °त्थंगदो, NORSU °च्छंगदो.

29[b] NOR डाहु°, T डाउ°. — COR °डुामरिदो, P °दाहुम्मरिदो, W °डामरिदो, N °डापकिदो. — C सहीहि, POR सहीहिं. — C हेलाई, P हेलाइं, NSU हेलाए, T हेलाअ. — C कठ्ठिज्जए, P कड्डिज्जए, WN °दि, OR कठ्ठिज्जदि.

29[c] TU देणावि. — N ण्टिसामअ omits गिरं. — CP संतोसवित्तासणि, W संतोसणं तासणिं, N संतोसविद्वेसिणीं, S संतोसणं तासहं, T संतोसिणीं ता.

29[d] C °वारिदिंदु°, P °वारेदंदु°, WNRU °वारिंदेंदु°, OT °वारिदेदु°. — PORTU वोलेइ, N वोल्लेइ. — C जामणिं, W जामिणं.

29[1] C अथ तक्कज्जसेसं, P अणं च क°. — PWOR कविंजलओ, STU कइंजलो. — C णिवेदिस्सदि, N णिवेदस्सदि.

29[2] P omits. — N इदं च, S तं एव्व. — C देवेण कट्टव्वं, WOR तए का°, N देवेण तधा का°, SU तह का°, T तहा का°.

29[3] C परिक्रम्य निष्क्रांता विचक्षणा, N °क्रमति, ST °क्रांता.

29[4] CPW राजा सरभसमुपसृत्य विदूषकं प्रति

विदूषकः । अज्ज हिन्दोलअचदुत्थी[5] । तहिं देवीए पुरदो कप्पूरमञ्जरी हिन्दोलए आरोविदव्वा[6] । ता मरगदपुञ्जट्ठिदेण देवेण कप्पूरमञ्जरी हिन्दोलअन्ती दट्ठव्वा[7] । एदं तं कज्जसेसं[8] ।

राजा । विचिन्त्य[9] । ता अदिक्खिणउत्ता वि छलिदा देवी[10] ।

विदूषकः । पाइदा जुण्णमज्जारिआ कञ्जिअं दुद्धं ति तक्केमि[11] ।

राजा । को अण्णो तुम्हाहिंतो मह कज्जसज्जो[12] । को अण्णो चन्दाहिंतो समुद्दवड्ढणविअड्ढो[13] ।

इति परिक्रम्य कदलीगृहप्रवेशं नाटयतः[14]

(C प्रत्याह, P omits वि° प्रति). — CWSU omit वअस्स; P भो वयस्स. — CPO पुण. — U omits तं. — C तक्कज्जस्स सेसं.

29[5] C भो अज्ज. — CW °चउत्थीए, P हिंडोलणचउत्थी, NR हिंदोलचउत्थी, O हिंदोलणचउत्थी, S °चउद्दहि त्ति. T हिंदोलचउद्दसी, U हिंदोलचउद्दहि त्ति. — C adds गोरी अच्चिदव्वा.

29[6] C तदो, P तेहिं, OR तत्थ, STU omit. — C omits देवीए; P देवीए गोरी, W गोरिं कदुअ देवीए, N देविए. — CPW NOR omit पुरदो. — P omits कप्पू°. —P हिंडोलए, O हिंडोलअं, RU हिंदोलअं, T हिंदोलिअं. — P आरोवदित्था, W आरोद्दव्वा, N आरोहिदव्वा, T आरोपइदव्वा, U आरोपिदव्वा.

29[7] CWNRU मरगअ°, P मरमय°, O मरगए°, S मरगआ°, T मरअज°. — P °पुंजेट्ठिदेण, W °पुजिट्ठदेण ज्जेव. N °पुलिट्ठिदेण. — S omits देवेण. — P हिंडोलयं, W हिंदोवालयंती. NS हिंदोलंती, OR हिंदोलए हिंदोलंती. — P दट्ठव्वा.

29[9] OR omit. N omits राजा.

29[10] PSTU omit ता. — CPWNST अद°, U गद्द°. — U omits वि. — SU दे° छ°. — W छल्लिदा सा, T चलिआ, U छलिआ.

29[11] WNO omit विदू°; R विद°. — W NORS पाइआ, T विदू ता अदक्खिणउत्ता वि देवी वंचिआ पाइदा. — C जुण्णमंजरी, P °मंजरी, W जुण्णमंजारिया, ST जिण्ण°, U जिज्जमाज्जारिआ. — CPW NSTU omit कंजिअं. — CPWNS तक्क. R तक्केमि.

29[12] C राजाह, W विदूषकं प्रति instead of राजा. — CW वयस्स को, S को उण. — C तुह्याहिंता, P तुमाहिंतो, OR °हिंतो, T तुम्हाहिंदो. — C अण्ण, W मे. TU कज्जसज्जो (T °सेवो) अण्णाणं.

29[13] OR जदो को. — ST चंदाहिंदो, U चंदादो. — C °वढ्ढणे तिविहको, P °वड्ढयातचिढो. W °वट्ठयातयिाट्ठो, N °वढ्ढदणे दिळ्ळो, O °वड्ढणयिाट्ठो but या is in the margin corrected to णदि: R °वळ्ळायायिाळ्ळो. T °वट्टयाविअड्ढो.

29[14] C परिक्रम्य कदलीनां गृहप्रवेसं. — N प्रवेशे. — WT नाटयति.

विदूषकः । इअं उत्तुङ्गा फलिहमणिवेदिआ[15] । ता इध उववि‌सदु वअस्सो[16] ।

राजा तथा करोति[17]

विदूषकः । हस्तमुद्यम्य[18] । भो दीसदु पुण्णिमाचन्दो[19] ।

राजा । विलोक्य[20] । अहो दोलाहिरूढाए मह वल्लहाए वअणं पुण्णिमाचन्दो त्ति णिह्रिसदि[21] । सम्यगवलोक्य[22] ।

विच्छाअन्तो णअररमणीमण्डलस्साणणाइं
  विच्छोलन्तो गअणकुहरं कन्तिजोण्हाजलेण ।
पेच्छन्तीणं हिअअणिहिअं णिद्दलन्तो अ दप्पं
  दोलालीलासरलतरलो दीसए से मुहेन्दू ॥ ३० ॥

अवि अ[1] ।

29[15] P जोगा इयमुत्तंगा, ORT omit इअं. — W अच्चुत्तमा, N उत्तुंग, OR जुग्गा अच्चुतुंग, ST तुंग, U omits. — C फलिकमणिवेदिका, P फलह°, NTU फलिअ°, O फडिअ° in the margin corrected to फलिह°, S °फलअ. — U °वेदो.

29[16] STU omit ता. — CPWNOR इह, STU एत्थ. — CP महाराओ, NOR पिअवअस्सो.

29[17] STU तथा कुरुतः.

29[18] T हस्तमुद्दिश्य. — C adds वक्ति.

29[19] C भो वयस्स, S भो भो, T एसो. — CN दीसदि, STU दीसइ. — CW °इंदो, PNOR °अंदो.

29[20] C वि° स्वगतं चिंतयति, PW वि° स्वगतं.

29[21] CW अइ, P अज्ज, NO अए, R आए, S तीए. — CPT दोलाधि°, WNOR दोलारू°, SU डोलाहिरूढाए कप्पूरमंजरीए, T मह कप्पूरमंजरीए. — C °इंदु, P °चंदं, W °इंद, N °अंदो. — P त्ति, N omits. — C निहिसीयदि, N णिदिस्सादि, S णिवेदीअदि, T णिह्रिसति, U णिह्रीसइ.

29[22] C समस्तमवलोक्य प्रकाशं वक्ति, PNO समंतादवलोक्य. — P adds प्रकाशं.

30[a] U विच्छाणंतो. — W नयणरमणीमंडलसा°, O °रमणि°, R omits णअर°—अ दप्पं.

30[b] C विक्कालंतो, P वित्थोलंतो, W विक्कालिंतो, N पक्कालंतो, U विच्छेलंतो. — T °कुहलं. — P °जलेणं, N °उलेण.

30[c] P पित्थतीणं, STU पेच्छंताणं. — Mss. °णिहिदं. — T णिहलं रूअदप्पं.

30[d] SU डोला°. — U °सरस°. — S °तरला. — W सोमदे. — P ण इ.

उच्चेहिं चामरेहिं धवलधअवडाडम्बरिल्लावलीहिं
घण्टाहिं विन्दुरिल्लासुरतरुणिविमाणाणुसारं लहन्ती।
पाआरं लङ्घअन्ती कुणइ रअवसा उण्णमन्ती णमन्ती
एन्ती जन्ती अ दोला जणमणहरणं बुड्डुणुब्बुड्डणेहिं ॥ ३१ ॥

अवि अ[1]।

रणन्तमणिणेउरं झणझणन्तहारच्छडं
कणक्कणिअकिङ्किणीमुहलमेहलाडम्बरं।
विलोलवलआवलीजणिअमञ्जुसिञ्जारवं
ण कस्स मणमोहणं ससिमुहीअ हिन्दोलणं ॥ ३२ ॥

विदूषकः। भो सुत्तआरो तुमं[1]। अहं उण विच्चिआरो भविअ वित्थरेण वण्णेमि[2]।

31ᵃ P गोपुरेहिं, W गोउरेहिं instead of चामरेहिं. — WO धुअधवलवडा°, R कअधवलवडा°, S °धअपडा°, T °पटा°, U °धडा°. — C °डबरोल्लासलोहिं, SU °डबरिल्लं चलेहिं, T °डंबरच्चंचलेहिं.

31ᵇ C वट्टरिल्ला°, PW विदुरिल्ला°, N बिंदुरिल्ला°, ST वित्थरिल्ला°, U पत्थरिल्ला°. — C °णाणुहारं, P °णाणुरूवं, N °णाणुआरे, OR °णाणरूअं. — N वहंती.

31ᶜ CPWOR कुणदि, N °दी. — COR °वसादुक्ख°. — T omits णमंती.

31ᵈ CP तोए दोला सलोलं (C °ला), W जंती दोला सलोलं, OR एंती दोला सलोलं, ST भंती. — SU डोला. — P जणणमण°. — S °हरणी. — C वट्टणुव्वट्टणेहिं, P कड्डणुक्कड्डणेहिं, W बुडुणुवुड्डणेहिं, N वुड्डणुव्वुड्डणेहिं, OR कंसणुक्कंसणेहिं, S बड्ड°, T बुड्डण-उड्डणेहिं. U पुड्ड°.

32ᵃ N °णेपुरं. — C रणन्तमणतहारछटं, P रणझणंतहारत्थणं, R झणंत°. — N °छदं, T °ज्झडं.

32ᵇ C झणझणिर°, P रणज्झणिर°, W कणक्कणिद°, N क्कणक्कणित°, O झणझणिद°, R झकलक्कऊणिद°, SU झणंझणिद°, T झणज्झणिह°. — C °मुहलमेहडा°, WORU °मुहर°, N °महुर°.

32ᶜ U विलोलमणिआवली°. — C °वणिद°, PWNOR °जणिद°.

32ᵈ STU ण कस्स खु मणोहरं. — CP °मुहोइ, WSTU °मुहोए. — P हिंडो°.

32¹ C विदू°। राजानमाह. — STU भो वअस्स. — P °कारो, T °अरो. — W तुवं.

32² P अम्ह. — CU पुण, P पुण्ण. — P °कारो, N वित्थरआरो, S पुत्ति°, T उत्ति°, U वुत्ति°. — C विक्कारिय, PS वित्थारिअ, N वित्थारइःसं, TU omit. — P वण्णमि, N omits, STU वण्णइस्सं.

उवरिट्ठिअथणपब्भारचम्पिअं चलणपङ्कआण जुअं ।
हक्कारइ व्व मअणं रणन्तमणिणेउररवेण ॥ ३३ ॥
हिन्दोलणलीलाइअमुहलं रहचक्कचक्कलं रमणं ।
किलकिलइ व्व सहरिसं मणिकञ्चीकिङ्किणिरवेण ॥ ३४ ॥
तारन्दोलणहेलासरन्तसरिअच्छलेण से हारो ।
विक्खरइ व कुसुमाउहणरवइणो कित्तिवल्लीओ ॥ ३५ ॥
संमुहपवणपणोल्लिअवरिल्लदरदाविआइँ अङ्गाइं ।
हक्कारिऊण मअणं पासम्मि णिवेसअन्ति व्व ॥ ३६ ॥

33ᵃ C राजाह, W राजा. — C °ट्ठिदत्थण-भारचंपियं, P °चंपियं, N °त्थणप्पभारंपीडिअं, R °रविअं, S °थणाहारंणमंतमज्झाए, T °थणभाराणमंतमज्झाए, U °थणाहारोणमंतमज्झाए. — P चलण°, N चरण°, OR °पंकजजुअं से, STU चरणकमलजुअं.

33ᵇ CW विदूषकः. — CPO पुक्कारइ, W पुक्कारय, N हक्कारई, R फक्कारइ, S हक्कारिइ, T हक्कारिच्छइ, U हंकारेइ. — T विअ, U च. — N रत्नमणि°. — P °णोउरमिसेणं, O °मिसेण, R °णिसेण, STU °णोउरारावं.

34ᵃ CW राजा, N अयं च, S अस्सं च वअंस, T अवयं च, U अस्सं च before the verse. — C हिंडोलयधरलीलालंपड, P अंदोलणलीलचलणलंपटं, WOR हिंदोलणलीलाललणलंपडं, N हिंदोलणलीलारंभलंपडं, S °लीलाए मुहलं, U °मुहरं. — C चक्कघदुलं, PWOR चक्कचक्कलं, N चक्कारं, T °चक्कसरिसं, U °चक्कलं.

34ᵇ C विदू° कलकलइ, W °किलिइ, S किलिकिलिइ, U °लए. — P त्थ, S च. — S सरिसं corrected to सरिसरिसं. — P °रावणं, W कंचमणि°, N मणिकंचचणकिंकिणी°, O कंचीमणि°, S कलकंची°, T चलकची°.

35ᵃ CW राजा, T अवि अ before the verse. — NORT दोलंदोलण°. — P °त्थलेण, W °पसरियसरियाणिहेण, N °सरिआछलेण, S °वसरंतसणच्छलेण, T °पसरतसरछलेण, U °वसरंतसरच्छलेण. — C हारा, WOR हारो से.

35ᵇ CW विदूषकः. — P विक्किरइ, W विक्खिरइ, N विक्किरई, OR विक्किरइ, S विकीरइ, TU विकरइ. — CNORT व्व, S अह, U विअ. — P कुसुम्भाओद°, W कुसुमाउट°, N कुसुमाजुह°, T उसुमाउह°. — U °वरवइणो. — P कित्तियवल्लीओ, OR कित्तिवीआइं.

36ᵃ C राजा. — W सम्मुपवण°. — N °पवल्लिअ°, U °पवणोल्लोलिअ°. — C °वरिल्लदरिसाविघाइं, SU °दलदंसिआइ (U °दल), T °वरिवल्लदरदाविआइ. — SU अंगाइ.

36ᵇ CW विदूषकः. — C हक्कारिऊय, W हक्कारिउ व्व, N हक्कारिनुण, T अक्कारिअ

ताडङ्कजुअं गण्डेसु बहलघुसिणेसु घडणलीलाहिं ।
देइ व दोलन्दोलणरेहाओ गअणकोट्टेण ॥ ३७ ॥
णअणाइ पसइसरिसाइ ज्ञत्ति फुल्लाइ कोउहल्लेण ।
अप्पेन्ति व कुवलअदलसिलीमुहे पञ्चबाणस्स ॥ ३८ ॥
दोलारअविच्छेओ कहं पि मा होहिइ त्ति पडइ व्व ।
पुट्ठीअ वेणिदण्डो वम्महचम्मट्ठिआअन्तो ॥ ३९ ॥
इअ एआइ विलासुज्जलाइँ दोलापवञ्चचरिआइं ।
कस्स ण लिहइ व चित्ते णिउणो कन्दप्पचित्तअरो ॥ ४० ॥

उण. — STU पासेसु. — W णिवेसियंति, U णिवेसिअंतीव.

37a C ततो राजा, W राजा. — STU ताडंग°. — TU °जुअलं. — T गंडसु. — CPS बहुल°. — CSTU °घुसुणेसु, N °घुस्सुणलीलाहि.

37b C विदू° । दिइ, NT देई. — CNORT व्व. — SU डोलं°. — C °लेहाउ, T °लेहा, U °लेहाओ. — CN गणाणा°, W गगण°, STU गअण°. — C °कुट्टेण, PN °कोढेण, O °कोट्टेण, R °को-ण, ST °कोढम्मि, U °कुट्टम्मि.

38a CW राजा. — PWNOR णअणाइं. — C पसरिसरिछाइं, PWNOR °साइं, N पसाइ°, SU पसरि°, T °सरिच्छाइ. — P omits ज्ञत्ति. — CPWNOR फुल्लाइं, T फुला. — C कोदुहिल्लेण, WOR कोदु°.

38b CW विदूषकः. — CP उप्पंति, W अप्पंति, N उप्पंखित्ति, STU उप्पत्ती. — CPWNOR व्व, ST विअ, U पिअ. — C कुलदल°, PW °सिलिंमुहे, N °मुहं, STU कुवलअसिलीमुहाणं अणंगस्स.

39a CW राजा. — SU डोला°. — P वित्थेउ, N °रसविच्छेओ. — CPN कहिं, R कइं. — ORT वि. — CPNOR होउ, W होहइ, S होदु, TU होइ. — C ज्ञत्ति, P इति, NORS इत्ति. — C पयडइ, N पदइ, T पहरइ, U पवइ.

39b CW विदूषकः. — C पुठ्ठोइ, P पिट्ठाए, W पिट्ठिम्मि, N पुछोअ, OR पुट्ठंमि, SU पुट्ठीए, T पुटे वेणी°. — NO मम्मह°, R मम्मट्ठिआअंतो, N °चम्मेट्ठि°, T °चम्मलटि°, U °चंमंटि°.

40a CW राजा. — N omits इअ; S इइ. — C याइं, P एया, W एसाइ, N एआइं, S एआए, TU एदाए. — O विलासो°. — C °लाइं, STU °लाइ. — SU डोला°. — N °प्पपंच°, OR °प्पवंच°, T °पपंच°. — STU °चरिदाइ.

40b CW विदूषकः. — STU कस्स खु ण, U कस्स वा खु ण. — CPN लिहेइ. — CPNSTU omit व; R व्व. — W णिउणं. — T कंदंपवित्तारो.

राजा । सविषादम्[1] । कधं ओदिण्णा कप्पूरमञ्जरी रित्ता दोला रित्तं मज्झ चित्तं रित्ताइं दंसणूसुअजणणअणाइं[2] ।

विदूषकः । ता विज्जुल्लेहाइदं खणदिट्ठणट्ठाए ताए[3] ।

राजा । मा एवं भण[4] । हरिअन्दपुरी विअ दिट्ठा पणट्ठा अ[5] । स्मृतिनाटितकेन[6] ।

मञ्जिट्ठी ओट्ठमुद्दा णवघडणसुवण्णुज्जला अङ्गलट्ठी
दिट्ठी बालेन्दुलेहाधवलिमजइणी कुन्तला कज्जलाहा ।
इत्थं वण्णाण रेहा विहरइ हरिणीचञ्चलच्छीअ एसा
कन्दप्पो जीअ दप्पी जुअजणजअणे पुक्खलक्खो विभाइ ॥४१॥

40[2] CPWSU omit कधं; T कहि. — CP ORT अवद्दण्णा, W अवयण्णा, N अवतिंणा, S ओइण्णा अ, U ओइण्णा. — After कप्पू° P adds दोलाहिंतो, W adds दोलाउ. — SU डोला. — W रित्तं च, OR रित्तं अ. — C मउ, O मज्ज. — SU रित्ताइ. — C दंसयसयजणस्स नयणाइं, P दंसणुच्छुय°, WN दंसणुस्सुअ°, OR दंसणूसुआइं मज्झ (O मज्ज) णअणाइं (O °इ), SU °णअणाइ, T दंसणोसुअ°.

40[3] P omits विदू°. — ORU omit ता. — C विज्जुल्लेहाइयं, P विज्जुलेहि व्व इयं, W विज्झुलेहा इव, N विज्जुलेहाविवअ, OR विज्जुल्लेह व्व इअं. — P खणुदिट्ठविहा, W °णट्ठा, N क्खणं दिट्ठा णट्ठा अ, OR खणदिट्ठा तक्खणे णट्ठा, T खणदिट्ठाए. — CT तोए, PWNOR omit; SU एदोए.

40[4] P वयस्स मा. — NORSTU एव्वं.

40[5] P वयस्स हरिचंदउरी, W हरयंदपुव्वरि, OR °पुरि, SU °उरि, T पुर.इ. — WORSTU व्व. — C दिठ्ठा ण पुण णठ्ठा य, SU खणदिट्ठा पणट्ठा अ.

40[6] C स्म° भूयो प्याह राजा.

41[a] N मंजिट्ठा. — P °घडव°, W °घड्यि°. — SU अंगअट्ठी, T °लट्ठी.

41[b] WOR वालिंदु°. — N °लेंहालवलिम°. — W °जयणो, NSTU °जणणी, OR °जिणणी. — N कुतला, TU कुंदला. — CPW °लाभा.

41[c] OR इच्छं.. — N वण्णाणं. — C विहरई, W वियरइ. — N हरिणा°. — CP °लच्छोइ, W °लत्थोइ, STU °लच्छोए. — C जोए, S तोए, U एसो.

41[d] CW जोइ, P जोय, N दोइ, ORTU जाद, S जाअ. — CPNORSTU दप्पो. — C जइजणजइणो, P जयिजणजयणो, W जगजण°, N जणमणदलणो, OR जुअजणजिणणो, STU तिहुवणविजई (T णिहुअण°, U तिभु°). — C फुल्ललक्खो, W वद्धलक्खु, N बद्ध°, OR °लक्खु. — C विहादि, P विठादि, W टुयदि, N °दि, OR व्व ठाइ, S इहाइ, U विहाइ.

विदूषकः । एदं तं मरगदपुञ्जं[1] । इध उववासिअ पिअवअस्सो पडिवालेदु तं[2] । संझा वि संणिहिदा वट्टदि[3] ।

तथा कुरुतः[4]

राजा । अदिसिसिरा वि जामिणी अदिसंताविणिं गिम्हमज्झण्हवेलं अणुहरदि[5] ।

विदूषकः । ता लच्छीसहअरो खणं चिट्ठदु देवो जाव अहं सिसिरोवआरसामग्गिं संपादेमि[6] । इति नाट्येन निष्क्रम्य पुरोऽवलोक्य[7] । किं उण एसा विअक्खणा इदो णिअडिआ आअच्छदि[8] ।

राजा । संणिहिदो संकेदकालो कधिदो सहीहिं[9] । स्मृत्वा मदनाकूतमभिनीय[10] ।

41[1] P एयं. — SU omit तं. — CPWNORSU मरगअ°.

41[2] CPN ता इह, WORTU इह, S जह. — P उपविसिय पि प्रियवि°, S उवसिअ वअस्सो; T omits पिअ°; U वअस्सो. — N °वाडेव, S °वालेउ, U °पालेदु. — CU omit तं.

41[3] W °हिदा ज्जेव, SU °हिदा एव्व. — STU वट्टइ.

41[4] C ततो राजा तथा कुरुते, P तथा कुरुते राजा, W तथा कुरुते, N उभौ तथा कु°.

41[5] CPN omit राजा; W राजा स्मरणमभिनीय. — C अयिसिसिर, PSU अइसिसिरा, W अइसिसि, NOR अइसिसिरं, T सिसिरा. — WNOR पि. — CP हिमाणीं, W हिमाणिं, NOR जामिणिं, T जामणि. — C संताविणीं, P संताविणीमणु°, WNOR संतावदाइणिं (OR संदाव°), S अइसंतापिणी, TU अइसंदाविणी. — CPWNOR omit गिम्ह°; S °मज्झण्ह°. — C अणुहहामि, PWOR अणुहवामि. N अणुभवामि, SU °हरइ, T °हर.

41[6] C ताव. — T °सहसरो. — P एगउ खणं. — SU चिट्ठउ. — COR देओ, N omits. — STU omit अहं. — W सिसिरोवयर°, OR °रोपआर°. — CPW संपाडेमि.

41[7] C परिःक्रम्य, P परि° निःक्रम्य, WOR परिक्रम्य. — C विलोक्य वक्ति विदूषकः, W विलोक्य, SU निष्क्रम्यावलोक्य, T परिक्रम्यावलोक्य; PNWS add च.

41[8] CPNOR पुण. — STU omit एसा. — STU इदो एव्व. — CP नियडी, N निअल्लि, SU विइक्खंती, T विअक्खअंति. CW आगच्छदि, SU आअच्छइ, T आआच्छदी.

41[9] P संणिट्ठिदो यं, N °हिदो अ. — CPWOR संकेअ°, N संझाकालो अ. — CPN कहिदो, S कहीओ, TU सहीहिं कहिदो. — CWNO मंतीहिं, P मंतीहि, R वंदीहिं, S omits; WNOR add पि. — STU add ता संभावणीओ, after which S adds अवि णाम तहेव्व भवे.

41[10] C omits स्म°; P तां स्म°. — C मदनातद्गतमभिनीय कर्पूरमंजरीस्वरूपमाश्रित्याह

किसलअकरचलणा वि हु कुवलअणअणा मिअङ्कवअणा वि।
अहह णवचम्पअङ्गी तह वि हु तावेइ अच्छरिअं ॥ ४२ ॥

विदूषकः । सम्यगवलोक्य[1] । अहो विअक्खणा सिसिरोवआरसामग्गीसहिदा आअदा[2] ।

ततः प्रविशति गृहीतशिशिरोपचारसामग्री विचक्षणा[3]

विचक्षणा । परिक्रम्य[4] । अहो पिअसहीए विरहदाहज्जरो[5] ।

विदूषकः । उपसृत्य[6] । भोदि किं एदं[7] ।

विचक्षणा । सिसिरोवआरसामग्गी[8] ।

विदूषकः । कस्स किदे[9] ।

विचक्षणा । पिअसहीए किदे[10] ।

विदूषकः । ता मह वि अद्धं देहि[11] ।

विचक्षणा । किं णिमित्तं[12] ।

विदूषकः । महाराअस्स किदे[13] ।

राजा, PN मदनाकृतिमभिनीय. — T adds अवि णाम तहा हु वे.

42[a] U °अर°. — Mss. °चरणा. — T omits वि. — NT omit हु; SU अ. — N कुवलअअणा. — C °मियंकवणा. — S च, TU अ.

42[b] STU omit अहह. — STU अहिणवचंपअअंगी (U अभि° S °अंगं). — T तअ. — T omits वि. — CP य, N कवु, STU omit. — SU तवेइ त्ति, T तेवेइ त्ति. — ORTU अच्चरिअं, S अच्छेरं.

42[1] C विलोक्य, P सम्यगवलोक्याय, WOR सम्यग्विलोक्य.

42[2] C कधं, P अयि, NOR अए, SU omit. — NSU विअ° वि. — S °रोअआर°. — W °सामग्गि°, OR omit °सामग्गी°. — P °सहिदहत्था, OR °गहिदहत्था. — CW omit आअदा; PN विअ, T अअदा.

42[3] C विच° शिशिरोपचारयुक्ता, PN शिशिरोपचारसामग्रीसहिता, S शिशिरोपचारसामग्रीकरा, TU यथोद्दिष्टा. — OU add च.

42[4] C परिक्रम्याह विचक्षणा, NOR omit विचक्षणा.

42[5] P °सही. — C महंतो दाह°, P महंतो वि°, N महंतो क्खु वि°. — ORS °डाह°, T विरहज्जरो.

42[6] C adds तामाह.

42[7] P भो, W भादो, OR विअक्खणे, STU भो विअक्खणे. — N किमिदं.

42[9, 10, 13] CPWNOR कदे. — U omits 42[10].

42[11] P मह्यं, W मज्झं, OR मम. — CPW पि. — P अट्ठं, S अड्ढं. T हत्थे दिहि.

42[12] C कस्स कदे.

विचक्षणा । किं उण कारणं[14] ।

विदूषकः । कप्पूरमञ्जरीए वि किं[15] ।

विचक्षणा । किं ण जाणासि महाराअस्स दंसणं[16] ।

विदूषकः । तुमं पि किं ण जाणासि महाराअस्स कप्पूरमञ्जरीए दंसणं[17] ।

इत्युभौ हसतः[18]

विचक्षणा । ता कहिं महाराओ[19] ।

विदूषकः । तुह वअणेण मरगदपुञ्जे[20] ।

विचक्षणा । ता महाराएण सह मरगदपुञ्जदुवारे चिट्ठ जेण उहअदंसणे जादे सिसिरोवआरसामग्गीए जलञ्जली दिज्जदि[21] ।

विदूषकः । तां परिष्वज्य[22] । तहिं गच्छ जदो णाअच्छसि[23] । इति चिपति[24] । तां प्रति[25] । ता कीस दुवारुद्देसे भविदव्वं[26] ।

42[14] C omits उण; PWNOR पुण. — NST कालणं. — POR add तस्स.

42[15] P °जरी. — CN omit वि. — S किं कप्पू°, TU किं उण कप्पू°. — N adds कलणं.

42[16] T तुमं कि. — W याणासि, N आणासि, T अणासि कप्पूरमंजरि महाराअस्स. — C दंसणं तीए, T दंसणं त्ति.

42[17] W उ तुवं, O तुअं. — OR वि, STU omit. — C न जानासि किं, TU किं उण ण. — W जाणासि, NSU आणासि. — T महाराअ, U कप्पू° महा°. — O दंसणे. — C adds कारणं.

42[18] CPWN इत्युभे. — P परस्परं ह°, N हसहेति ह°.

42[20] SU तुज्झ. — Mss. मरगअ°. — C °पुंजे ज्जेव. — PWOR add चिट्ठदि.

42[21] W °रायएण. — U omits सह — Mss. मरगअ°. — C °दुवारदेसे, P °दुआरोद्देसे, W °दुआरे. N °दुआरोदेसे. T °दुवारं. — C चिठ्ठदव्वं, N चिठ्ठ क्खणं. — T जं. — CPT उभअ°, O उअ°, SU उभआणं दं°. — T तिलजलंजली. — P दि, STU दिज्जइ.

42[22] C तामालिंग्योपसृत्याह, P तामुपसृत्य शिशिरोपचारसामग्रीमादाय, WOR तामुपसृत्य, N तामसृत्य.

42[23] CP जहिं पुण, NSTU जहिं. — CP नागच्छसि, W णागच्छदि, STU णाइआ चिट्ठइ. — OR add हे सिसिरोवआरसामग्गि.

42[24, 25] CU omit. — P विदू° तां प्रति.

42[26] N किस. STU केण. — CP दुवारदेसे, N दुआरठेसे. S दुवारुद्देसेण, T दुवारो-

विचक्षणा । देवीए आदेसेण[27] ।

विदूषकः । कीदिसो आदेसो[28] ।

विचक्षणा । तहिं देवीए बालतरुणो तिण्णि आरोविदा[29] ।

विदूषकः । के के[30] ।

विचक्षणा । कुरवअतिलअअसोआ[31] ।

विदूषकः । ता किं तेहिं[32] ।

विचक्षणा । भणिदा सा देवीए जधा[33] ।

कुरवअतिलअअसोआ आलिङ्गणदंसणग्गचलणहआ ।
विअसन्ति कामिणीणं ता ताणं देहि दोहलअं ॥ ४३ ॥

एण्हिं तं संपादइस्सदि[1] ।

विदूषकः । ता मरगदपुञ्जादो पिअवअस्सं आणिअ तमालविडवन्त-

द्देसेण, U दुवारदेसेण. — CP भोदव्वं, N होव्वं, SU omit.

42[27] N omits. — OR add कप्पूरमंजरी आगमिस्सदि (R आअस्सदि).

42[28] N omits. — CPW किं तीए, OR किं ति तीए, SU कीरिसो, T किरिसो.

42[29] N omits तहिं. — C बाणतरु, PSU °तरू, W वालतरु, N बालतरुआ, T वालतरवो. U वाल°. — C तिण्णि, N तीण्णीओ, U तिण्णी. — T आरोचिदा, U °पिदा.

42[30] NOR को को, ST ते के, U दे के.

42[31] N omits. — P कुरुबय°. W कुरु°. — C °लयआसोया, STU °लआसोआ.

42[32] N omits. — T ता किं. — S देहिं, T ते.

42[33] NO omit. — P भणिया. — T देवीए कप्पूरमंजरी. — WR omit जधा; SU जह, T जहा.

43ª N विचक्षणा before the verse. — O omits 43. — CPW कुरु°. — C °लयआसोया, R °तिलअसोआ, STU °तिलआसोआ. — N लिंगणदंसणचलणग्गहणसहा, RT °दंसणचलण°. — STU °हदा.

43ᵇ C वियासंति. — CWN सुंदरीणं. — W omits ता. — C दोहयलयं. — 43 is not reckoned as verse in C.

43[1] P Sanskrit only. — O omits एण्हिं. — C सा तं. T omits तं. — CPW OR संपाड°, S संपाइस्सदि. — N adds त्ति.

रिदं ठाविअ एदं पच्चक्खं करिस्सं[2]। तथा नाटयति[3]। राजानं प्रति[4]। भो भो उट्ठिअ पेक्ख णिअहिअअसमुद्दचन्दलेहं[5]।

राजा तथा करोति[6]

ततः प्रविशति विशेषभूषिता कर्पूरमञ्जरी[7]

कर्पूरमञ्जरी। कहिं उण विअक्खणा[8]।

विचक्षणा। तामनुसृत्य[9]। सहि करीअदु देवीए समादिट्ठं[10]।

राजा। वअस्स किं उण तं[11]।

विदूषकः। तमालविडवन्तरिदो जाण[12]।

विचक्षणा। एसो कुरवअतरू[13]।

कर्पूरमञ्जरी तमालिङ्गति[14]

43² CPWNORSU मरगअ°. — S °पुंजाहिंदो, T °पुंजिभाहिंदो, U °पुंजाहिंतो. — C °वयस्सो. — N आणीअ. — C °विडवंतरठ्ठिदं, P °वंतरविट्ठो, N °विलवंतरिदं, ORU °वंतरिअं, S °विडपतरिअट्ठिअं, T °वंतरिट्टिअं. — CPWNO ठविअ, R थविअ, STU करिअ. — W omits एदं. — P पच्चक्खं च, STU °क्खो. — COR करइस्सं, W करेइस्सं. S कारइस्सं, U काइस्सं.

43³ C विदू° तथा. — CPW नाटयित्वा.

43⁴ C राजानमाह.

43⁵ CO भो once only, STU omit. — STU उट्ठेहि २. — WOR संपेक्ख, S दक्खणीआ, U दक्ख. — P °चंदलिहियं. S हिअअसमुद्दचंदलेहा.

43⁷ C ततो विशति. — ST सविशेष°. — POR°भूषितांगी, W °भूतागी.

43⁸ C कर्पू° प्राह. — T कहं. — CWN पुण. P पि पुण.

43⁹ C तामनुसृत्याह, PWOR तामुपसृत्य.

43¹⁰ C omits सहि. — CPOR कीरदु, WS कीरउ, T किरइ, U किरउ. — C कं दे°. P तं जं देविए, WS देवी, OR देईए. — C समादिठ्ठि.

43¹¹ C राजा विदू° माह. — CPWN पुण. — T किं उण त वअस्स.

43¹² N तलंमाल°. — C °तरितो, OT °तरिओ, R °तरो, S °तरिट्ठिओ; W adds भविअ, S adds णिल्लक्को, T adds भवीअ णिलक्खो भविअ, U adds णिल्लक्को. — N जाणंनु. SU जाणाहि, T जाणेहि. — OR add राजा तथा करोति.

43¹³ C विच° तामाह। सहि एसो, P एस सो, WNORS एस, U omits; T एसो after कु°. — P कुरुबय°.

राजा ।

णवकुरवअवच्छो कुम्भयोरत्थणीए
रहसविरइएणं णिब्भरालिङ्गणेणं ।
तह कुसुमसमिद्धिं लम्भिओ सुन्दरीए
जह भसलकुलाणं एत्थ जत्ता समत्ता ॥ ४४ ॥

विदूषकः । भो पेक्ख पेक्ख महेन्दजालं[1] । जेण[2] ।

बालो वि कुरवअतरू तरुणीअ गाढमुवगूढो ।
सहस त्ति कुसुमणिअरं मअणसरे विअ समुग्गिरइ ॥ ४५ ॥

राजा । ईदिसो ज्जेव दोहलस्स पहावो[1] ।

विचक्षणा । अअं तिलअद्दुमो[2] ।

कर्पूरमञ्जरी चिरं तिर्यगवलोकयति[3]

44[a] CPWNOR विचक्खणा. — C °वत्थो, P °कुरुबयवच्छो, WNOR °ब्बच्छो, STU °लट्ठो,

44[b] SU रभस°. — CPW °ढेणं. N °ढेण. — NSU °लिंगणेण, T °लिंगण.

44[c] W कुसम°. — PST °समिद्धं, O °स-मद्धि. — CPWNOR लंभिदो, ST लं-भिआ.

44[d] C भमण°, U सहल°. — N °कुलुणं. — COR तत्थ, N तत्र. — S जाला, U जत्था. — N पउत्ता, O पडत्ता, R omits; ST समत्था.

44[1] P भो भो पेक्ख पेक, W भो भो पिक्ख, N भो पेक्ख २, OR पेक्ख भो. STU भो वअस्स पेक्ख २. — CNOR महिंद°, S इदं वम्महंमहिंद°, TU इदं (T एदं) वम्महेंद°.

45[a] P कुरुबयं°, RT कुरवतरु. — Mss. तरु-णीए (W तरीए). — WN गाढमव°, S °ऊढो, T °उठो.

45[b] N झत्ति, STU सहसा. — NSTU omit त्ति. — C पंफुल्लिदो, P पुफल्लिदो, N पफुल्लिदो, S फुल्लिओ, TU पुप्फिओ instead of कुसुम°—समुग्गिरइ. — OR फुल्लणिअरं मअणसरं.

45[1] CN इदिसो, S एआरिसो, TU ईरिसो. — P य्येव, O ज्जेच, R ज्जेव्व, SU एव्व, T जव्व. — POR दोहलअस्स, N दोह-अलअस्स. — CP प्पभावो, OR प्प-हाओ.

45[2] C सहि एसो, PN भद्द एस, OR भद्द एसो.

45[3] C ततः कर्पू° तर्जयति चिरमवलोकयति च तं, P कर्पू° चित्तं तर्ज्जयति अवलोकयति च, W omits चिरं; OR चिरं तर्जयति आलोकयति च, SU चिरं तर्जयन्त्यवलो-कयति.

राजा ।

तिक्खाणं तरलाणँ कज्जलकलासंवट्टिआणं पि से
पासे पञ्चसरं सिलीमुहधरं णिच्चं कुणन्ताणँ अ ।
णेत्ताणं तिलअट्ठुमे णिवडिआ धाडी मअच्छीअ जं
तं सो मञ्जरिपुञ्जदन्तुरसिरो रोमञ्चिओ ब्व ट्ठिओ ॥ ४६ ॥

विचक्खणा । एसो वि असोअसाही[1] ।

कर्पूरमञ्जरी चरणताडनं नाटयति[2]

राजा ।

असोअतरुताडणं रणिअणेउरेणंहिणा
कअं च मअलञ्छणच्छविमुहीअ हेलुल्लसं ।
सिहासु सअलासु वि त्थवअमण्डणाडम्बरं
ठिअं च गअणङ्गणे जणणिरिक्खणिज्जं सणं ॥ ४७ ॥

46a C omits राजा. — Mss. तरलाणा. — C °संवठ्ठिदाणं P °संसग्गिदाणं, WNOR °संवग्गिदाणा, S °संवट्ठिदाणं, TU °संपक्किदाणं. — ST वि, N अ.

46b N °सुरं, T °रसं. — P °मुहधो. — C भिच्चं. — Mss. °ताणा. — OR व, T वं.

46c PO °दुमे. — CWNOR णिवडिदा, P णिवणिदा, SU णिपडिआ. — N घाडी, STU पाली. — CPW मयच्छीए, N मअच्छीणा, OR मिअ°, STU मिअच्छीए.

46d C °दंतुररसो, N °दंदुर°. — CPWNOR रोमंचिदो. — CPO व्व ट्ठिदो, W वट्टिदि, N वट्ठदि, STU वट्टए.

46[1] C विच° तां पुनराह । सखि एसो, W एसे, N एस, S एसे पंचसरं । एसो. — CNSTU omit वि. — C असोयतरु, U °पाअवो.

46[2] C करताडनं, WOR चरणेन ताडयति.

47a CWNOR विअक्खणा. — CN रणित°, PWORSU रणिद°. — P °नेउंघ्रिणा, NSTU °णेउरेणंघिणा.

47b CWNOR कदं, PSTU किदं. — RSTU मिअ°. — CWOR °मुहीए, P STU °मुहीए, N °कतिमुहीणा. — S लोलुस्सं, U लोलुज्जलं.

47c ST सअलासु अ. — C कवियमंडलाडंबरं, W कवय°, N करिअ°, SU त्थवअ°, T थवक°.

47d CPNOSU ठिदं, W विट्ठं, R टिकजं, T टिदं. — C गणायंगणं, NOR गअणंगणं, STU सअलंगणा. — C °णिरिक्खणिज्जं, W °णिरक्ख°, N °निरक्खणंतक्खणंतक्खणं, P खणे, STU खणा.

विदूषकः । भो वअस्स जं सअं ण किदं दोहलदाणं देवीए जाणासि किं एत्थ कारणं[1] ।

राजा । णं तुमं जाणासि[2] ।

विदूषकः । भणामि जइ देवो ण कुप्पदि[3] ।

राजा । को एत्थ रोसावसरो[4] । भण उम्मुद्दिदजीहो[5] ।

विदूषकः ।

इह जइ वि कामिणीणं सुन्देरं धरइ अवअवाणँ सिरी ।
अहिदेवअ व्व विलसइ तह वि हु तारुण्णए लच्छी ॥ ४८ ॥

राजा । मुणिदो दे अहिप्पाओ[1] । किं उण किं पि भणामो[2] ।

बालाउ होन्ति कोऊहलेण एमेअ चवलचित्ताओ ।
दरलसिअथणीसु पुणो णिवसइ मअरद्धअरहस्सं ॥ ४९ ॥

47[1] W वअस्स. — C सयं जं तं संपदं, P जं ण संपदं सयं, OR सअं जं ण संपदं. — CPWNO कदं, R कअं. — P दोहल॰, NOR दोहलअ॰, U दोहलं दाणिं. — P दे॰, N एवीए. — COR जाणासि एत्थ किं कारणं, P एत्थ जाणासि किं कारणं, W एत्थ जाण किं कारणं, N एत्थ किं कारणं जाणेसि, SU जाणासि किं एत्थ कारणं (S कारणत्ति), T किं एत्थ जाणासि कारणं.

47[2] CWNOR omit णं, P न. — CW तुयं, N गुअं, OR तुअं, T तुमं ण, U तुमं णं. — CWNOR जाण.

47[3] U भणाइ. — WNU जदि, R जद. — C कुप्पसि, STU कुप्पइ.

47[4] ORT एत्थ को. — C रोसावरो, W ॰सारो, SU कोवावसरो.

47[5] ST मं भण, U ता भण. — CP उम्मुद्दिया जीहा, W उम्मुद्दिदा॰, N उद्दुदजीहाए, STU उम्मुद्दिअ जीहं.

48[a] S omits विदूषकः. — R इह जद, T जह जयि. — N कामियं, T कामिणीयं. — CPWU ॰वाण, ORST अवअआण.

48[b] W ॰देवद, SU ॰देवदे, T देवते. — S ल्ल. — CPR विभसइ, WN णिवसइ, O णिभसइ. — T omits हु; SU अ. — CPW तारुणयं तीए.

48[1] C जाणिदो, PNORT मुणिदो, S मुणिओ. — P omits दे. — CPWST अभि॰.

48[2] CPWN पुण, S किं दु किं वि, T उण ण किं वि. — N omits पि. — COR भणामि.

49[a] S होंति सव्वमेअ, T होंति मेव, U होंति एमेअ. — N कोउहलेण, SU कोउहल्लेण. — C एयमेय, W एमेव, N अमेअ, O पमअ, R घमअ, STU see above. — W चलणचित्ताउ, STU तरल॰.

49[b] C दरिहसिय॰, P दरहसिय॰, W दरल्लसियठणोउ, N दरमोमोअत्थणीणं, O दर-

विदूषकः । तरुणो वि रूवरेहारहस्सेण फुल्लन्ति[1] । ण उण रदिरहस्सं जाणन्ति[2] ।

नेपथ्ये[3]

वैतालिकः । सुहसंझा भोदु देवस्स[4] ।

लोआणं लोअणेहिं सह कमलवणं अद्धणिद्दं कुणन्तो
मुञ्चन्तो तिव्वभावं सह अ सरहसं माणिणीमाणसेहिं ।
मञ्जिट्ठारत्तसुत्तच्छविकिरणचओ चक्कवाएक्कमित्तो
जाओ अत्थाचलत्थो उवह दिणमणी पिक्कणारिङ्गपिङ्गो ॥ ५० ॥

राजा । संणिहिदो संझासमओ वट्टदि[1] ।

विदूषकः । संकेदकालो कधिदो सहीहिं[2] ।

उल्लसिअत्थयणीसु, R दार उण रदरहस्सं जानंति ल्लसिअत्थयणीसु, STU दरगलिअ°. — W पुण. — C वियसद्द, W धरंति, S विअडइ. — C °छ्रज°, N मअलद्धअ°, R मअरद्धर°. — S °विहस्सं.

49[1] U omits. — C विदू° वत्ति, S omits विदू°. — W ताऌणो, R तरुओ, T तरुणा. — C omits वि. — OR रू-अरेहारसेण, S °रहस्से, T °रेहरहस्से. — OR विअसंति.

49[2] U omits. — C पुणो. — CWORS रइ°, P रई°, T रयि°. — Instead of 49[1,2] N has only ल्यव जायंति.

49[4] C वैता° प्राह. — C °संज्झा, P °संजा, OR सुहा°, S सुहाअ संझा, T सुहं सन्झा, U सुसंझा. — S omits भोदु; T देउ, U होदु. — N देअस्स.

50[a] C लोचणेहिं, O °हि. — N °यणे. — STU बद्धणिद्दं. — OR करेंतो.

50[b] W मुच्चंतो. — OR तिव्वभावं. — P सुह, W सहि, N सुर. — P सहरसं, W सहरिसं, SU सरभसं. — P कामिणी°, R मणिणी°

50[c] N °सुत्तछव°. — O °चओ, S °चवो. — WORSTU °वाअक्क°. — STU °मित्तं.

50[d] Mss. जादो. — C अत्थावलंवो, P °त्थो, SU अत्थाअल°, T हत्थाचल°. — P उअह, U वहदि. — CPWNSTU पक्क°. — NSU °णारंग°, OR °णारंभ°.

50[1] C राजाह, P omits राजा; N राजा भो वअस्स. — C संणिहिदा संज्झा°. — SU वट्टइ.

50[2] CWOR संकेअ°, N संझाकालो. — CN SU कहिदो, P कहिंदो दो, T ते कहिदो; SU add मे. — CP मंतीहिं, W NOR अंदीहिं. — PW add पि, SU add ता कहं विअ, T adds ता.

कर्पूरमञ्जरी । सहि विअक्खणे गमिस्सं दाव[3] । विआलो संवुत्तो[4] ।

विचक्खणा । एवं करीअदु[5] ।

इति परिक्रम्य निष्क्रान्ताः सर्वे[6] ।

द्वितीयं जवनिकान्तरम्[7] ।

50[3] C कर्प्पूर॰ वक्ति. — T अणागमिस्सामि.

50[4] N विकलो, R विआले, S पओसआलो, T पदोसकालो, U पओसकालो. — WU संपत्तो, T पत्तो. — N adds वट्टदि.

50[5] C विचक्खणा प्राह । सहि एवं, SU एव्वं. — CPWO कीरदु, R कीर.

50[6] T omits परिक्रम्य.

50[7] PWSTU यवनिकांतरं.

ततः प्रविशति राजा विदूषकश्च[1]

राजा । तामनुसंधाय[2] ।

दूरे किज्जउ चम्पअस्स कलिआ कज्जं हलिद्दीअ किं
ओल्लोल्लाइ वि कञ्चणेण गणणा का णाम जच्चेण वि ।
लावण्णस्स णवुग्गएन्दुमहुरच्छाअस्स तिस्सा पुरो
पच्चग्गेहि वि केसरस्स कुसुमुक्केरेहि किं कारणं ॥ १ ॥

अवि अ[1] ।

मरगअमणिगुत्था हारलट्ठि व्व तारा
भमरकवलिअन्ता मालईमालिअ व्व ।
रहसवलिअकण्ठं तीअ दिट्ठी वरिट्ठा
सवणपहणिविट्ठा माणसं मे पविट्ठा ॥ २ ॥

1ª PWNOR किज्जदु, S किंचइ, T किज्ज पअस्स, U किज्जइ. — PW हलिद्दीइ, N हरिद्दाइ, OR हलिद्दाअ, S °द्दीए, T हलंद्दीए, U हलंतीए.

1ᵇ P अल्लोल्लाअ, N उल्लल्लेण, OR उत्तत्तेण, STU °ल्लेण अ. — W गणणा य का. — O जव्वेण. — N किं.

1ᶜ N अलाअंणःस, U लाअव्वस्स. — P णवु-ग्गदेंदु°, W णाउग्गदिंदुमहुयरछायस्सं, N णवोग्गदेंदु°, OR णवोदिदेंदु°, SU समु-ग्गदिंदुकिरण°, T सयुतादेंदुकिरणछाअस. — W तिस्स.

1ᵈ PORT °हिं, W पच्चुग्गेहि, N पच्चंगेहिं. — T वेकसरस्स, U केदअस्स. — P कुसुमुक्के-रेहिं, WR °हिं, N °मक्करेहिं, OU °मक्करेहिं, T कुसुमेक्केरिहि. — N कालयां, S कज्जाइ, TU कारिअं.

2ª POR °मणिपुंजा, WN °गुच्छा, T °गुटा. — NSU °लट्ठी. — SU व.

2ᵇ STU भसल°. — R °कवलिअंतः, S °क-वलअँता. — T मालदी. — P °मालियव, N °मलई, T °मलिए.

2ᶜ SU रभस°. — N °वलीअ°. — PWNOR °कंठी. — PW तीइ, NSU तीए, T तीआ.

2ᵈ PWN पइट्ठा.

विदूषकः । भो वअस्स किं तुमं भज्जाजिदो विअ किं पि किं पि कुरुकुराअन्तो चिट्ठसि[1]।

राजा । वअस्स सिविणअं दिट्ठं अणुसंधेमि[2]।

विदूषकः । ता कधेदु पिअवअस्सो[3]।

राजा ।

जाणे पङ्करुहाणणा सिविणए मं केलिसेज्जागअं
कन्दोट्टेण तडत्ति ताडिउमणा हत्थन्तरे संठिआ ।
ता कोड्डेण मए वि झत्ति धरिआ ढिल्ले वरिल्लञ्चले
तं मोत्तूण गअं च तीअ सहसा णट्ठा खु णिद्दा अ मे ॥ ३ ॥

विदूषकः । स्वगतम्[1] । होदु एवं दाव[2] । प्रकाशम्[3] । भो वअस्स अज्ज मए वि सिविणअं दिट्ठं[4]।

राजा । सप्रत्याशम्[5] । ता कधीअदु कीदिसं तं सिविणअं[6]।

2[1] P पियवयस्स. — STU अज्ज किं. — P तु, W तुवं, N तुमं पि, OR तुअं. — N भज्जाए जिदो, SU भज्जिजदो, T भंजिदो; PO add यद्द, W पिद्द, R पद्द. — P व, WOR व्व. — POR किं पि once only, S किं वि once only, TU omit. — PN कुरुकुरुअंतो, STU घुरुघुराअंतो.

2[2] N भो वअस्स omits सिविणअं—पंकरुहाणणा 3[a]. — W पियं सविणायं, R सिविणिअं, STU सिविणए. — P मायासमाणुसंधेह्मि, W समनुसंधामि, STU माणुसिं अणु°.

2[3] W inserts कीदिसं तं before ता, S omits ता. — P कधिदु, R कधे, STU कहेदु.

3[a] W सुविणाये. — NT °सज्जा . — PWNOR °गदं.

3[b] NU कंदोट्टेण. — PORT तडित्ति, N झटित्ति. — Mss. ताडिदु°. — N हत्थंतरे. — Mss. संठिदा.

3[c] P कोघेण, N केथेण, O कोडेण, R कोडेण, T कोढेण मये. — PNOR धरिदा, W गहिदा. — PWNOR ढिल्लं. — OR वरिल्लंचलं, N वरिल्लंचले.

3[d] W मत्तूण. — P गदा द्द, WOR गदं. — P तिय, W तीइ, NSTU तीए. — P WNOR णट्ठा अ. — W वि मे, O सम्मो.

3[2] STU होदु. — ORSTU एव्वं.

3[4] T omits वअस्स. — WSU omit वि. — P सिवयणं, W सुविणयं, N सिविणिअं, OR सिविणं.

3[5] P सप्रत्यासयं साभिलाषं, W सप्रकाशं, STU सोत्प्रासं.

3[6] PWNOR कहिज्जदु, SU कहिज्जउ, T कहिज्जद. — ORSU कीरिसं, T कि-

विदूषकः । अज्ज जाणे सिविणए सुरसरिदासोत्ते सुत्तो म्हि[7] ।

राजा । तदो तदो[8] ।

विदूषकः । ता हरसिरोवरि दिव्वलीलावलआए गङ्गाए पक्खालिदो म्हि तोएण[9] ।

राजा । तदो तदो[10] ।

विदूषकः । तदो सरअसमअवरिसिणा जलहरेण जधिच्छं पीदो म्हि[11] ।

राजा । अच्छरिअं अच्छरिअं[12] । तदो तदो[13] ।

विदूषकः । तदो चित्ताणक्खत्तगदे भअवदि मत्तण्डे तम्बवण्णीसंगदसमुद्दन्तेण गदो सो महामेहो[14] । जाणे अहं पि तस्स गब्भट्ठिदो गच्छामि[15] ।

राजा । तदो तदो[16] ।

रिसं. — N omits तं. — W सुविणयं, NR °णिअं, ST omit.

3[7] STU omit जाणे. — W सिवणए; R adds स. — P °सरिसोत्तो, WOR °स-रिसोत्ते, NSTU °सरिआ°. — STU पसुत्त.

3[8] NOR omit; PWS omit तदो तदो.

3[9] PWNORS omit विदूषकः. — STU omit ता. — P हरि°, N हरसिरस्सो-वरि. — P °लीलाचलणाए, N °लीलाए अपगाए omits गङ्गाए; O °लीलावेआए, S °पआए, TU °लीलावआराए. — W तोएण पक्खालिदो सि, S °लिओ सि corrected to म्हि. — STU omit तोएण.

3[10] P omits राजा. — R तदो once only.

3[11] P सरद°. — W °वरसिणा. — P अहि-त्थि, WNOR जहिच्छं, SU जहच्छं, T जहेत्थं.

3[12] NR अच्छरिअं once only, S अच्छेरं once only, U °रीअं २.

3[13] N तदो once only, ORSU omit.

3[14] P तदा चित्तन° भयवं, W भगवं, N भअव-ठि, OR °वइ, S omits; U भगवइ. — W मच्चंडे, S चंडसूए. — P तंवण्णीसंग-मेसंगतस्समुद्दंतेण, W तंबवण्णियादीसंगमेस-मुद्दं, N तंम्मवंणिसंगदं समुद्दं, O तम्मव-णियादीसंगससमुद्दं, R म्मवणिसाईसंगमस-मुद्दं, SU तंबपण्णि°, T तंबपण्णीसंगदस्स-समुद्दंतेण गओ. — ORT omit सो.

3[15] NSTU वि. — NOR omit तस्स. — P °ट्ठिदो ज्जेव, W °ठिदो, N मेहगब्भ°, OR तगाब्भट्ठिदो, SU °गभो, T °ट्ठियदो. N अच्छामि, T पेच्छामि. — STU add त्ति.

3[16] RS तदो once only.

विदूषकः । तदो तहिं सो थूलजलबिन्दूहिं वरिसिदुं पउत्तो[17] । अहं च रदणाअरसुत्तीहिं मुत्ताणामहेआहिं जलाहिंतो समुप्पडिअ पीदो म्हि ताणं च दसमासप्पमाणं मुत्ताहलं भविअ गब्भे संठिदो[18] ।

राजा । तदो तदो[19] ।

विदूषकः ।

तओ चउस्सट्ठिसु सुत्तिसु ट्ठिओ घणम्बुबिन्दू जिअवंसरोअणो
सुवत्तुलं णित्तलमच्छमुज्जलं कमेण पत्तो णवमोत्तिअत्तणं ॥ ४ ॥

तदो सो अहं अत्ताणअं ताणं सुत्तीणं गब्भगदं मुत्ताहलत्तणेण मक्खेमि[1] ।

राजा । तदो तदो[2] ।

3[17] OR सो तहिं, STU omit तहिं. — N त्थूलबिंदूहिं, SU बविर°, T धोर°. — P वरसि. — P पट्टो, WSU पअट्टो, T पउटो.

3[18] T अहं अ. — Mss. रअणाअर°. — O °सुत्तिहिं. — P मुत्ताहलनामधेयाहिं, W मुत्तासुत्तिणामधेयांहिं, N मोत्ताणामधेआहिं. — Instead of जलाहिंतो W तो, N संपुडं, S जलधाराहिं, TU जलधराहिं. — P समुप्पोड्डिय, W समुप्फड्डिय, N समुग्घाडिअ, OR समुप्फुरिअ, S संपडिओ, T समुपाडिदो, U संपाडिदो. — PWOR add जलबिंदूहिं (P °बिंदु) समं. — P अहित्थं पोदो, N जहिछं पोदो, T omits पोदो. — PWOR omit म्हि. — N तायं पि, STU तायं च अहं. — T दसमाप्पमाया, WOR °प्पमायो, N छमास°, T दहमास°. — P मोत्ताहले, WOR °हलो, N मोत्ताहलं, S °भलं, T °फलं. — OR हुविअ. — P संठिड्डो, SU सुसंठिओ, T सुसंट्ठिड्डो.

3[19] R तदो once only.

4[a] Mss. तदो. — WNOR चउस°. — P सुत्तिसंठिदो, WNT ट्ठिदो, OR ठिदो. — P घणंबुबिंदू हियबंधुरोद्धरो, WOR °बिंदू जिदवंसरोअणो, N °बिंदुड्ढिअअबंधरोअणो, S °बिंदुज्जिदपंसुरोअणं, TU °बिंदुज्जिअ-(T °द°)कंचुअंचिदो.

4[b] PS सुवट्टुलं, T सुवदुलं, U सुवत्थुलं. — P °मच्छमज्जलं, W णिच्चल°, OR णित्तुल°, S णित्थलमज्झमु°, T णिट्ठुलं णिट्ठुलमच्छमज्जलं, U णित्थलमच्छमु°. — OR वरमुत्ति°.

4[1] P inserts राजा । तदो तदो । विदूषकः before तदो. — STU तदो सुत्तीणं गब्भगदं अत्ताणं मुत्ताहलत्तणेण (T मुत्ताफ°) मक्खामि (U मुणामि). — OR omit तदो. — PWNOR हं. — PW अत्ताणं, N omits. — OR omit ताणं. — PW omit सुत्तीणं. — P गदं omits गब्भ; OR °गअं. — P मोत्ता° परिणादं, W मुत्ताफल°, N भोत्ताहल°. — P मक्खामि, N भणामि.

4[2] RU तदो once only.

विदूषकः । तदो परिणदिकाले समुद्दादो कड्ढिदाओ ताओ सुत्तीओ फाडिदाओ अ[3]। अहं चदुस्सट्ठिमुत्ताहलाणं मज्झट्ठिदो[4]। किणिदो अ एक्केण सेट्ठिणा सुवण्णलक्खं दइअ[5]।

राजा । अहो विचित्तदा सिविणअस्स[6]। तदो तदो[7]।

विदूषकः । तदो तेण आणिअ वेअडिअं विद्धाविदा मोत्तिआ[8]। मम वि ईसीस वेअणा समुप्पण्णा[9]।

राजा । तदो तदो[10]।

विदूषकः ।

तेणं च मुत्ताहलमण्डलेणं एक्केक्कआए दसमासिएणं।
एक्कावली लट्ठिकमेण गुत्था सा संठिआ कोडिसुवण्णमुल्ला ॥ ५ ॥

4[3] N omits विदूषकः. — PSU omit तदो; N तदो अ. — OR °काले अ. — PW समुद्दाउ, N समुद्दाहिंतो. — OR omit कड्ढि°. — P omits ताओ; W सुत्तीउ ताउ, P सुत्तीए, N सुत्तिआ. — P फोडिदाउ, N प्फालिदाओ, O दारिदा, R दारिदाओ, S ताडिताणाओ, T पोडिदाओ, U ताडिताओ. — WOR omit अ.

4[4] STU तदो अहं. — P च्चायडसट्ठि°, W चदुस°, N चउठ्ठि°, OR चउसट्ठि°, SU चउस्सट्ठि°, T चउरसट्टि°. — PWOR °मुत्ताहलत्तणं, N °मोत्ताहलत्ताणं, T °फलाणं, U °मोत्ताहलाणं. — PWNOR गदो ठिदो, S मज्झट्ठिओ, T मज्झकिदो टिदो. — U adds किदो अ.

4[5] PS कोदो, W कोहो, N कोरोदो, TU see below. — W हं, T तदो instead of अ; U omits. — P एकेण, STU साकेअणिलएण एक्केण. — P सुवणय°. — W देय, N देऊण, S दाऊण, T दयिअ. — O adds अहं, TU add कोदो म्हि.

4[7] R तदो once only.

4[8] W omits in the text. — OR तेण अ, TU देण आणीअ. — P वेगडियं, N वेधणआरं, OR वेधआरएहिं, SU वेअडिएहिं, T वेअकारीहिं. — P विधाविदा ते, N वेधिआ ते, OR वेधाविआइं, STU विद्धाविआ ता. — P मोत्तिदा, OR मोत्तिआइं (O °इ).

4[9] W omits in the text. — PN ममावि, STU मह वि तहिं वेलम्मि (U °लाए). — Mss. ईसोसि; S adds अ. — TU सोसवेअणा. — P संपत्ता, OR संपण्णा.

4[10] W omits; R तदो once only.

5[a] ORT विदू° तदो, SU omit वि°. — PW तेणं च, N तेणावि, O तेणोअ, R तेण अ, STU तेणो व्व. — PNU मोत्ता°. — TU °फल°. — WNT °मंडणेण (W °णं), SU °लेण. — P एक्केक्कियाए, WNORU °दाए, NU एक्कक्क°, T एक्कदाए. — WNT °सिएण, ORU °मासएण, S °मासिदाए

5[b] PW का°. — N गंठ्ठिक्कमेण, OR गंठि-

राजा । तदो तदो[1] ।

विदूषकः । तदो तं कररिडआए कटुअ साअरदत्तो गदो पञ्चालाहिवस्स सिरिवज्जाउहस्स णअरं कण्णउज्जं णाम[2] । तहिं सा विक्किणिदा कोडीए सुवण्णस्स[3] ।

राजा । तदो तदो[4] ।

विदूषकः । तदो अ[5] ।

दट्ठूण थोरत्थणतुङ्गिमाणं एक्कावलीए तह चङ्गिमाणं ।
सा तेण दिण्णा दइआइ कण्ठे रज्जन्ति छेआ समसंगमम्मि ॥ ६ ॥

अवि अ[1] ।

णहधवलिअजोण्हाणिब्भरे रत्तिमज्झे
कुसुमसरपहारुत्ताससंमीलिआणं ।

कमेण. — W गुञ्ठा, NR उत्था, T गुठा. — N omits सा; SU जा, T या. — PWNORST संठिदा. — S कोडिसुअण्ण°.

5[1] S omits; R तदो once only.

5[2] S omits विदू°. — ORU omit तदो. — PNO omit तं. — P तरंडियागदं, STU करंडए. — P कडुय, N कउअ, T करिअ. — POR सागर°, N सा° णाम वणिज्जो puts गदो after णाम; S गओ, T गवो. — STU वीर(T सिरिवीर°)-विज्जाहरमल्लदेवस्स. — O णअणं. — T कण्णकुंजं.

5[3] P तदो तेण तहिं च सा, W तदो सा, N तहिं च सा, OR तेण तहिं सा. — WNR विक्किणीदा, STU विक्किदा कोडिसुवण्णमुल्लेण (S °मूलेण), N सुवण्णअस्स.

5[4] RU तदो once only.

5[5] P तदा, ST omit तदो अ.

6[a] W तट्ठूण. — P थोरत्थण°.

6[b] U देण. — N दइआअ, SU दइआए, T दइएअ. — P रच्चंति, S रेज्जन्ति.

7[a] P °बहुलिद°, WOR °वहलिद°, S धवलिअ°, T धवलिअणवजोण्हा°, U धवलिअणह°. — O °मज्जे, R °मजे.

7[b] W कुसमसरहपत्तास°, N °प्पहारुत्तात°. — P °मंसौलिदाणं, WNOR °संमीलिदाणं.

णिह्नुवणपरिरम्भे णिब्भरुत्तुङ्गपीण-
त्थणकलसणिवेसा पीडिओ हं विबुद्धो ॥ ७ ॥

राजा । किंचिद्विहस्य विचिन्त्य[1] ।

सिविणअमिणं ण सच्चं तं पाणसमासमाअमं मुणसि ।
पडिसिविणएण तस्स वि णिवारणं तुह अहिप्पाओ ॥ ८ ॥

विदूषकः । भट्टो ठक्कुरो छुहाकिलन्तो बम्हणो अविणीदहिअआ बालरण्डा विरहिदो अ माणुसो मणोरधमोदएहिं अत्ताणअं विडम्बेदि[1]। अवि अ वअस्स पुच्छामि कस्स उण एसो पहावो[2]।

राजा । पेम्मस्स[3] ।

विदूषकः । भो देवीगदे पणअप्परूढे वि पेम्मे किं णु कप्पूरमञ्जरिं स-

---

7c P णिह्नुयणि° णिब्भरत्तुंग°, T णिब्भरोत्तुंग°.

7d N °त्थणत्थलणि°, STU °त्थणअलस°. — PWNRST पीडिदो, O पीठिदो.

7[1] S स्मृत्वा, T किंचित्स्मीत्वा, U किंचित स्मितं विधाय. — PNOR add च.

8a W सविण°. — P °मिणमसच्चं, WOR °मेणमसच्चं, N °मिसेण सव्वं, STU °मिमं. — PWNOR तं दिट्ठं मेणुसंधमाणस्स (W मेणुसंधिमाणस्स, N ममाणुसरत्तस्स). — U पाणसमाअमं.

8b P °सिविएण एयस्स, N एदस्स. — P omits वि; OR अ. — P वारणं, N णित्धारणे. — S ते, TU दे. — WST अभि°. — W adds सविणउ ण भोदि एसो सविणयमिणसो दिव्वो अदिट्ठे माणुसम्मि अणुराउ पडिसुविणएण तस्स व णिवारणं तुह अभिप्पाउ. पाठांतरं.

8[1] OR भट्टो, STU पब्भट्टो विअ (T णाड्ढो). — O ढक्करो. — W छुहकिलंतो य, ORSU खुहा°, SU °किलिट्ठो, T चुिहाकिलिढो; STU add विअ. — P बभणो. — N अविवीद°, OR अविणीअ°, S अविणअ°, U अविबाद°; STU add विअ. — P बालदंडा. — POR omit अ; STU विअ. — P मणुस्सो. — WNORTU मणोरह°, P मणोहरमोदएहि, S रहमोदसएहि, T °मोदअसएहिं, U °रहुम्मादसएहिं. — WT अत्ताणं, N अत्ताणं अ, OR अप्पाणअं, SU अप्पाणं. — W विडंबेइ, N विडंबअदि, SU विणोदेसि.

8[2] W पुछामि वयस्सं, PNSTU पुच्छेमि. — W omits उण; S मण. — PWORS एस. — PWNOR पहाओ, S पहावो.

8[3] U omits. — PS पेमस्स, T पेम्मणो.

ङ्गवित्थारिदलोअणो पिअन्तो विअ पुलोएसि[4]। किं तिस्सा परिहीअमाणगुणा देवी[5]।

राजा। मा एवं भण[6]।

> कीए वि संघडइ कस्स वि पेम्मगण्ठी
>
> एमेअ तत्थ ण हु कारणमत्थि रूवं।
>
> चङ्गत्तणं पुणु महिज्जइ जं तहिं पि
>
> तं दिज्जए पिसुणलोअमुहेसु मुद्दा॥ ९॥

विदूषकः। भो किं उण एदं पेम्मं पेम्मं ति भणन्ति[1]।

राजा। अस्सोखमिलिदस्स मिधुणस्स मअरद्धअसासणेण पढ्ढं पणअग्गण्ठिं पेम्मं ति छइल्ला भणन्ति[2]।

8[4] U omits विदू° भो.— P देई°, N देवीए गदे, S देवीपणअरूढे वि, T देवींदो आअदे, U देवीगए. — PW °परूढे. — PW T omit वि. — P किं इति, W omits किं ण; NOR किंत्ति, T किं णाम. — N °मंजरीं पि. — P सव्वालंकिदसच्चंगं वित्थारिय लोयणा पुणो पुणो, W °विआरिअ°, NORSTU °रिअ°, S सव्वंगे°. — S पीअंतो, T विज्जंतो, U पिज्जंतो. — PW पलोएसि, N अवलोअअसि, OR पलोअसि, U विलोएसि.

8[5] P तत्तो, W तत्तो, N तदो वि हीअमाण°. — NTU °गुणगणा.

8[6] ORSTU एव्वं. — T adds कए विअ चित्तं संघट्टअइ कस्स वि पेम्मंगटीय अभिपावो एव्वं जव्व तदो एत्थ ण हु कालणं रूवं सुंदेरत्तणं पुणो अतिरचइ अवि अ.

9[a] STU काए. — P संपडदि. WOR संघडदि. — T पेमंगंधी.

9[b] TU एव्वेअ. — W इत्थ. — NSTU कालण°. — OR °मेदि, STU °मेत्थ. — PWNOR रूअं, T रूपं.

9[c] P omits पुणु, NOR पुण, STU उण. — P अहिलिसज्जदि, WOR महिज्जदि, N लहिज्जदि. — SU वि.

9[d] P त दज्जए. — T विसुण° मुदं.

9[1] STU omit भो. — W पुण किं, PN पुण, OR पुणं, SU omit. — S णदं. — PTU पे° once only, N पेम्म पेम्मेत्ति, S पोमि पेम्मं ति, T पेम्मेति. — PW भणादि, N भणेदि, O मणंति, S भणिज्जइ, T भणंदि.

9[2] N omits राजा. — PWOR °मिलिदो, NT °मो°, S °मिलंद, U °मिलअस्स. — Mss. मिहु°. — P °सासणेणिं, N सअरद्धअसासणा, OR °सासणे. — P पणअपरूढगंठी, W पणायपरूढहियगंठी, N विरूढप्पणअगंठि, OR परूढो णेहगांटी, SU परूढं पणअगंठिं (U °थिं), T परूढप्पणअगंथि. — PW पेम, N पेम्म, ST

विदूषकः । कीदिसो सो[3] ।

राजा ।

जस्सिं विअप्पघडणाइकलङ्कमुक्को
अन्तो मणम्मि सरलत्तणमेइ भावो ।
एक्केक्कमस्स पसरन्तरसप्पवाहो
सिङ्गारवड्डिअमणोहवदिण्णसारो ॥ १० ॥

विदूषकः । कधं विअ सो लक्खीअदि[1] ।

राजा ।

जाणं सहावपसरन्तसुलोलदिट्ठी-
पेरन्तलुलिदअमणाणँ परोप्परेण ।
वड्ढन्ति वम्महविइण्णसरप्पसारा
ताणं पआसइ लहुं चिअ चित्तभेओ ॥ ११ ॥

पेम्मे. — WNT त्ति. — P भणेति, S भणंति, T omits छ° भ°.

9[3] ST कोरिसो, U केरिसे.

10[a] PNOSTU °घडणादि°. — U °मुत्तो.

10[b] N अन्तम्मि जस्स, OR अत्ताणअम्मि, STU अंते म°.

10[c] W एक्किक्कयस्स, N एक्कक्कमस्स, OR एक्कक्क-अस्स, STU एक्कक्कमस्स. — P °रसप्पहो, NR °प्पसारो, SU °समप्पसार, T पसरं-ससमप्पसार.

10[d] NR °वढ्ठिअमणोभव°, O °मणोभव°, SU °वड्ढिदमणोरह°, T °वढ्ढिदमणोरह°. — P °दृक्खसारे, N °दप्पसारोन, TU °दिट्ठसारो.

10[1] ORSTU कहं. — W वि च सो लक्खी-यदि.

11[a] N प्पहाव°, OR सहाअ°, T सहास°. — PST °सलोण°, WN °सलोल°, U °प-सण्ण°. — PU °दिट्ठि.

11[b] NR °लुंठिअ°, S °घोल्लिअ°, T °गुल्लिद°, U °गुल्लद°. — Mss. °मणाण. — W परोपरेण, NT परंपरेण, U परप्परेण.

11[c] P वट्टंतवम्महविलासंरसप्पसारो, W वड्ढंतव-म्महविअचरसप्पसारो, N वठ्ठंमम्महवि-तोक्खरसप्पसारो, O वढ्ढंतमम्महविक्खरस-प्पसारो, R वठ्ठंतमेम्मरविइस्सरस omits what follows as far as सो भणए म inclusive, see 12[b]; T वट्टंति वम्मह-विदिक्खसरप्पसारा, U वड्ढंतवम्महविइक्ख-सरप्पसारो.

11[d] P लहुं पि स, W लहू वि स, NS लहु व्विअ, O लहू विअ, TU लहु च्चिअ. — PW °हेऊ, N °भावो, O वित्तहेऊ corrected to °भाओ, S °भेदो, TU °भेओ. — S adds वि । वअं उण एदं जाणीमो । रा । वअस्स किं विअ.

विदूषकः ।

अन्तो णिविट्ठमणविब्भमडम्बरो जो
सो भण्णए मअणमण्डणमेत्थ पेम्मं ।
दुल्लक्खअं पि पअडेइ जणो जअम्मि
तं जाणिमो सुबहुलं मअणेन्दजालं ॥ १२ ॥

किं च[1]। जइ चित्तगदं पेम्मं अणुराअं उप्पादेदि ता किं कज्जं मण्डणाडम्बरविडम्बणाए[2]।

राजा । वअस्स सच्चं एदं[3]।

किं मेहलावलअसेहरणेउरेहिं
किं चङ्गिमाइ किमु मण्डणडम्बरेहिं ।
तं अत्थमत्थि इह किं पि णिअम्बिणीणं
जेणं लहन्ति सुहअत्तणमञ्जरीओ ॥ १३ ॥

अवि अ[1]।

किं गेअणट्टविहिणा किमु वारुणीए
धूवेण किं अगुरुणो किमु कुङ्कुमेण ।

12ᵃ NSU अंते, T अंत. — P णिविट्ठमाण°, T ब्बिविट्ठमविभम°.

12ᵇ N सो भणए. — W °मिळ, N °मंडलमेत्थ. — NT पेम्म.

12ᶜ T दुल्लक्खिअदं, U °क्खिअं. — STU वि. — T पअसेइ जणो जणम्मि.

12ᵈ N जणिमो, STU मण्णिमो. — P सबहुलं, T सुवहलं. — P मयणंदयालं, WNU मअणिंद°.

12[2] P यदि, WT जदि. — W त्तगदं, T चित्तटाअं, U °गअं. — TU पेम्म. — STU उप्पादेइ. — T तदो, U omits. — P कज्जयदि, WN किज्जदि, OR कज्जदि, TU omit.

12[3] T omits वअस्स. — PWOR इयं, N इदं, T जेव्व एदं.

13ᵃ W °सेहरेणउरेहिं, S °णेउरसेहरेहिं.

13ᵇ N चंगिमा, S चंगिमाए, TU चंगिमाणमुह. — PWN °अरेण.

13ᶜ T तं अत्थयमत्थिक इह. — ST वि. — PN णिअंबिणीओ, O °णीणं corrected to °णीओ.

13ᵈ T जणं. — N लिहंति. — R सुहत्तणण°.

13[1] W omits; S किं च.

14ᵃ S भेअरंगविहिणा, TU गेअरंगविहिणा.

14ᵇ P धूएण, W धूवेणं, N धूपेण, T धूमेण omits किं. — P अगुरुणा, W अगुरणा,

मिट्ठत्तणे महिअलम्मि ण किं पि अण्णं
  रच्छिस्स अत्थि सरिसं पुणु माणुसस्स ॥ १४ ॥

अवि अ[1]।

जा चक्कवट्टिघरिणी जणगेहिणी जा
  पेम्मम्मि ताण ण तिलं पि विसेसलम्भो।
जाणे सिरीअ जइ किज्जइ को वि भेओ
  माणिक्कभूसणणिअंसणकुङ्कुमेहिं ॥ १५ ॥

अवि अ[1] ।

किं लोअणेहिँ तरलेहिँ किमाणणेण
  चन्दोवमेण सिहिणेहिँ किमुण्णएहिं।
अण्णं णिमित्तमिह किं पि तमत्थि मण्णे
  जेणङ्गणाउ हिअआहि ण ओसरन्ति ॥ १६ ॥

विदूषकः। एवं णेदं[1]। किं उण अण्णं पि मे कधेसु जं कुमारत्तणे

N अगुरणो, STU अगरुणो. — P कुंकुमेणं.

14[c] S तिट्ठत्तणे, T दिटत्तणे, U सिंखागुणेन. — W महिअलं पि, U महिलासु. — NS TU वि.

14[d] P रच्छिस्स, W त्तरस्स, N रच्छिए. — P ORST पुण, N पाणु, U उण.

15[a] N चक्कवट्ट°. — PT °घरणी. — PN जा, O जाँ.

15[b] S ण हु को वि, TU ण हि किं पि (T वि). — U °लाहो.

15[c] P जाणा सिरीइ, W सरीइ, NSTU °रीए. — P जधि को वि भउव्वभावो. — OR जदि, S जइ. — W किज्जहि, N कज्जदि, OR किज्जदि. — W को हु भेदो, N भावो, S भेदो.

15[d] N °भूसणणिअसण°.

15[1] PU किं च, WS omit.

16[a] ST लोअणेहि तरलेहि.

16[b] T चंदोप°. — N त्थणेहिं, S सिहणेहि, TU थणएहिँ (T °हि). — PS किमुण्णएहि, N किमूणअएहिं, T किमुत्तणेहि.

16[c] WOR तं (W ता) किं पि अण्णमिह भूवलए णिमित्तं. — P कं पि, ST वि. — N तमिक, T तदत्थि.

16[d] NSTU जेणंगणाओ, OR जे अंगणाउ. — PWOR हिअआउ, N °हिं. — P उसरंति, W उत्तरंति, T वोसरंति.

16[1] U omits विदू°. — ORSTU एव्वं. — N णेदं, SU एदं.

माणुसस्स मणोजन्तणं तस्सिं पि तारुण्णए किं पि चङ्गत्तणं चडदि[2]।

राजा ।

णूणं दुवे इह पआवइणो जअम्मि
जे देहणिम्मवणजोव्वणदाणदक्खा ।
एक्को घडेइ पढमं कुमरीणमङ्गं
कण्डारिऊण पअडेइ पुणो दुईओ ॥ १७ ॥

तेण अ[1]।

समणिवलअकञ्चीणेउरा वेसलच्छी
मरगअमणिमाला गेरिआ हारलट्ठी ।
हिअअहरणतन्तं जोव्वणं कामिणीणं

16[2] PWNOR पुण. — WOR omit पि; ST वि. — WT omit मे. — SU कत्तेसु, T सुणोदु भवं. — U जं अंगं. — N कुमारीत्तणो, S कुमरित्तणेण, T माणुसस्स कुमारित्तणो, U कुमारत्तणेण omits माणुसस्स. — PW मे मणोज्जं, N अमणोज्जं, O मणुसाअत्तं corrected to मणुज्जअत्तं, R मणुस्सअत्तं, S मणोजंतणं रमणिज्जत्तणं, T अंगे मणोजतणं. — P omits पि; W तस्साबि, N जं तं पि, STU तं वि. — PST तारूण्णए, N तारूण्णए य, O तरुणत्तणेण, R तरुणत्तणे. — PNS omit किं पि; RTU किं वि. — TU सुंदरत्तणं. — P वट्टदि, W वड्ढइ, NU वड्ढदि, O वट्टुदि, R वठ्ठादि, S होइ, T आरोहइ.

17[a] O नुणं, STU जाणे. — W जइम्मि, O जअगम्मि.

17[b] P जं देहनिम्मव्वणदाण°, S देहियं वहण°, TU °णिव्वहण°.

17[c] PN घडेदि, T घटोइ. — SU पुढमं, T पडमं. — N °मंग, OR °रीण अंगं.

17[d] P कडारिऊण, N मुक्कारिण, S तं सारिऊण, TU तं दारिऊण. — T पअसेइ. — U उणो. — NORU दुदीओ, S दुदीवो, T दुद्दिवो.

17[1] P omits; W तेणे अ, OR अवि अ, U जेण अ.

18[a] P सुमणिवलयकंठे नेउरावेसलत्थी, W सुमिण°, N रणिअवलअकंचीणेउरावास°, O सुमणि°, R °णेउरारउलच्छी.

18[b] P °माली. — PWOR गोरिआ, SU हारिआ, T चंगीआ. — P °लत्थी.

18[c] S °भरण°. — WOR °मंतं, NT °मंतो.

जअइ मअणकराइं छट्ठअं लट्ठअं च ॥ १८ ॥

तधा अ[1]।

अङ्गं लावण्णपुण्णं सवणपरिसरे लोअणा फारतारा
वच्छं थोरत्थणिल्लं तिवलिवलइअं मुट्ठिगेज्झं च मज्झं।
चक्काआरो णिअम्बो तरुणिमसमए किं णु अण्णेण कज्जं
पञ्चेहिं चेअ बाला रइरमणमहावेज्जअन्तीउ होन्ति ॥ १९ ॥

नेपथ्ये[1]।

सहि कुरङ्गिए इमिणा सिसिरोवआरेण णलिणी विअ कामं किलम्मामि[2]।

18d PNOR जअदि. — N °कड्अं पट्ठअं च-ट्ठअं च, OR छ° लक्खअं अ, U छ° चोट्ठअं च.

18[1] PN तहा अ, W अदो अ, ORSU तह अ, T अवि अ.

19a PS लाअण्ण°. — SU सवणपसरिआ, T °पन्नरिआ. — PW लोयणो. — P फारतारे, W हारतारे, N रतारा. T फालतारा.

19b W वत्थं, T वत्सं. — P तिवलियवलइयं, N °वलअं, T तिवलिअवलिअं. — P °गज्जं NO °गेज्जं, STU °गज्झं. — OR अ, N omits. — NO मज्जं.

19c STU चक्कुच्छेहो. — W किं तु. — S अक्खेहि.

19d P वेय, O जेव्वं, R जेव्व, T एव्व. — N omits बाला. — PWOR मअणज्ज-अमहा°, N रहिरमणमहावेजअंतीअ, R °वजअंतीउ, STU रइरमणजए वेअअंती (S वेजअंती, T वेजसंति) व (T व्व, U वि). — P हुवंति, T होइ, U हाइ.

19[1] W नेपथ्ये कुरंगिका। विरहयगब्भन्धरसासेण सेयसलिलसित्तगत्तो संवुत्ता तत्तभोदि कप्पूरमंजरी ता वत्थंचलेण वीजिस्सं दाव तधा कुवंती भो भो वरिल्लपवणेण णिव्वुदो देहदाहो, see iii. 22[1] ff.; N नेपथ्ये चिलतरगब्भंविसिया स्सेदसलिलसित्तगत्ता तत्तभवदी वस्संतंचलेण वीजवस्सं वसणंचलाप-वणेण णिवुत्तो देहदाहो.

19[2] PW कर्पूरमंजरी सहि, TU अइ. — P कुरंगीए. — T सिसिरोवअरेण; U adds णोहारेण. — POSU णलिणि, W तालिणि. — Mss. व्व. — N इसए instead of कामं; T omits कामं. — P किलिंमिया, W कामिया किलिस्सामि, NSU किलमामि, OR किलिम्मामि, T किलिस्सामि. — P adds कुरंगिका। विरहयगब्भहरवासेण सेयसलिलसित्तगत्ता संभूदा तत्र भोदी कप्पूरमंजरी अवलेणं विजिस्सं दाव तथा कुवंती भो भो उवरिल्लपल्लवपवणेण णिव्वादो पदीवो। विचिंत्य स्वगतं ॥

विसं व बिसकन्दली विसहरो व्व हारच्छडा
वअस्समिव अत्तणो किरइ तालवेण्टाणिलो ।
तहा अ करणिग्गअं जलइ जन्तधाराजलं
ण चन्दणमहोसहं हरइ देहदाहं च मे ॥ २० ॥

विदूषकः । सुदं पिअवअस्सेण[1] । भरिदा कण्णा पेऊसगण्डूसेण[2] । ता किं अज्ज वि उवेक्खीअदि घणघम्मेण किलम्मन्ती मुणालिआ गाढक्कढिददूसहेण सलिलेण सिञ्चिज्जन्ती केलिकुङ्कुमपुत्तलिआ छम्मासिअमोत्तिआणं तडत्ति फुडन्ती एक्कावली गण्ठवणकेआरिआ लुण्ठिज्जन्ती गन्धहरिणेहिं[3] । ता सच्चं सिविणअं दे सं-

---

20a PWNORT विस व्व, S विसं अ. — T विसकंदलं. — PWORS °हर, T °धर. U °हरं व.

20b W वयंम°, O विसगिमिव अकणो, R विसग्गिमिव, STU परिस्समविवत्तणं (S °द्दणं). — P किरिदि, WN किरदि, SU कुणइ, T कणइ. — P तालत्रंतोनिन्लो, W तालविंता°, N तालवृंदणिलो. R तालवेपणिन्लो, S तालवुंता°, T तालउंदा°.

20c P तहा हि, SU तहा करविणिग्गअं, T तहा करभणिगदं, P °निगदं. — PN जलदि.

20d POR °महो, N °सधो. — PN हरदि. — O देहिदाहं. — OR अ.

20[2] PN जं भरिदा, WORTU भरिआ, S हरिआ. — P कसंगुलो, OR कसंजलो, S ते कस्सा, T दे क°, U देगा क°. — P पीऊसेहिं, WNS पीऊस°, N °गंडूसेहिं. O °गंसेयाढ्र, R °गंडमेण.

20[3] S तं. — N अज्ज वि किं. — PN उपेक्खी°, S उवक्खी°. — PW किलिंमंतो, NOR क्रिलंतो, U क्रिलमंतो. — SU मुणालिआ विअ, T मुणालिक्केव. — P गाढंकडुणदुसह, W °कढिण°, N °कथ्यिददुःसहेण, O °कड्ढणं°, R गाघ्वट्ठण°, S °कढिद°, T °कहिअदुम्महेण, U °क्कधिअ°. — W सिच्चंतो, OR सिंचंतो. — W केलिकुसुम°, NOR °कुंकुमत्थलो, T केलोकुंकुपुत्तिआ; STU add विअ टाहवेग्गण. — P म्मासियमोत्तिया, W °मुत्तियाण, N छमासिअमोत्तिआण, O छम्मसिअमोत्तिआण, R °मोत्तिआ, SU छम्मासमोत्तिआ, T तुट्टिज्जंतो छम्मासमोत्तिआ; TU add विअ. — PORS तडित्ति, N कुडिन्ति. T तट्टित्ति, U संति. — P टुंतो भावेण, W फुट्टंतो, N फुडति, OR तुटंतो, S तुट्टंतो. T पुटंतो, U फटंतो. — STU एक्कावलो विअ. — P गंधित्रक्ष्यकेयारया. W गंठिवक्षय°, N °कलिआ, OR °केदारिआ. T गंविवक्खकेदारिअ, U omits. — PW लूढिज्जंतो, N लुंठिज्जतो, S लुटि°, U omits; ST add विअ. —

पक्खं[4]। ता एहि पविसम्ह[5]। उब्भिज्जदु मअरद्धअपडाआ[6]। पवट्टदु कण्ठकुहरम्मि पञ्चमहुंकाराणं रिञ्छोली[7]। थक्कन्तु बाहप्पवाहा[8]। मन्थरिज्जन्तु णीसासप्पसरा[9]। लहदु लावण्णं पुणण्णवभावं[10]। खडक्किआदुवारेण पविसम्ह[11]।

इति प्रवेशं नाटयतः[12]

ततः प्रविशति नायिका कुरङ्गिका च[13]

नायिका। ससाध्वसं स्वगतम्[14]। अम्मो किं एसो सहसा गअणङ्गणादो ओदिण्णो पुण्णिमाहरिणङ्को[15]। किं वा तुट्ठेण णीलकण्ठेण णिअदेहं ल-

---

PNOR °हरिणेण, W °हरिणएहिं. — STU add णिब्भरमअणज्जरजज्जरिअविलुत्तगत्ता (T °जरविलुत्त°, U °ज्जरवड्ढअरविलुत्त°) संवुत्ता (S सा संवुत्ता, T संउत्ता).

20[4] S संवं. — ORTU दे सि°, S ते सि°. — W omits संपक्खं.

20[5] WNOR omit ता; T एताहि. — P पविसिम्ह. O यविसामो, R पविस्सम्हो.

20[6] W उब्भेदु. STU उत्तंभिज्जउ. — W °पडायं, N °पताआ, T मअणद्धअपआओ. U °पआआ.

20[7] PWOR पअट्टदु, N पअट्टउ, SU पवट्टउ. — P कण्ठकुहरम्मि. N कंठम्मि, O कण्णअहरम्मि. SU कलकंठकंठकु°, T कलकंठोकु°. — W °हुंकाराण. NT °हुंकारणं, OR °हुंकार. SU पंचमुग्गाराण (U °णं). — P रित्योली, NT रिछोली.

20[8] W थक्कंसु. N थकन्तु. O थक्कंदु. R थक्कदु. S ढक्किज्जंतु, T ठक्किज्जंदु, U ढक्किज्जंतु. — T °प्पवाहो.

20[9] P मधरिज्जत्तु, N संवरिज्जंदु. T मंदीकोज्जंदु. — PSU °प्पसारा, T °पसारा.

20[10] W लहंदु. N लहेदु, R वहदु. S लहाउ, TU लहउ. — PTU लाअण्णं. — P NOR पुणणव°, N °हावं, STU पुण्णभावं.

20[11] PWOR omit. — N खिडिक्किआदुआरेण. S कड°, TU किड°.

20[12] P खडक्कियापवेसेण, W खडक्किकोद्घाटनेन, O खडिक्कोद्घाटनेन. R खटिकोक्काटनेन instead of इति; N इति प्रविशतः

20[13] R तत विशति.

20[14] P omits नायिका. — P ससाध्वसा अवलोक्य स्व°, W ससाध्वसमात्मगतं. OR स्वगतं ससाध्वसं.

20[15] W अम्हे. S अंम्मो, U अम्हो. — PW NORST एस. — ORT omit सहसा. — W गयणंगणाहि, OR °गणाहिं. — PN अवइण्णो. W अवयणो, ORSU ओइण्णो, T ओइण्णो. — WS हरिणंको.

म्भिदो मणोहवो[16]। किं वा हिअअस्स दुज्जणो णअणाणं सज्जणो मं संभावइस्सदि[17]। प्रकाशम[18]। इदं इन्दआलं विअ पेक्खामि[19]।

विदूषकः। राजानं हस्ते गृहीत्वा[20]। भोदि सच्चं इन्दआलं संपण्णं[21]।

नायिका लज्जते[22]

कुरङ्गिका। सहि कप्पूरमञ्जरि अब्भुट्ठाणेण संभावेहि भट्टारअं[23]।

नायिका उत्थातुमिच्छति[24]

राजा। हस्ते गृहीत्वा[25]।

उट्ठिऊण घणभारभङ्गुरं मा मिअङ्कमुहि भञ्ज मज्झअं।
तुज्झ एरिसणिवेसदंसणे लोअणाण मअणो पसीअउ ॥ २१ ॥

अवि अ[1]।

जिस्सा पुरो हरइ णो हरिआललच्छी
रोसाणिअं ण कणअं ण अ चम्पआइं।

20[16] SU omit वा. — O मुट्ठेण, T किमुत्तुक्केण. — W णीलयंठेण णिअयदेहं. — STU लंभिओ. — PN मअणो, OR °हओ, S मणो, T °भवो.

20[17] WNOSTU णअणाण. — POR सज्जणो जणो. — WN omit मं. — WOR संभावेदि, N भावइस्सदि, OR सं° मं.

20[19] N यहि गुरंगिए, OR सहि कुरंगिए before इदं, WNSU omit इदं; T एदं. — N इंदलालमिव, T इंदजालं. — PSU व्व, WT omit; OR अ. — N पेक्कामि, SU दक्खामि.

20[20—22] N omits. — P सच्चं भो, W भोदो, STU होदि. — T सच्चमिदाणीं. — S °जालं.

20[23] N विद्दुत्थाणेण संलावेहि भट्टारअं. — R सहि कप्पूरमंजरिअं तुज्झ etc., see the following verse. — T अब्भुट्ठाणेण. — W संभावेह, O संभावअ. — W भट्टदारयं, STU भट्टारं.

21[a] S °भारमंथरं. — T भंग. — NO मज्जअं, SU मज्झमं.

21[b] N तुस्स, O तुज्ज. — PWNOR ईदिस°, S ईरिस°. — T °दंसणे. — P पसीयदु, WS पसीदतु, NOR °दतु, T °दउ, U °दद्द.

22[a] P जिस्सा, NSU अस्सा, OR जाए. — PWNOR हरदि, STU पुरइ. — P हरियाहलहट्टो, N दलिह्ना हरिह्ना; O हरिआहरिह्ना, and adds in the margin ललक्को; STU °लट्ठो.

22[b] T रोसणिअं. — N कणयं णवचंपकाइं.

ताइं सुवण्णकुसुमेहि विलोअणाइं
अच्चेमि जेहि हरिणच्छि तुमं सि दिट्ठा ॥ २२ ॥

विदूषकः । गब्भघरवासेण सेअसलिलसित्तगत्ता संवुत्ता तत्थभोदी कप्पूरमञ्जरी[1] । ता सिअअञ्चलेण वीजइस्सं दाव[2] । तथा कुर्वन्[3] । हा हा कधं वरिल्लपवणेण णिव्वाविदो पदीवो[4] । विचिन्त्य स्वगतम्[5] । भोदु लीलोज्जाणं जेव गच्छम्ह[6] । प्रकाशम्[7] । भो अन्धआरणच्चिदं वट्टदि[8] । ता णिक्कमम्ह सुरङ्गामुहेण ज्जेव पमदुज्जाणं दाव[9] ।

सर्वे निष्क्रमणं नाटयन्ति[10]

राजा । कर्पूरमञ्जरीं करे गृहीत्वा[11] ।

22^{c} PWR °मेहिं, T °कसमेहि, U सुभव°. — PU सुलोअणाइं, T सलोअणाइं.

22^{d} P अवंमि, W अंचेमि, N अच्चेम, T अच्चमि. — P जहिं, WOR जेहिं. — N हरिणच्छिअ. — P तुमं पविट्ठा, OR तुअं.

22^{1} PWNOR गब्भहर°, T °धर°. — S °वासेणे व्व, U °वासेण व्व. — P सलिलसित्त°. — STU °सित्तसव्वगत्ता. — P WNOR संभूदा, T संउत्ता. — PN तत्तभोदी, W तदो भोदि, SU तत्तहोदिं, T तदो होदि. — W कप्पूरमंजरि, SU °जरिं.

22^{2} WSTU omit ता; OR ता इमं. — P OR सिच°, WN अंचलेण. — PN विजिस्सं, W वज्जिअस्सं, SU वीजिस्सं, T विज्जइस्सं.

22^{4} S हा once. — W कथं, STU कहं. — P परिल्लवणेण, W वरिल्लंचलेण, OR वरिल्लपल्लवेण, STU वरिल्लपल्लवपवणेण. — P णिव्वादो, WN णिव्वाणो, OR विज्जाविओ, ST णिव्वाविओ, U णिव्वासिओ. — N प्पदीपो, R पदीओ, S पईओ, T पइव्वो, U दीवो.

$22^{5,6}$ OR omit. — ST omit भोदु; U होदु. — W °लुज्जाणे, SU °लुज्जाणं. — P ज्येव, WN ज्जेव, STU omit. — P गच्छामो, N गच्छेम्ह, STU गमिस्सामो; U adds दाव.

22^{8} N omits भो; U भो भो. — P अंधयारणिच्चिदं, W अंधारपणच्चिदं, N अंधआरेण णट्टिदं, STU अंधआरेण जिदं तिहुवणं (U भुवणं). — OR पहदि, STU वट्टइ.

22^{9} P णिक्कमंम्ह, S °मिअ, T °मिह्य. — PT सुरंग°, OR सुरंगा°. — P य्येव NO ज्जेव्व, R जेव्व, STU °मुहेणे व्व — OR omit दाव; ST पविसम्ह.

22^{10} N निष्क्रामं नाटयंतः, TU तहे (T तह) त्ति नि° (U परिक्रम्य निष्क्रामं).

22^{11} STU नायिकां हस्ते. — PNOR धृत्वा.

मज्झ हत्थठिअपाणिपल्लवा ईस संचरणचञ्चुरा हव।
जं चिराअ कलहंसमण्डली होउ केलिगमणम्मि दूहवा ॥ २३ ॥

स्पर्शसुखमभिनीय[1] ।

जे णवस्स तिमिसस्स कण्टआ जे कलम्बकुसुमस्स केसरा।
अज्ज तुज्झ करफंससक्खिणो ते हवन्तु मह अङ्गसङ्गिणो ॥ २४ ॥

नेपथ्ये[1]

वैतालिकः। सुहणिबन्धणो भोदु देवस्स चन्दुज्जोदो[2]।
भूगोले तिमिराणुबन्धमलिणे भूमीघरे व्व ट्ठिए
संजाआ णवभुज्जपिञ्जरमुही जोण्हाइ पुव्वा दिसा।
मुञ्चन्तो मुउउन्दकेसरसिहासोहाणुकारे करे
चन्दो एक्ककलाकमेण अ गओ संपुण्णबिम्बत्तणं ॥ २५ ॥

अवि अ[1]।

23ª P °त्थिद°, WORSTU °ठिद°, N हत्थ-ट्ठिद°. — Mss. ईसि (P ईसं). — N संचरणपल्लवा, O °बंधुरा, R °बंधुरा. — P हवं, WNO भव. — STU होत्थि (T होइ, U होदि) ईसि कलकंठिसंचरा.

23ᵇ OR तं, T जं अच्चिराअ. — PWOR भोदु. N omits; STU होइ. — N दुब्भआ, OR दहगा, SU दुब्भआ, T दुब्भआ.

23¹ P परस्परं स्पर्श°, T सुखस्पर्शमभि°..

24ª PO तिउसस्स, W तउसस्स, N तिउरस्स, R टिउसस्स, T फणिसस्स. — PNS कदंब°, W कयंब°. — P °मुकुलस्स, W °कुसमस्स, OR °मउलस्स.

24ᵇ NOR °फंससंगिणो, S °पंच°. — N उअंति, STU भवंतु. — P मुह अंगणिमादा, WO णणु णिज्जिआ धुवं (O धुअ), O in the margin मह देहसंगआ, R महोट्ठसंगआ, TU मम अंग°.

24² P वै° पठति, T वैतालिकपोरेकः, U omits वै°. — W सुहणुबं°, U सुभ°. — OR STU होदु. — P चंदुजोउ, WNSTU चंदुज्जोओ.

25ª PO °हरे, W °हर, N °धरे, R °घरे, U °घरा. — NOU व. — PWNRTU ट्ठिदे, O छिदे but in the margin ट्ठिदे.

25ᵇ P जं जादा, WNORTU संजादा, S °णा. — N जोह्णाअ, STU °ए.

25ᶜ P मुच्वंतो, W मुच्वंतो, ST मुंचंदो. — P मुचकुंद°, WORS मुचुकुंद°, N मुचुउंद°, T मुचुअंद°. — W °केसरि°. — OR °सिरोसोहा°, S °सिहारेहाणुराए, TU °सिहारेहाणुआरे.

25ᵈ POR पेक्ख, N पेक्ख instead of एक्क. — NOR °कलाक्कमेण, STU °कलक्कमेण. — OR व. — Mss. गदो. — N संपुण्ण°.

25¹ N omits.

अकुङ्कुममचन्दणं दसदिसावहूमण्डणं
अकङ्कणमकुण्डलं भुवणमण्डलीभूसणं।
असोसणममोहणं मअरलञ्छणस्साउहं
मिअङ्ककिरणावली णहअलम्मि पुञ्जिज्जइ॥ २६॥

विदूषकः। भो कञ्चणचण्डेण वण्णिदा चन्दुज्जोदलच्छी[1]। ता संपदं माणिक्कचण्डस्सावसरो[2]।

नेपथ्ये[3]

द्वितीयो बन्दी।

डज्झन्तागुरुधूववट्टिवलआ दिज्जन्तदीवुज्जला
लम्बिज्जन्तविचित्तमोत्तिअलआ मुच्चन्तपारावआ।
सज्जिज्जन्तमणोज्जकेलिसअणा जम्पन्तदूईसआ
सेज्जुच्छङ्गवलन्तमाणिणिजणा वट्टन्ति लीलाघरा॥ २७॥

अवि अ[1]।

26a OR place 26a after 26b. — TU अकुंकुममअंदणं. — N दहदिसावधूमंडलं. — W °बहू°.

26b T अकुंकुममकुंडलं. — P भवण°, N तुअण°, OR भुअण°, STU धरणि°. — OR °मंडलीमंडणं.

26c N असोसणमपोहणं. — T °लंकणसाउधं.

26d P नहयलंमि, T णहयलम्मि. — P पुंजस्सय, W पुंजिज्जदि.

26[1] U omits विदू°. — W एसा instead of भो, STU omit. — P कणचंडेण, O °चंदेण वण्णिआ. — P पढमोग्गयचंदु°. — Mss. °ज्जोअ°. — W °छली.

26[2] P ला, SU omit ता. — P सपदि, S संपइ, U संपढि.

26[3] OR नेपथ्यार्द्धे.

27a ORSTU omit बन्दी. — P adds पठति. — N ढज्जंता°, O उज्जंता°, R दुज्जता°, S संझ्झंतागरु°, T उझ्झंतागरु°, U डज्झंतागरु°. — PN °धूम°, R° धूअ°, TU °धूप°. — S °पट्टि°. — N °बहला. — P दिज्झंत°, N दीअंत°. — NORT °दीउज्जला.

27b OR धोइज्जंत°. — U °विद्दत्त°. — P WNOR °लदा. — N मुज्जंत°, ORSU मुंचंत°, T मुचंत°. — R °पादावआ.

27c T आसज्जत्त°. — O °मणुक्ख°, R °मणुण्ण°. — NSTU जप्पंत°, W जंपंतु°.

27d P सज्जोत्संग°, N सज्जूत्संगचलन्त°, TU सेज्जुस्संग°. — P मिज्जाजाहा, WOR सेज्जाहरा, N लीलाहरा, T °परा.

देन्ता कप्पूरपूरच्छुरणमिव दिसासुन्दरीणं मुहेसुं
लण्हं जोण्हं किरन्ता भुवणजणमणाणन्दणं चन्दणं व ।
जुम्हं कन्दप्पकन्दं णिहुवणकलणाकन्दलिल्लं कुणन्ता
जाआ एणङ्कपाआ सरअजलहरुम्मुक्कधाराणुकारा ॥ २८ ॥

विदूषकः ।

गिरिसुत्तंसो णहसरहंसो ।
णिहुवणकन्दो वट्टइ चन्दो ॥ २९ ॥

कुरङ्गिका ।

ससहररइअमरट्टो माणिणिमाणघरट्टो ।
णवचम्पअकोअण्डो मअणो जअइ पअण्डो ॥ ३० ॥

कर्पूरमञ्जरीं प्रति[1] । पिअसहि तए किदं चन्दवण्णणं महाराअस्स पुरदो पढिस्सं[2] ।

कर्पूरमञ्जरी लज्जते[3] । कुरङ्गिका पठति[4] ।

28a PS दंता. — T °पुंर° .— PO °सुंदराणं. — PST मुहेसु.

28b TU सिणहं. — WN किरंतो. — WN OR भुअण°. — R °मणाणं, S °मणो-णंदणं — P omits चंदणं; T चंदण. — PO वा, WN च, T व्व.

28c PSTU जिम्हं. — N कंदप्पमूल, SU कं-दप्पदप्पं, T कदप्प. — PWOR तिहु-अण°, N णिहुअण°. — S °कंदलल्लं. — P जणंता, W कुणंतो, S कुणंदा.

28d PWNT जादा. — P पादा सरद जलह-रुम्मुक्कधारानुकारो, W °हरोमुक्क°, N °धा-रानुआरा, O सरल°, STU सरअ (S ग-अण°) विसहरुम्मुक्कणिम्मोअचंगा.

29a P दिसुबहुतंसो, W दिसअवयंसो, N दि-संबहुतंम्पो, O दिसय्वहुतंसा, R दिसव-हुत्तंसो. — U णहहर°.

29b PN णिहुणअ°, WR णिहुअण°. — N पसरइ, O यवअट्टद्, R पअदद्, T प-वट्टइ.

30a P ससिहररयमरदो, W ससिहररइअ°, N ससहरपिअमरट्टो, S °रइव्वमरंटो. — W मामाणिणि°, U माणिणि°.

30b PNO °कोदंडो. — T अअणो. — NOR पचंडो.

30[2] NORSU तुए. — PWN कदं, OR कअं, SU किअं. — P चंदवल्लहंवण्णयं, O णवकव्वअभणअं, TU place चन्द° after पुरदो. — PO महाराअपुरदो, W तं म-हा° पुरउ, S पुरओ. — RSU पठिस्सं, T पट्टिस्सं.

30[3] STU नायिका. — P अधोमुखी तिष्टति instead of लज्जते.

मण्डले ससहरस्स गोरए दन्तपञ्जरविलासचोरए।

भाइ लञ्छणमओ फुरन्तओ केलिकोइलतुलं धरन्तओ॥ ३१॥

राजा। अहो कप्पूरमञ्जरीए अहिणववत्थुदंसणं उत्तिविचित्तत्तणं रमणीओ सद्दो रसणीसन्दो अ[1]। तां प्रति[2]।

मा कहं पि वअणेण विब्भमो होहिइ त्ति तुह णूणमिन्दुणा।

लञ्छणच्छलमसीविसेसओ पेच्छ बिम्बवलए णिए कओ॥३२॥

अवि अ[1]।

पण्डुरं जइ वि रज्जए मुहं कोमलङ्गि खडिआरसेण दे।

दिज्जए उण कवोलकज्जलं ता लहेज्ज ससिणो विडम्बणं॥३३॥

चन्द्रमुद्दिश्य[1]।

मुक्कसङ्क हरिणङ्क किं तुमं सुन्दरीपरिसरेण हिण्डसे।

31[a] P गोरः — N दंतिदंतणाहक्केअचोरण, T दंतपंचर°. — P °चोरय.

31[b] P ठाति. WOR भादि, T भा. — P लंत्यणमऊ, W °मउ, N °मिआ, OT °मिओ, R °णिओ, S °मुओ. — P फरंतऊ, W फुरंगउ, N फुडंतओ. — P °तुला, N °तुरं, STU °तणुं.

31[1] N omits अहो. — WOR अहिणवअत्थ°, N अहिणवत्थदंसणरमणीओ सदो, S अभि°. — N °विचित्तता, O °विचित्त, R विचित्तदा, S °विद्दत्त°, T °विभात्ततयां, U adds स. — STU omit रमणीओ. — WSU omit सद्दो. — PNT °णिस्संदो.

31[2] N omits.

32[a] PWN कहिं. — STU वि. — W विब्भउ. — PW होहइ, NT होइ, ORS होउ, U होदु. — P त्ति, N इत्थं, OSTU इत्ति, R इति.

32[b] STU लंछणच्छवि°. — N °मुसी°. — P पत्ये, T येक्ख. — NOR बिंबफलए. — P मिसो. — PWNOR कदो, S किओ, T किदो.

32[1] WNS किं च.

33[a] PWOR पंडुरंगि, N पंडरेण, SU पंडरं. — N जदि. — PWNOR omit वि. — N रज्यते, S रच्चए, T रज्जय. — P कोमलंग. — N खंडिआ°, S घसिआ°, T यडिआ°, U घडिआ°. — POR ते, T दो.

33[b] PW पुण. — P कउल°, NS कओल°. — POR लहिज्ज, W कहिज्ज, N लहेदु. — P सिसिणो. — W वेडं°

33[1] STU चंद्रं प्रति.

34[a] T मुक्कसंकट. — W तुवं, OR तुअं. — WU हिंडसि, N हिंडसि वा.

गोरग्गंडपरिपंडुरत्तणं पेच्छ दिक्खमिमिणा मुहेण दे ॥ ३४ ॥

नेपथ्ये महान्कलकलः[1] । सर्वे आकर्णितकेन[2]

राजा । किं उण एसो कोलाहलो[3] ।

कर्पूरमञ्जरी । ससाध्वसम्[4] । पिअसहि एदं अवगमिअ आअच्छ[5] ।

कुरङ्गिका निष्क्रम्य प्रविशति[6] ।

विदूषकः । एदं जेव पिअवअस्सं वञ्चणागदं अवगमिअ आअछदि देवी[7] ।

कुरङ्गिका । ता कुज्जवामणकिरादवरिसधरसोविदल्लाणं एसो हलबोलो[8] ।

कर्पूरमञ्जरी । ता मं पेसेदु महाराओ जेण अहं इमिणा सुरङ्गामुहेण

34[b] W तुज्झ बिंबपरिपंडु°, U गोरगंध°. — NU दिक्खममुणा, T दिक्खममिणा. — WORU ते.

34[1] POR महाकलकलः, WS कलकलः.

34[2] NSTU आकर्णायंति.

34[3] PWN पुण. — PWNOR एस. — W महाकोलाहलो.

34[4] PWNSTU °ध्वसा; STU add तिष्ठति.

34[5] SU omit. — T सहि एदं अविगमिअ. — PW आगछ.

34[6] WSU omit. — P कुरंगिका । जं पियसही याणवेदि । इति निःक्रम्य पुनः प्रविश्य च. T कुरं° तथा करोति प्रविश्य पुनरागत्य वदती.

34[7] PNT omit विदूषकः. — P सा अहं अवगमिऊण अगदा कधिस्सं । देवीए पियसहीए पियवयस्सस्स वंचणा कदमवगदमणां, W देवीए पियवयस्सस्स वंचणा कदमवग, N देवीए प्पिअवअस्सकिदं वंचणामवगमिदं । कुरंगिका । भट्टरअस्स वंचणं किदं तए सह संगमं जाणिअ आअछदि देवी, O देवीए पिअवस्सेण वंचणा कदे त्ति अवगमिअं, R देवीए पिअवअस्सेण वंचणा केद त्ति अवगमिअं कुरं पिअसहि भदारअस्स वंचणं कदुअ तए सह संगमं जाणिअ आछदि देवी, S पिअसहि एदं एव्व पविअवअस्सं वं° आअच्छइ अवगमिदुं देवी, T पिअसहि एदं एव्व पिअवअस्स वंचणागअं अव° आ° देवी, U पिअसहि एदं जेव्व पिअ° वंचणागअं अव° आ° देवी.

34[8] P कथयति कुरंगिका कधेदि कथयति कुरंगिका कधेदि कथयति, NR omit कुरङ्गिका see above; T विदू°. — POU omit ता; NR तेण. — N omits कुज्ज. — PWNTU °किराअ°, OR °किरात°. — P °वेरिस°, NSU °वरिसवर°, T °वरिसहर. — P °सोवेद°, NOR °सौविद°, T omits °सोविदल्लाणं. — PWNORS एस, T सो. — NOR हलहलो, T कोलाहलो.

ज्जेव पविसिअ रक्खाघरं गच्छामि जाव देवी महाराएण सह संगमं ण जाणादि[9]।

इति निष्क्रान्ताः सर्वे[10] ।

तृतीयं जवनिकान्तरम[11] ।

34[9] STU omit कर्पू°. — PORT पेसदु, N पोसदु, S पेसउ. — STU पे° कप्पूरमंजरिं महाराओ. — P जेणाहम्मिमिणा, W जेण ज्जेव इहागदा वि ण जाणीआमि omits अहं इमिणा. — N omits अहं; STU अहं वि. — OR सुरंगिआदुवारेण, TU °मुहेणे. — P य्येव, WS omit; NR जेव्व, O ज्जेव्व, TU व्व. — N पोवसिअ. — PW रक्खाहरं, N रक्खाहरअं, O रक्काघरं, R छोघरं, T रखाधरं. — N जात, OR जह, SU जेण, T तेण. — U omits देवी and सह; ST महाराएण संगमं देवी. — N omits ण. — W याणादि, S आणाइ, T आणादि. — W adds राजा। एवं कुणम्ह.

34[10] PN इति परिक्रम्य निष्क्रांताः सर्वे.

34[11] U इति तृतीयं. — PWSTU यवनिकांतरं.

ततः प्रविशति राजा विदूषकश्च[1]

राजा । अहो[2]

गाढअरुम्हो गिम्हो पवलो मअणो कहं णु सोढव्वो ।
सा उण सारङ्गच्छी एक्कघरे वि दुलहा विहिणा ॥ १ ॥

जदो[1]

इह कुसुमसरेक्कगोअराणं इदमुहअं पि हु दूसहं ति मख ।
जरढरइकरालिओ अ कालो सह अ जणेण पिएण विप्पलम्भो ॥ २ ॥

विदूषकः । एक्के मम्मधबाहणिज्जा अण्णे तावसोसणिज्जा[1] । अम्हा-

---

0[2] NS omit राजा.

1[a] PWNOR गाढअरो. — W अम्ह गिम्हो, N गिह्मपवणो, T omits गिम्हो. — P पवलो, W अहो पवलो, N प्पअंडो, T पअलो. — POR पवणो, W मलयपवणो, N omits. — P त कधं, W ता कहं, NOR ता कधं. — P omits णु. — PWNOR सहिदव्वो.

1[b] PWNOR omit. — SU omit वि. — SU दुल्लहा, T दुलाहा.

1[1] S omits.

2[a] PSTU omit इह. — S °सरसरंकगाअराणं. — PW इदमुभअं, N इदमुभरअं, O दुदअ तहा and in the margin as RU इदमुहअं, S इदमिह, T इदमुभवं. — ORTU वि, S कं पि. — O अ corrected to हु, STU omit हु. — W दूसयं, N दुस्सहं, SU सुदूसहं. — T मखो.

2[b] P जठ°, NR जरठ°, T जरट°. — PWNOR °रवि°. — PWOR °करालिदो, N °करछिदो. — U omits अ. — N आलो. — PWN सुहअ, OR तह अ, T सहज. — SU विप्पओओ, T विपवोवो.

2[1] N एक्को, OR एक्के दाव, STU भो एक्के; T adds ख्खु, U adds एव्व. — PW व-°म्मह°, NOR मम्मह°, ST वम्महस्स, U म्रम्महस्स. — PW °वहणिज्जा, N °बाहणिज्जो, O °तंवणिज्जा, R and O in the margin °हणाणिज्जा, T वाहणिज्जो वि अ किं उण कुहाए and omits the

रिसो उण जणो ण कामस्स बाहणिज्जो ण तावस्स सोसणिज्जो[1]।

नेपथ्ये[3]

शुकः । ता किं णु क्खु दे मूलुप्पाडिदचूलिअं सीसं करिस्सं[4]।

राजा । विहस्य[5] । वअस्स लीलावणसच्छन्दचारिणा केलिसुएण किं भणिदं[6]।

विदूषकः । सक्रोधम्[7] । आ दासीएपुत्त भुत्थल्लजोग्गो सि[8]।

नेपथ्ये[9] ।

सव्वं तुम्हारिसाहिंतो संभावीअदि जइ मे ण होन्ति पक्खावलीओ[10]।

राजा । कधं उड्डीणो विअ[11] । विदूषकं प्रति[12] ।

---

rest. — N अक्खो, U omits अक्खे ता°. — N °सोसणिज्जो, S तावससो°.

2[3] T omits. — P जणमणो. — N कामबाहणिज्जो omits the rest. — P वहणिज्जा, WO वहणिज्जो, R हणणिज्जो. — OR तावसोसणिज्जो. — SU add किं जणा छुहाए.

2[4] SU omit शुकः. — W किं न, S किं णा. — PWNTU खु, O कख, R क्खु, S सु. — N omits दे; STU एदं. — P °चूलियं, W समूलुप्पाडिय°, N मूलप्पालिअचूलिआविअलं, OR °चूडिआविअलं, RT °प्पाडिअ°, S आलुप्पाडिअ°, U °प्पालिअचूलाअं. — P विसरिसं सिरं, N सीसअं, SU ते सिरं, T दे सिरिकं. — P संपचं, WOR करइस्सं, N करिस्से विलसवरिसंपचं.

2[6] SU omit वअस्स — N °वणं स्स°, U °वणस्स°. — P केलीसयसउंतेण, W केलो°, TU °सउंदेण. — WT भणिअं.

2[7] W omits.

2[8] PORST आः. — OR °उत्त. — P भुंजिणायजोगे, W मुल्लयकरणजुग्गो, N भुत्तिजोग्गो, R भुत्थुल्ल°, STU आलिअभक्खणजोग्गो.

2[10] N शुकः सच्चं. — P °सेहिंतो, N तुम्हरिहिन्तो, S तुम्हाहिं, T तमाहिंतो, U तुम्हाहिंतो. — PNTU संभाविज्जदि (TU °ज्जइ), S संभावीजइ. — PWOR जदि. — OR मह. — W णा मे. — P होंतिउ, W हुंतीउए. — STU पक्खवालीओ, U पक्खपालीओ.

2[11] N राजावलोक्य, SU रा । विलोक्य. — WORSTU कहं. — P व्व, W omits; O विअइ, R विअदि.

णिसा तलिणवित्थरा तह दिणस्स वड्डत्तणं
ससी लहइ खण्डणं तह अखण्डबिम्बो रई।
णिदाहदिअहेसु विप्फुरइ जस्स एस क्कमो
कहं ण स विही तओ खुरसिहाहि खण्डिज्जइ ॥ ३ ॥

किं च णिउणं सलाहणिज्जो जइ सुहअसंगमो भोदि[1]। जदो[2]

मज्झण्हे सिरिखण्डपङ्ककलणा आ संझमोल्लंसुअं
लीलामज्जणमा पओससमअं साअं सुरा सीअला।
गिम्हे पच्छिमजामिणीणिहुवणं जं किं पि पञ्चेसुणो
एए पञ्च सिलीमुहा विजइणो सेसा सरा जज्जरा ॥ ४ ॥

विदूषकः। मा एवं भण[1]।

पण्डुच्छविच्छुरिअणाअलआदलाणं

3ᵃ N णिह्वा तह ण वित्थरा जह दिणेलु दीह-त्तणं. — WOR दिणेसु. — P वदुत्तणं and वट्टत्तणं, OR वड्डत्तणं, S पुड्डत्तणं, T उद°, U वुड्ढ°.

3ᵇ P लहरि, NOR लहदि. — P देवी instead of रई.

3ᶜ TU णिदाघ°. — P °दियाहसुं. W °दिअसेसु, N °दिअसेलु, ORT °दिवसेसु. — P विफुरदि, W विफुरइ, N °रंदि, OR °रदि. — STU कस्स एक्कक्कमो, P एस क्कम्मो.

3ᵈ WN कधं. — W स ण. — PWNO तदो, R तडो. — STU कहं ण विसमेसुणो. — PNO °हिं. W °सिंहाहिं, R °सिहांइं, SU °धराहि, T °धराए. — W °ज्जदु, N खंडज्जदि, OR °ज्जए.

3¹ N किं चा, R किं वा. — STU णिच्च. — PWN सेवणिज्जो, STU सहणिज्जो गिह्मो. — P जहि, WNOR जदि, T जइ ज. — W सुहिसंगमो, N लुहअजणसंगमो, STU पिअजणसमाअमो. — P WN होदि, S भविस्सइ, T हविस्सदि, U भविस्सदि.

4ᵃ P मज्झन्हे, NRSTU मन्झण्हे, O मज्जणे. — S सिरिकंठ°. — O °मुल्लंसुंअं, N °मोल्लंसअं.

4ᵇ P °मज्जणायं पउससमये, W पउस्स°, OR पदोस°, U °मज्झणामप्पओस°, STU °समआ. — WS सोलआ.

4ᶜ N मोयहे. T गिमे. — PN °णिहुअणं. — P omits पि; N च, ST वि.

4ᵈ P एदं, W एदो, NORSTU एदे.

4¹ NORSTU एव्वं.

5ᵃ P पंडुत्यविरिदिनाप°, W पंडुत्थवि°, SU °च्छद्द°. — WNORSTU °छुरिद°. — Mss. °लदा°. — S °णादाणं.

साहारतेल्लरसपेसलपोप्फलाणं ।
कप्पूरपंसुपरिवासिअचन्दणाणं
भद्दं णिदाहदिअहाणँ वअस्स होउ ॥ ५ ॥

राजा । एदं उण एत्थ रमणिज्जं[1] ।

सपञ्चमतरङ्गिणो सवणसीअला वेणुणो
समं सिसिरवारिणा वअणसीअला वारुणी ।
सचन्दणघणत्थणी फरिससीअला कामिणी
णिदाहदिअहोसहं सअलसीअलं कस्स वि ॥ ६ ॥

अवि अ[1] ।

लीलुत्तंसे सिरीसं सिहिणपरिसरे सिन्दुवाराण हारो
अङ्गे ओल्लं वरिल्लं रमणपणइणी मेहला उप्पलेहिं ।
दोसुं दोकन्दलीसुं णवबिसवलआ कामवेज्जोवणिज्जो
तावातङ्कक्कतन्तं महुसमअगमे एस वेसो ऽ बलाणं ॥ ७ ॥

5b W सहार°, N साहेर°, OR साहोडविल्ल°, STU साहाविभोल्ल°. — WNOR °परियेसल°, S °रसपेसण°. — PR °पोफलाणं, W °पुफलाणं, N °पोफहाणं, O °फोप्फुल्लाणं.

5c OR °फंस°, T °पूर°. — PWNOR °वासिद°, T °वःसिआ°. — S °चुम्नआणं. T °प्पोत्थंआणं, U °वत्थआणं.

5d PN °टिअसाण, W °दिवसाण. ORSTU °हाण. — PNOR भोदु, STU होदु.

5[1] O omits राजा. — WS इदं, OR गच्छं. — PWNOR पुण. — P अत्थ, W पिछ. — N रमणाज्जं.

6a N सणंचम°. — W वेणावो, N वेणुणा.

6b N °वारिणो.

6c OR °थणत्थलो, STU °रसत्थणी. — PNR सअणसीअला, W सायस°, O सअण° corrected to फरिस°. — T °सीदाला.

6d P °दियस्सोसहं, W °दिवसो°, NU °दिअसो°, T °दिहसो°. — PW भण ण सोयलं, T मआलसोअलं.

7a P लीलुत्तंसो, W लीलो°, OR लीलुत्तंसं. — N सरीसं त्थण°, ST सिहण°, U सिहर°. — N सिंधुवारण.

7b T जहणपणइणी मेहाला.

7c P °कुंदलीसुं, TU °कंदलेसुं. — P भदविमसनया. — P कामणिज्जो मणिज्जो, W °विज्जो मणुज्जो, N °वेड्डो मणुड्डो, O °वेज्जो मणोस्सः, R °वेज्जो मणोणो.

7d P तावत्तंकंरूवमाणं, W तावातंकिक्कतंतं, N

विदूषकः । अहं उण भणामि[1] ।

मज्झण्हहलण्हघणचन्दणपङ्किलाणं
साअं णिसेविअणिरन्तरमज्जणाणं ।
सामासु वीअणअवारिकणुक्खिआणं
दासत्तणं कुणइ पञ्चसरो वहूणं ॥ ८ ॥

राजा । स्मरणमभिनीय[1] ।

पच्चङ्गं णवरूवभङ्गिघडणारम्भे जणे संगमो
जाणं ताणँ खणं वं रत्तिदिअहा गच्छन्ति दीहा अवि ।
जाणं ते अ मणं पि देन्ति ण रइं चित्तस्स संताविणो
ताणं जन्ति मणोरहेक्कजणणा मासोवमा वासरा ॥ ९ ॥

भावो गिम्हेहिक्कतन्तो, OR तावातंकक्खमाणं, S तावुक्कंभेक्कतंते, TU तावुत्तंभेक्कतंतो (T ताउत्तं°). — WR °गदे, O °समए गदे. — N बलणं.

7[1] PW पुण, S omits.

8[a] W मज्झण्हसण्ह°, OR मज्जण्हए वहलचंदण°, ST मज्झण्हदिक्खणवचंदण°, U मज्झण्हदिक्खणवचंदण°. — TU °सोअलाणं

8[b] P निसेविद°, W णिवेसिय°, NOR णिवेसिद°, STU साअण्हसेविद° (S °सेविअ°). — TU °णिरंदर

8[c] N हसोसि, STU णोसासु. — N वोअणावा°, STU वोअणिअ°. — PWNORU °कणुक्खिदाणं, S °कणोल्लिदाणं, T °कणूखिदाणं.

8[d] PW कुणदि, N वहदि, R कुणघ. — W बहूणं, NO बलाणं, R वलाणं.

9[a] P पच्चपजो, W पंचम्मं, OT पच्चग्गं, R पच्चंग्गं. — NOR °रुअ°, STU °चूद°. — S °भंग°. — T दिणे. — WOR संगमं, O in the margin संगमो.

9[b] WOR वंकताणा मणम्मि होंति सहसा थे णाम हल्लोहला (W °हलो); O in the margin as our text. — PNOSTU ताणा. — PO खणा व झत्ति, N खणा भवंति, TU खणो व्व. — O दअहा. — P यच्चंति, N वदृढंति, O वट्टंति.

9[c] P जाणं सो ण खणं पि, WOR ते णिहुं ण खणं (W खणाणं omits ण) पि, NSTU जाणं ते (SU दो) अ मणंमि, O in the margin णिच्चं जाण खणं पि. — ST दंति. — P नि, T omits ण. — PW रई, T रइ. — SU रित्त व्व, T रित्तं च. — P ते तावियो, WOR संदाविणो, STU उत्ताविणो.

9[d] P जत्ति, N झन्ति, T ढ्िति, U ठंति. — P मणोरहेक°, WOR जअम्मि दोहरसमा. — NT मसोपमा. — S वसरा.

विदूषकं प्रति[1]। अत्थि तग्गदा का वि वत्ता[2]।

विदूषकः। अत्थि[3]। सुणादु पिअवअस्सो[4]। कधेमि सुहासिदं दे[5]। जा सा कप्पूरमञ्जरीए रक्खाभवणे सुरङ्गा दिण्णा सा देवीए दिट्ठा[6]। तदो तं सुरङ्गादुवारं देवीए पिहुलसिलासंचएण णीरन्धं कदुअ णिबद्धं[7]। अणङ्गसेणा कामसेणा कलिङ्गसेणा वसन्तसेणा विब्भमसेणा त्ति पञ्च चामरधारिणीओ सेणन्तणामहेआओ सहेण फरक्किदफरअकरवालहत्थाओ कारामन्दिरस्स रक्खाणिमित्तं पुव्वदिसाए णिउत्ताओ[8]। अणङ्गलेहा चन्दणलेहा चित्तलेहा मिअङ्कलेहा विब्भमलेह

9[1] P राजा विदू°, S omits.

9[2] PW अवि अ अत्थि, N वअस्स अत्थि, STU किं अत्थि after वत्ता. — N तग्गा, OR तत्थगदा.

9[4] P सुखेदु, W सुणादु. — STU वअस्सो.

9[5] PWSTU कहेमि. — P सुहासियं, W कसुहासियं. — P त, W ते, STU omit दे add राजा । कहेहि २ । (T omits २) विदू° ।.

9[6] P जं सा, W omits सा; N जदो प्पहुदि. OR जदो पहुदि सा. — PNOR °मंजरी. — P रक्खाभव्वण, N °भवणादो. — P सुरंगाद्दुवारं, N सुरंगादुआरे. O सुरंगा, R रंगा, T सुरंगदुवारेण. — PN omit दिण्णा; T गदा. — PNOR omit सा. — POR omit देवीए. — P दिट्ठं, OR omit. — WT add राजा । तदो तदो । विदूषकः.

9[7] P translation only. — N तदो प्पहुदि, OR तदो आरब्भिअ, SU तदो अ. — WT omit तं. — OR सुरंगा°. — W N °दुआरं, STU °कुहरं omit देवीए. — N बहलसिला°, STU पिंगलसिला°. — T णीरंधे. — W कदुय, S करिअ. — W णिवद्धं, NR पिहिदं, O omits; STU णिबंधिअ. — P देव्या पृथुरसिलासंचयेन बंधापितं नीरंध्रं कृत्वा.

9[8] W अवरं च before अणङ्ग°. — WOR कलिंगसेणा कामसेणा, N कलिंगसेणा वसंत° विब्भमसेणा चित्तसेणा णामधेआओ omits कामसेणा and त्ति पंच; ST विब्भमसेणो त्ति पंच. — PN omit सेणन्त°, WOR °सेणा त्ति णाम°, W °धेया, OR °हेआ. — P omits सहेण-हत्थाओ. — NOR omit सहेण; S सहेण वि. — W फरक्किदफरया करवालहत्था सहचारिणीउ, N फारकंपिदकरवालधारिणीओ, OR फरक्किदफारकरवालहत्थाओ (O कर°), S परप्परं किं पि कलवालहत्थाओ फलआवो, T परुप्परं कंपिदकरवालहत्थाओ सच्चंमावो, U परप्परं कंपिदकरवालहत्थाओ सफलाओ. — N कारमंदिररक्खा°, SU कारामंदिररक्खा°, T बंदिघररक्खा°. — P °देसाए, N °दिसाओ, T °दिसा. — S णिवुत्ताओ, T णिउव्वा.

त्ति लेहन्तणामहेआओ पञ्च सेरन्धीओ पुङ्खिदसिलीमुहधणुहत्था-ओ दक्खिणदिसाए णिवेसिदाओ[9]।

कुन्दमाला कञ्चणमाला बउलमाला मङ्गलमाला माणिक्क-माल त्ति मालन्तणामहेआओ कलिदकुन्तहत्थाओ तम्बोलकरङ्कवा-हिणीओ पच्छिमदिसाए ठाविदाओ[10]।

अणङ्गकेली बक्करकेली सुन्दरकेली राअकेली कन्दप्पकेलि त्ति केलीअन्तणामहेआओ फलअखग्गधारिणीओ मज्जणपाली-ओ उत्तरदिसाए आढत्ताओ[11]।

9[9] P ता अणंग°. — OR चित्तलेहा चंदलेहा. STU चंदणलेहा (U चंद्रलेहा) मिअंकलेहा इंदुलेहा. W मियंग°. — SU °लेहे त्ति. — PWORS omit लेहन्त°; N णामधेआओ. T णामहेआवो. — U omits पञ्च. — P पुंसिदसिलिमुहधणहहत्थेण निवडणिबद्धतोणीरट्टुद्धरधाणुक्कसस्सण समं सरंधीसत्थेण, W पुखितसिलीमुहधणुहत्था निविडसंनद्धमेरंधीसत्थेण, N °सिलीमुहहत्थाओ. OR °धणूहत्थेण णिवित्थ(R °ट्ठु°) सेरंधीमत्थेण सह (R omits सह), STU °धणुद्दंडहत्थाओ. — P दक्खिणाए दि°. N दक्षिणाए दि°. S दहिविहिणिमाए. — OR णिवेसिआओ. S णिउत्ताओवेसिओ, T णिउत्तावो.

9[10] P कुंद° कंचण° बउल° कुवलय° मंगलमाले. W कुंद° चंद° चंदण° मंगल° कंचणमाल. N कुंद° चंदण° कुवलअ° कंचण° मंगल° माणिक्कमाल. OR कुंद° बउल° चंदण° कुवलअ° माणिक्क° (R adds कंचण°) मंगलमाल, STU किंद° कंचण° बउल° (T बउल°) माणिक्क° रअणमाले (S °ला, T °लं). — PT ति, N त्ति सत्त — PW णामधेयाउ, N माल त्ति णामधेआओ, OR णामहेआओ, S मालणामहेओ पंव, T णाम. — P उहयहत्थकलिदकुंदेण परिससहस्सण परिवेडिदाओ, W तह कलिदकुंतहत्थाउ, N णवणिसिदकुंतहत्थपाइक्कसहस्सेण, OR कलिदकुंदहत्थाओ, S omits; T कंपिदकुदलट्ठीवो, U कड्ढिअकोदंडलट्ठीओ. — P तंबोलकरंडवाहिउं, W तंबोलकरंड°, R तंबोलकवाहिणीओ. S तंबोलकरंगवाहिणीओ दंडहंथाओ दक्षिविदणिसाडिककोअंडलट्ठीओ, T तंदूल°. U तब्बूल°. — PW ठविदाउ, N णिवेसिदाओ.

9[11] T अंगकेलि वबरक्कामराअकि त्ति. — W OT वक्कर°, N कर्कर°, R पुक्कर°, SU बब्बर°. — PW सुंदर° राअ° कंदप्पकेली, N कंदप्प° सुंदर° णीलुप्पलकेलि, OR राअ° सुंदर° कंदोदकेलि, S सुंदर° काम° राअकेलि, U काम° राअकेलि. — PW omit त्ति. — PS omit केली°; WN णामधेआओ, OR णामहेआओ, T केलिअंत°. — P चेडियक्कडत्तलाविदरिल्लेण भिच्चसहस्सेण समं, W फडयकडयल्लचि-

ताणं पि उण उवरि मन्दारवदी तरङ्गवदी कल्लोलवदी मदिरावदी केलिवदि त्ति पञ्च वदीणामहेआओ कणअचित्तदण्डहत्थाओ सुहासिदपाढिआओ अज्झक्खीकिदाओ[12] ।

राजा । अहो देवीए अन्तेउरस्स दासीसामग्गी[13] ।

विदूषकः । एसा देवीए सारङ्गिआ णाम सही किं पि विण्णवेदुं पेसिदा[14] ।

ततः प्रविशति सारङ्गिका[15]

सारङ्गिका । जअदु जअदु भट्टा[16] । देवी विण्णवेदि[17] । अज्ज वडसावित्तीमहूसवोवअरणाइं केलिविमाणं आरुहिअ देवेण पेक्खिदव्वाइं त्ति[18] ।

त्तला विबुणविदुरिल्लाउ, N फालअखम्भधारिणीओ पापिड्ङ्कसहस्सेण समं, OR फडअचक्कवेल्लणविज्जुरिल्ला, S सफलआसिलआ, T कणअवेत्तधारणीओ, U कणअवेत्तदंडहत्थाओ. — P मज्जणवालीउ. NTU omit; OR मज्जणकरीओ, S °पालिआ. — W केलीसट्टेण उत्तर°. — PS आणत्ताओ, W अठत्ताउ. T पच्चक्खिकिदावो, U पच्चक्खीकदा आणंताओ.

9[12] U omits. — ST अण्णं वि, N ताणं वि. — PO पुण, W मज्झे, R omits; T उणो. — ST उवरि मन्दिरस्स. — P मदिरावदी कल्लोल° तरंग° माण° केलिवदीदि, W मंदार° कल्लोल° तरंग मदिरा° केलिवदि, N मदिरा° केलि° कल्लोल° तरंग° माणवदी, OR मंदिरा° कल्लोल° अणंग° केलिवदि, S दार° तरंग° कल्लोल° मदिरा° केलिवदि. — PT त्ति, N पंच त्ति. — WOR omit पंच वदी°. N see below. – P °धेयाउ. — W कणयवित्त°. N परिहारकुमारीओ कणअ°. S कणअवेत्तंदोलिअकराओ, T omits, see iv. 9[11]. — P सुहासोयपढियाउ, W सुहासिअ°, NS सुहासिअपाठि°, O सुहसिअ°, R सुहास्यअपाठि°, T सुहासिहपाटि°. — P अद्धक्खीरदाओ, W अद्दक्खी°, N बंदीणामधेआओ अद्धक्खी°, OR अद्धक्खी°, T अज्झखीदावो. — WNOR °कदाओ. — PW add पंच वीणाकारीओ, N adds त्ति.

9[13] PWNOR अहो देवीए सामग्गी अंतेउरोचिदा.

9[14] N भो वअस्स देवीए एसा, SU एसा वि, T अहो instead of एसा. — W विमपि, T किं वि. — P विण्णवेदुमागदा, N णिवेदइदुं, OR विण्णविदुं किं पि, TU विण्णविदुं. — S पेसिआ. — P adds राजा । आगच्छदु.

9[15] STU प्रविश्य.

9[16] PN omit सार° — SU जेदु, T जेदु च. — WN महाराओ.

9[17] PN देव देवी. W भट्टारकं देवी. — N विण्णावेदी, U °वेद.

9[18] P भाउभूदमादावडमावित्तीमहोसवे पेक्खोव-

राजा । जं आदिसदि देवी[19] ।

चेटी निष्क्रान्ता[20] । उभौ परिक्रम्य प्रासादाधिरोहणं नाटयतः[21]
ततः प्रविशति चर्चरी[22]

विदूषकः ।

मुत्ताहलिल्लाहरणोच्चआओ लासावसाणे तलिणंसुआओ ।
सिञ्चन्ति अण्णोण्णमिमीउ पेच्छ जन्तज्जलेणं मणिवारएहिं ॥ १० ॥

इदो अ[1] ।

परिब्भमन्तीउ विचित्तबन्धं इमाउ दोसोलह णच्चणीओ ।
खेलन्ति तालाणुगअप्पआओ तुहङ्गणे दीसइ दण्डरासो ॥ ११ ॥
समंससीसा समबाहुहत्था रेहाविसुद्धं अवराउ देन्ति ।

णाई, W भाउयाइ महूसउवयरणाइं, N चउत्थदिअहे भविअ वटसावित्तिमहूसवोअकरणाइं, OR वडसाइत्तीमहूसवोवअरणाइं, S तडाअमहूसवोवरणाइ, T तटाअमहुसवोवकरणाइं, U तडाअमहू°. — P देवेण केलीविमाणपासादमारुहिअ, N देवेण केलिविमाणप्पसादमारुहिअ. — W देवेण देवी पिक्खिदव्वणि, N °दव्व, T °दव्वं. — P omits त्ति; W त्तित्ति, NR त्ति.

9[19] P आदेशे, NS देवी आणवेदि, TU द्रेवी आदिसदि.

9[21] NOR omit परि°. — P प्रासादरोहणं, W °ोहनाटितकेन, NU प्रासादारोहणं, T प्रासादावरोहणं.

9[22] PORSTU omit. — W चच्चरी.

10[a] N विदू° भो पेक्ख २ मोत्ता°. — S °भरणज्जलाओ, TU °भरणुज्जलाओ. — OR लास्सा°, T णच्चा°. — N चलिअंसुआओ, STU तरलंसु°.

10[b] P सिच्चंति, W सिंचिंति. — N अण्णोण्णमिमीअ, O °मिमीओ, SU °ममीओ, T °ममीअ पेक्ख. — P जंभज्जलेणं, N जंताज°, OR °लेहिं, STU जंतंजलं. — W मणिभाइणेहिं, N °वारणेहिं, OR °धारएहिं, STU जज्जरसिंगएहिं.

10[1] PWSU omit.

11[a] P इदो हसंठीउ, W °मंतीए, SU °मंतीओ. — WORSU इमा इदो, N विणिम्मि, T आमा इदो. — P दोसालह, WOR सोलह, N दोसोल्हसं, S सोडह, TU सोडस. — P णच्चिणीओ, S णंचईओ.

11[b] Mss. °गद°. — PNORU °प्पदाओ, S °प्पवाओ, T °पदावो. — S रंगणे, TU रंगकणे. — POR दीसदु, WN दीसदि, S omits. — P दंडरेसो, W डंड°, N दंतुरासे, S तड्डुओ सो, TU तंडवो सो.

12[a] P समंससीसमव्वाहुहत्थ, W सामंस°, N °सीसं. — N °हत्थं, S सहबाहुबंध, U °बाहुबंधा. — N रेह°, S रेखा°. — WOR °विसुद्धा. — N अवराओ, SU अपराओ, T अपरा. — PS दंति, N होति, T दअंती.

पंतीहिँ दोहिं लअतालबन्धं परोप्परं साहिमुहीउ चल्लिं ॥ १२ ॥
मोत्तूण अण्णा मणिवारआइं जन्तेहि धारासलिलं खिवन्ति ।
पडन्ति ताओ सहिआणमङ्गे मणोभुवो वारुणबाणचङ्गा ॥ १३ ॥
इमा मसीकज्जलकालकाआ तिकण्डचावाउ विलासिणीओ ।
पुलिन्दरूवेण जणस्स हासं समोरपिच्छाहरणा कुणन्ति ॥ १४ ॥
हत्थे महामंसबलीधराओ हुंकारफेक्काररवा रउद्दा ।
णिसाअरीणं पडिसीसएहिं अण्णा मसाणाहिणअं कुणन्ति ॥ १५ ॥
का वि वाइअकरालहुडुक्का रम्ममद्दलरवेण मअच्छी ।
दोल्लआहिँ परिवाडिचलाहिं चल्लिकम्मकरणम्मि पअट्टा ॥ १६ ॥

12[b] RSU पंतीहि, T पंतिहि. — P दोहि. — NSU परप्परं, T परुपरु. — WORS °मुहो, N °मुहा, TU °मुहोओ. — P वूलें, W चलंति, N हुवंति; OR अ केलि, S छं ॥ णं ॥ लिं, T सल्लो, U छल्लिं.

13[a] U मोक्कण. — P मणियारयाइं, OU °धारआइं, R °हारआइं, S °सारआइं, T मुकूखअम्मपिधारआइं. — N जन्तेहिं. OR जंतेण. — R विवंति, ST खिपंति.

13[b] T पंटंति. — P सहिआण अंगे, WO in the margin R महिलाण अंगे (W अंगो), N अ पिआण अंगे, O in the text अविआण अंगे, S वि पिआणमंगे, TU वि पआणमग्गे (T °मंगे). — P मणोभवे, W मणोहवा; OR °भुओ T °भवो. — P °बाणउक्का, W °वाणउक्का, N °बाणकप्पा, O °वाणजुक्का in the margin °जोग्गा. R वारुणजुक्का. T °वाणचंगो.

14[a] N समीकज्जलकालअंगा. OR °कालदेहा. S मसीमुज्जल°, T मसीकक्कजल°, U मसीमज्जल°. — P तिकंडवावाउ. N तिहंडहाराओ. OR तिक्कंडचावाओ. ST तिकखंडचावाओ. U तिखंडचावाओ.

14[b] WT °रूपेण, N °रूएण. — ORST °भरणा. — W करंति, T करेंति.

15[a] N omits. — P महामासविलीउ बाला, W °वलीधरीउ, O महावंस°, OR °बलीधराओ, STU महामंसधरीओ वक्क°(T बक्क°) हुंकारफेक्कार° (S °हिक्कार°, T °पेक्कार°). — OR °रवाउ. — P रउद्दा, °OR रुद्दा, SU अ रोद्दा, T अ रुंदा.

15[b] N omits. — W णिसायरीहिं, S °सरीणं, TU णोसाचरीणं. — P मासाणा°, S °भिणअं. — O करेंति, R करेंति end of the mss.

16[a] PNO वादिद°, WT वाइद°, S वाहिअ°. — P °हुडक्का, NT °हुडुका, O °हुंडुंक्का, S °हिढक्का. — PWO मंदमद्दल°. — WNT °लएण, U °रएण. — WST मिअच्छी.

16[b] PWNO भूलदाहिं (W °हि), SU दोलआहि. T दोल्लदाहि. — N पडिवाहिं

किङ्किणीकअझणज्झणमक्षा कण्ठगीइलअजन्तिअतालं ।
जोइणी व लअणच्चणलीलं तारणेउररवं विरअन्ति ॥ १७ ॥
कोउहल्लवसजङ्गमवेसा वेणुवाअणपरा अवराओ ।
कालवेसवसहासिअलोआ ओसरन्ति पणमन्ति हसन्ति ॥ १८ ॥

प्रविश्य[1]

सारङ्गिका । पुरो ऽवलोक्य[2] । एसो महाराओ मरगदपुञ्जादो कअलीघरं अणुप्पविट्ठो[3] । ता गदुअ देवीए विण्णाविदं णिवेदेमि[4] । उपसृत्य[5] । जअदु जअदु भट्टा[6] । देवी विण्णवेदि जधा साअंसमए तुम्हे मए परिणाइदव्व त्ति[7] ।

चलाहिं, SU परिपाढि°, T परिवाडिचहिं. — P वल्लिकम्म°, W चल्लि २ कम्म°, N णच्चकम्म°, O चारिकम्मकरणेहिं, STU चुल्लि°. S °करम्मि. — P पवट्ठा.

17ᵃ P खिंखिरीकदरणमक्खा, W °कदरणज्झण-सद्दं, NS °कद°, O °किदसणज्जणसद्दं, T किंकिणीए किदझंझणमणा. U °किद°. — P कंठगीहिलयजंतिदताणं, W °गीदि-लयजंतिद°, N °गीदलअजंतितताला, O °गादलअजंतितताणं, SU °गीअ°, T °गीइ°.

17ᵇ P योगिणी, N जोगिणी, O जोइणि, T जोअणि व्व. — P °कोलं, WO °केलिं, N °किल्लं, S लअणं-णलीलं. — W °र-वा, N तालणेउररअं, S °णेउण°. — P विरयंते, N विलअंति, O विरएंति.

18ᵃ PWO कोदु°. — P °हल्लजणणंगनिवेसा, N °जणणंगुलवेसो, S °वसगम्मिर , TU °गम्मिर°. — PWNO °वादण°.

18ᵇ P °नासियलोयं, W °भामिअ°, N °हासिद°, O °भामिअलोकं, S कालवेअरवहासिअ° corrected to कारवे°, T काअवेअरअ-भासिअ°, U राअवेअरअहासिद°. — PW उसरंति. — S असंति.

18¹ P omits. — WT add सारंगिका.

18² W विलोक्य.

18³ PWSTU एस; PN add पुणो. — S omits महाराओ, U puts it after म-रग°. — P मरगयपुंज य्येव, W मरगयपुंजे व गदो, NO मरगअकुंजं (O °पुंजं) जेव्व गदो, SU मरगअ°, T मरकअ°. — PS TU कदली°, N कंदली°. — PWN °हरअं, T °घरमज्झमणुपविटो, P अणुपइट्ठा, W अणुपयट्टो, N अणुपइट्ठो, O पइट्ठो, S पविट्ठो भट्टा, U °विट्ठो.

18⁴ P ता तग्गद पि, N ता तग्गदं पि गदुअ, O omits गदुअ. — N देवीविण्णावीविअं, O विणाविदं. STU देवीविण्णविदं. — P WNT विण्णवेमि.

18⁶ O जअदु once only, SU जेदु once only, T जेदु २. — W महाराउ, N देओ, O भट्टार.

18⁷ W भट्टारय देवी, PNO add एदं, W इदं. — STU जह; TU add अज्ज. — N

विदूषकः । भोदि किं एदं अकण्डकुम्भण्डपडणं[8] ।

राजा । सारङ्गिए सव्वं वित्थरेण कधेसु[9] ।

सारङ्गिका । एदं विण्णवीअदि[10] । अणन्तरादिक्कन्तचदुद्दसीदिवसे देवीए पोम्मराअमई गोरी भेरवाणन्देण कदुअ पडिट्ठाविदा[11] । अअं च दिक्खाविहिप्पविट्ठाए देवीए विण्णत्तो जोईसरो गुरुदक्खिणाणिमित्तं[12] । भणिदं च तेण[13] । जइ अवस्सं दक्खिणा दादव्वा ता एसा दीअदु[14] । तदो देवीए विण्णत्तं[15] । जं आदिसदि भअवं त्ति[16] । पुणो वि

संण्णासमए; S adds अज्ज. — N तूअं, SU तुम्मेहिं सा, T ठमं. — P मया परिणाविदबु, W °णावदव्व, N °णेदव्वा omits त्ति; S °णाहदेव्वो, T °णाइदव, U °णाइदव्वे.

18[8] W भोदी. N भो, ST omit; U होदि omits किं — P °कुम्हण्ड°, W °कुम्हडवरणं, N अकालकोहंड°, O अभंड°, S TU आआसादो णिवडिअं अहंडं (S अभंडं) गुप्फंडफलं (S कोहिंडफलं).

18[9] WO सवित्थरं omit सव्वं. — PS कहेहि, N कधेहि, T कहेस, U कहेसु. — P adds किं खेदं, W कं खेद त्ति, O किं एदं ति.

18[10] N एवं, O देव एद, SU सव्वं, T omits. — T कहिजइ.

18[11] P अणंतिरातिक्कंदव्वदउसोए दिवसे, W अदिक्कंतचउद्दसीदिअसे, N अणंतरातिक्कंतचउद्दसीदिअसे, O अणंतरं णिव्वत्तवउद्दसीदिअहे, S अणंतादक्कंदचउद्दईदिअहे, T अणंदराणीक्कंदचउद्दहिदिहमेसे, U °क्कंदचउद्दसीदिअहे. — P पोमरायमणिक्कमणी, W पोमरायमणिक्कमयं, N पम्मोराअमई, O पोम्मराअमाणिक्कमई, S मोम्मराअमरं. — W गोरिं, N गोरीं. — W कदुअ भेरवाणंदस्स पासे, N कदुअ भे°. — PT कदुअ. — P परित्थाविदा, W पदि°, N पडिट्ठाविदा, O पइट्ठा°, S पइट्ठाविआ, T पटाविदा, U पइ°.

18[12] PWNO सअं. — POT अ. — P विक्खा गिहाद, W दिक्खा गदोहा. NO दिक्खा गहिदा, S दक्खिणाविहिं पविट्ठाए, T दिखाविहिणिविट्ठाए, U दिक्खाविहिप्पविट्ठाए. — P तदो देवीए, W तदा तयापि. NTU omit देवीए; O तदो तए. — P विणाविदो य सो. N विण्णत्तो.

18[13] O तेण जोईसरेण, TU देण.

18[14] P दि, W जदि, OSTU जइ मे. — NO गुरुदक्खिणा. — PWSU दाअव्वा. — P एसा दीअदु, W पसादीकयदु, N पसादीअदु महाराअस्स, O अहिलहिदो अत्थो करीअद ता एसा दीअदु, S पसीद उप्पादीअदु एदं, TU उप्पादीअदु एदं.

18[15] PS omit तदो. — N विण्णत्तं, STU भणिदं.

18[16] W जं आ° तं कायव्वं, N आदिसति, S °सइ. — O भेरवाणंदो. — PWNSTU omit त्ति.

उल्लविदं तेण[17]। अत्थि एत्थ लाडदेसे चण्डसेणो णाम राआ[18]। तस्स दुहिदा घणसारमञ्जरि त्ति[19]। सा देवण्णएहिं णिद्दिट्ठा जधा एसा चक्कवट्टिघरिणी भविस्सदि त्ति[20]। तदो सा महाराएण परिणेदव्वा जेण गुरुस्स वि दक्खिणा दिण्णा भोदि[21]। भट्टा वि चक्कवट्टी किदो भोदि[22]। तदो देवीए विहसिअ भणिदं जं आदिसदि भअवं त्ति[23]। अहं च विण्णवेदुं पेसिदा[24]। गुरुदक्खिणा वि दिण्णा[25]।

विदूषकः । विहस्य[26]। एदं तं सीसे सप्पो देसन्तरे वेज्जो[27]। इध अज्ज विवाहो लाडदेसे घणसारमञ्जरी[28]।

18[17] P पुण्णो पुण्णो. — WO omit वि. — O भणिदं, STU उत्तं; PWO add च. — T तेण भेर°, U देण.

18[18] N अत्थि एत्थ. — P लाडसमंडले, W °देसम्मि, NT लाट°, O लाडदेसमंडले. — W °सेणे.

18[19] S दुहिआ. — P °मंजरी त्ति, N °मंजरी णाम.

18[20] P दिवण्णहि, WT °वुसुएहिं (T °हि), N देवण्णेहिं, O दवण्णहिं. — P दिट्ठा, W आइट्ठा, NO आदिट्ठा, T omits. — W NOT omit जधा; SU जह. — STU omit एसा. — P चक्कवट्टकारिणी, N चक्कवत्ति°, T °परिणी हविस्सदि. — P omits त्ति. — T adds णिव्वाहिदं.

18[21] P omits. — N omits सा; O मम. — PW °राअहत्थेण, N °राअस्स, O °राओ. — PW परिणाविदव्वा, N °णेतव्वा, O °णाविदव्वो त्ति. TU °णेदंव्वा — N तेण — NSTU गुरुदक्खिणा, O अम्ह गु°. — NU omit दिण्णा; S वि दिण्णा. — PW भविस्सदि. O भोदु, S होइ, TU होदि

18[22] WNO भत्ता. — NTU omit वि; OS अ. — O चक्कवत्ती. — PWNO कदो, SU omit; T कोदे. — P भोत्ति, WT होदि. O भोदु त्ति, SU होइ.

18[23] P omits तदो; W ता. — SU विह° दे°, T अवहसिअ दे°. — PNO भणिअं, T मणिदं. — P यदा. — O आणवेदि, S आदिसइ. — PWNOS omit त्ति. — W adds तं करेदि.

18[24] P तदो अहं च. — PNSTU °विदुं. — S पेसिआ.

18[25] P गुरुस्स वि गुरु°, WNO गुरुस्स गुरु° (O दक्खि°) SU तुह गुरुद°, N °दक्खिणाणिमित्तं. — PWNO omit वि. — W सा instead of दिण्णा, N omits; O दिण्णे त्ति. — U adds होइ.

18[26] O omits.

18[27] W ता उवक्खाणं एदं STU इदं. — PWT omit तं: N ते, U मा. — P उसीसे.

18[28] Mss. इह. — OS विआहो. — P लाडएसे. N लाट°, STU देसन्तरे. — TU °मंजरि त्ति

राजा। किं दे भेरवाणन्दस्स पहावो परोक्खो[29]।

सारङ्गिका। देवीए कारिदं पमदुज्जाणस्स मज्झट्ठिदवडतरुमूले चामुण्डाअदणं[30]। भेरवाणन्दो वि देवीए समं तहिं आगमिस्सदि[31]। तग्गदे अ तक्खणविहिदे कोदुअघरे विवाहो भविस्सदि[32]। इति परिक्रम्य निष्क्रान्ता[33]।

राजा। वअस्स सब्बं एदं भेरवाणन्दस्स विअम्भिदं ति तक्केमि[34]।

विदूषकः। एवं णेदं[35]। ण हु मअलञ्छणं अन्तरेण अण्णो मिअङ्कमणिपुत्तलिअं पज्झरावेदि सेहालिआकुसुमुक्करं वा करेदि[36]।

प्रविश्य[37]

18[29] P ते पुण, N ते, O omits; STU देव. — N भेरवाणंदप्पहावो. S भेरवाणंदपभावेण. P पहावा, TU पहावेण. — P परोखेवा, W परोक्खे, N ण पच्चक्खो. S अवरक्खो, T ण सक्कीअदि विदू, U अपरोक्खो. — O adds दे तां प्रति कहिं स संपदं भेरवाणंदो.

18[30] P देवी, STU omit. — PNO कारिद, W °दे. — W पमुज्जाणस्स. TU °ज्जाण. — POU °ट्ठिदे°. — P °तरुमूल, N °बउलतरु°, S °वट°. — P चामुंडाअदणे, WN °डाअअणे, O °डाभवणे, STU चामुंडाए आअदणं (S °तणं).

18[31] O भेर°. — PWNOS omit वि. — PWN देवी omit समं. — PWNOTU omit तहिं — SU आअमिस्सदि, T आमिसदि.

18[32] P उभौ अग्गदो, W अग्गदो, N ता अज्ज. O ता सज्ज, TU तग्गए. — NO TU omit अ. — W तक्खिणविहिदा, NO दक्खिणाविहिदो, S तंकाल°, TU तक्काल°. U °विहिए. — P कोटूहलम. W केअईलदाहरए, N कोऊहडघरे, O कोऊहलेना. — PNOSU omit भविस्सदि; T हविस्सदि. — PWNO add ता इह ज्जेव (P य्येव, O ज्जेव्व) देवेण ठादव्वं (P गंदव्वं, W गंतव्वं).

18[33] P omits इति. — ST omit परिक्रम्य.

18[34] W राजा साकूतं. — WNU सच्चं. — W वियंभिय, N विज्जंभिअं, O विअंभिअं ST भेरवाणंदविहिदं, U भइरवाणंदविहिअं. – PS omit ति; WT त्ति. — P तक्कोमि.

18[35] OSTU एव्वं. — N सेदं, SU एदं.

18[36] NU मिअंकल°, OST मिअल°. — P मयंक°, W मियंकपुत्तलियं, O °पुत्तलिं. — PO पज्जरावेदि, W पळअवेदि, N पसाएदि, S °वेइ, U पज्झरिवेदि. — W ण हु सरअसमीरमंतरेण सेहा°, N ण हु कदुसमअमंतरेण सेहा°. — P °कुसुमक्कोरं, W °कुसुमुक्करो, TU °कुसुमफुक्कारं. — PO विकरेदि, WN किरेदि. S करेइ, U करोदि.

18[37] NO ततः प्रविशति.

भैरवानन्दः । इअं सा वडतरुमूले णिब्भिण्णस्स सुरङ्गादुवारस्स पिधाणं चामुण्डा[38] । तां हस्तेन प्रणम्य[39] ।

कप्पन्तकेलिभवणे कालस्स पुरो ऽ सुराण रुहिरसुरं ।
जअइ पिअन्ती काली परमेट्ठिकवालचसएण ॥ १९ ॥

प्रविश्योपविश्य च[1] । अज्ज वि ण णिग्गच्छदि सुरङ्गादुवारेण कप्पूरमञ्जरी[2] ।

ततः प्रविशति सुरङ्गाद्वारोद्घाटितकेन कर्पूरमञ्जरी[3]

कर्पूरमञ्जरी । भअवं पणमामि[4] ।

भैरवानन्दः । उइदं वरं लहसु[5] । इध ज्जेव उवविस[6] ।

कर्पूरमञ्जरी उपविशति[7]

भैरवानन्दः । स्वगतम्[8] । अज्ज वि ण एदि देवी[9] ।

प्रविश्य[10]

18[38] P एदं तं, O इदं वडतरुमूलणिब्भिन्नस्स, SU वडअरु°, T वउसाहि°. — W णिकंतस्स, N विनिंहिदस्स. — O सुरुंगा°. — N °दुआरस्स. — P पिधाण, W विधाने, N पिहाण, OSU पिहाणं, T पिथाणं. — W चामुंडास्ते, O omits; T चामुंडाअदणं. — WO add इह (O एत्थ) ज्जेव (O ज्जेव्व) खणामेत्तं चिट्ठामि.

18[39] PN omit तां; W चामुंडा, O चामुंडां. — SU कृतांजलिः प्रणम्य. — N adds पठति.

19[a] P °भुवणा कोलस्स. — WNS omit पुरो. — P सुराराण, WN पुराण, O सुरासुर, ST सुरासुराण (T °णां). — W रुहिरसुरपुरं, N रुहिरसंपूअं.

19[b] PNO जअदि. — N चंडी परमेठ्ठी. — T °कपालचसएण.

19[1] P प्रविस्योपवि व. OSTU °श्योपसृत्य. — NO omit च.

19[2] O कहं अज्ज वि. — P निगच्छदि, N आअछदि, S णिग्गच्छइ. — O सुरुंगा°. — NO °दुआरेण.

19[3] U omits ततः. — W °द्घाटननाटितकेन, NSU सुरंगोद्घाटितकेम, T सुरंगोटितकेन.

19[4] TU कर्पू° पुरोवलोक्य. — P पणविज्जसि, WO पणमिज्जसि, N पणबिज्जसि.

19[5] P उच्चिदं, W पुत्ति इच्छियं, N उचिदं, S वच्छे इमं, T उदइं. — P वर. — W लह, OT लहेसु. S लहेहि, U लहस्सु.

19[6] N omits. — Mss. इह. — P य्येव, O ज्जेव्व, SU एव्व, T यव्व. — P उपसमु. W उपविस, O उवविससु, SU उवविसीअदु (S उप°), T उवविसडि.

19[7] PNSU omit. — W कर्पू° तथा कृत्वा. — T omits उपविशति.

19[8] PNOSTU omit भैर°; W स्व° भैर°. — OS omit स्वगतम्.

19[9] O कहं अज्ज. — STU ण एदि अज्ज

राजा । परिक्रम्य पुरोऽवलोक्य च[11] । इअं भअवदी चामुण्डा[12] । प्रणम्यावलोक्य च[13] । इअं कप्पूरमञ्जरी[14] । ता किं णेदं[15] । भैरवानन्दं प्रति[16] । इदं विअवीअदि णिअभवणे विवाहसामग्गिं कदुअ आअद म्हि[17] । ता गेण्हिअ आगमिस्सं[18] ।

भैरवानन्दः । वच्छे एवं करीअदु[19] ।

राजा व्यावृत्य परिक्रामति[20]

भैरवानन्दः । विहस्य स्वगतम्[21] । इअं कप्पूरमञ्जरीठाणं अण्णेसिदुं गदा[22] । प्रकाशम्[23] । पुत्ति कप्पूरमञ्जरि सुरङ्गादुवारेण ज्जेव तुरिदपदं गदुअ सट्ठाणे चिट्ठ[24] । देवीए आगमणे पुणो आगन्तव्वं[25] ।

कर्पूरमञ्जरी तथा करोति[26]

वि॰ — N णो गच्छदि॰ — P कलावदी देवी॰

19[11] WT राजा २, S देवी and omits the rest. — TU omit परिक्रम्य॰ — W विलोक्य॰ — P omits च; TU स्व॰

19[12, 13] O भअवं पणामामि । भैर । विरं जीअ उवविससु । देवी॰

19[12] P भयं, W अए इयं॰ — P भगवती देवी चा॰, W भवदी, SU ॰वई॰

19[13] PN प्रविश्यावलोक्य च, STU omit.

19[14] P अए इअं, W अध इयं, N इदो इअं, O अए कप्पू॰ इअं, T इअं अ॰

19[15] NSTU एदं, O खेदं॰

19[16] T प्रकाशं भैर॰ प्रति॰

19[17] W इयं, O भअवं इदं॰ — P विणावीयसि णियभुवणे, O ॰भवणं॰ — P कडुय विवाहसामगियं, N कदुअ वि॰, O गदुअ वि॰. — WT ॰सामग्गी, S विआह॰. — PW आगद म्हि. O omits; T आदंम्हि॰

19[18] P ततो, WN तदो तं. O omits; SU तं. — PO गेण्हाविअ, N गण्हाविअ, S गाहिअं॰ — ST आअमिस्सं॰

19[19] PNOT वत्से॰ — SU इदं, T एव्वं॰ — WO कोरदु, S करइ, TU किरदु॰

19[20] P व्यावृत्ति, S omits.

19[21] TU omit विहस्य॰

19[22] P omits इअं॰ — P कर्पूरमंजरी इति गेहमण्णेसिदुं, W ॰मंजरीघरं, SU ॰जरिट्ठाणं — W गदा इति निःक्रांता॰

19[23] O प्रकाशं कर्पूरमंजरीं प्रति॰

19[24] NOT ॰मंजरी॰ — P त्वं सुरंगाद्वारेण, N ॰दुआरेण, O सुरंगादवीरं॰ — P य्येव, N जेव्व, O ज्जेव्व, STU omit. — P तुरिदपद, N तुरिदं पदं, SU तुवरिअ॰, T तुरिअ॰. — P गडुय, W गदुअ. — P पंगणे, W णिअभवणे, T संगणे॰ — P विट्ठ

19[25] PWS देवी॰ — O आगमणेण, STU आअमणे॰ — O पुणो वि, S इह पुणो वि, TU पुणो इह॰ — W आतंतव्वं, STU आअं॰, TU ॰दव्वं॰

19[26] PU omit. — W कर्पू॰ । ठं भअवं आणवेदि । इति निष्क्रांता, N कर्पू॰ टुक्करं

राज्ञी । इदं रक्खाघरं[27] । प्रविश्यावलोक्य च स्वगतम्[28] । अए इअं कप्पूरमञ्जरी[29] । सा का वि सारिक्खा दिट्ठा[30] । प्रकाशम्[31] । वच्छे कप्पूरमञ्जरि कीदिसं दे सरीरं[32] । आकाशे[33] । किं भणासि[34] । मह सिरोवेअणा समुप्पण्ण त्ति[35] । स्वगतम्[36] । ता पुणो तहिं गमिस्सं[37] । प्रविश्य पार्श्वान्यवलोक्य[38] । हला सहीओ विवाहोवअरणाइं लहुं गेण्हिअ आअच्छध[39] । इति परिक्रामति[40] ।

प्रविश्य कर्पूरमञ्जरी तथैवास्ते[41]

राज्ञी । पुरोऽवलोक्य[42] । इअं कप्पूरमञ्जरी[43] ।

भैरवानन्दः । वच्छे विब्भमलेहे आणीदाइं विवाहोवअरणाइं[44] ।

करोदि, O कर्पू° । जं भवं आणावेदि त्ति निष्क्रांता.

19[27] PNS देवी, O राज्ञी निरूप्य. — NST एदं. — P रखगेहं, N रक्खागेहं, O रक्खाभवणं.

19[28] S omits च. — PWNO omit स्व°.

19[29] TU omit अए.

19[30] N omits सा; P adds पुणा. — P साक्खा, W सारक्खिआ, N सदिक्खा, O रस्सा सारिक्खए, S सारिच्छी, T सरिछि, U सरिच्छी. — P पिक्खिदा, W अक्खा, N मए पि, O चिट्ठदि.

19[31] PWNO omit.

19[32] PN वत्से. — PNOT °मंजरी. — N किदिसं, S कीरिसं, TU केरिसं.

19[34] WNSTU भणासि.

19[35] N सच्चा मह, TU omit मह. — P सिरोवेणा, W सिरेवेअणा N सरीरवेअणा. O °वेअणा. — PWNO omit समु°, TU °ण्णो. — PWN omit त्ति. — S adds ता खेरं सुप्पीअदु, TU खेरं सुप्पीअद.

19[36] P देवी, WO राज्ञी, NU राज्ञी स्व°, S omits.

19[37] TU omit ता. — U पुणो वि.

19[38] S omits प्रविश्य; T प्रका°. — PN पार्श्वतोवलोक्य O पार्श्वम°, STU पश्चादव°; O adds च.

19[39] W हेला. — PS omit सहीओ; N सुखीओ. — P °गरणाइं, W °णाइ, N °करणाइं, S विआहो°, T °होवरणं, U °होवअरणं. — P इह. WN लहु, STU omit. — W गिण्हअ, SU गण्हिअ. — P आगच्छध, W आगछध, N आअध, O आगमिस्सध. STU आअच्छह.

19[41] P omits प्रविश्य; O कर्पू° प्रविश्य.

19[42] S देवी. — PN add च. S adds स्व.

19[44] P कालवदि. TU मिअंकलेहे: SU add किं. — WO आणिदाइं, S आणिआइ. — P °वगरणाइं. N °पकरणाइं, S विआहो°, SU °णाइ. T °करणाइं.

राज्ञी । अध इं[45] । किं उण घणसारमञ्जरीसमुइदाइं आहरणाइं विसुमरिदाइं[46] । ता पुणो गमिस्सं[47] ।

भैरवानन्दः । एवं भोदु[48] ।

देवी निष्क्रामति नाटितकेन[49]

भैरवानन्दः । पुत्ति कप्पूरमञ्जरि तं जेव करीअदु[50] ।

कर्पूरमञ्जरी निष्क्रान्ता[51]

राज्ञी । रक्षागृहप्रवेशं नाटयति कर्पूरमञ्जरीं दृष्ट्वा[52] । अए सारिक्खदाए विणडिद म्हि[53] । स्वगतम्[54] । झाणविमाणेण णिव्विग्घं परिसप्पिणा तं आणेदि जोईसरो[55] । प्रकाशम्[56] । महीओ जं जं णिवेदिदं तं गेण्हिअ आअच्छध[57] । चामुण्डायतनप्रवेशनाटितकेन तामवलोक्य[58] । अहो सारिक्खदा[59] ।

19[45] WNSTU देवी. — PNO आणीदाइं, W omits; STU अह इं.

19[46] PWO पुण. — P °मंज्ञरीए समुचिताइं, WNO °समुचि°, S °दाइ, T समुचिआदं, U °इआइ. — PNSU आभरणाइं (SU °इ), T आभलणाइं. — P वीसरि°, W वीसरियाइं, SU °दाइ.

19[48] STU एव्वं. — PO कीरदु, N करीअदु, STU omit भोदु.

19[49] P omits देवी; WOTU राज्ञी. — W निक्रम्य, ST निष्क्रमणं, U निष्क्रामं. — S नाटयति.

19[50] STU omit पुत्ति. — P तं ज्येव, W तं ज्जेव, N तह ज्जेव, O तह ज्जेव्व, S तुए वि तहिं, T तुमं वि तं जेव्व, U तुए वि तं चेअ. — PWO कीरदु, S गंतंव, TU करिअदु.

19[51] S नायिका पूर्ववदाचरति, TU नायिका निष्क्रांता.

19[52] WOU देवी, N राज्ञी राजा च. S omits. — W °गृहे. — N नाटयतः. — STU नायिकां दृष्ट्वा. — S adds स्व.

19[53] P सारिच्छएण, W सिरिक्खएण, N सारिक्खिएण, STU सारिच्छेण. — N विणदिद, O विदंविद, STU विप्पलद्ध.

19[54] S omits

19[55] O णिव्विग्घपरिसप्पिणा झाण°, S °विमादेण, TU °विमाणेण. — P णिव्विग्घपरिसप्पिणा, W णिविग्घं परिसरे अप्पणो, N णिदिठ्ठं परिसप्पणं, STU णिव्विग्घेण. — PO तामाणेदि, W तं तमाणेदि, N तमाणेदि, S तं आणेइ, TU पुरिसं (T पुरुसं) इत्थिअं वा आणेदि (U °णेइ). — P महाज़ोगीसरो, W महाजोई, N महाजोओ.

19[56] WNSTU omit.

19[57–59] WNSTU omit महीओ. — N जं once only, ST omit; U जो. — W णिवेदिदव्वं, ST विवाहोइदाइं (S °इ), U विवाहोइदो. — PO तं तं, W तं लहुअं NST omit. — O गेण्हिअ, S

भैरवानन्दः । देवि उवविस महाराओ वि आअदो ज्जेव वट्टदि[60] ।

ततः प्रविशति राजा विदूषकः कुरङ्गिका च[61]

भैरवानन्दः । आसणं आसणं महाराअस्स[62] ।

सर्वे यथोचितमुपविशन्ति[63]

राजा । एसा सरीरिणी मअरद्धअपालिच्चिआ देहन्तरसंठिदा सिङ्गारसवरचावलट्ठी दिवससंचारिणी पुण्णिमाचन्दचन्दिआ[64] । अवि अ गुणगणमाणिक्कमञ्जूसा रदणमई बाउल्लिआ[65] । तधा अ एसा विसारिणी कुसुमणिब्भरा महुलच्छी[66] । किं च[67] ।

गणिहअ, U गणिहआ. — P आगदा, W गछध. S आअच्छत्म, T आअछह्म, U आअंछम्ह. — W °यतनेप्र°, N °यतननाटितकेन, S चामुंडागृहं प्रविश्य तामव° स्व, TU चामुंडामंटपप्रवेशं नाटयति प्रविश्य कर्पूरमंजरी पूर्ववदास्ते. — W तामलोक्य. TU राज्ञी तामव°. — W सारक्खिदा २. N सरिछअं, SU सारिच्छं. T सरिछं.

19[60] P वत्से कलावदि, W देवी. — WO उयविससु. — WTU omit वि. — PW आगदो. — P य्येव, NO ज्जेव्व, STU एव्व and omit वट्टदि.

19[61] T विदूषकश्च. — O सारंगिका च.

19[62] N omits भैर°. — WNS आसणं once only. — PSTU omit महाराअस्स.

19[64] N राजा नायिकां प्रति. TU राजा स्व. — WO एमा सा. — W कपूरमंजरी सारक्खिवया विलासचरणी instead of सरीरिणी. — P °च्छयापालिया, W °च्छियपरिच्छिआ, N मअद्धअपालिच्छिआ, O मअरद्धअस्स सव्वाधिआ सत्ती, STU °पालित्तआ. — P देहंतरं संट्ठिद, N देहंतरेण संट्ठिआ, STU omit. — P °सबधणुलट्ठी. W °सबर°, N सिंगाररसचावलिठ्ठी, O °संचअवावलट्ठी, STU सिंगाररसमर°, T °चाप°. — N दिअस°, ST दिअह°. — P पुणमुदिया, W पुण्णिमाइंद°, NO °अंद°, STU पुस्सचंद°.

19[65] S मखे, TU अवि अ मखे. — P पच्च्रयगुणमाणिक्कमंजूसा, W एसा गुणगणमाणिक्कसुन्निया, N प्पगुणगुण°, O प्पगुणगण°, S गुणगणण°. — BNOSTU रअण°. P णमयी, W मग्गिऊण मणस्स. — BPO अंजणस्स सलाआ, W वाउणिआ, N अंजणस्सलाआ, STU पुत्तलिआ.

19[66] P omits. — W जधा सु, N जधा अ, O जधा, SU जहा, T omits. — STU omit एसा. — B आरणकुसुममाणिप्पचा. W लावणकुसुमणिसणा, N रअणोकुसुमणिउणा, O अरणकुसुमणिप्फणा, STU विसारिणी कुसुमणिब्भरा. — O महुलट्ठी.

भुवणजअपडाआ रूवरेहा इमीए
जह तह णअणाणं गोअरं जस्स जाइ ।
वसइ मअरकेऊ तस्स चित्ते विचित्ते
वलइअधणुदण्डो पुङ्खिएहिं सरेहिं ॥ २० ॥

विदूषकः । जनान्तिकम[1] । सच्चं किदं तए आहाणअं[2] । तडं गदाए वि णावाए ण वीससीअदि[3] । ता तुण्हिक्को चिट्ठ[4] ।

राज्ञी । कुरङ्गिकां प्रति[5] । कुरङ्गिए तुमं महाराअस्स विवाहणेवच्छं कुण सारङ्गिआ वि घणसारमञ्जरीए करेदु[6] ।

20^{a} P °जणपडाया, W भुअणजयपडीया, N °जणवताआ, O °वडाआ, T °पदाआ. — WN रूअ°, STU रूवसोहा.

20^{b} BPO जह जह, T तह तह. — B गोअरे, N गोरसं. — BWNO जादि. P दि.

20^{c} PSTU णअणवल्लणसक्षा (P वयण°, PT °चलण°) पेसिदो तस्स मज्झे. — O वसदि. — B मयरधो, W मयरद्धो, N °केतु, O °केदु. — N विचित्तो.

20^{d} W वलईय°, N वलइद°. — B पुंदेहिं, P पुंखिदोसू, WNO पुंखिदेहिं, STU पुंखिदेसू. — PSTU अणंगो, W सरेहिं.

20^{1} B जनांतिकं । एकांते, PN जनांतिकेन.

20^{2} O वअस्स सच्चं, P सत्वं, T सच्वं. — B कयं, PW कदं, O omits, S एदाए गहिदं, U एआए गहिदं. — P ते, OSU omit; T तोए. — P आहणायं, O आहणअं सुणासु, S आभलणं, TU आभरणं; S adds कि दु, TU किं तु.

20^{3} B तड्डंगिदाए, PN तडंगदाए, W महाणयतडगदाए, O तडगदाए, ST तग्गदेण. U तग्गएण. — NSTU omit वि. — B णोकाए, PW णावाए, N णोआए, O णाविआए, SU विआरेण, T विआए. — B वोससदि, WOSU विस्ससीअदि, T विससिअदि.

20^{4} O omits. — S तं. — PWNSTU तुण्हीको. — P चिट्ठ, STU चिट्ठामि. — WO add पियवयस्स (W only) तुमं मअणसरप्पहारजज्जरिद(O °ज्जरिअ°)हिअअं एवं कुरूकुराअंतं (O कुरूकुरुअंतं) सुणिअ देवी तुम्ह अहिप्पाअं मुणिस्सदि (O सुणिस्सदि । तुण्हिक्कअं चिट्ठ) । भैरवानंदः । वच्छे (W only) पत्तं विवाहमंगलमुहुत्तं ता महाराअस्स किज्जदु जधोचिदं तए पडिवयां (W जहोचिदप्पडि°)

20^{5} U omits राज्ञी. — BO omit कुर° प्रति.

20^{6} B कुरंगीए, STU omit. — N तुअं. — B णोवत्थं, P °निवत्थं, N णोवच्छं, OS विआह°. — PWNO कुरु, S कु. — B

इत्युभे अप्युभयोर्विवाहघटनां नाटयतः[7]

भैरवानन्दः । उवज्झाओ हक्कारीअदु[8] ।

राज्ञी । एसो सअलसोत्तिअमोलिमण्डणं अज्जउत्तस्स उवज्झाओ अज्जकविञ्जलो चिट्ठदि[9] । ता करेदु अग्गिआरिअं[10] ।

विदूषकः । एस सज्जो म्हि[11] । भो वअस्स उत्तरीए गण्ठिं दाइस्सं दाव[12] । हत्थेण हत्थं गेण्ह कप्पूरमञ्जरीए[13] ।

राज्ञी चमत्कृत्य सविषादमवलोकयति[14]

सारंगीया, P सारंगिए. — PNSTU omit वि. — NT करोदु, O कोरदु.

20[7] BO इत्युभयोर्विवाह°, PN °वाहकरणं, STU उभे तह इत्युभयोर्विवाहालंकारं (S तहे त्ति उभ°, T °वाहनेपथ्यं) कुरुतः.

20[8] WO भैर° वच्छे. — B उवज्झाय, O उवज्जाओ. — B हक्कारियदु, T अक्कारिअदु.

20[9] BS omit राज्ञी; TU देवी. — B उपाध्याय आर्यकपिंजलस्तिष्टति. — PWNO read अज्जउत्त एसो वि (O omits) and omit सअल° अज्ज°; S सअलसोत्तिअमोलिमंडणं अज्जउत्तस्स एस, TU एस सअलसोत्तिअमोलिमंडणं अज्जउत्तस्स. — P उज्जाउ, O उव्वज्जाओ. — PN °कविंजलओ, STU °कइंजलो; S adds त्ति. — T चिटइ.

20[10] P भैरवानंद ता करेदु, O कोरदु, STU करीअदु. — B अग्गारियं, P अग्गिग्गारियं, N अग्गिआरिअ, STU अग्गिकज्जं.

20[11] O विदू° त्वरितमुत्थाय. — BPWO omit एस सज्जोम्हि, TU omit एस. — S omits म्हि.

20[12] ST omit भो वअस्स; U ता वअस्स. — N उत्तोरीए. O उत्तरीअयपडस्स, S उत्तरीअ, T उतरिवछे, U omits उत्त°-दाव. — B गठिं, N गंठी, T गथिं. — B दयस्स, N देविस्सं. O दइस्सं, S omits; T वयहामि. — N ताव, S omits.

20[13] B हस्ते हस्तं गृहाण कर्पूरमंजर्याः, W परिणेटु महाराउ कप्पूरमंजरिं इति हस्ते हस्तं ग्राहयति कर्पूरमंजर्याः, O तुमं हत्थेण, T वअस्स हत्थेण, U गहाण हत्थेण. — N हत्थं, SU हत्थंगुट्ठं. — P गेण्हे, N गेण्हिअ, SU omit; T कप्पूर° गिदाण.

20[14] BP इति राज्ञी चमत्कृत्य (P °ता), W राज्ञी इत्याकर्ण्य स्वगतं किं नेदं इति चमत्कृत्य, N इति भन्ता संमुहे इत्थमण्णअदि इति संस्कृत्य, O इति चमत्कृत्य कधं भुल्लो हं, S राज्ञी च° सविषादमालो°, TU देवी etc.

भैरवानन्दः । सुट्ठुदरं भुल्लो सि[15] । जदो कप्पूरमञ्जरीए घणसारमञ्जरि त्ति णामन्तरं[16] ।

राजा । करमादाय[17] ।

जे कण्टआ तिमिसमुद्धफलाण सन्ति
जे केअईकुसुमगब्भदलावलीसु ।
फंसेण णूण तुह मज्झ सरीरदिण्णा
ते सुन्दरीअ बहला पुलअङ्कुराली ॥ २१ ॥

विदूषकः । भो वअस्स भामरीओ दिज्जन्तु हुदवहे लाआमोक्खो करीअदु[1] ।

20[15] B omits भैर°; O भैर° तस्य भावमुपलभ्य विदूषकं प्रति; S reads भैर° वच्छे पडिसिद्ध, and then follows a lacuna which a second hand has filled out as in U; TU भैर° । वच्छे किं णु पडिसिद्धादरं विअ पुलोएसि (T विलोएसि). — SU omit सुट्ठु°-सि. — B सुट्ठदरं, W उव्वज्झाअ सुट्ठुदरं, N तुअं सुठ्ठुतरं, T सुट्ठुअरं. — P भल्लो, N भोलो, T भता. — W सखि, T सो.

20[16] O जादं, T अदो. — SU कप्पूरमंजरि त्ति. — BPSU घणसारमंजरीए, W °मंजर, NO °मंजरी, T omits. — B इत्ति, POSTU omit. — B नामधेयांतरं, P किमंतरं, W अपरं नामंतरं, STU णामंतरं एदं.

20[17] ST add स्वगतं.

21 B केअइतिउसस्स कंटया ते सुंदरीए करफंसरोमांचावलीसिक्खिदा धुवं.

21[a] P जे क वि धात्तिसस्स फले वसंति. W जे के वि ते तिउसमुद्धफलेसु हुंति. N तिउसमुद्धफले ण सति, O तिउसमुद्धफलाण होंति, S तिमिसबधफलाण.

21[b] P ये, N ते. — PWN °गंधदला°, O °गुच्छदलावलीसुं, SU °लीए.

21[c] ST पंसेण. — P नूह तुह मंजुसरीरजाया, W नूण तुह मज्झ सरीरतुल्ला, N तुज्झ पुण मज्झ सरारतुल्ला, O णूणमिह मज्झ सरीरओअस्स, STU ताण तह (T इह) मज्झ सरीरदिण्णा.

21[d] T दे. — PNO सुंदरीए. — P बहुपुलयंकुराए, W बहलं पुलअंकुरिल्ला, NSTU बहला (NT व°) पुलअंकुराली, O पुलआ बहला धउला.

21[1] B भो वयस्स । ता भामरीउ दिज्जउ । हुयवहे लाजा खिप्पंउ, P भामरियाउ दिज्जंतु. हुयासे लज्जामोखकं कीरदु. W भो वयस्स भामरीउ दिज्जंतु हुयवहे लाजा खिपिज्जतु. N भो वअस्स पज्जलिअहुअवहभमरीओ दिज्जदु हुअवहे जलांज-

राजा सर्वं तथैव नाटयति[2] । नायिका सलज्जा तिष्ठति[3] । राजा विवाहं निर्वर्त्य सोत्साहं यथार्हं सर्वान्समभ्यर्च्य चक्रवर्त्ती भूत्वा आसां चक्रे[4] ।

नेपथ्ये[5]

लोओ क्खिवदु, O भो वअस्स भामरिओ दिज्जंतु वहूलाजंजलोओ खिप्पदु:, S वअस्स पज्जलिए हुअवहे आहुदी दिज्जइ । (lacuna) क्खो । तुवरिअपदं दिज्जउ भमरीओ, TU वअस्स पज्जलिदे (U °र्ण) हुदवहे आहुदी दिज्जउ (T °ई) करउ लाआमोक्खो । तुवरिअपदं करीअदु सत्तपदी परिक्कमो.

21[2–4] B भ्रामर्य्यां नाटयंति । नायका धूमेन व्यावृतमुखी । राज्ञी सपरिवारा निःक्रांता, P भ्रामर्यौ नाटयतः । नायिका धूमेन विमुखी । राज्ञी परिवारा निःक्रांता । राजा सर्वं करोति विवादं निवर्त्य सोत्साहं सर्व्वानपि यथार्हमभ्यर्च्य विसर्ज्य चा चक्रवर्त्ती भूत्वा तया सह आसां चक्रे सहर्षां, W भ्रामर्या नाटयंति नायका धूमेन व्यावृत्तमुखी । राज्ञी सपरिवारा निःक्रांता । सव्वाणं पच्चक्खं परिणीदा कप्पूरमंजरी. N राजा भमणं नाटयति । नायिका धूमेन व्यावृतमुखी तिष्टति । राज्ञी सपरिवारा निःक्रांता, O राजा तथा करोति, S इति परिणयति.

21[5]–24 BPW omit. — N भैरवा । विवाहे दक्खिणा दिज्जदु आचरिअस्स । राजा । दिज्जदु । वअस्स णामणअं ते दिस्सं । विदू । सुत्थि होदु त्ति नतन्ति । भैरवा । महाराअ किं ते पुणो वि पिअं कुणोमि । राजा जोईस्सर कि अवरं प्पिअं वट्टदि end of the ms. The translation adds यतः कुंतलेश्वरसुताकरस्पर्शस्फारसौख्यशिथिलीकृतः स्वर्गः । पालयामि वसुधातलराज्यं चक्रवर्तिपदवीरमणीयम । तथाप्येतद्भवतु तावत् । सार्थो नन्दतु सज्जनानां सकलो वर्गः खलानां पुनर्नित्यं खिद्यतां भवतु ब्राह्मणजनः सत्याशीः सर्वदा । येघो मुंचतु संचितमपि सलिलं सस्योचितं भूतले लोको लोभपराङ्मुखो ऽनुदिवसं धर्मे मतिं बिभर्तु. — O भैर° राजानं प्रति किं ते भूओ प्पियमुवकरेमि राजा भअवं तुह प्पसादेण एसा लद्धा राज्ञी परिणेदु महाराओ सव्वाणं पच्चक्खं नेपथ्ये वैतालिकः पठति सुहणिवधो भोदु विवाहमहूसवो देवस्स तहा अमअणमिव रई सा वासुदेवं व लच्छी हरमिव गिरिपुत्ती साहिलासं पउत्ता सुहअदु सह अ त्तं चक्कवत्ती पहूदं सिरिरिव किंदवंसा सामरज्जस्स वीआ राजा विवाहं निर्वर्त्य योगिनं प्रति तथा वि इदं भोदु भरदवअणं २ । णिच्चं वट्ठदु सज्जणाण सअलो वग्गो खलाणं पुणो णिच्चं खिज्जदु भोदु बंभणजणो सच्चासिहा सव्वदा । मेहो मुंचदु संचिअं पि सलिलं सस्सप्पिअं भूअले लोओ लोहपरम्मुहो णुदिअहं धम्मे मदिं पावस दुस्कृतमाश्रित्य स्वामिंस्त्वच्चरणारविंदवशतः श्रृंगारसंजीविनी लब्धा पंचशरप्रिया ननु मया कर्पूरमंजर्यसौ तल्लाभेन च चक्रवर्त्तिपदवी लोके समासादिता किं किं नेह करोति हंत महतां संदर्शनं जतुषु.

वैतालिकः । सुहाअ भोदु विवाहमहूसवो देवस्स[6] ।

जं मुद्धं तिमिसं णवं च पणसं जे पारिभद्दुमा
जे दण्डा कमलाण किं च कुसुमं जं केअईसंभवं ।
सव्वं तुज्झ कलेवरे गुणगणं लद्धं बला तारिसा
रोमञ्चा फुडपुट्ठकण्टअमिसा मेल्लन्ति णिच्चुल्लसा ॥ २२ ॥

भैरवानन्दः । अण्णं किं दे पिअं करीअदु[1] ।

राजा । इदो वि परं किं पिअं[2] । जदो[3] ।

देवी रोसकसाअमाणसवई णो होइ सावत्तए
लद्धा पुण्णससङ्कमण्डलमुही सिङ्गारसंजीविणी ।
संजाआ अवि चक्कवट्टिपअवी किं अण्णमब्भत्थणं
सव्वं तुज्झ अणुग्गहेण भरिअं जं माणुसे लब्भइ ॥ २३ ॥

तधा वि इदं भोदु[1] ।

भरतवाक्यम्[2]

21[6] T वैतालिकयोरेकः. — SU सुहो. — Mss. होदु — After देवस्स T adds सुहोवणादसअलमहो सुरमंडलविरइदसोत्थित्ताअणम्मुहलिददसदिसावह विवाहसवो संउत्तो.

22[a] T जं मुतंधं तिणीसं. — TU ण. — S दे पारिभद्द (lacuna).

22[b] S जो दंडो.

22[c] T संते तुज्झ करम्स तं. SU कलेबरे. — T लद्धं. — K मंगे तव करस्य यत् गुणगणं लब्धुंफलास्ताट्टशा.

22[d] SU रोमंचप्फुड°. T रोमंचे फुठपुट्ट. — TU मेलंति. — K रोमांचेरितकंटकमिषात मेलंति नित्योज्ज्वलाः.

22[1] SU पिअं ते (U दे). — T करिअदु.

22[2] S इदो परं किं पिअं. — TU किं अवरं वि.

22[3] SU omit; T अदो.

23 S omits.

23[c] T चक्कवट्टी°. — TU °पदवी. — T अणमब्भत्थं.

23[d] TU भरिदं. — TU लंभइ. K लभ्यते.

23[1] S तथापीदमस्तु. — T भैर । तधि. U तह. — T मदं. — TU होदु.

अणुदिअहं विफुरन्तो मणीसिजणसअलगुणविणासअरो
रिन्नत्तणदावग्गी विरमउ कमलाकडक्खवरिसेण ॥ २४ ॥

इति निष्क्रान्ताः सर्वे[1] ।

चतुर्थं जवनिकान्तरम्[2] ।

---

24 TU अणुपमगुणं कईणं परिमलमहिअं मुहेसु विभरंति (T विभरदि) कप्पूरमंजरीअं तिभुवणतिलअं पुणो जलइ. — K as S. — S °दिअह विप्फु°. — T adds राजा कर्पूरमंजरीं हस्ते गृहीत्वा कौतुकागारं विवेश.

24[1] BS omit; O इति परिक्रम्य निष्क्रांताः सर्वे.

24[2] B इति चतुर्थं, STU इति चतुर्थं. — P WSU यव°.

Part II

GLOSSARIAL INDEX

TO THE

KARPŪRA-MAÑJARĪ

BY

STEN KONOW

GLOSSARIAL INDEX

Abbreviations:—ts. = **tatsama.** — H. = Hemacandra's Grammatik der Prâkritsprachen (Siddhahemacandram, Adhyâya VIII) mit kritischen und erläuternden Anmerkungen herausgegeben von Richard Pischel. Theil I. II. Halle, 1877, 1880. — HD. = The Deśînâmamâlâ of Hemachandra. Edited with critical notes, a glossary, and a historical introduction, by R. Pischel and G. Bühler. Part I. Bombay, 1880 (Bombay Sanskrit Series, No. XVII.).

अ *after anusvāra* **च** [च] *and.* **a**, i. 1^{1}, 3^{1}, 5^{b}, 12^{3}, 17^{1}, 20^{27}, 22^{1}, 23^{b}, 26^{1}, 33^{1}, $34^{d, 33}$; ii. 4^{1}, 5^{2}, 6^{c}, 9^{d}, $11^{c, 5}$, 23^{d}, $27^{b, 1}$, 28^{c}, $30^{c, 1}$, $31^{d, 1}$, 40^{5}, 46^{b}, 50^{b}; iii. 1^{1}, 3^{d}, $4^{3, 5}$, 5^{5}, 6^{1}, $8^{1, 2}$, 13^{1}, 14^{1}, 15^{1}, 17^{1}, 18^{1}, 20^{c}, 21^{1}, 22^{b}, $25^{d, 1}$, 27^{1}, 31^{1}, 32^{1}; iv. 2^{b}, 6^{1}, 9^{c}, 10^{1}, 18^{32}, $19^{65, 66}$. **ca**, i. 1^{c}, 11^{1}, 18^{7}, 19^{d}, $20^{15, 26, 29, 31}$, $22^{a, b}$, $23^{c, 1}$, 34^{30}, 35^{c}; ii. $6^{24\ 26}$, 10^{c}, 23^{d}, 24^{d}, 29^{2}, $47^{b, d}$; iii. $3^{d, 18}$, 5^{a}, 12^{1}, 18^{d}, 19^{b}, 20^{d}; iv. 3^{1}, $18^{12, 13, 24}$, 19^{67}, $22^{a, b}$.

अअं *see* **इदम्.**

अइ [अयि] *a vocative particle, O, prithee,* ii. 6^{4}.

अइदीह [अतिदीर्घ] *very long,* i. 21^{d}.

अए [अये] *a vocative particle, O, ah,* i. 5^{2}; iv. $19^{29, 53}$.

अंस ts. *a shoulder,* iv. 12^{a}.

अंसुअ [अंशुक] *a garment, cloth,* i. 28^{b}; iv. 4^{a}, 10^{a}.

अंहि [अंह्रि] *a foot,* ii. 47^{a}.

अकङ्कणा [°न] *without bracelets,* iii. 26^{b}.

अकण्ड [अकाण्ड] *unexpected, sudden,* iv. 18^{d}.

अकधिद *untold, see* **कथ्.**

अकलिअ *not performed, see* **कल्**

अकालजलद ts. *name of a man,* i. 18^{2}.

अकुङ्कुम ts. *without saffron,* iii. 26^{a}.

अकुण्डल ts. *without earrings,* iii. 26^{b}.

अक्खर [°क्षर] *a letter,* i. 20^{14}; ii. 1^{2}, 8^{2}, 10^{6}.

अखण्ड ts. *unbroken, whole, entire,* iv. 3^{b}.

अखण्डिद [°त] *unbroken,* i. 16^{3}.

अगुरु ts. *aloe,* iii. 14^{b}, 27^{a}.

अग्ग [अग्र] *first, foremost; front, foremost point,* i. 16^{c}, 26^{a}; ii. 6^{a}, 14^{b}, 20^{a}, 43^{a}.

अग्गहत्थ [अग्रहस्त] *forepart of the hand or arm,* i. 4^{c}.

अग्गिआरिआ [अग्निकारिका] *arranging of the sacred fire,* iv. 20^{10}.

अग्गिम [अग्रिम] *first*, i. 29^{b}.

अग्घ [अर्घ्य] *a respectful offering*, i. 4^{d}.

अघडिअ *not performed, see* घट्.

अङ्क ts. *act of a drama*, i. 6^{b}.

अङ्कुर ts. *a sprout, shoot, blade*, iv. 21^{d}.

अङ्ग ts. *a body, limb*, i. 13^{b}, 14^{2}, $20^{15, 16, 31}$, 33^{a}; ii. 10^{c}, 12^{a}, $28^{b, c}$, 36^{a}, 41^{a}, 42^{b}; iii. 8^{4}, 17^{c}, 19^{a}, 24^{b}, 33^{a}; iv. 7^{b}, 13^{b}.

अङ्गण [°न] *a place, courtyard*, ii. 47^{d}; iii. 20^{15}; iv. 11^{b}.

अङ्गणा [°ना] *a woman, female*, i. 14^{2}, 25^{c}, 36^{d}; iii. 16^{d}.

अङ्गुलि ts. *a finger*, i. 36^{c}.

अचन्दण [°न] *without sandal*, iii. 26^{a}.

अच्चब्भुद [अत्यद्भुत] *very wonderful, supernatural*, i. 21^{b}.

अच्चहम [अत्यधम] *exceedingly inferior*, i. 20^{4}.

अच्चुत्तम [अत्युत्तम] *exceedingly superior*, i. 20^{4}.

अच्छ ts. *clear, transparent*, iii. 4^{b}.

अच्छरिअ [आश्चर्य] *marvellous, wonderful; a wonder*, i. 24^{5}, 25^{13}; ii. 42^{b}; iii. 3^{12}.

अच्छि [अक्षि] *eye*, i. 16^{3}; ii. 3^{2}, 27^{a}, 41^{c}; iv. 1^{b}.

अजणिअ *not produced, see* जन्.

अज्ज [अद्य] *to-day*, i. 20^{34}, 34^{25}; ii. 1^{2}, $6^{14, 23}$, 29^{5}; iii. $3^{4, 7}$, 20^{3}, 24^{b}; iv. 9^{18}, 18^{28}, $19^{2, 9}$.

अज्ज [आर्य] *an honorable man, master*, i. 12^{5}, $20^{5, 11, 36}$, 34^{1}; ii. 6^{7}; iv. 20^{9}.

अज्जउत्त [आर्यपुत्र] *honorific designation of the husband*, i. 19^{6}, 34^{38}; iv. 20^{9}.

अज्झक्ख [अध्यक्ष] *superintendent, head*. ajjhakkhikidāo, iv. 9^{12}.

अञ्चल ts. *border, end, skirt*, i. 26^{c}, 27^{b}; iii. 3^{c}, 22^{2}.

अञ्जण [°न] *collyrium*, i. 20^{36}, 26^{a}; ii. 19^{a}.

अञ्जलि *see* जलञ्जलि.

°अण *see* सुरअण.

अणङ्ग [अन°] *Cupid*, i. 2^{b}, 33^{d}; ii. 6^{d}.

अणङ्गकेली [अन°] *name of a woman*, iv. 9^{11}.

अणङ्गलेहा [अनङ्गलेखा] *name of a woman*, iv. 9^{9}.

अणङ्गसेणा [अनङ्गसेना] *name of a woman*, iv. 9^{8}.

अणन्तर [अन°] *without interval, immediately adjoining*, i. 12^{2}; iv. 18^{11}.

अणिल [अनिल] *wind*, i. 16^{4}, 17^{d}, 20^{c}; iii. 20^{b}.

अणुकार [अनु°] *resembling*, iii. 25^{c}, 28^{d}.

अणुग्गह [अनुग्रह] *favor*, iv. 23^{d}.

अणुणअ [अनुनय] *conciliation*, i. 20^{43}.

अणुदिअहं [अनुदिवसम्] *day after day*, iv. 24^{a}.

अणुबन्ध [अनु°] *continuity, sequence*, iii. 25^{a}.

अणुराअ [अनुराग] *love*, iii. 12^{2}.

अणुसार [अनु°] *conformity to*, ii. 31^{b}.

अण्ण [अन्य] *other*. aṇṇo, i. 20^{39}; ii. 6^{8}, $29^{12, 13}$; iv. 18^{36}. aṇṇā, i. 4^{5}. aṇṇaṁ, i. 18^{7}, $20^{2, 31}$; ii. $6^{24, 26}$; iii. 13^{c}, 14^{c}, $16^{c, 2}$; iv. 22^{1}, 23^{c}. aṇṇaṁ ca, *moreover*, i. 18^{7}, 20^{31}. aṇṇeṇa, i. 27^{d}; iii. 19^{c}. aṇṇe, iv. 2^{1}. aṇṇā, iv. 13^{a}, 15^{b}, 17^{a}. aṇṇāṇaṁ, i. 1^{b}.

°अण्ण [कर्ण] *ear, see* आ[अण्ण].

अण्णोण्ण [अन्योन्य] *each other*, iii. 9^{2}; iv. 10^{b}.

अत्त- [आत्मन्] *self, oneself*. appā, i. 8^{1}. attāṇaaṁ, iii. 4^{1}, 8^{1}. **attaṇo, ii. 10^{6}**; iii. 20^{b}.

अत्थ [अर्थ] *object, meaning*, i. 8[a], 20[7, 8].

अत्थाचल [अस्ता॰] *the western mountain behind which the sun is supposed to set*, ii. 50[d].

अत्थाणी [आस्थानी] *an assembly-room*, ii. 3[a].

अदस् *that, yonder.* amuṇā, i. 26[d].

अदिणिउण [अतिनिपुण] *very clever*, ii. 29[10].

अदिसंताविं- [अतिसंतापिन्] *very burning, hot*, ii. 41[5].

अदिसिसिर [अतिशिशिर] *very cold*, ii. 41[5].

अद्द [आर्द्र] *wet, moist*, ii. 11[c].

अद्ध [अर्ध] *half, half portion, side*, i. 25[b], 28; ii. 42[11].

अद्धणारीसर [अर्धनारीश्वर] *Çiva as half female*, i. 28[4].

अद्धणिद्द [अर्धनिद्र] *half asleep*, ii. 50[a].

अध [अथ] *now, then*, ii. 11[3]. adha iṁ [atha kiṁ], *what else, yes, certainly*, i. 4[17], 21[6]; iv. 19[45]. adha vā [atha vā] *or, or rather*, i. 18[10], 30[2]. *Cp.* अह.

अन्त ts. *end*, i. 14[d]; iii. 2[b]; iv. 9[8, 9, 10, 11].

अन्तर ts. *interior; interval; different, another*, i. 7[b], 12[3], 29[a, d], 34[34], 35[b]; ii. 1[a]; iii. 3[b]; iv. 18[27], 19[64], 20[16].

अन्तरिद [॰त] *gone within, hidden*, ii. 43[2, 12].

अन्तरेण ts. *without, except*, i. 34[17, 18]; iv. 18[36].

अन्तेउर [॰पुर] *inner apartments, harem*, i. 34[38]; ii. 11[3]; iv. 9[13].

अन्तो [अन्तर्] *internally, within*, iii. 10[b], 12[a].

॰अन्द [चन्द्र] *the moon.* muhaanda, ii. 17[b].

अन्दोल- *to swing, wave, shake.* andolia, i. 17[b]. andolida, i. 16[3].

अन्दोलण [॰न] *swinging*, ii. 35[a], 37[b].

अन्धआर [॰कार] *darkness*, iii. 22[8].

अपुव्व [अपूर्व] *not having existed before, quite new, wonderful*, i. 25[4], 34[25].

अप्प- *see* अत्त-.

अबला ts. *a woman*, i. 15[a]; iv. 7[d].

अब्भत्थणा [अभ्यर्थन] *request*, iv. 23[c].

अब्भुअ [अद्भुत] *wonder*, i. 26[d].

अब्भुट्ठाण [अभ्युत्थान] *rising from a seat in honor of*, iii. 20[23].

अमुणा *see* अदस्.

अमोहण [॰न] *not bewildering*, iii. 26[c].

अम्बु ts. *water*, iii. 4[a].

अम्महे H. 4. 284. *a particle expressing joy*, i. 34[24].

अम्मो H. 2. 208. *a particle expressing surprise*, iii. 20[15].

अम्हारिस [अस्मादृश] *like me*, iv. 2[2].

॰अर [कर] *causing, performing*, i. 15[b], 34[33]; ii. 28[d]; iv. 24[a].

अर्च् *to honor, praise.* accemi, iii. 22[d]. accido, i. 34[33]. accidā, ii. 6[23, 25].

अलअ [॰क] *a curl, lock of hair*, i. 26[a]; ii. 20[a].

अलंकार ts. *decoration, ornament*, i. 31[a]; ii. 24[2].

अलंकिअ, ॰किद *see* कृ.

अवअव [॰यव] *a limb*, i. 33[c]; ii. 48[a].

अवदृध *see* तृ + अव.

अवत्था [॰स्था] *state, condition*, ii. 8[3], 9[1].

अवदारेदि *see* तृ + अव.

अवन्तिसुन्दरी ts. *name of the wife of Rājaçekhara*, i. 11[b].

अवर [अपर] *another*, iv. 12[a], 18[a].

अवराइद [अपराजित] *name of a poet*, i. 8[3].

अवसर ts. *occasion, turn,* ii. 0[5], 47[4]; iii. 26[2].

अवसाण [°न] *stopping, end,* iv. 10[a].

अवस्सं [°श्यम्] *necessarily,* iv. 18[14].

अवि [अपि] *and, also; though,* i. 1[1], 3[1], 17[1], 22[1], 26[1], 33[1]; ii. 4[1], 5[2], 27[1], 29[c], 30[1], 31[1]; iii. 1[1], 6[1], 8[2], 13[1], 14[1], 15[1], 21[1], 25[1], 27[1], 32[1]; iv. 6[1], 9[b], 19[65], 23[c].

अविणीद [°नीत] *immodest, insolent,* iii. 8[1].

अस *to be.* mhi, i. 29[d]; ii. 28[2]; iii. 3[7, 9, 11, 18]; iv. 19[17, 53], 20[11]. si, ii. 6[13], 11[1]; iii. 22[d]; iv. 2[8], 20[15]. atthi, i. 25[d, 5], 34[8]; iii. 9[b], 13[c], 14[d], 16[c]; iv. 9[2, 3], 18[18]. santi, iv. 21[a]. āsi, i. 18[2, 8].

असुर ts. *a demon,* ii. 31[b]; iv. 19[a].

असोअ [°शोक] *a tree with red flowers, Jonesia Açoka,* i. 20[27]; ii. 42[31], 43[a], 46[1], 47[a].

असोसण [अशोषण] *not drying up, not withering up,* iii. 26[c].

अह [°थ] *then,* ii. 3[d]. *Cp.* **अध.**

अहं *I.* ahaṁ, i. 13[1], 16[1], 18[1, 6], 20[14, 16, 30, 41], 34[15, 30, 38]; ii. 6[6], 28[4], 32[2], 41[6]; iii. 3[15, 18], 4[1, 4], 34[9]; iv. 7[1], 18[24]. haṁ, iii. 7[d]. maṁ, i. 20[15, 28], 28[8], 32[d], 34[22, 38]; ii. 1[d]; iii. 3[a], 20[17], 34[9]. mae, i. 25[6], 34[25]; ii. 6[14], 8[3], 24[2]; iii. 3[c, 4]; iv. 18[7]. majjha, i. 16[1]; ii. 40[2]; iii. 23[a]; iv. 21[c]. mama, iii. 4[9]. maha, i. 18[8], 19[b], 20[29, 40], 25[d], 30[d], 34[10]; ii. 3[c], 6[20], 8[c], 9[1], 29[12, 21], 42[11]; iii. 24[b]; iv. 19[35]. me, i. 18[2], 20[23, 25], 34[5, 13]; iii. 2[d], 3[d], 16[2], 20[d]; iv. 2[10]. amhe, i. 16[2], 34[30], 36[1]. amhāṇaṁ, i. 4[2], 19[5], 20[20]. ṇo, i. 1[c].

अहह ts. *a particle implying sorrow or surprise, alas,* i. 25[13]; ii. 42[b].

अहिणअ [अभिनय] *acting, gesticulation,* iv. 15[b].

अहिणव [अभिनव] *new, original,* iii. 31[1].

अहिदेवआ [अधिदेवता] *presiding deity,* ii. 48[b].

अहिप्पाअ [अभिप्राय] *intention,* ii. 48[1]; iii. 8[b].

अहिव [अधिप] *a king,* i. 12[b, 8]; iii. 5[2].

अहो ts. *a particle expressing surprise,* i. 29[2]; ii. 29[21], 42[2, 5]; iii. 4[6], 31[1]; iv. 0[2], 9[13], 19[59].

अहोमुह [अधोमुख] *having the face downwards,* ii. 13[b].

आ [आस] *a particle expressing pain or anger,* i. 18[6], 20[28]; iv. 2[8].

आ *prep., to, until,* iv. 4[a, b]. āaṇṇaṁ [ākarṇam] *up to the ear,* ii. 6[d]. āmūlaṁ, *to the ground,* i. 4[b].

आअड्ढिअ *see* **कृष.**

आअदण [आयतन] *a sanctuary, altar,* iv. 18[30].

आअर [आदर] *attention, care,* i. 13[c].

आअर [°कर] *see* **कुसुमाअर.**

आअल्लअ [°यल्लक] HD. 1. 75. *impatience, longing,* ii. 10[6].

आइ [°दि] *first; beginning with,* i. 1[a]; iii. 10[a].

आउह [°युध] *weapon,* iii. 26[c].

आगमण [°न] *coming, return,* iv. 19[25].

आडम्बर ts. *show, display,* ii. 24[b], 32[b], 47[c]; iii. 12[2].

आडम्बरिल्ल H. 2. 159. *ostentatious, imposing,* ii. 31[a].

आढत्त H. 2. 138. *applied,* iv. 9[11].

आणण [°नन] *mouth*, *face*, ii. 1[c], 30[a]; iii. 3[a], 16[a].

आणन्दण [°नन्दन] *pleasing*, *delighting*, iii. 28[b]

आणावेदि *see* **ज्ञा + आ.**

आणा [°ज्ञा] *an order*, *command*, i. 18[d].

आतङ्क ts. *disease*, *pain*, iv. 7[d].

आदेस [°श] *an order*, *command*, ii. 42[27, 28].

आप + प्र *to get*, *obtain*, *arrive*. patto, i. 13[d]; iii. 4[b]. pattā, i. 20[b]; ii. 28[3]. pattammi, i. 35[b].

+ सम *to complete*; *to arrive*, *come*. samattā, ii. 44[d].

आरम्भ ts. *beginning*, i. 12[8].

आलवाल ts. *a basin or trench for water round the root of a tree*, i. 34[39].

आलिङ्गण [°न] *embracing*, ii. 1[c], 43[a], 44[b].

आली ts. *row*, *series*, ii. 11[c]; iv. 21[d].

आवली ts. *line*, *row*, *range*, i. 4[4], 20[b, 8, 25]; ii. 16[a], 31[a], 32[c]; iii. 26[d]; iv. 2[10], 21[b].

आविल ts. *turbid*, *greasy*, i. 13[a].

आवेस [°श] *entering into*, *devotedness*, *passion*, ii. 1[3].

आसण [°न] *a seat*, i. 21[2], 24[1], 34[4]; iv. 19[62].

आसम [°श्रम] *a hermitage*, i. 17[a].

आसा [°शा] *hope*, ii. 9[d].

आहरण [आभ°] *an ornament*, i. 20[26], 28[a]; iv. 10[a], 14[b], 19[45].

आहा [°भा] *light*, *appearance*, ii. 41[b].

आहाणअ [°भाणक] *a proverb*, iv. 20[2].

इ *to go*. ei, iii. 10[b]. edu, ii. 0[3].

+ आ *to come*. edi, iv. 19[9]. enti, i. 15[d]. ehi, i. 12[1], 34[3, 22]; iii. 20[5]. entī, ii. 31[d].

इं [किम्] *see* **अध इं.**

इअ [इति] H. 1. 91. *thus*, i. 9[b]; ii. 22[a], 40[a].

इणं *see* **इदम्.**

इत्थं ts. *thus*, i. 18[c], 33[c]; ii. 41[c].

इदम् *this*, *that*. aaṁ, ii. 45[2]; iv. 18[12]. iaṁ, i. 4[3], 26[d], 35[c]; ii. 29[15]; iv. 18[38], 19[12, 14, 22, 29, 43]. iṇaṁ, ii. 27[d]; iii. 8[a]. idaṁ, i. 24[1]; ii. 22[1], 28[1]; iii. 20[19]; iv. 2[a], 19[17, 27], 23[1]. imaṁ, ii. 29[c]. imiṇā, i. 12[8], 28[2]; iii. 19[2], 34[b, 9]. assa, i. 10[a]. imāe, i. 34[4]. imīe, ii. 24[c]; iv. 20[a]. imīa, i. 28[b]. ime, i. 4[9]. imā, iv. 14[a]. imāu, iv. 11[a]. imāo, i. 34[32]. imīu, iv. 10[b]. imāṇam, i. 7[b].

इदर [इतर] *another*, i. 4[4].

इदो [इतस्] *hence*, *this way*, *further*, ii. 0[3], 41[8]; iv. 10[1], 22[2].

इध [इह] *here*, i. 14[3], 20[27], 25[7]; ii. 29[16], 41[2]; iv. 18[28], 19[6]. *Cp.* **इह.**

इन्दआल [इन्द्रजाल] *jugglery*, iii. 20[19, 21].

इन्दजाल *the same*, ii. 44[1]; iii. 12[d].

इन्दीवर ts. *a blue lotus*, ii. 3[c].

इन्दु ts. *the moon*, ii. 1[c], 29[d], 30[d], 41[b]; iii. 1[c], 32[a].

इव ts. *like*, *as*, *as it were*, iii. 20[b], 28[a].

इष् *to wish*. icchāmi, i. 24[5]. icchaï, i. 11[b]. icchanti, ii. 28[d]. icchidā, i. 34[35].

+ अनु *to search*. aṇṇesīadu, i. 20[39]. aṇṇesiduṁ, iv. 19[22].

+ प्र *to dismiss*, *send*. pesehi, i. 34[38]. pesedu, iii. 34[9]. pesiaṁ, ii. 7[a]. pesida, ii. 6[17]. pesidā, iv. 9[14], 18[24].

इह ts. *here*, i. 7[b]; ii. 48[a]; iii 13[c], 16[c], 17[a]; iv. 2[a]. *Cp.* इध.

ईक्ख्+उप *to neglect, overlook, disregard.* uvekkhīadi, iii. 20[3].

+प्र *to see.* pekkhāmi, iii. 20[19]. peccha, i. 14[d]; iii. 32[b], 34[b]; iv. 10[b]. pekkha, i. 18[9]; ii. 43[5], 44[1]. pekkhadu, i. 16[3]. pecchantīṇaṁ, ii. 30[c]. pekkhidavvāiṁ, iv. 9[18].

ईदिस [°दृश], *fem.* °sī, *such*, i. 18[5], 20[26, 33], 34[17]; ii. 45[1].

ईस [ईषत्] *slightly*, iii. 23[a]. īsīsa, i. 14[b]; iii. 4[9]. īsīsi°, ii. 1[5].

ईसर [°श्वर] *see* जोईसर.

ईसारोस [ईर्ष्यारोष] *jealous anger*, i. 4[a].

उ ts. *an expletive particle*, iii. 13[b], 14[a, b].

उअर [°दर] *the belly*, ii. 1[b].

उआर [°दार] *noble, exalted*, i. 19[3].

उइद [°चित] *fit, proper*, i. 4[3]; ii. 10[6]; iv. 19[5].

उक्कर [°त्कर] *a heap, multitude*, i. 19[a]; iv. 18[36].

उक्केर H. 1. 58. *the same*, iii. 1[d].

उक्ख् *to sprinkle, wet, moisten.* ukkhiāṇaṁ, iv. 8[c].

उच्च ts. *high, elevated*, ii. 31[a].

उच्चअ [°य] *a collection, heap*, i. 28[a]; ii. 21[a]; iv. 10[a].

उच्चोड [√चुट्] *withering*, ii. 10[a].

उच्छङ्ग [उत्सं°] *lap, interior*, ii. 29[a]; iii. 27[d].

उज्जल [उज्ज्वल] *bright, shining, beautiful*, i. 34[d]; ii. 40[a], 41[a]; iii. 4[b], 27[a].

उज्जाण [°द्यान] *pleasure-garden, park*, ii. 6[22]; iii. 22[6, 9]; iv. 18[30].

उज्जुअं [ऋजुकम्] *directly, straightforwardly*, i. 20[4, 20].

उज्जोद [उद्द्योत] *light, lustre*, iii. 24[2], 26[1].

उडु ts. *a star.* uḍusamaa, *evening*, i. 36[b].

उड्डामरिअ [°त] *terrified*, ii. 29[b].

उण [पुनर्] *again, however*, i. 4[2, 16, 19], 6[b], 16[2], 20[8, 14, 25, 30, 41], 28[6], 33[b], 34[33]; ii. 1[c], 6[24], 8[3], 10[6], 24[3], 29[4], 32[2], 41[8], 42[14], 43[8, 11], 48[2], 49[2]; iii. 8[2], 9[1], 16[2], 33[b], 34[3]; iv. 1[b], 2[2], 5[1], 7[1], 9[12], 19[46]. *Cp.* पुणो.

उण्णअ [उन्नत] *high, elevated*, iii. 16[b].

उण्ह [उष्ण] *hot, warm*, ii. 11[a].

उत्तंस ts. *crest, chaplet*, iii. 29[a]; iv. 7[a].

उत्तर ts. *northern; accompanied with, consisting chiefly of*, i. 18[a]; iv. 9[11].

उत्तरफग्गुणी [°फल्गुनी] *the 12th lunar mansion, preceding Hasta, which word means also hand*, i. 20[16].

उत्तरासाढा [°षाढा] *the 21st lunar mansion; preceding Çravaṇa, which word means also ear*, i. 20[31].

उत्तरीअ [°य] *an upper garment*, i. 34[5]; iv. 20[12].

उत्ताण [°न] *stretched out, conceited*, i. 19[5].

उत्तास [उत्त्रास] *fear, terror*, iii. 7[b].

उत्ति [उक्ति] *speech, expression*, i. 8[b], 20[1]; iii. 31[1].

उत्तुङ्ग ts. *lofty, high, tall*, ii. 29[15]; iii. 7[c].

उत्थम्भण [उत्तम्भन] *raising*, i. 18[b].

उद्देस [°श] *place, region*, ii. 42[26].

उप्पत्ति [उत्पत्ति] *birth, origin*, i. 34[17].

उप्पल [उत्पल] *a blue lotus*, i. 34[c]; iv. 7[b].

उप्पिउ *see* ऋ *Caus.*

उप्फुल्ल [उत्फु°] *opened, swollen,* i. 20[b].

उब्बिम्बिर HD. 1. 127. *fem.* °rī, *afflicted, dejected,* ii. 9[c].

उब्बुड्डुण H. 4. 101. *emerging, rising,* ii. 31[d].

उब्भिज्जदि *see* भिद् + उद्.

उमा ts. *name of the wife of Çiva,* i. 24[c].

उम्मत्त [उन्म°] *drunken, mad,* ii. 2[d].

उम्मुक्क *see* मुच् + उद्.

उम्मुद्दिद [उन्मुद्रित] *unsealed, opened,* ii. 47[5].

उम्ह- [उष्मन्] *heat,* iv. 1[a].

उरई [°गी] *a female snake,* i. 20[a].

उल्लस ts. *sport, play; splendor,* ii. 47[b]; iv. 22[d].

उल्लासि- [°सिन्] *shining,* i. 28[b].

उवअरण [उपक°] *instrument, means,* iv 9[18], 19[39, 44].

उवआर [उपचा°] *procedure, (remedial) treatment,* ii. 41[6], 42[2, 8, 21]; iii. 19[2].

उवज्झाअ [उपाध्याय] *teacher,* i. 9[a]; iv. 20[8,9].

उवमा [उप°] *resemblance; as last member of a compound, like to,* i. 32[b]; iii. 16[b]; iv. 9[d].

उवमाण [उपमान] *comparison,* i. 30[c].

उवरि [उप°] *above, over,* ii. 20[b], 33[?]; iii. 3[?]; iv. 9[12].

उवह H. 2. 211; HD. 1. 98 *see lo,* ii. 50[d]

उव्वेल्ल [उद्वेल] H. 4. 223. *overflowing,* ii. 1[b].

उहअ [उभय] *both,* ii. 18[?], 42[21]; iv 2[?].

ऊसव [उत्स°] *festival, pleasure,* i. 13[d], 16[3], 18[d]; iv. 21[6].

ऊसुअ [उत्सुक] *desirous, eagerly expecting,* ii. 40[2].

ऋ *Caus., to give, offer.* appenti, ii. 38[b]. uppiu, ii. 19[b].

एक्क [एक] *one.* ekka, i. 26[d]; iii. 25[d]; iv. 1[b], 2[a], 7[d], 9[d]. ekko, i. 18[1], 20[41]; ii. 6[22]; iii. 17[c]. ekkā, i. 4[3]. ekkaṁ, i. 25[6], 26[c]. ekkeṇa, i. 24[c], 27[a]; ii. 6[25]; iii. 4[5]. ekkassiṁ, i. 20[26]. ekke, iv. 2[1].

एक्कत्थ [एकस्थ] *near,* ii. 8[d].

एक्कमित्त [एकमित्र] *the one or only friend,* ii. 50[c].

एक्कावली [एका°] *a single string of pearls,* i. 20[7]; iii. 5[b], 6[a], 20[3].

एक्केक्कआ [एकैकता] *the being one-by-one.* °āe, *one by one, singly,* iii. 5[a].

एक्केक्कम HD. 1. 145. *one another,* iii. 10[a].

एण ts. *a black antelope,* ii. 21[b].

एणङ्क [एणा°] *the moon,* iii. 28[d].

एणणाहि [°नाभि] *musk,* ii. 7[b].

एण्हिं H. 2. 134. *here, now,* i. 14[c], 20[c]; ii. 43[1].

एतद् *this, that.* esa, i. 4[10], 28[6]; ii. 27[1]; iv. 3[c], 7[d], 20[11]. eso, i. 4[7], 28[2, 5], 34[24], ii. 6[10, 20], 43[13], 46[1]; iii. 8[2], 20[15], 34[3, 8]; iv. 18[3], 20[9]. esā, i. 20[2, 18, 40], 28[3], 30[d], 32[c], 34[1, 34]; ii. 6[17], 8[b], 10[2, 3], 41[c, 8]; iv. 9[14], 18[14, 20], 19[64, 66] eaṁ, i. 5[a], 11[b], 35[a]; ii. 8[c]. edaṁ, i. 4[11], 5[2], 31[1], 34[5]; ii. 6[4], 10[8], 29[8], 41[1], 42[7], 43[2]; iii. 9[1], 12[3], 34[5, 7]; iv. 5[1], 18[8, 10, 27, 34, 35]. edassa, i. 5[6], 28[3, 8]. eāi, ii. 40[a]. edāe, i. 31[1],

33[2]; ii. 9[1], 10[4]. ee, iv. 4[d]. edaiṁ, ii. 8[2]. edāhiṁ, ii. 10[5]. edāṇaṁ, i. 34[31, 33].

एत्तिअ H. 2. 157. *so much, so great*, ii. 6[15].

एत्थ [अत्र] *here*, i. 12[b], 25[5], 34[8]; ii. 8[3], 9[1], 44[d], 47[1, 4]; iii. 12[b]; iv. 5[1], 18[18]. etthantare, *in the meantime*. i. 29[d].

एदावत्थ [एतदवस्थ] *being in that condition*, i. 34[38].

एमेअ [एवमेव] H. 1. 271. *just so*, ii. 49[a]; iii. 9[b].

एरिस [ईदृश] *such*, iii. 21[b].

एवं ts. *thus, so*, i. 18[12], 20[15, 17, 28, 30]; ii. 6[7], 40[4], 50[5]; iii. 3[2], 8[6], 16[1]; iv. 4[1], 18[35], 19[19, 48].

ओट्ठ [°ष्ठ] *lip*, i. 13[a]; ii. 41[a].

ओदिस्स *see* तृ+अव.

ओलग्गाविआ HD. 1. 164. *a female servant*, ii. 9[1], 28[4].

ओल्ल [आर्द्र] H. 1. 82. *wet, moistened, juicy, fresh, new*, i. 28[b]; iii. 1[b]; iv. 4[a], 7[b].

ओसह [औषध] *a medicament*, iv. 6[d].

कअली [कद°] *the plantain tree*, ii. 14[b]; iv. 18[3].

कइ [°वि] *a poet*, i. 1[a], 4[19], 5[5], 6[2], 8[3], 9[a], 10[a], 20[2].

कइत्तण [कवित्व] *poetry, office of poet*, i. 19[5], 20[6, 18], ii. 10[2].

कइन्द [कवीन्द्र] *a king of poets, a honorific epithet of a poet*, i. 11[a].

कइराअ [कविराज] *the same*, i. 9[a].

कउ [क्रतु] *a sacrifice*, i. 24[b].

कक्कस [कर्कश] *hard, rough, merciless*, i. 20[43].

कङ्कण ts. *a bracelet*, i. 18[10].

कङ्केल्ली ts. HD. 2. 12. *the Açoka tree*, i. 17[c].

कच्च [काच] *glass, crystal*, i. 20[26].

कज्ज [कार्य] *work, affair, business*, ii. 6[8], 28[4], 29[1, 4, 8, 12]. kiṁ kajjaṁ, *what is the use of*, ii. 28[a]; iii. 1[a], 12[2], 19[c].

कज्जल ts. *lampblack, used as a collyrium*, i. 20[7]; ii. 23[a], 41[b], 46[a]; iii. 33[b]; iv. 14[a].

कञ्चण [काञ्चन] *gold*, i. 32[a]; ii. 12[b]; iii. 1[b].

कञ्चणचयड [काञ्चन°] *name of a bard*, i. 16[2]; iii. 26[1].

कञ्चणमाला [काञ्चन°] *name of a woman*, iv. 9[10].

कञ्चणसेल [काञ्चनशैल] *mount Meru*, ii. 15[b].

कञ्ची [काञ्ची] *name of a town in Southern India, Conjevaram*. i. 15[a].

कञ्ची [काञ्ची] *a girdle*, i. 34[a]; ii. 15[a], 23[c], 34[b], iii. 18[a].

कञ्चुलिआ [°का] *a bodice*, i. 20[7].

कञ्जिअ [काञ्जिक] *sour gruel*, ii. 29[11].

कड् + प्र *to show, display, manifest*. paaḍei, iii. 12[c], 17[d]

कडक्ख [कटाक्ष] *a glance, a side-long look*, i. 29[a]; iv. 24[b].

कडिल्ल HD. 2. 52. *a cloth girt round the loins*, i. 27[d].

कडिसुत्तअ [कटिसूत्र] *a girdle*, i. 20[9].

कढिद *see* क्वथ्.

कण ts. *a drop*, iv. 8[c].

कणअ [कनक] *gold*, i. 20[9]; iii. 22[b]; iv. 9[12].

कणक्कणिअ [क्वणक्वणित] *tinkling*. ii. 32[b].

कणिट्ठ [°निष्ठ] *youngest*, ii. 6^{24}.

कण्टअ [°क] *a thorn, prickle, sting*, iii. 24^{a}; iv. 21^{a}, 22^{d}.

कण्ठ ts. *the throat*, i. 16^{3}, 20^{27}; ii. 1^{b}, 2^{a}, 17^{a}; iii. 2^{c}, 6^{b}, 20^{7}; iv. 17^{a}.

कण्ड [का°] *an arrow*, i. 16^{3}; iii. 18^{d}.

कण्डारेद्ग *to excavate; carve, sculpture.* °riūṇa, iii. 17^{d}. *According to O* = utkīrya. *Cp. Marāṭhī*, kaṁḍāraṇeṁ.

कण्ण [°र्ण] *ear*, i. 20^{40}, 32^{b}; ii. 27^{a}; iii. 20^{2}.

कण्णउज्ज [कान्यकुब्ज] *name of a city, Kanouj*, iii. 5^{2}.

कण्णऊर [कर्णपूर] *an ornament worn in the ear, an ear-ring*, i. 14^{2}.

कण्णा [कन्या] *a young girl*, i. 25^{6}.

कण्णाडी [कर्णाटी] *a Karṇāṭa woman*, i. 15^{c}.

कण्णुप्पल [कर्णोत्पल] *an ear-lotus*, i. 34^{c}.

कत्थूरिआ [कस्तूरिका] *musk*, i. 18^{18}, 34^{39}.

कध् *to tell, say.* kadhemi, i. 32^{4}; iv. 9^{5}. kadhehi, ii. 11^{2}. kadhedu, iii. 2^{3}. kadhesu, iii. 16^{2}; iv. 18^{9}. kahijjau, i. 5^{a}. kadhīadu, i. 34^{7}; iii. 3^{6}. kadhido, ii. 41^{9}, 50^{2}. akadhidā, i. 28^{4}. kadhidaṁ, i. 5^{7}.

कधं [कथम्] *how, why*, i. 18^{15}, 30^{1}; ii. 1^{2}, $6^{15, 21}$, 11^{6}, 40^{2}; iii. 10^{1}, 22^{4}; iv. 2^{11}. *Cp.* कहं.

कन्नारत्तण *wretchedness, imbecility* (*K*, kārpaṇya), i. 19^{2}, 20^{7}.

कन्ति [का°] *loveliness, beauty*, ii. 27^{b}, 30^{b}.

कन्द ts. *a root, bulb, garlic*, iii. 28^{c}, 29^{b}.

कन्दप्प [°र्प] *Cupid*, i. 16^{3}; ii. 40^{b}, 41^{d}; iii. 28^{c}.

कन्दप्पकेली [°र्पकेली] *name of a woman*, iv. 9^{11}.

कन्दलिद [°त] *richly or suddenly produced*, i. 16^{3}.

कन्दलिल्ल H. 2. 159. *shooting, sprouting*, iii. 28^{c}.

कन्दली *the plantain tree; a new shoot, sprig*, ii. 14^{b}; iii. 20^{a}; iv. 7^{e}.

कन्दोट्ट HD. 2. 9. *a blue lotus*, iii. 3^{b}.

कप्पन्त [°ल्पान्त] *end of the world, universal destruction*, iv. 19^{a}.

कप्पूर [°र्पूर] *camphor*, i. 17^{b}, 29^{c}, 34^{39}; iii. 28^{a}; iv. 5^{c}.

कप्पूरमञ्जरी [कर्पू°] *name of the heroine of our play*, i. $34^{20, 24}$; ii. 6^{24}, 28^{3}, $29^{6,7}$, 40^{2}, $42^{15,17}$; iii. 8^{4}, 20^{23}, 22^{1}, 31^{1}; iv. 9^{6}, $19^{2, 14, 22, 24, 29, 32, 43, 50}$, $20^{13, 16}$.

कम [क्र°] *succession, regular course, manner*, iii. 4^{b}, 5^{b}, 25^{d}; iv. 3^{c}.

कमल ts. *a lotus*, ii. 11^{d}, 16^{a}, 50^{a}; iv. 22^{b}.

कमला ts. *a name of Lakṣmī*, iv. 24^{b}.

कम्पि- [°म्पिन्] *shaking, agitating*, i. 17^{c}.

कम्म- [°र्मन्] *action, performance*, iv. 16^{b}.

कम्मण [कार्मण] *magic, witchcraft*, ii. 26^{b}.

कर ts. *hand; ray, beam*, ii. 16^{a}, 42^{a}; iii. 20^{c}, 24^{b}, 25^{c}.

करण्ड ts. *a box*, iv. 9^{10}.

करण ts. *doing, making*, ii. 6^{15}; iv. 16^{b}.

करण्डिआ [°का] *a small box*, iii. 5^{2}.

करवाल ts. *a sword*, iv. 9^{8},

कराल ts. *gaping; terrible; fem. a terrible form of Durgā*, i. 18^{8}, 20^{28}; iv. 16^{a}.

करालिअ [°त] *made terrible*, iv. 2^{b}.

करि- [°रिन्] *an elephant*, ii. 6^{10}.

कल् *to hold, do, notice.* akalia, i. 2^{a}. kalida, iv. 9^{10}.

कलकण्ठ- [°ण्ठिन्] *the cuckoo*, i. 16^{3}.

कलङ्क ts. *stain, fault*, iii. 10ª.

कलण [°ना] *doing, putting on*, iii. 28ᶜ; iv. 4ª.

कलम ts. *rice*, i. 19ª.

कलम्ब ts. *the Kadamba tree*, iii. 24ª.

कलस [°श] *a water-pot.* thaṇakalasa, *a breast like a water-pot*, ii. 24ᵇ; iii. 7ᵈ. thaṇakalasiṇī, *a woman having such breasts*, ii. 23ᵇ.

कलहंस ts. *a swan*, iii. 23ᵇ.

कला ts. 1. *a small part; a digit of the moon*, i. 4ᵇ; ii. 10ᶜ, 46ª; iii. 25ᵈ. 2. *any practical art*, ii. 27ᶜ.

कलिआ [°का] *a flower, bud*, ii. 27ª; iii. 1ª.

कलिङ्गसेणा [°ना] *name of a woman*, iv. 9⁹.

कलेवर ts. *body*, iv. 22ᶜ.

कल्लोलवदी [°ती] *name of a woman*, iv. 9¹².

कल्लोलिणी [°नी] *a river*, ii. 3ª.

कवलण [°न] *eating, swallowing*, i. 20ᵇ.

कवलिअ [°त] *eaten, chewed*, iii. 2ᵇ.

कवाल [°पाल] *the skull*, iv. 19ᵇ.

कविञ्जल [कपि°] *name of the Vidūṣaka*, i. 20⁴˒ ³⁶˒ ⁴³, 34¹; ii. 27¹, 29¹; iv. 20⁹.

कवोल [°पोल] *the cheek*, i. 32ᵇ; iii. 33ᵇ.

कव्व [काव्य] *a poem, poetry, a Kāvya*, i. 1ᵈ, 8ᵇ, 19⁶˒ ⁷, 20⁴˒ ⁶; ii. 4ᶜ.

कष् *to rub, test, try.* kasīadi, i. 18¹⁸.

कस + वि *to open, bloom.* viasanti, ii. 43ᵇ.

कसवट्टिआ [कषपट्टिका] *a touch-stone*, i. 18¹⁸, 19⁷.

कसाअ [कषाय] *red, affected*, iv. 23ª.

कहं [कथम्] *how*, iv. 1ª, 3ᵈ. kahaṁ pi [kathamapi] *somehow, in any way*, ii. 39ª; iii. 32ª. *Cp.* कधं.

कहिं H. 3. 60. *where*, i. 35ᵇ; ii. 42¹⁹, 43³. kahiṁ pi, *somewhere, anywhere*, i. 24⁵, 25⁴.

काअ [°य] *body*, iv. 14ª.

काण ts. *one-eyed*, i. 20⁷.

काणण [°नन] *a forest, park*, ii. 22ᵇ.

काम ts. *love, Cupid*, ii. 5ᵇ; iv. 2², 7ᶜ.

कामं ts. *well, forsooth*, iii. 19².

कामरूव [°प] *Assam*, i. 14².

कामसेणा [°ना] *name of a woman*, iv. 9ᵈ.

कामिणी [°नी] *a loving, beautiful woman*, i. 33ª; ii. 43ᵇ, 48ª; iii. 18ᶜ; iv. 6ᶜ.

कार ts. (*at the end of comp.*) *author*, i. 8³.

कारण ts. *reason, cause*, ii. 27ᵈ, 42¹⁴, 47¹; iii. 1ᵈ, 9ᵇ.

कारामन्दिर ts. *a prison-house, jail*, iv. 9⁸.

कारि- [°रिन्] *doing, causing*, ii. 10ª.

काल ts. *time; death, the destroying god*, i. 8³; ii. 6⁸, 28ᵈ, 41⁹, 50²; iii. 4³; iv. 2ᵇ, 19ª.

काल ts. *black*, iv. 14ª, 18ᵇ.

कालक्खरिअ [°लाक्षरिक] *a scholar*, i. 18¹.

कालन्तर [°लान्तर] *opportunity*, i. 35ᵇ.

काली ts. *a name of Durgā*, iv. 19ᵇ.

काश् + प्र *to appear, become manifest.* paāsai, iii. 11ᵈ.

किआ [क्रिया] *performance, a religious rite*, i. 24ᵇ.

किद [कृति] *work, composition*, i. 11ᵇ.

किंसुअ [°शुक] *a tree, Butea frondosa, having red blossoms*, i. 16ᶜ.

किंकरी ts. *a female servant*, i. 36ᵇ.

किङ्किणी ts. *a bell*, i. 20⁹; ii. 32ᵇ, 34ᵇ; iv. 17ª.

कित्ति [कीर्ति] *fame*, ii. 35ᵇ.

कित्तिम [कृत्रिम] *artificial*, ii. 28ª.

किम *the interrogative pronoun, who, what, which; with* vi, pi, *it is indefinite, some one, a certain. The neuter* kiṁ *is used with instr. in the sense, what is the use of?* kiṁ *is used also as an interrogative particle.* kiṁ ca, *moreover, further.* ko, i. 4^{19}, $5^{a, b}$, 16^{1}, 20^{39}, 28^{2}, 35^{b}; ii. 23^{c}, 27^{c}, $29^{12, 13}$, 47^{4}; iii. 15^{c}. kā, i. 4^{6}, 16^{1}, 20^{12}, 33^{c}, $34^{1, 3}$; ii. 25^{b}, 27^{d}; iii. 1^{b}; iv. 9^{2}, 6^{a}, 19^{30}. kiṁ, i. 1^{c}, $4^{2, 12, 16}$, $6^{b, 2}$, 8^{1}, 11^{1}, 16^{2}, $18^{8, 10, 13, 16}$, $19^{d, 6}$, $20^{2, 4, 20}$, $21^{3, 5}$, 22^{a}, 23^{1}, 24^{4}, 25^{1}, 28^{8}, 34^{c}, 35^{c}; ii. 6^{16}, $10^{c, 2, 6}$, $11^{3, 4}$, 16^{b}, 24^{4}, $28^{a, d}$, $29^{c, 4}$, 41^{8}, $42^{7, 12, 14, 15, 16, 17, 32}$, 43^{11}, 47^{1}, 48^{2}; iii. $1^{a, d}$, 2^{1}, $8^{4, 5}$, 9^{1}, $12^{1, 2}$, $13^{a, b, c}$, $14^{a, b, c}$, $16^{a, b, c, 2}$, 19^{c}, $20^{3, 15, 16, 17}$, $34^{a, 3}$; iv. $2^{4, 6}$, 3^{1}, 4^{c}, 9^{14}, $18^{8, 29}$, $19^{15, 34, 46, 67}$, $22^{b, 1, 2}$, 23^{c}. kaṁ, ii. 11^{2}. keṇa, i. 10^{1}. kassa, i. 23^{d}, 27^{c}; ii. 32^{d}, 40^{b}, 42^{9}; iii. 8^{2}, 9^{a}; iv. 6^{d}. kie, iii. 9^{a}. ke ii. 42^{30}.

किरण ts. *a ray, beam,* ii. 29^{d}, 50^{c}; iii. 26^{d}.

किराद [°त] *a Kirāta; a dwarf,* iii. 34^{8}.

किल ts. *certainly, I think,* ii. 8^{b}.

किलकिल- *to sound, jubilate, laugh.* °lai, ii. 34^{b}

किलम्मइ *see* **क्लम**.

किसलअ [°य] *a young and tender shoot,* ii. 42^{a}.

कीदिस [°दृश] *of what kind,* i. 20^{36}; ii. 42^{28}; iii. 3^{6}, 9^{3}; iv. 19^{32}.

कीस H. 3. 68. *why,* ii. 42^{26}.

कुग्गाम [°ग्राम] *a petty village or hamlet,* i. 18^{18}.

कुङ्कुम ts. *saffron,* i. 13^{c}, 16^{a}; ii. 8^{a}, 12^{a} iii. 14^{b}, 15^{d}, 20^{3}.

कुच्च [कूर्च] *beard,* i. 20^{40}.

कुज्ज [°ब्ज] *humpbacked, crooked,* iii. 34^{8}.

कुट्टिणी [°नी] ts. *a bawd,* i. 18^{6}, 34^{34}.

कुडिल [°टिल] *crooked, curled,* ii. 20^{a}.

कुडुम्ब [°टुम्ब] *family, household, relationship,* i. 4^{12}, 34^{31}.

कुण्डल ts. *an ear-ring,* ii. 18^{a}.

कुण्डलिअ [°त] *bowed, bent,* ii. 6^{d}.

कुन्त ts. *a lance,* iv. 9^{10}.

कुन्तल ts. *the hair of the head,* ii. 41^{b}.

कुन्तल ts. *name of a country,* i. 12^{b}, 34^{8}. kuntalī, *a Kuntala woman,* i. 15^{c}.

कुन्दमाला ts. *name of a woman,* iv. 9^{10}.

कुप *to be angry.* kuppadi, ii. 47^{3}. kuppa, i. $20^{5, 11}$.

कुप्पासअ [कूर्पासक] *a sort of bodice,* i. 13^{b}.

कुमरी [°मारी] *a girl,* ii. 22^{a}; iii. 17^{c}.

कुमारत्तण [°त्व] *childhood, the age from 10 to 12,* iii. 16^{2}.

कुम्भ ts. *a pitcher, water-pot, jar,* ii. 44^{a}.

कुम्भअड [°ष्माण्ड] *a white gourd,* iv. 18^{8}.

कुम्भुब्भव [°म्भोद्भव] *an epithet of Agastya,* i. 17^{a}.

कुरङ्गच्छी [°ङ्गाक्षी] *a deer-eyed woman,* ii. 3^{2}.

कुरङ्गिआ [°का] *name of a woman, the confidential servant of Karpūramañjarī,* iii. 19^{2}; iv. 20^{6}.

कुरल ts. *a lock of hair,* i. 15^{a}.

कुरवअ [°क] *a species of amaranth* ii. 42^{31}, $43^{a, 13}$, 44^{a}, 45^{a}.

कुरुकुराअ- *to croon, grumble, growl.* °rā-anto, iii. 2^{1}. °rāantī, i. 18^{15}.

कुल ts. *family, herd, collection,* i. 11^{a}, 17^{c}, 19^{7}; ii. 2^{d}, 44^{d}.

कुलमग्ग [°मार्ग] *the doctrine and practices of left-hand Çāktas,* i. 22^{b}.

कुल्ला [°ल्या] *a river, stream,* ii. 10^{d}.

कुवलअ [°य] *the blue water-lily,* ii. 19^{b}, 38^{b}, 42^{a}.

कुसल [°शल] *skilful, clever,* i. 1^{d}.

कुसीलव [°शीलव] *an actor,* i. 4^{2}.

कुसुम ts. *a flower,* i. 4^{4}, 16^{b}; ii. $6^{19, 21}$, 7^{a}, 21^{a}, 44^{c}, 45^{b}; iii. 1^{d}, 22^{c}, 24^{a}; iv. 18^{36}, 19^{66}, 21^{b}, 22^{b}.

कुसुमसर [°शर] *Cupid,* iii. 7^{b}; iv. 2^{a}.

कुसुमाअर [°कर] *the spring,* ii. 1^{5}.

कुसुमाउह [°युध] *Cupid,* ii. 35^{b}.

कुहर ts. *a cavity,* ii. 30^{b}; iii. 20^{7}.

कूर ts. *food, boiled rice,* i. 19^{a}.

कृ *to make, do, prepare. Caus., to cause to do.* kuṇai, ii. 31^{c}; iv. 8^{d}. karedi, i. 20^{33}; iv. 18^{36}. kuṇanti, i. 14^{b}; iv. 14^{b}, 15^{b}. karissaṁ, ii. 10^{5}, 43^{2}; iv. 2^{4}. kuṇa, iv. 20^{6}. karedu, iv. $20^{6, 10}$. kuṇanto, ii. 50^{a}. kuṇantā, i. 15^{c}; iii. 28^{c}. kuṇantāṇã, ii. 46^{b}. kāduṁ, ii. 6^{14}. kāūṇa, ii. 8^{a}. kadua, ii. 8^{3}; iii. 5^{2}; iv. 9^{7}, 18^{11}, 19^{17}. kijjai, ii. 27^{c}; iii. 15^{c}. karīadi, i. 20^{26}. kijjau, iii. 1^{a}. karīadu, i. 20^{40}, 25^{1}; ii. 43^{10}, 50^{5}; iv. $19^{19, 50}$, 21^{1}, 22^{1}. kaa, iv. 17^{a}. kida, ii. 6^{15}. kao, iii. 32^{b}. kido, ii. 9^{1}; iv. 18^{22}. kaaṁ, ii. 47^{b}. kidaṁ, i. 19^{6}; ii. 6^{24}, $11^{3, 4}$, 47^{1}; iii. 30^{2}; iv. 20^{2}. kae, ii. 10^{d}. kide, ii. $42^{9, 10, 13}$. kidāo, iv. 9^{12}. kaāī, ii. 19^{a}. karaṇijjaṁ, i. 12^{2}. kādavvā, i. 34^{35}. kādavvaṁ, i. 24^{4}; ii. 29^{2}. kārio, ii. 15^{b}. kāridaṁ, iv. 18^{30}.

+ अलम् *to decorate.* °kiaṁ, i. 33^{a}. °kidā, ii. 24^{2}.

कृष् *to draw, drag away, bend.* kaḍḍhijjai, ii. 29^{b}. kaḍḍhia, i. 32^{c}. kaḍḍhidāo, iii. 4^{3}.

+ आ *to draw, pull, snatch.* āaḍḍhia, i. 29^{b}.

कॄ *to spread, scatter* kirai, iii. 20^{b}. kirantā, iii. 28^{b}.

केअअ *fem.* **केअई** [°तक] *name of a plant,* i. 29^{b}; ii. 7^{a}; iv. 21^{b}, 22^{b}.

केआरिआ [°दारिका] *a meadow,* iii. 20^{3}.

केदई [°तकी] *name of a plant,* ii. $6^{19, 20, 21, 22}$.

केलि ts. *play, sport, amorous sport,* i. 24^{d}, 26^{c}; iii. 20^{3}, 23^{b}, 31^{b}; iv. 2^{6}, 9^{11}.

केलिआर [°कार] *causing pastime,* i. 14^{2}.

केलिकाणण [°नन] *a pleasure-park,* ii. 22^{b}.

केलिभवण [°न] *a pleasure-house,* iv. 19^{a}.

केलिवदी [°ती] *name of a woman,* iv. 9^{12}.

केलिविमाण [°न] *a pleasure-palace,* iv. 9^{18}.

केलिसअण [°शयन] *a pleasure-couch,* iii. 27^{c}.

केलिसेज्जा [°शय्या] *the same,* iii. 3^{a}.

केवलं ts. *only,* i. 6^{b}, 24^{c}; ii. 28^{2}.

केस [°श] *hair,* i. 26^{b}.

केसर ts. *the filament of a flower, fibre; the Bakula tree,* iii. 1^{d}, 24^{a}, 25^{c}.

कोअण्ड [°दण्ड] *a bow,* i. 16^{3}; iii. 30^{b}.

कोइल [°किल] *the cuckoo,* i. 18^{c}; iii. 31^{b}.

कोउहल्ल [कौतूहल्य] *desire, curiosity,* ii. 38^{a}; iv. 18^{a}.

कोऊहल *the same*, ii. 49^{a}.

कोडि [°टि] *ten millions*, iii. 5$^{b, 3}$.

कोडु HD. 2. 33. *desire, curiosity*, ii. 37^{b}; iii. 3^{c}.

कोदुअघर [कौतुकगृह] *a pleasure-house*, iv. 18^{32}.

कोमल ts. *tender, soft*, ii. 10^{c}; iii. 33^{a}.

कोल [कौ°] *belonging to the left-hand Çāktas*, i. 23^{d}.

कोलाहल ts. *a loud and confused noise*, iii. 34^{3}.

कोस [°श] *membrum virile*, i. 20^{28}.

क्खु, हु, *after* ā *and anusvāra* खु [खलु] *indeed, methinks*. kkhu, i. 20^{43}; iv. 2^{4}. hu, i. 4^{6}, 20^{38}, 34$^{b, 17, 18}$; ii. 42$^{a, b}$, 48^{b}; iii. 9^{b}; iv. 2^{a}, 18^{36}. khu, i. 5^{2}; ii. 0^{5}, 6^{6}, 10^{2}; iii. 3^{d}.

क्रम *intens. Caus., to cause to go.* caṅkamio, ii. 18^{b}.

+अति *to pass.* adikkanta, iv. 18^{11}.

+आ *to attack, subdue.* akkanta, i. 14^{2}.

+निस् *to go away, to leave.* ṇikkamamha, iii. 22^{9}.

क्री *to buy.* kiṇido, iii. 4^{5}. kiṇidā, i. 34^{15}.

+वि *to sell.* vikkiṇīadi, i. 18^{18}. vikkiṇidā, iii. 5^{3}.

क्लम *to be tired out, exhausted.* kilammāmi, iii. 19^{2}. kilammantī, iii. 20^{3}. kilanto, iii. 8^{1}.

क्वथ् *to boil.* kaḍhia, ii. 6^{b}. kaḍhida, iii. 20^{3}.

क्षल्+प्र *Caus., to wash, wipe away.* pakkhālido, iii. 3^{9}.

क्षिप *to throw, cast.* khivanti, iv. 13^{a}.

खअ [क्षत] *hurt, torn, broken; a wound*, i. 28^{a}; ii. 11^{b}.

खग्ग [°ड्ग] *a sword*, iv. 9^{11}.

खञ्ज् *to limp, halt.* khañjia, i. 21^{c}.

खडक्किआ HD. 2. 71. *a side-door, back-door*, iii. 20^{11}.

खडिआ [°टिका] *chalk*, iii. 33^{a}.

खण [क्षण] *an instant, moment*, ii. 3^{2}, 40^{3}, 41^{c}, 47^{d}; iv. 9^{b}, 18^{32}.

खण्ड- *to break, cut, crush.* khaṇḍissaṁ, i. 20^{16}. khaṇḍijjaï, iv. 3^{d}. khaṇḍaanta, i. 15^{b}.

खण्ड ts. *a piece, part*, i. 23^{c}.

खण्डणा [°ना] *breaking, cutting, frustrating*, ii. 27^{d}; iv. 3^{b}.

खलखण्ड *a kind of cake? jest, joke?* (*K*, kalikhaṇḍa apūpaviçeṣaḥ, *N*, deçyāṁ khaḍikhaṇḍaçabdaḥ krīḍāvācakaḥ), i. 34^{15}.

खाद् *to eat.* khajjae, i. 23^{b}.

खाम [क्षाम] *thin, emaciated*, ii. 6^{10}.

खार [क्षार] *salt*, ii. 11^{b}.

खिण्ण [°न्न] *afflicted, tired*, i. 20^{a}.

खिवइ *see* क्षिप.

खु *see* क्खु.

खुट्टइ H. 4. 116. *to fall short*, ii. 4^{a}.

खुर [क्षुर] *a razor*, iv. 3^{d}.

खेलइ *to play, move to and fro.* khelanti, iv. 11^{b}.

गअण [गगन] *the sky*, ii. 30^{b}, 47^{d}; iii. 20^{15}.

गङ्गा ts. *the Ganges*, i. 4^{a}; iii. 3^{9}.

गण ts. *a flock, multitude; certain demigods who are the attendants of Çiva*, i. 25^{c}, 33^{a}; ii. 28^{c}; iv. 19^{65}, 22^{c}.

गणणा [°न] *counting,* ii. 37^{b}.

गणणा [°ना] *regard.* kā g., *what need we say of,* iii. 1^{b}.

गण्ठि [ग्रन्थि] *a knot, tie,* i. 15^{d}, 20^{43}; iii. $9^{a,2}$; iv. 20^{12}.

गण्ठिवण्ण [ग्रन्थिपर्ण] *name of a fragrant shrub, according to P = Tabernaemontana coronaria,* iii. 20^{3}.

गण्ड ts. *the cheek,* i. 15^{a}, 16^{a}; ii. 37^{a}; iii. 34^{b}.

गण्डूस [°ष] *a mouthful, handful,* iii. 20^{2}.

गत्त [गात्र] *a limb, body,* ii. 27^{b}; iii. 22^{1}.

गन्ध ts. *smell, odor,* ii. 6^{19}.

गन्धतेल्ल [°तैल] *a fragrant oil.* i. 13^{a}.

गन्धहरिण ts. *the musk-deer,* iii. 20^{3}.

गब्भ [°र्भ] *womb, belly, interior,* i. 34^{17}; iii. $3^{15,18}$, 4^{1}; iv. 21^{b}.

गब्भहर [°र्भगृह] *inner apartment,* iii. 22^{1}.

गम् *to go, pass.* gacchāmi, iii. 3^{15}, 34^{9}. gacchanti, iv. 9^{b}. gaccha, i. $20^{23,25}$; ii. 42^{23}. gacchamha, iii. 22^{6}. gamissaṁ, i. 34^{38}; ii. 50^{3}; iv. $19^{37,47}$. gamissāmo, i. 36^{1}. gao, iii. 25^{d}. gado, iii. 3^{14}, 5^{2}. gaā, i. 33^{c}. gadā, i. 18^{15}, $20^{23,25}$; iv. 9^{2}, 19^{22}. gaaṁ, i. 35^{b}; iii. $3^{a,d}$. gadaṁ, ii. 1^{3}, 11^{2}; iii. 4^{1}, 12^{2}. gadāe, iv. 20^{3}. gae, i. 14^{a}, 35^{c}. gade, iii. 3^{14}, 8^{4}; iv. 18^{32}. gadua, iv. 18^{4}, 19^{24}.

+**अनु** *to accompany.* aṇugaa, iv. 11^{b}. aṇugadā, ii. 28^{2}.

+**अव** *to know, learn.* avagamia, iii. $34^{5,7}$.

+**आ** *to come.* āacchasi, ii. 42^{23}. āacchadi, ii. 41^{8}; iii. 34^{7}. āaccha, iii. 34^{5}. āacchadha, iv. $19^{39,57}$. agamissaṁ, i. 20^{38}; iv. 19^{18}. āgamissadi, iv. 18^{31}. āgantavvaṁ, iv. 19^{25}. āado, iv. 19^{60}. āadā, ii. $6^{14,17}$, 42^{2}; iv. 19^{17}. āgadaṁ, i. 18^{4}; iii. 34^{7}.

+**उद्** *to rise, ascend.* uggaa, iii. 1^{c}.

+**निस्** *to come out, part.* ṇiggacchadi, iv. 19^{2}. ṇiggaaṁ, iii. 20^{c}.

+**सम्** *to join, meet.* saṁgada, iii. 3^{14}.

गम ts. *going away,* iv. 7^{d}.

गमण [°न] *going, motion,* iii. 23^{b}.

गम्भीर ts. *deep, solemn,* i. 28^{2}.

गरल ts. *poison,* ii. 11^{a}.

गल् *to drop, fall. Caus., to pour out, filter, strain.* galanti, ii. 9^{b}. gāliassa, i. 19^{c}.

+**वि** *to vanish, disappear.* vialida, ii. 6^{10}.

गलिबइल्ल [°बलीवर्द] HD. 6. 91. *a strong but lazy bull,* i. 20^{29}.

गव्व [°र्व] *pride,* i. 19^{5}.

गाढ ts. *strong, vehement, intense,* i. 19^{5}, 20^{43}; ii. 45^{a}; iii. 20^{3}; iv. 1^{a}.

गिम्ह [ग्रीष्म] *summer,* ii. 41^{5}; iv. 1^{a}, 4^{c}.

गिरा [गिर्] *speech, voice, words,* ii. 29^{c}.

गिरि ts. *a mountain,* i. 20^{a}.

गिरिन्द [°रीन्द्र] *the king of mountains, Himavant, the father of Pārvatī,* i. 3^{b}.

गिरिस [°श] *Çiva,* i. 3^{b}; iii. 29^{a}.

गिरिसुआ [°ता] *Pārvatī,* i. 4^{d}.

गीद [°त] *song, singing,* iv. 17^{a}.

गुण ts. *quality virtue; thread, string, cord,* i. 10^{b}, 20^{43}, 33^{a}; ii. 2^{b}, 4^{a}, 26^{b}, 27^{c}, 28^{c}; iii. 8^{5}; iv. 19^{65}, 22^{c}, 24^{a}

गुत्थ *see* गुम्फ्.

गुम्फ् *to string, tie, arrange.* gumphedi, i. 4^{4}. gumphantā, i. 15^{d}. guttha, iii. 2^{a}, 5^{b}.

गुरु ts. *a teacher, spiritual preceptor,* i. 5^{b}, 22^{a}; iv. $18^{12, 21, 25}$.

गुह् *to hide.* gūḍha, ii. 21^{a}.

+उप *to embrace.* uvagūḍho, ii. 45^{a}.

गॄ+समुद् *to throw out, put forth.* samuggiraï, ii. 45^{b}.

गेअ [°य] *song,* iii. 14^{a}.

गेज्झ [ग्राह्य] *what can be grasped,* i. 30^{a}; iii. 19^{b}.

गेरिआ [गैरिका] *red chalk,* iii. 18^{b}.

गेहिणी [गृ°] *wife,* i. 11^{a}; iii. 15^{a}.

गै *to sing.* gāanta, i. 21^{a}.

गोअर [°चर] *range of the organs of sense, grip, hold, influence,* iv. 2^{a}, 20^{b}.

गोट्ठी [°ष्ठी] *conversation,* i. 20^{36}.

गोर [गौर] *white, yellowish,* iii. 34^{b}.

गोरअ *the same,* iii. 31^{a}.

गोरङ्ग [गौराङ्ग] *fem.* °ṅgī, *having a pale-red body,* i. 20^{9}.

गोरी [गौ°] *Pārvatī,* i. 28^{4}; ii. 6^{25}; iv. 18^{11}.

गोवअ [°पक] *a cow-herd,* i. 21^{a}.

ग्रह् *to seize, take.* geṇha, iv. 20^{13}. ghettūṇa, i. 12^{3}. geṇhia, iv. $19^{18, 39, 57}$.

घट् *Caus., to join, accomplish, form.* ghaḍeï, iii. 17^{c}. aghaḍia, i. 2^{b}.

+उद् *Caus., to open.* ugghāḍijjanti, i. 36^{a}.

+सम् *to be united, joined.* saṁghaḍaï, iii. 9^{a}. saṁghaḍide, i. 18^{8}.

घट्ट् *to rub.* ghaṭṭedi, i. 4^{6}.

घडण, °णा [घटन, °ना] *forming, joining; contact; coining, stamping,* ii. 37^{a}, 41^{a}; iii. 10^{a}; iv. 9^{a}.

घण [°न] 1. *compact, dense, strong,* i. 13^{c}, 27^{b}, 29^{d}; ii. 6^{10}, 12^{a}; iii. 20^{3}; iv. 6^{c}, 8^{a}. 2. *a cloud,* iii. 4^{a}.

घणसार [घन°] *camphor,* ii. 21^{a}.

घणसारमञ्जरी [घन°] *name of a woman, synonymous with Karpūramañjarī,* iv. $18^{19, 28}$, 19^{46}, $20^{6, 16}$.

घण्टा ts. *a bell,* ii. 31^{b}.

घम्म [°र्म] *heat, warmth,* ii. 6^{10}; iii. 20^{3}.

घर H. 2. 144. *a house,* i. 14^{c}, 18^{2}, 20^{34}; ii. 2^{d}; iv. 1^{b}, 18^{3}.

घरट्ट ts. *a grinding-stone,* iii. 30^{a}.

घरिणी [गृहिणी] *a wife,* i. 19^{7}, 34^{11}; ii. 8^{b}; iii. 15^{a}; iv. 18^{20}.

घल्ल् H. 4. 334. *to throw, cast.* ghallissaṁ, i. 20^{31}.

घुसिण [°सृण] *saffron,* ii. 37^{a}.

घेत्तूण *see* ग्रह्.

च *see* अ.

चअ [°य] *collection, heap, mass,* i. 26^{b}; ii. 50^{c}.

चउव्विह [चतुर्विध] *of four kind, fourfold,* ii. 1^{d}.

चउस्सट्ठी [चतुःषष्टि] *sixty-four,* iii. 4^{a}.

चओर [चकोर] *the Greek partridge (said to feed on moonbeams),* i. 1^{d}.

चक्क [चक्र] *a wheel,* ii. 18^{b}, 23^{c}, 34^{a}.

चक्कल HD. 3. 20. *round,* ii. 34^{a}.

चक्कवट्टि- [चक्रवर्तिन्] *an emperor,* i. 12^{a}; iii. 15^{a}; iv. $18^{20, 22}$, 23^{c}.

चक्कवाअ [चक्रवाक] *ruddy goose,* ii. 8^{b}, 50^{c}.

चक्काआर [चक्राकार] *wheel-like,* ii. 23^{c}; iii. 19^{c}.

चक्खु [चक्षुस्] *an eye*, ii. 5^{a}.

चङ्कम- *see* **क्रम**.

चङ्कमण [चङ्क्र°] *going, walking*, i. 27^{d}.

चङ्ग HD. 3. 1. *beautiful*, i. 31^{b}, 33^{a}; ii. 25^{a}. 28^{b}; iv. 13^{b}.

चङ्गत्तण *beauty*, i. 14^{2}, 20^{9}; iii. 9^{c}, 16^{2}.

चङ्गिम- H. 1. 35; 2. 154. *beauty*, ii. 24^{d}, 26^{c}; iii. 6^{a}, 13^{b}.

चच्चा [चर्चा] *smearing, anointing*, i. 20^{9}.

चञ्चल ts. *trembling, tremulous*, ii. 41^{c}.

चञ्चुर ts. *waddling*, iii. 23^{a}.

चट्ट- *licking, cp. Marāṭhī* caṭaṇeṁ, i. 20^{28}

चड् H. 4. 206. ***to rise, increase.*** caḍadi, iii. 16^{2}.

चण्ड ts. *wild, **impetuous, angry***, i. 17^{d}, 23^{a}; ii. 10^{b}.

चण्डंसु [चण्डांशु] *the sun*, i. 35^{a}.

चण्डवाल [°पाल] *name of a king*, i. 12^{a}.

चण्डसेण [°न] *name of a king*, iv. 18^{18}.

चण्डिम- H. 2. 154. *impetuosity*, i. 16^{3}.

चदुत्थी [चतुर्थी] *the fourth day (e. g., of a lunar fortnight)*, ii. 6^{23}, 29^{5}.

चदुद्दसी [चतुर्दशी] *the fourteenth day of a lunar fortnight*, iv. 18^{11}.

चदुर [चतुर] *skilful, conversant with*, i. 7^{1}.

चदुरत्तण *skill, loveliness*, i. 20^{1}.

चदुस्सट्ठि [चतुःषष्टि] *sixty-four*, iii. 4^{4}.

चन्द [चन्द्र] *the moon*, i. 32^{b}; ii. 5^{b}, 6^{10}, 27^{b}, 29$^{13, 19, 21}$, 43^{5}; iii. 16^{b}, 24^{2}, 25^{d}, 26^{1}, 29^{b}, 30^{2}; iv. 19^{64}.

चन्दण [°न] *sandal*, i. 14^{b}, 17^{b}, 20^{9}; ii. 10^{a}, 11$^{a, 1}$; iii. 20^{d}, 28^{b}; iv. 5^{c}, 6^{c}, 8^{a}.

चन्दणलेहा [°नलेखा] *name of a woman*, iv. 9^{9}.

चन्दिआ [चन्द्रिका] *moonlight*, iv. 19^{64}.

चम्प् H. 4. 395. ***to compress, squeeze.*** campiaṁ (*P translates* pīḍitaṁ), ii. 33^{a}.

चम्पअ [°क] *name of a tree and its flowers*, i. 14^{2}, 16^{a}, 34^{39}; ii. 42^{b}; iii. 1^{a}, 22^{b}, 30^{b}.

चम्पा ts. *name of a town, Campā*, i. 14^{2}.

चम्म- [चर्मन्] *skin*, i. 23^{c}.

चम्मट्ठि [चर्मयष्टि] *a whip.* cammaṭṭhiā-anto, *looking like a whip*, ii. 39^{b}.

चर् + सम् *Caus., to communicate.* saṁcārentā, ii. 2^{c}.

चरिअ [°त] *acting, behaviour, acts*, ii. 40^{a}.

चल् *to stir, move; to get loose.* caliā, ii. 1^{a}. caliaṁ, i. 27^{d}.

चल ts. *tremulous, rolling*, ii. 5^{a}; iv. 16^{b}.

चलण [°रण] *a foot*, i. 20^{34}; ii. 13^{a}, 33^{a}, 42^{a}, 43^{a}.

चलण [°न] *moving, shaking*, i. 36^{c}.

चल्लि [चारी] *the motion of the feet in the dance*, iv. 12^{b}, 16^{b}.

चवल [°पल] *unsteady, wavering*, i. 15^{a}; ii. 49^{a}.

चसअ [°षक] *a drinking-vessel*, iv. 19^{b}.

चामर ts. *a chowry, fan*, ii. 31^{a}; iv. 9^{8}.

चामुण्डा ts. *a terrific form of Durgā*, iv. 18$^{30, 38}$, 19^{12}.

चारि- [°रिन्] *wandering, moving*, iv. 2^{6}.

चारु ts. *lovely*, i. 16^{3}.

चाव [°प] *a bow*, ii. 6^{d}; iv. 14^{a}, 19^{64}.

चाहुआण [°चान] *the Cāuhan family*, i. 11^{a}.

चि + उद् *to gather, arrange.* uccinedi, i. 4^{3}.

चिअ *see* **चेअ.**

चित्त ts. *mind, heart*, ii. $40^{b, 2}$, 49^{a}; iii. 11^{d}, 12^{2}; iv. 9^{c}, 20^{c}.

चित्त [°त्र] 1. *bright, variegated, spotted*, iv. 9^{12}. 2. *a picture*, i. 27^{c}, 30^{d}; ii. 4^{a}.

चित्तअर [°त्रकर] *a painter*, ii. 40^{b}.

चित्तभित्ति [चित्र°] *a painted wall, a wall-picture*, i. 36^{a}.

चित्तलेहा [चित्रलेखा] *name of a woman*, iv. 9^{9}.

चित्ता [°त्रा] *the fourteenth lunar mansion*, iii. 3^{14}.

चिर *long.* ciraṁ, *for a long time*, ii. 4^{d}. ciraa, *at last*, iii. 23^{b}.

चिराअ- [°य-] *to tarry.* cirāadi, ii. 6^{2}.

चिहुर H. 1. 186. *the hair of the head*, ii. 21^{a}.

चुम्ब् *to kiss.* cumbia, i. 17^{d}.

चुम्बण [°न] *kissing*, i. 2^{a}.

चूडामणि ts. *a crest-jewel; best, excellent*, i. 5^{b}. °ttaṇa [°tva], i. 20^{2}.

चूर्ण् *to crush.* cūraïssaṁ, i. 20^{30}. cūrïadu, i. 20^{27}.

चूलिआ [°का] *top-knot*, iv. 2^{4}.

चेअ, चिअ, च्च H. 2. 184. *restrictive or strengthening particle; used with* tad (*like* tad eva) *to mean 'the same'*; i. 8^{a}, 21^{d}; iii. 11^{d}, 19^{d}.

चेडिआ [°टिका] *a female slave or servant*, i. $20^{20, 26}$.

चेत्त [चैत्र] *a lunar month, March-April*, i. 17^{d}, 18^{d}.

चोरअ [°क] *a thief, robber*, iii. 31^{a}.

चोल ts. *name of a country*, i. 15^{b}.

च्च *see* **चेअ.**

छइल्ल HD. 3. 24. *clever*, i. 1^{c}, 5^{7}; iii. 9^{a}.

छट्ठअ [षष्ठक] *the sixth*, iii. 18^{d}.

छडा [°टा] *mass, lustre, splendor, flash*, i. 29^{a}; ii. 32^{a}; iii. 20^{a}.

छत्त [°त्र] *a parasol, umbrella*, ii. 29^{d}.

छद् + प्र *to hide, conceal.* pacchāanti, i. 33^{b}.

छप्पअ [षट्पद] *a bee*, ii. 2^{b}.

छम्मुह [षण्मुख] *a name of Kārttikeya*, i. 3^{a}.

छम्मासिअ [षण्मासिक] *weighing six māṣa*, ii. 17^{a}; iii. 20^{3}.

छल ts. *deception, guise, semblance*, ii. 35^{a}; iii. 32^{b}.

छल- *to deceive, cheat.* chalidā, ii. 29^{10}.

छवि ts. *color, splendor, shimmer*, i. 29^{b}; ii. 47^{b}, 50^{c}; iv. 5^{1}.

छाआ [°या] *reflection, light*, ii. 6^{10}; iii. 1^{c}.

छुर् *to cover, smear, envelop.* churia, iv. 5^{a}. churio, i. 29^{d}.

छुरण ts. *smearing, anointing*, iii. 28^{a}.

छुहा [क्षुध्] *hunger*, iii. 8^{1}.

छेअ [°क] *clever*, ii. 26^{c}; iii. 6^{b}.

छेत्त [क्षेत्र] *field, width*, i. 30^{c}.

छोल्ल् H. 4. 395. *to cleanse, rub.* chollanti, i. 14^{a}.

ज *see* **यद्.**

जअ [°य] *conquest, triumph*, iv. 20^{a}.

जअ- [जगत्] *the world*, iii. 12^{c}, 17^{a}.

जअण [°यन] *subduing*, ii. 41^{d}.

जइ [यदि] *if*, ii. 47^{3}, 48^{a}; iii. 12^{3}, 15^{e}, 33^{a}; iv. 2^{10}, 3^{1}, 18^{14}.

जइ- [जयिन्] *fem.* °iṇī. *conquering, vanquishing,* ii. 41^{b}.

जक्ख [यक्ष] *one of a class of demigods,* i. 25^{c}.

जङ्गम ts. *moving,* iv. 18^{a}.

जच्च [जात्य] *noble, well-born, genuine,* i. 14^{2}, 32^{a}; ii. 19^{a}, 25^{b}; iii. 1^{b}.

जज्जर [जर्जर] *old, decayed,* iv. 4^{d}.

जण [°न] *people, man; common people,* i. 4^{2}, 18^{a}, 21^{5}, 34^{8}; ii. 3^{a}, 6^{17}, 28^{b}, 31^{d}, 40^{2}, 41^{d}, 47^{d}; iii. 12^{c}, 15^{a}, 27^{d}, 28^{b}; iv. 2$^{b, 2}$, 9^{a}, 14^{b}, 24^{a}.

जणण [°नन] *fem.* °ṇī, *producing, causing; fem. a mother,* i. 26^{d}; iv. 9^{d}.

जत्ता [यात्रा] *festival, procession,* ii. 44^{d}.

जदो [यतस्] *from whence, from which time; because,* i. 4^{3}, 12$^{3, 9}$, 18^{18}, 19^{7}, 20$^{7, 13}$, 31^{2}, 34$^{31, 32}$; ii. 6^{6}, 42^{23}; iv. 1^{1}, 3^{2}, 20^{16}, 22^{3}.

जधा [यथा] *as, as follows,* i. 7^{3}, 8^{4}, 13^{2}, 16^{4}; ii. 26^{1}, 42^{33}; iv. 18$^{7, 20}$. *See* जह.

जधिच्छं [यथे°] *at will,* i. 16^{3}; iii. 3^{11}. *Cp.* जहिच्छं.

जन् *to be produced, be, become, happen. Caus., to produce.* jāo, i. 29^{d}; ii. 50^{d}. jāā, i. 20^{d}, 35^{c}; ii. 1^{d}, 3^{d}; iii. 28^{d}. jāaṁ, i. 16^{a}. jāde, ii. 42^{21}. jaṇia, i. 2^{a}; ii. 19^{a}, 32^{c}.

+ सम् *to grow, become.* saṁjāā, iii. 25^{b}; iv. 23^{c}.

जन्त [यन्त्र] *an instrument, machine,* iv. 13^{a}. °jjala, *an artificial stream of water, showerbath,* iv. 10^{b}. °dhārā, *the same,* iii. 20^{c}.

जम्पिअ [जल्पित] *speech, murmur,* ii. 2^{b}.

जर [ज्वर] *fever,* ii. 42^{5}.

जरढ [°ठ] *hard, solid,* iv. 2^{b}. jaraḍhāamāṇa, *growing old, ripe, matured,* ii. 1^{5}.

जल ts. *water,* i. 4^{a}; ii. 11^{c}, 24$^{c, 3}$, 30^{b}; iii. 3$^{17, 18}$, 20^{c}.

जलञ्जलि [जला°] *a libation of water presented to the manes of a deceased person,* ii. 5^{d}, 42^{21}.

जलहर [°धर] *a cloud,* iii. 3^{11}, 28^{d}.

जल्प् *to speak, talk.* jampanta, iii. 27^{c}.

जवणिअन्तर [°निकान्तर] *the tiring-room,* i. 12^{3}.

जह [यथा] *as, that,* i. 34$^{a, b, c}$; ii. 44^{d}; iv. 20^{b}. jahā, *the same,* i. 34^{d}. *See* जधा.

जहिं [यत्र] H. 3. 60. *where,* i. 20$^{23, 25, 26, 33}$.

जहिच्छं [यथे°] *at will,* ii. 22^{a}. *See* जधिच्छं.

जामिणी [यामिनी] *night,* ii. 29^{d}, 41^{5}; iv. 4^{c}.

जाव [यावत्] *as far as, till, in the meantime,* ii. 41^{6}; iii. 34^{9}.

जि *to conquer, surpass, curb, restrain, be victorious.* jaaï, i. 4^{d}; iii. 18^{d}, 30^{b}; iv. 19^{b}. jaa, i. 14^{2}. jaadu, ii. 6^{12}; iv. 9^{16}, 18^{6}. jia, iii. 4^{a}. jido, iii. 2^{1}.

+ निस् *to conquer.* ṇijjida, i. 14^{2}.

+ विनिस् *to conquer, defeat.* viṇijjia, i. 13^{d}.

जीव् *to live.* jīvadha, i. 20^{41}.

जीव ts. *life, soul,* i. 35^{a}.

जीविअ [°त] *life,* ii. 9^{d}.

जीहा [जिह्वा] *tongue,* ii. 47^{5}.

जुअ [युग] *a pair, couple,* i. 26^{a}; ii. 13^{a}, 18^{a}, 33^{a}, 37^{a}.

जुअ- [युवन्] *young,* ii. 41^{d}.

जुअल [युगल] *a pair, couple,* i. 20^{31}; ii. 6^{24}, 7^{b}, 13^{b}, 16^{a}.

जुअलअ [युगलक] *the same*, ii. 14^{a}.

जुज्झ [युद्ध] *see* मल्लजुज्झ.

जुण्ण [जीर्ण] *old, wasted, decayed*, ii. 29^{11}; iii. 28^{c}.

जुहिट्ठिर [युधिष्ठिर] *name of the eldest Pāṇḍava prince. His eldest brother, the son of Kuntī, was Karṇa, which word means also ear*, i. 20^{15}.

जेट्ठ [ज्येष्ठ] *eldest*, i. 20^{15}, 34^{35}; ii. $10^{2,4}$.

जेत्तिअ H. 2. 157. *so much as*, i. 7^{b}.

जेव [एव] H. 4. 280. *a particle used to strengthen the sense, just, quite. If anusvāra or* ā, ī, ū *precedes, we find the form* jeva; *otherwise*, jjeva. jeva, i. 5^{7}, 7^{1}, 16^{4}, $20^{4,6,20}$, 34^{34}; ii. 6^{25}, 24^{3}; iii. 22^{6}, 34^{7}; iv. 19^{50}. jjeva, i. 8^{3}, 20^{34}; ii. 1^{2}, 9^{1}, 45^{1}; iii. 22^{9}, 34^{9}; iv. $19^{6,24,60}$.

जोइणी [योगिनी] *a witch, sorceress*, iv. 17^{b}.

जोईसर [योगेश्वर] *a sorcerer*, i. 26^{d}, 28^{5}; iv. 18^{12}, 19^{55}.

जोग्ग [योग्य] *fit, appropriate*, i. 19^{2}; ii. 5^{d}, 23^{a}; iv. 2^{a}.

जोण्हा [ज्योत्स्ना] *moonlight*, i. 1^{d}, 4^{e}, 29^{e}; ii. 11^{a}, 30^{b}; iii. 7^{a}, 25^{b}, 28^{b}.

जोव्वण [यौवन] *youth*, iii. 17^{b}, 18^{c}.

ज्ञा *to know*. jāṇāsi, i. 18^{16}; ii. $42^{16,17}$, $47^{1,2}$. jāṇāï, i. 35^{b}. jāṇādi, i. 32^{2}; iii. 34^{9}. jāṇimo, iii. 12^{d}. jāṇanti, ii. 49^{2}. jāṇa, i. 34^{1}; ii. 43^{12}. jāṇe, i. 22^{a}; iii. $3^{a,7,15}$, 15^{c}. jāṇīadi, i. 28^{2}.

+आ *to order, command.* āṇavedi, i. 19^{8}, 34^{36}. āṇavedu, i. 4^{15}.

+वि *to communicate, speak, tell.* viṇṇavedi, iv. 9^{17}, 18^{7}. viṇṇavedum̐, iv. 9^{14}, 18^{24}. viṇṇavīadi, ii. 28^{1}; iv. 18^{10}, 19^{17}. viṇṇatto, iv. 18^{12}. viṇṇattam̐, iv. 18^{15}. viṇṇāvidam̐, iv. 18^{4}.

ज्वल् *to burn, be hot.* jalaï, ii. 11^{c}; iii. 20^{c}.

+उद् *Caus., to make illustrious.* ujjaledi, i. 19^{7}.

झणज्झण ts. *a jingling sound*, iv. 17^{a}.

झणझण- *to sound, jingle.* °ṇanta, ii. 32^{a}.

झत्ति [झटिति] *quickly, suddenly, at once*, i. 20^{d}, 36^{b}; ii. 38^{a}; iii. 3^{c}. *Cp.* तडत्ति.

झर् + प्र H. 4. 173. *Caus., to cause to drop, ooze.* pajjharāvedi, iv. 18^{36}.

झाण [ध्यान] *meditation, contemplation*, i. 22^{a}, 24^{b}, 34^{27}; ii. 4^{d}; iv. 19^{55}.

टप्पर HD. 4. 2. *gaping, large, uneven*, i. 20^{40}.

टिक्किद HD. 4. 3. *adorned with a tilaka or mark made with san al wood or unguents*, ii. 11^{5}.

टेण्टा 1. *a scar, see* bhamaraṭeṇṭā. 2. HD. 4. 3. *a gambling-place.* ṭeṇṭākarālā, *terrible in the gambling-places or a Durgā of the gambling-places* (*K*, uraḥkiṇopalakṣitacaṇḍikā), i. 18^{8}, 20^{28}.

ठक्कुर ts. *a lord, chief*, iii. 8^{1}.

ठाण [स्थान] *place; tone, modulation,* i. 4[7], 20[40]; ii. 1[a]; iv. 19[22, 24].

डज्झन्त *see* दह्.

डम्ब् + वि *to cheat, deceive, mock.* viḍambedi, iii. 8[1].

डम्बर ts. *mass, show, pomp, empty noise,* i. 2[a]; iii. 12[a], 13[b].

डिम्भ ts. *a young child,* i. 30[a].

डी + उद् *to fly up.* uḍḍīṇo, iv. 2[11].

ढिल्ल [शिथिल] *loose, relaxed, careless,* i. 13[c]; iii. 3[c].

ण [न] *not,* i. 6[b], 8[1], 13[a, b], 18[16, 18], 20[4, 7, 8, 9, 14, 20, 38], 22[a], 25[d], 27[c], 30[d], 34[a, b, c, 17, 18]; ii. 1[a], 4[a, d], 6[6], 8[d], 10[5], 16[b], 24[4], 26[d], 28[d, 2], 32[d], 40[b], 42[16, 17, 23], 47[1, 3], 49[2]; iii. 8[a], 9[b], 14[c], 15[b], 16[d], 20[d], 22[b], 34[9]; iv. 2[2, 10], 3[d], 9[c], 18[36], 19[2, 9], 20[3].

णअण [नयन] *eye,* i. 20[36], 34[c]; ii. 6[a], 19[a], 21[a, b], 38[a], 40[2], 42[a]; iii. 20[17]; iv. 20[b].

णअर [नगर] *a town,* i. 25[5]; ii. 30[a]; iii. 5[2].

णअरी [नगरी] *the same,* ii. 3[b].

णं H. 4. 283. *surely (as used half questioningly),* i. 29[c], 34[20]; ii. 47[2].

णक्खत्त [नक्षत्र] *a lunar mansion,* i. 20[16, 31]; iii. 3[14].

णच्चण [नर्तन] *dancing,* iv. 17[b].

णच्चणी [नर्तनी] *a female dancer,* i. 16[3]; iv. 11[a].

णच्चिद [नर्तित] *dancing,* iii. 22[8].

णट्ट [नृत्य] *dancing, acting,* i. 4[2, 16]; ii. 15[b]; iii. 14[a].

णट्टावअ [नर्तापक] *causing to dance, move, shake,* i. 16[3], 17[c].

णड् + वि H. 4. 150. *to confuse, mystify, delude.* viṇaḍida, iv. 19[53].

णडी [नटी] *an actress, courtesan,* ii. 28[a].

णन्दिउड्ढ [नन्दिवृद्ध] *name of a poet,* i. 20[20].

णन्दिणी [नन्दिनी] *a daughter,* i. 12[8].

णरवइ [नरपति] *a king,* ii. 35[b].

णरिन्द [नरेन्द्र] *the same,* i. 12[a].

णलिण [नलिन] *a lotus flower,* i. 27[a].

णलिणी [नलिनी] *a lotus plant, a pond abounding in lotuses,* i. 35[d]; iii. 19[2].

णव [नव] *new,* i. 32[a]; ii. 2[c], 19[b], 41[a], 42[b], 44[a]; iii. 1[c], 4[b], 24[a], 25[b], 30[b]; iv. 7[c], 9[a], 22[a].

णह- [नभस्] *the sky,* iii. 7[a], -29[a]. ṇahaddhe [nabho'rdhe] *in the midst of the sky,* i. 25[b].

णहअल [नभस्तल] *the sky,* iii. 26[d].

णाअलआ [नागलता] *Piper betle,* iv. 5[a].

णाडिआ [नाटिका] *a short or light domestic comedy in four acts, such as the Ratnāvalī,* i. 6[a].

णाणा [नाना] *manifold, various,* ii. 3[b].

णाम [नाम] *name; by name; indeed,* i. 25[5], 34[8, 11]; ii. 26[a]; iii. 1[b]. 5[2]; iv. 9[14], 18[18].

णामन्तर [नामा°] *another name,* iv. 20[16].

णामहेअ [नामधेय] *name,* i. 20[15, 16, 31]; iii. 3[18]; iv. 9[8, 9, 10, 11, 12].

णाराअ [नाराच] *an iron staff on the goldsmith's scales,* i. 20[13].

णारिङ्ग [नारङ्ग] *an orange,* ii. 50[d].

णाल [नाल] *a lotus-stalk,* ii. 16[a].

णावा [नौ] *a ship,* iv. 20[3].

णास [न्यास] *a deposit, pledge of love,* i. 3[a].

णाह [नाथ] *lord, husband,* i. 35[c].

णाहि [नाभि] *the navel,* i. 34[b]; ii. 24[a].

णिअ [निज] *own, one's own,* i. 19[2], 20[34], 33[a], 34[35]; ii. 28[b], 43[5]; iii. 20[16], 32[b]; iv. 19[17].

णिअंसण HD. 4. 38. *a garment, cloth,* iii. 15[d].

णिअडिअ [निकटिक] *near, at hand,* ii. 41[8].

णिअत्थ *see* वस + नि.

णिअम्ब [नित॰] *the buttocks, the circumference of the hips,* ii. 1[a], 15[a], 24[b]; iii. 19[c].

णिअम्बिणी [नितम्बिनी] *a woman with large and handsome hips,* ii. 26[b]; iii. 13[c].

णिअर [निकर] *a multitude, collection,* ii. 17[b], 45[b].

णिउण [निपुण] *clever, skilful, careful,* ii. 40[b]; iv. 3[1].

णिएइ H. 4. 181; 3. 56. *to see,* i. 34[b].

णिओअ [नियोग] *injunction, command,* ii. 28[2].

णिक्कलङ्क [निष्क॰] *stainless,* i. 10[b].

णिच्च [नित्य] *continual, perpetual, constant; always,* i. 2[b], 33[d]; ii. 10[d], 46[b]; iv. 22[d].

णिडाल [ललाट] H. 1. 47, 257. *the forehead,* ii. 20[a].

णित्तल [निस्तल] *round, globular,* iii. 4[b].

णिदाह [निदाघ] *heat, summer,* iv. 3[c], 5[d], 6[d].

णिद्दा [निद्रा] *sleep,* ii. 50[a]; iii. 3[d].

णिन्दणिज्ज [निन्दनीय] *worthy of blame,* i. 20[7].

णिप्पट्ट HD. 4. 31. *abundant, exceeding; very much,* i. 17[c]. *Cp. Marāṭhī* nipaṭa *or* nippaṭa.

णिबन्धण [निबन्धन] *causing,* iii. 24[2].

णिब्भर [निर्भर] *vehement(ly), exceedingly; close; full of;* ii. 44[b]; iii. 7[a, c]; iv. 19[16].

णिब्भरराअ [निर्भरराज] *another name of Mahendrapāla,* i. 9[a].

णिमित्त [नि॰] *cause, motive; at the end of a compound, in order to, for the sake of,* i. 12[a], 34[38]; ii. 42[12]; iii. 16[c]; iv. 9[3], 18[12].

णिम्मवण [निर्मापण] *cp.* H. 4. 19. *building, forming,* iii. 17[b].

णिरक्खर [निरक्षर] *without letters, illiterate,* i. 20[13].

णिरन्तर [नि॰] *uninterrupted,* iv. 8[b].

णिरिक्खणिज्ज [निरीक्षणीय] *what can be seen,* ii. 47[d].

णिरिक्खिअ [निरीक्षित] *look,* ii. 6[c].

णिल्लक्खण [निर्लक्षण] *undistinguished, unimportant,* i. 18[6].

णिवडिअ *see* पत + नि.

णिवारण [नि॰] *preventing, warding off,* iii. 8[5].

णिविड [निबिड] *close, compact,* ii. 24[e].

णिवेदअ [निवेदक] *telling, indicating,* ii. 8[3].

णिवेस [निवेश] *entrance; expanse, contour,* i. 36[a]; iii. 7[d], 21[b].

णिव्वड H. 4. 62. *to become clear.* ṇivvaḍadi, i. 19[7].

णिव्विग्घ [निर्विघ्न] *without hindrance,* iv. 19[55].

णिसग्ग [निसर्ग] *nature,* i. 31[b]; ii. 25[a].

णिसा [निशा] *night; by night,* ii. 9[a]; iv. 3[a].

णिसाअर [निशाचर] *fem.* °rī, *a fiend, Rākṣasa,* iv. 15[b].

णिह [निभ] *like, similar,* i. 32[a].

णिहित्त *see* धा + नि.

णिहुवण [निधुवन] *coitus,* iii. 7[c], 28[c], 29[b]; iv. 4[c].

णीरन्ध [नीरन्ध्र] *without interstices, close,* iv. 9[7].

णील [नी°] *black,* ii. 14[a].

णीलकण्ठ [नी°] *a name of Çiva,* iii. 20[16].

णीसन्द [निःस्यन्द] *flowing, streaming,* iii. 31[1].

णीसास [निश्वास] *a sighing, sigh,* i. 20[c]; ii. 10[a]; iii. 20[9].

णु [नु] *an interrogative particle,* iii. 8[4], 19[c]; iv. 1[a], 2[4].

णूणं [नूनम्] *certainly,* iii. 17[a], 32[a]. ṇūṇa, iv. 21[c].

णेउर [नूपुर] *an anklet,* i. 20[30]; ii. 32[a], 33[b], 47[a]; iii. 13[a], 18[a]; iv. 17[b].

णेत्त [नेत्र] *eye,* i. 30[c], 32[a]; ii. 3[c], 46[c].

णेदं [नु + एतद्] H. 4. 279. *that. A form used only after anusvāra,* i. 18[12]; iii. 16[1]; iv. 18[35], 19[15].

णेवच्छ [नेपथ्य] *decoration, attire, dress,* i. 33[b], 34[38]; ii. 26[b], 27[c], 28[d]; iv. 20[3].

णेह [स्नेह] *affection, love,* i. 15[d].

णो *see* अहम्.

णो [नो] *not,* i. 13[a], 22[a], 23[d], 30[b]; iii. 22[a]; iv. 23[a].

णोल्ल् + प्र H. 4. 143. *to toss.* paṇollia, ii. 14[b], 36[a].

ण्हाण [स्नान] *bathing, bath,* i. 26[c], 28[a], 30[1]; ii. 24[c].

तओ [ततस्] *thence, thereafter, then,* iii. 4[a]; iv. 3[d]. *Cp.* तदो.

तंस [त्र्यस्र] *triangular, oblique.* ii. 1[d], 6[c].

तड् *Caus., to beat.* tāḍiumaṇa- [tāḍitumanas] *having the intention to beat,* iii. 3[b].

तड [°ट] *a shore, bank,* iv. 20[3].

तडत्ति [तडदिति] *quickly, at once,* i. 20[15, 16]; iii. 3[b], 20[3]. *Cp.* झत्ति.

तणु [°नु] *body,* i. 33[b]; ii. 8[a], 24[d]. °laā [latā] *body,* ii. 1[d], 9[d], 11[c]. °llaā, *the same,* i. 28[b].

तत्थ [°त्र] *there, here,* ii. 27[d]; iii. 9[b].

तत्थभोदी [तत्रभवती] *her honor, a respectful title,* iii. 22[1].

तद *this, that, he, she, it.* sa, iv. 3[d]. so, i. 5[5], 6[a], 10[a], 19[7], 21[5]; ii. 1[2], 28[a, c], 46[d]; iii. 3[14, 17], 4[1], 9[3], 10[1], 12[b]. sā, i. 1[c], 8[b], 11[b], 19[7], 34[13]; ii. 4[a], 11[d], 14[a], 29[d], 42[33]; iii. 5[b, 3], 6[b]; iv. 1[b], 9[3], 18[20, 21, 38], 19[30]. taṁ, i. 13[d], 19[7], 20[27, 29], 25[a, d, 7], 26[c], 29[c]; ii. 8[c], 9[1], 27[c], 28[b], 29[2, 4, 8], 41[1, 2], 43[1, 11], 46[d]; iii. 3[d, 6], 5[2], 8[a], 9[d], 12[d], 13[c], 16[c]; iv. 9[7], 18[27], 19[50, 55, 57]. tad *as first part of a compound in* takkajja [tatkārya], ii. 28[4]; takkāla [tatkāla], i. 8[3]; takkhaṇa [tatkṣaṇa], iv. 18[32]; taggada [tadgata], ii. 1[3], 11[2]; iv. 9[2], 18[32]; tabbhattā [tadbhartṛ], ii. 8[b]. teṇa, i. 7[1], 8[1], 20[27], 21[d, 3]; ii. 28[b, 4], 29[c]; iii. 4[8], 6[b], 17[1]; iv. 18[13, 17]. teṇaṁ, iii. 5[a]. tassa, i. 4[19], 25[b], 34[11]; ii. 6[23]; iii. 3[15], 8[b]; iv. 18[19], 20[c]. tie, ii. 6[a], 10[c], 15[a], 19[a]. tīa, ii. 1[d], 5[a], 9[c], 17[a], 23[a, b];

iii. 2[c], 3[d]. tāe, ii. 6[15, 25], 28[2], 40[3]. tissā, ii. 11[3], 12[a], 23[d], 29[a]; iii. 1[c], 8[5] tassiṁ, ii. 28[d]; iii. 16[2]. te, i. 8[a], 19[b, d], 20[c]; ii. 5[b, d]; iii. 24[b]; iv. 9[c], 21[d]. tāo, ii. 1[2]; iii. 4[3]; iv. 13[b]. tāiṁ, ii. 8[2]; iii. 22[c]. tehiṁ, i. 34[15]; ii. 42[32]. tāṇa, iii. 15[b]. tāṇã, iv. 9[b]. tāṇaṁ, i. 31[a], 33[d]; ii. 43[b]; iii. 3[18], 4[1], 11[d]; iv. 9[d, 12].

तदो [ततस्] *thence, therefore, thereafter, then*, i. 18[4]; iii. 3[9, 10, 11, 13, 14, 16, 17, 19], 4[1, 2, 3, 7, 8, 10], 5[1, 2, 4, 5]; iv. 9[7], 18[15, 21, 23]. *Cp.* तओ.

तधा [°था] *so, thus.* tadhā vi, *even then, still, yet*, i. 16[5], 20[10]; ii. 29[2]; iii. 18[1]; iv. 19[66], 23[1]. *Cp.* तह.

तन्त [°न्त्र] *a certain kind of religious treatises; chief remedy or charm*, i. 22[a]; iii. 18[c]; iv. 7[d].

तव *Caus., to burn.* tāvei, ii. 42[b].

तमाल ts. *name of a tree*, ii. 43[2, 12].

तम्बवण्णी [ताम्रपर्णी] *name of a river*, i. 17[d]; iii. 3[14].

तम्बोल [ताम्बूल] *the leaf of piper betle*, iv. 9[10].

तरङ्ग ts. *a wave, unsteady motion*, i. 18[a], 28[a]; ii. 1[b], 6[b].

तरङ्गवदी [°ती] *a woman's name*, iv. 9[12].

तरङ्गि- [°ङ्गिन्] *waving, tremulous*, iv. 6[a].

तरट्टी *a bold young woman*, i. 16[3]; ii. 4[d].

तरल ts. *trembling, sparkling, unsteady*, ii. 30[d], 46[a]; iii. 16[a].

तरलण *waving, shaking*, i. 15[c].

तरलि- [°लिन्] *shaking*, i. 17[a].

तरु ts. *a tree*, i. 20[27]; ii. 42[29], 43[13], 45[a], 47[a], 49[1]; iv. 18[30, 38].

तरुणी ts. *fem.* °ṇī, *young, a young man or girl*, i. 30[c]; ii. 4[d], 31[b], 45[a].

तरुणिम- H. 2. 154. *youth*, iii. 19[c].

तक्क *to suppose, guess, reason.* takkemi, ii. 29[11]; iv. 18[34]. takkīadi, i. 28[3].

तलिण [°न] *thin, small, little*, iv. 3[a], 10[a].

तवण [°पन] *burning*, ii. 11[b].

तसर [*Marāṭhī* तसर] *a kind of coarse silk*, i. 20[9].

तह [°था] *so, thus, and also;* taha vi, *even then, still, yet*, i. 1[c], 9[a]; ii. 42[b], 44[c], 48[b]; iii. 6[a]; iv. 3[a, b], 20[b]. tahā, i. 13[b], 34[a, b, c, d]; iii. 20[c]. *Cp.* तधा.

तहिं H. 3. 60. *there*, i. 20[23, 25], 25[6]; ii. 0[5], 29[6], 42[23, 29]; iii. 3[17], 5[3], 9[c]; iv. 18[31], 19[37].

ता [तात्] *therefore, then*, i. 4[12], 6[2], 8[1], 10[1], 12[1], 16[3], 18[14, 17], 19[3, 6], 20[2, 4, 20, 29, 34], 25[1], 28[8], 30[d], 34[26]; ii. 1[3], 10[5], 11[2], 12[b], 13[b], 14[b], 15[b], 16[b], 17[b], 18[b], 19[b], 20[b], 21[b], 22[b], 24[4], 29[7, 10, 16], 40[3], 41[6], 42[11, 19, 21, 26, 32], 43[b, 2]; iii. 2[3], 3[c, 6, 9], 12[2], 20[3, 4, 5], 22[2, 9], 26[2], 33[b], 34[3, 9]; iv. 2[4], 18[4], 19[15, 18, 37, 47], 20[4, 10].

ताडङ्क [ताट°] *an ear-ring*, ii. 37[a].

ताडण [°न] *beating*, i. 2[b]; ii. 47[a].

ताडिउमणा *see* तड्.

तार ts. *loud, shrill, radiant, clear, shining*, ii. 21[a], 35[a]; iii. 2[a]; iv. 17[b].

तारआ [°का] *a star*, ii. 17[b]

तारा ts. *the pupil of the eye*, iii. 19[a].

तारामेत्ती [°मैत्री] *unselfish friendship*, ii. 28[3].

तारिस [°दृश] *such*, iv. 22[c].

तारुण्ण [°ण्य] *youth*, i. 18[b], 20[d]; iii. 16[2].

तारुण्णअ *the same*, ii. 48[b].

ताल ts. *clapping hands*, *beating time*, *time (in music)*, iv. 11[b], 12[b], 17[a].

तालवेण्ट [°वृन्त] *a fan*, iii. 20[b].

ताव [°प] *heat, glow, pain*, ii. 29[a], iv. 2[1, 2], 7[d].

तासि- [त्रासिन्] *fem.* tāsiṇī, *terrifying, alarming*, ii. 29[c].

ति, त्ति [इति] *a particle used to report the very words spoken by some one. The form* ti *occurs only after anusvāra.* tti, i. 6[a], 20[1, 20], 34[1, 15]; ii. 8[b], 29[21], 39[a], 45[b]; iii. 32[a]; iv. 9[8, 9, 10, 11, 12], 18[7, 19, 20], 19[35], 20[16]. ti, i. 6[2], 28[9], 34[3]; ii. 29[11]; iii. 9[1, 2]; iv. 2[a], 9[18], 18[16, 23, 34].

तिकण्ड [त्रिकाण्ड] *having three joints, consisting of three parts*, iv. 14[a].

तिक्ख [तीक्ष्ण] *sharp, strong, severe, hot*, i. 29[a]; ii. 3[d], 5[a], 46[a].

तिण्णि [त्रि] *three*, i. 4[9]; ii. 42[29].

तिमिर ts. *darkness*, iii. 25[a].

तिमिस [°ष] *a certain plant*, *Benincasa cerifera*, iii. 24[a]; iv. 21[a], 22[a].

तिरिच्छि [तिर्यक्] H. 2. 143. *obliquely*, ii. 1[b].

तिल ts. *the seed of the sesamum plant*, iii. 15[b]. °jala, *water with sesamum seed, offered to the dead as a libation*, ii. 5[d]. °antaraṁ, *so much as a sesamum seed*, ii. 1[a].

तिलअ [°क] *a certain tree*, *Clerodendrum phlomoides*, ii. 42[31], 43[a], 45[2], 46[c].

तिलोअण [त्रिलोचन] *an epithet of Çiva, who has on his head the half moon, ardhacandra, which word means also a clenched fist*, i. 20[27].

तिवलि [त्रि°] *the three folds of skin above the navel of a woman*, i. 30[a]; ii. 24[a]; iii. 19[b].

तिव्व [तीव्र] *acute, hot, warm*, ii. 50[b].

तिहाअ [त्रिभाग] *the third part (of the eye, used in the side-long look of women)*, ii. 5[a], 8[d].

तिहुवण [त्रिभुवन] *the three worlds*, i. 10[a]; ii. 10[1].

तुङ्गिम- H. 2. 154. *height, elevation*, i. 34[b]; iii. 6[a].

तुट्ठ *see* तुष्.

तुण्हिक्क [तूष्णीक] HD. 5. 15. *quiet, silent*, iv. 20[4].

तुन्दिल ts *having a protuberant belly, corpulent*, i. 20[7].

तुमं *see* त्वम्.

तुम्हारिस [त्वादृश] *similar to you*, iv. 2[10].

तुरङ्ग, °म ts. *a horse*, i. 18[13], 21[c].

तुरिदपदं [त्वरित°] *quickly*, iv. 19[24].

तुलण [°न] *weighing*, i. 20[14].

तुला ts. *a balance, scales; resemblance*, i. 20[13, 14]; iii. 31[b].

तुल्ल [°ल्य] *like*, ii. 10[d].

तुष् *to be pleased. Caus., to please, satisfy.* tuṭṭha, i. 36[d]. tuṭṭheṇa, iii. 20[16]. tosidā, ii. 11[5].

तुसार [°षार] *frost, ice, snow*, i. 14[a].

तुहिणाअर [तुहिन°] *the moon*, i. 4[b].

तॄ + अव *to descend. Caus., to bring down.* odiṇṇo, iii. 20[15]. odiṇṇā, ii. 40[2]. avaiṇṇaṁ, i. 25[a]. avadāriadu, i. 25[9].

तृ + वि *to give, bestow.* viiṇṇa, iii. 11[c]. + समुद् *to put away.* samuttārida, i. 30[1].

तेत्तिअ H. 2. 157. *so much*, i. 7[b].

तेल्ल [तैल] *oil*, iv. 5[b].

तोअ [°य] *water*, iii. 3[9].

तोणीर [तू°] H. 1. 124. *a quiver*, ii. 16[b].

तोरण ts. *an arched doorway*, i. 17[a].

त्ति *see* ति.

°त्थ [°स्थ] *staying, abiding*, ii. 50[d].

त्रुट् *to fall asunder, be parted.* tuṭṭaï, ii. 4[d]. tuḍida, *broken, ruined*, i. 18[8].

त्वम् *thou, you.* tumaṁ, i. 16[1], 19[3, 5], 20[10, 13, 25, 29], 34[3, 20, 30]; ii. 6[6], 11[1], 24[3], 32[1], 42[17], 47[2]; iii. 2[1], 22[d], 34[a]; iv. 20[6]. tae, i. 18[6]; iii. 30[2]; iv. 20[2]. tujjha, i. 16[1], 20[8], 34[25]; iii. 21[b], 24[b]; iv. 22[c], 23[d]. tuha, i. 20[15, 16, 30]; ii. 7[a], 9[c], 10[d, 2], 42[20]; iii. 8[b], 32[a]; iv. 11[b], 21[c]. de, i. 14[2], 18[4], 19[2], 20[6, 7, 27], 32[1]; ii. 48[1]; iii. 20[4], 33[a], 34[b]; iv. 2[4], 9[5], 18[29], 19[32], 22[1]. tumhe, i. 20[41]; iv. 18[7]. tumhehiṁ, i. 20[12]. tumhāhiṁto, ii. 29[12]. tumhāṇaṁ, i. 18[1], 20[41]. vo, i. 3[b].

थक्क् H. 4. 16. *to stay, cease.* thakkantu, iii. 20[8].

थण [स्तन] *the female breast*, i. 2[b], 18[b], 27[b]; ii. 1[c], 23[b], 24[b], 29[a], 33[a], 44[a], 49[b]; iii. 6[a], 7[d], 21[a]; iv. 6[c].

थणाअ *the same*, ii. 27[a].

थणिल्ल H. 2. 159. *having breasts*, iii. 19[b].

थल [स्थ°] *raised or rounded surface*, i. 27[b].

थली [स्थ°] *the same*, ii. 1[a].

थवअ [स्तबक] *a bunch, cluster of blossoms*, ii. 47[c].

थूल [स्थू°] *large, great*, iii. 3[17].

थोअ [स्तोक] *little, small; a little*, i. 16[b]; ii. 1[b], 11[1].

थोर H. 1. 124, 255. *large; great, big*, ii. 27[a], 44[a]; iii. 6[a], 19[b].

दइअ [°यित] *lover, husband*, i. 24[c]. *Fem.* °ā, *wife*, iii. 6[b]. daidā, *wife*, i. 28[8].

दंसण [दर्शन] *looking, seeing, showing*, i. 34[25]; ii. 3[2], 40[2], 42[16, 17, 21], 43[a]; iii. 21[b], 31[1].

दक्ख [°क्ष] *able, skilful*, iii. 17[b].

दक्खारस [द्राक्षा°] *grape-juice*, ii. 26[d].

दक्खिण [दक्षिण] *right, southern*, i. 20[15]; iv. 9[9].

दक्खिणा [दक्षिणा] *the Dekkhan*, i. 12[9]. °vadha [°patha] *the Dekkhan*, i. 25[5], 34[8].

दक्खिणा [दक्षिणा] *present, gift, remuneration*, iv. 18[12, 14, 21, 25].

दण्ड ts. *a stick, staff, stalk, handle*, i. 16[3], 32[c]; ii. 6[10], 9[a], 39[b]; iv. 9[12], 20[d], 22[b].

दण्डरास ts. *a kind of dance*, iv. 11[b].

दन्त ts. *a tooth, ivory*, i. 14[a], 20[25]; iii. 31[a].

दन्तुर *rising, bristling*, ii. 46[d]. ts.

दप्प [दर्प] *pride, haughtiness*, ii. 30[c].

दप्पण [दर्पण] *a mirror*, i. 18[10].

दप्पि- [दर्पिन्] *proud, arrogant*, ii. 41[d].

दर ts. H. 2. 215. *a little, slightly*, ii. 14[b], 36[a], 49[b].

दरिद्दत्तण [°द्रत्व] *poverty, indigence*, i. 20^{b}.

दल् *to split, cleave.* dalantā, ii. 2^{a}.

+ **निस्** *to cut, break.* ṇiddalanto, ii. 30^{c}.

दल ts. *leaf, petal*, i. 29^{b}; ii. 6$^{20, 23, 24, 25}$, 14^{b}, 38^{b}; iv. 5^{a}, 21^{b}.

दस [°श] *ten*, iii. 3^{18}, 26^{a}. *Cp.* **दह**.

दसमासिअ [दशमाषक] *weighing ten māṣa*, iii. 5^{a}.

दह् *to burn.* ḍajjhanta, iii. 27^{a}.

दह [°श] *ten*, i. 18^{b}. *Cp.* **दस**.

दहि [°धि] *milk*, i. 19^{c}.

दा *to give.* deï, ii. 37^{b}. denti, i. 13^{a}; iv. 9^{c}, 12^{a}. dehi, ii. 42^{11}, 43^{b}. deu, i. 3^{b}. dedu, ii. 1^{5}. deha, i 18^{a}. dāïssaṁ, iv. 20^{12}. daia, i. 20^{40}; iii. 4^{5}. dādavvā, iv. 18^{14}. dento, i. 4^{d}. dentā, ii. 2^{b}; iii. 28^{a}. dijjae, iii. 9^{d}, 33^{b}. dijjadi, ii. 42^{21}. dīadu, iv. 18^{14}. dijjantu, iv. 21^{1}. dijjanta, iii. 27^{a}. dijjamāṇa, i. 30^{c}. diṇṇa, ii. 6$^{10, 22}$; iii. 3^{9}, 10^{d}. diṇṇā, i. 18^{d}; iii. 6^{b}; iv. 9^{6}, 18$^{21, 25}$, 21^{c}. diṇṇaṁ, iii. 34^{b}. diṇṇā, ii. 16^{a}.

दाण [°न] *giving, gift, donation*, ii. 5^{d}, 47^{1}; iii. 17^{b}.

दारा [°राः] *a wife*, i. 23^{a}.

दाव् H. 4. 32. *to show.* dāviaï, ii. 36^{a}.

दाव [तावत्] *just, now, truly, indeed*, i. 31^{1}, 34^{26}; ii. 6^{22}, 50^{3}; iii. 3^{2}, 22$^{2, 9}$; iv. 20^{12}.

दावग्गि [°वाग्नि] *a forest-conflagration*, iv. 24^{b}.

दासत्तण [°स्त्व] *slavery, service*, iv. 8^{d}.

दासी ts. *a female slave*, i. 18^{6}, 20$^{28, 33, 40}$; iv. 2^{8}, 9^{13}.

दाह ts. *burning*, ii. 10^{b}, 29^{b}, 42^{5}; iii. 20^{d}.

दिअह [दिवस] *a day*, i. 18^{b}, 21^{d}; ii. 9^{a}, 10^{c}; iv. 3^{c}, 5^{d}, 6^{d}, 9^{b}.

दिक्खा [दीक्षा] *initiation*, iv. 18^{12}.

दिक्खिअ *see* **दीक्ख्**.

दिट्ठि [दृष्टि] *a look, glance, eye*, i. 18^{a}, 21^{b}, 28$^{b, 8}$; ii. 1^{5}, 5^{e}, 8^{d}, 23^{a}, 41^{b}; iii. 2^{c}, 11^{a}.

दिण [°न] *day*, ii. 6^{10}; iv. 3^{a}.

दिणमणि [दिन°] *the sun*, ii. 50^{d}.

दिणेस [दिनेश] *the same*, i. 21^{c}.

दिंमुह [दिङ्मुख] *quarter of the sky*, ii. 4^{b}.

दिवस ts. *day*, i. 34^{26}; iv. 18^{11}, 19^{64}.

दिश् *to point out, show.* diṭṭho, i. 24^{c}.

+ **आ** *to point out, show, order.* ādisadi, iv. 9^{19}, 18$^{16, 23}$. ādiṭṭhaṁ, ii 26^{1}.

+ **निस्** *to point out, show.* ṇiddisadi, ii. 29^{21}. ṇiddiṭṭhā, iv. 18^{30}.

+ **समा** *to command, direct, instruct.* samādiṭṭhā, i. 10^{1}. samādiṭṭhaṁ, ii. 43^{10}.

दिसा [दिश्] *direction, quarter of the sky*, i. 14^{2}; iii. 25^{b}, 26^{a}, 28^{a}; iv. 9$^{c, 9, 10, 11}$.

दिसाभाअ [दिग्भाग] *quarter of the sky, direction*, i. 16^{d}.

दीक्ख् *to consecrate, initiate.* dikkhiā, i. 23^{a}.

दीव [°प] *a lamp, light*, ii. 6^{10}; iii. 27^{a}.

दीह [°र्घ] *long*, i. 21^{d}, 35^{c}; ii. 2^{b}; iv. 9^{b}.

दीहत्तण [°र्घत्व] *length*, i. 32^{a}.

दीहर H. 2. 171. *long*, ii. 9^{a}.

दीहिआ [दीर्घिका] *a long lake*, ii. 3^{c}.

दुइअ [द्वितीय] *second, other,* iii. 17[d].

दुक्कअ [दुष्कृत] *a sin, misdeed,* ii. 8[c].

दुक्ख [दुःख] *sorrow, distress,* ii. 8[c].

दुज्जण [दुर्जन] *a wicked, malicious person,* iii. 20[17].

दुट्ठ [दुष्ट] *wicked,* i. 20[40].

दुविअ [द्वितीय] *second, other,* ii. 8[3].

दुद्ध [दुग्ध] *milk, milky juice,* i. 16[b]; ii. 6[b], 29[11].

दुब्बल [दुर्बल] *weak, feeble,* ii. 9[d].

दुम [द्रुम] *a tree,* i. 17[b]; ii. 45[2], 46[c]; iv. 22[a].

दुलह [दुर्लभ] H. 1. 115. *difficult to be attained,* iv. 1[b].

दुल्लक्खअ [दुर्लक्ष्य] *difficult to be seen,* iii. 12[c].

दुवार [द्वार] *a door,* i. 21[4]; ii. 42[21, 26]; iii. 20[11]; iv. 9[7], 18[38], 19[3; 24].

दुवे *see* **द्वि**.

दुससि- [द्विशशिन्] *having two moons,* i. 34[d].

दुहिदा [°तृ] *a daughter,* i. 34[15]; iv. 18[19].

दूई [°ती] *a female messenger, a confidante,* iii. 27[c].

दूर ts. *distant, far. Adv., to a distance, highly, entirely,* i. 2[a], 6[a], 20[33]; iii. 1[a].

दूसण [दूष°] *spoiling, disfiguration, defect,* i 18[c]; ii. 23[d].

दूसह [दुः°] *insupportable, intolerable,* iii. 20[3]; iv. 2[a].

दूहव [दुर्भग] H. 1. 192. *ugly, hideous,* iii. 23[b].

दृश् *to see. Caus. to show. Pass., to appear.* daṭṭhuṁ, i. 24[5]. daṭṭhūṇa, iii. 6[a]. daṭṭhavvā, ii. 29[7]. daṁsemi, i. 25[a]. daṁsido, ii. 6[22]. daṁsiaṁ, ii. 21[b]. dīsaï, iv. 11[b]. dīsadi, i. 4[2], 20[26]. dīsae, ii. 30[d]. dīsadha, i. 4[16]. dīsanti, i. 6[b]. dīsadu, ii. 29[19]. diṭṭha, ii. 40[3]. diṭṭhā, ii. 11[d], 40[5]; iii. 22[d]; iv. 9[6], 19[30]. diṭṭhaṁ, i. 25[4, 6]; iii. 2[2], 3[4]. diṭṭhā, ii. 5[a].

देव ts. *a god; a king,* i. 18[c], 24[a], 34[44]; ii. 11[5], 22[1], 24[4], 26[1], 28[1], 29[7], 41[6], 47[3], 49[1]; iii. 24[2]; iv. 9[18], 21[6].

देवी ts. *a queen; Pārvatī,* i. 12[3, 8], 16[3], 18[17], 19[8], 34[28, 34, 36]; ii. 6[22, 23], 11[3], 22[a], 28[2], 29[7, 10], 42[27, 29, 33], 43[10], 47[1]; iii. 8[4, 5], 34[7, 9]; iv. 9[6, 7, 13, 14, 17, 19], 18[4, 7, 11, 12, 15, 23, 30, 31], 19[9, 25, 60], 23[a].

देव्वण्णअ [दैवज्ञ] *an astrologer,* iv. 18[20].

देसन्तर [देशा°] *another place, foreign parts,* iv. 18[27].

देह ts. *body,* ii. 10[b], 11[b]; iii. 17[b], 20[d, 18]. dehantara, *another body,* i. 34[34]; iv. 19[64].

दोकन्दली [दोः°] *a plantain-like arm,* iv. 7[c].

दोखण्ड [द्वि°] *having both halves, i. e. full (of the moon),* i. 32[b].

दोखण्ड- [द्वि°] *to cut in two, to break.* dokhaṇḍaantā, i. 15[b].

दोणी [द्रो°] *a bucket, cavity,* i. 29[b].

दोल् *to swing, oscillate.* dolanti, i. 26[b].

दोला ts. *a swing, hammock,* i. 21[b]; ii. 29[21], 30[d], 31[d], 37[b], 39[a], 40[a, 2].

दोल्लआ [दोर्लता] *a creeper-like arm,* iv. 16[b].

दोसोलह [द्विषोडश] *thirty-two,* iv. 11[a].

दोहल ts. *the longing of a pregnant woman, the desire of plants at budding time*, i. 20[27, 29]; ii. 45[1], 47[1].

दोहलअ [°क] *the same*, ii. 43[b].

द्वि *two.* duve, i. 16[2], 34[30, 32]; iii. 17[a]. dohiṁ, i. 4[c], 30[b]; iv. 12[b]. dohi, ii. 18[b]. dosu, i. 16[d]. dosuṁ, iv. 7[c].

धअवड [ध्वजपट] *a flag, banner*, ii. 31[a].

धणु [°नुस्] *a bow*, i. 32[c], 33[d]; iv. 9[9], 20[d].

धणुह H. 1. 22. *a bow*, ii. 3[d].

धम्म [°र्म] *religion, custom*, i. 23[d].

धम्मदारा [धर्मदाराः] *lawful wife*, i. 23[a].

धर ts. *holding, carrying*, ii. 46[b]; iv. 15[a].

धरणी ts. *earth, country*, i. 12[a]. °dala [°tala] *the surface of the earth, the earth*, i. 25[9].

धवल ts. *white, handsome*, ii. 23[a], 31[a].

धवल- *to make white or resplendent.* dhavalenti, i. 10[a]. dhavalia, iii. 7[a]. dhavalio, i. 29[c].

धवलिम- H. 2. 154. *whiteness*, ii. 41[b].

धा + अनुसम *to think over; make peace with.* aṇusaṁdhemi, iii. 2[2]. aṇusaṁdhedha, i. 20[42].

+ नि *to place, put.* ṇihio, ii. 29[a]. ṇihiaṁ, ii. 30[c]. ṇihitta, i. 4[c].

+ वि *to bring about, arrange.* vihide, iv. 18[32].

धाडी [°टी] *assault, attacking*, ii. 46[c].

धारा ts. *a stream, current*, ii. 9[b]; iii. 20[c], 28[d]; iv. 13[a].

धारि- [°रिन्] *carrying*, iv. 9[9, 11].

धाव् *to run.* dhāvantassa, i. 18[13].

धुवागोद [ध्रुवागीत] *introductory stanza*, i. 4[11].

धूदा H. 2. 126. *a daughter*, i. 18[6].

धूव [°प] *incense, perfume*, iii. 14[b].

धूववट्टि [°पवर्ति] *a pillar or cloud of smoke*, iii. 27[a].

धृ *to hold, carry, contain, stop.* dharaï, ii. 48[a]. dharantao, iii. 31[b]. dhariā, iii. 3[c].

धोअ [धौत] *washed, washed off*, i. 26[a].

धोद *the same*, i. 30[1].

नन्द् *to be delighted, rejoice.* ṇandantu, i. 1[a].

नम *to bow, make obeisance to; to sink.* ṇamaha, i. 2[b]. ṇamanti, ii. 31[c]. ṇaa, i. 4[c].

+ उद् *to rise, ascend.* uṇṇamantī, ii. 31[c].

+ परि *to be changed, ripe.* pariṇamantā, i. 8[a]. pariṇaaṁ, ii. 8[c].

+ प्र *to bow down.* paṇamāmi, iv. 19[4]. paṇamanti, iv. 18[b].

नश् *to disappear.* ṇaṭṭhā, iii. 3[d]. ṇaṭṭhāe, ii. 40[3].

+ प्र *to disappear, be lost.* paṇaṭṭhā, ii. 40[5].

नी *to carry, bring, conduct.* ṇaissadha, i. 34[27]. ṇaia, ii. 11[3].

+ आ *to bring.* āṇemi, i. 25[c]. āṇedi, iv. 19[55]. āṇia, ii. 43[2]; iii. 4[8]. āṇīadi, i. 25[8]. āṇīadu, i. 25[7]. āṇīā, i. 26[d]. āṇīdāiṁ, iv. 19[44].

+ उप *to offer, present.* uvaṇijjo, iv. 7[c].

+ परि *to marry. Caus., to cause to*

marry. pariṇeï, i. 12^{b}. pariṇedavvā, iv. 18^{21}. pariṇāïdavvā, iv. 18^{7}.

णृत *to play, act.* ṇaccidavvaṁ, i. 4^{18}.

पअ [°द] *foot; pace; dignity, rank,* i. 9^{b}, 12^{a}, 21^{a}; iv. 11^{b}.

पअइ [प्रकृति] *nature, natural condition,* ii. 26^{c}.

पअट्टावअ [प्रवर्तापक] *producing,* i. 16^{3}.

पअट्टइ *see* वृत + प्र.

पअडेइ *see* कट् + प्र.

पअण्ड [प्रच°] *impetuous,* iii. 30^{b}.

पअवी [पद°] *position, rank,* iv. 23^{c}.

पआवइ [प्रजापति] *the god Prajāpati, the creator,* iii. 17^{a}.

पआसइ *see* काश् + प्र.

पओट्ठ [प्रकोष्ठ] *the fore-arm,* ii. 16^{a}.

पओस [प्रदोष] *evening,* iv. 4^{b}.

पंसु [पांसु] *dust,* iv. 5^{c}.

पक्ख [पक्ष] *a wing,* iv. 2^{10}.

पक्खाउज्ज [पक्षातोद्य] *a kind of drum, cp. Hindī* pakhāüj, i. 4^{10}.

पक्खालिद *see* क्षल् + प्र.

पङ्क ts. *mud, paste,* i. 16^{a}; ii. 8^{a}, 12^{a}; iv. 4^{a}.

पङ्कअ [°ज] *a lotus,* ii. 13^{b}, 33^{a}.

पङ्करुह ts. *the same,* iii. 3^{a}.

पङ्किल ts. *turbid, smeared, anointed,* iv. 8^{a}.

पङ्केरुह ts. *a lotus,* i. 4^{d}, 35^{d}.

पच्चक्खं [प्रत्यक्षम्] *clearly, openly,* i. 30^{d}; ii. 43^{2}.

पच्चग्ग [प्रत्यग्र] *fresh, new,* iii. 1^{d}.

पच्चङ्गं [प्रत्यङ्गम्] *on every limb,* iv. 9^{a}.

पच्छा [पश्चात्] *behind, from behind; afterwards,* i. 34^{27}; ii. 6^{c}.

पच्छिम [पश्चिम] *last; western,* iv. 4^{c}, 9^{10}.

पज्झरावेदि *see* क्षर् + प्र.

पञ्च ts. *five.* pañca, i. 18^{b}; iv. 4^{d}, $9^{8, 9, 12}$. pañcehiṁ, iii. 19^{d}.

पञ्चगव्व [°व्य] *the five products of the cow,* i. 20^{26}.

पञ्चदस [°श] *fifteen,* i. 34^{26}.

पञ्चबाण ts. *Cupid,* ii. 19^{b}, 38^{b}.

पञ्चम ts. *the fifth note of the gamut, said to be produced by the cuckoo; name of a musical mode,* i. 16^{3}; ii. 2^{c}, 5^{b}; iii. 20^{7}; iv. 6^{a}.

पञ्चसर [°शर] *Cupid,* i. 32^{c}; ii. 46^{b}; iv. 8^{d}.

पञ्चाल ts. *name of the country between the Yamunā and the Ganges, the Doab,* iii. 5^{2}.

पञ्चालिआ [°का] *a doll,* ii. 12^{b}.

पञ्चालिआ [पाञ्चालिका] *the Pāñcālikā style in poetry,* i. 1^{c}.

पञ्चेसु [°षु] *Cupid,* i. 18^{c}; iv. 4^{c}.

पञ्जर ts. *a cage,* i. 18^{15}; iii. 31^{a}.

पट् + उद् *Caus., to tear out, eradicate.* uppāḍaissaṁ, i. 20^{15}. uppāḍia, i. 20^{31}. uppāḍida, iv. 2^{4}.

पट्ट ts. *a garment, silk cloth,* i. 36^{c}.

पट्टअ [°क] *a tablet, palette,* i. 4^{6}.

पट्टंसुअ [पट्टांशुक] *a silk garment,* ii. 14^{a}.

पठ् *to recite.* paḍhissaṁ, i. 18^{17}; iii. 30^{2}. paḍha, i. $19^{3, 8}$; ii. 10^{7}. paḍhiadi, i. 19^{7}.

पड [°ट] *a garment, cloth,* i. 14^{d}.

पडण [पतन] *falling,* iv. 18^{8}.

पडाआ [पटाका] *a flag, banner,* iii. 20[6]; iv. 20[a].

पडिवट्टअ [प्रतिपट्टक] *a silk cloth,* i. 20[9].

पडिवड्डाविआ [प्रतिवर्धापिका] *speaking agreeably or congratulating in her turn,* i. 13[1].

पडिसिविणअ [प्रतिस्वप्नक] *a dream in return,* iii. 8[b].

पडिसीसअ [प्रतिशीर्षक] *a mask,* i. 4[5], 20[40]; iv. 15[b]. [*K*, anukāryānurūpavarṇanāmukha].

पढण [पठन] *reading, reciting,* i. 24[b].

पढम [प्रथम] *first,* i. 20[23, 25], 34[24]; iii. 17[c].

पणअ [प्रणय] *attachment,* iii. 8[4], 9[2].

पणइ [प्रणति] *a bow, courtesy,* i. 4[a].

पणइ- [प्रणयिन्] *attached to, joined to,* iv. 7[b].

पणस [पनस] *the bread-fruit,* iv. 22[a].

पणाम [प्रणाम] *a bow, salutation.* i. 34[24].

पणोल्लिअ *see* **णोल्ल् + प्र.**

पण्डिच्च [पाण्डित्य] *erudition, Punditship,* i. 18[4, 8, 9].

पण्डी *a Pāṇḍya woman,* i. 15[a].

पण्डु [पा°] *pale, yellowish,* ii. 10[c]; iv. 5[a].

पण्डुर [पा°] *pale-white, yellowish-white,* ii. 6[10]; iii. 33[a].

पण्होत्तर [प्रश्नोत्तर] *riddle and answer,* i. 5[2].

पत् *to fall.* paḍaï, ii. 39[a]. paḍanti, iv. 13[b].

+ नि *to fall down, to be cast at.* ṇivaḍiā, ii. 5[c], 46[c].

+ समुद् *to jump up, to emerge.* samuppaḍia, iii. 3[18].

पत्त [°त्र] *a leaf,* ii. 1[2], 7[a].

पत्त [पात्र] *a dramatis persona,* i. 4[3].

पत्त *see* **आप् + प्र.**

पत्तिआमि *see* **या + प्रति.**

पद् + उद् *Caus., to produce.* uppādedi, iii. 12[2].

+ निस् *to be produced.* ṇippajjadi, i. 34[18].

+ सम् *to become. Caus., to accomplish, produce.* saṁpaṇṇaṁ, iii. 20[4, 21]. saṁpādemi, ii. 41[6]. saṁpādemha, i. 12[2]. saṁpādaissadi, ii. 43[1].

+ समुद् *to be produced.* samuppaṇṇā, iii. 4[9]; iv. 19[35].

पदि [°ति] *a husband,* i. 19[7].

पदीव [प्रदीप] *a lamp,* iii. 22[4].

पंति [पङ्क्ति] *a line, row, series.* ii. 1[2], 17[b]; iv. 12[b].

पब्भार [प्राग्भार] HD. 6. 66. *a mass, large quantity,* ii. 33[a].

पभाद [प्रभात] *day-break, dawn,* ii. 6[10].

पमदुज्जाण [प्रमदोद्यान] *pleasure-grounds,* iii. 22[9]; iv. 18[30].

पमाण [प्र°] *measure, size, extent,* i. 16[3]; iii. 3[18].

पर ts. *other, different; intent on,* i. 18[2, 8]; iv. 18[a], 22[2]. paraṁ, *however, excessively, at the utmost,* i. 1[b], 34[30]; ii. 11[a].

परम ts. *highest, best,* ii. 28[d].

परमत्थ [°मार्थ] *truth, reality,* ii. 22[1].

परमेट्ठि- [°ष्ठिन्] *an epithet of Brahmā,* iv. 19[b].

परंपरा ts. *an uninterrupted series, succession,* i. 9[b], 18[4, 8, 9].

परहुअ [°भृत] *the cuckoo,* ii. 2[a].

परिअण [°जन] *attendants, suite,* i. 28[6].

परिक्खण [परीक्षण] *testing, examining*, ii. 29[a].

परिक्खीण [°क्षीण] *emaciated, diminished*, ii. 6[10].

परिणदि [°ति] *maturity*, iii. 4[3].

परिपण्डुरत्तण [°पाण्डुरत्व] *dazzling whiteness*, iii. 34[b].

परिरम्भ ts. *embracing*, i. 2[a]; iii. 7[c].

परिवाडि [°पाटि] *order, succession*, iv. 16[b].

परिसप्पि- [°सर्पिन्] *moving about*, iv. 19[55].

परिसर ts. *neighborhood, environs*, iii. 19[a], 34[a]; iv. 7[a].

परिहास ts. *joking, merriment*, ii. 6[6].

परुस [°ष] *hard, harsh*, i. 7[a].

पअट्ट *see* वृत् + प्र.

परोक्ख [°क्ष] *invisible, unknown*, iv. 18[29].

परोप्पर [परस्पर] *each other, mutual*, iii. 11[b]; iv. 12[b].

पल्लङ्क [पर्यङ्क] *a bed, couch*, i. 36[b].

पल्लव ts. *a sprout*, i. 26[b]; iii. 23[a].

पवञ्च [प्रपञ्च] *display, diversity*, ii. 40[a].

पवञ्च- [प्रपञ्चय-] *to display, show, expand.* pavañcida, i. 16[3].

पवण [°न] *the wind*, ii. 11[b], 14[b], 36[a]; iii. 22[4].

पवल [प्रबल] *violent*, iv. 1[a].

पवाह [प्र°] *a stream, current*, ii. 10[d]; iii. 10[c], 20[8].

पवेस [प्रवेशक] *an interlude in a drama*, i. 6[c].

पसअ [प्रसृति] *the palm of the hand*, i. 30[c]; ii. 38[a].

पसदि *the same*, i. 16[b].

पसर [प्र°] *outbreak, course*, iii. 20[9].

पसरण [प्र°] *going, streaming forth*, ii. 10[a].

पसव [प्र°] *blossom*, ii. 6[22].

पसाअ [प्रसाद] *propitiatory offering, propitiation, favor*, i. 4[a], 22[a], 34[25].

पसादी + कृ [प्र°] *to present.* °kidaṁ, ii. 6[24].

पसार [प्र°] *spreading*, iii. 11[c].

पसाहण [प्रसाधन] *decoration, toilet*, i. 20[36]; ii. 19[a], 22[a], 24[3].

पसूण [प्रसून] *a bud, flower*, i. 19[a].

पह [°थ] *way; reach*, iii. 2[d].

पहा [प्रभा] *light, splendor, similarity*, i. 16[a].

पहार [प्र°] *striking, shooting*, iii. 7[b].

पहाव [प्रभाव] *power, efficacy*, ii. 6[22], 45[1]; iii. 8[2]; iv. 18[29].

पहुद [प्रभृति] *beginning, beginning with*, i. 32[d].

पप्फुट्ट *see* स्फुट् + प्र.

पहुदि [प्रभृति] *beginning, beginning with, from, ever since*, i. 20[20, 34]; ii. 3[2].

पा *to drink. Caus., to cause to drink.* piāmo, i. 22[b]. pianto, iii. 8[4]. pianti, iv. 19[b]. pijjae, i. 23[b]. pijjantaṁ, i. 16[d]. pīdo, iii. 3[11, 18] pāidā, ii. 29[11].

पाअ [°द] *foot; beam*, i. 4[d], 20[30]; iii. 28[d].

पाअन्त [पादान्त] *the extremity of the feet*, i. 14[d].

पाआर [प्राकार] *a rampart, wall*, ii. 31[c].

पाउअ [प्राकृत] *the Prakrit language*, i. 7[a].

पाउद *the same*, i. 6[2].

पाडिसिद्धी HD. 6. 77. *emulation, rivalry*, i. 10[b], 20[12, 33]; ii. 10[6].

पाठिआ [पाठिका] *a reciting or reading woman*, iv. 9[12].

पाण [प्राण] *life, soul*, iii. 8[a].

पाणि ts. *hand*, i. 27[a]; iii. 23[a].

पामर ts. *a low-caste man*, i. 20[39].

पारावअ [°त] *a pigeon*, iii. 27[b].

पारिभद्द [°द्र] *the coral tree*, iv. 22[a].

पाल् + प्रति *to guard, observe.* paḍivāledu, ii. 41[2].

पालित्तिआ *capital; a treasure; a paragon of*, ii. 3[b]; iv. 19[14]. (*K*, bhaṅgīprakāraḥ pālayitṛkā; yadvā pālittaā iti deçīpadaṁ mūlanīvyāṁ vartata iti sampradāyaḥ.)

पास [°र्श्व] *side, flank*, ii. 36[b], 46[b].

पाहुड [प्राभृत] *a present, gift*, ii. 7[a].

पि *see* वि.

पिअ [प्रिय] *dear, beloved, agreeable*, i. 1[b], 3[a], 15[c], 16[1]; ii. 27[c]; iv. 2[b], 22[1, 2].

पिअवअस्स [प्रियवयस्य] *a dear friend*, i. 18[17], 20[39], 32[1]; ii. 6[10], 10[6], 41[2], 43[2]; iii. 2[3], 20[1], 34[7]; iv. 9[4].

पिअसही [प्रियसखी] *a female friend, a lady's confidante*, ii. 8[3], 42[5, 10]; iii. 30[2], 34[5].

पिक्क [पक्व] *ripe*, ii. 50[d].

पिङ्ग ts. *yellow-red*, ii. 50[d]

पिच्छ ts. *tail-feather*, ii. 14[a]; iv. 14[b].

पिञ्जर ts. *reddish-yellow, tawny, gold-colored*, ii. 8[a], 12[a]; iii. 25[b].

पिण्ड ts. *mass, ball*, i. 35[a].

पिधाण [°न] *covering*, iv. 18[38].

पिसुण [°शुन] *slanderous*, iii. 9[d].

पिसुण- [°शुनय-] *to indicate.* pisuṇaï, ii. 24[d]. pisuṇedi, i. 20[6].

पिहुल [पृथुल] *broad, large*, iv. 9[7].

पीड् *to press, squeeze.* pīḍio, iii. 7[d].

पीण [°न] *fat, round*, i. 18[b]; iii. 7[c].

पुङ्खिअ [°त] *furnished with feathers*, ii. 3[d]; iv. 20[d].

पुङ्खिद *the same*, iv. 9[9].

पुञ्ज् *to heap up, collect.* puñjijjaï, iii. 26[d]. puñjia, i. 14[d].

पुञ्ज ts. *heap, multitude*, i. 19[d]; ii. 46[d].

पुट्ठ *see* स्पृश्.

पुट्ठी [पृष्ठ] *the back*, ii. 39[b].

पुणण्णव [पुनर्नव] *revived, refreshed*, iii. 20[10].

पुणो [पुनर्] *again, back; on the other hand*, i. 34[27]; ii. 3[c], 5[c], 6[b, 13], 26[c], 28[4], 49[b]; iii. 17[d]; iv. 18[17], 19[25, 37, 47]. puṇu, ii. 23[d]; iii. 9[c], 14[d]. *Cp.* उण.

पुण्ण [पूर्ण] *filled, full, accomplished, fulfilled*, i. 20[d]; ii. 41[d]; iii. 19[a]; iv. 23[b].

पुण्णिमा [पूर्णिमा] *the day of full moon*, i. 25[9], 34[d]; ii. 6[10], 29[19, 21]; iii. 20[15]; iv. 19[64].

पुत्त [°त्र] *a son*, i. 18[8], 19[7]; iv. 2[8].

पुत्तलिआ [°लिका] *a doll*, iii. 20[3]; iv. 18[36].

पुत्ती [°त्री] *a daughter*, i. 20[28]; iv. 19[24, 50].

पुरदो [°तस्] *before, in the presence of*, i. 18[17], 19[5, 6], 20[20]; ii. 10[6], 29[6]; iii. 30[2].

पुरन्धी [°न्ध्री] *an elderly married woman*, i. 16[3].

पुरस्सर [पुरः°] *preceding*, i. 20[16, 31].

पुरिस [°रुष] *a man*, i. 7[b].

पुरो [पुरस्] *before; formerly*, iii. 1[c], 22[a]; iv. 19[a].

पुलअ [°क] *horripilation, thrill of joy*, iv. 21[d].

पुलअ-, पुलोअ-, H. 4. 181. *to look, behold.* puloesi, iii. 8[4]. pulantīa, ii. 1[d].

पुलअण [°कन] *horripilation,* i. 15[a].

पुलिन्द ts. *a man of a certain barbarous tribe, a mountaineer,* iv. 14[b].

पुव्व [पूर्व] *eastern,* i. 14[2]; iii. 25[b]; iv. 9[3].

पूर ts. *a stream, flood,* iii. 28[a].

पूरण ts. *filling,* i. 34[39].

पृ *to fill.* pūriāe, i. 4[b].

पेऊस [पीयूष] *nectar,* iii. 20[2].

पेक्ख, पेच्छ *see* **ईक्ष्.**

पेङ्खिअ [प्रेङ्खित] *swung, shaken,* i. 21[a].

पेम्म [प्रेमन्] *love, affection,* iii. 8[3, 4], 9[a, 1, 2], 12[b, 2], 15[b].

पेरन्त [पर्यन्त] *circuit, border,* iii. 11[b].

पेसल [पेशल] *artificially made pleasant, seasoned,* iv. 5[b].

पोट्टिस *name of a poet,* i. 20[20].

पोत्त *a garment, cloth,* i. 27[b]; ii. 24[c].

पोत्थअ [पुस्तक] *a book,* i. 18[2].

पोप्फल [पूगफल] H. 1. 170. *the areca nut,* iv. 5[b].

पोम्मराअ [पद्मराग] *a ruby,* ii. 15[a]; iv. 18[11].

प्रछ् *to ask.* pucchāmi, iii. 8[2]. pucchissaṁ, i. 4[12]. pucchia, i. 34[1]. pucchīanti, i. 18[13].

फंस [स्पर्श] *touch, contact,* iii. 24[b]; iv. 21[c].

फग्गुण [फाल्गुन] *a Hindu month corresponding to February-March,* i. 20[29].

फण ts. *the hood of a serpent,* i. 20[b].

फणिलआ [°ता] *the betel plant,* i. 17[c].

फरअ HD. 6. 82. *a shield,* iv. 9[3].

फरक्किद [स्फारीकृत] *shaken, swung,* iv. 9[3].

फरिस [स्पर्श] *touch, contact,* iv. 6[c].

फल ts. *fruit, result,* ii. 6[16]; iv. 21[a].

फलअ [°क] *plank, shield, expanse;* i. 30[b], 32[b]; ii. 15[a], 23[c]; iv. 9[11].

फलिहमणि [स्फटिक°] *a crystal-stone,* ii. 29[15].

फड् *see* **स्फट्.**

फार [स्फार] *large, great,* i. 20[b]; iii. 19[a].

फुड् *see* **स्फुट्.**

फुड [स्फुट] *clear, white, clearly, evidently,* ii. 12[b]; iv. 22[d].

फुल्ल् *to open, blow, blossom. Intens., the same.* phullanti, ii. 9[1]. phullāi, ii. 38[a]. pamphulliā, i. 16[b].

फुल्ल ts. *a flower,* i. 19[a].

फेक्कार [फेत्कार] *a shriek, howl,* iv. 15[a].

बइल्ल *see* **गलिबइल्ल.** *Cp. Marāṭhī* baila.

बउलमाला [बकु°] *name of a woman,* iv. 9[10].

बक्कर [बर्कर] HD. 6. 89. *a jest,* ii. 6[8].

बक्करकेली *name of a woman,* iv. 9[11].

बन्दि- [°न्दिन्] *a panegyrist, bard,* i. 16[2, 4].

बन्ध् + नि *to bind, close.* ṇibaddhaṁ, iv. 9[7].

बन्ध ts. *arrangement, literary composition, posture,* i. 6[2], 7[a]; ii. 4[c]; iv. 11[a], 12[b].

बन्धव [बा°] *a kinsman, friend,* i. 16[3].

बम्ह- [ब्रह्मन्] *the god Brahmā,* i. 24[a].

बम्हण [ब्राह्मण] *fem.* °ṇī, *a Brāhmaṇa, fem. the wife of a Brāhmaṇa,* i. 20[4, 26, 33, 43]; iii. 8[1]. *fem.* i. 20[34].

बरिहि- [बर्हिन्] *a peacock,* ii. 15[b].

बला [°लात्] *perforce, violently*, i. 13^d; iv. 22^c.

बलि ts. *an oblation*, iv. 15^a.

बहल ts. *copious, abundant*, i. 13^a, 20^d; ii. 3^a, 37^a; iv. 21^d.

बहिणिआ [भगिनिका] *a sister*, i. 34^{22,25,32,35,38}; ii. 6^{24}, 9^1, 10^{2,4}.

बहु + मन *to value, esteem.* °mannedi, i. 28^c.

बहुसो [°शस्] *often*, i. 4^a; ii. 29^b.

बाउल्लिआ HD. 6. 92. *a doll*, iv. 19^{65}.

बाण ts. *an arrow*, ii. 11^c; iv. 13^b.

बाध् *to harrass, torment.* bāhaṇijjo, iv. 2^2. bāhaṇijjā, iv. 2^1.

बाल ts. *young, new*, i. 13^c, 15^a; ii. 41^b, 42^{29}, 45^a, 49^a; iii. 8^1, 19^d.

बालकइ [°वि] *a young poet*, i. 9^a.

बाह [°ष्प] *a tear*, ii. 9^b, 10^d; iii. 20^8.

बाहिर [बहिस्] H. 2. 140. *external*, i. 34^{30}.

बाहु ts. *an arm*, i. 30^b; iv. 12^a.

बाहुमूल ts. *a shoulder*, ii. 24^a.

बिन्दु ts. *a drop*, i. 26^b; iii. 3^{17}, 4^a.

बिम्ब ts. *the Bimba fruit; the disk of the sun or moon*, i. 13^a; ii. 20^b; iii. 25^d, 32^b; iv. 3^b. saṁpuṇṇabimbattaṇa [saṁpūrṇabimbatva], *fullness of disk*, iii. 25^d.

बिस ts. *the fibre, fibrous stalk of a lotus*, iii. 20^a; iv. 7^c.

बुड्डण H. 4. 101. *sinking, inclining*, ii. 31^d.

बुध् + वि *awaken.* vibuddho, iii. 7^d.

बोल् H. 4. 162. *Caus., to pass.* boleï, ii. 29^d.

बोल H. 4. 2. *speech, words*, ii. 4^c.

भअव- [भगवत्] *fem.* °vadī, *favored, exalted, venerable, holy*, i. 20^{27}; ii. 6^{25}; iii. 3^{14}; iv. 18^{16,23}, 19^{4,12}.

भङ्ग ts. *breaking*, i. 28^a.

भङ्गि ts. *bending*, iv. 9^a.

भङ्गुर ts. *fragile*, iii. 21^a.

भज्जाजिद [भार्याजित] *enslaved by women, a hen-pecked husband*, iii. 2^1.

भञ्ज् *to break.* bhañja, iii. 21^a.

भट्ट- [भर्तृ] *a lord, master*, iv. 9^{16}, 18^{6,22}.

भट्टारअ [°क] *venerable, worshipful*, iii. 20^{23}.

भण् *to say, speak; name, call.* bhaṇāmi, ii. 47^3; iv. 7^1. bhaṇāsi, i. 20^{28}; iv. 19^{34}. bhaṇādi, i. 34^{28}. bhaṇimo, ii. 23^d. bhaṇāmo, ii. 48^2. bhaṇanti, i. 24^a; iii. 9^{1,2}. bhaṇa, i. 20^{17}, 25^{1,8}; ii. 6^7, 40^4, 47^5; iii. 8^6; iv. 4^1. bhaṇaha, ii. 16^b. bhaṇia, i. 34^{35}. bhaṇantassa, i. 20^{30}. bhaṇṇaï, i. 5^a, 6^a. bhaṇīadi, i. 20^{4,20}; ii. 10^2. bhaṇṇae, iii. 12^b. bhaṇidā, ii. 42^{33}. bhaṇidaṁ, i. 7^1; iv. 2^6, 18^{13,23}.

भण्डअ [भाण्डक] *a small vessel, cup*, i. 20^{26}.

भत्त- [भर्तृ] *husband*, i. 11^b; ii. 8^b.

भद्द [°द्र] *happiness, blessing*, i. 1^a, 20^{26}; iv. 5^d.

भमण [भ्र°] *shaking, moving*, ii. 1^c.

भमर [भ्र°] *a bee*, ii. 13^b; iii. 2^b.

भमरटेण्टा [भ्र°] *having an unsteady character, or, having a scar like a bee*, i. 18^8. (*BNJ*, bhramaṇaçīlā; *P*, bhramaravat ṭiṭo yasyāḥ. ṭeṭo ni madhyasthito[!] maṇiviçeṣaḥ. ṭiṭā bhīṣaṇā; *O*, bhramarasadṛçena ṭeṭākhyaguhyāgeṇa[!]. ṭeṭā akṣigolakam iti kecit; *K*, bhamaraṭeṁte ity etad deçīpadaṁ muṣṭiprahāraprarūḍhe veçyorahkiṇe vartate. bhramaravarṇakiṇamaṇāu. tathā ca prayogaḥ. ṭeṁṭāvalokanakutūhalabhaṁgabhīrur iti. yadvā bhramarāṇāṁ viṭānāṁ ṭeṁṭā bhūyate.)

भवण [°न] *abode, dwelling, house*, ii. 6^{22}; iv. $19^{a, 17}$.

भविस्स [°ष्य] *what is to be, the future*, i. 18^{3}.

भसल HD. 6. 101. *a bee*, i. $16^{c, d}$; ii. 44^{d}.

भा *to shine, seem, appear*. bhāī, i. 23^{d}, 33^{b}; iii. 31^{b}.

+ **वि** *the same.* vibhāī, ii. 41^{d}.

भादर [भ्रातृ] *a brother*, i. 20^{15}.

भामरी [भ्रा°] *walking round from left to right*, iv. 21^{1}.

भार ts. *a burden, weight, mass*, i. 18^{2}; ii. 21^{a}; iii. 21^{a}.

भारिआ [भार्या] *a wife*, i. 12^{3}.

भाव ts. *being, condition; feeling, sentiment; a venerable, worthy man (term of address)*, i. 4^{15}, 5^{a}; ii. 10^{c}, 50^{b}; iii. 10^{b}, 20^{10}.

भावणिज्ज *see* **भू**

भासा [°षा] *language, dialect*, i. 7^{1}, 8^{b}.

भिक्खा [°क्षा] *alms*, i. 23^{c}.

भिङ्ग [भृ°] *a bee*, i. 29^{b}; ii. 6^{a}.

भिच्च [भृत्य] *a servant, slave*, i. 33^{d}.

भिद् + उद् *pass. to shoot up, be raised.* ubbhijjadu, iii. 20^{6}.

+ **निस्** *to tear up, break through.* ṇibbhiṇṇassa, iv. 18^{38}.

भुअङ्ग [भुजङ्ग] *a paramour, gallant*, i. 14^{2}.

भुज्ज [भूर्ज] *the birch tree*, iii. 25^{b}.

भुत्थल्ल *food for a cat*, iv. 2^{8}. (*O*, bhutthallaḥ majjārīe bhutti. bhūmipātanayogyaḥ; bharitrayogya iti vā bhūthir iti bhāṣāyāṁ.)

भुल्ल H. 4. 177. *erring, oblivious*, iv. 20^{15}.

भुवण [°न] *the world*, iii. 26^{b}, 28^{b}; iv. 20^{a}.

भू *to be, become. Caus., to cherish, affect, win.* hosi, i. 19^{5}. hoi, i. 7^{a}, 8^{b}; iv. 23^{a}. bhodi, i. 20^{43}, 34^{10}; iv. 3^{1}, $18^{21, 22}$. honti, i. 21^{d}; ii. 10^{d}, 49^{a}; iii. 19^{d}; iv. 2^{10}. hava, iii. 23^{a}. hou, i. 1^{a}, 8^{b}; iii. 23^{b}; iv. 5^{d}. bhodu, i. 14^{2}, $20^{26, 27}$, 34^{41}; ii. 49^{4}; iii. 3^{2}, 22^{6}, 24^{2}; iv. 19^{48}, 21^{6}, 23^{1}. havantu, iii. 24^{b}. bhavissaṁ, i. 13^{1}; ii. 28^{4}. hohii, ii. 39^{a}; iii. 32^{a}. bhavissadi, iv. $18^{20, 32}$. bhavia, i. 20^{34}; ii. 9^{1}, 32^{2}; iii. 3^{18}. bhavidavvaṁ, ii. 42^{26}. bhāvaṇijjā, ii. 26^{c}.

+ **अनु** *to enjoy, experience, feel.* aṇubhavidaṁ, i. 34^{25}.

+ **सम्** *to arise, be born. Caus., to honor, show respect to; to fancy, imagine.* saṁbhūdāṇaṁ, i. 18^{9}. saṁbhāvehi, iii. 20^{23}. saṁbhāvaissadi, iii. 20^{17}. saṁbhāvīadi, iv. 2^{10}.

भूगोल ts. *terrestrial globe*, iii. 25^{a}.

भूचन्द [°न्द्र] *an earth-moon*, ii. 27[b].
भूमि ts. *earth; ground*, i. 25[d], 34[18].
भूमिआ [°का] *character, costume in a play*, i. 12[3].
भूमीघर [°गृह] *cellar, underground chamber*, iii. 25[a].
भूष् *to adorn, decorate.* bhūsidā, ii. 11[5].
+ वि *the same.* vihūsaanti, i. 31[a]. vihūsiā, ii. 22[b].
भूसणा [°षणा] *ornament, decoration*, i. 30[1], 31[b]; ii. 23[d], 25[a]; iii. 15[d], 26[b].
भृ *to fill, pervade; have, possess.* bhariaṁ, iv. 23[d]. bharidā, iii. 20[3].
भेअ [°द] 1. *splitting, wound*, iii. 11[d]. 2. *difference*, iii. 15[c].
भेरवाणन्द [भैरवानन्द] *name of a yogin*, i. 21[4], 24[3], 34[25, 33, 35]; ii. 6[22]; iv. 18[11, 29, 31, 34].
भो [भोस्] *a vocative particle, O, sir*, i. 18[1], 34[30]; ii. 24[2], 29[19], 32[1], 43[5], 44[1], 47[1]; iii. 2[1], 3[4], 8[4], 9[1], 22[8], 26[1]; iv. 20[12], 21[1].
भोज्ज [°ज्य] *food, meal*, i. 23[c].
भोदी [भवती] *honorific pronoun, used as term of respectful address to women*, ii. 42[7]; iii. 20[21]; iv. 18[8].
भ्रंश् *to fall, decline, decay.* bhaṭṭho, iii. 8[1].
भ्रम् *to whirl, swarm round.* bhamiaṁ, ii. 13[b].
+ परि *to wander about, turn round.* paribbhamantīu, iv. 11[a].

———

मअ [°द] *madness, rut*, ii. 6[10].
°मअ [°य] *fem.* °maī, *made of, consisting of*, i. 36[a]; iv. 18[11], 19[65].
मअच्छी [मृगाक्षी] *a deer-eyed woman*, ii. 46[c]; iv. 16[a].
मअणा [°दन] *beeswax*, i. 13[a]. (*K*, himavraṇopaçamanārthaṁ hi madhūcchiṣṭam adhare dadhatīti lokaprasiddhiḥ.)
मअणा [°दन] *love, Cupid*, ii. 10[6], 16[b], 33[b], 36[b], 45[b]; iii. 12[b, d], 18[d], 21[b], 30[b]; iv. 1[a].
मअरकेउ [मकरकेतु] *the same*, iv. 20[c].
मअरद्धअ [मकरध्वज] *the same*, ii. 49[b]; iii. 9[2], 20[6]; iv. 19[64].
मअरलञ्छणा [मकरलाञ्छन] *the same*, iii. 26[c].
मअलञ्छणा [मृगलाञ्छन] *the moon*, ii. 47[b]; iv. 18[36].
मइरा [मदि°] *spirituous liquor*, i. 20[26].
मउलि [मौ°] *head*, i. 4[c].
मंस [मां°] *flesh, meat*, i. 23[b].
मग्ग [मार्ग] *way, doctrine*, i. 22[b].
मग्गणा [मार्ग°] *an arrow*, i. 32[d].
मङ्गलमाला ts. *name of a woman*, iv. 9[10].
मज्ज [°द्य] *spirituous liquor, wine*, i. 22[b], 23[b].
मज्जणा [°न] *bathing*, iv. 4[b], 8[b].
मज्जणापाल [मज्जन°] *fem.* °lī, *keeper of a bath*, iv. 9[11].
मज्जारिआ [मार्जारिका] *a cat*, ii. 29[11].
मज्झ [°ध्य] *the middle, centre; the waist*, majjhe, *between, among*, i. 8[3], 18[1], 20[41], 30[a]; ii. 6[b], 20[b]; iii. 4[1], 7[a], 19[b]; iv. 18[30].
मज्झअ [°ध्यक] *the same*, iii. 21[a].

मज्झण्ह [°ध्याह्न] *midday*, ii. 41^{5}; iv. 4^{a}, 8^{a}.

मज्झिम [°ध्यम] *central*, i. 14^{c}.

मञ्जरि ts. *a shoot, sprout, flower-bud*, ii. 46^{d}; iii. 13^{d}.

मञ्जिट्ठ [माञ्जिष्ठ] *fem.* °ṭṭhī, *red as madder*, ii. 41^{a}.

मञ्जिट्ठा [°ष्ठा] *munjeet or madder*, ii. 50^{c}.

मञ्जीर ts. *an anklet*, ii. 13^{a}.

मञ्जु ts. *lovely, sweet*, i. 18^{c}; ii. 32^{c}.

मञ्जूसा [°षा] *a box, casket*, iv. 19^{15}.

मण- [°नस्] *mind, thought, desire*, i. 14^{b}; ii. 32^{d}; iii. 10^{b}, 11^{b}, 12^{a}, 28^{b}.

मणं [°नाक्] *a little, slightly*, iv. 9^{c}.

मणहरण [मनो°] *fascinating; fascination*, ii. 28^{b}, 31^{d}.

मणि ts. *a gem, jewel*, i. 34^{18}, 36^{a}; ii. 9^{b}, 15^{a}, 25^{b}, 29^{15}, 32^{a}, 33^{b}, 34^{b}; iii. 2^{a}, 18^{a,b}; iv. 10^{b}, 1[illegible].

मणीसि- [°नीषिन्] *clever, wise*, iv. 24^{a}.

मणोजन्तण [°नोयन्त्रण] *checking the mind*, iii. 16^{2}.

मणोज्ज [°नोज्ञ] *beautiful*, iii. 27^{c}.

मणोभु [°नोभु] *Cupid*, iv. 13^{b}.

मणोरध [°नोरथ] *wish, desire*, iii. 8^{1}.

मणोरह *the same*, iv. 9^{d}.

मणोहव [°नोभव] *Cupid*, iii. 10^{d}, 20^{16}.

मण्डण [°न] *an ornament, embellishment, trimmings*, i. 3^{a}, 28^{a}; ii. 47^{c}; iii. 12^{b,2}, 13^{b}, 26^{a}; iv. 20^{9}.

मण्डल ts. *a globe, ring, disk; a group, collection*, i. 35^{a}; ii. 30^{a}; iii. 5^{a}, 31^{a}; iv. 23^{b}.

मण्डली ts. *the same*, iii. 23^{b}, 26^{b}.

मण्डव [°प] *a hall, arbor*, i. 36^{d}.

मत्तण्ड [मार्त°] *the sun*, iii. 3^{14}.

मदिरावदी [°ती] *name of a woman*, iv. 9^{12}.

मद्दल [मर्दल] *a kind of drum*, iv. 16^{a}.

मन्न *to be minded, think.* maṇṇemi, iii. 4^{1}. maṇṇe, i. 13^{d}, 30^{a}, 33^{d}; iii. 16^{c}; iv. 2^{a}. maṇṇedi, i. 28^{8}. maṇṇantao, ii. 8^{b}.

+अभि *to honor, belove.* ahimada, ii. 6^{17}.

+अव *to despise, disregard.* avamaṇṇida, i. 14^{2}.

मन्त [°न्त्र] *a Vedic hymn; a charm, spell*, i. 22^{a}; ii. 6^{22}.

मन्त- [मन्त्रय-] *to consult, deliberate, talk.* mantaantassa, ii. 6^{15}.

मन्थर- *to grow slow, to decrease.* mantharijjantu, iii. 20^{9}.

मन्द ts. *soft, gentle*, i. 17^{b}.

मन्दारवदी [°ती] *name of a woman*, iv. 9^{12}.

मम्मध [°न्मथ] *Cupid*, iv. 2^{1}. *Cp.* वम्मह.

मरगअ [°कत] *an emerald*, ii. 13^{a}; iii. 2^{a}, 18^{b}.

मरगदपुञ्ज [°कत°] *a place or seat adorned with emeralds, emerald-arbor*, ii. 29^{7}, 41^{1}, 42^{20,21}, 43^{2}; iv. 18^{3}.

मरट्ट HD. 6. 120. *pride, elegance, charm*, ii. 23^{c}; iii. 30^{a}. (*K*, ii. 23^{c} vilāsa.)

मरढी *a Marāṭha woman*, i. 16^{a}.

मलअ [°य] *name of a mountain-range of South-western India*, i. 15^{d}, 16^{3,4}, 20^{c}.

मलिण [°न] *black, dark*, iii. 25^{a}.

मल्लिआ [°का] *a kind of jasmin*, i. 16^{b}.

मल्लजुज्झ [°युद्ध] *a boxing-match*, ii. 21^{b}.

मसाण [श्मशान] *a cemetery*, iv. 15^{b}.

मसि ts. *lamp-black, a black powder used*

to paint the eyes, ii. 7^{b}; iii. 32^{b}; iv. 14^{a}.

मह् H. 4. 192. *to wish, long for.* mahijjaï, iii. 9^{c}.

महग्घिद [°हार्घित] *praised*, i. 34^{33}.

महल्ल HD. 6. 143. *old, elder*, ii. 9^{1}.

महादेवी ts. *a great queen, queen-consort*, i. 28^{3}.

महाबम्हण [°ब्राह्मण] *a great Brāhmaṇa*, i. 20^{29}.

महामंस [°मांस] *dainty flesh, especially human flesh*, iv. 15^{a}.

महामेह [°घ] *a great cloud*, iii. 3^{14}.

महाराअ [°ज] *a great king*, i. 12^{3}, 28^{2}; ii. 0^{3}, 1^{5}, 6^{12}, 9^{1}, $42^{13, 16, 17, 19, 21}$; iii. 30^{2}, 34^{9}; iv. $18^{3, 21}$, $19^{60, 62}$, 20^{6}.

महावेजअन्ती [°वैजयन्ती] *a great banner of victory*, iii. 19^{d}.

महिअल [°हीतल] *the face of the earth, the earth*, iii. 14^{c}.

महिन्दवाल [°हेन्द्रपाल] *the king Mahendrapāla*, i. 5^{b}.

महिला ts. *a woman*, i. 7^{b}, 22^{b}, 25^{4}.

महिसी [°षी] *a buffalo-cow*, i. 19^{c}.

मही ts. *the earth*, ii. 22^{b}.

महीअल [°तल] *the surface of the earth, the earth*, i. 34^{34}; ii. 10^{3}.

महु [°धु] *the spring*, ii. 5^{b}, 6^{21}; iv. 7^{d}, 19^{66}. mahūsava [°dhūtsava], *the spring festival*, i. 16^{3}.

महुर [°धुर] *sweet, charming*, i. 28^{2}, 36^{d}; iii. 1^{c}.

महुर- [मधुराय-] *to become sweet.* mahurijjaï, ii. 26^{d}.

महुरिम- H. 2. 154. *sweetness, beauty*, ii. 2^{b}.

महूसव [महोत्सव] *a great festival*, i. 18^{d}; iv. 9^{1}, 21^{6}.

महेन्दजाल [महेन्द्र°] *jugglery*, ii. 44^{1}.

महोसह [°हौषध] *a great, efficacious herb*, iii. 20^{d}.

मा ts. *a prohibitive particle, not*, i. $20^{5, 11, 17, 42}$; ii. 6^{7}, 39^{a}, 40^{4}; iii. 8^{6}, 21^{a}, 32^{a}; iv. 4^{1}.

माअही [°गधी] *the Māgadhī style in poetry*, i. 1^{c}.

माण [°न] *pride, jealous anger*, i. 15^{b}, 18^{a}; iii. 30^{a}.

माणस [°नस] *mind, heart; name of a sacred lake*, ii. 6^{10}, 50^{b}; iii. 2^{d}; iv. 23^{a} (rosakasāamāṇasavaī [roṣakaṣāyamānasavatī], *having her mind affected by anger*).

माणिक्क [°क्य] *a ruby*, i. 20^{26}; iii. 15^{d}; iv. 19^{65}.

माणिक्कचण्ड [°क्यचण्ड] *name of a bard*, iii. 26^{2}.

माणिक्कमाला [°क्यमाला] *name of a woman*, iv. 9^{10}.

माणिणी [°निनी] *an angry, jealous woman*, ii. 50^{b}; iii. 27^{d}, 30^{a}.

माणुस [°नुष] *a man; mankind, the world of men*, i. 31^{b}; ii. 25^{a}; iii. 8^{1}, 14^{d}, 16^{2}; iv. 23^{d}.

मादा [°तृ] *a mother*, i. 20^{25}.

मादुच्छअ *fem.* °cchiā. H. 2. 142. *a maternal uncle, fem. aunt*, i. $34^{10, 13}$.

मारुद [°त] *wind*, i. 16^{3}.

मालई [°ती] *a great-flowered jasmin*, iii. 2^{b}.

माला ts. *a garland, chaplet, row, string*, i. 20^{9}; ii. 6^{b}, 13^{b}, 20^{a}; iii. 18^{b}; iv. 9^{10}.

मालिआ [°का] *the same*, i. 11[a], 17[a]; iii. 2[b].

मास [°ष] *a weight of gold*, iii. 3[18].

मास ts. *a month*, iv. 9[d].

माहप्प [°हात्म्य] *majesty, dignity*, i. 9[b].

मिअङ्क [मृगा°] *the moon*, ii. 42[a]; iii. 21[a], 26[d].

मिअङ्कमणि [मृगा°] *the moon-gem, supposed to ooze away under the moon's rays*, iv. 18[36].

मिअङ्कलेहा [°गाङ्कलेखा] *name of a woman*, iv. 9[9]. °kadhā [°kathā], *the story of Mṛgāñkalekhā, a poem of Aparājita*, i. 8[3].

मिअङ्ग [मृद°] *a kind of drum*, i. 4[9].

मिट्ठत्तण [मृष्टत्व] *sweetness*, iii. 14[c].

मिधुण [°थुन] *a pair, couple*, iii. 9[2].

मिल् *to join, combine.* milido, ii. 6[13]. milidaṁ, i. 34[31]. milidassa, iii. 9[2].

मिलाण [म्लान] *faded, withered*, ii. 6[10]

मिसा [°षात्] *under the pretext of, in the disguise of*, i. 18[c]; iv. 22[d].

मिहुण [°थुन] *a pair, couple*, i. 14[d].

मील् *to be closed.* mīlanta, i. 35[d].

+सम *to close the eyes.* sammīliāṇaṁ, iii. 7[b].

+समुद् *to become manifest.* samummīlaï, i. 31[b]; ii. 25[a].

मुउउन्द [°चुकुन्द] *name of a tree*, iii. 25[c].

मुक्ख [मूर्ख] *foolish*, i. 18[6].

मुच् *to loose, let go, quit.* muñcaha, i. 18[a]. muñcanto, ii. 50[b]; iii. 25[c]. muccanta, iii. 27[b]. mottūṇa, iii. 3[d]; iv. 13[a]. mukka, ii. 6[10]; iii. 34[a]. mukko, iii 10[a]. mukkā, i. 29[a], 31[a].

+अव *to loosen, take off.* avamukka, i. 28[a].

+उद् *to loosen, shed.* ummukka, iii. 28[d].

मुच्छा [मूर्छा] *fainting, swooning*, i. 35[d].

मुट्ठि [°ष्टि] *the clenched hand, fist*, i. 30[a]; iii. 19[b].

मुण H. 4. 7. *to know, think, understand.* muṇasi, iii. 8[a]. muṇīadi, i. 28[4]. muṇido, ii. 48[1].

मुणाल [मृ°] *fem.* °lī, °liā, *a lotus-fibre*, ii. 6[10], 11[c]; iii. 20[3].

मुत्ता [मुक्ता] *a pearl, pearl-oyster*, i. 20[d]; iii. 3[18].

मुत्ताहल [°क्ताफल] *a pearl*, iii. 3[18], 4[4], 5[a]. °ttaṇa [°tva], *condition of being a pearl*, iii. 4[1].

मुत्ताहलिल्ल [°क्ताफलवत्] *abounding in, or consisting of pearls*, i. 4[c]; iv. 10[a].

मुत्ति [°क्ति] *release, final emancipation*, i. 24[a].

मुद्दा [°द्रा] *a seal, stamp, token*, i. 33[c]; ii. 2[a], 41[a]; iii. 9[d].

मुद्दिअ [°द्रित] *sealed, closed*, i. 35[d].

मुद्ध [°ग्ध] *foolish, innocent; charming, lovely*, i. 16[b], 19[d], 34[3]; ii. 26[a]; iv. 21[a], 22[a].

मुल्ल [मूल्य] *price*, iii. 5[b].

मुह [°ख] *fem.* °muhī, *face, mouth, opening; beginning with*, i. 13[c], 20[27, 30], 24[a], 26[a], 34[d, 3]; ii. 10[b], 17[b], 27[b], 32[d], 47[b]; iii. 9[d], 21[a], 22[9], 25[b], 28[a], 33[a], 34[b, 9]; iv. 23[b].

मुहल [°खर] *noisy, tinkling*, ii. 32[b], 34[a].

मुहेन्दु [°खेन्दु] *a moon-like face*, ii. 30[d].

मूल ts. *root, ground*, i. 4[b], 16[c]; ii. 2[a], 24[a]; iv. 2[1], 18[30, 38].

मृ *to die. Caus., to kill.* mudo, i. 20[41]. māraṇijjā, ii. 5[b].

मज *to purify, cleanse.* majjidā, ii. 11[5].

मेल्ल् H. 4. 91. *to loosen, emit, to be emitted.* mellanti, iv. 22[d].

मेहला [°खला] *a girdle, flank of a mountain*, i. 20[a]; ii. 32[b]; iii. 13[a]; iv. 7[b].

मोक्ख [°क्ष] *final emancipation; scattering, strewing*, i. 22[b], 24[d]; iv. 21[1].

मोत्तिअ [मौक्तिक] *a pearl*, ii. 17[a]; iii. 4[9], 20[3], 27[b]. °ttaṇa [°tva], *condition of being a pearl*, iii. 4[b].

मोदअ [°क] *sweetmeat*, iii. 8[1].

मोर [मयूर] *a peacock*, iv. 14[b].

मोलि [मौ°] *head*, i. 11[a]; iv. 20[7].

मोहण [°न] *bewildering, one of the five arrows of Cupid; coitus, love*, i. 2[b], 32[d]; ii. 32[d]; iii. 26[c].

यद् *who, which, what; that, when, because, in order that.* jo, i. 6[a], 19[7], 21[5], 34[10]; iii. 12[a]. jā, i. 8[b], 19[7]; ii. 23[b]; iii. 15[a]; iv. 9[6]. jaṁ, i. 13[c], 19[7, 8], 20[27, 29], 21[c], 25[d], 26[a, b, c], 29[a], 34[28, 36]; ii. 3[d], 6[17], 7[b], 8[a], 11[d], 27[c], 28[b], 46[c], 47[1]; iii. 9[c], 16[2], 23[b]; iv. 4[c], 9[19], 18[16, 23], 19[57], 22[a, b], 23[d]. jeṇa, i. 18[6], 20[27], 34[38]; ii. 8[d], 42[21], 44[2]; iii. 16[d], 34[9]; iv. 18[21]. jeṇaṁ, i. 32[d]; iii. 13[d]. jīa, ii. 41[d]. jassa, i. 9[b], 10[b], 18[2]; iv. 3[c], 20[b]. jissā, ii. 23[a, d]; iii. 22[a]. jassiṁ, ii. 28[c]; iii. 10[a]. je, i. 19[b, c], 20[a]; ii. 5[a]; iii. 17[b], 24[a]; iv. 21[a, b], 22[a, b]. jehi, iii. 22[d]. jāṇaṁ, i. 33[c]; iii. 11[a]; iv. 9[b, c]. jesuṁ, ii. 5[c].

यन्त्र- *to restrain, regulate.* jantia, iv. 17[a].

यम + सम *to restrain, bind, gather.* saṁjamantī, i. 27[c].

या *to go, happen, be possible.* jāsi, ii. 8[d]. jāï, i. 21[c], 30[b, d]; iv. 20[b]. jāmo, i. 22[b]. janti, iv. 9[d]. jantī, ii. 31[d].

+ प्रति *to believe, trust.* pattiāmi, ii. 6[6].

युज *to be proper, fit.* juj̣jadi, i. 34[39].

+ नि *to appoint, use.* ṇiuñjīāmi, i. 20[14]. ṇiuñjīasi, i. 20[13]. ṇiuttāo, iv. 9[8].

+ प्र *to represent on the stage, act, perform; to use, employ.* pauñjadha, i. 10[1]. pauñjaïum, i. 11[b]. pauñjīadi, i. 20[26].

रअ [°य] *force, speed*, ii. 31[c], 39[a].

रअण [°त्न] *a gem, jewel*, i. 14[a]; ii. 18[a].

रअणि [°जनि] *night*, ii. 11[b].

रअणिवल्लह [°जनिवल्लभ] *the lover of the night, the moon, which is also called* rājā, i. 5[a].

रइ [°वि] *the sun*, i. 25[b]; iv. 2[b], 3[b].

रइ [°ति] *sexual pleasure; the wife of Cupid*, i. 2[b], 15[b]; ii. 2[d]; iv. 9[c].

रइरमण [रति°] *Cupid*, iii. 19[d].

रउद्द [रौद्र] *violent, wild*, iv. 15[a].

रक्खा [°क्षा] *guarding*, iv. 9[8]. °ghara [°gṛha] *a prison*, iii. 34[9]; iv. 19[27]. °bhavaṇa [°na] *the same*, iv. 9[6].

रक्ष् *to guard, watch.* rakkhijjae, i. 32[c].

रअ् *to arrange, produce.* raïa, iii. 30^{a}. raïā, ii. 20^{a}.

+वि *to arrange, effect, perform, make.* viraanti, i. 13^{b}; iv. 17^{b}. viraïeṇaṁ, ii. 44^{b}.

रच्छा [°थ्या] *a high-way, main road,* i. 20^{29}, 32^{2}.

रज *to be colored, pleased. Caus., to please, satisfy.* rajjae, iii. 33^{a}. rajjanti, iii. 6^{b}. ratta, ii. 50^{c}. rañjedi, i. 19^{7}.

रण *to sound, tinkle.* raṇanta, ii. 32^{a}, 33^{b}. raṇia, ii. 47^{a}.

रण्डा ts. *a slut, whore, widow,* i. 23^{a}; iii. 8^{1}.

रत्त *see* **रज**.

रत्ति [रात्रि] *the night,* iii. 7^{a}; iv. 9^{b}.

रदण [°त्न] *a gem, jewel,* i. 20^{13}, $25^{4,6}$; iv. 19^{65}.

रदणचण्ड [रत्न°] *name of a bard,* i. 16^{2}.

रदणाअर [रत्नाक°] *the ocean,* iii. 3^{18}.

रदि [°ति] *sexual pleasure,* ii. 49^{2}.

रम *to rejoice at, have sexual intercourse with.* ramāmo, i. 22^{b}.

+वि *to come to an end, to cease.* viramaü, iv. 24^{b}.

रमण ts. *the hip and the loins,* i. 30^{b}, 34^{a}; ii. 23^{c}, 34^{a}; iv. 7^{b}.

रमणिज्ज [°णीय] *pleasant, charming,* i. 14^{2}, $20^{7,8}$, 30^{1}; iv. 5^{1}.

रमणी ts. *a lovely young woman,* ii. 30^{a}.

रमणीअ [°य] *pleasant, charming,* iii. 31^{1}.

रम्म [°म्य] *pleasing, agreeable, lovely,* i. 23^{d}; iv. 9^{a}, 16^{a}.

रव ts. *a cry, yell, noise, sound,* ii. 32^{c}, 33^{b}, 34^{b}; iv. 15^{a}, 16^{a}, 17^{b}.

रस ts. *sap, juice, flavor, desire, love, sentiment (in poetry),* i. 12^{b}, 14^{b}, 24^{d}, 29^{c}; ii. $11^{a,1}$, 12^{a}; iii. 10^{c}, 31^{1}, 33^{a}; iv. 5^{b}.

रसाअण [°यन] *an elixir of life,* ii. 8^{2}.

रह्+वि *to quit, leave.* virahido, iii. 8^{1}.

रह [°थ] *a carriage,* i. 21^{c}, 25^{b}; ii. 18^{b}, 34^{a}.

रहस [°भस] *impetuosity,* i. 15^{b}; ii. 44^{b}; iii. 2^{c}.

रहस्स [°स्य] *secret, mystery, esoteric teaching,* ii. $49^{b,1,2}$.

रहुउल [°घुकुल] *the Raghu-family,* i. 5^{b}.

राअ [°ग] *passion; a melody,* ii. 2^{d}. rāarāa [rāgarāja], *the king of melodies, the best musical mode,* ii. 2^{c}.

राअ- [°जन्] *a king,* i. 34^{8}; iv. 18^{18}.

राअउल [°जकुल] *a royal family, court,* i. $20^{26,27,33}$.

राअकेली [राज°] *name of a woman,* iv. 9^{11}.

राअसुअ [°जशुक] *a king-parrot,* ii. 14^{a}.

राअसेहर [°जशेखर] *the poet Rājaçekhara,* i. 5^{4}, 10^{a}, 11^{a}.

राढा ts. *lustre; name of a district in Bengal,* i. 14^{2}.

राहु ts. *name of a demon,* ii. 21^{b}.

रिञ्छोली HD. 7. 7. *a row, line, series,* iii. 20^{7}.

रित्त [°क्त] *empty, void,* ii. 40^{2}. °ttaṇa [°tva], *indigence,* iv. 24^{b}.

रीइ [°ति] *style, diction,* i. 1^{d}.

रीदि *the same,* i. 20^{1}.

रुच्चि [°चि] *wish, passion, liking,* iii. 14^{d}.

रुट्ठ [°ष्ट] *angry,* i. 36^{d}.

रुद्द [°द्र] *the god Çiva,* i. 4^{b}.

रुप्प [रूप्य] *silver*, i. 4^{b}.

रुह् + **अधि** *to ascend*. ahirūḍhāe, ii. 29^{21}.

+ **आ** *to ascend, obtain. Caus., to raise, place; to plant.* āruhia, iv. 9^{18}. ārūḍhaṁ, i. 9^{b}. ārovidā, ii. 42^{29}. ārovidavvā, ii. 29^{6}.

+ **प्र** *to develop, rise, grow.* parūḍha, iii. 9^{3}. parūḍhe, iii. 8^{4}.

रुहिर [°धिर] *blood*, iv. 19^{a}.

रुढि ts. *growth, natural production, custom or habit (which, according to a well-known saying, prevails even over precept)*, ii. 27^{d}.

रूव [°प] *form, figure, beauty*, i. 29^{2}, 31^{a}, 34^{17}; ii. 12^{b}, 49^{1}; iii. 9^{b}; iv. 9^{a}, 14^{b}, 20^{a}.

रे *a vocative particle, ho*, i. 18^{8}.

रेणु ts. *dust*, i. 29^{d}.

रेह् H. 4. 100. *to shine, appear beautiful.* rehaï, ii. 16^{b}. rehae, ii. 23^{b}.

रेहा *shine, beauty* (*K*, ii. 41^{c} çobhā), ii. 41^{c}, 49^{1}; iv. 20^{a}.

रेहा [°खा] *line, streak*, ii. 37^{b}; iv. 12^{a},

रोमञ्च [°माञ्च] *horripilation*, iv. 22^{d}.

रोमञ्चिअ [°माञ्चित] *with the hair erect, thrilled*, ii. 46^{d}.

रोस [°ष] *anger, wrath*, ii. 47^{4}; iv. 23^{a}.

रोसाण- H. 4. 105. *to polish.* rosāṇiaṁ, ii. 12^{b}; iii. 22^{b}.

लअ [°य] *time in music*, iv. 12^{b}, $17^{a,\,b}$.

लआ [°ता] *a creeper, creeping plant*, i. 28^{b}, 34^{a}; ii. 1^{d}, 9^{d}, 11^{c}; iii. 27^{b}.

लक्ख [°क्ष] *one hundred thousand*, iii. 4^{5}.

लक्ख [°क्ष्य] *aim, mark*, ii. 41^{d}.

लक्ख् *to see, behold.* lakkhijjae, i. 16^{c}. lakkhīadi, iii. 10^{1}.

लग् *to adhere, cling to, to follow, elapse.* laggaï, ii. 25^{b}. lagga, i. 16^{c}, 26^{a}. laggā, i. 22^{b}; ii. 6^{15}. laggaṁ, ii. 24^{a}. laggassa, i. 20^{30}. laggehi, i. 16^{d}.

लङ्का ts. *name of Ceylon and its capital*, i. 17^{a}, 20^{a}.

लङ्किम- [°मन्] *youth, freshness*, ii. 24^{d}.

लङ्घ् *to leap, jump over.* laṅghaantī, ii. 31^{c}.

लङ्घि- [°ङ्घिन्] *mounting, transgressing*, ii. 27^{a}.

लच्छी [°क्ष्मी] *success, splendor, the goddess of fortune*, i. 20^{36}, 33^{b}, 34^{38}; ii. 22^{b}, 25^{b}, 28^{d}, 41^{6}, 48^{b}; iii. 18^{a}, 22^{a}, 26^{1}; iv. 19^{66}.

लञ्छण [लाञ्छन] *the (moon) mark, or spot on the moon*, iii. 32^{b}.

लञ्छणमअ [लाञ्छनमृग] *the spot on the moon, which is held to resemble a deer*, iii. 31^{b}.

लञ्छिअ [लाञ्छित] *marked, furnished with*, ii. 7^{b}.

लडहअ HD. 7. 26. *charming*, iii. 18^{d}.

लट्ठि [यष्टि] *a stick, stem, stalk; liana; a string of pearls adorned with a gem; anything thin or slender (at the end of compounds after words meaning body)*, ii. 6^{22}, 10^{a}, 24^{d}, 41^{a}; iii. 2^{a}, 5^{b}, 18^{b}; iv. 19^{64}.

लण्ह [श्लक्ष्ण] *soft, smooth, fine, charming*, iii. 28^{b}; iv. 8^{a}. laṇhaa, *the same*, ii. 24^{c}.

लदा [°ता] *a creeper, creeping plant*, i. 16^{3}, 34^{39}.

लप + आ *to speak.* ālavīadi, i. 4^{11}.

+ उद् *to speak, say.* ullavidaṁ, iv. 18^{17}.

लभ् *to take, get, obtain. Caus., to cause to take, to give.* lahaï, iv. 3^{b}. lahadi, i. $20^{27, 29}$. lahanti, iii. 13^{d}. laha, i. 20^{29}. lahasu, iv. 19^{5}. lahadu, iii. 20^{10}. lahejja, iii. 33^{b}. lahantī, ii. 31^{b}. labbhaï, iv. 23^{d}. laddha, i. 20^{14}. laddhā, iv. 23^{b}. laddhaṁ, ii. 1^{c}; iv. 22^{c}. lambhio, ii. 44^{c}. lambhido, iii. 20^{16}. lambhiā, ii. 13^{a}.

+ समा *to touch, anoint.* samālambhaṇīo, ii. 11^{1}.

लम्ब् *to hang down.* lambijjanta, iii. 27^{b}.

+ अव *to resort to, partake in.* avalambedi, i. 20^{9}.

+ आ *to support.* ālambia, i. 26^{b}.

लम्ब ts. *hanging down*, i. 20^{10}.

लम्बत्थणी [°स्तनी] *a woman with large, pendulous breasts*, i. 20^{7}.

लम्भ ts. *attainment, obtaining*, ii. 28^{c}; iii. 15^{b}.

लस् *to appear, come to light.* lasia, ii. 49^{b}.

+ वि *to shine, become manifest.* vilasaï, i. 36^{d}; ii. 48^{b}.

लहुं [°घु] *quickly, easily*, iii. 11^{d}; iv. 19^{39}.

ला H. 4. 238. *to put on.* lenti, i. 13^{b}.

लाआ [°जा] *parched or fried grain*, iv. 21^{1}.

लाडदेस [°टदेश] *name of a country, part of Gujarāt*, iv. $18^{18, 23}$.

लावण्ण [°ण्य] *beauty, loveliness*, i. 32^{a}; ii. 3^{a}; iii. 1^{c}, 19^{a}, 20^{10}.

लास [°स्य] *dancing, dance*, iv. 10^{a}.

लाह [°भ] *gaining, obtaining*, i. 12^{a}.

लिख् *to write, engrave, paint.* lihaï, ii. 40^{b}. lihijjaï, i. 27^{c}. lihido, ii. 8^{1}.

+ वि *to engrave, paint.* vilihiuṁ, i. 30^{d}.

लिङ्ग् + आ *to embrace.* āliṅgasu, i 34^{22}.

लिह् *to lick, grind, rub.* līḍha, i. 16^{a}.

+ वि *to lick, to delight in.* vilihantu, i. 1^{d}.

लीला ts. *play, sport, beauty, ease, grace*, i. 34^{38}, 36^{a}; ii. 30^{d}, 37^{a}; iii. 3^{9}; iv. 4^{b}, 7^{a}, 17^{b}. līlāghara [°gṛha], *a pleasure-house*, iii. 27^{d}. līlāvaṇa [°na], *a pleasure-garden*, iv. 2^{6}. līlōjjāṇa [°dyāna], *the same*, iii. 22^{6}.

लीलाइअ [°यित] *play, sport*, ii. 34^{a}.

लुण्ट् *to rob, plunder.* luṇṭijjantī, iii. 20^{3}. luṇṭia, iii. 11^{b}.

लुप + वि *to tear off.* viluṭta, ii. 24^{3}.

लुम्बी HD. 7. 28. *a creeping plant, liana*, i. 32^{2}.

लेह [°ख] *a letter, writing*, ii. $6^{17, 20}$.

लेहा [°खा] *a line, streak, the moon's crescent*, ii. 20^{a}, 41^{b}, 43^{5}; iv. 9^{1}.

लोअ [°क] *the world, mankind, men*, ii. 50^{a}; iii. 9^{d}; iv. 18^{b}.

लोअण [°चन] *an eye*, i. 26^{a}, 35^{d}; ii. 3^{a}, 50^{a}; iii. 8^{4}, 16^{a}, 19^{a}, 21^{b}.

लोट्ट H. 4. 146. *to sleep; to roll on the ground.* loṭṭaï, ii. 4^{b}.

लोट्टण *rolling on the ground.* racchā-loṭṭaṇī, *street-walker, strumpet,* i. 20[28].

लोल ts. *shaking, quivering,* i. 36[c].

लोह ts. *copper,* i. 20[9].

व् *see* **व्व.**

°वअ [पद] *foot,* iii. 3[9].

वअंस [°यस्य] *fem.* °ṁsī, *friend, companion,* ii. 13[a].

वअण [°चन] *voice, speech, words,* i. 19[2, 3], 20[29], 21[5]; ii. 42[20].

वअण [°दन] *face,* ii. 11[d], 18[b], 29[21], 42[a]; iii. 32[a]; iv. 6[b].

वअस्स [°यस्य] *fem.* °ssī, *friend, companion,* i. 20[17], 25[3]; ii. 6[2, 13], 11[1], 29[4, 16], 43[11], 47[1]; iii. 2[1, 2], 3[4], 8[2], 12[3], 20[b]; iv. 2[6], 5[d], 18[34], 20[12], 21[1].

वंस [°श] *family, flute,* i. 4[7], 18[9].

वंसरोअणा [°शरोचना] *bamboo-manna, Tabasheer (whose lustre is similar to that of the opal),* iii. 4[a].

वच् *to speak, call.* vuccāmi, i. 34[15].

वच्छ [वृक्ष] *a tree,* ii. 44[a].

वच्छ- [°क्षस्] *the breast, bosom,* iii. 19[b].

वच्छा [°त्सा] *a girl, young woman,* iv. 19[19, 32, 44].

वच्छोम *name of a town, the capital of Kuntala, according to the commentaries, Vidarbhā,* i. 25[5].

वच्छोमी *the Vāidarbhī style in poetry,* i. 1[c].

वञ्च् *to deceive, dupe.* vañcio, ii. 8[a].

वञ्चणा [°ना] *fraud,* iii. 34[7].

वड [°ट] *the fig-tree,* iv. 18[30, 38].

वडसावित्ती [°टसावित्री] *the divinity fancied to be in the Vaṭa-tree during the Vaṭasāvitrīvrata, an observance among women on the day of the full moon of Jyāiṣṭha,* iv. 9[18].

वड्ढत्तण [वड्ढत्व] HD. 7. 29. *growth,* iv. 3[a].

वड्ढण [°र्धन] *growth, increase,* ii. 29[13].

वड्ढावअ [वर्धापक] *fem.* °viā, *congratulating,* i. 16[1].

वड्ढिम- [वृद्धि] H. 2. 154. *growth, length,* i. 34[c].

वण [°न] *a forest,* i. 17[b], 18[18]; ii. 50[a].

वण्ण [°र्ण] *color, beauty,* i. 14[2]; ii. 7[b], 41[c].

वण्णण [°र्णन] *description, praise,* ii. 1[3]; iii. 30[2].

वण्णिआ [°र्णिका] *a color, paint,* i. 4[6].

वत्ता [वार्ता] *tidings, news,* iv. 9[2].

वत्थु [°स्तु] *an object,* iii. 31[1].

वद् *Caus., to cause to sound, to play.* vāïa, iv. 16[a].

वदी [°ती] *the suffix* vatī, iv. 9[12].

वन्द् *to salute, pay homage to, to worship.* vandiduṁ, i. 36[1]. vandïadi, i. 20[33].

वम्मह [मन्मथ] H. 1. 242. *Cupid,* ii. 3[d], 18[b], 39[b]; iii. 11[c]. *Cp.* **मम्मध.**

वर ts. *best, excellent; a boon, favor; a bridegroom,* i. 1[b], 12[b]; ii. 17[a]; iv. 19[5].

वरिट्ठ [°ष्ठ] *best, most excellent, preeminent,* ii. 11[d]; iii. 2[c].

वरिल्ल *a cloth, garment,* ii. 36[a]; iii. 3[c] 22[4]; iv. 7[b].

वरिस [वर्ष] *rain; a year,* i. 20[41]; iv. 24[b].

वरिसधर [वर्ष°] *a eunuch,* iii. 34[8].

वरिसि- [°र्षिन्] *raining,* iii. 3[11].

वर्ण्- *to describe, praise.* vaṇṇemi, ii. 32[2]. vaṇṇaa, i. 18[14]. vaṇṇīasi, i. 20[10]. vaṇṇido, i. 8[1, 3]. vaṇṇidā, ii. 24[2]; iii. 26[1].

वल् *to turn round, surround; appear.* valanta, iii. 27[d]. valia, i. 30[a]; ii. 24[a]; iii. 2[c].

वलअ [°य] *a bracelet; a circle*, i. 25[d]; ii. 9[b], 16[a], 32[c]; iii. 13[a], 18[a], 27[a], 32[b]; iv. 7[c].

वलइअ [°यित] *surrounded, encircled; bowed, curved*, i. 33[d]; iii. 19[b]; iv. 20[d].

वलही [°भी] *the sloping roof*, i. 36[a].

वली *a fold of skin on the belly*, ii. 1[b].

वल्लह [°भ] *dear, beloved; lover, husband*, i. 18[a], 19[b], 34[8]; ii. 6[23], 29[21].

वल्लहराअ [°भराज] *name of a king*, i. 34[8].

वल्ली ts. *a creeping, winding plant*, ii. 35[b].

वस् *to dwell.* vasaï, iv. 20[c].

+ नि *to dwell, stay.* ṇivasaï, ii. 49[b].

वस् + नि *to put on, wear; to attire.* ṇiatthā, ii. 14[a]. ṇivasiaṁ, i. 26[c].

वस [°श] *influence; used in the instrumental case with the sense, on account of*, i. 31[a], 36[c]; ii. 31[c]; iv. 18[a, b].

वसन्त ts. *the spring*, i. 12[8], 13[d], 18[14]; ii. 1[3].

वसन्तसेणा [°ना] *name of a woman*, iv. 9[9].

वसुंधरा ts. 1. *the earth*, i. 16[3]. 2. *name of the wife of the Vidūṣaka*, i. 20[34].

वसुहा [°धा] *the earth*, i. 25[a].

वह् *to bear, carry.* vahanti, i. 19[a]. vahanto, i. 18[2].

+ समुद् *the same.* samuvvahadi, i. 20[27].

वहू [°धू] *a wife*, i. 21[a]; ii. 2[a]; iii. 26[a]; iv. 8[d].

वा ts. *or*, i. 18[b, 10, 18], 20[40], 30[2]; ii. 27[a]; iii. 20[16, 17]; iv. 18[36].

वा *to blow.* vāanti, i. 17[d].

+ निस् *Caus., to blow out.* ṇivvāvido, iii. 22[4].

वाअ [°त] *wind*, i. 15[d].

वाअण [°दन] *sounding, playing*, iv. 18[a].

वाणी ts. *speech, voice*, i. 1[b], 20[7].

वाद [°त] *wind*, i. 32[2].

वाम ts. *left*, i. 20[15], 28[4].

वामण [°न] *a dwarf, pigmy*, iii. 34[8].

वारअ [°क] *a vessel, cup*, iv. 10[b], 13[a].

वारि ts. *water*, iv. 6[b], 8[c].

वारुण ts. *consisting of water*, iv. 13[b].

वारुणी ts. *spirituous liquor*, iii. 14[a]; iv. 6[b].

°वाली [पा°] *edge*, i. 15[a].

वास् + परि *to make fragrant.* parivāsia, iv. 5[c].

वास ts. *dwelling, abode*, ii. 3[b]; iii. 22[1].

वास [व्या°] *the poet Vyasa*, i. 1[a].

वासर ts. *the day*, i. 35[a]; ii. 2[d]; iv. 9[d].

वाहि- [°हिन्] *fem.* °hiṇī, *bearing, carrying*, iv. 9[10].

वि, *after anusvāra* **पि**, [अपि] *though, also, cp.* kiṁ. vi, i. 4[6, 9], 7[a], 8[a],

13[c], 16[d, 2], 18[6], 20[d, 7, 8, 10, 13, 14, 39], 24[a], 25[b], 27[c], 28[2, 3, 4, 5, 8], 30[1], 31[a, b], 33[c], 34[13, 30, 32, 34], 36[1]; ii. 1[2], 5[c], 6[13, 25], 8[d], 10[4], 18[a, b], 23[c], 25[a, b], 28[3], 29[10], 41[3, 5], 42[a, b, 11, 15], 45[a], 46[1], 47[c], 48[a, b], 49[1]; iii. 1[b, d], 3[c, 4], 4[9], 8[b, 4], 9[a], 15[c], 20[3], 33[a]; iv. 1[b], 6[d], 9[2], 16[a], 18[17, 21, 22, 25, 31], 19[2, 9, 30, 60], 20[3, 6], 22[2], 23[1]. pi, i. 1[b], 4[12], 10[a], 13[1], 16[1], 18[16], 19[6], 20[16, 20], 22[a], 24[5], 25[a, 4], 34[c], 35[b, c]; ii. 1[a], 11[1, 2], 27[c], 28[d], 39[a], 42[17], 46[a], 48[2]; iii. 2[1], 3[15], 9[c], 12[c], 13[c], 14[c], 15[b], 16[c, 2], 32[a]; iv. 2[a], 4[c], 9[c, 12, 14].

विअ [इव] *as, like,* i. 1[d], 4[2, 16], 18[15], 20[d, 7, 9, 13, 30, 43]; ii. 6[10, 19], 11[6], 40[5], 45[b]; iii. 2[1], 8[4], 10[1], 19[2], 20[19]; iv. 2[11]. *Cp.* व्व.

विअइल्ल [°चकिल] *a kind of jasmin*, i. 19[d].

विअक्खण [°चक्षण] *circumspect, wise, clever,* i. 20[1].

विअक्खणा [°चक्षणा] *name of the queen's female servant,* i. 18[6], 19[5], 20[1, 4], 34[35]; ii. 6[4, 13, 14, 17], 10[3], 11[4], 41[8], 42[2], 43[3], 50[3].

विअड्ढ [°दग्ध] *clever, experienced,* ii. 29[13].

विअप्प [°कल्प] *doubt, hesitation, suspicion,* iii. 10[a].

विअम्भिद [°जृम्भित] *gaping, opening, display, machination,* iv. 18[34].

विअलिद *see* गल् + वि.

विअसइ *see* कस + वि.

विआर [°चार] *consideration,* ii. 6[8].

विआल [°काल] *evening,* ii. 50[4].

विओअ [°योग] *separation, absence,* ii. 9[c].

विक्कम [°क्रम] *force, prowess, valor,* i. 14[2].

विक्खम्भ [°ष्कम्भ] *an interlude between the acts of a drama,* i. 6[b].

विक्खरइ [*Marāṭhī* विखरणें] *to scatter,* ii. 35[b].

विचित्त [°त्र] *various,* iii. 27[b]; iv. 11[a], 20[c]. °ttaṇa [°tva] *variety, strikingness,* iii. 31[1]. °dā [°tā] *the same,* i. 20[1]; iii. 4[6].

विच्छाअ- [°य-] *to make pale, outshine.* vicchāanto, ii. 30[a].

विच्छेअ [°द] *interruption,* ii. 39[a].

विच्छोल- H. 4. 46. *to cause to quiver.* viccholanto, ii. 30[b].

विजइ- [°यिन] *victorious,* iv. 4[d].

विज्जुल्लेह- [°द्युल्लेख-] *to act as lightning.* vijjullehāïdaṁ, ii. 40[3].

विट्टालि- H. 4. 422. *fem.* °liṇī, *polluting,* i. 18[3].

विडम्ब ts. *deception, fraud,* ii. 28[a].

विडम्बणा [°ना] *disguise, imitation, mockery,* iii. 12[2], 33[b].

विडव [°टप] *a branch, bush, thicket,* i. 19[b]; ii. 43[2, 12].

विडूर [°दूर] *name of a mountain or country from which the Vāiḍūrya jewel is brought,* i. 34[18].

विणडिद *see* णड् + वि.

विणा [°ना] *without,* i. 18[18], 20[36].

विणास [°नाश] *destruction,* iv. 24[a].

विण्णवेदि *see* ज्ञा + वि.

वित्तिआर [वृत्तिकार] *a commentator,* ii. 32[2].

वित्थर [°स्तर] *extension, minute details,* i. 34[a]; ii. 32[2]; iv. 3[a], 18[9].

वित्थिण्ण [°स्तीर्ण] *large, wide,* ii. 23[b].

विद् + **नि** *to tell, announce.* ṇivedemi, ii. 10[6]; iv. 18[4]. ṇivedehi, i. 34[3]. ṇivedaïssadi, ii. 29[1]. ṇivedīadi, ii. 22[1]. ṇivedidaṁ, i. 16[4]; iv. 19[57].

विन्दुरिल्ल [?] *resplendent? tinkling?* [*K*, ujjvala; *J*, mañjughoṣa; *R*, vidrāṇa; *U*, vistārav̤at; *in the Bālarāmāyaṇa, translated* vyatikara, sadṛça, *and* miçra], ii. 31[b].

विप्पलम्भ [विप्र°] *separation,* iv. 2[b].

विब्भम [°भ्रम] *perturbation, flurry of mind caused by love, amorous play,* i. 2[a], 16[3]; ii. 3[b]; iii. 12[a], 32[a].

विब्भमलेहा [°भ्रमलेखा] *name of the queen; name of a woman,* i. 16[1]; iv. 9[9], 19[44].

विब्भमवन्त [°भ्रमवत्] *fem.* °vaī, *whirling round, swinging,* i. 21[b].

विब्भमसेणा [°भ्रमसेना] *name of a woman,* iv. 9[8].

विमाण [°न] *a car, vehicle,* i. 34[27]; ii. 31[b]; iv. 19[55].

विरअण, °णा [°चन] *arrangement, dressing, embellishment.* i. 20[?]; ii. 28[a].

विरह ts. *separation,* i. 35[c]; ii. 42[5].

विरहि- [°हिन्] *fem.* °hiṇī, *separated from the lover or mistress,* i. 20[c]; ii. 2[c].

विलास ts. *coquetry, grace, beauty,* ii. 40[a]; iii. 31[a].

विलासिणी [°नी] *a coquettish woman, a woman,* iv. 14[a].

विलुत्त *see* लुप + वि.

विलेवण [°पन] *ointment, unguent, cosmetic,* i. 30[1].

विलोअण [°चन] *an eye,* iii. 22[c].

विलोल ts. *rolling, unsteady,* ii. 32[c].

विवरीअ [°परीत] *inverted,* ii. 16[b].

विवाह ts. *marriage,* iv. 18[28, 32], 19[17, 39, 44], 20[6], 21[6].

विश् + **अनुप्र** *to enter.* aṇuppaviṭṭho, iv. 18[3].

\+ **उप** *to sit down.* uvavisa, iv. 19[6, 60]. uvavisadu, i. 24[2]; ii. 29[16]. uvavisia, i. 34[3]; ii. 41[2].

\+ **नि** *to enter, fix. Caus., to fix, apply, place, arrange.* ṇiviṭṭha, i. 21[b]; iii. 12[a]. ṇiviṭṭhā, iii. 2[d]. ṇivesaanti, ii. 36[b]. ṇivesaantī, i. 27[a]. ṇivesiā, ii. 15[a]. ṇivesiaṁ, ii. 18[a]. ṇivesidāo, iv. 9[9].

\+ **प्र** *to enter. Caus., to introduce.* pavisamha, iii. 20[5, 11]. pavisia, iii. 34[9]. paviṭṭhā, iii. 2[d]. paviṭṭhāe, iv. 18[12]. pavesaa, i. 21[7].

विस [°ष] *poison,* iii. 20[a].

विसअ [°षय] *an object, matter; range, reach,* i. 24[5]; ii. 8[d].

विसट्ट H. 4. 176. *to burst open, be expanded,* ii. 4[b].

विसहर [°षधर] *a snake,* iii. 20

विसारि- [°रिन्] *fem.* °riṇī *wandering about,* iv. 19[66].

विसुद्ध [°शुद्ध] *correct, accurate,* iv. 12[a].

विसेस [°शेष] *difference, mode, variety,* i. 8[a, b]; iii. 15[b].

विसेसअ [°शेषक] *a mark on the forehead with sandal etc.*, iii. 32b.

विहि [°धि] *performance, manner, conduct, rule, fate, destiny*, ii. 28a; iii. 14a; iv. 1b, 3d, 1812.

विहूसण [°भूषण] *ornament, decoration*, ii. 25b.

वीअणअ [°जनज] *produced by fanning*, iv. 8c.

वीज *to fan.* vījaïssaṁ, iii. 222.

वीणा ts. *a lute*, i. 48.

वुत्तन्त [वृत्तान्त] *news, tidings*, ii. 112.

+**नि** *Caus., to ward off.* ṇivāria, ii 29d.

वृत *to be, abide, stay.* vaṭṭaï, ii. 4c, 20b; iii. 29b. vaṭṭadi, i. 3431; ii. 413, 501; iii. 22d; iv. 1960. vaṭṭanti, i. 121, 13c; ii. 5d; iii. 27d.

+**आ** *Caus., to stir, churn.* āvaṭṭia, i. 16b.

+**उद्** *Caus., to rub, clean, anoint.* uvvaṭṭiaṁ, ii. 12a.

+**प्र** *to go forward, proceed; to arise, be produced; to begin; to be occupied with.* paaṭṭaï, ii. 4c. paaṭṭaü, i. 1b. pavaṭṭadu, iii. 207. paaṭṭo, i. 36c. paaṭṭā, iv. 16b. paütto, i. 42, 62; iii. 317. paüttā, i. 416, 164.

+**सम्** *to become, arrive. Caus., to anoint.* saṁvutto, ii. 504. saṁvuttā, iii. 221. saṁvaṭṭiāṇaṁ, ii. 46a.

वृध् *to increase. Caus., to augment; to congratulate.* vaḍḍhanti, iii. 11c. vaḍḍhia, iii. 10d. vaḍḍhāvīasi, i. 12a. vaḍḍhāvidā, i. 162.

वृष् *to rain.* varisiduṁ, iii. 317.

वेअ [°द] *the Veda*, i. 24b.

वेअडिअ [वैकटिक] *a jeweller*, iii. 48.

वेअणा [°दना] *feeling, pain*, iii. 49; iv. 1935.

वेज्ज [वैद्य] *a physician*, iv. 7c, 1827.

वेणी ts. *a braid of hair*, i. 13b; ii. 1c, 39b.

वेणु ts. *a flute*, iv. 6a, 18a.

वेदिआ [°का] *an altar, raised seat*, ii. 2915.

वेरुलिअ [वैडूर्य] H. 2. 133. *the Vāiḍūrya jewel, cat's eye*, i. 3418.

वेला ts. *time, opportunity*, ii. 615, 415.

वेष्ट *to surround, enclose, embrace.* veḍhium, i. 30b.

वेस [°ष] *dress, apparel*, iii. 18a; iv. 7d, 18a, b.

वो *see* **त्वम्**.

व्यध् *to pierce. Caus., to cut, perforate, bore.* vindhanti, i. 32d. viddhāvidā, iii. 48.

व्व, व [इव] *like, as.* vva, i. 18d, 29d, 35d; ii. 33b, 34b, 36b, 39a, 46d, 48b; iii. 2a, b, 20a, 25a. va, i. 4d, 16d; ii. 35b, 37b, 38b, 40b; iii. 20a, 28b; iv. 9b, 17b. *Cp.* **विअ**.

— —

शङ्क् *to fancy.* saṅke, iv. 22c.

शम+**नि** *Caus., to hear, listen to.* ṇisāmaa, ii. 29c.

शिक्ष् *Caus., to teach, instruct.* sikkhāvīasi, ii. 271.

शुष् *Caus., to wither, emaciate.* sosaṇijjo, iv. 22. sosaṇijjā, iv. 21.

श्रु *to hear.* suṇa, ii. 27[d]. suṇasu, i. 8[2]. suṇādu, ii. 9[1]; iv. 9[4]. soūṇa, i. 35[c]. suṇīadi, i. 4[10], 21[5]; ii. 10[8]. suvvantaṁ, ii. 27[d]. sudaṁ, ii. 24[4]; iii. 20[1].

श्लाघ् *to praise.* salāhaṇijjo, iv. 3[1].

श्वस + उद् *to be loosened, relaxed.* ūsasantaṁ, ii. 24[b].

+ वि *to trust, confide, rely.* vīsasīadi, iv. 20[3].

स [स्व] *one's own,* iv. 19[24].

सअ [शत] *a hundred,* iii. 27[c]. *Cp.* सद.

सअं [स्वयम्] *self,* ii. 47[1].

सअंकिद [स्वयंकृत] *self-made,* i. 19[6].

सअण [शयन] *a bed, couch,* iii. 27[c].

सअल [सकल] *all, entire,* i. 34[8]; ii. 5[c], 28[c], 47[c]; iv. 6[d], 20[9], 24[a].

संविहाणअ [°धानक] *arrangement of incidents,* i. 34[25].

सक्कअ [संस्कृत] *the Sanskrit language,* i. 7[a].

सक्कद *the same,* i. 6[2].

सक्करा [शर्करा] *sugar,* ii. 26[d].

सक्खि- [साक्षिन्] *an eye-witness,* i. 18[13]; iii. 24[b].

सग्ग [स्वर्ग] *heaven,* i. 4[a].

सङ्का [श°] *hesitation, scruple, fear,* iii. 34[a].

संकेद [°त] *a rendezvous,* ii. 41[9], 50[2].

सङ्ग ts. *touch, contact,* ii. 28[c].

संगम ts. *meeting, union, intercourse,* iii. 6[b], 34[9]; iv. 3[1], 9[a].

सङ्गि- [°ङ्गिन्] *fem.* °giṇī, *touching, meeting, attached to,* ii. 20[a]; iii. 24[b].

संघाडी [°टिका] HD. 8. 7. *a couple, union, contact,* i. 3[b].

सचन्दण [°न] *with sandal, rubbed with sandal,* iv. 6[c].

सच्च [°त्य] *true, real; adv. indeed, forsooth,* i. 20[1]; ii. 6[4]; iii. 8[a], 12[3], 20[4, 21]; iv. 20[2]. *Compar.,* saccadara, ii. 6[5].

सच्छन्द [स्व°] *at one's own will,* iv. 2[6].

सज्ज ts. *ready, prepared,* ii. 28[4], 29[12]; iv. 20[11].

सज्जण [°न] *a good person,* iii. 20[17].

सज्जी- *to be prepared, made ready.* sajjīanti, i. 4[9]. sajjijjanta, iii. 27[c].

सज्झ [साध्य] *to be accomplished, attainable, possible,* i. 25[d].

संचअ [°य] *heaping up, collection,* ii. 1[2]; iv. 9[7].

संचरण ts. *going, motion,* iii. 23[a].

संचारि- [°रिन्] *fem.* °riṇī, *moving, wandering,* iv. 19[64].

संजीवि- [°विन्] *fem.* °viṇī, *bringing to life, resuscitating,* ii. 3[c]; iv. 23[b].

संजोअअर [°योगकर] *uniting, bringing together,* i. 34[33].

संझा [°ध्या] *evening,* i. 34[41], 36[1]; ii. 41[3], 50[1]; iv. 4[a].

सट्टअ [°क] *a kind of drama,* i. 4[18], 6[a], 12[b].

सण [श°] *hemp,* i. 20[43].

संणिहिद [°निहित] *near,* ii. 41[3, 9], 50[1].

सद् + प *to be pleased, propitious.* pasīaü, iii. 21[b].

सद [शत] *a hundred,* i. 20[28, 41]. *Cp.* सअ

सद्द [शब्द] *a word, sound, speech, noise,* i. 8[a], 20[3], 36[c]; iii. 31[1]; iv. 9[3].

संतावि- [°पिन्] *fem.* °viṇī, *burning, afflicted;* iv. 9[c].

संतोसि- [°षिन्] *fem.* °siṇī, *pleasing, comforting,* ii. 29[c].

संधि ts. *union, friendship, peace,* ii. 6[14, 15, 16]

सपञ्चम ts. *with the Pañcama mode,* iv. 6[a].

सप्प [°र्प] *a snake,* iv. 18[27].

सम ts. *same, equal, like, even, plain; adv., together, with,* i. 19[a], 20[12, 26, 33], 24[d]; ii. 10[5]; iii. 6[b], 8[a]; iv. 6[b], 12[a].

समअ [°य] *time,* 20[29], 36[b]; ii. 6[21], 50[1]; iii. 3[11], 19[c]; iv. 4[b], 7[d], 18[7].

समणि ts. *adorned with jewels,* iii. 18[a].

समत्त *see* **आप + सम.**

समसीसिआ [°शीर्षिका] *a setting on a par with, equality,* i. 20[26].

समाअम [°गम] *meeting, arrival,* iii. 8[a].

समारम्भ ts. *beginning,* i. 14[2].

समिद्धि [°मृद्धि] *abundance,* ii. 44[c].

समुइद [°चित] *fit, appropriate,* iv. 19[16].

समुदअ [°य] *collection, multitude,* i. 28[2].

समुद्द [°द्र] *the ocean,* ii. 29[13], 43[5]; iii. 4[3].

समुद्दन्त [°द्रान्त] *sea-shore,* iii. 3[14].

समोरपिच्छ [समयूर°] *with peacocks' tail-feathers,* iv. 14[b].

संपइ [°प्रति] *now,* i. 35[b].

संपक्कि- [°क्किन्] *mixed with, having contact with,* i. 17[b], 20[c].

संपदं [सांप्रतम्] *now,* i. 19[6], 34[7]; iii. 26[2].

संपुड [°ट] *a cavity, fold,* ii. 6[23, 24, 25], 7[a].

संपुण्ण [°पूर्ण] *full,* iii. 25[d].

संभव ts. *birth, origination,* iv. 22[b].

संभोअ [°ग] *copulation,* i. 20[a]; ii. 28[c].

संमुह [°ख] *facing, opposite,* ii. 36[a].

सर- [°रस्] *a lake, pond,* iii. 29[a].

सर [श°] *an arrow,* ii. 3[d], 45[b]; iii. 11[c]; iv. 4[d], 20[d].

सरअ [शरद्] *the autumn,* iii. 3[11], 28[d].

सरण [श°] *refuge,* ii. 10[b].

सरणी ts. *a path, line, row, swarm,* ii. 6[a].

सरल ts. *straight, honest,* ii. 23[a], 30[d]. °ttaṇa [°tva], *sincerity,* iii. 10[b].

सरस्सई [°स्वती] *the goddess of poetry,* i. 1[a].

सरस्सदी *the same,* i. 34[34]; ii. 10[3, 4].

सरहसं [°भसम्] *impetuously,* ii. 50[b].

सरिआ [°रित्] *a river,* ii. 27[b], 35[a].

सरिच्छ [°दृक्ष] *equal, like,* i. 19[c], 29[b].

सरिस [°दृश] *the same,* i. 35[a]; ii. 10[a], 11[a], 38[a]; iii. 14[d].

सरीर [श°] *body,* iv. 19[32], 21[c].

सरीरि- [शरीरिन्] *fem.* °riṇī, *embodied,* iv. 19[64].

सलाआ [शलाका] *a pin, stick used as a brush or pencil,* i. 20[7], 34[18].

सलिल ts. *water,* i. 17[d], 20[43]; iii. 20[3], 22[1]; iv. 13[a].

सवज्जा [°पर्या] *worship, attendance,* i. 34[35].

सवण [श्र°] *an ear,* i. 29[a]; ii. 8[2], 18[a]; iii. 2[d], 19[a]; iv. 6[a].

सवर [शब°] *a mountaineer, savage,* iv. 19[64].

सव्व [सर्व] *every, each, all,* i. 7[1], 14[2],

18¹; ii. 6⁴˒⁵, 24², 27ᶜ, 28ᶜ; iii. 8⁴; iv. 2¹⁰, 18⁹˒³⁴, 23ᵈ.

सव्वंकस [सर्वंकष] *all-scratching, i. e. very galling or exciting*, i. 18ᵈ.

सव्वस्स [सर्वस्व] *the very essence*, i. 28ᵇ.

ससङ्क [शशा°] *the moon*, iv. 23ᵇ.

ससहर [शशध°] *the same*, iii. 30ᵃ, 31ᵃ.

ससि- [शशिन्] *the same*, i. 25ᵃ; ii. 10ᶜ, 20ᵇ, 21ᵇ, 32ᵈ; iv. 3ᵇ.

ससिआ *the same*, iii. 33ᵇ.

ससिप्पहा [शशिप्रभा] *name of a queen, the mother of Karpūramañjarī*, i. 34¹¹˒¹⁷.

ससिहण्ड [शशिख°] *a digit of the moon*, i. 3ᵃ.

ससुर [श्वशुर] *a father-in-law*, i. 18².

सह् *to endure*. soḍhavvo, iv. 1ᵃ.

सह ts. *together with; at the same time*, ii. 6¹⁴˒¹⁵, 9ᵃ˒ᵇ˒ᵈ, 42²¹, 50ᵃ˒ᵇ; iii. 34⁹; iv. 2ᵇ.

सहअर [°चर] *a companion, friend, husband*, ii. 41⁶.

सहरिसं [°र्षम्] *with joy*, ii. 34ᵇ.

सहसा ts. *forcibly, suddenly*, i. 18ᵈ, 29ᵃ; ii. 45ᵇ; iii. 3ᵈ, 20¹⁵.

सहा [°भा] *an assembly*, i. 19⁷.

सहाव [स्वभाव] *innate disposition, nature*, iii. 11ᵃ.

सहिआ [°खी] *a female friend*, iv. 13ᵇ.

सहित्तण [°खित्व] *friendship*, ii. 28³.

सहिद [°त] *accompanied by, together with*, i. 28⁸; ii. 42².

सही [°खी] *a female friend*, i. 19⁵; ii. 7ᵃ, 29ᵇ, 41⁹, 43¹⁰, 50²˒³; iii. 19², 20²³; iv. 9¹⁴, 19³⁹˒⁵⁷.

साअं [°यम्] *in the evening*, iv. 4ᵇ, 8ᵇ, 18⁷.

साअरदत्त [साग°] *name of a merchant*, iii. 5².

साध्+प्र *to adorn, decorate*. pasāhiā, ii. 22ᵃ.

सामग्गी [°ग्री] *completeness of outfit, outfit, the requisites*, ii. 41⁶, 42²˒⁸˒²¹; iv. 9¹³, 19¹⁷.

सामल [श्या°] *blackish*, i. 16ᶜ.

सामा [श्या°] *night*, iv. 8ᶜ.

सार ts. *essence, vigor*, iii. 10ᵈ.

सारङ्ग ts. *an antelope*, ii. 20ᵇ; iv. 1ᵇ.

सारङ्गिआ [°का] *name of a female servant of the queen*, iv. 9¹⁴, 18⁹, 20⁶.

सारिआ [°का] *a kind of bird, Maina, Acridotheres tristis*, i. 18¹⁵.

सारिक्ख [सदृक्ष] H. 1. 44. *like, similar*, iv. 19³⁰. °dā [sadṛkṣatā] *likeness, resemblance*, iv. 19⁵³˒⁵⁹.

सालिआ [शालिका] *an apartment, room*, i. 14ᶜ.

सावत्तअ [°पत्न्य] *the position of a rival wife*, iv. 23ᵃ.

सास [श्वा°] *a sigh*, ii. 9ᵃ.

सासण [शासन] *direction, order*, iii. 9².

साहार [साहकार] *produced from the mango*, iv. 5ᵇ.

साहि- [शाखिन्] *a tree*, ii. 46¹.

साहिमुह [°भिमुख] *fem.* °hī, *facing one another*, iv. 12ᵇ.

साहुलिआ HD. 8. 52. *a garment, cloth*, i. 20²³.

सिअअ [°चय] *a cloth, garment*, i. 4³, 26ᶜ; iii. 22².

सिक्खावणा [शिक्षापणा] *teaching*, ii. 8^{c}.

सिग्घं [शीघ्रम्] *quickly*, i. 4^{d}.

सिग्घत्तणा [शीघ्रत्व] *speed*, i. 18^{13}.

सिङ्गार [शृ°] *love, passion*, ii. 3^{c}; iii. 10^{d}; iv. 19^{64}, 23^{b}.

सिच् *to sprinkle.* siñcanti, iv. 10^{b}. siñcijjantī, iii. 20^{3}. sitta, iii. 22^{1}. sitto, i. 20^{13}.

सिञ्जा [शि°] *tinkle, jingle*, ii. 32^{c}.

सिञ्जिअ [शिञ्जित] *tinkling, singing*, i. 18^{c}.

सिढिल- [शिथिलय-] *to relax, loosen.* siḍhilaāmi, ii. 1^{3}.

सिणिद्ध [स्निग्ध] *affectionate*, i. 16^{3}.

सिद्ध ts. *a kind of supernatural being*, i. 25^{c}.

सिद्धि ts. *witchcraft, magic power*, i. 21^{5}.

सिन्दुवार *name of a tree* (*Vitex negundo*) *and its flower*, i. 19^{b}; iv. 7^{a}.

सिप्पि H. 2. 138. *a conch-shell*, i. 4^{b}.

सिर- [शिरस्] *head, top, summit*, ii. 46^{d}; iii. 3^{9}; iv. 19^{35}.

सिरिखण्ड [श्री°] *sandal-wood*, iv. 4^{a}.

सिरिताली [श्री°] *a kind of toddy-palm*, ii. 1^{2}.

सिरिराअसेहर [श्रीराजशेखर] *the renowned Rājaçekhara*, i. 10^{a}.

सिरिवज्जाउह [श्रीवज्रायुध] *name of a king*, iii. 5^{2}.

सिरी [श्री] *wealth, dignity, beauty*, i. 33^{b}; ii. 48^{a}; iii. 15^{c}.

सिरीस [शिरीष] *the flower of Acacia sirissa*, iv. 7^{a}.

सिला [शि°] *a stone, rock*, ii. 15^{b}; iv. 9^{7}.

सिलीमुह [शिलीमुख] *an arrow*, ii. 19^{b}, 38^{b}, 46^{b}; iv. 4^{d}, 9^{9}.

सिलोअ [श्लोक] *a verse*, ii. 7^{b}, 8^{3}, 9^{1}.

सिविणअ [स्वप्न] *a dream*, iii. 2^{2}, $3^{a,4,6,7}$, 4^{6}, 8^{a}, 20^{1}.

सिसिर [शिशि°] *cold; the cold season*, i. 13^{d}; iv. 6^{b}.

सिसिरोवआर [शिशिरोपचार] *artificial refrigeration, means for cooling*, ii. 41^{6}, $42^{2,8,21}$; iii. 19^{2}.

सिसुत्तणा [शिशुत्व] *childhood, infancy*, i. 20^{d}.

सिहण्ड [शिख°] *a lock of hair left on the crown of the head* (*used as synonymous with* çekhara), i. 5^{a}.

सिहरि- [शिखरिन्] *a mountain*, i. 15^{d}.

सिहा [शिखा] *top, tip; edge*, ii. 47^{c}; iii. 25^{c}; iv. 3^{d}.

सिहिण HD. 8. 31. *the female breasts*, i. 34^{b}; iii. 16^{b}; iv. 7^{a}.

सीअल [शीतल] *cool, cold*, i. 15^{d}; iv. 4^{b}, $6^{a,b,c,d}$.

सीमन्तिणी [°न्ती] *a woman*, i. 15^{b}; ii. 28^{b}.

सील [शी°] *nature, disposition*, ii. 6^{6}.

सीस [शीर्ष] *head*, i. 20^{27}; iv. 2^{4}, 12^{a}, 18^{27}.

सुअ [शुक] *a parrot*, iv. 2^{6}.

सुआ [°ता] *a daughter*, i. 3^{b}, 12^{b}.

सुउमार [°कुमार] *very delicate or soft*, i. 7^{a}, 20^{7}.

सुकइ [°वि] *an excellent poet*, i. 20^{20}.

सुट्ठुदरं [सुष्टुतरम्] *excellently, exceedingly*, i. 20^{7}; iv. 20^{15}.

सुणअण [°नयन] *having beautiful eyes*, ii. 11^{d}.

सुत्त [सूत्र] *a thread, fibre*, ii. 50^{c}.

सुत्तआर [सूत्रकार] *an author of Sūtras*, ii. 32^{1}.

सुत्ति [शुक्ति] *a pearl-oyster*, iii. 3[18], 4[a, 1, 3].

सुत्थ [सुस्थ] *well-conditioned*, ii. 1[a].

सुन्दर ts. *fem.* °rī, *beautiful, lovely*, i. 20[8]; ii. 44[c]; iii. 28[a], 34[a]; iv. 21[d].

सुन्दरकेली ts. *name of a woman*, iv. 9[11].

सुन्दरत्तण [°त्व] *beauty, loveliness*, i. 14[2].

सुन्देर [सौन्दर्य] *the same*, i. 28[b], 33[c]; ii. 48[a].

सुप्पज्जल [°प्राञ्जल] *very straight, honest, sincere*, ii. 27[1].

सुबहुल ts. *very great*, iii. 12[d].

सुमरण [स्म°] *remembering, recollection*, ii. 10[b].

सुर ts. *a god*, i. 25[c]. sura-aṇa [-jana], *the gods*, i. 3[a].

सुरअ [°त] *copulation, sexual intercourse*, i. 24[d].

सुरङ्गा ts. *a subterranean passage*, iii. 22[9], 34[9]; iv. 9[6, 7], 18[38], 19[2, 24].

सुरसरिदा [°रित्] *the Ganges*, iii. 3[7].

सुरहि [°भि] *the spring*, i. 14[2]; ii. 22[b].

सुरा ts. *spirituous liquor*, i. 24[d]; iv. 4[b], 19[a].

सुलक्खणा [°क्षणा] *name of a woman*, i. 34[35]; ii. 9[1].

सुलोल ts. *very waving, unsteady*, iii. 11[a].

सुवण्ण [°र्ण] *gold, a golden coin*, i. 14[2], 18[18], 19[7], 20[14]; ii. 41[a]; iii. 4[5], 5[b, 3], 22[c].

सुवट्टुल [°र्तुल] *very round*, iii. 4[b].

सुस्सूसअ [शुश्रूषक] *attentive, obedient*, i. 20[34].

सुह [°ख] *happy, agreeable; happiness, ease, joy*, i. 3[b], 14[2], 34[41], 36[b]; ii. 28[d]; iii. 24[2]; iv. 21[6].

सुहअ [°भग] *blessed, beloved, beautiful*, ii. 9[c], 10[d]; iv. 3[1]. -ttaṇa [-tva], *beauty, loveliness*, iii. 13[d].

सुहसंझा [°खसंध्या] *a happy evening*, ii. 49[4].

सुहासिद [°भाषित] *a witty saying, good counsel*, iv. 9[5, 12].

सृ ts. *go, proceed, flow.* saraï, ii. 6[c]. saranta, ii. 35[a].

+ अप *to go away, to vanish.* osaranti, iii. 16[d]; iv. 18[b].

+ प्र *to flow forth, to grow. Caus., to extend.* pasaranta, iii. 10[c], 11[a]. pasārida, i. 16[3].

+ प्रति *Caus., to arrange.* paḍisāredi, i. 4[5]. paḍisārīadi, i. 4[8].

से H. 3. 81. *his, her*, i. 29[2]; ii. 1[3], 6[c], 13[a], 18[a], 30[d], 35[a], 46[a].

सेअसलिल [स्वेद°] *sweat, perspiration*, iii. 22[1].

सेज्जा [शय्या] *a bed, couch*, i. 23[c]; ii. 4[b]; iii. 3[a], 27[d].

सेट्ठि- [श्रेष्ठिन्] *a merchant*, iii. 4[5].

सेणा [°ना] *the word* senā, iv. 9[8].

सेरन्धी [सैरन्ध्री] *a female attendant in the women's apartments*, i. 36[c]; iv. 9[9].

सेव् *to attend upon, frequent.* sevaï, ii. 17[b].

+ नि *to practice, enjoy.* ṇisevia, iv. 8[b].

सेस [शेष] *remaining; rest*, ii. 29[1, 4, 8]; iv. 4[d].

सेहर [शेखर] *a crest; chaplet, diadem*, iii. 13[a].

सेहालिआ [शेफालिका] *a kind of flower supposed to blossom by moon-light*, iv. 18[36].

सोडीरत्तण [शौटीर्य] *valor*, i. 32[2].

सोढव्व *see* सह्.

सोण [शो°] *red*, i. 26[a].

सोत्त [स्रोतस्] *a stream*, i. 12[b]; ii. 27[b]; iii. 3[7].

सोत्तिअ [श्रोत्रिय] *a learned Brāhmaṇa*, iv. 20[9].

सोविदल्ल [सौ°] *a harem-keeper*, iii. 34[8].

सोसण [शोष°] *emaciating, name of one of the arrows of Cupid*, i. 32[d]; iii. 26[c].

सोहग्ग [सौभाग्य] *beauty, charm*, ii. 3[b].

सोहञ्जण [शोभाञ्जन] HD. 8. 37. *horse-radish*, i. 20[29]. (*K*, phalgunamāsi tatkandaṁ khaṇḍayanti; *J*, puṣpanimittaṁ çākhānāṁ troṭanam ity arthaḥ.)

सोहा [शोभा] *light, splendor*, i. 28[2], 29[2], 31[a, b], 34[17]; ii. 10[b], 25[a]; iii. 25[c].

सोहि- [शोभिन्] *shining, lovely*, ii. 7[b].

स्खल् *to tumble, fall down, end.* khaliā, i. 20[a]. khaliam, i. 32[b].

स्तम्भ् *Caus., to stop, arrest.* thambhemi, i. 25[b].

स्तृ+प्र *to spread, to make a bed.* pattharijjanti, i. 36[b].

+**वि** *to increase. Caus., to spread, extend.* vittharanti, ii. 2[d]. vittharida, iii. 8[4].

स्था *to stand, remain, find place. Caus., to place, arrange.* ciṭṭhasi, i. 18[15]; iii. 2[1]. ṭhāï, i. 34[a]. ciṭṭhadi, i. 21[4]; ii. 6[10]; iv. 20[9]. ciṭṭha, ii. 42[21]; iv. 19[24], 20[4]. ciṭṭhadu, i. 34[26]; ii. 41[6]. ciṭṭhissaṁ, i. 20[34]. ṭhia, ii. 33[a]; iii. 23[a]. ṭhida, iv. 18[30]. ṭhio, ii. 1[b], 46[d]; iii. 4[a]. ṭhido, iii. 3[15], 4[4]. ṭhiā, i. 26[c]. ṭhidā, i. 20[2, 18]. ṭhiaṁ, ii. 47[d]. ṭhidaṁ, i. 20[27]. ṭhideṇa, ii. 29[7]. ṭhie, iii. 25[a]. ṭhāvia, ii. 43[2]. ṭhavio, ii. 17[a]. ṭhāvido, i. 4[7]. ṭhāvidāo, iv. 9[10].

+**उद्** *to stand up, rise.* uṭṭhiūṇa, iii. 21[a]. uṭṭhia, ii. 43[5].

+**प्रति** *Caus., to place, establish.* paḍiṭṭhāvidā, iv. 18[11].

+**सम्** *to stand, to be settled, fixed.* saṁṭhido, iii. 3[18]. saṁṭhiā, iii. 3[b], 5[b]. saṁṭhidā, iv. 19[64].

स्ना *Caus., to wash, bathe.* ṇhāvio, i. 29[c].

स्पृश् *to touch.* puṭṭha, iv. 22[d].

स्फद् *Caus., to split, cleave.* phāḍidāo, iii. 4[3].

स्फुट् H. 4. 177. *to break, fall asunder.* phuḍantī, iii. 20[3].

+**प्र** *to open, become manifest.* pahuṭṭaï, ii. 4[a].

स्फुर् *to appear, become manifest, to quiver, vibrate.* phuraü, i. 1[c]. phurantao, iii. 31[b].

+**वि** *to quiver, shine, blaze out.* vipphuraï, iv. 3[c]. vipphuranto, iv. 24[a].

स्मृ *to remember.* sumarasi, ii. 24[3].

+**वि** *to forget.* visumaridāiṁ, iv. 19[46].

स्रंस् *to fall down.* saṁsamāṇaṁ, i. 27[b].

स्वप् *to sleep.* suvanti, i. 14^{c}. sutto, iii. 3^{7}.

हं *see* **अहम्.**

हंस ts. *fem.* °sī, *a swan, flamingo,* ii. 6^{10}, 8^{a}; iii. 29^{a}.

हक्कार- *to call, summon.* hakkārai, ii. 33^{b}. hakkāriūṇa, ii. 36^{b}. hakkāria, i. 4^{12}. hakkārīadu, iv. 20^{8}.

हत्थ [°स्त] *a hand,* i. 18^{10}, 26^{b}, 36^{c}; ii. 6$^{17, 20}$, 29$^{a, d}$; iii. 3^{b}, 23^{a}; iv. 9$^{8, 9, 10, 12}$, 12^{a}, 15^{a}, 20^{13}.

हन *to strike, beat.* haā, ii. 43^{a}.

हन्त *exclam., go to! mind you!* ii. 26^{a}.

°हर [°धर] *carrying,* ii. 6^{d}.

हर ts. *a name of Çiva,* ii. 6^{23}; iii. 3^{9}.

हरण ts. *stealing, fascinating,* ii. 28^{b}, 31^{d}; iii. 18^{e}.

हरि ts. *a name of Viṣṇu,* i. 24^{a}.

हरिअन्दपुरी [हरिश्चन्द्र°] H. 2. 87. *the city of Hariçcandra, supposed to be situated in mid-air, a fata morgana,* ii. 40^{5}.

हरिआल [°ताल] *yellow orpiment,* iii. 22^{a}.

हरिउड्ढ [°वृद्ध] *name of a poet,* i. 20^{20}.

हरिकेली ts. *a name of Bengal,* i. 14^{2}.

हरिणङ्क [°णाङ्क] *the moon,* i. 10^{b}, 12^{a}, 25^{9}; iii. 20^{15}, 34^{a}.

हरिणच्छ [°णाक्ष] *fem.* °cchī, *deer-eyed,* iii. 22^{d}.

हरिणी st. *a doe, female antelope,* ii. 41^{c}.

हलबोल HD. 8. 64. *murmuring, noise,* i. 4^{10}; iii. 34^{8}.

हला ts. *a vocative particle used in addressing a female friend,* iv. 19^{39}.

हलिद्दी [°रिद्रा] *turmeric,* iii. 1^{a}.

हस *to laugh, mock. Caus., to cause to smile, laugh.* hasanti, iv. 18^{b}. hasantīe, i. 20^{15}. hāsia, iv. 18^{b}.

+ उप *to deride, ridicule.* uvahasīāmi, i. 18^{6}.

+ वि *to smile.* vihasia, iv. 18^{23}.

हा *ah, alas,* iii. 22^{4}.

हा + परि *to be inferior to.* parihīamāṇa, iii. 8^{5}.

हार ts. *a garland, necklace,* ii. 10^{a}, 11^{b}, 17^{a}, 23^{b}, 32^{a}, 35^{a}; iii. 2^{a}, 18^{b}, 20^{a}; iv. 7^{a}.

हाल ts. *name of a poet,* i. 20^{20}.

हास ts. *laughter, merriment,* ii. 3^{b}, 10^{b}; iv. 14^{b}.

हि ts. *because, for,* i. 14^{3}, 16^{5}.

हिअअ [हृदय] *heart,* i. 34^{35}; ii. 26^{a}, 30^{c}, 43^{5}; iii. 8^{1}, 16^{d}, 18^{c}, 20^{17}.

हिण्ड् *to go, wander.* hiṇḍase, iii. 34^{a}.

हिन्दोल- *to swing.* hindolaantī, ii. 29

हिन्दोलअ [°क] *a swing,* ii. 29$^{5, 6}$.

हिन्दोलअप्पभञ्जणी [°कप्रभञ्जनी] *the swing-breaker, the swing-festival,* ii. 6^{23}.

हिन्दोलण [°न] *swinging,* ii. 32^{d}, 34^{a}.

हीरअ [°क] *a diamond,* ii. 25^{b}.

हु *see* **खु.**

हुंकार ts. *the sound* hum, *murmur, humming,* i. 36^{d}; iii. 20^{7}; iv. 15^{a}.

हुडुक्क ts. *a small musical instrument, perhaps timbrel, drum*, iv. 16[a].

हुदवह [हुत°] *fire*, iv. 21[1].

हृ *to carry, carry away, captivate, to enchant.* haraï, iii. 20[d], 22[a]. haranti, ii. 26[a].

+ अनु *to imitate, resemble.* aṇuharaï, i. 6[a]. aṇuharadi, ii. 41[5].

+ परि *to avoid.* pariharia, i. 6[2].

+ वि *to sport, play.* viharaï, ii. 41[c].

हेला ts. *ease, facility*, ii. 29[b]. 35[a], 47[b].

Part III

ESSAY

ON

RĀJAÇEKHARA'S LIFE AND WRITINGS

BY

STEN KONOW

1. Chronological List of Books and Papers Concerning Rājaçekhara.

1827. Wilson, H. H. Select specimens of the theatre of the Hindus. 3 vols. Calcutta, 1826–27. References to 3d ed., 2 vols., London, 1871.

1862. Hall, Fitz-Edward. Vestiges of three royal lines of Kanyakubja, or Kanauj, with indications of its literature. Journal of the Asiatic Society of Bengal, xxxi. 1 ff.

1869. Govinda Deva S'ástri. The Bálarámáyaṇa. A drama by Rájaśekhara. Edited etc. Benares. Reprinted from the Pandit, a monthly journal of the Benares college, devoted to Sanskrit literature, old series, vol. iii., nos. 25–35.

1871. Vāmanācārya. The Viddhaśálabhañjiká edited etc. The Pandit, old series, vols. vi. and vii., nos. 65–73.

1872. Vāmanācārya. The Karpúramañjarí edited etc. The Pandit, old series, vol. vii., nos. 73–76.

1873. (Jīvānanda Vidyāsāgara.) Biddhashala Bhanjika, a drama by Rajashekhara, with a commentary by Satyavrata Samasrami. Calcutta.

1873. Aufrecht, Theodor. Ueber die Paddhati von Çārngadhara. Zeitschrift der deutschen morgenländischen Gesellschaft, xxvii. 1–120.

1878. Borooah, Anundoram. Bhavabhuti and his place in Sanskrit literature. Calcutta.

1879. Cunningham, A. Report of a tour in the Central Provinces in 1873–74 and 1874–75. Archaeological survey of India, ix. 85. Calcutta.

1881. Borooah, Anundoram. Practical English-Sanskrit Dictionary. Vol. 3. With a prefatory essay on the ancient geography of India. Calcutta. See especially §§ 134 and the following.

1883. Müller, F. Max. India: what can it teach us? London.

1883. Pischel, R. [Review of] Kausika's Zorn (Tschandakauçika). Ein indisches Drama von Kschemisvara. Zum ersten Male und metrisch übersetzt von Ludwig Fritze. Göttingische gelehrte Anzeigen. 1883, pages 1217-41.

1883. Hariçcandra. Karpūr Maṁjarī, saṭṭak (Yah nāṭak çuddha prākṛt bhāṣā meṁ Rājaçeṣara kabi kā banāyā huā hai . . .) Bānāras: Āryayantrālaya sambat 1939.

1883. Jībānanda Vidyāsāgara. Biddhashala bhanjika, a drama by Rajasekharakabi. Edited with a commentary. Calcutta. "Dvitīyasaṁskaraṇam."

1884. Bhandarkar, R. G. Report on the search for Sanskrit mss. in the Bombay Presidency during the year 1882–83. Bombay.

1884. Peterson, Peter. A second report of operations in search of Sanskrit mss. Journal of the Bombay Branch of the Royal Asiatic Society, no. xliv. Pages 59f, 63f.

1884. Jīvānanda Vidyāsāgara. Bālarāmāyaṇa nāma nāṭakam mahākavi çrī Rājaçekhara viracitam . . . vyākhyayānvitam. Calcutta.

1885. Cappeller, Carl. Pracaṇḍapâṇḍava [or Bālabhārata] ein Drama des Râjaçekhara. Strassburg.

1886. Apte, Vaman Shivram. Râjaśekhara: his life and writings. Poona: "Arya-Bhushana" Press. Pages 54.

1886. Bhâskar Râmchandra Ârte. The Viddhasâlabhanjikâ of Râjasekhara: with the commentary of Narayana Dixit . . . To which is added the Ritusamhâra of Kâlidâsa with a close English translation and various readings by Keshava Râoji Godbole. Poona.

1886. Peterson, Peter, and Durgâprasâda. The Subhâshitâvali of Vallabhadeva. Bombay Sanskrit Series, no. xxxi. Bombay.

1887. Durgâprasâda and Kâśînâtha Pâṇḍuranga Paraba. The Karpûramanjarî (with the commentary of Vâsudeva) and the Bâlabhârata of Râjaśekhara. Bombay. Kâvyamâlâ. 4.

1887. Fleet, John F. The date of the poet Râjaśekhara. Indian Antiquary, xvi. 175–178.

1889. Kielhorn, F. Siyadoni stone inscription. Epigraphia Indica, i. 162–179.

1890. Lévi, Sylvain. Le théâtre Indien. Paris.

1890. Vaman Shastri Islampurkar. A lucky wife or Karpoormanjari. Composed from Prakrita or Maharashtri dialect. Bombay: "Tattva-vivechaka" Press. Vāgvilāsa-ratnākara, ratna 1.

[This seems to be the most convenient place for the names of a few books (1. Dictionaries; 2. Grammars; 3. Texts; 4. Books on plants, minerals, etc.) to which I have made more or less frequent reference in the Notes to the Translation. The list includes only works whose titles have been abbreviated or about the precise edition of which there might be some doubt. — C. R. L.]

BR. = Sanskrit-Wörterbuch von Böhtlingk und Roth. St. Petersburg, 1855–75.

OB. = Sanskrit-Wörterbuch in kürzerer Fassung von Otto Böhtlingk. St. Petersburg, 1879–89.

Molesworth = Dictionary, Marāṭhī and English, by James T. Molesworth. 2d ed. Bombay, 1857.

Hemachandra = Hemak'andra's Abhidhānak'intāmaṇi, ein systematisch angeordnetes synonymisches Lexicon. Herausgegeben, übersetzt und mit Anmerkungen begleitet von Otto Böhtlingk und Charles Rieu. St. Petersburg, 1847.

HD. = The Des'īnāmamālā of Hemachandra. Part I. Text and critical notes. By R. Pischel. Bombay, 1880. (See p. 117.)

H. = Hemacandra's Grammatik der Prākritsprachen, herausgegeben von R. Pischel. Halle, 1877–80. (See p. 117.)

Vararuchi = The Prākṛita-Prakās'a, or the Prākṛit Grammar of Vararuchi. Edited and translated by E. B. Cowell. Hertford, 1854.

Jacobi = Ausgewählte Erzählungen in Māhārāshṭrī. Zur Einführung in das Studium des Prākṛit. Grammatik. Text. Wörterbuch. Von Hermann Jacobi. Leipzig, 1886. Appended is a sketch of the Çaurasenī.

Whitney = A Sanskrit Grammar. By William D. Whitney. 2d ed. Leipzig, 1889.

Çakuntalā = S'akuntalā . . . by Kālidāsa. Edited by Monier Williams. 2d ed. Oxford, 1876. Cited on account of the annotations.

Meghadūta = Meghadūta . . . von Kālidāsa. Herausgegeben von A. F. Stenzler. Breslau, 1874.

Kādambarī = The Kādambarī of Bāṇa. Edited by Kāçināth Pāṇḍurang Parab. Bombay, Nirṇaya Sāgara Press, 1890. The references are to page and line of the text; but may be found with equal facility in the translation of Miss C. M. Ridding, London, 1896.

Harshacharita = The Harshacharita of Bāṇa. Edited by K. P. Parab and Dh. P. Vaze. Bombay, Nirṇaya Sāgara Press, 1892. The text references (as before) will serve also for the translation of Cowell and Thomas, London, 1897.

Parab, Subh. = Subhāshita-ratna-bhāṇḍāgāram, or Gems of Sanskrit Poetry. Selected and arranged by K. P. Parab. 2d ed. Bombay, Nirṇaya Sāgara Press, 1886.

Sprüche = Indische Sprüche. Herausgegeben von O. Böhtlingk. 2d ed. St. Petersburg, 1870–73.

Roxburgh = Flora Indica, or Descriptions of Indian Plants. By William Roxburgh. Calcutta, 1874. Reprinted from Carey's ed. of 1832.

Rājanighaṇṭu = Rājanighaṇṭu-sahito Dhanvantarīya-nighaṇṭuḥ. Poona, 1896. Ānandaāçrama Series, no. 33.

SR. = Saṁgīta-ratnākara. Same Series, no. 35.

Griffiths = The Paintings in the Buddhist Cave-Temples of Ajantâ, Khandesh, India. By John Griffiths. 2 vols., folio. London, 1896–97. The references to this work were added by me in the proofs. Hence their extreme brevity. It is to be hoped that some one with a good knowledge of the artificial poetry may make a careful study of these pictures.

2. Rājaçekhara's Life.

Earlier Opinions as to Rājaçekhara's Date. — The name of Rājaçekhara has been known to Indian scholars ever since the beginning of our century. Extracts from two of his works were published by the late H. H. Wilson. That critic also tried to fix as his date the end of the eleventh or the beginning of the twelfth century A.D.

Aufrecht, in his treatise on the Çārṅgadharapaddhati, collected the different verses ascribed in that anthology to the name of Rājaçekhara and expressed himself (p. 77) to the effect that, in his opinion, the poet was the immediate predecessor of Jayadeva.

Anundoram Boroosh is of opinion that the tradition according to which Rājaçekhara is said to have been a contemporary of Çaṁkara should be trusted, and that, accordingly, "we can safely fix the seventh century as his probable date."

I pass by the opinion of F. Max Müller that Rājaçekhara lived in the fourteenth century, as being founded on a confusion of our poet with a younger Rājaçekhara who wrote the Prabandhakoça, about 1347 A.D. (see p. 196).

The different allusions made by the poet himself in his works were discussed by Pischel, who came to the conclusion that Rājaçekhara must have lived at the end of the tenth or the beginning of the eleventh century.

Peterson and Durgāprasāda assure us that Rājaçekhara's real date is the middle of the eighth century; which, according to them, is shown by the fact that Kṣīrasvāmin, who was the teacher of Jayasiṁha of Kashmir (A.D. 750), quotes a verse from the Viddhaçālabhañjikā, and that the king Mahendrapāla, to whom Rājaçekhara himself refers as being a pupil of his own, was reigning in 761 A.D.

Vaman Shivram Apte, in discussing these various views, comes to the conclusion that Rājaçekhara lived between the end of the seventh and the middle of the tenth century, most probably about the end of the eighth, because he quotes Bhavabhūti and is himself quoted in the Daçarūpa.

Durgāprasāda and Paraba place our poet between 884 and 959 A.D.

Rājaçekhara's Relations to Mahendrapāla, and to the Latter's Son, Mahīpāla. — Rājaçekhara, in all his four extant plays, declares himself to be the spiritual teacher of a king Mahendrapāla or Nirbhayarāja. Cp. Viddh. i. 6 (ed. Arte), Raghukulatilako Mahendrapālaḥ sakalakalānilayaḥ sa yasya çiṣyaḥ; Karp. i. 5, Mahindavālassa ko a gurū; i. 9, Ṇibbhararāassa taha uvajjhāo; Bālar. i. 5, Nirbhayaguruḥ; Bālabh. i. 11, devo yasya Mahendrapālanṛpatiḥ çiṣyo Raghugrāmaṇīḥ.

Aufrecht had declared Mahendrapāla and Nirbhaya to be one and the same person, and their identity was proved by Pischel, p. 1221. Nirbhaya, accordingly, is a *biruda* or *ὄνομα πανηγυρικόν* of Mahendrapāla. The mss. of the Karpūramañjarī are in favor of the form Ṇibbhara (only the Jaina mss. read Ṇibbhaya), and Nirbhaya may be a false Sanskrit translation of this name.

Mahendrapāla's son was Mahīpāla, the paramount sovereign of

Āryāvarta, i.e., according to Bālar. vi. 52[1] (p. 170.6, ed. Govinda), the country to the north of the Narmadā. Cp. Bālabh. i. 7[1] (p. 2. 16, ed. Cappeller), tena (Mahīpāladevena) ca Raghuvaṁçamuktāmaṇin Āryāvarta-mahārājādhirājena çrīNirbhayanarendranandanenārādhitāḥ sabhāsadaḥ. Cp. C. Mabel Duff's Chronology of India, p. 296 and 82 ff.

Rājaçekhara lived about 900 A.D. — Now Fleet has shown that this Mahīpāla must be identified with the king Mahīpāla of the Asni inscription, dated Vikrama saṁvat 974 = A.D. 917, and has thus proved that Rājaçekhara lived at the beginning of the tenth century A.D. As pointed out by Pischel and Fleet, the Bālabhārata was performed in Mahodaya, and Mahodaya is another name of Kānyakubja (Bālar. x. 87[1], 89[c] = p. 306. 6, 15), with which town Mahendrapāla and Mahīpāla are connected in the Siyadoni inscription. See Kielhorn, p. 170 f. For Mahendrapāla we have the dates 903–4 and 907–8. Fleet was not aware of the fact that Mahendrapāla and Nirbhaya are one and the same, and thought that Mahendrapāla must be another son or a grandson of Nirbhayanarendra, whose real name, according to him, was Mahiṣapāla. But this form of the word is rather suspicious, and the published photograph of the Asni inscription is in favor of Mahindrapāla, as pointed out by Kielhorn, p. 171[16]. As for this form, see Bühler, Epigraphia Indica, i. 244.

Kielhorn's summing up of the names of the four sovereigns of Mahodaya or Kānyakubja or Kanauj, as presented to us by the Siyadoni inscription, together with their known dates, may here be repeated for the reader's convenience from Epigraphia Indica, i. 171 :

1. Bhoja, A.D. 862, 876, and 882.
2. Mahendrapāla or Nirbhayanarendra or Mahiṣapāla, A.D. 903 and 907; pupil of the poet Rājaçekhara.
3. His son Kṣitipāla or Mahīpāla or Herambapāla, A.D. 917; patron of Rājaçekhara.
4. His son Devapāla, A.D. 948.

Fleet, Indian Antiquary, xv. 105 ff., has edited an inscription from Dighwa-Dubauli, of the Mahārāja Mahendrapāla of Mahodaya, dated Harṣa saṁvat 155 = A.D. 761–2. As shown by Fleet, xvi. 175 ff., this feudatory Mahārāja must be quite a different person from the pupil of Rājaçekhara, but may possibly have been one of his ancestors. Peterson and Durgāprasāda confounded both, and thus arrived at the false date mentioned above.

The historical facts being thus finally established, it is no longer necessary to comment upon other suggestions or conjectures respecting the poet's date. Nor can any authority be attributed to the traditional account that Rājaçekhara was a contemporary of Çaṁkarācārya. This opinion is founded on the Çaṁkaradigvijaya, a work which is, in every respect, very untrustworthy. The same must be said about the South Indian tradition according to which Rājaçekhara was king of Malabar, his real name being Kulaçekhara Perumāl. This king, according to the Keraḷotpatti or Keralaviçeṣamāhātmya lived in 322 A.D. (!) See Apte, p. 13, note.

Rājaçekhara's Personal History. A Yāyāvara Brahman, of the Çaiva Sect. — Rājaçekhara gives more details about himself and his family than most Indian authors. According to Bālar. i. 6^b, 13^d; Viddh. i. 5^2, he belonged to a Yāyāvara family. Hall, p. 14, note, translates yāyāvara with 'maintainer of a sacrificial hearth'; and Nārāyaṇa Dīkṣita, in his commentary on Viddh. i. 5^2, quotes Devala to show that yāyāvara means a kind of gṛhastha: dvividho gṛhastho yāyāvaraḥ çālīnaç ca, 'there are two kinds of gṛhastha, the yāyāvara and the çālīna.' But probably yāyāvara is the name of the family. The Yāyāvaras were brahmans. Apte, p. 18, justly remarks that Rājaçekhara must also be presumed to have been a brahman because he is said to be an incarnation of Bhavabhūti and because it is not becoming for a kṣatriya to be a guru or upādhyāya. On the other hand, Rājaçekhara's wife, Avantisundarī, is called, at Karp. i. 11^a, "The crest-garland of the Chauhan family," and was accordingly a Rajput princess. [Conjectures about her name in Pischel's Prākrit-grammatik, p. 39–40.]

Rājaçekhara seems to have been a Çaiva. This, as pointed out by Apte, p. 19, is rendered probable by the introductory stanzas to his works. Thus two of the four introductory stanzas in the Karpūramañjarī are in praise of Çiva and Pārvatī, as are also Viddh. i. 3 and Bālabh. i. 1, 2; whereas, in the Bālarāmāyaṇa, the abstract deity "vāṇīnāṁ gumpha" is extolled. But he cannot have been a bigot; for in the third āçvāsa of the Yaçastilakacampū we are told that he, like many other poets, when occasion arose, did honor to the religion of the Jains. See Peterson, A second report, 1884, p. 45 f.

Rājaçekhara's Place of Origin the Western Deccan. — Rājaçekhara's family seems to originate from Mahārāṣṭra, that is (cp. Bālar. x. 73$^{1 ff.}$, p. 302. 18 ff.), from Vidarbha and Kuntala. His great-grandfather, Akālajalada, is called, in the Bālar. i. 13^1, p. 9. 1, Mahārāṣṭracūḍāmaṇi, 'a crest-jewel of Mahārāṣṭra.' Nārāyaṇa Dīkṣita, in the introduction to his commentary on the Viddhaçālabhañjikā, tells us that Rājaçekhara in the Bālarāmāyaṇa declares himself to be from Mahārāṣṭra, and that he made use of the language of that country to a great extent. And in the colophon to the Benares edition of the Karpūramañjarī, the poet is styled Mahārāṣṭracūḍāmaṇi 'a crest-jewel of Mahārāṣṭra.' On the other hand, in the Sūktimuktāvali, Rājaçekhara's ancestor, Surānanda, is called Cedimaṇḍalamaṇḍanam, 'an ornament of the country of the Cedis.'

Apte has pointed out that our poet is especially acquainted with Southern customs and places and often alludes to Southern rivers, such as Kāverī, Tāmraparṇī, Narmadā, etc. He knows "the black cheeks, the pure smile, and the teeth rubbed white with the rind of betel, of the Draviḍa women, the curling ringlets of Karnatic maidens, the pleasure-seeking propensities of Lāṭa," etc. See Apte, p. 20 f. In the Āucityavicāracarcā, v. 27, a stanza by Rājaçekhara is quoted which does not occur in any of his known works:

> karṇāṭīdaçanāñkitaḥ çitamahārāṣṭrīkaṭākṣāhataḥ
> prāuḍhāndhrīstanapīḍitaḥ praṇayinībhrūbhañgavitrāsitaḥ |
> lāṭībāhuviveṣṭitaç ca malayastrītarjanītarjitaḥ
> so 'yaṁ saṁprati Rājaçekharakavir Vārāṇasīṁ vāñchati ‖

'Marked by the teeth of the Karṇāṭa maidens, hurt by the sharp glances of the Mahārāṣṭra women, pressed by the voluptuous breasts of the Āndhrīs, frightened by the frown of his beloved friend, embraced by the arms of the Lāṭa maidens, menaced by the fore-finger of the women from Malaya, the poet Rājaçekhara nowadays is longing for Benares.' As the stanza is given by Kṣemendra, the Rājaçekhara here mentioned is presumably no other than our poet. The countries that are named range from Cambay to Comorin, and justify little more than the conjecture that Rājaçekhara was from the Western Deccan. And as we find him in the position of court-poet at Kanauj, far to the north, we must suppose that he, like Bilhaṇa, left his native country to seek wealth and fame at foreign courts.

Rājaçekhara at the Court of Kanauj. — Rājaçekhara seems to have been very proud of his position as the guru of king Mahendrapāla, and he mentions this fact in all his plays. In the Sūktimuktāvali we find a stanza by a pupil (antevāsin) of Rājaçekhara, beginning āgaskāriṇi kāiṭabhapramathane. It would of course be impossible to tell whether this antevāsin was the king Mahendrapāla.

The poet's connection with the court of Kanauj seems to have continued on into the reign of Mahendrapāla's son and successor, Mahīpāla; for it was at the request of the latter that the Bālabhārata was represented. But we do not know how long Rājaçekhara remained at Mahīpāla's court.

Rājaçekhara at the Court of Cedi. — Rājaçekhara seems also to have had some connection with the Cedi princes. His name occurs in verse

85 of the Bilhari inscription of the rulers of Cedi, published by Kielhorn in the Epigraphia Indica, i. 251 ff. The verse runs:

suçliṣṭabandhaghaṭanā vismitakavirājaçekharastutyā |
āstām iyam ākalpaṁ kṛtiç ca kīrtiç ca pūrvvā ca ||

'May this composition, the several parts of which are well-joined, and which would deserve praise even from the wonder-struck poet Rājaçekhara, last to the end of the world, as well as the preceding eulogy.' (Kielhorn.) The reference to our poet in a Cedi inscription gains somewhat in its significance from a stanza in the Sūktimuktāvali, which is attributed to the name of Rājaçekhara, and which may perhaps be of interest in this connection:

nadīnāṁ Mekalasutā nṛpāṇāṁ Raṇavigrahaḥ |
kavīnāṁ ca Surānandaç Cedimaṇḍalamaṇḍanam ||

'The Narmadā among rivers, Raṇavigraha among kings, and Surānanda among poets adorn the country of the Cedis.' This verse seems to be written in praise of Raṇavigraha, and if that be the case, it cannot belong to the younger Rājaçekhara. As shown by Fleet,[1] Raṇavigraha is a *biruda* of the Cedi prince Çaṁkaragaṇa, who lived about the middle of the tenth century. We may therefore, perhaps, conclude that Rājaçekhara at some time of his life had connection with the Cedi court.

Rājaçekhara's Ancestry. — Some details about Rājaçekhara's ancestry are given in his works. His father was a high minister, mahāmantrin (Bālar. i. 7²; Bālabh. i. 8¹⁸), Durduka (Bālar. i. 13¹), or Duhika (Viddh. i. 5²); and his mother's name was Çīlavatī (Bālar. i. 13¹). Poetical skill appears to have been traditional in the family. In a well-known stanza, Bālar. i. 13, we read:

sa mūrtto yatrāsīd guṇagaṇa ivākālajaladaḥ
Surānandaḥ so 'pi çravaṇapuṭapeyena vacasā |
na cānye gaṇyante Tarala-Kavirāja-prabhṛtayo
mahābhāgas tasminn ayam ajani yāyāvarakule ||

'This illustrious man (Rājaçekhara) was born in the Yāyāvara family; to which belonged Akālajalada, like a host of virtues incarnate; and Surānanda, whose words are worthy of being drunk in by the ears; not to speak of others, such as Tarala and Kavirāja.' See Aufrecht, p. 77. Pischel, p. 1223, gives a slightly different translation, and remarks that the verse does not prove that Tarala and Kavirāja belonged to Rājaçekhara's family.

[1] The dynasties of the Kanarese districts of the Bombay Presidency from the earliest historical times to the Musalman conquest of A.D. 1318. Gazetteer of the Bombay Presidency. Vol. i., Part ii., Bombay 1896, p. 414.

But in a stanza, given by Peterson in his Second Report, p. 59, and probably written by the younger Rājaçekhara, it is expressly stated that Tarala was a yāyāvara.

Akālajalada was the great-grandfather of Rājaçekhara: see Bālar. i. 13[1]; Viddh. i. 5[8]; Aufrecht, p. 4. Stanza 777 of Çārṅgadhara's Paddhati is attributed to Akālajalada; and as his name is ingeniously woven into the stanza, with a double or hidden meaning (see Aufrecht, p. 4), we can hardly doubt the correctness of the attribution. The Subhāṣitāvali contains the same stanza, as no. 843; and here it is attributed to a "Southerner," dākṣiṇātya.[1] But whether this Southern poet, Akālajalada, the author of the stanza, is identical with the ancestor of Rājaçekhara is not yet proved. According to a stanza ascribed to Rājaçekhara in the Sūktimuktāvali, the dramatist Kādambarīrāma plagiarized from Akālajalada and thereby achieved fame as an excellent writer. See Peterson's introduction to the Subhāṣitāvali, p. 102.

Surānanda must also have been a poet, as may be inferred from the epithets given to him by Rājaçekhara, in the Raṇavigraha stanza (above, p. 182), and as is directly stated in the stanza just quoted (p. 182).

Tarala's name occurs in a stanza which, in the Sūktimuktāvali and the Harihārāvali, is given under Rājaçekhara's name:

> Yāyāvarakulaçreṇer hārayaṣṭeç ca maṇḍanam |
> suvarṇabandharuciras Taralas taralo yathā ||

'As the central gem, brilliant with golden setting, adorns the necklace, thus Tarala, illustrious on account of his Suvarṇabandha, adorns the Yāyāvara family.' Suvarṇabandha, with its double meaning, seems to contain an allusion to some work of Tarala.

As for Kavirāja, this must mean a different person from the author of the Rāghavapāṇḍavīya, if indeed the word is here used as a proper name. It is, of course, often merely a honorific title, and is applied to various poets. Thus Rājaçekhara himself, according to Karp. i. 9[a], was successively called bālakavi and kavirāja; and, at Viddh. i. 5[2], he calls himself Kavirājaçekhara — cp. Bilhari inscription, p. 182. See Pischel, Die Hofdichter, p. 37.

[1] The Padyāvalī contains a stanza (or more) ascribed to a poet "of the Deccan": see Pischel, Die Hofdichter des Lakṣmaṇasena, Göttingen, 1893, p. 10.

3. Rājaçekhara's Extant Writings.

Four plays are extant which are ascribed to Rājaçekhara. Their names are as follows:

1. Karpūra-mañjarī.
2. Viddha-çālabhañjikā, or 'The Statue.'
3. Bāla-rāmāyaṇa.
4. Bāla-bhārata or Pracaṇḍa-pāṇḍava.

Karpūra-mañjarī [= Camphor-cluster]. — This is, in my opinion, the oldest of our poet's plays: see below. It is called a Saṭṭaka. This word is said, at i. 6, to mean a kind of Nāṭikā where the praveçakas and viṣkambhakas are wanting. The Sāhityadarpaṇa (no. 542) adds that it is written entirely in Prākrit; that the "marvellous flavor" (adbhuta rasa) prevails in it; that its acts are named javanikā; and that it, in other particulars, is like the Nāṭikā; further (no. 429), that the title of a Saṭṭaka, as well as that of a Nāṭikā, is to be taken from the name of the heroine. And the Karpūramañjarī and the Ratnāvalī are cited as titles exemplifying the rule.

The Karpūramañjarī contains four acts called javanikāntara. It tells us how the king Caṇḍapāla marries Karpūramañjarī, the daughter of the Kuntala king, and thus becomes a paramount sovereign. The jealousy of the queen, and the machinations that bring the king and the heroine together, form the plot of the play. The adbhuta rasa is represented by the sorcerer Bhāiravānanda and his tricks. See Apte, p. 22 f.; Lévi, p. 249 f.

That the Karpūramañjarī is the oldest of Rājaçekhara's known plays I am inclined to infer from the circumstance that it was not, like the other plays, acted at the request of the king, but by the wish of the poet's wife Avantisundarī.

The Karpūramañjarī was edited for the first time by Vāmanācārya in The Pandit, 1866–72. Then follows the edition by Durgāprasāda and Paraba, 1887.

I have seen two paraphrases of the Karpūramañjarī in modern vernaculars. The first is a Hindī translation by the well-known poet Hariçcandra (cp. Grierson, The modern vernacular literature of Hindustan, Calcutta, 1889, no. 581), and was printed in the year 1883. The other is a Marāṭhī translation, Bombay, 1890. See the chronological list under 1883 and 1890.

Of the existing commentaries, the best known is that of Vāsudeva, which Durgāprasāda and Paraba have subjoined in their edition. It is hardly more than a Sanskrit paraphrase, and is of relatively small value. Much better is the South Indian commentary of Kṛṣṇasūnu. Pītāmbara's Jalpatiratnamañjarī is also of some use. The commentary of Dharmadāsa is known to me by name only. It is quoted by Durgāprasāda and Paraba in their edition of the play. For further information, see the critical account of the mss., p. xxiii ff.

Viddha-çālabhañjikā. — The next production of our poet seems to have been the Viddha-çālabhañjikā or The Statue. This is a Nāṭikā in four acts, and the author seems, in several points, to have imitated the Ratnāvalī. In one passage (iv. 1^{19} = p. 113. 12 ff. in the edition of Ārte) the plays of Çrīharṣa are perhaps directly alluded to. The plot is quite similar to that of the Karpūramañjarī. The King Candravarman of Lāṭa has no son. He therefore tries to pass off as a boy his only daughter Mṛgāñkāvalī, and sends her under the name of Mṛgāñkavarman to the Queen of King Vidyādharamalla.

In the first act, Vidyādharamalla tells the Vidūṣaka that he has, in a dream, seen a beautiful girl ; but that, as he tried to catch her, she escaped, leaving her necklace. This was, as we learn in the third act, no dream, but an actual fact brought about by the contrivings of the King's minister, who knew who the disguised "boy" in the Queen's apartment was. An attendant persuades "the boy" to enter the King's sleeping-room, telling her that she would there meet the god of love. A seer had already foretold that whoever should take Mṛgāñkāvalī to wife would become a universal emperor. And on this account the minister desired to bring it about that his royal master and Mṛgāñkāvalī should fall in love with each other. Afterwards, the King sees in the garden some maidens amusing themselves at swinging, and among them recognizes the face he saw in his dream. He is now thoroughly enamored. In a pleasure house he beholds a picture and a statue of Mṛgāñkāvalī, and puts the necklace on the statue. At last he gets a glance of the girl herself, but she immediately disappears.

In the second act, after some irrelevant incidents, the King again beholds his beloved, and learns that she is, in her turn, enamored of him.

In the third act, after a long dialogue, and a trick played by the Vidūṣaka upon the Queen's confidante Mekhalā, we find the King and the Heroine together in the garden. But their meeting is brought to a sudden end by the announcement of the approach of the Queen.

In the fourth act, the Vidūṣaka and his wife appear on the stage, the latter, asleep. In her sleep, she discloses the fact that the Queen is intending to make the King marry Mṛgāñkavarman in the disguise of a woman, in order to get her revenge for the trick played upon Mekhalā. Further on, the wedding takes place; and now a messenger comes from Candravarman to announce that his master has got a son, and that the supposed Mṛgāñkavarman is in fact the daughter of Candravarman.

A good résumé of the play is given by Wilson, ii. 354–60. See also Apte, p. 24; Lévi, p. 245. Apte passes judgment on the literary merit of the play at p. 28.[1]

The play was represented at the request of çrīyuvarājadeva (i. 5[4]), that is, according to Wilson, the heir-apparent, probably at his installation in the joint administration of the government. The heir-apparent must be Mahīpāla. But, as shown above (p. 181), there is some evidence that Rājaçekhara was connected with the Cedi princes. It is therefore possible that Yuvarājadeva may be one of the Cedi princes, either Keyūravarṣa Yuvarājadeva I., who reigned about the middle of the tenth century, or Yuvarājadeva II., who was a contemporary of king Vākpati of Mālava. See Kielhorn, Epigraphia Indica, ii. 304; and cp. C. Mabel Duff, Chronology of India, p. 293.

The Viddhaçālabhañjikā was edited by Vāmanācārya (1866–71), Jīvānanda Vidyāsāgara (1873 and 1883), and Bhāskar Rāmchandra Ārte (1886). Ārte has subjoined the commentary of Nārāyaṇa Dīkṣita, the son of Rañganātha Dīkṣita and a pupil of Dāmodara. Nārāyaṇa was a native of Mahārāṣṭra; according to Aufrecht, he lived in the eighteenth century.

Bāla-rāmāyaṇa. — This is a Nāṭaka in ten acts. Of all Indian dramas it is probably the greatest in bulk. The prologue alone, as Apte observes, is as long as an act, and each act has the bulk of a Nāṭikā like the Ratnāvalī. The number of stanzas is 741. It is hard to see how so lengthy a play could well have been brought out upon the stage. And the author himself seems to have felt this difficulty; for he says (at i. 12): "If some wise critic should find it to be a fault of this Bālarāmāyaṇa that it is too long, that acute critic should be asked whether or not some virtue is to be found in the *diction*. And if this be the case, well then, let him *read* and enjoy my six compositions." It is here of no importance whether the prologue is a later addition to the play, as is made probable by Pischel, p. 1227. On the other hand, we may conclude from the words of i. 1[2] that the play was really represented at the request of the king Mahendrapāla.

[1] [Without unfairness to Rājaçekhara, non-Sanskritists can hardly accept Apte's strictures until some one has made a sympathetic translation and interpretation of the piece. Such a treatment is in prospect from the pen of Mr. Montgomery Schuyler, Jr., a pupil of my friend, Professor Jackson of Columbia University. — C. R. L.]

The Bālarāmāyaṇa relates the whole history of Rāma from Sītā's svayaṁvara to the slaying of Rāvaṇa and the return to Ayodhyā after Sītā had passed through the ordeal of fire. Rāvaṇa is from the very beginning represented as the jealous rival of Rāma and as taking a part in the svayaṁvara; and his love and longing play a much more prominent rôle than his ferocity and cruelty. The banishment of Rāma is, in the Bālarāmāyaṇa, brought about by Çūrpaṇakhā and other demons under the disguise of Daçaratha and Kāikeyī.

A full analysis of the play is hardly called for. It would involve a repetition of well-known incidents. The reader may consult Lévi, p. 272 ff.; Apte, p. 31 ff.; and Baumgartner, Das Rāmāyaṇa und die Rāma-literatur der Inder, Freiburg im Breisgau, 1894, p. 126.

As for his sources, the poet seems to give some hints concerning them in the stanza at Bālar. i. 16 and Bālabh. i. 12, which is ascribed to Dāivajña:

babhūva Valmīkabhavaḥ purā kavis
tataḥ prapede bhuvi Bhartṛmeṇṭhatām |
sthitaḥ punar yo Bhavabhūtirekhayā
sa vartate saṁprati Rājaçekharaḥ ||

'He who in former days was the poet sprung from the ant-hill (Vālmīki) and subsequently assumed on earth the form of Bhartṛmeṇṭha and who again appeared in the person of Bhavabhūti, the same is now Rājaçekhara.'

That our poet is largely indebted to the works of Vālmīki and Bhavabhūti is clearly shown by Apte. For the most part he drew upon the Rāmāyaṇa of Vālmīki; and where he deviated, "he clearly imitated Bhavabhūti; and there are unmistakable signs that he had the Mahávíracharita before him at the time of writing this play [cp. e.g. Bālar. x. 65 and Mahāv. i. 55]. . . . In the sixth act, he follows Bhavabhúti in exculpating Daçaratha's wife. . . . The scene of Lanka and Alaka is a clear imitation of Bhavabhúti etc." See Apte, p. 37, 38. Lévi (p. 292 f.) speaks of Rājaçekhara's relation to Bhavabhūti, and shows (Appendice, p. 37) that the former occasionally imitated Kālidāsa.

Bhartṛmeṇṭha is less known. Cp. Peterson and Durgāprasāda, Introduction, p. 92; Bühler, Detailed report of a tour in search of Sanskrit mss., Bombay, 1877, p. 42; Aufrecht, ZDMG. 36. 368; Lévi, p. 183. Bhartṛmeṇṭha seems also to be called Hastipaka, which word is equivalent to Meṇṭha. His kāvya, Hayagrīvavadha, is known from the Rājataraṅgiṇī and from quotations. Now I think that Lévi was right in inferring from the verse before us that Bhartṛmeṇṭha has, in some way or other, treated the history of Rāma. But I cannot deem Lévi's supposition (Appendice, p. 47), that the work in which Bhartṛmeṇṭha did so may be the Bhaṭṭikāvya, to be a probable one. The same opinion that Lévi held, had been previously expressed by Borooah, p. 20.

Burnell's opinion of the Bālarāmāyaṇa is that "it has nothing remarkable about it but its prosy length." See Classified Index, p. 169. But it must be admitted that there are several passages of great lyrical beauty in it, and that the poet's mastery of the several languages is better shown in the Bālarāmāyaṇa than in any other of his plays.

The Bālarāmāyaṇa was edited by Govinda Deva, Benares, 1869, and by Jīvānanda, Calcutta, 1884. No complete commentary is known to exist.

Bāla-bhārata. — Rājaçekhara's last work is the Bāla-bhārata, or, as it is sometimes called, the Pracaṇḍa-pāṇḍava. Both names are used in the play itself: see i. 8[b] and [d]. It is a Nāṭaka (see text, i. 8); and as such, it ought to contain at least five acts. In fact, however, it has only two. It seems accordingly to be incomplete, and was very likely "projected on the same plan as the Bāla-rāmāyaṇa" (Apte, p. 39).

As the poet himself tells us, the Bāla-bhārata is founded on the Mahābhārata. See i. 4, where Rājaçekhara implores Vyāsa to grant him the help of his muse. The play has three stanzas taken directly from the Mahā-bhārata. These are: i. 18 = MBh. i. 62. 53 (=2333); ii. 5 = MBh. i. 1. 111 (= 109) or v. 29. 53 (= 861); and ii. 6 = i. 1. 110 (=108) or v. 29. 52 (=860).

In the first act, the svayaṁvara of Drāupadī is described. In the second act we learn how Yudhiṣṭhira lost everything in gambling; how Duḥçāsana dragged Drāupadī by the hair of the head; and how at last the Pāṇḍavas depart to the forest.

For an account of the contents, see Apte, p. 40–41. See also Wilson, ii. 361. "The story is not very interestingly told; . . . but the verses are smooth and flowing," says Apte.

The play was represented at Mahodaya (Kanauj) before Mahīpāla, then paramount sovereign over Āryāvarta, and it appears to have been the last work of our poet.

The Bāla-bhārata was edited by Cappeller, Strassburg, 1885. See A. Weber's notice of the edition in Indische Studien, xviii. 481–3. It was also edited by Durgāprasād and Parab, Bombay, 1887, in the Kāvya-mālā. In this latter edition, after stanza i. 32, only the chāyā of the Prākrit passages is given.

4. Lost Works and the Anthologies.

A Tradition of More than Four Works. — Rājaçekhara speaks of "our six works" at Bālar. i. 12, as we saw, p. 186. Four of these have been discussed. Of the other two we have at present no knowledge. If we may trust the statement made at Karp. i. 9, that the poet had already achieved eminence when he wrote the Karpūramañjarī, it may be that these other two works preceded the Karpūramañjarī and were his earliest productions. And it is of course possible that they are still extant under some other author-name (such, for instance, as Candra-cūḍa), equivalent in meaning to "Rājaçekhara," but quite unlike it in form.

Fragments in the Anthologies. — The Anthologies give a considerable number of stanzas which they ascribe to Rājaçekhara. It may be that some of these are taken from "these other two works." And it is worth while to assemble them here, either as a help for future students in the identification of the two works, if they are still extant; or else as fragments, if they are lost.

My collections are made from two anthologies: the Paddhati of Çārṅgadhara, and the Subhāṣitāvali of Vallabhadeva. It is convenient to have their dates given here. Çārṅgadhara's work was written about 1363 A.D. (Grierson, Modern Vernacular Literature of Hindustan, p. 6). Vallabhadeva flourished probably between 1400 and 1450 A.D. (Bühler, Kunstpoesie, p. 71). I give first the twenty-five pratīkas of the twenty-four stanzas which I have identified as parts of Rājaçekhara's four known plays; and then those of the ten stanzas which I have not been able to trace in Rājaçekhara's writings.

The few stanzas from Vallabhadeva's collection are marked "Val."; the rest are from Çārṅgadhara's. In order to avoid "overrunning" of lines, I abbreviate Viddh. by V.; Bāla-r. by R.; Bāla-bh. by Bh.; and Karp. by K.

Anthology-stanzas (24) identified in Rājaçekhara's Writings. — We will first examine the stanzas given by the Anthologies with or without explicit statement of authorship, and traceable to the writings of our poet.

The following eleven are ascribed by the Anthologist to Rājaçekhara, either expressly by name, or else by reference to one of his plays, and are found in his writings:

3659. taraṁgaya dṛço. = V. iii. 27; R. iii. 25; Bh. i. 31.
3750. nirvyājā dayite. = R. iv. 44.
3757. abhyutthānam upāgate. = R. iv. 43.
3837. dhatte pañkajinītale. = V. i. 43.
3928. vaktraçrījita-. = V. ii. 11.
3936. vahneḥ çaktir. = R. v. 35.

Val. 322. udanvacchinnā. = R. i. 8. See Bhartṛhari, and below, p. **190.**
Val. 1411. dāhombhaḥ. = V. ii. 21. Cp. K. ii. 29.
Val. 2223. bhindānaḥ sundarīṇām. = V. i. 12. See below.
Val. 2281 = Val. 3446. lokottaraṁ caritam. = R. ii. 51.
Val. 2282. = pṛthvi sthirā bhava. = R. i. 48.

The following eleven, accredited by the anthologist, Çārṅgadhara, to "Somebody" (*Kasyacit*, or the like), that is, given as anonymous verses, are found in Rājaçekhara's writings :

1099. yasya vajramaṇer bhede. = R. iii. 66.
3077. kulagurur abalānām. "kasyāpi." = V. i. 1.
3282. padbhyām muktās. = Bh. i. 28.
3373. tad vaktraṁ yadi. = V. i. 14 ; R. ii. 17.
3516. upaprākārāgram. = V. i. 31.
3591. sāirandhrīkarakṛṣṭa-. = V. ii. 23.
3719. vrajaty aparavāridhim. = V. iv. 1.
[3722. (=Val. 2223, above.) bhindāno māninīnām. = V. i. 12.]
3816. ye dolākelikārāḥ. = V. i. 27 ; cp. R. x. 55.
3912. celāñcalena. = V. ii. 9.
3929. amandamaṇi-. = V. ii. 6.

The stanza *dṛçā dagdham* is given as an anonymous one by Vallabhadeva, no. 1309 ; while Çārṅgadhara (no. 3078) ascribes it to Kṣemendra (about 1037 A.D. !). As a matter of fact, it is found more than a century earlier, at Viddh. i. 2. (See also Sprüche.)

Three of Rājaçekhara's stanzas occur in one recension or another of the Çatakas of Bhartṛhari (about 650 A.D.?). Did our dramatist take them from his predecessor? or were they taken from Rājaçekhara by some later redactor of the Çatakas and added thereto (as was the case with Kālidāsa's *anāghrātam puṣpam*)? Apte discusses the question at p. 52 and deems the latter alternative the more likely. Vallabhadeva ascribes the first to **Rājaçekhara, see above.** For detailed references, see Sprüche, where all **three are given.** The stanzas are :–

Bālar. i. 8, udanvacchinnā bhūḥ (see above) ;
Bālar. iii. 17, sthitiḥ puṇye 'raṇye ;
Bālar. vii. 40, vahati bhuvanaçreṇīm.

Anthology-Stanzas (10), **"of Rājaçekhara," not yet traced.**—There remain a few stanzas which the anthologies ascribe to Rājaçekhara, but which have not yet been traced by me to any of his known works. They are :

85. taṁ vande padmasadmānam.
251. nūnaṁ dugdhābdhi-. (See Indische Sprüche, 3806.)

3423. āhāre viratiḥ. (Sprüche, 1079.) = Val. 3485, as anonymous.
3926. cañcallolāñcalāni.
Val. 2563. indor lakṣma.
Val. 3046. dātur vāridharasya.
174. trayo 'gnayas trayo vedāḥ.
188. Bhāso Rāmila-Somilāu.
189. aho prabhāvo vāgdevyāḥ.
190. Sarasvatīpavitrāṇām.

The first of these ten looks like the introductory stanza of some lost work. The Rājaçekhara to whom the last four are ascribed is, I opine, the younger Rājaçekhara, of later date than our dramatist (see p. 196).

5. Rājaçekhara and the Prākrit Literature.

The Literary Prākrits and the Real Vernaculars. — Rājaçekhara's writings would probably be of less importance to us if we were better informed about the history of Prākrit literature. But on this subject our knowledge is exceedingly limited. The word Prākrit itself has different meanings. Thus in modern Indian books, we find it used in the sense of vernacular; but its general use is to designate the literary dialcets described by the Prākrit grammarians. These dialects were not real vernaculars, and are clearly distinguished from them by native writers, the literary dialects being called Prākrits, while the spoken vernaculars are called Apabhrançās or Deçībhāṣās.

The Prākrits are, of course, developed from Apabhrançās, and the first beginnings of Prākrit literature must therefore be traced back to the old literature in the vernaculars; but this task still lies beyond the reach of our abilities. From a comparative analysis of the ancient literary remains of India, it must be concluded that, from the earliest times, there were many stanzas current among the people, relating old legends and traditional tales, and that many of those stanzas were current in the old vernaculars. Most of them are probably incorporated in the great Indian epics, and our principal knowledge of them must be derived from those sources. Such stanzas are alluded to and quoted as early as in the time of the Brāhmaṇas; and several Vedic hymns must be reckoned to that branch of literature. But this question is connected with the history of Indian literature in general and cannot be discussed here. Our present inquiries must be restricted to the poetical literature in Prākrit proper, and I must therefore leave out of account the large Pāli literature, which has a history of its own, and also the literature of the Jainas, though this sect has exerted the preponderating influence upon the development of Prākrit literature in general. Thus most of the authors who have written on Prākrit grammar and lexicography are Jainas. And the circumstance that the Jainas chose the Māhārāṣṭrī for their literary compositions, contributed greatly to the development of that language for literary uses.

On the other hand, the Jainas cannot be supposed to have written in a language not before used in literature, and modern inquiries point to the conclusion that a large poetical literature existed in Prākrit, though only a small portion of it has come down to us. The reason for this fact is not very hard to find. The golden age of Prākrit literature falls in the time before the Sanskrit literature had reached its classical perfection. The great gap in the history of that literature, between the end of the epic period and the epoch which Max Müller called the renaissance of Sanskrit literature, has proved to be partly an illusion, and we now know that Sanskrit literature dates much farther back than was formerly supposed. But its fuller development at the hands of the great mediæval poets of India absorbed all the interest of the educated classes, and to this day the systematic searches for mss. in India have often had Sanskrit literature chiefly in view.

Early Prākrit Lyrics. — The oldest poetry of India is contained in the Vedic hymns and belongs to the religious branch of lyrics. In later times, we find this branch of literature represented by the poems of the different Indian sects, the religious çatakas, the stotras, and stutis. A good deal of this literature is written in Prākrit, but must be treated in connection with the religious history of India, especially that of the Jains. It is in the secular lyrics that the Indian literature has reached its highest perfection. This literature has not produced many complete works, but is generally contained in numerous detached verses, each giving a little genre-picture of Indian life. Most of these verses are erotic, and are generally admired by the critics.

Hāla's "Seven Centuries." — Such verses were, in early times, collected into anthologies, often called çatakas or centuries. The most ancient extant anthology that we know is the Sattasaī or the "Seven Centuries" of Hāla. This work is entirely written in Māhārāṣṭrī Prākrit, and we have no knowledge of the existence of any work, of that kind and of equal age, written in Sanskrit. Hāla is another name of Sātavāhana, a name which often occurs in the Andhrabhṛtya dynasty. Hāla was probably not himself the compiler of the Sattasaī, but only the compiler's patron. The time of his life cannot be fixed with certainty, but he probably belongs to the first centuries of our era, and he must have lived a long time before Bāṇa, who, in his Harṣacarita, Introduction, verse 13, praises the Sattasaī. In Hāla's anthology, the author's name is quoted after many of the verses, and from this fact we may conclude that Prākrit lyrics have a history which goes back to a time long before Hāla. Unfortunately we do not know anything but the names of some of these poets. Nor are we much better informed as to the later development of this branch of Prākrit literature.

Jayavallabha's Vajjālagga. — Bhaṇḍarkar, Report for 1883–84, p. 17, notices a second anthology, the Vajjālagga, composed by the Çvetāmbara Jain, Jayavallabha. I cannot, from the materials at my disposal, fix his time; but the commentary of Ratnadeva is dated in the year 1393, which must, according to Bhaṇḍarkar, be of the Vikrama era, and the same scholar has found verses from the Gauḍavaho in the collection. The name Vajjālagga is derived from the systematic arrangement in vrajyās or chapters, each treating a different subject. There are 48 such chapters, which are enumerated in 5 gāthās. The total number of verses is 704; and, judging by the specimen given by Bhaṇḍarkar, the Vajjālagga must be much like to the Sattasaī. For the form of the title, cp. Bhaṇḍarkar, l.c., p. 324, comm. on stanza 4; and HD. 7. 17. The language is the Māhārāṣṭrī.

I am not aware of the existence of other poetical anthologies in Prākrit.

Ānandavardhana's Visamabāṇalīlā. — Ānandavardhana, who, according to the Rājataraṅgiṇī, v. 34, obtained fame under the king Avantivarman of Kashmir (855–84), wrote a Prākrit poem, the Visamabāṇalīlā. We know this work from quotations in the author's rhetorical work, the Dhvanyāloka. These quotations seem to show that the Visamabāṇalīlā was also an anthology, probably written for the use of poets (kavivyutpattaye, Dhvanyāloka, iv. 7).

Ānandavardhana quotes verses in Apabhraṅça and may have composed his anthology also in Apabhraṅça. The quotations by Hemacandra must be taken from some such work, but we do not know anything more about it, and the Apabhraṅça literature lies outside of our subject. Nor can I here dwell on works such as the Ṛṣabhapañcāçikā of Dhanapāla (tenth century), because it belongs to the religious literature of the Jains.

Guṇāḍhya's Bṛhatkathā. — The lyrical Prākrit literature is, for the most part, written in Māhārāṣṭrī. But the first name which occurs in the poetical Prākrit literature, is connected with another dialect, the Pāiçācī.

The poet Guṇāḍhya is said to have written his Bṛhatkathā in that language. Guṇāḍhya is commonly supposed to have lived in the first centuries of our era. See Bühler, Report, p. 47. The Bṛhatkathā was not an original work of Guṇāḍhya, but a compilation of folk-tales then current, such as the Pañcatantra and the Vetālapañcaviñçati, which collections are, to this day, widely spread in the modern vernaculars of India. The work itself has not been found, but we know it pretty well from the two translations, one by Kṣemendra, the Bṛhatkathāmañjarī, and the other by Somadeva, the Kathāsaritsāgara. According to the testimony of those authors and of Daṇḍin, it was written in the Pāiçācī language. This dialect is described by Hemacandra in his Prākrit grammar, iv. 303 ff., and it is probable that Hemacandra made actual use of a copy of the Bṛhatkathā. See Pischel, De Grammaticis Prācriticis, Vratislaviae, 1874, p. 33. Bühler, also, when in India, was told that manuscripts of the work were still extant.

The Pāiçācī seems to be more closely connected with the really spoken vernaculars of ancient India than is any other literary Prākrit. And that branch of literature which is represented by the Bṛhatkathā must always have been popular. In some of the Sanskrit collections of folk-tales we also find verses in the old vernaculars, the Apabhrañças. But the history of this literature is too closely connected with the general literary and linguistic history of India to be dealt with here, and we shall only state the fact that the earliest collection of folk-tales of which we have certain knowledge was written in Prākrit.

In the Mahākāvya, on the other hand, the priority must unquestionably be assigned to the Sanskrit literature. Aside from the Rāmāyaṇa, no Prākrit kāvya can claim an antiquity equal to that of the Buddhacarita of Açvaghoṣa.

Prākrit Kāvyas. Rāvaṇa-vaha. — The oldest Prākrit kāvya is the Setubandha. This poem, whose Prākrit name is Rāvaṇavaha or Dahamuhavaha, contains in 15 Sargas the story of Rāma, from the starting of the monkey army to the slaying of Rāvaṇa. It was formerly ascribed to Kālidāsa; so by the commentator Rāmadāsa, who lived under the emperor Akbar. And also in the colophons the name of Kālidāsa occurs. But tradition generally ascribes the poem to Pravarasena. Thus Bāṇa does, in the Harṣacarita. Introduction, verse 14, and Kṣemendra, in the Aucityavicāracarcā, verse 16. According to Rāvaṇavaha, i. 9, the work seems to have been completed at the request of a king by some poet. Pravarasena was therefore probably a king. We know four kings by that name. As the Rāvaṇavaha is mentioned by Daṇḍin and Bāṇa, it cannot be later than the sixth century. Tradition seems to point to one of the two Kashmirian kings of that name. The poem was perhaps written on the occasion of the building of a great bridge over the Vitastā or Jehlam by Pravarasena II. See Rājataraṅgiṇī, iii. 354. This king is now commonly placed in the sixth century after Christ.

It is likely that Pravarasena was not himself the author, but that the work was merely dedicated to him. We cannot ascertain who the real author was. But it is not probable that we have to do with a work by Kālidāsa. The excessive use of compounds is not in accord with Kālidāsa's style; and it would be difficult to understand why Bāṇa and Kṣemendra did not ascribe the work to Kālidāsa, if it were really written by him.

Bappai-rāa's Gauḍa-vaha. — Another Prākrit kāvya is the Gauḍavaha of Bappai-rāa, written about 750 A.D. and in celebration of the poet's patron, king Yaçovarman of Kanauj. This poem seems to have come down to us in mutilated form. The different parts of it are very loosely connected, and the theme itself, the slaying of the Gauḍa king, is hardly more than vaguely alluded to. The king Yaçovarman was subjugated by the king Lalitāditya of Kashmir (about 726 A.D.), and Bappairāa therefore was a contemporary of Bhavabhūti. See Rājataraṅgiṇī, iv. 144 His Sanskrit name is Vākpatirājā, probably a translation of the Prākrit name.

Ānandavardhana, in his Dhvanyāloka, quotes verses from a third Prākrit kāvya, the Harivijaya of Sarvasena, which work is not otherwise known.

Rājaçekhara is not known to have written other works than dramas.

Prākrit Drama: Saṭṭakas. — The Indian drama seems to have its root partly in Sanskrit, partly in Prākrit literature. The one play which is written in Prākrit exclusively is the Karpūramañjarī. But we are, I think, right in concluding from the definition of the word saṭṭaka, given in the work itself, that the Karpūramañjarī was not the first composition of its kind And the word saṭṭaka occurs, in the form sāḍaka, as early as on the Bharhut stūpa. The quotation from Tagore, given by Lévi, ii. 5, may help us to understand the origin of the saṭṭaka. In most characteristics it agrees with the Nāṭikā, but was perhaps classed separately, not only because it was written entirely in Prākrit, but also because a distinct kind of dancing was used in it.

Karpūra-mañjarī the only Saṭṭaka Extant. — At all events, Rājaçekhara's work is the only extant pure Prākrit drama; and his chief importance in the history of Prākrit literature lies in the fact that he has given to us a unique specimen of a kind of literature which has perhaps a history of its own.

This Play Important for the History of the Drama.—The Karpūramañjarī is also of importance for the history of the Indian drama in general. To judge from some indications in the rhetorical literature, we must suppose that, in early times, a sthāpaka (as well as the sūtradhāra) had something to do with the arrangement of the play. But in most of the known plays, the sthāpaka has disappeared. In his recension of Lévi's book, Le théâtre Indien, in the Göttingische Gelehrte Anzeigen, 1891, p. 361, Pischel has suggested that this fact is owing to a reformation by Bhāsa (cp. Pischel, ibidem, 1883, p. 1234).

In the Karpūramañjarī we still find the sthāpaka in action. Most of the mss., it is true, have substituted the more usual word sūtradhāra for sthāpaka, where the latter occurs; but it clearly appears from the whole arrangement of the introduction that this proceeding is false. In i. 12^3, we learn that the "ajjo" is busy with his wife in the tiring-room. There is no question that the word ajja or ārya in this passage means the sūtradhāra. It therefore follows that the sūtradhāra was not on the stage between the end of the nāndī and that of the prastāvanā. We must accordingly conclude that those manuscripts are right which represent a sthāpaka as coming on the stage immediately after the nāndī.

It may also be noted here that this same passage, i. 12^3, clearly shows that the female rôles were sometimes played by female actors.

The nāndī itself is of interest in the Karpūramañjarī, because verses are recited after it. This is a curious fact. We find the same again in the Pārvatīpariṇayanāṭaka (Pischel, l.c., p. 360.) The Karpūramañjarī, accordingly, may be consulted with profit by the student of the general history of the Indian drama; and it is not unlikely that the Saṭṭaka has on this point preserved traces of a more ancient stage of development in this branch of literature.

6 Other Poets mentioned by Rājaçekhara.

Several Other Poets are occasionally mentioned in the Writings of Rājaçekhara.—Many of the memorial verses which occur in the anthologies, and are ascribed to him, were most probably not written by our poet. Some of them are, according to the Harihārāvali, taken from the "Bhojaprabandha of Rājaçekhara." It is, accordingly, probable that they are extracts from the Prabandhakoça of the *younger* Rājaçekhara, which was written in 1347. Most of those verses are collected in alphabetical arrangement, after the name of the poets mentioned, in the introduction to the edition of the Karpūramañjarī in the Kāvyamālā. In this place I can only take notice of the poets alluded to in Rājaçekhara's plays.

Hariuḍḍha, Ṇandiuḍḍha, Poṭṭisa, and Hāla are mentioned as poets at Karp. i. 20[20]. The Tanjore mss. of this passage, however, have, instead, the names Haribamhasiddhi (?), Oḍḍīsa, Pālittaa, Campaarāa, and Mallasehara. With reference to these names, see Pischel, Göttingische Gelehrte Anzeigen, 1891, p. 365.

Aparājita is mentioned at Karp. i. 8[3], as a poet contemporary with Rājaçekhara, and as speaking in terms of highest praise of the merits and achievements of Rājaçekhara. In the Tanjore mss., Aparājita bears the surname Babbararāa. He is said to be the author of a Mṛgāṅkalekhākathā. This work is not otherwise known, but was probably a composition founded on a tale like that of Kathāsaritsāgara 65. 221 ff. Stanzas by Bhaṭṭāparājita occur as no. 1024 of the Subhāṣitāvali (see also the Introduction thereto, p. 103) and in the Padyāvali.

Çaṁkaravarman or Kṛṣṇaçaṁkaraçarman was another contemporary poet. His name is mentioned in the first form at Bālar. i. 16[2]; and in the second at Viddh. i. 6[1]. He is called sabhya in the Bālarāmāyaṇa, and goṣṭhīgariṣṭha in the Viddhaçālabhañjikā; but he is not otherwise known. A Çaṁkaravarman occurs among the poets of the Sūktimuktāvali

Dāivajña is mentioned at Bālar. i. 15[2] and Bālabh. i. 11[1]. This may be a proper name and refer to some contemporary poet. Or it may be a simple appellative, to be rendered by 'fortune-teller' (so Fleet, p. 176).

7. Mentions of Rājaçekhara in the Literature.

By Vasukalpa, Abhinanda, and Somadeva. — According to Aufrecht in the Catalogus catalogorum, p. 502, Rājaçekhara is mentioned in the Sūktimuktāvali as a contemporary poet by Vasukalpa and Abhinanda. We do not know anything about Vasukalpa, but we have two poets named Abhinanda. The one is known as the author of a kāvya, the Rāmacarita, and was the son of Çatānanda The other was called Gāuḍābhinanda, and was a son of Jayanta Vṛttikāra. His great-great-grandfather lived under king Muktāpīḍa Lalitāditya of Kashmir, whose accession, according to Bühler, cannot have taken place before 724. Gāuḍābhinanda must therefore have lived about the middle of the ninth century. He is known as the author of the Kādambarīkathāsāra and of the Yogavāsiṣṭhasāra. Bühler, Indian Antiquary, ii. 102 ff., thought the two Abhinandas to be one and the same. On that point, cp. Durgāprasāda and Paraba, Kāvyamālā, Part ii. 50. Abhinanda is also quoted, Suvṛttatilaka iii. 16, 29.

Rājaçekhara's name is further mentioned in Somadeva's Yaçastilaka-campū. According to the colophon, this work was written çaka 882 = A.D. 960. As mentioned above, we are told in the third āçvāsa that Rājaçekhara occasionally pays honor to the religion of the Jains. As far as I can see, these words cannot apply to the known works of the poet.

In the Daçarūpa and the Sarasvatī-kaṇṭhābharaṇa. — The Daçarūpa quotes Karp. i. 23 (iii. 14 = p. 117 in Hall's edition), Viddh. i. 31 (iv. 50 = p. 182), and Bālar. iv. 60 (ii. 2 = p. 62). The last passage is said to be taken from the Hanumannāṭaka — see Jīvānanda's ed., ii. 14.

From the Sarasvatī-kaṇṭhābharaṇa (ed. by Anundoram Borooah, Calcutta, 1883), I have noted the following quotations: Bālar. i. 42 (p 224); Bālar. iii. 25 = Viddh. iii. 27 = Bālabh. i. 31 (p. 214); Bālar. v. 8 = Viddh. iii. 2 (p. 315); Bālar. vi. 19 (p. 81); Bālar. vi. 34 (p. 26); Karp. i. 1 (p. 138); Karp. i. 19 (p. 348); Karp. i. 25 (p. 348); Karp. ii. 11 (p. 108); Karp. ii. 42 (p. 194); Viddh. i. 3 (p. 149); Viddh. i. 8 = Bālabh. i. 9 (p. 67); Viddh. i. 14 = Bālar. ii. 17 (p. 215) ; Viddh. i. 15 (p. 179); Viddh. i. 19 (p. 367); Viddh. i. 20 (p. 72); Viddh. i. 31 (p. 223); Viddh. iii. 5 (p. 104 and 214); Viddh. iii. 14 (p. 72). Cp. Colonel G. A. Jacob, Journal of the Royal Asiatic Society, 1897, p. 304 ff.

In Works of Kṣemendra. — Kṣemendra, also, in several of his works gives references from Rājaçekhara's plays. In the Āucityavicāracarcā, we find Bālar. i. 39 (v. 13); ii. 20 (v. 20); iv. 1 (v. 36); v. 11 (v. 14); x. 41 (v. 12); Bālabh. ii. 11 (v. 12); Karp. i. 18 (v. 18); and likewise the following stanzas which I cannot trace: citācakraṁ candraḥ (v. 15); strīṇāṁ madhye (v. 16); Karṇātīdaçanāñkitaḥ (v. 27). In the Kavikaṇṭhābharaṇa only one stanza by Rājaçekhara is quoted (nakhadalitaharidrāgranthigāure, 5. 1), and this one is not from his known works. In the Suvṛttatilaka, iii. 35, Rājaçekhara is praised for his ability in the Çārdūlavikrīdita metre; and from his works the following two passages are given, namely, Viddh. i. 30 (at ii. 23) and Bālar. i. 63 (at ii. 41).

In the Kāvya-prakāça, Prākṛta-piñgala, etc. — The Kāvya-prakāça also contains a number of citations from Rājaçekhara. Thus we find there Karp. i. 19, 20: ii 4, 9; Viddh. i. 2; etc. (cp. Jacob, l.c., 1898, pp. 294, 303, 305, 313). Further quotations from Rājaçekhara, and mentions of him, are found in the Prākṛtapiñgala (Karp. i. 4, 20. 22, 23, 26; ii. 5); Ganaratnamahodadhi (see Pischel, p. 1223); Hemacandra's Prākrit grammar (see Pischel, l.c.); Mañkha's Çrīkaṇṭhacarita (xxv 74); Abhinavagupta (see Jacob, l.c., 1897, p. 297); Ruyyaka (see Jacob, l.c., 1897.

p. 307); and in later works, such as the Kuvalayānanda, the Sāhityadarpaṇa, and Mārkaṇḍeya's Prākrit grammar; also in Kāleyakutūhala.

A special interest has been attached to the quotation in Kṣīrasvāmin's commentary on Amara i. 8[4], where, in speaking of the form gonasa, he quotes Viddh. i. 3 to show that the form gonāsa also is used in the same sense. Kṣīrasvāmin further quotes Viddh. i. 11 to show that tāraka is neuter as well as feminine. Cp. Apte, p. 6. Peterson identified the commentator Kṣīrasvāmin with Kṣīra, who is mentioned, Rājatar. iv. 489, as the tutor of king Jayāpīḍa; and thus he came to the conclusion that Rājaçekhara was much older than we now know him to be. Aufrecht on the other hand had already stated (ZDMG. 28. 104) that Kṣīrasvāmin must have lived in the eleventh century, since he quotes Bhoja and is himself quoted by Vardhamāna.

8. Rājaçekhara's Prākrit.

Rājaçekhara was, to use Apte's words, "a poet of great learning and much information." The poet himself seems to be very proud of his linguistic skill, as he directly calls himself sarvabhāṣāvicakṣaṇa (Bālar. i. 10[1]) or savvabhāsācadura (Karp. i. 7[1]). Bālar. i. 11, he mentions the different languages used in literary compositions: Sanskrit, Prākrit, Apabhrança, and Bhūtabhāṣā. As far as we know, he himself wrote only in Sanskrit and Prākrit. It would be out of place here to discuss his knowledge of Sanskrit. It must suffice to state that he shows a great proficiency in that language. I must here be contented to examine his Prākrit. The Prākrits of the plays, it must be remembered, were no really spoken vernaculars; but rather, essentially literary fictions founded on the vernaculars. They were perpetually influenced, not only by the Sanskrit, but also by the spoken languages. Most of the so-called deçī-words must be derived from this last source. Cp. S. P. Pandit's note to Dhruva's article on the Rise of the Drama, Transactions of the Ninth International Congress of Orientalists, i. 313.

Çaurasenī and Māhārāṣṭrī. — These are the only Prākrit dialects which occur in the writings of Rājaçekhara. Herein, therefore, he has not evinced a breadth of linguistic knowledge comparable with that of the author of the Mṛcchakaṭikā.

[Addition by the General Editor. — In order that this volume may be of service to students of Prākrit in America, to whom, for the most part, no help from a teacher and no elementary books will be accessible, I am constrained to make the following Addition. For a good general account of Prākrit, see Jacobi's article, "Prākrit Languages," in Johnson's Universal Cyclopædia.

The Çauraseni is used as the conversational dialect, that is, in the prose passages; while the Māhārāṣṭrī is regularly used in the stanzas. Upon this point the beginner should consult Jacobi, Introduction, §§ 9, 10. The chief distinctive peculiarities of the Çāurasenī are succinctly stated by Jacobi, pages LXX–LXXII. These the learner should study. I am convinced that the best basis for a clear understanding of the differences between the two dialects is afforded by some concrete examples. I have therefore thought it worth while to devote a little space to a collection of some of the doublets which actually occur in this play. In the first column is given the Sanskrit form; in the second, its Çāurasenī counterpart; and in the third, the Māhārāṣṭrī form.

Çāurasenī-Māhārāṣṭrī Doublets used in this Play.—

Sanskrit.	Çāurasenī. (Prose.)	Māhārāṣṭrī. (Verse.)
atha	adha	aha
tathā	tadhā	taha
yathā	jadhā	jahā
katham	kadhaṁ	kahaṁ
iha	idha	iha
tatas	tado	tao
etad	edaṁ	eaṁ
eti	edi	ei
jānāti	jāṇādi	jāṇāi
dadātu	dedu	deu
bhavati, -tu	bhodi, -du	hoi, hou
bhaviṣyati	bhavissadi	hohii
labhate	lahadi	lahai
vartate	vaṭṭadi	vaṭṭai
-vartatām	pavaṭṭadu	paaṭṭau
tiṣṭhati	ciṭṭhadi	ṭhāi
harati	haradi	harai
kathyatām	kadhīadu	kahijjau
kriyatām	karīadu	kijjau
dṛçyate	dīsadi	dīsai
bhaṇyate	bhaṇīadi	bhaṇṇai
kṛta	kida	kaa
gata	gada	gaa
jāta	jāda	jāa
jita	jida	jia
hita	hida	hia
ā-nīta	ā-ṇīda	ā-ṇīa

Sanskrit.	Çāurasenī. (Prose.)	Māhārāṣṭrī. (Verse.)
sthita	ṭhida	ṭhia
sthāpita	ṭhāvida	ṭhāvia
kalita	kalida	kalia
kvathita	kaḍhida	kaḍhia
ghaṭita	ghaḍida	ghaḍia
dayitā	daidā	daiā
puñkhita	puñkhida	puñkhia
bhūṣitā	bhūsidā	vi-hūsiā
bhṛta	bharida	bharia
ni-veçita	ṇi-vesida	ṇi-vesia
ava-tīrṇa	odiṇṇa	ava-iṇṇa
adbhuta	acc-abbhuda	abbhua
prasṛti	pasadi	pasai
prabhṛti	pahudi	pahui
prākṛta	pāuda	pāua
saṁskṛta	sakkada	sakkaa
manoratha	maṇoradha	maṇoraha
marakata	maragada	maragaa
mithuna	midhuṇa	mihuṇa
ratna	radaṇa	raaṇa
rati	radi	rai
rīti	rīdi	rīi
latā	ladā	laā
vāta	vāda	vāa
çata	sada	saa
sarasvatī	sarassadī	sarassaī
sarit	sura-saridā	sariā
manmatha	mammadha	vammaha
divasa	divasa	diaha

These forms can all be easily found in the Glossarial Index: and from the Index it appears at a glance which of the citations are prose and which are poetry, the exponential part of the citation being a number for the prose and a letter for the verse. By the help of this table it will be easy to form a clear idea of the extent to which the manuscripts, as we have them, conform to the prescriptions of the native grammarians or disregard them.] [END OF THE ADDITION.]

Rare and Provincial Words. — The most striking feature of Rājaçekhara's Prākrits is his abundant use of rare and provincial words. We give some instances from the Karpūramañjarī:

ubbimbira	**caṅgima-**	**taraṭṭī**	**bhasala**	**bakkara**
olaggāviā	**caṭṭi-**	**tasara**	**bhutthalla**[1]	**vacchoma**
olla	**campia**	**timisa**	**bhulla**	**vacchomī**
kaṅkellī	**calli**	**pakkhāujja**	**maraṭṭa**	**varilla**
kaṇḍāriūṇa	**chailla**	**pāḍisiddhi**	**maraḍhī**	**vindurilla**
kandoṭṭa	**chollai**	**pālittiā**	**mahalla**	**sāhuliā**
koḍḍa	**ṭapparakaṇṇa**	**potta**	**mahilā**	**sippī**
khaḍakkiā	**ṭikkida**	**bāulliā**	**riñcholī**	**sihiṇa**
khalakhaṇḍ..	**ṭeṇṭākarāla**	**buḍḍaṇa**	**rosāṇia**	**hakkārai**
galibailla	**ṭhakkura**	**bola**	**laṅgima-**	**etc.**
caṅga	**ḍhilla**	**bolei**	**laṭṭhaa**	
caṅgattaṇa	**ṇiei**	**bhamaraṭeṇṭā**	**lumbī**	

In Rājaçekhara's other works, also, many such words occur. Most of them are explained in the Prākrit grammars and lexicons; some of them have equivalents only in modern vernaculars.

[The student who uses diligently the smaller St. Petersburg Lexicon in the reading of this play cannot fail to be struck by the frequency with which the writings of Rājaçekhara, notably the Bālar., have furnished to Böhtlingk his first authentication of many words. The starred kālākṣarika is supported by i. 18[1]. The word dhāṭī (cp. ii. 46) is one of four synonyms for 'sudden attack' (prapāta, abhyavaskanda, dhāṭī, abhyāsādana, see Hemachandra, 800), for not one of which, in this sense, had a quotation been hitherto adduced, save a single one from Sāyaṇa (BR. v. 1524). — C. R. L.]

Marāṭhīcisms. — Marāṭhī words are used on a large scale by Rājaçekhara, according to Nārāyaṇa Dīkshita and Apte. And indeed, on the whole, our poet seems to be largely indebted to the vernaculars. Forms such as kaṇḍāriūṇa, caṭṭi-, tasara, pakkhāujja, etc., are known only from

[1] This word is rather dubious: but as the various readings all seem to be glosses, I was obliged to adopt it.

modern dialects, and a form like ḍhilla represents a more advanced stage of phonetic development than the literary Prākrits in general. Compare Pischel on Hemacandra i. 89. I cannot here enter into the question concerning Rājaçekhara's relation to the spoken vernaculars, from want of sufficient materials.

The Poet sometimes confused his Two Dialects. — I must be content to touch upon the following question: Was Rājaçekhara able to distinguish correctly the two Prākrit dialects which he used in his plays? The question is difficult on account of the miserable condition of the mss. The Indian editions cannot be trusted; and the Prākrit passages in the critically edited Bālabhārata are not extensive enough to be made the basis of the inquiry. Moreover, a mere glance at the various readings suffices to show that, in most instances, the text has been restored conjecturally.

There remains the Karpūramañjarī. The mss. of this work are by no means correct nor consistent in their readings. Words such as ratna, sarasvatī, iha, manoratha, mithuna, etc., are constantly written raaṇa, sarassaī, iha, maṇoraha, mihuṇa, in the prose as well as in the verses. And at i. 20^{13}, the form raaṇa in the Cāurasenī is also supported by Kṛṣṇasūnu, who gives the two translations ratna and racana. On the other hand, in all mss., we find forms like idaṁ in verses (e.g. iv. 2^{a}). But generally some of the mss. have the correct form. It is therefore necessary to examine critically the practice of Rājaçekhara, and to test his forms upon the touchstone of the native grammarians where they give distinct rules for dialectic usage.

Rājaçekhara's Usage tested by Mārkaṇḍeya's Prākrit Grammar. — Mārkaṇḍeya, in his Prākṛtasarvasva, gives a fuller description of the Cāurasenī than the other grammarians; and I shall try in the following paragraphs to show how some of his rules are practised by Rājaçekhara. I quote Mārkaṇḍeya after the ms. Wilson 158^{b} in the Bodleyana (Aufrecht no. 412).[1] The chapter on the Çāurasenī begins fol. 51^{a} and contains nine prakaraṇas.

In the fourth prakaraṇa we find a sūtra, kṣaṇakṣīrasadṛkṣāṇāṁ cchaḥ na syāt, 'cch should not be substituted [for kṣ] in kṣaṇa, kṣīra, sadṛkṣa.' In accordance with this rule I have adopted the reading sārikkha in iv. $19^{30, 53, 59}$.

According to a sūtra in the third prakaraṇa, l should not be substituted for y in yaṣṭi (yaṣṭyāṁ laç ca na syāt). But at Karp. ii. 6^{22} and iv. 19^{64},

[1] It is a pity that this ms. is insufficient as the basis for an edition of the text. I have tried to procure new material from Southern India through Professor G. Oppert, but in vain.

all mss. read laṭṭhī. Cp. Pischel on Hemacandra 1. 247, where several instances of laṭṭhī are quoted from the Çāurasenī. It is not without interest that all these quotations are taken from Rājaçekhara's writings.

Mārk. vi. has the sūtra, ata uttarasya ñer e syāt . . . idudbhyām uttarasya ñer mmi vā syāt, 'in words ending in -a, -e is substituted for the affix of the locative singular; in words ending in -i and -u, -mmi may be substituted.' But in the Karpūramañjarī we find the following instances of -mmi in a-themes: majjhammi i. 8^{3}, kuharammi iii. 20^{7}.

Another sūtra in the same prakaraṇa runs thus: do ñasaḥ | ḍo eva syāt . . . ād ataḥ kvacid | ato ñaser āt syāt kvacit, 'for the ablative sing. only the affix do is substituted. . . . In words ending in -a sometimes ā is substituted.' Accordingly the forms ending in -hiṁto ought not to be used in the Çāurasenī. Still in the Karpūramañjarī, forms occur such as pāmarāhiṁto i. 20^{29}; tumhāhiṁto ii. 29^{12}; candāhiṁto ii. 29^{13}, jalāhiṁto iii. 3^{18}, tumhārisāhiṁto iv. 2^{10}.

In the nominative sing. masc. of the pronoun etad, Mārkaṇḍeya forbids the use of the form esa in the Çāurasenī: na esa etadaḥ | sunā etada esa na syāt. This rule is in accordance with the general practice in all critical editions. But at Karp. i. 4^{10} and ii. 27^{1} and iv. 20^{11}, all mss. read esa, instead of the correct eso.

As for the verbal inflexion, the form ghettūṇa in the Çāurasenī, i. 12^{3}, is of interest compared with the regular geṇhia, iv. $19^{18, 39, 57}$.

Of less importance is the use of the dhātvādeça muṇ = jñā in prose. Cp. Pischel on Hemacandra iv. 7, etc.

These instances point to the conclusion that Rājaçekhara's linguistic skill was not so remarkable as he likes to tell us. For some important questions in Prākrit phonology and inflexion, his writings are of no importance. I shall only mention two cases.

The question whether we have to assume a cerebral ḻ for the Prākrits is as dubious as before. The South Indian mss. of the Karpūramañjarī always have cerebral ḻ. the others generally l.

Nor is the use of the Anunāsika elucidated by these manuscripts. The very probable supposition that in the nom. plur. neutr. and instr. plur. the Anunāsika *must* be used when the final syllable is short, is neither strengthened nor weakened by the mss. Most of them write the Anusvāra or nothing. Only R sometimes uses the Anunāsika, but very irregularly, to denote a long as well as a short syllable, and U in one place (iii. 16) has the Anunāsika correctly.

After all we must therefore state that Rājaçekhara is more important for our knowledge of the Prākrit lexicography than of the phonology an inflexion.

Possible Inference as to Obsolescence of Said Dialects. — Finally, from the fact that Rājaçekhara, "who knew all languages" (i. 7[1]), did not correctly distinguish the different Prākrits, we may infer that the living knowledge of those dialects was, at that time, considerably diminished. This supposition is not disproved by the fact that Somadeva, the author of the Lalitavigraharājanāṭaka (Kielhorn, Indian Antiquary, xx. 201 ff.; Göttinger Nachrichten, 1893, 552) writes a Prākrit which is in close accordance with the rules of Hemacandra. Hemacandra's grammar is dedicated to king Jayasiṁha of Anhilvād (1094–1143), and is therefore older than the Lalitavigraharājanāṭaka, which was written in Sāmbhar, 1153. The late Dr. Bühler, some years ago, drew my attention to the close connection between the courts of Anhilvād and Sāmbhar. (Cp. also Gazetteer of the Bombay Presidency, Vol. i., Part i., 179 ff.) And it is quite probable that Jayasiṁha sent copies of Hemacandra's grammar to Sāmbhar. If such is the case, the fact would sufficiently account for the correct Prākrit in Somadeva's work.

9. Rājaçekhara's Literary Characteristics.

Pischel's Estimate of the Poet. — Pischel has given a brief statement p. 1227 f., which it may be well to reprint: Rājaçekhara war ein Meister des Wortes und seine Dramen sind überaus wichtig für die Kenntnis des Sanskrit und noch mehr des Prākrit. Seine Verse sind elegant und fliessend und selbst in dem entsetzlich langweiligen Bālarāmāyaṇa wird man manche Scene wegen des Wohllauts der Verse, wegen der Sprichwörter und der Anspielungen auf Sitten und Gebräuche nicht ohne Interesse und Genuss lesen. Aber als Dramatiker steht Rājaçekhara nicht hoch. Im Bālarāmāyaṇa erweist er sich als starken Nachahmer[1] des Kālidāsa und Bhavabhūti, in der Viddhaçālabhañjikā und der Karpūramañjarī als Nachahmer des Dichters der unter Çrīharṣa's Namen gehenden Stücke, ohne dessen Witz zu erreichen. Nur im 2. und 3. Akte der Viddh. sind zwei launige Scenen eingelegt, deren Grundzüge man aber unschwer in der ersten Scene des 3. Aktes des Nāgānanda erkennt. Eine unglaubliche Geschmacklosigkeit ist die Scene im 5. Akt des Bālar. (p. 119 ff.), wo die künstliche Sītā und Sindūrikā mit den Drosseln im Munde, die Sanskrit und Prākrit sprechen, auftreten.

Apte also discusses our poet's literary characteristics at length, pages 41–44. [The poet's works ought, as I think, to be translated and inter-

[1] A systematic study of our poet's writings, with a view to determine the extent to which he imitated his predecessors, would be, I am persuaded, a fruitful one. The açoka scene of our present play recalls that of the 3. act of Mālavikā. — C. R. L.

preted by some Western scholar before a judgment is passed upon them which the Occident may fairly accept. See my notes to ii. 30, 31, 32. Native judgment sometimes goes too far in condemnation; and it often goes too far in praise. Of the latter error, the following stanza (attributed to a certain "highly cultured Çaṁkaravarman," at Bālar. i. 17 = Viddh. i. 7) is an example:

> pātuṁ çrotrarasāyanaṁ, racayituṁ vācaḥ satāṁ sammatā,
> vyutpattim paramām avāptum, avadhiṁ labdhuṁ rasasrotasaḥ, |
> bhoktuṁ svādu phalaṁ ca jīvitataror, yady asti te kāutukaṁ,
> tad bhrātaḥ çṛṇu Rājaçekharakaveḥ sūktīḥ sudhāsyandinīḥ‖ — C. R. L.]

The Poet's Skill in Metres. — Rājaçekhara's masterly command of the more elaborate metres is one of his most notable characteristics. He especially excelled in Sragdharā and (as has indeed been pointed out by the Indian critic, Kṣemendra, p. 198: cp. p. 209, where the metres of the present play are given) in Çārdūlavikrīḍita. Our poet's metrical skill is by no means restricted to Sanskrit; in Prākrit versification also he has shown a really remarkable power. His predecessors usually contented themselves with an occasional Anuṣṭubh or Āryā in the Prākrit portions of their plays; while Rājaçekhara (as Apte observes, p. 44) has given us nearly forty Prākrit stanzas in the highly artificial Çārdūlavikrīḍita alone (they number 33). This is a matter of no mean importance to the student of Indian metres. See below, p. 206; and cp. Stenzler's metrical notes, published after his death, ZDMG. xliv. 1–82.

Rime. — Rime forms an essential element of versification in the poetry of the modern Indian vernaculars, and also in Prākrit; but not in Sanskrit. Where rime occurs in Sanskrit poetry, as, for instance, in that of Jayadeva, we may assume that the influence of the vernacular or of Prākrit poetry has been at work. It is of interest to note that Rājaçekhara makes occasional use of rime. Instances are: Viddh. i. 4, 5; iii. 8; Karp. iii. 29, 30, 31. [It may be added that two of the Magician's ribald songs, i. 22, 23, are full of internal rimes. So ii. 11.— Rime, *Antya-anuprāsa*, is freely used, for example, in the Gīta-govinda and Moha-mudgara. Cp. Sāhitya-darpaṇa, no. 637; Ch. P. Brown, Sanskrit Prosody, p. 21; Pischel, H., p. 208. — C. R. L.]

Proverbial Expressions. — Another prominent literary characteristic of Rājaçekhara is his fondness for the use of proverbial expressions. [In our present play, I have noted saws or proverbs or proverbial expressions at the following places: i. $18^{10,13,18}$; ii. 1^{2}; iii. 6^{b}; iv. $18^{8,27}$; 20^{3}; and perhaps

ii. 26^d, 29^{11}, and iv. 20^{12}(?) ought to be added. Apte has collected a good many on p. 45 of his essay.

The Indian form of "A bird in the hand is worth two in the bush" may be mentioned, since our poet gives it at Viddh. i. 22^2: it reads, "Better a partridge to-day than a pea-hen to-morrow," varaṁ takkālovaṇadā tittirī ṇa uṇa diahantaridā morī. A far older form of the saw is given by Vātsyāyana, in the Kāmasūtra, p. 19^7, ed. Bombay, who, in a most interesting carpe-diem-argument, says, "Better a dove to-day than a peacock to-morrow," varam adya kapotaḥ çvo mayūrāt. In Manwaring's Marāṭhī Proverbs, no. 516, we find "Why do you want a mirror in which to see your bracelet?" From i. 18^{10} it appears that the saying is at least a thousand years old.

Colonel George A. Jacob informs me that he has a "Handful of Popular Maxims current in Sanskrit Literature" now (Feb., 1900) in press in Bombay. — C. R. L.]

Rājaçekhara Repeats Himself. — Cappeller has already drawn attention (p. vi f.) to the fact that Rājaçekhara frequently repeats himself. These repetitions extend sometimes over a whole stanza, sometimes only over a part. I give the following list, which is not exhaustive:

Bālar. i. 9 = Bālabh. i. 15.
Bālar. i. 10 = Bālabh. i. 5.
Bālar. i. 14 = Bālabh. i. 3.
Bālar. i. 16 = Bālabh. i. 12.
Bālar. i. 17 = Viddh. i. 7.
Bālar. i. 18 = Bālabh. i. 11.
Bālar. i. 20 = Bālabh. i. 14.
Bālar. ii. 17 = Viddh. i. 14.
Bālar. iii. 23 = Viddh. ii. 5.
Bālar. iii. 25 = { Bālabh. i. 31. / Viddh. iii. 27.
Bālar. iii. 39 = Bālabh. i. 65.
Bālar. iii. 54 = Bālar. vii. 68.
Bālar. v. 5, cp. Bālar. vii. 77.
Bālar. v. 8 = Viddh. iii. 2.
Bālar. v. 25 = Viddh. iv. 6, cp. Karp. iv. 2.
Bālar. v. 39 = Viddh. i. 24.
Bālar. v. 73 = Viddh. iii. 15.
Bālar. vi. 11 = Bālar. vi. 16.
Bālar. vii. 31, cp. Bālar. x. 43.
Bālar. vii. 38 = Bālar. x. 44.
Bālar. vii. 39 = Bālar. x. 46.
Bālar. viii. 11, cp. Viddh. iv. 20.
Bālar. x. 40 = Viddh. iii. 11.
Bālar. x. 58, cp. Bālabh. i. 19.

Bālabh. i. 9 = Viddh. i. 8.
Bālabh. i. 22 = Viddh. ii. 22.
Bālabh. i. 27 = Viddh. iii. 16.
Bālabh. ii. 3, cp. Karp. ii. 32.
Bālabh. ii. 7 = Bālabh. ii. 13.
Bālabh. ii. 15, cp. Viddh. i. 17.
Karp. iii. 26 = Viddh. iii. 12.

10. Rājaçekhara's Favorite Metres.

1. Çārdūlavikrīḍita; 2. Vasantatilaka; 3. Çloka; 4. Sragdharā. — In the Suvṛttatilaka, iii. 35, Kṣemendra praises Rājaçekhara for his ability in the Çārdūlavikrīḍita; and this metre is, in fact, used to a great extent in his works. Thus I have noted 208 instances from the Bālarāmāyaṇa, 41 from the Bālabhārata, 36 from the Viddhaçālabhañjikā, and 24 from the Karpūramañjarī. The second place in frequency must be attributed to the Vasantatilaka, which metre occurs 159 times in the Bālar., 25 in the Bālabh., 11 in the Viddh., and 23 in the Karp. The third place in frequency is held by the Çloka. Of this there are 126 instances in the Bālar., 25 in the Bālabh., and 3 in the Viddh. To the Sragdharā belongs the fourth place, with 94 occurrences in the Bālar., 12 in the Bālabh., 10 in the Viddh., and 11 in the Karp.

5. Āryā; then Triṣṭubh; etc., etc.—Of other metres, the following occur more or less frequently:

Āryā	Pṛthvī	Vaṅçastha
Upagīti	Praharṣiṇī	Vasantamālikā
Gīti	Mandākrāntā	Çālinī
Triṣṭubh	Mālinī	Çikhariṇī
Drutavilambita	Rathoddhatā	Svāgatā
Puṣpitāgrā	Rucirā	Hariṇī

To these must be added some very free Prākrit metres, such, for instance, as Viddh. i. 4, 5; ii. 7; iii. 8, and Karp. iii. 29, 30. The two stanzas last mentioned are of a form not known from other sources. The stanza iii. 29 forms the half of a Mātrāsamaka, but is shown by the rime to be intended as a complete stanza. Each pāda consists of 8 syllabic instants. The following stanza, iii. 30, is constructed on a similar scheme, each pāda containing 12 syllabic instants.

11. Metres of the Karpūra-mañjarī.

The Metres in the Order of Their Frequency.—In the Karpūramañjarī, the metres, listed in the order of their frequency, and each with the number of its occurrences, are given in the subjoined table. Under "Triṣṭubh" are included Indravajrā, Upendravajrā, and Upajāti.

Āryā[1]	32	Svāgatā	4
Çārdūlavikrīḍita	24	Gīti	2
Vasantatilaka	23	Puṣpitāgrā	2
Triṣṭubh	12	Upagīti	1
Sragdharā	11	Vaṅçastha	1
Rathoddhatā	9	Çālinī	1
Pṛthvī	7	Çikhariṇī	1
Mālinī	7	iii. 29, 30 (above, p. 207)	2
Mandākrāntā	5	Sum	144

[1] Note that, in the amphibrach which forms the sixth foot of the first half of the Āryā, the resolution of the long into two shorts is permitted if a new word begin with the second syllable of that foot: e.g. i. 3, 8, 9; ii. 37, 48, 49.

[**Scene-groups.** — There are four considerable passages in this play in which metres of the same kind are, so to say, "bunched," and in which, accordingly, the unity of thought of the passage is reflected in the unity of its metrical form. The passages are: in act ii., stanzas 12–22, eleven āryā stanzas, forming the "Tiring-scene"; again in act ii., stanzas 33–40, eight āryā stanzas, forming the "Swing-scene"; then in act iv., stanzas 10–18, nine stanzas of hendecasyllabics, being six triṣṭubh and three svāgatā stanzas, describing the Banyan festival scene. Finally, in act iii., the passage 9–17, consisting of nine vasantatilaka stanzas, forms the bulk of the "lengthy and vapid discussion of love."

It is worth noting that a Çārdūlavikrīḍita serves as the initial stanza of the Prologue, of act i. proper (i. 13), of the love-scene in the first act (i. 26), of act ii., and of act iii.; see the Table, p. 209. The same metrical form is especially employed for the more elevated passages of description: for example, i. 16–18, the spring; i. 35, the evening; iii. 25, moonrise; iii. 27, the garden scene. And it is also used at the climax of some gravely emotional passages, as at iv. 9. — L.]

The Metres in the Order of Their Occurrence. — The following table (p. 209) gives the metres of the Karpūra-mañjarī in the order of their occurrence in the text. See also p. 289, note to iv. 19[64].

Metres of the Karpūra-mañjarī.

Act I.		Act II.		Act III.		Act IV.	
i. 1	Çārdūlavikrīḍita	ii. 1	Çārdūlavikrīḍita	iii. 1	Çārdūlavikrīḍita	iv. 1	Āryā
i. 2	Puṣpitāgrā	ii. 2	Mandākrāntā	iii. 2	Mālinī	iv. 2	Puṣpitāgrā
i. 3	Āryā	ii. 3	Çārdūlavikrīḍita	iii. 3	Çārdūlavikrīḍita	iv. 3	Pṛthvī
i. 4	Sragdharā	ii. 4	Vasantatilaka	iii. 4	Vaṅçastha	iv. 4	Çārdūlavikrīḍita
i. 5	Āryā	ii. 5	"	iii. 5	Indravajrā	iv. 5	Vasantatilaka
i. 6	Gīti	ii. 6	"	iii. 6	"	iv. 6	Pṛthvī
i. 7	Āryā	ii. 7	Rathoddhatā	iii. 7	Mālinī	iv. 7	Sragdharā
i. 8	"	ii. 8	Çārdūlavikrīḍita	iii. 8	Āryā	iv. 8	Vasantatilaka
i. 9	"	ii. 9	Mālinī	iii. 9	Vasantatilaka	iv. 9	Çārdūlavikrīḍita
i. 10	"	ii. 10	Sragdharā	iii. 10	"	iv. 10	Indravajrā
i. 11	Rathoddhatā	ii. 11	Çikharinī	iii. 11	"	iv. 11	Upajāti
i. 12	Svāgatā	ii. 12	Āryā	iii. 12	"	iv. 12	"
i. 13	Çārdūlavikrīḍita	ii. 13	"	iii. 13	"	iv. 13	"
i. 14	Vasantatilaka	ii. 14	"	iii. 14	"	iv. 14	Upendravajrā
i. 15	Sragdharā	ii. 15	"	iii. 15	"	iv. 15	Upajāti
i. 16	Çārdūlavikrīḍita	ii. 16	"	iii. 16	"	iv. 16	Svāgatā
i. 17	"	ii. 17	"	iii. 17	"	iv. 17	"
i. 18	"	ii. 18	"	iii. 18	Mālinī	iv. 18	"
i. 19	Vasantatilaka	ii. 19	"	iii. 19	Sragdharā	iv. 19	Āryā
i. 20	Çārdūlavikrīḍita	ii. 20	"	iii. 20	Pṛthvī	iv. 20	Mālinī
i. 21	Vasantatilaka	ii. 21	"	iii. 21	Rathoddhatā	iv. 21	Vasantatilaka
i. 22	Indravajrā	ii. 22	"	iii. 22	Vasantatilaka	iv. 22	Çārdūlavikrīḍita
i. 23	Çālinī	ii. 23	Mandākrāntā	iii. 23	Rathoddhatā	iv. 23	"
i. 24	Vasantatilaka	ii. 24	Mālinī	iii. 24	"	iv. 24	Gīti
i. 25	"	ii. 25	Upajāti	iii. 25	Çārdūlavikrīḍita		
i. 26	Çārdūlavikrīḍita	ii. 26	Vasantatilaka	iii. 26	Pṛthvī		
i. 27	Vasantatilaka	ii. 27	Çārdūlavikrīḍita	iii. 27	Çārdūlavikrīḍita		
i. 28	Upajāti	ii. 28	Sragdharā	iii. 28	Sragdharā		
i. 29	Çārdūlavikrīḍita	ii. 29	Çārdūlavikrīḍita	iii. 29	[See p. 207]		
i. 30	Mandākrāntā	ii. 30	Mandākrāntā	iii. 30	"		
i. 31	Upajāti	ii. 31	Sragdharā	iii. 31	Rathoddhatā		
i. 32	Çārdūlavikrīḍita	ii. 32	Pṛthvī	iii. 32	"		
i. 33	Mandākrāntā	ii. 33	Āryā	iii. 33	"		
i. 34	Pṛthvī	ii. 34	"	iii. 34	"		
i. 35	Çārdūlavikrīḍita	ii. 35	"				
i. 36	Sragdharā	ii. 36	"				
		ii. 37	"				
		ii. 38	"				
		ii. 39	"				
		ii. 40	"				
		ii. 41	Sragdharā				
		ii. 42	Āryā				
		ii. 43	"				
		ii. 44	Mālinī				
		ii. 45	Upagīti				
		ii. 46	Çārdūlavikrīḍita				
		ii. 47	Pṛthvī				
		ii. 48	Āryā				
		ii. 49	"				
		ii. 50	Sragdharā				

Summation of Stanzas.

Act i.	has	36
" ii.	"	50
" iii.	"	34
" iv.	"	24
Sum		144

PART IV

TRANSLATION

OF THE

KARPŪRA-MAÑJARĪ

WITH

AN INTRODUCTION AND NOTES

BY

C. R. LANMAN

Mulier est hominis confusio ;
Madame, the sentence of this Latin is—
Womman is mannes joye and al his blis.

—CHAUCER. "The Nonne Preestes Tale," 344.

1. Geography of the Play in General.

The geography of the play in general and the geographical allusions of the text demand some notice. The action of the play[1] is at the court of King Chaṇḍapāla, that is, in his palace and palace gardens. I do not know that this name designates an historical personage; but the poet plainly intended that we should imagine the general scene of the play to be in the Deccan (cp. "Here in the Deccan," i. 25^5, 34^8). Chaṇḍapāla addresses his queen as "daughter of the [a] sovereign of the Deccan," i. 12^8. And the fact that the king of Kuntala and Chaṇḍapāla are represented as marrying aunt and niece (i. 34^8) would lead us to imagine Chaṇḍapāla's "kingdom in the Deccan" as not far from that of his father-in-law (which is undefined) nor from that of Kuntala. Moreover, the allusions[2] of i. 15 and 17 (cp. 20) point with clearness to the Deccan or Southern India (cp. i. 36, note 3).

Kuntala seems to have included parts of the region that is drained by the upper Kistna and the Tungabhadra.[3] It covered what is now the southernmost part of the Bombay Presidency and of Haiderabad, and the northwest corner of Madras, with part of Mysore[4] — say the Districts of North Kanara, of Belgaum, and of Bellary; and perhaps it reached even farther east. The inscription of Kurugode[5] names as capital of Kuntala the town of Kurugode, which is fourteen miles from Bellary town, north and west.

Vidarbha seems to have reached from the Kistna north nearly to the Narbadā. It is included in Mahārāṣṭra.[6] And Kuntala seems also to have been so included.[7] This may throw light on the statement of the commentators (Konow, p. 160) about Vacchoma as capital of Kuntala.

Lāṭa designated, in the time of our poet, the region north of the lower Narbadā and east of the Gulf of Cambay, modern Broach or Central and Southern Gujarāt, Ptolemy's Λαρική. See Epigraphia Indica, i. 274, iv.

[1] The place where the play was first *represented* or brought out, may have been the court of Nirbhara: see i. 9 and p. 217.

[2] The allusions to Bengal and Assam etc. (i. 14^2) are not such as to yield data for geographical inferences.

[3] See Duff, Chronology of India, under A.D. 973, and Borooah's Essay, § 145.

[4] Including the once important Banavasi, Ptolemy's Βανανασεί; cp. Ind. Ant. xiii. 367.

[5] Colebrooke's Essays, ii. [272], [273].

[6] See Borooah, § 146–8; Bālar. x. 74.

[7] According to passages in Bālar., which Borooah (note 3) does not specify. According to Daçakumāracharita, viii., p. 59, ed. Peterson, the Lords of Vanavāsin and of Kuntala seem to have been vassals of Vidarbha.

246; and Borooah's Essay, § 154. The statement of iv. 18[28], "the wedding is set for here and today, while the bride is in the country of Lāṭa," indicates that Chaṇḍapāla's realm was not Lāṭa.[1] Another northern place is Kanauj, mentioned in the Jester's dream (iii. 5[2]) as if distant. I imagine Chaṇḍapāla's realm as south or southeast of Kuntala.

2. Hindu Seasons, Months, and Asterisms.

In the Prākrit text above, and in the sequel also, there is a considerable number of allusions to the Hindu seasons and months and asterisms. Convenient tables of the months, etc., are so rare in this country that I am confident that the American student will welcome the ensuing table.

SEASON	MONTH	TIME	ASTERISMS IN WHICH FULL MOON MAY OCCUR
Vasanta Spring	Chāitra Vāiçākha	March–April April–May	14, Chitrā; 15, Svātī 16, Viçākhā; 17, Anurādhā
Grishma Summer	Jyāishṭha Āshāḍha	May–June June–July	18, Jyeshṭhā; 19, Mūla 20, P.-Ashāḍhā; 21, U.-Ashāḍhā
Varsha Rains	Çrāvaṇa Bhādrapada	July–August Aug.–Sept.	23, Çravaṇa; 24, Çravishṭhā 25, Çata-bhishaj; 26, P.-Bh.; 27, U.-Bh.
Çarad Autumn	Āçvina Kārttika	Sept.–Oct. Oct.–Nov.	28, Revatī; 1, Açvinī; 2, Bharaṇī 3, Kṛttikā; 4, Rohiṇī
Hemanta Winter	Mārgaçīrsha Pāusha	Nov.–Dec. Dec.–Jan.	5, Mṛga-çīrsha; 6, Ārdrā 7, Punar-vasu; 8, Pushya
Çiçira Cool season	Māgha Phālguna	Jan.–Feb. Feb.–Mar.	9, Āçleshā; 10, Maghā 11, P.-Phalgunī; 12, U.-Ph.; 13, Hasta

Whitney's Sūryasiddhānta, Journal of American Oriental Society, vi. 414 and 468, may be consulted; also his essay on the Lunar Zodiac, Oriental and Linguistic Studies, i. 341 f. For the older division into three seasons, Hot, Wet, and Cold, which is still in popular use, see Bühler, Epigraphia Indica, ii, 262, and Manwaring's Marāṭhī Proverbs, no. 1279. Older month-names: Whitney, Journal, vi. 414; or Sewell and Dīkshita, Indian Calendar, p. 24. Very instructive is Part X (*c*) of Manwaring.

I abbreviate Pūrva, 'former,' by P.; Uttara, 'latter,' by U.; Phalgunī by Ph.; and Bhādrapadā by Bh. The 22d asterism is Abhijit: see note to i. 20[31], and Whitney's Zodiac, p. 409.

[1] It is true that at iv. 18[18] the text says, "Here (? ettha) in the Lāṭa country." But as this is in palpable conflict with iv. 18[27, 28], it may be ettha = 'there.'

3. Time-allusions of the Play and Time of the Action.

For the determination of the time of the action, we have one datum which is both certain and precise, that of the Banyan festival (act iv.). It synchronizes with the full moon of Jyāiṣṭha. — The second datum, that of the Swing festival of Gāurī (act ii.), if I have identified it aright, is no less certain and precise. The fourth day of that festival falls on the sixth lunar day of the bright half of Chāitra. — The third datum is drawn from the allusions to the beginning of spring (act i.). These are entirely certain. Whether we may take them as intending precision, is a question rather of common sense than of erudition.[1] The evidence is in favor of interpreting them precisely.

The action of the play, accordingly, covers a period of just two and one-half lunations: that is, all of Chāitra, all of Vāiçākha, and the light half of Jyāiṣṭha. The scene of the play being in the south, we may suppose the lunar months to be reckoned as from new moon to new moon,[2] rather than as from full to full.[3] — There remains act iii. Its action takes place at a full moon: is it that of Chāitra or of Vāiçākha?

Act I. — The initial motif of the play proper is the advent of spring. The month is Chāitra, i. 17[d], 18[d]; the frost is gone, i. 14[a]; the Malabar winds, from the southwest, have set in, i. 15[d], 16[3, 4], 20[c]; the spring has begun, i. 12[8], 14[2], 18[14], with all its beauties, i. 16[3]. — The act ends with evening, i. 35, and at least one night intervenes between acts i. and ii. And since the time of act ii. is the sixth of the bright fortnight of Chāitra, the latest date for act i. is the fifth of that fortnight.

But it appears, from act ii. 4,[4] that a considerable number of days must have elapsed since act i. During that time, but not after the beginning of act ii.,[5] King and Heroine have seen each other, ii. 42[16, 17], and become deeply enamored. We can hardly make the interval less than five days, and would therefore set the time of act i. on the first of the bright fortnight of Chāitra. The duration of act i. is part of one day.

1 There is great discordance between popular usage and the statements of the learned bookmakers of India in regard to seasonal divisions: see Bühler, Epigraphia Indica, ii. 262. So here in New England, we speak of one of our characteristic blustering vernal winds as "a regular March wind," even if it be a little before or after the calendar month of March.

2 The **amā-anta** system. In this, the bright fortnight (**çukla**), or fortnight of the waxing moon, comes first, and then the dark fortnight (**kṛṣṇa**), or that of the waning moon. See Ep. Ind., i. 404; or The Indian Calendar, p. 4. Thus: <>.

3 The **pūrṇimā-anta** system, diminuendo-crescendo, thus: ><.

4 So too from ii. 8, 9. Perhaps also from ii. 1[2]. Certainly not from i. 34[26]. It is odd that the King waits five days to propound his question, ii. 11[3]; but the playwright needed it as introduction to his tiring scene.

5 In the Swing scene, although the King sees the Heroine, she does not see him.

Act II. — The time is still Madhu, ii. 6[21], or Chāitra, and the spring "is very gently coming on," ii. 1[5]. The nights are still chilly, ii. 41[5]. We read at ii. 29[5], "Today is the fourth day of the Swing festival." The allusions to the worship of Gāurī that accompanied the festival (see ii. 6[23, 25], ii. 29[6]) indicate that the *gāuryā dolotsava* is intended (see note to ii. 6[23], and additional note thereto, on p. 289), and this begins on the third of the bright half of Chāitra. The date of act ii. is therefore the sixth of waxing Chāitra. — The act lasts part of one day. When the Swing scene ends, evening is near, ii. 41[3]. The açoka scene is somewhat later in the same evening, for the Heroine has in the meantime been "exquisitely decorated," ii. 43[7].

Act III. — The action is on the evening of the night of a full moon, iii. 25[d], 32[b], which must be that of either Chāitra or Vāiçākha. The allusions to punkahs and shower-baths, iii. 20, and to the "intense heat" (*ghaṇa-ghamma*, iii. 20[3]), indicate that the hot weather (March to May, inclusive) is far advanced. I therefore deem the latter alternative the more probable one, and place the action of act iii. at the full moon of Vāiçākha. This date allows ample time for the Queen's jealousy (cp. p. 247, note 7, with p. 289, note to ii. 41[9]) to drive her to the drastic measure of imprisoning the Heroine, and time for the construction of the subterranean passage (p. 219). And it still falls within the limits of spring (*vasanta*) — cp. the next paragraph.

Act IV. — The spring (*mahu-samaa*) has now gone, iv. 7[d]; the summer (*gimha*, iv. 1) is come, iv. 4[c], 5[d], 6[d]. The time of the action is explicitly defined, iv. 9[18], as the "Banyan festival." This falls on the day of the full moon of Jyāiṣṭha, iv. 9[18] note. In substantial accordance herewith is the allusion, iv. 3[a], to the length of the days, which reaches its maximum a little later; and so is the statement, iv. 18[11], that the image of Gāurī was set up "on the fourteenth day just past," that is, the fourteenth of the light half of Jyāiṣṭha. — The action of the merry-making (p. 221, scene 3) runs over a part of the day-time. The wedding takes place in the evening, iv. 18[7].

Synoptic Table of the Time of the Action.

Act I.: beginning of spring, first of Chāitra, bright half . . . . [Say March 15].
Interval of five days.

Act II.: fourth day of Swing festival of Gāurī, sixth of Chāitra, ditto . . [Say March 20].
Interval of about ten days + just one lunation.

Act III.: full moon of Vāiçākha . . . . [Say May 1].
Interval of one lunation.

Act IV.: Banyan festival, full moon of Jyāiṣṭha . . . . [Say June 1].

4. Synoptic Analysis of the Play.

The purpose of this synopsis is to make clear 1. the places or scenes of the action in detail, and 2. the details of the stage-business. Since the references to the text are given throughout, it will also serve 3. as a useful finding-table. For greater convenience, I have divided the synopsis into scenes, guided partly by the entrances and exits and partly by the places of the action, but without special reference to the canons of the native dramaturgy.

Several scenes are double or even multiple scenes: that is, the stage represents simultaneously the scene of the principal action and also the King in some place of observation or concealment near by (such are scenes 4 and 7 of act ii.: cp. note to iii. 34^1); or the stage is imagined to represent successively (as in act iii., scene 2, and act iv., scene 5) several places in which the players have to be, during the course of that scene. In the latter case, the place comes to the actor instead of the actor's going to the place. His going, however, is mimetically indicated by a "stepping about."

By "palace garden" or "palace," as used in the sequel, is meant of course the palace garden or palace of King Chaṇḍapāla.

Prologue, I. 1 to I. 12^5.

During the prologue, the stage represents the play-house (or *nāṭya-çālā*, Lévi, p. 371) of the King for whom the play is enacted. The first performance may have been for King Ṇibbhara, i. 9, 11.

Scene 1. Enters the Director (*sūtradhāra*) and recites the benediction, i. 1–2 [Then exit.]

Scene 2. Enters the Stage-manager (*sthāpaka*) and praises Çiva, i. 3–4, and describes the preparations for the play, i. 4^2.

Scene 3. Enters the Assistant (*pāripārçvika*) of the Stage-manager, i. 4^{14}. They discuss the play, the author, why he writes in Prākrit, at whose instance the piece is given, and the gist of the plot, i. 4^{14}–12^3. Exeunt.

Act I.

Scene 1 (the advent of spring): the palace garden. Enter King and Queen, with retinue, i. 12^6. They congratulate each other on the arrival of spring, and describe the season in stanzas, i. 13–14.

Behind the stage, two Bards describe the beauties of spring, i. 15–16, and are followed in the same strain by the royal pair, i. 16^3–18.

Scene 2 (comic intermezzo): place and actors as before. Jester and Vichakshaṇā quarrel, i. 18^1. Retorts, sharp and coarse, follow; then rival stanzas, i. 19–20; then threats, i. 20[15]. General laughter, i. 20[35]. Exit Jester, i. 20[41].

Scene 3 (the tipsy Magician): place and actors as before. Reënters Jester, i. 21[1], announcing the Magician, who follows, i. 21[8], tipsy, singing ribald songs. He offers to show a specimen of his powers to the King, i. 25[1]. The latter suggests that he produce on the stage a lovely girl. The wizard sets about it, i. 25[10]. Thereupon—

Scene 4 (love scene): place and actors as before. Enters the Heroine, i. 25[11]. Rapturous stanzas from the King, i. 26–27. She gives the King a coquettish glance, i. 28[9]. He is deeply enamored, i. 29–34. She tells her story, i. 34[8-21]. The Queen asks that the Heroine may remain a fortnight, i. 34[26], and conducts her to the gynæceum, i. 34[38].

Behind the stage, two Bards in descriptive stanzas announce the evening, i. 35–36, and the King goes to prayer.

Act II.

Scene 1 (the love-sick King): the palace garden. Enter King and Porteress. ii. 0[1]. Enamored stanzas, ii. 1–6.

Scene 2 (the billet-doux): place and actors as before. Enter Jester and Vichakshaṇā, ii. 6[3]. They discuss briefly the King's condition, ii. 6[4-10], unheard by him.

They address the King, ii. 6[12]. It transpires that Vichakshaṇā bears a love-letter, ii. 6[20], from the Heroine to the King. This the King reads, ii. 8. Stanzas from Vichakshaṇā, from her sister, and from the Jester, ii. 9–11.

The King asks, ii. 11[2], what happened to the Heroine after the Queen conducted her (at i. 34[38]) to the gynæceum. Properly the replies form no new scene; but they have such dramatic unity that it is well to treat them as a scene.

Scene 3 (the tiring scene, a duo between Vichaksnaṇā and King): place and actors as before. Introductory questions and answers, ii. 11[2-6]. In eleven half-stanzas, ii. 12–22, Vichakshaṇā describes how the Heroine was arrayed and adorned in the gynæceum. The King caps each half-stanza with one of his own, in which he interprets the description with some fanciful conceit. Exit Vichakshaṇā, ii. 29[3].

It now transpires that she and the Jester have arranged that the Heroine shall swing in a swing set up before the idol of Pārvatī, and that the King shall have an opportunity to observe her from an arbor near by, ii. 29[6-7]. With the Jester, the King "makes as if entering" the Plantain Arbor, ii. 29[14].

Scene 4 (the swing scene): the palace garden; the Heroine in the swing; King and Jester concealed in the Plantain Arbor. The King pours forth his soul in rapturous stanzas, ii. 30–32.

Then follows, in eight stanzas, ii. 33–40, the Jester's description of the Heroine's swinging. It is filled with pretty conceits and forms a pendant to the tiring scene. — The Heroine quits the swing, ii. 40^{2}.

Scene 5 (serio-comic intermezzo): the gardens. The King at the Plantain Arbor laments her departure in tragic strains, and the Jester gives mocking response, ii. 40^{2}–41. Evening approaches, ii. 41^{3}; but night's coolness avails not to attemper the King's amorous fever, ii. 41^{5}.

The Jester leaves the King "alone" on the Emerald Seat, ii. 41^{6}, and makes as if leaving the stage to get something to cool him off, ii. 41^{7}. The King continues his amorous plaint, ii. 42.

Scene 6 ("stage-traffick"): a part, near by, of the gardens. Reënters Vichakshaṇā with refrigerants, ii. 42^{3}. She and the Jester, ii. 43^{2}, arrange it so that the King shall witness the coming açoka scene.

The King is imagined to secrete himself behind a shrub, ii. 43^{3}.

Scene 7 (the açoka scene): the garden. Enters the Heroine, ii. 43^{7}. She embraces a young amaranth, looks at a tilaka, and touches with the tip of her foot an açoka tree; whereupon all three burst into gorgeous bloom, ii. 43^{14}–47.

King and Jester discuss the matter, ii. 47^{1}–49^{2}.

Behind the scene a Bard describes the evening, ii. 50. Exeunt all. See also p. 289, n. 2.

Act III.

From iii. 34^{9} we infer that, between the last act and this, jealousy has prompted the Queen to imprison the Heroine in some room in the Queen's section of the palace; and that, unknown to the Queen, a secret subterranean passage has been made from this room to the palace garden.

The room where the lovers meet (iii. 20^{12}) and the lamp-incident occurs (iii. 22^{4}) adjoins the prison room, as I think; for the lovers go from their meeting-room to the garden by the subterranean passage, and they must enter the passage from the prison room or near it. This meeting-room has a "back-door" entrance, perhaps from some obscure court-yard.

The prison room is an "inner room," close and sweat-provoking, iii. 22^{1}. That it is near the Queen's I infer from iv. 19^{37-39} and $^{52-57}$.

Scene 1 (the King's vision): a place outside the palace (perhaps an obscure court-yard?) near the lovers' meeting-room. Enter King and Jester. The King describes a vision in which he met the Heroine, iii. 2^{2}–3. To divert him, the Jester tells an elaborate counter-vision, iii. 3^{4}–7. The two engage in a lengthy and vapid discussion of love, iii. 8^{1}–19.

From behind the stage they hear the enamored plaints of the Heroine, iii. 19^{2}. The Jester indulges himself in much badinage with the King, iii. 20^{1}. Both "make as if entering," by a "back-door," the meeting-room, iii. 20^{12}, that is, they "step about" by way of intimation to the spectators that they are entering it, though remaining, of course, on the stage.

Scene 2 (the lovers' meeting): [part 1] a room near the prison room (see above). Enters the Heroine, with her friend, to meet King and Jester, iii. 20^{13}. The King takes the Heroine's hand, iii. 20^{25}. She has just come from a close "inner-room," so the Jester fans her, and in so doing puts out the lamp, iii. 22^{1-4}.

King and Heroine hand in hand,—the four now grope their way [part 2] through the prison room (? see above), and then [part 3] through the dark passage, iii. 22^{9}, to the gardens [part 4].

Scene 3 (the moonrise scene): the palace garden. A continuation of the last part of the foregoing scene. Stanzas of admiration and delight from the King, iii. 23–24. Behind the stage, Bards describe the rise of the full moon, iii. 25–28. Then follow stanzas by the Jester, Kurañgikā, and the Heroine, iii. 29–31, and the King, iii. 32–34.

Sudden uproar, iii. 34^{1}. The Queen has heard of her consort's tricks and is coming, iii. 34^{7}. The Heroine escapes, by the secret passage, to her prison, iii. 34^{9}. Exeunt omnes.

Act IV.

From iv. 9^{6-7}, it appears that the Queen has now learned of the subterranean passage and blocked up its entrance. We are forced to assume that this closure of the passage is made *at the garden end* thereof. For the Heroine, the passage thus becomes a cul-de-sac: its prison end is open; she can enter it and traverse its entire length; but she cannot get out at the garden end.

Accordingly, somewhere near the garden end, a new branch passage has been excavated from the main passage to the sanctuary of Chāmuṇḍā near the Banyan, the mouth of this branch passage being concealed behind the idol, iv. 18^{38}. Between the entrance of the Magician and that of the King (scene 5), the Heroine traverses the passage that connects the prison and the sanctuary five times.

Scene 1 (the love-sick King): presumably, the King's apartments. Enters, with his Jester, the King, and bemoans the ardor of summer and of love. Episode of the tame parrot, iv. 2^{4}. More stanzas of love and summer, iv. 3–9.

The Jester now tells the King how the Queen has closed up the entrance to [the garden end of] the subterranean passage, and tells of the guards that have been set all about that entrance, iv. 9^{6-12}.

Scene 2 ("stage-traffick"): place and actors the same. Enters Sārañgikā, iv. 9^{15}, with a message from the Queen: "The King must mount the palace roof today to see the Banyan festival," iv. 9^{18}. Exit Sāraṅgikā, iv. 9^{20}.

Scene 3 (the Banyan festival): from the palace roof, iv. 9^{21}, King and Jester look down on an elaborate dance. In nine stanzas, iv. 10–18, the Jester describes the dance, the merry-makings, and the off-hand theatre play (impersonations with masks, etc.).

We must here imagine a slight interval in which King and Jester come down from the palace terrace and go to the Emerald Seat, and thence to the Plantain Arbor. But see note to ii. 29^{7}.

Scene 4 ("some necessary question of the play"): the Plantain Arbor, palace garden, iv. 18^{3}. Reënters Sāraṅgikā, iv. 18^{1}, with a message from the Queen: "The Queen has arranged that the King, this very evening, shall take to wife yet another princess, iv. 18^{7}, a princess of Lāṭa, named Ghanasāra-mañjarī," iv. 18^{18-19}. The messenger, furthermore, narrates that the Magician induced the Queen to assent to this arrangement on the ground that her husband, the King, would become an Emperor by contracting this new marital alliance, iv. 18^{22}. The ceremony is to take place in a sanctuary near the Banyan, presumably the festival Banyan, iv. 18^{30-32}. Exit Sāraṅgikā.

After exchanging suspicions (iv. 18^{34-36}) that the Magician is at the bottom of this affair, exeunt King and Jester. The mention of their exit is omitted in the stage directions.

Scene 5 (the wedding): the sanctuary of Chāmuṇḍā, in the palace garden, near the Banyan. With two episodes:

> **Episode 1^{a}, the prison room ; 1^{b}, the Queen's apartment.**
> **Episode 2^{a}, the prison room ; 2^{b}, the Queen's apartment.**

Enters the Magician, iv. 18^{37}, and does homage to the Goddess, iv. 19, whose idol screens the mouth of the new branch passage, iv. 18^{38}.

Enters the Heroine, iv. 19^{3}, coming from her prison, and issuing forth from the passage by a small opening behind the idol.

Enters the Queen, iv. 19^{10}, coming from the garden, and is dumfounded at seeing the Heroine, whose escape from the prison she thought she had at last effectually blocked. The Queen cannot believe her own eyes, iv. 19^{14-15}. Accordingly,

Episode 1^{a}. The Queen, iv. 19^{20}, on pretext of returning to her apartments to get some things for the wedding (iv. 19^{18}), "steps about" on the stage, to indicate that she is leaving. We are to imagine that she goes by way of the garden to the prison room. The Magician sees through her pretext and sends the Heroine hurriedly back, iv. 19^{24}, by the new branch passage, to her prison, which she is of course imagined to reach before the Queen. The Queen is again no less astonished to find the Heroine quietly seated in the prison, iv. 19^{29}, and, after a few words with her, "starts" to return to the sanctuary,

iv. 19^{37}. Thereupon, the Heroine returns thither by the secret passage, with speed (see iv. 19^{41}).

Episode 1^b. The Queen, on her way back, to make good her pretext, stops at her own apartment for a moment while she and her friends pick up the things for the wedding, iv. 19^{38-39}. Arriving at the sanctuary, she is again dumfounded, iv. 19^{43}, at seeing the Heroine as before.

Episodes 2^a and 2^b are simply repetitions of the same manœuvres, iv. 19^{49-55} and iv. 19^{56-60}.

Enters the King, with his Jester and Kurañgikā, iv. 19^{61}. Effusive admiration on the part of the King, iv. 19^{64}–20. The Jester shuts him up, iv. 20^4. The attendants proceed to arrange the wedding costume for the King and for "Ghanasāra-mañjarī," iv. 20^6. It now transpires, iv. 20^{13}, that the latter is no other than Karpūra-mañjarī. The ceremony is performed, iv. 21^2, and the King "takes his seat as an Emperor," iv. 21^4.

Behind the stage, a Bard congratulates him, iv. 21^6; the King felicitates himself, iv. 23; and the play closes with the usual benediction.

5. Dramatis Personæ.

Chaṇḍa-pāla, the King.

Kapiñjala, his Jester (Vidūshaka), a **Brahman.**

Vibhrama-lekhā, the Queen.

Vichakshaṇā and Sārañgikā, her attendants.

Bhāiravānanda, a master magician.

Kāñchana-chaṇḍa and Ratna-chaṇḍa, two bards.

Porteress, an unnamed woman, who serves as door-keeper.

A tame parrot.

Karpūra-mañjarī, the Heroine.

Kurañgikā, her confidante.

Note.—The Heroine is the daughter of Vallabha-rāja, King of Kuntala, and of his wife, Çaçi-prabhā (p. 240). The latter is the sister of Vibhrama-lekhā's mother. The Heroine and the Queen of our play are therefore first cousins (daughters of sisters).

Abbreviations.—For abbreviated titles of books and papers cited, see pages 175–177.

KARPŪRAMAÑJARĪ.

ACT I.

PROLOGUE.

INVOCATION.

ALL hail to Sarasvatī ! [1] joy to the poets, Vyāsa [2] and the rest ! may the most excellent words of others too [3] turn out highly acceptable to the critics ! may the Vāidarbhī style of writing [4] flash like a revelation upon us, -- so too the Māgadhī and also the Pāñchālikā ! may the connoisseurs of poetry let these styles melt on their tongue, as do Chakora birds with the moon-beams ! [5] **1**

Moreover :

Ever cherish ye deep reverence for [6] the loves of Cupid and [his wife] Rati, in which no flurried embraces are noticed, no noisy kissing is going on, nor amorous beating of the breasts.[7] **2**

[*End of the invocation.*[8]]

STAGE-MANAGER. May the union of Çiva and [Pārvatī, his wife,] the Daughter of Himālaya, who are dear to the hosts of the Gods, whose pledge of love is [their son,] the Six-faced [God, Kārttikeya], and who are adorned with a crescent moon [on their brows], yield you happiness **3**

And again :

Victorious is Rudra,[9] who often, as he bows low [10] to assuage [his Pār-

[1] The Goddess of Speech.

[2] Reputed author of the Mahā-bhārata.

[3] That is, of this dramatic company, no less than those of the more famous poets.

[4] The styles (rīti) are enumerated at Sāhitya-darpaṇa, no. 625 f. See Kāvyādarça, i. 40 f.

[5] On which they are said to feed.

[6] 'Bow down (far, i.e.) low before.

[7] 'Loves, not possessing noticed embrace-flurries, nor produced kissing-noise, nor performed breast-beatings.'

[8] Recited presumably by the sūtra-dhāra or Director (who here makes his exit); and, if so, an interesting survival of older dramatic usage. See Konow's Essay, p. 196; and Lévi, pp. 379, 135. The "Director's" first subordinate seems to have been the "Stage-manager"; and subordinate in turn to the latter was his "Assistant." See p. 217.

[9] Tantamount to Çiva.

[10] 'In his bowings.'

vatī's] jealous anger, lays — a bit quickly[1] — at the lotus-like feet of the Daughter of Himālaya his offering of pearly moon-beams,[2] together with a silvery conch made of the moon's slender crescent and filled to the brim[3] with waters of the Ganges of Heaven, and places his two hands the while [in token of reverence] on his bowed head. 4

[*Walks about the stage and looks toward the tiring-room.*]

But our players seem [already] to be busy about their acting: for one actress is getting together such costumes as suit the rôles; another is twining garlands of flowers; [4] a third is putting the masks in order; some one seems to be rubbing colors on a palette; here they are tuning[4] a flute; there a lute is being strung; [8] and here they are making ready three drums; here the noise of timbrels is heard; [10] there they are rehearsing the introductory stanza. So I'll call some attendant and inquire.

[*Looks toward the tiring-room and beckons.*] [13]

[*Enters the Assistant of the Stage-manager.*]

ASSISTANT. Sir, your commands. [15]

STAGE-MANAGER. You seem to be busy about a play, are you not?

ASSISTANT. To be sure. We are going to enact a Saṭṭaka.

STAGE-MANAGER. But who is the author of it?

ASSISTANT. Your worship, let this be answered: who is called "Moon-crowned"?[5] and who is the teacher of Mahendrapāla, the crest-jewel of the race of Raghu? 5

STAGE-MANAGER. [*Reflecting.*] Aha! that, I think, is an answer in the form of a question: [*aloud*] Rāja - - - çekhara!

ASSISTANT. [Yes,] he *is* the author of it.

STAGE-MANAGER. [*Recollecting.*] It has been said by the connoisseurs:

"Saṭṭaka" is the name of a play which much resembles a Nāṭikā, excepting only that Praveçakas, Vishkambhakas, and Aṅkas do not occur. 6

[*Reflecting.*] Then why has the poet abandoned the Sanskrit language and undertaken a composition in Prākrit?

[1] For fear lest her anger increase.

[2] 'Of moon-light pearls.'

[3] See under ā. Literally, 'to the root,' and so, 'radically, completely.' Similarly at ii. 2[a].

[4] See OB. under sthāna 1 (w).

[5] Literally, 'Having the night's beloved (raaṇivallaha) [i.e. the moon, which is also called rāja] as his crown' (sihaṇḍa) [Sanskrit, çikhaṇḍa, used as an equivalent for çekhara]. That is, the assistant's reply is couched in the form of a charade.

ASSISTANT. Sanskrit poems are harsh; but a Prākrit poem is very smooth; the difference between them in this respect is as great as that between man and woman. **7**

And he who is expert in all languages[1] has said:

The various themes remain the same; the words remain the same, although undergoing [certain phonetic] modifications[2]: a poem is a peculiar way of expression,[3] be the language whichsoever it may. **8**

STAGE-MANAGER. And has he then [the poet] made no statement about himself?

ASSISTANT. Listen. A statement has indeed been made by one of his poet contemporaries, the author of the story of Mṛgāñkalekhā, by Aparājita,[4] namely, as follows:

He who has risen to lofty dignity by the successive steps of young poet, chief poet, and teacher of King Ṇibbhara,[5] [i.e. Mahendrapāla], — **9**

He is the author of it, the famous Rājaçekhara, whose merits make resplendent the three worlds even, [and] are left unblemished [even] by the rivalry of the moon. **10**

STAGE-MANAGER. At whose instance then are you enacting the play?

ASSISTANT. The crest-garland of the Chauhan family,[6] the wife of the chief poet Rājaçekhara, the lady whose husband wrote the play, Avantisundarī, — *she* desires us to enact it.[7] **11**

Moreover:

In this excellent Saṭṭaka, which is a river of poetic flavors, [King] Chaṇḍapāla, the moon of our earth, in order to achieve the rank of an Emperor, takes to wife the daughter of the Lord of Kuntala. **12**

STAGE-MANAGER. Come, then! what we have at once to do let us accomplish; for the Director and his wife, who have taken the parts of the King and the Queen, are waiting in the tiring-room.

[*The two walk about the stage and exeunt.*] [4]

[*End of the Prologue.*]

[1] This seems to refer to Rājaçekhara. — The following jadhā is like the Greek "recitative ὅτι."

[2] Such namely as obtain between Prākrit words and the corresponding Sanskrit ones.

[3] That is, its distinctive character lies in its mode of expression. The definition is, in the original and as we give it, loose.

[4] See p. 197. [5] See p. 178.

[6] See p. 180, and C. M. Duff's Chronology of India, p. 277, and Journal of the Royal Asiatic Society, 1899, p. 546.

[7] Lit., 'it, the work of her husband.'

[*Then enter the King, the Queen, the Jester, and, according to rank, the attendants. All walk about the stage and take seats in due order.*] [7]

KING. O Queen, daughter of the sovereign of the Deccan, I congratulate you that the spring is begun.[1] For,

Inasmuch as the maidens no longer put much wax on their lips,[2] and do not in arranging their braids anoint them with fragrant oil, and do not put on a bodice, and are indifferent even as to the use of the thick saffron[3] for their mouths,—therefore I think the festal spring-time is at hand and has overcome by its power the cold. **13**

QUEEN. I too, in my turn, will congratulate you.

Now that the frosts are gone, [again fair maidens] rub their pearly teeth.[4] Little by little [again] they set their hearts on extract of sandal.[5] At this season, behold, couples sleep on the verandas of their dwellings,[6] the blankets heaped [unused] at the foot [of their couches]. **14**

FIRST BARD. [*Behind the stage.*] Victory, victory to thee, [O King]! Thou gallant of the women of the East, thou champak-bloom ear-ornament of the town of Champā,[7] thou whose lustre (*rāḍhā*) transcends the loveliness of Rāḍhā,[8] who hast conquered Assam by thy prowess, who

[1] See p. 214-215.

[2] As they would in the cold weather to prevent chapping.

[3] In the Indian materia medica (see Dhanvantarīya Nighaṇṭu, p. 96) saffron is esteemed fragrant and pungent and hot and as a specific for cough, phlegm, and sore throat. Hence pretty girls have less need of it at the end of the season of cold and of colds.

[4] With rind of betel (cp. p. 181). Konow cites Viddh., p. 75[2] (**chollida = gharṣita**), and H. 4.395 (**choll = takṣ**): 'Fair maidens (do, i.e. putzen, **un-mrjanti**) cleanse their teeth.' This too is a sign of returning spring: for in the cold weather, it was actually painful to cleanse them because of cracked lips. — Vāsudeva renders **chollanti** by **sphuranti**: 'the teeth-jewels flash,' i.e. girls show their pearly teeth in laughing, which they could not bear to do while their lips were so chapped. Cp. Ṛtu-saṁhāra, iv. 6.

[5] Esteemed as the most eminent refrigerant (Dhanvantari, p. 93), and so the exact opposite of the calefacient saffron. Cp. Indische Sprüche, 1763, 2215.

[6] **Ghara** seems to include the whole dwelling-place, i.e. the central bungalow and all the adjoining compound. In cold weather, people slept, for the sake of warmth, in the **antar-gṛha**, the innermost apartment or perhaps the central bungalow. Now, on account of the heat, they have left off doing so, and sleep in the **sāliās**: these may be thatch-roofed sheds without walls (to secure shade and allow circulation of air), or else verandas around the **antar-gṛha**; and might, in either case, be called **majjhima** as being 'between' the **antargṛha** and the walls of the compound.

Vātsyāyana, Kāmasūtra, ed. Bombay, 1891, p. 44, 45, speaks of a dwelling with spacious court, and with two sleeping-rooms (**bhavanam dvi-vāsagṛham**), an inner (**ābhyantaram**) and an outer (**bāhyam**); the comment refers also to the **vāstuvidyā**.

[7] The champak-tree has a very fragrant golden flower much used as a decoration for the hair and ears. The far-fetched metaphor of the bombastic panegyrist is chosen here in part for the sake of the pun.

[8] Literally, 'O thou, having the loveliness of **Rāḍhā** [a district of western Bengal]

providest merry-makings (*keli*) for Hari-kelī,[1] who mayst well make light of[2] the beauty of genuine gold, who delightest us by the comeliness of all thy person! — May the beginning of the fragrant season [spring] be a joy to thee! For now,

> Cool from the Malabar mountains, are coming the [vernal] breezes.[3]
> Wanton they ruffle the down on the cheeks[4] of the Pāṇḍian women,
> Breaking the jealous pride[5] of the tender maidens of Kāñchī,
> Filling the matrons of Chola with passion for love's embraces,
> Waving the tresses [fair] of the beauties that dwell in Karṇāṭa,
> Tying the knots of love 'twixt the Kuntala girls and their lovers. **15**

SECOND BARD. [*Behind the stage.*] The champak bloom has become like to a Marātha girl's cheek when rubbed with saffron-paste.[6] The jasmines, with blossoms as fair as slightly churned milk, are bursting and bursting.[7] The dhak-tree,[8] blackish at the root,[9] and with bees clinging to its tips, looks as if bees were clinging to it from head to foot[10] and drinking its juices. **16**

KING. Dear Vibhramalekhā, say not that I have congratulated thee, nor that thou hast congratulated me; but rather that both of us have been congratulated by the two bards, Kāñchana-chaṇḍa and Ratna-chaṇḍa.[11] [2] So now to her heart's content let my Queen with eyes as big as [her]

surpassed by thy (rāḍhā or) lustre' — again a pun.

1 A name for Bengal (Hemachandra, 957) — again a pun.

2 Literally, 'hast made light of,' i.e. art so handsome that thou canst well afford to do so. — When it comes to the version of Indian panegyric, English is poor indeed.

3 Cp. Madanikā's song kusumāuha-piadūao, near the beginning of act i. of Ratnāvalī (translated, Wilson, ii. 270). Also, Kādambarī, p. 437⁵. Similarly Tennyson, Locksley Hall, line 20, "In the Spring" etc.

4 Literally, 'Wanton in causing horripilation on the edges of the cheeks.'

5 So that they yield to the seductions of love. The same idea at ii. 50ᵇ and iii. 30ᵃ.

6 Of saffron it is also said that it will make the face as fair as the full moon's disk — Yogaratnākara, under kṣudrarogacikitsā, p. 382²² of Poona ed. The tertium comparationis appears to be the color common to the golden-hued champak blossom and to the flesh-tint of the cheek when somewhat yellowed by the overlaying of saffron.

7 The flowers of most varieties are very fragrant and of pure milky whiteness — cp. i. 19ᶜ.

8 The Butea frondosa, a middle-sized tree, its trunk crooked and covered with ash-colored, spongy, scabrous bark. Lac insects [Coccidæ] are frequent on its small branches and leaf-stalks. So Roxburgh, p. 540 f. The lac exudes from the punctures made by the coccus. — See Griffiths, fig. 72 and pl. 63.

9 So that this too (see preceding looks as if bees were swarming upon it.

10 Literally, 'appears (notatur) as if quaffed by bees that cling [to it] even in two directions or points, i.e. even at top and bottom.' — Perhaps bhasala (here rendered 'bee') refers (inaccurately?) to the coccus insects.

11 He is called by the equivalent name Māṇikya-chaṇḍa at iii. 26².

open palm,[1] contemplate this festal season of spring :[2] — [of spring,] that quickens bold maids unto amorous flurry ; that sets a-dancing like dance-girls the creepers that sway in the Malabar breezes ; that sweetly recites its pañchama-note in the throats of the soft-throated [cuckoos] ;[3] that brings forth in ample measure the rods for the bows of Cupid and speedeth the arrows of love with vehemence none may hinder ;[4] [of spring,] the loved friend of [that] matron staid, [the Earth,] the Keeper of Treasure. [3]

QUEEN. The Malabar-breezes have indeed begun, as the bards have said. For,

Waving the garlands that hang in the doorways of Lañkā,[5] slowly swaying the sandal-tree thickets in the hermitage of Agastya,[6] blended with odors of camphor, making to tremble the clumps of açoka,[7] setting completely a-dancing the creepers of betel, impetuously kissing the waters of Tāmraparṇī,[8] [hither at last] are blowing the breezes of Chāitra.[9] **17**

And again:

" Your jealous pride quit ye, [fair maids]! give [each] to your darling a glance, be it never so restless![10] [for] tender youth, that plumps your swelling breasts, by days is measured,[11] five [perchance], or ten! " — such is, as it were, the Five-arrowed God's[12] all-galling command, disguised

[1] Cp. note to i. 32.

[2] I take mahūsava (madhu-utsava) as an instance of rūpaka (Daṇḍin's Poetics, ii. 66) and interpret it, not as 'spring-festival,' but rather as 'the spring which is like to a festival,' and so, 'the festal season of spring.' Similarly, 'creeper dance-girls,' i.e. 'creepers that are like dance-girls.'

[3] Literally, [spring,] 'possessing the note, sweet and recited (or sweetly recited), in the throats of the soft-throated [kokilas or kouls].'

[4] I take this as a copulative compound (Whitney, Grammar, § 1257) made up of two possessive compounds: literally [spring,] 'possessing - abundantly-produced Cupid's-bow-rods and possessing unbroken arrow-impetuosity.' — The exceedingly long word is notable for its excessive alliterative use of nd's.

[5] Ceylon.

[6] Located on a crest of the Malabar range by the Rāmāyaṇa, ed. Bombay, iv. 41. 15; but a later stanza (34) of the same canto inconsistently puts his dwelling on Mount Kuñjara in Ceylon. — The canto contains many of the geographical allusions which occur in this play. Cp. Lassen, Indische Alterthumskunde, i. 153 f.

[7] Kañkellī, a name for the açoka-tree — see my notes to 1. 20[27].

[8] A river rising near the southern end of the Western Ghauts and flowing generally south and east to the gulf of Manar. At present the name Malaya is hardly applied to the Ghauts so far south.

[9] The first month of spring, March–April, p. 214.

[10] Literally, 'a glance, followed by unsteady movements (of the eyes).'

[11] Literally, 'youth [is] for days.'

[12] Cupid's. — For 20 names of Cupid and for names of his belongings, see Hemachandra, 227 ff.

under the melodious warblings of the cuckoo, which the festal season of Chāitra [just now] hath suddenly given.[1] 18

JESTER. Hi there! among you all, I'm the only one that's a bit of a scholar: for my father-in-law's father-in-law used to lug around books at another man's house.

ATTENDANT [Vichakshaṇā]. [*Bursts out laughing.*] Got your learning by direct inheritance, then, didn't you? [4]

JESTER. [*Rather nettled.*] Ha, you slave-girl's child, who'll be a bawd in your next birth, you Vichakshaṇa, Small-Fraction-er![2] am I such a fool as to be laughed at even by you? [6] And besides, — O you polluter of other men's sons, you light-o'-love,[3] you terror of the gambling-hells, hand and glove with ruined folk![4] — what have *you* got to say against my inheriting my learning?[5] please take notice that they who are born in Akāla-jalada's family do get their learning by inheritance! but there's no use in talking.— "Bangle on your wrist, no need of a mirror."[6] [10]

VICHAKSHAṆĀ. [*Reflecting.*] Right you are! — Nor of asking[7] the bystanders if a horse is speeding, when you see him on the dead run. — Come now, give us a description of spring. [14]

JESTER. How do you come to be standing there chattering like a caged starling?[8] *You* don't know anything. — So I'll give my recitation

[1] I find a very similar thought in Kāvyaprakāça, x. 105, p. 705, ed. Bombay (given also by Böhtlingk, Sprüche, 2021, **kṣīṇaḥ**, etc.).

[2] I coin this word to reproduce the jingling and riming billingsgate of the original — **ṇillakkhaṇe viakkhaṇe**, 'insignificant Vichakshaṇā'; and neglect the **-ā**.

[3] An unclear word; perhaps 'having the character of a bee' (in its flight), i.e. 'unsteady, capricious.'

[4] 'O thou, united with ruined folk,' root **truṭ**.

[5] 'Was the inheriting of my learning a discredit?'

[6] The fact is as plain without talk as is a bangle on your wrist without a mirror. This last seems to be a proverb (p. 206) and in abrupt form.

[7] That is, 'and no need of asking' etc. — Apparently a second proverb of the same purport as the foregoing.

[8] 'Caged **sāriā**.' The same as the **maaṇasāriā**, Skt. **madana-sārikā**. From **maaṇā** or **mayaṇā** Platts derives **mainā**, the name of the mina bird: see his Hindústání Dic'y, under **mainā**, p. 1108a. The mina is the talking starling or religious grackle of India, the Eulabes religiosa: see Century Dic'y, under Eulabes, and picture.

As Dr. Konow tells me, the **sārikā** is mentioned with the parrot (**suke sālikā**) as early as Açoka's reign, namely in Edict 5 of the Delhi Pillar: see Senart, Les édits des piliers, p. 44, 65, or Bühler, ZDMG. xlvi. 64, 69, or Bühler, Epigraphia Indica, ii. 259.

The birds are habitual companions in literature and in life. A caged parrot and the mina are mentioned together. Mṛcchakaṭikā, ed. Stenzler, p. 71[16], the latter as chattering (**kurukurāadi**) like a saucy house-maid. Cp. the whole scene with the caged **sāriā**, Ratnāvalī, beginning of act ii.; and parrot before my old man[1] and the Queen: for musk isn't sold in a petty hamlet or a jungle; nor is gold tested without a touchstone.[2] [18]

[*So saying, he recites.*]

The Sinduvāra shrubs that bear a quantity of blossoms like to rice-pudding,[3] — my favorites are they; and also the multitudes of fair jasmine blooms, like to strained buffalo-milk.[3] 19

VICHAKSHAṆĀ. [*Derisively.*] Your words are as paltry as you yourself are.[4]

JESTER. Well then, Miss Noble-Words, do *you* give a recital.

QUEEN. [*Smiling a bit.*] Friend Vichakshaṇā, you're rather puffed up[5] with pride before us on account of your strong poetic ability. [5]. So then, do you recite now, before my lord, [the King], a bit of poetry of your own making: for that is true poetry which will bear recital[6] in the assemblies; that is pure gold which proves clear[7] on the touchstone; she is a true wife who gladdens her husband; he is a true son who makes his family illustrious. [7]

VICHAKSHAṆĀ. As the Queen commands. [*So saying, she recites.*]

episode of this play, iv. 4. In KSS. 77, parrot and mina tell stories. — Caged birds in frescoes, Griffiths, pl. 45.

The Indian exquisite (nāgarika) spent the time between his forenoon meal and his midday nap in teaching his parrots and starlings to talk: see Kāmasūtra, ed. Bombay, 1891, p. 48[11], 49[18]; Bāṇa's Kādambarī, p. 356 end. For this accomplishment both birds have great capacity. They can rattle off at a great rate the Vedas and Çāstras, which they incessantly overheard: Kādambarī, p. 81[1], 38; cp. Harshacharita, p. 244[7], 221 end; also, above, p. 204, Pischel. Secrets must not be told in their presence: comm. to Manu vii. 149. A very learned parrot appears at KSS. lix. 28 ff. Both birds alike come to grief for their much talk, Sprüche, 899.

See T. C. Jerdon, Birds of India, Calcutta, 1863, ii. p. 320–340; R. C. Temple has a valuable paper about the bird, Panjābī Shārak, Indian Antiquary, xi. 291–3: cp. xiv. 305 (Aelian's description). See also Wilson, Hindu Theatre, ii. 277; and Index to Ridding's Kādambarī, p. 225, under maina. While I am studying this subject, my friend Rouse, of Rugby School, sends me his charming book, The Talking Thrush, London, 1899. And Bloomfield refers me to Kāuçika, x. 2, etc. (very pretty symbolism).

[1] The Sāhitya-darpaṇa, no. 431, allows vaassa, 'comrade,' as a form of address to the king, to be used by royal sages and by the jester. When so used by the jester, with pia-, it seems to me to connote no less familiarity than our colloquial "Old Man." — The chief of police uses it when he offers to treat the low-caste fisherman, who, after finding Çakuntalā's ring, gives part of the money-reward to the officers (end of prelude to act vi.). Cp. preface, p. xix

[2] I mustn't cast my pearls before swine, nor seek the applause of "the unskilful." Only "the judicious" must pass upon my verses. — Proverbial expressions again.

[3] In whiteness. Cp i. 16[b] and Kādambarī, p. 100, 261. — The Jester's verses smack of the kitchen.

[4] 'Your words match your own paltriness,' taking kantārattaṇa as = kārpaṇya.

[5] For uttāṇā. Konow cites Pāiyalacchī, st. 75.

[6] 'That is poetry which is recited' etc.

[7] Sub voce ṇivvaḍ: cp. H. 4. 62.

The winds that had almost died on[1] the flanks of the mountains of Lankā, that had grown weak from filling wide-expanded hood after hood of the serpents,[2] wearied with dalliance,[3] — at this season, they, as Malabar-winds, mingling with the sighs of maids whose lovers have left them, have become, suddenly, although in their childhood,[4] strong, filled as it were with freshness. **20**

KING. Truly, Vichakshaṇā is clever (*vichakshaṇā*) by reason of her skill in expression and her variety of diction. And so, she stands — what else? — as a crest-jewel of poets.

JESTER. [*Nettled.*] Then why don't you say it straight out: "Vichakshaṇā's at the tip-top in poetry, [and I,] Kapiñjala, a Brahman, at the very bottom"? [4]

VICHAKSHAṆĀ. My good man, don't get excited. It's your poem that betrays your poetic ability:[5] for your words, fine [enough in themselves], although [spent] on a matter blameable for paltriness, — like a string of pearls on a flabby-breasted [old hag], like a [trig] bodice on a pot-bellied creature, like the collyrium pencil[6] on a one-eyed woman, — are not over and above charming. [7]

[1] Root **skhal**: 'stumbled,' or (as we say of the wind) 'fallen'; and so, 'checked by.'

[2] Literally, 'had come to impoverishment in the wide-expanded hood-row's (subjective genitive!) swallowing.' The ranks of expanded hoods of the female serpents have swallowed so much of the wind that its force has slackened! Characteristic exaggeration! Quite similar is the idea of Daṇḍin, who calls the slack south-wind the "leavings from the repasts of the serpents of the Malabar hills," Daçakumāra-charita, I. v., beginning. — "The snakes, 'tis said, on wind are fed." Sprüche, 4873, **phaṇī pavanabhuk**: cp. 4376. "The Cobras . . . prefer taking their food at dusk or in the night." — Fayrer, p. 6.

My colleague, Mr. Samuel Garman, Herpetologist of the Agassiz Museum, kindly refers me to Sir Joseph Fayrer's Thanatophidia of India, 2d ed., London, 1874. Plates 1–6 of this magnificent folio are devoted to the very deadly Naja tripudians, the Naga, or Cobra di Capello. I quote from page 7: "Some of the snake-catchers have a curious notion concerning the sex of the Cobra. They say that the hooded snakes are all females and poisonous; and that the males are all hoodless and innocent." It is not venturesome to assume that this belief, albeit unfounded, was current a thousand years ago and accepted by our poet. Hence the significance of his specific mention of the female serpents. The males are in fact smaller than the females, Mr. Garman tells me. — If Fayrer is not accessible, the reader may consult Joseph Ewart's Poisonous Snakes of India, London, 1878.

[3] Cp. Bhartṛhari's **ardhaṁ nītvā**.

[4] Because the season in which they blow has only just begun. — The whole stanza is commented in Jhalkīkar's ed. of Kāvyaprakāça, iv. 41, p. 157.

[5] That is, if you have any: and here, yours show that you haven't. — I purposely use 'betray,' as having, like **pisuṇedi**, a sinister connotation.

[6] That is, the strokes of the pencil with which women applied the collyrium to blacken their eyelids and eyebrows by way of adornment.

JESTER. With you, on the contrary, although your matter was charming, — it wasn't pretty, the way you strung the words together. [8] Like a row of copper bells on a golden girdle, like trimmings of coarse silk on a [fine] silken fabric, like sandal-ointment on a girl of loveliest tint,[1] — it [your language] doesn't partake of the elegance [of your ideas].[2] But in spite of all that, you do get praised. [10]

VICHAKSHAṆĀ. My good man, don't get excited. There's no rivaling you: for you, though unlettered as the iron beam of a goldsmith's balance, are employed [in a, *that is*] as part of a [still finer] balance for weighing jewels; while I, though lettered like a [common] balance, am not employed in the weighing of gold.[3] [14]

JESTER. If you ridicule me that way, I'll tear off that part of you that goes by the name of Yudhishṭhira's eldest brother,[4] your left one, and your right one too, in a hurry. [15]

VICHAKSHAṆĀ. And I'll break that part of you that goes by the name of the asterism[5] following Latter Phalgunī, in a hurry. [16]

KING. Man, don't talk that way. She has some standing[6] in the line of poetry. [18]

JESTER. [*Nettled.*] Then why don't you say it straight out: "Our little hussy's a first-rate poet, ahead even of Harivṛddha, Nandivṛddha, Poṭṭisa, Hāla, and the rest"? [*So saying, he prances around on the stage.*] [21]

VICHAKSHAṆĀ. [*Derisively.*] You take yourself off to where my first swaddling-clothes went.[7] [23]

[1] To an Occidental, gāura, 'yellowish' is a doubtful compliment: it is applied to a beautiful woman of golden flesh-tint, at Rāmāyaṇa v. 10. 52, ed. Bombay, and is used similarly here, as I think.

[2] Or, your uncouth words do not support or keep from falling (avalambedi), that is, do not keep from appearing ridiculous, the elegance of your ideas. — The jester's words are good and his subject bad (like pearls on a hag): Vichakshaṇā's words are bad and her subject good (like a coarse patch on a fine fabric). I am not sure about avalambedi. If I am right, the sandal-ointment seems out of place.

[3] Presumably, the beam of the common balance, for bulky things like cotton, had its divisions marked by letters (akṣaras); while the beam of the balance for weighing gold or finer objects was not lettered. At any rate, the play of words on "unlettered" (= 'unmarked' and 'illiterate') and "lettered" (= 'marked' and 'literate') is palpable. — She means, "you, jester, are a rough stick; but are employed on work (poetry) as fine as gem-weighing — that is, royal favor gives you a chance at 'high art': while with me the case is reversed."

[4] Karṇa: karṇa, as appellative, means 'ear.'

[5] Hasta: hasta means also 'hand.' See p. 214.

[6] Compare BR. vii. 1330, under k).

[7] That is, "to the devil knows where!"

JESTER. [*Turning his head to look back.*] And you — to where my mother's first set of teeth went.[1] [25] Here's luck to such a royal court as this, where a hussy appears [to be set] on a par with a Brahman, where strong drink and the five products of the [sacred] cow are put in one and the same dish, where glass and ruby are employed together on the [same] parure. [26]

VICHAKSHAṆĀ. In this royal court may you have that[2] put on your neck [namely, a half-wring, as we might say], which the Exalted Triple-eyed God [Çiva] wears on his head [namely, the half-ring of the moon]; and may your head be well bruised by that [namely, the touch of a foot] by which[3] the longings of the açoka tree are satisfied [namely, the touch of a maiden's foot]. [27]

JESTER. Ha, you slave-girl's child, you terror of the gambling-hells, you wholesale polluter of young men,[4] you street-walker! that's the way you talk to me, [is it?] well then, as sure as I'm a great Brahman,[5] you shall get that by which, about February or March, the longings[6] of the horse-radish tree[7] are satisfied; and that which a strong but lazy bull gets from the outcastes.[8] [29]

VICHAKSHAṆĀ. While I, if you go rattling on that way, like the [jingling] bangles on my foot,[9] with my foot I'll smash your face. And

1 "To the devil knows where."

2 The **ardha-candra**, literally, 'half-moon,' serves as Çiva's diadem (cp. i. 3[a]); but the word means also 'the hand bent like the crescent moon for clutching.' 'To (give, i.e.) put a half-moon on a man's neck' = 'to wring his neck.'

3 Literally, 'by which the açoka tree gets its **dohada**:' **dohada**, 'the whimsical longing of a pregnant woman,' is here the desire of the budding tree to bloom. This is accomplished by the touch of a fair maid's foot. The "touch" as applied to the jester would be a rude kick.

The açoka is one of the loveliest of Indian trees. It blooms at the beginning of the hot weather, say the botanists; when touched by a fair maiden's foot, say the poets. — The latter have very much to say about it; compare ii. 43, below, and Vāsudeva's Scholion thereto, and see especially ii. 47. Indeed, the Sāhitya-darpaṇa makes the matter to be one of "common notoriety" — see no. 576, under **khyāti- . . . viruddhatā**, and p. 228 end. See also Paul Elmer More's "Century of Indian Epigrams," no. XI; and Sprüche, 5693, **raktāçoka**, a stanza which some Mss. insert in the Vikramorvaçī immediately after **raktakadamba**, iv. 30. The flowers are of a beautiful orange color, changing gradually to red.

4 Seems to mean the same as **para-putta-viṭṭālini**, i. 18[8]. — But Vāsudeva, p. 17[18], explains it as 'getting your living by perjury,' taking **kosa** as 'false oath.'

5 'By the word of me, a great Brahman.'

6 Sarcastically here.

7 Moringa pterygosperma, called **dançamūla** at Rājanighaṇṭu, p. 142, Poona. The bulbs are cut up for a pungent sauce and the limbs are torn off for their flowers.

8 A cut in his nose, for the insertion of a nose-ring (cp. Manwaring, Marāṭhī Proverbs, no. 201). — Cp. Hemachandra, 1268, and Marāṭhī *baila*. — For ablative, see p. 203.

9 The point of comparison between the jester and the bangles is the senseless noise

what's more, I'll tear off from you the pair of parts [your ears] that go by the name of the asterism [1] that follows Latter Ashāḍhā, and chuck 'em away. [31]

JESTER. [*Walking testily about the stage — then in a rather loud voice, behind the curtain* —] Commend me to such a royal court as this — when [2] it's a devil of a way off! [a court] where a slave-girl sets up a rivalry with a Brahman! Well, from this day on, *I* propose — obediently paying my humble duty to my worshipful spouse Vasuṁdharā — to stay just at home! [*Laughter all round.*] [35]

QUEEN. What sort of fun can we have without our worthy Kapiñjala? [or] how adorn our eyes beautifully without collyrium? [36]

JESTER. [*From the tiring room.*] Oh no, you won't get me to come back, not by a long shot! better look out for somebody else to be your "old man": or perhaps you might put this mean little wench in my place, after giving her a mask with a long beard, and awful ears.[3] — I'm the only one among you that's dead and done for; but you — here's life to you for a hundred years! [41]

VICHAKSHAṆĀ. Don't try to make up with [4] the Brahman Kapiñjala: conciliation only makes him all the harsher, just as sprinkling water on a knot in a hempen rope makes it all the tighter. [43]

QUEEN. [*Looking in every direction around her.*] For that the God of Day, resting his glance on the unsteady swings that are tossed to and fro by the feet of the singing wives of the herdsmen, driveth his car with halting coursers,[5] — therefore are the days very, very long.[6] **21**

JESTER. [*Reëntering hurriedly.*[7]] Give place, give place![8]

KING. For whom?[9]

JESTER. Bhāiravānanda is standing at the door.

that both make. **Pāda-lagga**, 'attached to my foot' = 'on my foot.'

[1] Strictly speaking, Abhijit (containing α Lyrae) comes next after Latter Ashāḍhā, but it is so far from the ecliptic as hardly to count. Then comes Çravaṇa: çravaṇa means also 'ear.' See p. 214, and Whitney's Essay on the Lunar Zodiac, there cited, pages 410, 409, and 355.

[2] Literally, 'such a court is praised when' . . ., like the German *das lobe ich mir.*

[3] "Ears like a bamboo cup" — says the Scholiast.

[4] I take **aṇu-saṁdhedha** as a Prākrit counterpart of **aṇu-saṁdhayata**, from **saṁdhay** as denominative of **saṁdhi**.

[5] Literally, 'goes, having a limping-steed car, a car with limping steeds.'

[6] This stanza is a covert hint (**dhvanyate**) at the fact that she greatly misses her jester. — Scholiast.

[7] See Lévi, Théâtre, p. 374.

[8] Although this English phrase means 'make way *or* room,' it is perhaps the nearest feasible equivalent for what is literally 'a seat, a seat!'

[9] 'What (purpose is there) with it (the seat)?'

QUEEN. The one who is popularly reported to be a wonderful master magician? [5]

JESTER. Yes, to be sure.

KING. Have him enter.

[*The Jester goes out, and reënters with the Magician.*]

BHĀIRAVĀNANDA. [*As if a little boozy.*] [1]

As for black-book and spell, — they may all go to hell! [2]
My teacher's excused me from practice for trance.[3]
With drink and with women we fare mighty well,
As on — to salvation — we merrily dance! [4] **22**

Moreover:

A fiery young wench to the altar I've led.[5]
Good meat I consume, and I guzzle strong drink;
And it all comes as alms, — with a pelt for my bed.
What better religion could any one think? [6] **23**

And again:

Gods Vishṇu and Brahm and the others may preach
Of salvation by trance, holy rites, and the Vedies.[7]
'Twas Umā's fond lover [8] alone that could teach
Us salvation plus brandy plus fun with the ladies **24**

[1] See A. V. W. Jackson on tipsy episodes in plays, Am. J'n'l of Philology, xix. 250.

[2] Literally, 'I know nothing of (= I ignore) spells [and] Tantras.' The latter I take here to be the treatises called Tantras — cp. Aufrecht, Bodleian Catalogue, 91–95.

[3] The intent contemplation which was very anciently and widely practised in order to bring on a state of hypnotic trance.

[4] Literally, 'unto salvation we go, following the Kula way.' The "Kula way" is so called because its followers (Kāulas) refer to a Kula Upanishad as scriptural authority for their practices (Williams). — The union of the male principle in nature with the female is typified in the androgynous form of Çiva in which the right side is male and the left is female. The latter represents the personified 'Power' of nature (çakti = 'power'), and her worshippers are called Çāktas or Followers of the Left-hand Way. This worship degenerated into the most indescribable licentiousness. It was ostensibly practised in order to attain, in the manner prescribed by the Tantras, the supernatural powers such as the Magician is here supposed to possess. — The reader may consult Monier-Williams, Brahmanism and Hinduism,[4] p. 180–186.

For the doubtless satirical juxtaposition of sensuality and salvation, cp. a lampoon on the Buddhists, cited by Leumann, Wiener Zeitschrift für die Kunde des Morgenlandes, iii. 332, which I render as follows:

A good soft bed; an early drink on rising;
Dinner at noon; his toddy in the evening;
Sweetmeats at night; — to crown it all, salvation!
See? that's the way your Çākya-son would work it!

[5] 'A hot strumpet has been consecrated (see dīkṣ) as lawful wife.'

[6] Literally, 'to whom does the Kāula religion not appear charming?'

[7] I have assumed "Vedy" (riming with "lady") as a colloquially humorous mispronunciation of "Veda," the name of the oldest holy scripture of India. It will seem natural enough to any Yankee.

[8] Çiva, as god of the Left-hand Çāktas.

KING. Here is a seat. Let Bhāiravānanda take it.

BHĀIRAVĀNANDA. [*Seating himself.*] What'll you have me do?

KING. Glad to see a wonder in 'most any line you please.

BHĀIRAVĀNANDA.

> I can bring down the moon to the ground
> And show you its rabbit-face [1] round.
> The car of the sun I can stop in mid-sky.
> Wives of sprites, gods, or Siddhas through heaven that fly,
> Or of Çiva's retainers, — I fetch 'em anigh.
> Lord knows what on earth I can't do if I try. **25**

So tell me what you'll have done.

KING. [*Looking at the Jester.*] Say, man, has a peerless gem of a woman been seen [2] anywhere?

JESTER. There is here in the Deccan [3] a town named Vidarbhā. There I have seen one gem of a girl. Her let him "fetch anigh" [to us] here. [7]

BHĀIRAVĀNANDA. I *am* fetching her anigh.

KING. Bring down the full moon [4] to the ground.

[*Bhāiravānanda represents in pantomime* [5] *the practice for trance.*] [10]

[*Then enters, with a hurried toss of the curtain, the Heroine. — All gaze.*] [12]

KING. Oh, wonderful, wonderful!

Since the tips of her curly locks yet stick to her face, since her eyes are red with the washed-off collyrium, since drops are a-tremble on the massy tresses she holds in her hand,[6] since she has but a single garment and that but half put on,[7] — therefore I think this girl, who alone can fill me with wonder,[8] was busied with her play in the bath [9] [at the moment when she was] "fetched anigh" by yonder master Magician. **26**

And again:

With one lily-hand arranging the border of the garment that falls on

[1] The Hindu sees, not a "man in the moon," but a rabbit (cp. H. C. Warren, Buddhism in Translations, p. 274), or a black-antelope (cp. note to ii. 20 below).

[2] We miss the tae or tue ('have you seen') which appears in the variants, and is answered by mae, i. 25[6].

[3] See page 213.

[4] Literally, 'the moon on the night of the full,' — in palpable allusion to the first line of the Magician's stanza (25), but with covert allusion to any full-moon-faced beauty whom the king would be glad now to see.

[5] See Lévi, Théâtre, p. 387.

[6] Literally, 'hand-supported mass of sprays of hair.'

[7] 'Since a single garment-border (or garment-skirt) has been put on.' — She had no time to put it all on properly.

[8] Literally, 'sole-producer of marvels.'

[9] Cp. ii. 24 and note to ii. 24[8].

her rounded breasts so firm,[1] with the other restraining[2] the sari[3] that flutters as she walks,[4] — who in a picture could her grace portray?[5] **27**

JESTER. For her bath she had doffed her ample parure. Her adornments were spoiled by the breaking of the waves.[6] Her slender form shows neath her dripping vesture.[7] This maiden's glance is the sum and substance of loveliness. **28**

HEROINE. [*As she looks at them all — aside.*] That this is some great King is made manifest by the way in which he plainly unites the graces of dignity and charm.[8] Of this one too I have an opinion, [namely,] that she is his First-Queen — you don't need to be told, in order to recognize Gāurī[9] at the left side of the Half-woman God.[10] And this is the master Magician. [5] Here again are the attendants. [*Stops to reflect.*] Then why does his look seem to make so much of me, even in the presence of his wife? [*So saying, she gives a coquettish glance.*[11]] [9]

KING. [*Aside—to the Jester.*] When she suddenly, past my ear, shot a sidelong glance sharply flashing, [a flashing glance] whose brilliancy was like that of the cavities of the petals on the tips of the ketakas where the bee sucks,[12] — then was I whitened surely with the best of camphor

[1] Literally, 'on her firm-breast-hills': **thala** is used of parts of the body which may be considered as raised or elevated or projecting or rounded above or beyond its general surface — so of buttocks (ii. 1ª), of cheeks, of breasts. Cp. BR., s.v. **sthala** (3ª, 4ª).

[2] Dr. Konow books the word, of course, under root **yam**.

[3] The **kaḍilla** (defined by HD. as **kaṭīvastra**) is doubtless the sari (or saree or sary), a long piece of silk or cotton wrapped about the hips, with one end falling nearly to the feet and the other thrown over the head, and here the same as the **potta** or 'garment' of line b — since she wore but "one."

[4] Literally, 'the **kaḍilla** which was moved (from the, i.e.) by the walking,' **caṅkramaṇatas**, Whitney, § 1098.

[5] Literally, 'she is not portrayed in any one's picture.'

[6] Of the pool or river in which she had been bathing.

[7] Literally, (the glance of this one) 'having a body-liana (**laā**) coming into sight (**ullāsin**) from her dripping vesture,' **ollaṅsua-ullāsi-taṇu-llaāe**: or, **ullāsin** might be 'radiant,' i.e. 'radiantly beautiful'— see BR. under **las** + **ud**.

[8] Literally, 'This one is known as a king by this (**iminā**) profound-and-charming grace-union.' Here **iminā** means 'this which you plainly see, this plain *or* manifest' (union), reminding us a little of Latin **ille**. As used of the character, **gambhīra** is 'deep, solemn, dignified.'

[9] Literally, 'Gāurī, even untold, is known:' — and it's just as easy, even without help, to recognize the Queen.

[10] See note to i. 22ᵈ.

[11] Vāsudeva defines **try-açram** as **tiryag-udañcitam**, (she looks a look) 'bent sideways.' The king refers to this glance at ii. 1ᵈ. — See notes on the coquettish glance, ii. 6ª, iii. 2ᵈ.

[12] Literally, 'when a sharp sideglance-flash was shot ear-nigh suddenly, — [a flash] possessing brilliancy (**chavi**) like [that of] bee-sucked ketaka-tip-petal cavities.' I take **sav-** as 'with an ear-interval,' not hitting. **Kaṭākṣachaṭā** occurs in the 2d example to Sāhitya-darpaṇa, no. 100, cited by BR. ii. 1072. The pple **āaḍḍhia**, 'pulled at' by bees, is booked under **kṛṣ** + **ā**.

(*karpūra*),[1] bathed surely with moonlight. Meantime I am become overlaid as it were with dense pearl-dust. 29

[*As before, aside — to the Jester.*]

Oh, the splendor of her beauty!

Methinks her waist, circled with triple folds, were easily grasped even by a baby's fist, while to compass the expanse of her hips is not possible[2] even with the two arms.[3] A tender child's hand suggests a comparison for the bigness of her eyes.[4] And so [by reason of her beauty], it is not possible in a picture to portray her as she really is.[5] 30

JESTER. Albeit her adornments are stripped off for the bath and her cosmetics are washed away by it, [yet] how lovely she is! or rather, let me say,

Even women who are devoid of ⌊natural⌋ beauty put on adornments, [for] they win a certain comeliness by such embellishment; [but] adornments make the comeliness even of a person who is naturally handsome to unfold itself [to still greater beauty].[6] 31

KING. That's true of *this* girl, at any rate. For

Her loveliness is like to gold, untarnished, unalloyed.[7] Her almond-eyes reach even to her ears.[8] The expanse of her cheeks is like to the full-orbed moon. That she is under the protection of the Five-arrowed God, [who guards her] with bended bow,[9] [is clear], because

[1] Or, with a pun of which the King is not consciously guilty, 'then was I irradiated with love for Karpūra (-mañjarī).'

[2] The phrase ṇo jāi (yāti) seems to be used like *es geht nicht*, *that won't go*, etc. 'The expanse is not possible to be embraced' (veṣṭ). For the use of the infinitive here and in d, see Jacobi, § 116. — "Expanse:" cp. i. 32[b].

[3] The style of beauty here exaggeratedly described is abundantly illustrated by the sculptures of ancient Indian monuments. They out-Rubens Rubens in his most drastic avalanches of buttocks. See A. Cunningham's Bharhut, Plate xxiii. Hindu painters show more self-restraint than the sculptors and poets: see Griffiths, i. p. 9[a].

[4] 'The bigness has a comparison (given, i.e.) suggested by the hand.' Cp. i. 32[a].

[5] Paccakkhaṁ.

[6] Literally, 'even of a person nature-handsome, the comeliness opens its eyes by [aid of] adornments.' Repeated at ii. 25.

[7] Literally, 'gold, new (*or* fresh) and genuine.' The two adjectives are not without appropriateness of reference to girlish loveliness also.

[8] A strange bit of racial psychology underlies the varying national ideals of beauty of person (cp. note to ii. 46). — Literally, 'Of her eyes the length is brought to a stop (skhalitam, 'stumbled, fallen,' — or as pple of the causative) by her ears.' Cp. i. 16[3]; 30[c]; 34[c]; ii. 27[a]. Of a handsome young ascetic, Bāṇa says, "his eyes were so long that he seemed to wear them as a chaplet," Kādambarī, p. 280. See Griffiths, i. 8[b].

[9] Dhaṇuddaṇḍa is 'bow-stock;' but *stock* in this connection (see Century Dict'y, s.v. *stock*, sense 9) is superfluous in English.

his arrows,[1] "Parcher," "Bewilderer," and the rest,[2] are piercing me through. **32**

JESTER. [*With a smile.*] The wind of the highway knows the liana's power of resistance.[3]

KING. [*With a smile.*] I tell you, old man:

The embellishment effected by their own manifold excellences makes handsome the person of women;[4] while splendor of attire seems [rather] to conceal[5] their beauty of form. Accordingly, for those on whose limbs is imprinted the seal of a certain loveliness,[6] Cupid, methinks, with bended bow, stands as the ever-ready servant.[7] **33**

Moreover: Of this maiden

The spread of the hips is such that no creeper-like girdle is on them; the breast-hills are so towering as to hide from her sight her waist;[8] the eyes are so long that there is no [room for a] lotus on her ear;[9] and the face beams forth with such radiance that it seems like a second moon on the night of full moon.[10] **34**

QUEEN. Worthy Kapiñjala, find out[11] who she is.

JESTER. [*To the Heroine.*] Come, sweet-faced girl, sit down and tell me who you are.

QUEEN. A seat for her!

Although we say *bow-string* when we mean the *string*, we say simply *bow* when we mean the *bow-stock*. Cp. **vana-antare** etc.

1 Literally his 'seekers.' The verb is listed under **vyadh**.

2 Namely, "Inflamer," "Ruiner," and "Ҫrazer" — **saṁdīpana, uccāṭana, unmādana**: see Uhle's Vetāla, p. 8^{12}. Or cp. Maheçvara's comment on Amarakoça, i. 1. 27. The two here mentioned are punned upon at iii. 26, see note.

3 Sodīrattaṇa, 'manliness, pride, self-respect.' For this passage, Dr. Konow suggests 'power of resistance.' Cupid knows how hard it is to conquer the King and so is shooting at him with great energy.

I give with diffidence the following interpretation: By i. 32, the King means, "Cupid guards this fascinating girl, and I fear I may not win her." "Never fear," says the Jester, reassuringly; "the wind knows how little resistance the swaying creeper offers."

4 'The person of women is beautiful [when] embellished by the host of their own excellences.'

5 In Index under **chad**. — Cp. ii. 26, 27.

6 'To whose limbs a certain imprint of loveliness is gone.'

7 Ready to read from their coquettish glances their unspoken commands and to enthrall their lovers accordingly. — Scholion.

8 Literally, 'the breast elevation (or prominence) is so that she sees not her navel at all.'

9 Cp. note to i. 32^b.

10 'And so outshining is the face that the night of full moon [is] possessing two moons.' Rājaçekhara repeats this idea (see p. 206) in his three other plays, Viddh. iii. 27, Bālar. iii. 25, Bālabh. i. 31; cp. Çārṅgadhara 3659 and p. 189: **udañcaya mukham manāg; bhavatu ca dvicandraṁ nabhaḥ.**

11 'Know thou by asking,' 'πυθοῦ.'

JESTER. Here is my over-garment. [5]

[*The Jester gives the Heroine the garment, and she sits down upon it.*]

JESTER. *Now* tell me.

HEROINE. There is here in the Deccan, at Kuntala,[1] a king named Vallabha-rāja, beloved (*vallabha*) by all his people.

QUEEN. [*Aside, to herself.*] Yes, and he's my aunt's husband. [10]

HEROINE. His consort is named Çaçi-prabhā.

QUEEN. [*Aside, as before.*] And she's my mother's sister.

HEROINE. [*Smiling.*] They call me by way of joke [?] their "bought daughter." [15]

QUEEN. [*Aside.*] Such splendor of beauty, surely, was not produced save from the loins of Çaçi-prabhā; nor are[2] pencils of precious beryl,[3] save from Beryl Mountain. [*Aloud.*] You are Karpūra-mañjarī, aren't you! [20]

[*The Heroine stands abashed.*]

QUEEN. Come, little sister, embrace me. [*So saying the Queen puts her arms around her.*]

HEROINE. Oh joy! here at last Karpūra-mañjarī has begun to receive recognition![4] [24]

QUEEN. Today, Bhāiravānanda, by your kindness, I have been made to enjoy an uncommonly neat [but] queer little arrangement in seeing [this] little sister.[5] So let her stay now for a fortnight. Afterwards you shall carry[6] her back by your magic power.[7] [27]

BHĀIRAVĀNANDA. As the Queen says.

JESTER. [*To the King.*] Say! we're everlastingly[8] — both of us — left out in the cold, you and I, since *they* have got together in a cosey family circle.[9] For these two women are "little sister" each to the other;

[1] See p. 213.

[2] The verbal idea in each of these two clauses is expressed by a derivative of the same root pad, with ud or with nis.

[3] Literally, 'beryl-gem-pencils.' The beryl occurs in hexagonal prisms; hence the appropriateness of the word "pencil." Some varieties are very beautiful (the emerald is one of them), while others are very little worth; hence the need of the word "gem."

[4] Literally, 'of K. this is the first salutation:' but if put thus, it might imply that she is glad she has received none before.

[5] Literally, 'today an unprecedented (= uncommonly neat) queer-little-arrangement (= saṁvihāṇaa, cp. OB. vii. 5ᵇ), with the sight of the little-sister, has been caused by your kindness to be enjoyed by me.'

[6] In the Prākrit, the verb is plural, — "honoris causa," says the Scholiast.

[7] Literally, 'contemplation-car;' that is, the supernatural power which you will attain by trance-practice will serve you to carry her home through the air to Kuntala.

[8] In rendering param, I venture to use this English vulgarism because it suits the Jester.

[9] 'Since of them (Queen, Heroine, Vi-

while Bhāiravānanda is praised and made much of for bringing them together. [33] And here a terrestrial Goddess of Speech, a go-between, [is parading about,] reincarnated as a downright Queen.[1] [34]

QUEEN. Vichakshaṇā, to Bhāiravānanda must be shown every attention his heart can wish, and you may go to your eldest sister, Sulakshaṇā, and tell her so.[2] [35]

VICHAKSHAṆĀ. As the Queen commands.

QUEEN. [*To the King.*] My lord, pray let me take my leave;[3] for you see the state the little sister is in,[4] and I'm going to the women's apartments[5] to arrange her attire with beauty and grace. [38]

KING. [Of course you may go; for] it is quite proper to fill the runnels about the roots of the champaka creeper with musk and camphor.[6]

FIRST BARD. [*Behind the stage.*] May twilight bring its gladness to my King. [41]

The hot-rayed sun's round orb, like to the body[7] of the soul of day,—who knows where that in all the world is gone,[8] now that the time for day to die[9] is come? And even this lotus-pool,[10] as if her eyes were sealed in a swoon on hearing of the long separation [that awaits her,] now that her lord is departed, hath shut fast the lids of all her lily-eyes.[11] **35**

chakshaṇā, and Magician) there is an assembled family.'

[1] Dr. Konow refers the allusion (sarcastic, says the Scholiast) of this sentence to Vichakshaṇā, comparing ii. 10^{8}; and takes **dehantareṇa** with **devī**, as the reading of W suggests. It vexes the Jester to see Vichakshaṇā so honored.

[2] 'Attention is to be paid . . ., telling your sister.'

[3] See Index, under **iṣ**.

[4] 'I am going . . . on account of the beauty and grace of attire of the little sister who has this condition,' which you plainly see.—She had been snatched from the bath by the Magician (cp. i. 26 and 28).

[5] The action is taken up again at ii. 11^{8}.

[6] The Scholiast takes this as a case of **samāsa-ukti**, citing for it Kāvya-prakāça, x. 97, p. 671, Bombay ed.,—cp. Sāhitya-darpaṇa, p. 309^{10-11}, transl., p. 398. The "champaka creeper" suggests a slender, lovely woman,—here the Heroine. It is proper to bestow thereon all needful attention.

[7] Taking **piṇḍa** as 'body'; but Dr. Konow takes **jīva-piṇḍa** as 'Lebens-masse,' 'Lebens-hauch.'

[8] Literally, 'who knows where (**kahiṁ**) in the world (**pi**) that is gone?'—In other words, I think that **pi**, although *adding* an indefinite idea to the interrogative, *does not* convert the interrogative into an indefinite ('somewhere') in this passage.

[9] 'The occasion for the death (**kāla**) [of the day] having arrived' (**āp**): Vāsudeva, "**sāyaṁsamaye.**"

[10] In Prākrit this is feminine (**ṇalinī**), and so I refer to it by the feminine pronoun in English.—Literally, 'the pool has become (**jāā**, under **jan**) having lilies shut ("shut," as used of the eyes).'—**Soūṇa**, under **çru**, Jacobi, § 61.

[11] The pool (feminine) of day-blooming lotuses closes her "eyes" (the blossoms on her "face") in a swoon of grief when her

SECOND BARD.

Opened [now] for our pleasure are jewelled roof-terraces and the picture-galleries.[1] By the attendants, couches, delightful in the starlight,[2] are hastily[3] spread. Silks begin to rustle as the fingers of the restless hands of the ladies in waiting move over them.[4] The pleasant murmur of the voices of women who have made up their quarrels[5] is heard in the arbors. **36**

KING. And we will go to our evening worship.[6]

[*At these words, exeunt omnes.*]

[*End of the First Act.*]

beloved lord (the sun) leaves her. The sun's departure is hinted at in the first half-stanza; and the second half-stanza is of course in clear allegorical allusion to the Heroine, and to her grief at being separated from the King. — This is a case of "transfer" (samādhi, Kāvyādarça, i. 93): "because the ways of the Heroine are here transferred to the lotus-pool," says the Scholiast. For day-blooming and night-blooming lotuses, see nôte to ii. 50, with which stanza this may be compared.

[1] 'The pleasure-terraces-and-galleries.'— Such places serve as rendezvous for lovers, says the Scholiast. Open roofs are much used in the East as a kind of pleasance at night. With Vāsudeva, I take citta-bhittī-ṇivesā as = citra-gṛhās.

[2] 'In the star-time.'

[3] "Hastily:" there is scarcely any twilight in Southern India.— See root stṛ.

[4] 'The sound (rustle) of silk has begun by reason of the moving of the fingers' etc.

[5] 'The hum of women angry and tranquillized.'

[6] 'To pay worship, [namely, our] evening-prayer,' somewhat like ἀγωνίζεσθαι πάλην

ACT II.

[*Then enter the King and the Porteress.*]

PORTERESS. [*Walking around a bit on the stage.*] This way, this way, O King!

KING. [*Takes several steps, and then, with his thoughts on her —*[1]]

On *that* occasion[2]

Not from their places[3] moved even the breadth of a sesamum seed her fair rounded buttocks;[4] her belly seemed as if slightly overflowing with wavy folds;[5] her neck she bent aside; while the braided tress, that from her moon-like face did stray,[6] was clasped within the folding of her breasts:[7] [thus] in fourfold wise her slender form she showed, as on me sideways she her glance did bend.[8] **1**

PORTERESS. [*To herself, aside.*] How now — even today — piling up the same old palm-leaves? — the same old stock phrases?[9] — Well, I must sing the praises of spring-time to him and so slacken his passion for her. [*Aloud.*] Contemplate, O King, the flowery season,[10] which is very gently coming on.[11] [5]

[Now] are lengthening the days that break completely[12] the seal of the throat of the cuckoo's mate, that make the bees to hum with sweetness

[1] That is, of course, on the heroine. Supply "says."

[2] The occasion described at i. 28^9, when she gave him the coquettish glance which he now recalls in line **d**.

[3] For the form of the ablative, see H. 3. 9.

[4] Properly, 'well-conditioned buttock-hill' — cp. i. 27^b, note.

[5] '(Was) possessing slightly overflowing fold-waves.' Cp. ii. 6^b.

[6] 'The braid in straying from her face-moon;' or 'the braid, in the nodding to and fro of her face-moon:' either **veṇī** or **āṇaṇendu** might be the subject of **bhamaṇa**.

[7] 'By her braid a breast-embrace was got.'

[8] 'Of her, looking-coquettishly at me, the body-liana became (jan) having-four-disposals *or* -arrangings (-vidhā):' that is, four dispositions or attitudes of as many parts of her liana-like body presented themselves to my notice as she glanced etc.

[9] 'The same piling together of palm-leaves, the same word-series:' proverbial equivalent for threshing the same old straw.

[10] 'Give a glance at the flowery season.' The Scholiast seems to think the form of expression a little forced. And I certainly do.

[11] 'Which is maturing a very little.' This is vague as a time-datum; but the statement at ii. 6^23 seems more definite.

[12] See i. 4^b note. Cp. also p. 203.

long drawn out,[1] that among forsaken lovers waken anew the Pañchama note,[2] the king of melodies, — [the days that are] crazy with passion, [days that are] the abodes of the troops of loves. 2

KING. [*Giving no ear to it. — In impassioned style.*]

When, to the eyes of all in the place of assembly, she appeared as[3] an abounding stream of loveliness, as a city of the manifold dwellings of laughter and amorous delight,[4] as a paragon[5] of comeliness, as a lake whose blue lotuses were eyes, but withal as the enlivener of my passion, — then did Cupid fix a sharp piercing arrow on the string of his bow.[6] 3

[*As if crazed with love.*] From the very instant that I first saw her, — the fawn-eyed[7] girl, —

If I paint a picture, she flashes forth upon it;[8] she falls not short in [any] excellencies;[9] on [my] couch, [meseems,] she slumbers; but I see her face like a full-blown flower in every quarter of the sky;[10] of my talk she is the subject; of my verses, she the theme;[11] from my brooding thoughts ne'er parted[12] for long is the tender wanton maid.[13] 4

And again:

They whom the coquettish half-glance of her piercing restless eye hath smit,[14] will [soon] to death be done by koïl's note[15] and spring and moon

[1] 'Giving a prolonged quality of sweetness to the hum of the bees.'

[2] 'That set agoing (**saṁ-car, caus.**) the Pañchama note.' Cp. i. 16[3]; also Çārñgadhara's Paddhati, no. 2048 (in the season of flowers, the koïl utters the fifth or Pañchama note, our G; the frog, A; the elephant, B).

[3] 'When she became the beauty-stream (of the eyes of, i.e.) in the eyes of the people of' etc. [4] Cp. ii. 22[b].

[5] I am in doubt about this word. And the Scholia are not fully clear to me.

[6] **Puñkha** is the arrow's notched and feathered end which is fixed on the string. (See Raghuvaṅça ii. 31.) "The arrow was '**puñkha**-ed' on the bow" means "the arrow's notch was fixed on the bow-string." This action is called **saṁdhāna**. So iv. 20[d].

[7] Properly 'gazelle-eyed.' The gazelle is a small and graceful antelope, with large liquid eyes. The reader should see the beautiful pictures of P. L. Sclater and O. Thomas's Book of Antelopes, London, 1894 —, if he would know the full force of this epithet.

[8] 'On a picture she bursts forth.' If I amuse myself with painting, my pictures always turn out to be portraits of her.

[9] This clause seems strangely inept.

[10] 'She blossoms out [like a flower] in' etc.

[11] 'In [my] talk she is present; in [my] poetry, she comes forward *or* makes her appearance *or* (if the author will forgive me) bobs up.'

[12] 'In [my] meditation, not separated is' etc.

[13] Dr. Konow books the verbs under **sphuṭ**. **khuṭṭai, loṭṭ, visaṭṭai** (Skt. **çaṭ**), **vṛt, truṭ**; see his references to Pischel's Hemachandra. Skt. **truṭ** is 'to part' (intrans.), as we say of a rope. Cp. Marāṭhī **tuṭaṇeṁ**, and Molesworth, p. 383b: "whilst of **moḍaṇeṁ** the sense is 'to break,' with the ever-inherent implication of destruction of form or state, the sense of **tuṭaṇeṁ** is 'to break,' with the implication of parting or separating."

[14] 'They who have been looked at (**diṭṭhā**) by a third-part of her eye.' Cp. Hāla's Saptaçataka, no. 505.

[15] Cp. note to ii. 2[c] and cp. i. 16[3]. Cp. Sāhitya-darpaṇa, no. 215.

and love;[1] while they on whom hath fallen her full glance[2] are dead and ready for our last farewells.[3] 5

[*As if lost in pensive remembrance.*] And again:

Before[4] her, [flies] a glance, [like] a line of bees, [straight and stinging];[5] while [in the middle,[6] *or*] about her waist there is a garland of milk-white wavy folds;[7] and behind her proceeds, amid her coquettish peepings, Cupid, holding his bow bent so nearly round that the string touches his ear.[8] 6

[*Stops to think.*] My man is long coming back. [2]

[*The Jester and Vichakshaṇā enter and walk about.*]

JESTER. Say, Vichakshaṇā, is this all true?

VICHAKSHAṆĀ. Yes, it's all true, only more so. [5]

JESTER. I don't believe you — you are so awful funny!

VICHAKSHAṆĀ. My good man, don't talk that way: there's one time for joking, and another for the consideration of business.

JESTER. [*Looking before him.*] Here's my old man, as out of spirits (*mukka-māṇasa*)[9] as a gander that's quit Lake Mānasa (*mukka-māṇasa*),[10] emaciated with the fever-of-love (*mada*) as an elephant with rut (*mada*),

[1] For the Moon as Love's ally, see Kādambarī, p. 559[12], **kusuma-çara-sahāyaç candramāḥ**. Cp. note to iii. 30.

[2] 'Full look' (**diṭṭhī**), in contrast with the "third-part-look" of line **a**.

[3] 'Are fit for the gift of the two handfuls of sesamum-water,' the customary libation to the departed.

[4] The metaphoric language is here so "bold" (**prāudha**, as Vāsudeva justly observes), that no bare English version suffices to reproduce the thought.

[5] 'Before [her] is the bee-row of her eyes.' Kālidāsa speaks (Meghadūta, 35) of the temple girls and their eyes, "Whose glances gleam, like bees, along the sky," a free but good rendering of **madhukara-çreṇi-dīrghān kaṭākṣān**. This last is precisely what Rājaçekhara seems here to have in mind. Coquettish glances may reach far, like the bee's long flight; are straight as a "bee-line;" like the bees, they leave a sting; perhaps also they are bright as the bees' shining wings, for bees are described as **sphurant** or 'flashing' at Sprüche, 1986d. — See H. H. Wilson's comment on the Meghadūta passage; cp. Sprüche, 2463, where the **kaṭākṣa** is likened to a swarm of bees. — See iii. 2[d].

The "row" or "string" (**çreṇi**) in which the wild geese fly is mentioned even in the Rigveda (iii. 8. 9); and a "string" of bees forms the "bow-string" of Cupid's sugar-cane bow (Megh., 71). **Bhiñga-saraṇī** is here about the same as **bhramara-pañkti** or **madhukara-çreṇi**. — Correction in proof: Konow takes **bhiñga-saraṇī** here rather as the dark eyebrows.

[6] "Before," "in the middle," and "behind" are in evident contrast, — **majjhe**, with double meaning, signifying here 'on her belly.'

[7] 'There is a boiled-milk wave-garland' — cp. ii. 1[b] note. See **kvath** in Index.

[8] 'Holding his bow rounded to the ear.' See under **ā**. — Cp. iv. 20[d].

[9] Here is a series of elaborate puns.

[10] His true and glorious home in the Himālayas, in order to return (about the end of November) to the every-day waters of India — see C. R. L. in Journal Am. Or. Soc'y, xix., p. 155–6.

languishing (*milāṇa*) from his violent inner-ardor[1] (*ghaṇa-ghamma*) like a stick of lotus-root wilted (*milāṇa*) in the strong heat (*ghaṇa-ghamma*), his color (*chāā*) lost like the brightness (*chāā*) of a lamp that they give you by day-time, pale and wasted (*paṇḍura-parikkhīṇa*) like the moon which is pale and wasted (*paṇḍura-parikkhīṇa*) [by the sun's splendor] at day-break at the end of the night of the full.[2] [10]

BOTH. [*Stepping about.*] Victory, victory to the King!

KING. Man! how have you gone so far as even again to meet Vichakshaṇā?

JESTER. This time Vichakshaṇā did the "going," for she came to make it all up with me. And when she had made up, I stopped to talk with her till ever so much time went by.[3] [15]

KING. "Making up!" — what's the use?

JESTER. [The use is] that (*jaṁ*) here, with a letter in her hand[4] from a regular little dear, is — Vichakshaṇā! [17]

KING. [*Acting as if he noticed a pleasant odor.*] It seems to me as if I smelt the fragrance of ketaka blossoms.

VICHAKSHAṆĀ. Here in my hand is a letter on ketaka flower-leaves. [20]

KING. How do there come to be ketaka flowers in March?[5]

VICHAKSHAṆĀ. Bhāiravānanda has imparted to us a spell by whose power one blossom already has been made to appear on the ketaka-stock in the Queen's palace-garden. [22] With some of its hollow flower-leaves, today, the fourth day of the "Swing-breaker,"[6] the Queen has paid

[1] So, despite OB., s.v. **gharma**, end, as against BR., s.v. **gharma**, 1, end.

[2] 'Like the daybreak full-moon-night moon.' [3] See BR. vi. 477 top.

[4] See A. V. Williams Jackson's notes on billets-doux in plays, American Journal of Philology, xix. 252. Further interesting allusions may be found at Kumāra-sambhava, i. 7; and in Kādambarī, p. 433[6]. The last passage speaks of scratching a message with the finger nails, and, as here, on petals of ketakī.

[5] 'In Madhu,' the older name of Chāitra = March-April: see Whitney, JAOS. vi. 413–4. The Screw-pine or ketaka does not flower till the rainy season, says Roxburgh, p. 707, i.e., some three months later. Roxburgh adds: "The tender white leaves of the flowers . . . yield that most delightful fragrance . . . ; of all the perfumes in the world it must be the richest and most powerful." See *Pandanus* in Century Dic'y, and note to iv. 21[b]. Also Griffiths, i. p. 36[b], and pl. 63.

[6] There are various Swing festivals. The most famous is the dola-yātrā (culminating with the Phālguna full moon), during which images of Krishṇa are placed on a swing and swung. The weight of the idols often broke the swing: hence the name in the text. — Again, on the eleventh of the bright half of Chāitra, Vishṇu and Lakshmī are swung. — The context of the passage before us (cp. ii. 29[5]) indicates that here the Swing festival of Gāurī (and Çiva) is intended, the **gāuryā dolotsava**. This **āndolana-vrata** is a rite observed by women and begins on the third of the bright half of Chāitra. Herein agree

homage to Pārvatī, the beloved of Çiva. And again, a couple more of them she has [taken and] bestowed as a mark of favor on her "little sister," Karpūra-mañjarī. And the latter has paid homage to the same exalted Gāurī[1] with one of her two flower-leaves; [25] and the other

Hollow flower-leaf of the ketaka blossom as a present to you your friend hath sent; and it is inscribed with a couplet[2] which is lovely with its words (*vaṇṇa*) [written] in musk-ink, [*or*, *punning*] which is lovely with the color[3] (*vaṇṇa*) of the musk-ink.[4] 7

[*With that, she hands him the billet-doux.*]

KING. [*Opens out*[5] (the somewhat folded leaf) *and reads it.*]

By staining a white goose with saffron-paste till her feathers were ruddy (*piñjara*), I suppose (*kila*) that I cheated her gander into thinking "She must be the mate of a Ruddy Goose" (*cakravāka*). To pay for it now, my misdeed is making me to know misfortune,[6] in that (*jeṇa*), although near,[7] thou comest not within range of even my half-glance. 8

Hemādri, the Vratārka, Nirṇaya-sindhu, and Dharma-sindhu. ☞ See p. 289 and 216.

[1] Pārvatī.

[2] 'And it (jaṁ) is inscribed with a çloka-couplet,' that is, a couplet which forms a çloka (= stanza 8). — With this interpretation, each of the two members of the couplet would be a half of stanza 8. — Otherwise, we may assume that siloa is used as equivalent to "verse," and with the same looseness as in English, and meaning 'line' or 'half-stanza' here, and 'stanza' at ii. 8³, 9¹.

[3] Colored chalks and brilliant miniums (red lead, etc.) were used as surrogates for ink. At Jātaka, iv. 489¹⁷, words are written on a wall with vermilion or "native cinnabar," jāti-hiṅgulaka. Cp. Horace, Satires, ii. 7. 98. See Bühler, Palæography, p. 92, 93; and my note to iii. 18 below. Any color would show well on the white floral leaves of the ketaka.

[4] Eṇa-ṇāhi, 'antelope navel,' is one of the many names for 'musk' or kastūrikā. This is reddish-yellow, overpowers the intense odor of ketakas, and provokes even elephants to rut. — Rājanighaṇṭu, p. 100.

In the same volume, p. 439, sahasravedhin is said to be a name for three things, sorrel, musk (kastūrikā), and asafetida (hiṅgu). The last is a gum from the Ferula alliacea. It may be that the drug sambul or sumbul, the musk-root of commerce (a product of Ferula Sumbul, see Ferula and sumbul in Century Dic'y), which is a fair substitute for musk, is here intended instead of the genuine animal secretion, and that it was used to make a colored "ink." This is the less unlikely since the radically identical hiṅgu and hiṅgula are names, one for the plant and the other for the pigment! — If not, then we must render, "lovely with the ink-words [*or* ink-color] and lovely with musk": in this case it is not incredible that the Heroine added a dash of the drastic perfume to her missive to make sure that her royal lover's passion should not flag.

[5] Or, 'reaches his hand (sc. karam) for it.'

[6] 'Because (jaṁ) her husband (tab-bhattā, under tad) was cheated [into] thinking . . . [by me], making (kṛ) a female haṅsa [which is naturally white] [to be] possessing a saffron-paste-ruddy body, therefore this misdeed of mine has turned out (pari-nam) as a teacher of misfortunes,' etc. Her misdeed, like bad karma, bears appropriate fruit (Manu xii. 62) in a separation like that of Ruddy Goose and mate (p. 262, n. 3).

[7] I.e., 'in the same palace': so iv. 1ᵇ. The Queen is already jealous (cp. ii. 29¹⁰), and compels this separation (cp. ii. 9ᶜ).

[*Reads it a second and a third time.*] *These* words indeed are an elixir of life to my ears!

VICHAKSHAṆĀ. I too have made a stanza, — a second one, which describes the plight of my dear friend, — and written it down. Here it is.

KING. [*Reads it.*]

At endless length, like to her days and nights, her [love-lorn] sighs go [slowly] trooping by.[1] With her bejewelled bracelets,[2] fall her streams of tears. And in thy absence, O fair lover, the hope of life for that dejected maid hath grown as feeble as her slender form. **9**

VICHAKSHAṆĀ. [And] *here*[3] is a stanza about her plight, composed by my elder sister, Sulakshaṇā, who is serving her as lady in waiting: listen to this, O King!

Her sighs escape like pearls from off their string,[4] and make the sandal to wither.[5] Hotly her body burns [with love's fever]. The beauty of the laugh on her face is naught save a memory.[6] Moreover, the pale tint of her limbs is as faint[7] as the moon's slender sickle by day. Ever her floods of tears for thee,[8] O fair lover, are like to rivers. **10**

KING. [*Sighing.*] What is there to say? in poetry she's your "elder sister," sure enough.

JESTER. This Vichakshaṇā is Goddess of Poetry for the earth, and her "elder sister" is Goddess of Poetry for the three worlds. So I'll set up no rivalry with them. [5] But [as I'm] before my old man, I'll describe, with such words as befit me, the longings of love.

VICHAKSHAṆĀ. Recite. We're listening.

JESTER. Moonlight[9] is excessively hot, like to poison is sandal-water,

[1] 'With the days and nights, long [are her] sigh-columns.' Her sighs are like an army, passing in long drawn out "columns" (daṇḍa, used in the sense of **daṇḍa-vyūha**). Cp. daṇḍa at iv. 11.

[2] The bracelets slip from her arms because she is so emaciated with love's fever. This is a frequent motif: see Çakuntalā, st. 66 (Williams) or 67 (Pischel), and Meghadūta, 2.— Kāvya-prakāça, x. 112, p. 735, Bombay, cites this stanza to illustrate **sahokti**.

[3] The function of **jeva** is slightly to emphasize the gesture which distinguishes this deictically used **ettha** from that of ii. 8[3].

[4] 'Are possessing a pearl-string-ḷike escape.'

[5] They are so hot that they (are sandal-**uccoḍa**-causing, i.e.) shrivel up even the cool sandal. Is this right? if so, the juxtaposition of the pearls is incongruous. Root **cuṭ** is said to mean 'become small.'

[6] 'Has memory as its refuge,' has need to be remembered (cp. Sprüche, 2253d), since it can no more be seen. This seems to me to be a distinct reminiscence of Kālidāsa's beautiful phrase **saṁsmaraṇīya-çobhā**, Çak., near beginning of act iv.

[7] Properly, 'tender, soft.'

[8] 'For the sake of thee,' **tuha kae** = **tava kṛte**.

[9] Moonlight, sandal, pearls, night winds, lotus-root, and water are all refrigerants or

a pearl-necklace is like caustic potash on a wound, the night winds burn my body, a fibrous lotus-root bristles like arrows,[1] and ablaze is my slim body, albeit wet with water, — because I've seen the choicest maid, with lotus-face, and eyes so fair. 11

KING. I say, man, you too need rubbing down with a drop of sandal-water yourself.[2]

Accordingly, tell me some circumstance about *her*. What next did the Queen do with her after taking her[3] to the women's apartments? [3]

JESTER. Vichakshaṇā, you tell what was done.

VICHAKSHAṆĀ. They made her toilet, sire, and decorated her with her sectarial mark and her ornaments, and entertained her. [5]

KING. How so?

VICHAKSHAṆĀ. Her firm limbs were anointed[4] with paste of saffron-essence until they were yellow.[5]

KING. That was burnishing a golden doll till it was beautifully bright.[6] 12

VICHAKSHAṆĀ. Her companions put on her feet a pair[7] of emerald anklets.

KING. That was surrounding a pair of shamefaced lotuses with swarms of bees.[8] 13

VICHAKSHAṆĀ. She was arrayed in a couple of silken garments as blue as the tail-feathers of a king-parrot.

KING. That was tipping out the stems of the plantain with leaves that are gently tossed in the breeze.[9] 14

are esteemed as such (see Sprüche, 3260; Rāja-nighaṇṭu, p. 167; and cp. Ṛtu-saṁhāra i. 2, 4 and iv. 2): even they bring no coolness to one burning with love's fever. Similar ideas, Sprüche, 2246, 1081. — The stanza is full of internal rimes.

[1] 'Is an arrow-series.'

[2] To cool your apparent fervor of love.

[3] As mentioned at i. 34^{38}.

[4] For the meaning, BR. vi. 761, compare udvartana — see Amarakoça ii. 6. 121.

[5] Until her natural flesh-tint became still more beautifully yellow.

[6] 'Accordingly (tā) the beauty of a golden doll was polished bright.' Similarly the tā of the next ten stanzas.

[7] 'Her feet were caused to receive a pair' etc.

[8] Root bhram = 'roam, range' (trans., as in *roam the woods* — see BR. bhram 2, for examples), and so 'stray around, surround'; causative, 'cause to surround.' — Active construction, "They caused bees to surround the pair of lotuses": passive, "The pair was caused to be surrounded with bees." — Cp. the note on ii. 19^{b}; cp. also ali-mālā, and my note on āvalī at iii. 26^{d}.

[9] 'Then the shoot of the plantain [became] possessing slightly wind-tossed leaf-tips.' Her thighs are likened to the stems of a plantain and her wavy silks to its leaves. — Scholion. Rāja-nighaṇṭu, xi. 107, p. 149, gives ūru-

VICHAKSHAṆĀ. Over the expanse of her buttocks was placed a girdle bejewelled with rubies.

KING. That was making a peacock dance on the cliffs of Golden
Mountain.[1] **15**

VICHAKSHAṆĀ. Upon her two fore-arms, — as it were, the stalks of her lotus-like hands,[2] — were put rows of bracelets.

KING. That was — tell me[3] — was it not making them as lovely as an
inverted quiver of Cupid! **16**

VICHAKSHAṆĀ. A choice necklace of monster-pearls[4] was placed on her neck.

KING. That was giving to the moon of her face an ample retinue of
stars, ranged in ranks about it.[5] **17**

VICHAKSHAṆĀ. And a pair of ear-rings, studded with gems, was put in her ears.

KING. That was transforming her face into a chariot of Cupid and
furnishing it with two wheels to drive it to and fro.[6] **18**

VICHAKSHAṆĀ. With native collyrium they adorned her eyes.[7]

KING. That was putting[8] a bee on the fresh blue-lotus[9] that serves as

stambhā, 'thigh-pillared' or 'thigh-stemmed,' as one of 16 names for plantain. Kālidāsa has the same comparison at Meghadūta 93; and so has Amaru, as cited by BR. under kadala. Parab, Subh., p. 449, çl. 396, has lambhitāḥ kadalī-stambhās tad-ūrubhyām parābhavam. Cp. rambhoru; also iv. 7^c below.

[1] Mount Meru, to whose rocky steeps her buttocks firm are likened here. Cp. ii. 34 n.

[2] 'On her handlotus-forearmstalk-pair.'

[3] 'Then, tell me, does it [the "pair"] not look like [*or* appear beautiful as *or* glitter as] a reversed Cupid's quiver?' — The forearm and the quiver have the same general shape. See Griffiths, i. p. 15 a, b, and pl. 73, 83. The synonyms for quiver stand at Amarakoça ii. 8. 88; but I cannot cite any special description of Cupid's quiver. The nose is compared to an inverted quiver, Parab's Subh., p. 435, çl. 121.

[4] 'Six-māṣika-pearls.' If a māṣaka or 'bean' was 4½ grains, these would weigh over a pennyweight apiece and be worth each some 27 × 27 or 729 times as much as a one-grain pearl! Cp. iii. 3^{18} below.

[5] 'Then a multitude of stars in ranks [*or* rows — as the pearls strung on their several parallel strings are in rows] attends upon her face-moon.'

[6] 'Then her face-Cupid-car with two wheels was driven to and fro.' Ear-rings like veritable wheels: Griffiths, figs. 12, 50, 52, 54, 55!

[7] 'Her eyes were made possessing native-collyrium-produced decoration.'

[8] 'Then a fresh-bluelotus-bee was given to the Five-arrowed God.' — See root ṛ: uppiu = uppio (Jacobi, § 2, line 5, Lautlehre) = arpito. — Konow thinks I am wrong, and that silīmuha here means only 'arrow.' Cp. ii. 38.

[9] The blue-lotus (kuvalaya, utpala) is one of the five flowers that serve as Cupid's arrows. A fair maid's eyes are often likened (as here) to such a lotus (see Sprüche, 3702, 3818, 3838); or, the face is a lotus, and the restless eyes are bees (2658, 2660).

The fondness of the bees for the lotus is a common-place of the poets. The dark collyrium is here likened to the dark bees that swarm about the blossoms. Cp. Raghuvança, iii. 8.

one of the arrows of the Five-arrowed God. [*Or,*] That was giving a fresh lotus-arrow[1] to the Five-arrowed God.[2] **19**

VICHAKSHAṆĀ. The wreath of curly locks that fringes the crescent of her forehead[3] was arranged.

KING. That was the spotted antelope appearing on the moon's disk.[4] **20**

VICHAKSHAṆĀ. Upon the temples of the bright-eyed maid they heaped the flowers her tressy burden hid.[5]

KING. That was letting you see a contest between Rāhu and the Moon, on the part of the fawn-eyed girl.[6] **21**

VICHAKSHAṆĀ. Thus the Queen decorated the girl with decorations to her heart's content.

KING. That was an adorning of the ground of a pleasure grove[7] by the beauty of spring.[8] **22**

JESTER. This, O King, is very truth that I tell you:

The maid whose look is straight and bright,—collyrium befits her [eyes]. Whose breasts are like to ample jars,—a pearl necklace becomes her. But if upon the round expanse of her buttocks you place a gorgeous girdle, we may call *this* adorning and *dis*-adorning her.[9] **23**

[1] As in Sprüche, 5691^{b}, **çilīmukha** (see BR.) means not only 'bee,' but also 'arrow.'

[2] That is, the renewal (implied in **nava**) of the decoration of her eyes was like renewing that one of Cupid's five arrows which consists of a blue lotus.

[3] 'Clinging to the edge of her forehead-mooncrescent.'—See **rac**.

[4] 'Accordingly, the black-spotted antelope is (**vṛt**) on the moon's disk in the middle.'—**Majjhāu** (= **-āo**, i.e. **madhyāt**), abl. sing., used adverbially.—The face is the moon's disk and the locks are the dark spots upon it.

The dark spot or fleck on the moon greatly enhances its beauty (Çakuntalā, **sarasijam**, i. 20, Williams), and is often likened to the black or dappled antelope (Kāvyādarça, ii. 35). Hence the moon is called **mṛgāṅka** and **hariṇa-lakṣaṇa** or **-lāñchana**. Rājaçekhara calls it **hariṇa-lakṣman** twice, and calls it **eṇaṅka** and **miaṅka** and **hariṇaṅka** in this play. Cp. Hāla, no. 14.—For the names of the "fleck," see Hemachandra, 106.—For the name "rabbit-marked," see i. 25 and note.

[5] 'Of the maid with eyes bright as camphor-gum the tress-burden was possessing a hidden flower-heap.'—Let the reader notice, with reference to the sequel (iv. 18^{19}, 20^{16}), that **ghaṇa-sāra** is one of eleven synonyms for camphor (**karpūra**, which see, Rāja-nighaṇṭu, p. 101).

[6] 'Then a boxing-match between Rāhu and Moon was shown [you] by the gazelle-eyed one.'—Rāhu, the demon who causes eclipses by "swallowing" or "hiding" the moon, is here likened to the heavy tresses; and the blossoms, to the moon.

Tresses and flowers have a strife to see which shall cover or hide the other. Her lovely tresses win—they eclipse the flowers.

[7] 'Sport-grove-ground.'—Or else, 'sport-grove-earth,' that is an earth or world of places or opportunities for amorous delights. In either case the Heroine is meant. Cp. ii. 3^{b}.

[8] This means the Queen.—Scholion.

[9] 'And, on the other hand, on whose wheel-like buttock-expanse is a certain girdle-pride, of her we call *this* adornment and *dis*-adornment'—if I may venture so to

KING. [*Again*[1] *with his thoughts on her.*]

Her soft bathing garment, wet and clinging closely[2] to her waist with its triple folds, and to her shoulders,[3] [but] loose upon her magnificent buttocks[4] and jar-like breasts,[5] betrays the tenderness[6] of her liana-like form and its beauty. **24**

JESTER. [*As if vexed.*] Ho you! I described her as adorned with all her ornaments: while you, — you won't remember her except[7] as robbed of all her decorations by the water.[8] — Well, hasn't my lord ever heard this?[9]

Adornments make the comeliness even of a person who is naturally handsome to unfold itself [to still greater beauty]. A certain splendor results from adorning even genuine precious stones with diamonds. **25**

KING. 'Tis only the hearts of fools, mind you,[10] that fair women[11] rob by the bewitching accessories of attire;[12] while clever men have to be won[13] by natural beauty. Grape-juice isn't sweetened with sugar.[14] **26**

VICHAKSHAṆĀ. As the King has intimated:[15]

To swelling breasts, or eyes that to the budding ears do reach,[16] [or] face that serves as moon unto the earth, and body that is a stream of the rivers of loveliness,[17] what excellence is imparted by[18] the art of dress and adornment? [Very little, perhaps. But] why[19] [then] is even that

reproduce the paronomasia of **bhūsaṇaṁ dūsaṇaṁ.**

[1] Cp. ii. 0[4].

[2] 'Adhering (**laggaṁ**), water-close' (i.e. skin-tight with the water, **jala-ṇividaṁ**).

[3] 'On triple-fold-provided-navel and on arm-roots': cp. Amarakoça, ii. 6. 79.

[4] 'Getting loose on her paragons of buttocks and breasts.' See **çvas + ud**, 'sich lösen,' in BR. [5] Cp. ii. 44[a].

[6] Perhaps **lañgima-** is connected with **lañgh**, 'spring,' and means 'springiness, elasticity,' and so 'litheness.' That is not far from Vāsudev's definition, **tāruṇya**, 'youthfulness, tenderness.'

[7] "Not . . . except" renders **jeva.**

[8] He had already so described her, i. 26.

[9] It wasn't the Jester's fault if the King hadn't heard the first half — see i. 31[b].

[10] **Hanta.**

[11] Καλλίπυγοι.

[12] Or, 'excellence (**guṇa**) of the witchery of attire.'

[13] **Bhāvaṇijjā**: we must take the causative of **bhū** as = 'cause to come *or* yield,' colloquial 'fetch' ("that'll fetch him"), slang 'fetch' (= 'allure, attract').

[14] It must be sweet by nature, if at all. Cp. Sprüche, 3316. [15] At i. 33[ab].

[16] Cp. i. 32[ab]. — Or, 'that reach to the ear-buds' (the flowers placed as ornaments over or in the ears). [17] Cp. ii. 3[a].

[18] 'What merit of breasts etc. is made by the art etc.?'

[19] 'Listen to this (**iṇaṁ**) reason . . . for this fact (**tattha** — see Whitney, § 303a), that (**jaṁ**) even that (**taṁ pi** — the toilet adornment just mentioned) is all (**savvaṁ**) agreeable: What (frustration *or*) impairment of natural growth is there?' The reason is put in the form of a rhetorical question. I take **tattha** and **jaṁ** as correlatives. — **Rūḍhi** outmatches artifice (**yoga**) and has a power [for better, for worse] quite independent of the tricks of the toilet — says the Scholiast.

all agreeable? Listen while I tell you the reason[1] for it now: You cannot spoil natural beauty! **27**

KING. Moreover, my honest Kapiñjala, here's a point for you:[2]

What is the use of artificial ways of adornment? Those are the tricks of actresses. The person itself that takes the heart of a man,[3] *that* is lovely. Therefore, matrons, at that supremely happy moment in which they are united with their husbands, and in which the joy of love that brings a whole host of excellences is attained, do not wish at all for splendid attire. **28**

VICHAKSHAṆĀ. Sire, this I may tell you: not only by the Queen's orders did I follow Karpūra-mañjarī,[4] but also because I had come to terms of close friendship[5] with her. Therefore, as I'm ready at her need, I will, again [as before] make myself her attendant.

For the purpose of testing the heat of her [love-fever], their hand was laid in the fold between her breasts[6] by her friends, and was often astonished out of it[7] by the burning and quickly[8] withdrawn.—[But] what of that even? Give ear to these words, pleasing, yet alarming:[9] Warding off the moonbeams with her hand for a shade, she passes the night.[10] **29**

The rest of the business Kapiñjala will tell you. And [as he says], so it should be done.

[*At this, she steps about the stage, and then exit.*] [3]

KING. But, man, what is that "rest of the business"?

JESTER. Today is the fourth day of the Swing festival.[11] [5] And ere it close, Karpūra-mañjarī is going to be put in the swing in front of the [image of] Pārvatī. So my lord is going to wait at the Emerald

[1] 'Listen to the reason, being heard (**suvvantaṁ**, passive of **çru**, Jacobi, § 69. 3), i.e. the reason, while I tell it.'

[2] 'You, this one, are instructed.'

[3] 'What own-person (**ṇia-aṅgaṁ**) is man-heart-captivating.'

[4] **Tāe**: loosely used genitive with **aṇugadā**.

[5] 'Had come to the amity of apple-of-the-eye-friendship.' Cp. Psalm xvii. 8.

[6] 'The hand, laid on *or* in, was withdrawn from the depression (**utsaṅga-tas**) between her breasts.'—For the dative in **-āa** cp. Jacobi, § 38, and i. 14^{2}, 34^{41}, iv. 21^{6}.

[7] See BR., **ḍāmara**, 'a very astounding thing.' The hand is spoken of—boldly—as astounded.

[8] **Helāi** (**helāe**), 'without more ado.'—See root **kṛṣ**.

[9] The reason for the alarm makes the Scholiast much trouble.—Her behavior seems to indicate that she is love-sick (cp. ii. 5^{b}, **canda-māraṇijja**), if not also a bit moon-struck.

[10] Cp. Vallabhadeva, no. 1411, and Konow's Essay, p. 190.

[11] Cp. ii. 6^{23} and note.

Seat[1] and watch Karpūra-mañjarī while she swings. This is "that rest of the business." [8]

KING. [*Reflecting.*] Well, you *have* scored one on the old lady, keen as she is. [10]

JESTER. Made the old cat drink sour gruel and think it was milk[2] — I *guess.*

KING. Who else but you[3] is ready at my need? What else but the moon is clever enough to raise the tides of the ocean? [13]

[*At that, they step about and make as if they were entering the Plantain Arbor.*] [14]

JESTER. Here is the raised seat begemmed with crystal. And so, man, sit down on it. [16]

[*The King does so.*]

JESTER. [*Raising his hand.*] O King, behold the moon at the full! [19]

KING. [*Looking.*] Oh! it's the face of my beloved in the swing that he's pointing out to me when he says "moon at the full." [*Regards her attentively.*] [22]

Paling the face of every beauty here,[4] making the sky's hollow vault to ripple[5] with the liquid moonlight of her loveliness, and breaking the haughty pride in the hearts of maids that regard her,[6] appeareth the moon-like orb of her face as she moves straight to and fro in her sport on the swing. [*Or,*] appeareth the moon-like orb of her face, artless and mobile, as she plays at swing.[7] **30**

[1] Literally "Emerald-Heap." This is, I think, a jocosely exaggerating nickname for a seat, liberally ornamented, as we may presume, with gems. The scholion to this passage calls it "a kind of raised seat"; and to such a seat allusion is made at ii. 29^{15}. The name appears to include not only the seat, but also an arbor (called "Plantain Arbor" at ii. 29^{14}) or other shelter in which it was placed, since a door is mentioned at ii. 42^{21}. To judge from iv. 18^{3}, the "Seat" and the "Arbor" would seem to be in two different localities. I cannot reconcile the apparent contradiction. Of course, we might render the name by "Emerald Arbor."

[2] [By me] 'she, thinking (ti) [This is] "milk" (duddhaṁ), was made to drink sour gruel — [thus] I conjecture.' — Proverbial. Konow cites Viddh., p. 114^{6}, and Hāsyārṇava, 38^{22}.

[3] For the ablatives, see p. 203.

[4] 'Making colorless (vicchāa) the faces of the (circle, i.e.) entire collection of beauties in the town.' [5] See under vicchola.

[6] 'That regard (īkṣ) her,' with envy of her beauty, namely.

[7] 'Appears her face-moon, straightly (sarala) moving-to-and-fro (tarala) in her swing-sport.' Or, 'Appears her face, artless (straight, not crooked) and mobile.'

The two adjectives are used of a look, in like collocation, in Bhartṛhari's smitaṁ kiṁcit. Tarala, used of winds, waves, lightning, of eyes, glances, faces a-tremble

And again:

With [waving] chowries[1] raised aloft, with showy rows of banners dazzling-white, [and] with bells,—assuming a likeness to the resplendent (?) Asura-maidens' cars,[2] [now] mounting the rampart, in its course, ascending, descending, coming, and going, the swing captivates[3] the heart of men with its sinkings and risings.[4] **31**

And again:

With the tinkling jewelled anklets,[5]
With the flashing jingling necklace,
With the show of girdles garrulous
From their ringing, ringing bells,[6]
With the sound of lovely jingles
From the rows of rolling bangles,—
[Pray] whose heart is not bewildered
While the moon-faced maiden swings?[7] **32**

JESTER. Oh! you're an aphorist;[8] but I'll be your commentator and describe her with all prolixity.

Pained neath the pressure of her towering breasts,
Her rosy feet cry out to Love for help,—
Their voice her tinkling anklets set with gems.[9] **33**

with angry tears, means 'mobile, bright, flashing,' etc.

Note the uncommonly effective employment of alliteration and of well-balanced paronomasia in the swing-line, which is an admirable bit of word-painting. The metre of Kālidāsa's lyrical master-piece suits it to perfection. The following verse may give some idea of the rhythm and the internal rime:

Moves to | and fro, | swinging high, | swinging low, || now a rise, | then a sink | ing.

[1] A kind of fan-like brush, made of the yak's tail, often with bejewelled handle, and serving as one of the insignia of royalty. Pictured in Griffiths, pl. 5, 7; Banners, i. p. 15 b.

[2] The order of words in my version is ambiguous, as it is in the original: the uncertain "resplendent" may qualify "Asura-maidens" (**asura-taruṇi**) or "cars."—The Asuras are the foes of the gods.

[3] 'Makes(**kuṇai**) captivation (**-haraṇaṁ**) by (**-vasā**) its coursing (**raa**).' **Raa, raya,** from **rī**, 'run, currere,' as used of the motion of liquids, is not an unfit word.

[4] What was said of the foregoing stanza applies in large measure to this.

[5] The four adjectives that fill up lines *abc* are bahuvrīhis to **hindolaṇaṁ**: 'a swinging which possesses (i.e. in which become manifest) tinkling-jewelled-anklets, jingling-necklace-flash, ringing-bell-mouthy-girdle-display, [and] rolling-bangle-row-produced-sweet-jingle-sound.'

[6] Little bells were attached to the girdles. See Bhartṛhari's **etāç calad**, or Sprüche, 1456; with which—in general, also—our stanza may be compared.

[7] 'To the heart of whom is her swinging not bewildering (heart-bewildering)?'

Note again the beautiful appropriateness of the rhythm: it is that of the **pṛthvī**, with its κῶλα of jingling tribrachs and bell-like, chiming cretics. The stanza is a *tour de force* in the use of imitative words (onomatopœia). Compare Edgar A. Poe's "The Bells." Rājaçekhara repeats the first half of the stanza at Bālabh. ii. 3.

☞ For pictorial illustration of a swing-scene, see Griffiths, figure 66.

[8] You express yourself with all the exaggerated concision of a writer of aphorisms (cp. Max Müller's Sanskrit Literature, p. 71f.)

[9] 'The pair of her foot-lotuses, pressed by the superposed-breast-mountain-slopes, calls as it were to Love with the sound of the tinkling jewelled anklets.'

Her rounded buttocks, as she plays at swing,
For joy are laughing, laughing once again,—
Their voice the chiming of her jewelled zone.[1] 34

The stream of pearls adown her neck that flows,
Bright undulating with the moving swing,
Bears far and wide King Cupid's name and fame,
As if they hung like creepers o'er its flood [2] 35

Her garments tossed, as gainst the wind[3] she swings,
Reveal some glimpses of her lovely form,
Which calls to Love to nestle by her side.[4] 36

Her earrings, striking gainst her saffroned cheeks,
Mark lines that do a playful tally keep,
To count each oscillation of the swing.[5] 37

Sudden she opes her eager bloomy eyes,
Big as her palm, and Cupid's quiver fills
With piercing shafts of lotus-petals blue.[6] 38

And on the downward glide, behind her head
Stands out her braid, like stock of Cupid's whip,
And says "Stay not the coursing of the swing!"[7] 39

Thus all this maiden's winsome-graceful ways,
Displayed in swinging, form a picture bright,
Which Love, sly limner, paints in every heart![8] 40

[1] 'Her chariot-wheel-rounded buttocks, swing-play-voiceful (i.e. -jingling), seem to laugh for joy, with the sound of the bells of her bejewelled girdle.' — Bejewelled girdle: Griffiths, pl. 55. Bells on bracelets, fig. 6; on trappings, pl. 6.

[2] 'Her pearl-necklace, with the semblance of a bright (**tāra**) river (**sariā**), flowing with the sport of the swinging, seems as if scattering afar the fame-creepers of the Flower-weaponed King.' Her necklace of magnificent (cp. ii. 17[a]) pearls is compared to a stream which snatches and carries far and wide Cupid's fame. This again is likened — in boldest metaphor — to a vine swaying loosely over the stream; the impetuosity of the stream tears the vine from its support and carries it far away; or it spreads his fame far and wide. (In short, her ornate beauty is a "card" for Cupid.) Bhartṛhari, in his **abhimata** (Sprüche, 494), speaks of "cutting the creeper of shame."

[3] Produced by her motion through the air.

[4] 'Revealed slightly by her garments tossed by the envisaged wind, her limbs, calling upon Love, make him, as it were, to settle down beside them.'

[5] 'Her earring-pair, by its contact-plays upon her thick-besaffroned cheeks, seems (to give marks for the oscillations, i.e.) to make a mark for each oscillation of the swing, with an eagerness of counting.'

[6] 'Her eyes, like her palm [in size — cp. i. 16[3], 30[c]], on a sudden blossomed-open with curiosity, seem to deliver bluelotus-petal-arrows to the Five-arrowed God.'

[7] 'The braid-stock behind her, acting the part of Cupid's whip, (goes downward, as it were, saying, i.e.) seems to say [threateningly] as she sinks or is on the downward oscillation, "There shall in no wise be an interruption of the course of the swing."'

I take **paḍai** of the first half of the forward oscillation, when the braid stands out. Of course it may refer to the first half of the backward oscillation; and if so, we must render, 'the braid falls on her back.'

[8] 'Thus this maiden's winsome-grace-

KING. [*Dejectedly.*] Ah, Karpūra-mañjarī has dismounted! Empty is the swing; empty my heart; empty the eyes of one who fain would gaze.

JESTER. She's come it on you like a streak o' lightning,[1] eh? in a wink — seen — vanished? [3]

KING. Speak thou not thus. [Say rather,] like the mirage[2] — seen and evanishèd.[3] [*He makes as if recalling something.*] [6]

As red as madder are her close-sealed lips; like fresh-wrought gold bright is her slender form; her glance outdoes in dazzling lustrousness *or* in whiteness,[4] the new moon's slender crescent; her jet-black hair is like collyrium. Thus o'er the maid, with tremulous fawn-like eyes, there plays this beauty of colors;[5] and by them,[6] arrogant Cupid in enthralling youthful hearts, seems to have fulfilled his purpose. **41**

JESTER. Here's the Emerald Seat. Sit down on it,[7] old man, and wait for her. [2] Besides, the evening is at hand. [*They do so.*] [4]

KING. The night, though very chill, [to me] seems like the very scorching hour of a summer's midday. [5]

JESTER. Well then, with [the remembrance of her] Loveliness as his [sole] companion, let the King just wait a jiffy while I fetch the various refrigerants to cool him off. [*At that, he makes as if he were leaving the stage,*[8] *and looks before him.*] Why, but here's Vichakshaṇā coming this way [and already] quite near by. [8]

radiant swing-display-ways, — in whose heart (citta) does not the skilful picture-maker (citta-ara, Skt. citra-kara), Love, as it were, depict [them]?'

Vilāsa is 'grace,' but also 'merry play' with a connotation of coquetry. Ujjala, 'blazing out, bright.' — To pavañca I assign the meaning āḍambara given by Halāyudha. — Caria has a vague meaning for which even the word "acts" is too precise: "ways" is perhaps its best English counterpart. — The Prākrit makes a pun on citta, which is lost in Sanskrit. — Properly, ṇiuṇa is 'skilful, clever.' I take it as '(playfully) skilful,' thereby straining it a little, I fear, in the direction of vidagdha, 'sly.'

[1] 'Then it was lightning-streaked (impersonal passive of denominative) by her.'

[2] 'Like the town of Hariçchandra.' — He was expelled from heaven for pride; but, repenting during his fall, he was forgiven and was stayed in mid-air, where he and his are now sometimes seen in their aerial city.

[3] Note the striking contrast between the King's love-lorn solemnity and the Jester's facetiousness. The difference between ṇaṭṭha and pa-ṇaṭṭha seems to be intentional and I have reproduced it in my version.

[4] Dhavalima- is applicable both to the radiance of a glance and to the whiteness of the moon.

[5] For rehā, see note to iv. 20[a].

[6] 'By which (jīa, scilicet rehāe) Cupid appears as possessing an accomplished object.'

[7] I suppose that the King had risen from it in his excitement. He does not seem to have left the Arbor since ii. 29[14].

[8] We have therefore now to imagine the stage as representing simultaneously two different scenes: 1. the "Emerald Seat" with

KING. At hand is

The time appointed, as her friends have told it.[1]

[*As if recollecting; and betraying by his manner the eagerness of love.*]

Thy hands and feet are shoots of tenderest growth;
Thine eyes, meseems, are water-lilies blue;
Thy face, albeit like the [cool-rayed] moon;—
Although thy form is like a champak fresh;—
Alas, oh marvel! how they me inflame![2] 42

JESTER. [*Looking attentively.*] Ah, here's Vichakshaṇā, with various refrigerants.

[*Then enters Vichakshaṇā carrying the refrigerants.*[3]]

VICHAKSHAṆĀ. [*Stepping about.*] Oh, how my dear girl suffers from the burning fever of separation!

JESTER. [*Approaching her.*] Lady, what have you here?

VICHAKSHAṆĀ. Various refrigerants.

JESTER. Whom are they for?

VICHAKSHAṆĀ. My dear girl.

JESTER. Well then, give me half.

VICHAKSHAṆĀ. What for?

JESTER. For the King.

VICHAKSHAṆĀ. But, [I mean,] for what reason?

JESTER. And what's the reason in Karpūra-mañjarī's case?

VICHAKSHAṆĀ. Don't you know she's seen the King?

JESTER. And you—don't you know the King's seen Karpūra-mañjarī?

[*At that, they both laugh.*]

the King seated, "alone"; and 2. the meeting-place (near by, to be sure) of the Jester and Vichakshaṇā. Cp. the Analysis, p. 219.

We are to suppose that the King does not hear the Jester's remarks (ii. 41^{8} and ii. 42^{2}) nor the ensuing colloquy (ii. 42^{5} as far as ii. 43^{2}); and that, in strictness, the Jester does not hear the King's remark, ii. 41^{9}.

And yet, curiously enough, the Jester does turn this last phrase to account by quoting it, mockingly, at ii. 50^{2}, as if he had legitimately overheard it. See ii. 50^{2} and note.

[1] The King here lapses into rhythm, although the forms are Çaurasenī: see preceding note. The appointment refers, I think, to a nocturnal meeting immediately following the close of act ii. ☞ See additional note upon p. 289.

[2] "Inflame," with literal and with metaphorical meaning, as in Prākrit. One expects green shoots, water-lilies, etc., to be cooling, not inflammatory. Similarly iii. 20.

[3] 'Possessing a taken coolness-contrivance totality.' See OB., **çiçiropacāra. Sāmagrī**, 'totality of the needful requisites.'

Bāṇa gives a most interesting list of the means used to allay the heat of the body at Harsha-charita, p. 177–178.

VIÇHAKSHAṆĀ. Where is the King, then?

JESTER. At the Emerald Seat, as you[1] directed. [20]

VICHAKSHAṆĀ. Well then, stay with the King near the door of the Emerald Seat, in order that, since each has seen the other, the last farewell may now be said to all refrigerants![2]

JESTER. [*Puts his arms around her. Then, throwing away the refrigerants, he says to them:*] Be off to the land of Never-come-back! [*And addressing her:*] Why then must we stay in the neighborhood of the door? [26]

VICHAKSHAṆĀ. On account of the Queen's directions.

JESTER. Why such directions?[3]

VICHAKSHAṆĀ. The Queen has planted there[4] three young trees.

JESTER. What trees? What trees? [30]

VICHAKSHAṆĀ. An amaranth, a tilaka, and an açoka.

JESTER. Pray what is she going to do with them?

VICHAKSHAṆĀ. The Queen said to Karpūra-mañjarī:

When a maiden who is in love, embraces an amaranth, or looks at a tilaka, or touches with the tip of her foot an açoka, then they burst into bloom. So do thou satisfy for them their longings.[5] 43

And now Karpūra-mañjarī is going to do it.

JESTER. Well then, I'll fetch the old man from the Emerald Seat, station him where he'll be hidden by the tamāla shrub, and let him witness the affair with his own eyes.[6] [2] [*He makes as if doing so.*[7] *To the King.*] Ho there, up and behold the moon's crescent [beaming] over the ocean of your heart.[8] [5]

[*The King rises and looks.*]

[*Then enters exquisitely adorned, Karpūra-mañjarī.*] [7]

KARPŪRA-MAÑJARĪ. But where's Vichakshaṇā?

[1] At ii. $29^{1\,ff}$. There he seems to have remained since ii. 29^{14}. Cp. ii. 41^{2} and note.

[2] Cp. ii. 5^{d}. The ardor of the two lovers is now such that nothing will any longer avail to cool them.

[3] 'Of what nature (significance) are the directions?'

[4] In the palace garden, near the door of the Plantain Arbor (with its "Emerald Seat") and the scene of the swinging.

[5] Do thou satisfy for them their longings to bring forth flowers, by doing these several acts: cp. i. 20^{27} and see my notes thereto.

[6] 'I will make this thing to be before his eyes.'

[7] See note to ii. 41^{7}.

[8] Compare Raghuvança, xii. 36, where Sītā's laugh is likened to the moon rising from the ocean.

VICHAKSHAṆĀ. [*Coming up to her from behind.*] My dear, now do as the Queen directed. [10]

KING. But man! what's this?

JESTER. Just you keep behind the tamāla bush and you'll find out.

VICHAKSHAṆĀ. Here's the amaranth. [13]

[*Karpūra-mañjarī puts her arms around it.*]

KING. This lovely maiden, whose swelling breasts are ample as a water-jar,[1] by her impetuous, close embrace, hath made the young amaranth tree to blossom with such a profusion of flowers that a [veritable] procession of swarms of bees has [already] arrived here! **44**

JESTER. Ah see, ah see, the mighty jugglery! For

The amaranth tree, young though it is, just now close enfolded in her tender arms, all on a sudden shoots forth a multitude of flowers, — Love's arrows, as it were. **45**

KING. Yes, not one whit less is the power[2] of longing.

VICHAKSHAṆĀ. Here is the tilaka tree.

[*Karpūra-mañjarī stands a good while looking at it with sidelong glances.*]

KING. Piercing, restless, and just touched with jet-black collyrium,[3] and having ever as their ready helper the Five-arrowed God[4] who bears the [flowery] shafts, — such are her eyes; and when[5] with them upon the tilak tree the fawn-eyed girl a sudden onset[6] makes, then it stands as if thrilled with delight,[7] its crown all bristling[8] with masses of clustering blossoms. **46**

VICHAKSHAṆĀ. And here's the açoka tree.

[*Karpūra-mañjarī makes as if she were giving it a dainty kick.*]

[1] Cp. ii. 24[b].

[2] 'Precisely such is the power.' The tree's longing (and the girl's?) must have been so powerful as to produce this magic effect.

[3] 'Anointed with a small portion of collyrium.'

[4] 'Ever making *or* putting (**kṛ**) Cupid at her side.'

[5] Literally 'When (**jaṁ**) the attack of the fawn-eyed girl's eyes, piercing, etc., fell on (was precipitated on) the tilaka-tree, then (**taṁ**) it stood thrilled as it were, etc.'

[6] Hemachandra, 800, gives **dhāṭī** as one of four synonyms (see above, p. 201) for "sudden attack," "surprise," — for that which, "if it happen by night, is called **sāuptika**," so familiar as main incident and as title of book x. of the Mahā-bhārata.

[7] Properly, 'horripilated, bristling.' Hindu poets constantly make allusion to horripilation or bristling of the hair as caused by emotions of pleasure. This again (see note to i. 32) is a curious fact of racial psychology; we think of it chiefly as a sign of terror. Cp. iii. 24 and note and iv. 21.

[8] **Dantura**, 'toothed, tusked,' and so 'thickly beset,' or 'bristling,' and in evident rapport with **romañcio**.

KING.

No sooner[1] had the maid, whose face is fair
As is the radiance of the dapple moon,[2]
In graceful play, to the açoka given,
With [rosy] foot[3] whose [jewelled] anklets rang,
A [dainty] touch, — than[1] in an instant burst
Forth into blossom, e'en from every spray
In all its crown, a gorgeous show of flowers —
A sight for all the denizens of heaven! **47**

JESTER. Say, man, do you know the reason why the Queen[4] didn't satisfy the longings of the trees herself?

KING. I suppose of course *you* know? [2]

JESTER. I'll tell, if the King won't get wrathy.

KING. What occasion is there for anger? unseal your tongue and speak. [5]

JESTER. Although in this world comeliness of person does maintain the attractiveness of doting matrons,[5] nevertheless, methinks, it is in youth's tenderest prime that Lakshmī (*or* Loveliness *personified*) manifests herself as presiding deity. **48**

KING. I catch your drift;[6] and, what's more, have something to say [on that point] myself.

In spite of the fact that[7] [very] young maidens,[8] by reason of their eager curiosity,[9] are [a bit] fickle-minded, nevertheless,[7] it is with them, — their breasts just budding into view, — that the mystery of the Dolphin-bannered [God of Love] doth abide. **49**

JESTER. [Yes,] even trees blossom out with the mystery of the beauty of form; but they know not the mystery of love.[10]

1 The two ca's hint at the fact that the touching with the foot and the bursting into bloom occurred simultaneously. — Scholiast. Cp. iii. 3[d].

2 'Deer-spotted [moon], [moon] flecked like the black antelope,' — see ii. 20 note.

3 **Aṅhiṇā.**

4 'Do you know what is the reason (in this, **ettha**, Whitney, § 303 a, i.e.) for this, that (**jaṁ**) the Queen, etc.?'

5 It seems to me licit to assign this connotation to **kāmiṇī**, which I take as antithetical to both **tāruṇṇae** and **bālāu.**

6 'Understood is your intention — I see what you mean,' namely, that the Queen is a trifle passée as compared with this tender bud, Karpūra-mañjarī. The form of the Jester's statement was purposely vague.

7 'Maidens are fickle — just so (**emea**)! — but (**puṇo**) the mystery abides with etc.' For **emea**, see Weber's Hāla, no. 865.

8 Like Karpūra-mañjarī, as contrasted with the oldish Queen.

9 Which is still unrestrained by the experiences and the sophistications of life.

10 A staid matron like the Queen may continue to bear lovely children, as the trees bear lovely blossoms; but she no longer knows the keenness of youthful passion.

[*Behind the stage.*]

ONE OF THE BARDS. A pleasant evening to the King!

Behold, [the sun,] the jewel of the day,[1]
His face red-yellow, like an orange ripe,[2]
Hangs on the crest of yonder sunset-hill.
Now Ruddy Goose and mate, alas, must part:[3]
Their only friend hath left them — he whose rays
Are myriad strings dyed gorgeous, madder-red.[4]
He slackens now his fierce impetuous heat,
And with it quick the pride of jealous maids;[5]
Lulls half to sleep the eyes of all the world[6]
And drowsy lilies that bestud the pool.[7] **50**

KING. At hand is now the even-tide —

JESTER. "The time appointed, as her friends have told it."[8] [2]

KARPŪRA-MAÑJARĪ. Vichakshaṇā dear, I'll go now; it's evening.

VICHAKSHAṆĀ. So let us do.

[*Thereupon, they step about, and exeunt omnes.*]

[*End of the Second Act.*]

[1] The stanza in outline reads: 'The su. (**diṇamaṇī**), making . . . , relaxing . . . , possessing a madder . . . ray multitude, sole friend . . . , has become (**jāo**) sunset-hill-situated,' etc. I have reversed the sequence of the clauses.

[2] One is tempted to think that *a *norange : an orange* : : *a naddre* : *an adder* : : *a numpire* : *an umpire*; but it appears that the **n** of **nāranj**, **ṇāriṅga**, was lost before the word was adopted into English speech. See C. P. G. Scott, Transactions of the American Philological Association, xxiii. 278, 272.

[3] The love and constancy of the Ruddy Goose and her mate are proverbial. They are doomed to pass the night in most pitiful separation. Hence the sun is their "sole friend." See Wilson's Meghadūta, note to 82.

[4] 'Possessing a multitude of rays which have the color (or gorgeousness) of madder-dyed-strings.'

[5] 'And at the same time (**saha a**) relaxing *or* making to relent (**muñcanto**) speedily (**sarahasaṁ**) his impetuousness (**tivva-bhāvaṁ**), together with the hearts of jealous-proud-maids.' — Night and moonlight (cp. ii. 5ᵇ) put an end to their pouting (as do the breezes of spring, i. 15ᵇ), so that they yield to the gentle influences of love. The same idea at iii. 30ᵃ.

[6] 'With the eyes of people at the same time (**saha**) making the lotus-group to be possessing half-sleep.' There is here a slight laxity of expression.

[7] The day-blooming lotuses (**kamala's**) that close their eyes (**nimīlanti**) at evening, as opposed to the night-blooming lotuses (**kumuda's**), that open their eyes (**unmiṣanti**) at evening — see Kāvyādarça, i. 94, and Ṛtusaṁhāra, iii. 23.

The latter are white and close their eyes at dawn, as appears from what is perhaps the loveliest of all the stanzas of Kālidāsa, to wit, **antarhite** etc., near the beginning of act iv. of Çak. — Cp. his Urvaçī, iii. 16. — See Böhtlingk's Hemachandra, 1160–1165, p. 217. — With this stanza, cp. i. 35 and iv. 18³⁰.

[8] The Jester mockingly takes his words from the King's own mouth (see ii. 41⁹). The part that he quotes forms an indravajrā line, but in the dialect of prose. See p. 257, note 8, and ☞ p. 289.

ACT III.

[*Then enters the King with the Jester.*]

King. [*With his thoughts on her.*]

Put far away from me the champak[1] bud!
What use have I for juicy turmeric?[2]
Of what esteem is gold though ne'er so pure?
Before her loveliness, whose radiance sweet,
Is likest that of newly risen moon,
What need of bakul blooms, profuse and fresh?[3] 1

And again:

Bright as a necklace strung with emerald gems,
Or wreath of jasmines where the bees have sucked,
Her lovely glance, as quick she bent her neck,[4]
Shot sidelong by,[5] and pierced my very heart.[6] 2

Jester. Say, man, what do you stand there for, reeling off your twaddle like an uxorious husband?[7]

[1] See i. 14[2], 16[a], and notes.

[2] The rhizome of Curcuma longa, a plant of the ginger family. It is used as a condiment; as a dye-stuff, it yields lovely shades of yellow; and when chewed, affects the saliva as would saffron. See Pliny, N. H. xxi. 70, cited by BR.: Indica herba, zingiberis effigie, conmanducata croci vim reddit. — In oll-ollāi (instr. s. fem. with hal-), the stem is doubled.

[3] 'What occasion is there (with, i.e.) for heaps of blooms of bakul, though fresh?' The bakul, Mimusops Elengi, Roxburgh, p. 318, has flowers that are white and fragrant.

[4] 'With an impetuously bended neck' — as **avyayībhāva.**

[5] 'Glance, directed towards (see **viç + ni** 7) in BR.) the region of her ear.' The coquettish glance is usually sidelong and comes as it were from the outer corner of the eye (**apāñga**). In darting such a glance, the girl may bend her neck or turn her head and so look by the place where, with her head in its natural position, her ear would be. —

One might suspect here a reminiscence of Bhartṛhari, who, in his **san-mārge**, q.v., speaks of "glance arrows" (**dṛṣṭi-bāṇās**) which are **çravaṇa-patha-gatās.**

[6] The "Sidelong glance," **kaṭākṣa**, etc.— Daṇḍin, in his Poetics, ii. 327, gives, as example of **viçeṣokti**, a stanza which says: The women have no battle-cars, elephants, cavalry, nor foot-soldiers; and yet with their sidelong glance (**apāñga-dṛṣṭi**) they conquer the three worlds. — Parab, Subh., p. 434–5, has some 19 stanzas on the **kaṭākṣa**. — See Bhartṛhari's stanza, just cited, = Sprüche 6824. Further, Hāla's Saptaçataka, 505. — See also ii. 5 and my note on ii. 6[a].

[7] **Bhajjājida**, literally, 'wife-conquered,' seems to me in this connection necessarily to suggest the doting, foolish, overfond husband, rather than the hen-pecked one. For the contempt in which the latter was held, see Sprüche, 4066.

KING. My thoughts, man, are on a vision that I've seen in sleep.

JESTER. Well then, old man, tell it to me.

KING. Methinks a maid with a lily-face stood in my vision within reach of my hand, and was about to strike me quickly with a blue lotus as I lay on my pleasure-couch. And then with eager haste did I catch hold upon the loose end[1] of her garment. No sooner[2] did she, leaving it in my hand, depart, than[2] my sleep, as it seemed, suddenly vanished too. 3

JESTER. [*Aside, to himself.*] Should think it might have! [*Aloud.*] Say, man, I too saw a vision last night.[3] [4]

KING. [*Expectantly.*] Tell me then, what was the vision?

JESTER. Methinks, last night in my vision I fell asleep by the Ganges. [7]

KING. And then, and then?

JESTER. Well, then the Ganges put her graceful little foot on the head of Çiva and washed me clean away with her water. [9]

KING. And then, and then?

JESTER. Then by a cloud that was raining at the autumn season to [its *or* my] heart's content[4] I was absorbed. [11]

KING. A marvel, a marvel! — And then, and then?

JESTER. And then, when the lordly sun had entered the asterism of Chitrā,[5] the great cloud went near(?)[6] the place where the Tāmraparṇī[7]

1 'With eagerness by me hastily she was held *or* caught on the loose end.'

2 **Ca . . . a**: cp. ii. 47 note. — Root muc.

3 **Adya**. — Modern English distinguishes by "last night" and "to-night" what in Sanskrit is contextually distinguished: thus, **adya‿ asmābhir atra‿ uṣitvā, prātaḥ**, etc., 'to-night we'll stop here, and early to-morrow morning,' etc.

4 Is **jadhicchaṁ** used *ἀπὸ κοινοῦ* (**kākākṣivat**, as the Hindus say)? I see no great pertinence in it in either case.

5 At the time of Rājaçekhara, the autumnal equinoctial colure would be less than ten degrees west of Spica, and the sun would be "in Chitrā" in "autumn" (iii. 3[11]).

For the transformation of rain-drops into pearls, see Sprüche, 344, 1544, 4029. According to the stanza **saṁtaptāyasi** (Ind. Ant. xiv. 323; Sprüche, 6781; and elsewhere), the transformation takes place under Svātī: see p. 214, above. So in Manwaring's Marāṭhī proverbs, no. 1291: "If the Svāti rain fall, there will be a crop of rubies and pearls, but you will not get cotton enough for a lamp-wick." Now Chitrā and Svātī have as their principal stars respectively Spica and Arcturus, and at the time of Rājaçekhara, the approximate longitude of these two stars was respectively 188° 32′ and 188° ·55′, that is practically the same. The author's mention of Chitrā, therefore, is not fortuitous, but significant. — My thanks are due to my honored colleague, Dr. Asaph Hall, for his kind help in matters of this nature. Cp. Whitney, Oriental and Linguistic Studies, ii. 377, and his chart of the zodiac.

6 Is **anteṇa** used "prepositionally" (like **antareṇa**), here compounded with its "governed" word-stem, and in the sense of **ante**, 'near'?

7 Cp. i. 17[d] note.

empties into the ocean. I, too, as I think, am within the cloud and go with it. [15]

KING. And then, and then?

JESTER. Then the cloud started to rain there with great big drops of water; and the sea-oysters, such as they call pearl-oysters, emerged from the waters[1] and absorbed me; and I was within them and became a monster pearl.[2] [18]

KING. And then, and then?

JESTER. Then in four-and-sixty pearl-oysters [successively] I was a drop of cloud-water, surpassing the opal[3] in hue, [and then,] in due course, I attained once more to the condition of being a pearl, one of perfect roundness,[4] clear, and flashing. **4**

So I, whom you see before you,[5] fancy that my own self in the shape of a pearl,[6] was inside of those pearl-oysters. [1]

KING. And then, and then?

JESTER. Then those pearl-oysters were taken from the ocean as soon as they were mature, and they were opened. And I was among the four-and-sixty pearls. And a certain merchant bought me, giving [for me] a hundred thousand gold pieces. [5]

KING. Oh, what a wonderful vision! And then, and then?

JESTER. Then the merchant sent for the jeweller and had him bore a hole through me.[7] And that gave me a little something of a pain. [9]

KING. And then, and then?

JESTER. And with the pearls of that lot,[8] weighing ten *māshakas* apiece, a single row was strung in necklace style,[9] and it was priced at ten million gold pieces. **5**

KING. And then, and then?

1 For the form, see p. 203.

2 This time it is a pearl of ten **māṣakas** —see my note to ii. 17[a]. See note 5, p. 264.

3 The tabasheer is a variety of opal found in the joints of the bamboo.

4 'I arrived at new-pearl-ness, very round, without any flat surfaces' etc., i.e. 'I arrived anew at' etc.

5 Thus I would express the force of **so aham**.

6 'With *or* by (my) pearl-ness.' For **attāṇaaṁ**, see Pischel on H. 3. 56.

7 'Then by him, fetching the jeweller, the pearl was caused to be drilled.'

8 'With that pearl-lot (of 64 pearls), weighing 10 **māṣakas** apiece.' The expression is loose; the adjective is logically an adjunct of **muttāhala** and not of **maṇḍala**.

9 That is, so as to form a necklace rather than a bracelet or what not: cp. **hāra-laṭṭhi**, iii. 18[b]; and **maṇi-yaṣṭi, Urvaçī**, iii. 10, and Kale's note.

JESTER. Then [the merchant, whose name was] Sāgaradatta, put it in his casket and went to the capital of Vajrāyudha, the king of Pañchāla, to Kanauj; and there he sold it for the ten million. **[3]**

KING. And then, and then?

JESTER. And then,

As he, [the King of Kanauj,] considered her towering ample breasts, and also the beauty of the single string of pearls, he put it on the neck of his beloved. — Men of sense are pleased to see like meet with like. **6**

Moreover:

At midnight's hour, which was full of moonlight resplendent throughout the sky, in love's embrace the royal pair had closed their eyes for terror at the shaft[1] of the Flower-arrowed God. Then by the plumpness[2] of her exceedingly towering, full, and jar-like breasts was I sore beset — [and so] awoke! **7**

KING. [*With a faint smile, and then reflecting.*]

You knew that this vision of mine, in which I met with her whom I love as my life (*pāṇa-samā-*), was unreal; and so you thought you could dismiss it from my mind by your counter-vision.[3] **8**

JESTER. A decayed chieftain, a brahman exhausted with hunger, a naughty young wench, and a forsaken man, — these beguile themselves with the sweetmeats of wishes.[4] And I ask you, man, whose power, now, is that?[5]

KING. Love's. **[3]**

JESTER. Although your love for the Queen has grown by [long] attachment, why, pray, do you, sir, fairly spreading your eyes over all of Karpūra-mañjarī's person, gaze at her as if you were absorbing her? are the Queen's good points inferior to hers? **[5]**

KING. Speak not thus!

Suppose the knot of love is tied betwixt some man and some maid; for all that, beauty, I think, is not the [sole] cause of it.[6] But if, even in that

[1] Strictly, 'blows,' 'shots.'

[2] Konow refers me to Kirātārjunīya, iv. 8, where Mallināth glosses **niveça** by 'largeness, plumpness' [of the breasts].

[3] 'This vision, not real, — it, possessing a meeting with the life-equal-girl, thou knowest. And by [thy] counter-vision, the warding-off *or* dismissal of it [of my vision] is thy intention.'

[4] Konow compares Viddh. i. 22^1.

[5] That is, Of whose power are these wishes and longings a manifestation? For the first two of the four cases, **pemmaṁ** seems to be too specific.

[6] 'Just under those circumstances (**emea**, cp. ii. 49^a), beauty, methinks, is not the [sole] cause of it' (**tattha**): but rather, says the Scholiast, the working out of the inborn nature.

case,[1] the [girl's] loveliness is much praised,[2] that is done to put a seal on[3] the mouths of unkind-spoken people. **9**

JESTER. But what, sir, is that which they call "Love, love"?

KING. The knot of attachment which exists between a mutually united pair, and which has grown strong under the dispensation of the Dolphin-bannered God, — that the connoisseurs call "Love." **[2]**

JESTER. And of what sort is it?

KING. [Love is that] in which the feeling within the heart attains[4] to sincerity and is devoid of the blemishes of suspicious behavior and so forth;[5] in which there is an on-flowing stream of longing of each for the other; whose very essence is imparted by Cupid and enhanced by amorous play. **10**

JESTER. And how might it be recognized?

KING. They whose hearts are set, each toward the other, in utter commotion by the unforced flow of very restless glances; who speed ever, more and more, the arrows that Cupid gives them; — of such persons[6] the heart-wound becomes very easily manifest. **11**

JESTER. That which has the outward beauty of a deeply seated disturbance of heart, — that the world calls "Love with Cupid's adornment." Hard as it may be to recognize, a person does manifest it among people. That we know to be Cupid's very mighty jugglery. **12**

Moreover, if the love that is in the heart[7] [of the one] awakens [in the other a corresponding] attachment, what occasion is there in that case for the trickery of the bravery of ornaments?

KING. That's true, man!

What need of girdles, bracelets, diadems, anklets? what need of beauty?[8] and what need of the shows of ornament? [There is no need

[1] Where beauty is not the sole cause of the attachment.

[2] As an ostensible reason for the love. — Since **mah** is not necessarily = **kāṅkṣ** (see Pischel, H. 4. 192), I suppose I am justified in connecting **mahijjai** here with Vedic **mah** ('is extolled, is magnified'), and not with **manth**, Marāṭhī **mathaṇeṁ** ('is revolved, considered, taken into account').

[3] 'Then (**taṁ**, correlative to **jaṁ**, 'if') a seal is put on' etc.

[4] **Ei**, that is, **eti**.

[5] 'Of suspicion-behavior and so forth,' **viappa-ghaḍaṇā-āi-**.

[6] 'Of what persons, possessing hearts completely agitated by glances which are nature-flowing and very restless, the sendings-forth of the Cupid-given-arrows increase, — of *them*' etc.

In this version I follow NR, reading (instead of **luṇṭia**, 'robbed') **luṇṭhia**, 'agitated.' I take **peranta-luṇṭhia** as 'boundary-agitated,' 'agitated to their very limits.' — See OB. under **tar** + **vi** 5).

[7] For **maṇa** and **citta**, occurring together at iii. $12^{a,1}$ and iii. 11, there seems to be but one available English word, namely 'heart.'

[8] Neither gewgaws nor beauty signify much where the passion is mutual. **Caṅga** and its

of all that.] And so,[1] in this world, it is something else[2] which puts the flowers of happiness in the grasp of fair maidens. **13**

And again :

What need of the performance of song and dance? and what need of strong drink? what need of incense of aloes? and what need of saffron? — On all the earth in daintiness naught else can equal man's tender passion.[3] **14**

And again :

The consort of an emperor and the wife of a common man, — in the matter of love there is not even a grain of distinction between them to be found, methinks, [even] if a certain difference in outward splendor is effected by rubies and decorations and garments and saffron. **15**

And again :

Why speak of restless eyes — of face like to the moon — of towering breasts? There is some other reason here, I think, why women from our hearts[4] do ne'er withdraw. **16**

JESTER. That is so. But explain to me another thing : [Even in that] which during childhood is unattractive to the heart of a man, — even in that, with [the attainment of] adolescence, a certain beauty develops itself. **[2]**

KING. Surely there must be here in the world two Creators who are skilful in building the body and in giving it the bloom of youth: the one fashions the first girlish form ; while the second, by giving it the finishing touches,[5] brings out its loveliness.[6] **17**

And therefore :

Bejewelled bracelets and girdles and anklets, beauty of dress, strings of emerald gems, mineral rouge,[7] a necklace of pearls, — [all those things]

derivatives are used of natural beauty — cp. **ṇisagga-caṅga**, ii. 25ᵃ, and **paai-caṅgima**, ii. 26ᶜ. As to the form (instr. s. fem., from Skt. **an**-stem !), cp. **umhā** cited by Jacobi, § 42, ²⁾.

[1] I take **taṁ** as 'and so.'

[2] 'There is of fair-waisted maids something else [than gewgaws — namely, native attractiveness], by which they get the flowers of happiness.' Or, **suhaattaṇa** may be the ensemble of womanly charms that draw and hold fast her lover's heart.

[3] I am not sure that I have hit just the right meaning of **ruccissa** : nor do I see the appositeness of **puṇu**.

[4] Ablative singular or plural, H. 3. 8, 9.

[5] 'By carving it *or* sculpturing it (Scholiast, **utkīrya**), by putting on the nicer touches' as contrasted with the first or rougher "fashioning" (**ghaḍaṇā**). The Marāṭhī **kaṇḍāraṇeṁ**, cited by Dr. Konow, is an instrument used for the finer work of goldsmiths and others.

[6] 'Makes fully manifest (the form), displays it to advantage.'

[7] Properly, **gāirikā**, which is usually defined as 'ruddle, red chalk.' But Hemachandra, 1036, makes it a synonym of **dhātu**, and this is a liquid mineral which wells up

are surpassed by the youthful bloom of maidens,[1] which is the spell that fascinates the heart, and is a sixth arrow of Cupid,[2] and a charming one.

Moreover : **18**

A form full of loveliness, eyes that reach almost to the ear and have large pupils, a bosom with ample breasts, a waist that has the triple folds and may yet be grasped by the fist, wheel-like buttocks,[3] — pray what need of aught else in the time of tender youth ? Just these five things put into maidens' hands Cupid's great banner of victory.[4] **19**

[*Behind the stage* (is heard the Heroine, saying :)]

Friend Kurañgikā, I am really languishing by reason of these refrigerants, as a lotus [languishes by reason of the arrival of the torrid season that calls for the use of refrigerants].

A shoot of lotus-root [to me] seems like poison; a string of pearls seems like a poisonous serpent; the breeze from the palm-leaf fan seems to spread flames ;[5] likewise the water from the jets of the shower-bath as it comes out on my hand is hot; and not the sandal, that sovereign remedy [against heat], allays the burning of my frame.[6] **20**

JESTER. Did the old man hear? are his ears loaded with a jowl-full of the nectar ?[7] [2] will he then even today take no notice of his lotus root[8] that is languishing by reason of the intense heat? of his saffron dolly that he has to play with,[9] that is being sprinkled with most intolerably scalding water ?[10] of his single string of monster pearls that [now]

from the ground. The wounded Çalya is said to run blood as the mountain runs **gāirika**, MBh., ix. 13. 14 = 669. It is mentioned at Meghadūta, 102, as a pigment (**dhātu-rāga**); and at Kumāra-sambhava, i. 7, as a sort of liquid mineral color (**dhātu-rasa**), such as might be used to inscribe love-letters on birch bark. Cp. my note on ii. 7, above. From the same poem, i. 4, we may infer that it was used as a cosmetic, since it is there mentioned as a decoration for the nymphs of heaven. So here.

[1] The five words of lines *ab* are nominatives absolute, with anacoluthon. We must repeat them in accusative form in *d* as objects of **jaai**.

[2] He regularly has five : cp. **pañca-bāṇa**, **pañcesu**, **pañca-sara**, in Index, and p. 239, n. 2.

[3] We have had most of these most fleshly details already at i. 32 and 30 and ii. 23.

[4] 'By just these five things maids become possessing Cupid's banner.'

[5] 'The wind spreads as it were its friend.' The friend of the wind is the fire, — Hemachandra, 1099, p. 444. OB. cites **anila-sārathi** as a name for fire from MBh. i. 15. 1 = 1058.

[6] Similar thoughts at ii. 42.

[7] Nectar of the Heroine's words. — The ludicrous incongruity of the metaphors is doubtless intentional.

[8] **Muṇāliā**, properly 'little lotus-root.' Is it used in the sense of **mṛṇālinī**, 'lotus-plant,' *pars pro toto?* At any rate, it must be rendered so as to bring out the jocose allusion to the Heroine's own words at iii. 19^c. — Mṛṇālikā is used as a girl's name (with many others) in the Kādambarī, p. 356^3.

[9] 'Play + saffron-dolly,' — cp. ii. 12.

[10] 'Water intensely boiled and intolerable,' in allusion to iii. 20^c.

in a trice is parting?[1] of his meadow of rose-bay,[2] that the musk-deer are plundering?[3] [3]— Well, your vision has turned out true.[4] Come, let us go in. [5] Let Cupid's banner be exalted. Let the strains of cuckoo-warblings start up in your wind-pipe. [7] Ease up with the floods of tears. Slow down with the torrents of sighs. [9] Let loveliness renew itself. Let us go in by the back door.[5]

[*At that, they make as if they were going in.*] [12]

[*Then enters the Heroine, with Kuraṅgikā.*]

HEROINE. [*Timidly — to herself.*] Why! is this the full moon suddenly descended from the court of heaven? [15] or has the Blue-necked God [Çiva], well-pleased, allowed Cupid to resume his own bodily form?[6] or is some one who is a rascally foe of my heart and a kindly friend of my eyes about to show me special favor? [*Aloud.*] This I regard as a piece of jugglery. [19]

JESTER. [*Taking the King's hand.*] Lady, the jugglery has become real. [21]

[*The Heroine stands abashed.*]

KURAṄGIKĀ. Dear Karpūra-mañjarī, rise to meet your lord and salute him. [23]

[*The Heroine is on the point of rising.*]

KING. [*Taking her hand.*]

Thy waist is ready to break neath the burden of thy bosom: break it not, O moon-faced maiden, by rising! — Cupid have mercy on my eyes after the sight of such ampleness [of breasts]![7] 21

Moreover:

In presence of whom, not the beauty of orpiment hath any charm, nor

[1] The allusions to lotus and doll were pat enough. But the tertium comparationis of this figure and the next, Konow thinks, is merely the Heroine's anguish.

[2] The Tabernæmontana (see this in Century Dic'y) coronaria, known as Adam's apple or East Indian rose-bay. It is a very fragrant shrub, having shining dark-green leathery leaves, "with elevations above the veins" (Roxburgh, p. 249). Its Prākrit name, "knot-leaf," may refer to this.

[3] No jealous rival of the King has turned up thus far. — But see Konow's view, note 1.

[4] Only in the most general way (cp. iii. 3): he met her in the dream, and now he meets her in fact.

[5] For the full significance of this clause and the following stage-directions, as I understand them, see p. 219–220.

[6] Cupid was burned by the fire of Çiva's wrathful glance and is therefore called "Bodiless" or An-aṅga. The story is told at Rāmāyaṇa, i. 23. 10–14, Bombay; or Kumāra-sambhava, iii. 71.

[7] For their beauty is enough to blind me! — See note on ṇivesa, iii. 7[d].

burnished gold, nor champak blooms, — with golden flowers I pay homage to those eyes with which thou, O fawn-eyed girl, hast been beheld.[1] **22**

JESTER. Her ladyship, Karpūra-mañjarī, by staying in the inner room, has become moist with perspiration. So now I will fan her with the border of my robe. [*So doing.*] Oh dear! I've put out the light with the wind from my garment. [4] [*Reflecting. — To himself.*] Never mind. We'll just go to the pleasure-garden. [*Aloud.*] Say, this *is* dancing around in the dark! so let's go out now to the pleasure-grounds, just by the subterranean exit. [9]

[*All make as if they were going out.*] [10]

KING. [*Holding Karpūra-mañjarī by the hand.*]

Keeping thy hand, which is like a tender spray, within mine, assume thou, [I pray,] a little unsteadiness[2] as thou movest along; in order that the kala-haṅsas, as they go about in their play, may at last find a rival who outmatches them in comeliness.[3] **23**

[*Showing by his demeanor his delight at the touch of her hand.*]

The prickles of the young gourd-melon,[4] the filaments of the cadamba flower, which today are witnesses of the touch of thy hand, — these will remain as if fastening themselves to my limbs.[5] **24**

[*Behind the stage.*]

A BARD. May the rising moon bring pleasure to the King.

[1] To whose eyes? to his own? if so, the stanza is flat indeed!

[2] **Cañcura** seems to be an intensive adjective from **car**: cp. **cañcūryate**, and Whitney, § 1148 k (**jañjapa**, **tartura**, etc.). The purpose of the "unsteadiness" or "waddling" is, as I suppose, to enhance the similitude of the girl to the much belauded teal.

[3] 'In order that at last the kala-haṅsa-group, in its play-going, may be uncomely.'

The **kala-haṅsa** or **kādamba** seems to be a kind of white teal with gray wings (Hemachandra, 1327). Its cry is often spoken of as most agreeable (**kala** — see the examples in BR., s.v. (1a), and Hemachandra, 1409). It was tamed and held in high esteem. Bāṇa often mentions it — see Index to Ridding's Kādambarī, p. 224.

[4] Benincasa cerifera, like the pumpkin, but with a waxy coat. I do not find this in Roxburgh; but at p. 700, under Cucurbita Pepo, he says of the fruit, that it is, "when young, exceedingly hairy." Note that of our common Cucurbitaceæ (cucumber, pumpkin), the fruits are often sharp-prickly and the vines hairy.

[5] That is, the delight which I feel at the touch of thy hand causes such horripilation that the asperities of these plants seem to have transferred themselves to my limbs for good and all. Cp. note to ii. 46[d].

This conceit of Rājaçekhara recurs at iv. 21 and iv. 22; see the notes. One is tempted to query whether it is not a reminiscence of Bāṇa: cp. Harsha-charita, text p. 26^{7-8}, **utkaṇṭakita- kapola-phalakena, lagna-karṇotpala-kesara-pakṣma-çakalena iva mukha-çaçinā.** ☞ See p. 220.

While the round ball of the earth is as black by reason of the darkness as if it were in a subterranean chamber, the face of the eastern quarter of the sky has become as yellow as a young birch with the moonlight; and the moon, sending forth rays that are like in beauty to the tufts of the stamens of the wing-seed,[1] has risen, digit by digit, till at last the full disk is above the horizon.[2] **25**

And again:

Without saffron, without sandal,[3] is the embellishment of the ten bride-like regions of heaven;[4] without bracelets, without ear-rings, is the decoration of the round earth;[5] without withering, without fainting, are the flowers[6] (*or* without "Parcher," without "Bewilderer," is the weapon of the God with the Dolphin-ensign);[7] a garland of moon-beams is massed in the sky.[8] **26**

[1] **Muuunda,** Pterospermum suberifolium, Roxburgh, p. 512, a middling sized tree. The flowers are white and fragrant and very long, and show a prominent column of united stamens. — I use "tufts" advisedly for **sihā**.

[2] 'The moon has gone to full-diskedness in the one-digit-manner.'

[3] That is, All the heaven is made lovely by the new-risen moon, "the cool-rayed one": it makes the sky yellow, and that without the help of saffron; it makes the air seem cool, and that without the help of sandal. — This stanza recurs at Viddh. iii. 12.

[4] The "ten points" or "regions" are the four cardinal points, the four intermediate points (NE. etc.), the zenith and nadir.

These are likened to brides. So Bhartṛhari, in his **bhūḥ paryaṅkaḥ**, describing the ascetic, says: "His couch is the ground; the blue sky above is his roof; and the moonbeams he hath for his candle; north, east, south, and west are the maidens (**dik-kanyās**) that fan him with breezes for chowries." Rājaçekhara has the same bold metaphor two stanzas later, iii. 28[a], in **disā-sundarī** (if not also in a variant of iii. 29, "**dig-vadhū**"); and it recurs as **dik-sundarī** in Jayadeva, Gīt. vii. 1. Bāṇa speaks of the "regions," **āçās**, as maidens, Kādambarī, p. 390[6-7].

[5] I take **bhuvaṇa-maṇḍalī** as 'round of the earth,' = **mahī-maṇḍala** or **bhū-maṇḍala**. Viddh. reads **dharaṇi-** for **bhuvaṇa-**.

[6] That is, In the cool moon-light, the flowers are recovering from the intense heat, which "parched" or "withered" them (**açoṣayat**) and which "bewildered" them or "made them faint" (? **amohayat**), in the day-time.

Since the stanza is a description of the loveliness of the night at moon-rise (iii. 26[1]), of its tones of color and its reviving flowers, it must be that the prior interpretation of line c is also the one primarily intended by the poet.

[7] From Cupid's equipment are missing "Parcher" and "Bewilderer": these are the names of two of Love's arrows — see note to i. 32[d]. Both of these names are included among those of the celestial weapons, partly allegorical, partly fanciful, which are rehearsed in the Rāmāyaṇa, cantos 27 and 56 of book i.; see especially i. 27. 14, 15 and i. 56. 7, 8, ed. Bombay. — Love's arrows, his bow, and his missiles are all formed of flowers: **puṣpāṇy asya‿iṣu-cāpa‿astrāṇi**, Hemachandra, 228.

I cannot help feeling that this alternative interpretation, although secondary in the intention of the poet, is the key to the whole wretched difficulty of this line. The chance for a pun has seduced the author into using **mohana** of flowers — a use which I cannot deem unforced. — BR., under **çuṣ**, cite **na mlāyanti na çuṣyanti kusumāni**.

[8] The area of denotation of **āvalī** and **ālī** is not coincident with that of any English word. See Hemachandra, 1423, for their

Jester. Well, Kāñchana-chaṇḍa has described the loveliness of moonrise; so now it's Māṇikya-chaṇḍa's [1] turn.

[*Behind the stage.*]

The Second Bard. The pleasure-pavilions show circling wreaths of incense rising from burning aloes; they are ablaze with the lighted lamps; [2] they have pendent festoons of lustrous (*or* rarest) pearls; [3] they swarm with doves let loose; in them are prepared charming pleasure-couches, and hundreds of confidantes are talking; while on the divans appear the pouting women-folk.[4] **27**

And again:

The moon-beams seem as if overspreading profusely with camphor the faces of those beauties, the quarters of the sky; [5] they scatter soft moonlight which rejoices the heart of the people of the earth as does sandal; they make the withered bulb of Love to sprout anew with amorous doings; and are like to jets sent forth from an autumn cloud. **28**

Jester.

White swan of heaven's pool,[6]
Of Çiva's crest, the jew'l,[7]
A bulb [8] of love
'S the moon above! **29**

synonyms, among which is **mālā**. 'Row,' 'string,' and 'streak' are among the more serviceable English versions of the words.

We find **āvalī** used of a 'string' of pearls; and of a 'wreath' of tresses; but also of a 'set' of teeth; and, humorously, even of a parrot's two wings, a 'set' of wings, iv. 2[10]. Like its synonym **rāji**, it is used with **dhūma** of a 'column' of smoke. **Mālā** is used of bees, ii. 13; of curly locks, ii. 20. — ☞ See Konow's version, p. 289.

[1] This designation is nearly tantamount to Ratna-chaṇḍa, the name he bore at i. 16[2].

[2] 'Ablaze with given *or* brought-in lamps.'

[3] See additional note, p. 289.

[4] 'The pavilions are possessing-divan-surface-appearing-jealous-women-folk.' **Uc-chaṅga**, 'on the surface,' = 'on,' with attenuated meaning, as in the case of **tala** = 'on' and **antara** = 'in.'

[5] 'The moon-beams (**eṇaṅka-pāā**) are giving as it were an overspreading (see **chur** in OB.) with floods of camphor to the faces of the sky-quarter beauties.' They flood things in every quarter with a pale whiteness like that of camphor-gum. — For **dik-sundarī**, see iii. 26[a] note.

[6] Similarly the sun is so called, e.g. Daça-kumāra-charita, p. 1[16].

[7] For the moon as Çiva's crest-jewel cp. i. 3. — The pronunciation of jewel so as to rime with pool is an inelegance which accords, as I think, with the tone of this brief doggerel as intended by the author.

[8] **Kanda**, 'bulb': more specifically, an 'onion.' One can hardly doubt that the Jester takes this particular word out of the Bard's mouth in order to make fun of it. — In the Bard's stanza, it would have been a little less prosaic if we had said "withered root;" but it is hardly competent to the translator to let the Jester's allusion disappear. Cp. p. 262, note 8.

Concerning the rimes in this and the following two stanzas, see p. 205. — For metre of 29 and 30, see p. 207

KURAÑGIKĀ. Proud of his ally, the moon,[1] crushing the pride of jealous maids,[2] with bow of fresh champak blossoms, Cupid is victor, the impetuous. **30**

[*To Karpūra-mañjarī.*] My dear girl, I'm going to recite to the King the verses which you made describing the moon.

[*Karpūra-mañjarī stands abashed. Kurañgikā recites.*]

On the moon's yellowish disk, which seems to have stolen its charming hue from some ivory cage,[3] appears in all its beauty,[4] manifest,[5] the antelope with which the disk is marked,[6] bearing a likeness to a playful koïl. **31**

KING. Oh, what an intuition for quite new conceits[7] has Karpūra-mañjarī! what charm in expression and pleasing words! and what flow of sentiment! [*Addressing the Heroine.*]

It must be that the moon, for fear lest thy [lovely] face be mistaken for its own, hath made — behold! — upon its own round disk a black collyrium-mark, disguised as its "Fleck."[8] **32**

And again:

If, O tender-limbed one, thy face were colored palish with chalk-water, [and if,] besides, black collyrium for the cheeks were put [on it], — then it might mock at the moon (*or*, then its likeness to the moon would be complete).[9] **33**

1 'Possessing pride made by the moon.' The moon is Love's most potent coadjutor — cp. notes to ii. 5[b] and 50[b], and especially Kādambarī, p. 559[12].

2 Gharaṭṭa, is a 'hand-mill' such as the women turn in India — see the excellent kaṭākṣa-verse, re re gharaṭṭa, Parab's Subh. p. 434, 105, for which Peterson, Subhāshitāvalī, 2388, has re re yantraka. Vāsudeva says "crusher," peṣaṇa-kartā.

3 Vilāsa is 'outside looks' and also 'beauty' — such as old ivory might have. Cp. Kādambarī, p. 390[11].

4 Thus I render bhāi.

5 And thus phurantao.

6 'The fleck-antelope': cp. ii. 20, note.

7 Vatthu, 'the substance' (as distinguished from the form, utti) is in this case little more than a 'conceit,' that is 'ingenious thought *or* fancy.'

8 'Surely by the moon, thinking to itself (tti) [with a touch of jealousy], "Not in any wise shall there be an error (vibbhama) [occasioned] by the face of thee," a black-collyrium-distinguisher (visesaa) has been made on its own disk-round, with "Fleck" disguise.' — For the well-known antelope-spot, see note to ii. 20. — The position of tuha after the tti is exceptional.

9 Either, 1. 'Then it would attain to derision of the moon (genitive), would get a chance to mock at the moon' on account of its superior beauty.

Or else, 2. 'Then the moon (nominative) would get a mocking, i.e. would incur contempt.'

Or else, 3. 'Then it would attain to the assumption-of-the-appearance of the moon.'

Cp. Bhartṛhari's vaktraṁ candra-viḍambi, pañkaja-parīhāsa-kṣame locane. Here the parallelism of parīhāsa, and Böhtlingk's interpretation of his conjectural -viḍambi

[*To the moon.*]

O antelope-flecked one, why wanderest thou, nonchalant, so near this beauty? Lo, here is the face that gave to thee the exceeding paleness of its own white cheeks! 34

[*Tremendous racket behind the stage. All listen.*] [1]

KING. But what is this uproar?

KARPŪRA-MAÑJARĪ. [*With some trepidation.*] My dear girl, [go and] find out what it is and come back to me. [5]

[*Kurañgikā goes out and reënters.*]

JESTER. Just this: the Queen has found out that my old man has tricked her,[2] and is coming.

KURAÑGIKĀ. Well, it's hunchbacks and dwarfs[3] and pigmies and eunuchs and harem-keepers that are making the hullabaloo. [8]

KARPŪRA-MAÑJARĪ. Then let the King excuse me, so that I, before the Queen finds out about my meeting with the King, may go to my prison by the same subterranean passage by which I came.[4]

[*Thereupon, exeunt omnes.*]

[*End of the Third Act.*]

(see BR. s.v., and Sprüche, 5896), support the first of the above versions.

The second version amounts to about the same thing as the first, and is supported by Sprüche, 453.

Mahābala Krishṇa Çāstrin, in his edition of the Çṛñgāra-çataka, 22 (Nirṇaya Sāgara Press, 1888), supports B's conjecture, but renders it by candra-anukāri etc., as in the third version.

Since the chalk-water and collyrium only enhance the beauty of her face and its likeness to the moon, I am unable to translate the vi of jai vi.

1 We may suppose that the actors now fall into two groups, King and Jester forming the one, Heroine and her friend forming the other. And the two sets of questions and answers that follow in dovetail, may be thought of as proceeding each independently of the other.

2 'Has resorted to trickery' (vañcanā-gadam), or 'has come here by a trick' (vañcanā-āgadam).

3 Griffiths, i., p. 10 b, speaks of dwarfs as favorite subjects of painting and sculpture. "Then, as now in India, they served to amuse persons of rank." Plates 29, 55, 85. — Concerning the inmates of the seraglio, see Sāhitya-darpaṇa, § 81.

4 'May go to my prison, entering by this same subterranean opening.'

ACT IV.

[*Then enters the King with the Jester.*]

KING. Alas!

The summer's heat is very intense;[1] mighty is love; **how pray is it to** be borne? Yet that fawn-eyed girl, albeit in one and the same palace with me, is hard to reach, as fate will have it. **1**

For,

In this world, by those who are under the power of the Flower-arrowed God alone, both these things indeed are very hard to bear, I think: the time that is made terrible by the intense sun, and separation from the beloved.[2]

2

JESTER. Some folks are harassed by Cupid, and others are wilted by the heat; but a chap of my stripe is neither harassed by Love nor wilted by the heat.

[*Behind the stage.*]

A PARROT. Well, won't Polly tear out your top-knot by the roots —*I* guess! **[4]**

KING. [*Laughing.*] Man, was the pet parrot talking which was roaming about at will in the pleasure-grove?

JESTER. [*Angrily.*] Ah, you wretch of a bird, you'll be cat's meat next. **[8]**

[(The parrot again) *behind the stage.*]

There's nothing I mightn't expect from the like of you[3] — if I hadn't a set of wings.[4] **[10]**

KING. Why! I believe it has flown. [*To the Jester.*]

The nights are of short duration and the days are waxing long. The round of the moon is broken[5] and the disk of the sun is unbroken. Why

[1] **Gāḍhaar'**, i.e. **gāḍhatara-**.

[2] The thought of this stanza is repeated in different language at Bālar. v. 25 and Viddh. iv. 6, as Dr. Konow points out. p. 206.

[3] 'Every thing (any thing) is deemed possible from the like of you.' This speech, iv. 2[10], seems also to come from the parrot. For the ablative, see p. 203. — Cp. Viddh. p. 29[4].

[4] "Set" seems to be used humorously; see note to iii. 26[d].

[5] 'The moon attains diminution' — so that it yields less coolness, as I suppose.

should not an arrangement whose course appears to be this in summer days, — why should it not be broken, then, with knife-points?[1] **3**

Moreover,[2] it is altogether to be praised[3] if it bring me a meeting with my beloved. For

At midday, the touch of sandal-paste; until twilight, moistened garments;[4] play in the bathing-pools until night-fall; in the evening, cool liquor;[5] and love's embraces in the last watch of a summer night;[6] these are the five arrows with which Cupid wins his victories: his other shafts are split and broken. **4**

JESTER. Say not so. [Say rather:]

A blessing on the summer days, O friend, because[7] in them the betel[8] leaves are overlaid with a palish shimmer, and the areca nuts are delightful with the flavor of mango oil, and the sandal is made [still more] fragrant with powdered camphor. **5**

KING. [Yes.] And this too is pleasant about them:[9]

Flutes, tremulous as if with koïl notes,[10] are cooling to the ears; liquor with cold water is cooling to the mouth; a sweetheart with massive breasts anointed with sandal is cooling to the touch: for any one there is for the summer days an antidote that is altogether cooling. **6**

And again:

In the graceful chaplet, an acacia bloom; near the breast, a necklace of sinduvāra berries; on the limbs, a moistened garment;[11] attached to the waist, a girdle with blue lotuses; on the two plantain-like arms,[12] bracelets of fresh lotus-roots: such is the apparel for [enamored] women that is

[1] **Khaṇḍa** is 'broken, incomplete,' or (of the moon) 'not full, gibbous'; **a-khaṇḍa** is 'not incomplete,' 'complete' in form and perhaps also in power; **khaṇḍijjai** is 'be broken, cut, brought to nought.' The "knife-points" are congruous enough with "cut," hardly so with "arrangement."

[2] An adversative conjunction (**kiṁ tu**?) would be much more appropriate here.

[3] 'It [the arrangement] is altogether (**ṇiuṇaṁ**) to be praised' (**çlāgh**).

[4] **Oll-aṅsuaṁ**: cp. iv. 7[b].

[5] Cp. my note to i. 22 and the lampoon there quoted.

[6] Cp. Rāvaṇa-vaha, ed. Goldschmidt, xii. 13. — **Jaṁ kiṁ pi** = 'some, a little,' with **ṇihuvaṇaṁ**.

[7] The three long bahu-vrīhis are "adjectives that contain reasons" — **hetu-garbha-viçeṣaṇāni.**

[8] *Piper betle*, a perennial creeper, Roxburgh, p. 53, 569. "The leaves are used as a wrapper for the little pellets of areca nut and lime which are extensively chewed in the East." The pellets are carried in boxes (cp. iv. 9[10]) commonly made of silver filigree. See Century Dic'y, under *betel* and *betel box*. — Areca palm, Griffiths, fig. 60.

[9] 'About them' (ettha), i.e. the summer days.

[10] 'Having koïl-notes and wavy.' The "waviness" or tremolo effect that may be given to the music of the flute may be supposed to suggest liquidity and so coolness.

[11] Cp. iv. 4[a].

[12] Cp. my note to ii. 14[b].

likely to be prescribed[1] by the physician [who treats the disease] of love,[2] as the sole charm against the pains of the heat when the spring season melts into summer.[3] **7**

JESTER. And I say, moreover :

Of women who at midday are anointed with smooth, thick, sandal-paste, who bathe the whole evening through,[4] who in the nights are besprinkled with drops of water that come from the punkahs, — of such, the Five-arrowed God accomplishes the enslavement. **8**

KING. [*Making as if he were recollecting something.*]

For those, to whom is given complete union with a person lovely with the combination of garb and fresh beauty,[5] — for them the nights and days, though long, go by like a twinkling ; and to whose sore-pained heart these [days][6] bring not even to a small degree the delights of love, — for them the days give birth to [vain] wishes only and drag by as if they were each a month long. **9**

[*Addressing the Jester.*] Is there any news about *her?*

JESTER. Yes, there is. Listen, old man ! Here's a joke for you. [5] The subterranean passage that was made to Karpūra-mañjarī's prison, was discovered by the Queen. Then, with a pile of huge stones, she closed up the entrance to the passage so that no one could slip through.[7] [7]

Five chowry-holders, girls with names ending in *senā*, Anañga-senā, Kāma-senā, Kaliñga-senā, Vasanta-senā, and Vibhrama-senā, with noisily brandished swords and shields in their hands, were appointed to keep guard over her prison on the east side. [8]

Five ladies in waiting, with names ending in *lekhā*, Anañga-lekhā, Chandana-lekhā, Chitra-lekhā, Mṛgāñka-lekhā, and Vibhrama-lekhā, with bows in their hands and arrows on the string, were set [to keep guard] on the south side. [9]

[1] 'To be offered *or* brought into service' — root **nī + upa**.

[2] Or, 'by the Cupid-physician,' 'by Dr. Cupid.' But perhaps this would be too jocose for the King in his present mood. "He's got it bad."

[3] 'At the going of the season of **Madhu**,' i.e. of the season of spring or **vasanta**. This consisted of the months March-April and April-May, whose older names were **Madhu** and **Mādhava** (see p. 214, or Whitney, JAOS. vi. 414, and cp. note to ii. 6^{21}). **Vasanta** is followed by **grīsma**. 'summer,' but the text does not show here how far the summer has progressed. — This costume, at all events, is light.

[4] 'Possessing practised interval-less bathings in the evening.'

[5] I take **ghaḍaṇā** as 'combination' — see OB. And to **bhañgi** I assign the meaning 'Art und Weise sich zu kleiden' (= 'garb'.) given it by OB., s.v., with a citation for it in that sense from our poet.

[6] Or, 'These burning days,' **saṁtāviṇo**.

[7] 'The entrance was closed by the Queen making (**kṛ**) it hole-less.' · See p. 220.

Betel-box bearers,[1] girls with names ending in *mālā*, Kunda-mālā, Kāñchana-mālā, Bakula-mālā, Mañgala-mālā, and Māṇikya-mālā, carrying lances in their hands, were stationed [to keep guard] on the west side. [10]

Bath-keepers, girls with names ending in *kelī*, Anañga-kelī, Barkara-kelī,[2] Sundara-kelī, Rāja-kelī, and Kandarpa-kelī, holding shields and swords, took their places[3] on the north side. [11]

And over [all] those, five reciters of witty sayings, girls with names ending in *vatī*, Mandāravatī, Tarañgavatī, Kallolavatī, Madirāvatī, and Kelivatī, were appointed as overseers, each with a bright golden staff in her hand. [12]

KING. Well, well! that's the entire personnel of the Queen's apartments!

JESTER. Here's the Queen's friend, Sārañgikā, sent with some message from her. [14] [*Then enters Sārañgikā.*] [15]

SĀRAÑGIKĀ. Victory, victory to my lord! The Queen's message is that today the King must mount to the terrace of his pleasure-palace and inspect the preparations and accessories[4] for the great festival of the Deity of the Banyan.[5] [18]

KING. As the Queen directs!

[*Exit the attendant.*] [20]

[*King and Jester step about, making as if they were ascending to the terrace. Then begins the charcharī.*[6]] [22]

JESTER. Behold, these maidens,[7] richly adorned with pearls,[8] at the close of the dance but scantily attired, are sprinkling each other with

[1] The royal betel-box, umbrella, etc., were often borne by regularly appointed officers. See for example, in BR., the compounds of tāmbūla; and cp. note to iv. 5[a].

[2] See Zachariae, Mañkhakoça, Nachträge.

[3] I suppose āḍhatta (= ārabdha, H. 2. 138) means 'fassten Fuss.'

[4] Uvaaraṇa seems to imply all this.

[5] The deity supposed to reside therein during the vaṭa-sāvitrī-vrata. The time of this observance is given as the full moon of Jyāiṣṭha by the Vratārka. I have a lithographed edition of the Vratārka, Benares, 1931 (A.D. 1875); and its treatment of the matter begins on folio 121, reverse, line 11. — Or see Nirṇaya-sindhu, II., folio 11 a. 3 — Or see Hemādri, Chaturvarga-chintāmaṇi, Vratakhaṇḍa, xxi., p. 273[4]. — My pupil, Mr. Albert Henry Allen of San Francisco, has prepared a well-digested account of this observance which will, I trust, be published in vol. xxi. of the Journal of the American Oriental Society, pages 53–66.

[6] The carcarī is a peculiar dance (cp. Vikramorvaçī, act iv.), accompanied by various poses as mentioned in the next verse. — Root viç + pra, in the sense of 'makes its début, begins, *geht los*'?

[7] Whom they see as they look down from the palace roof.

[8] 'Possessing pearly-ornament-accumulations.'

water which they take with jewelled cups from the jets of the shower-
bath. 10
And here [1]
Circling around with charmingly-varied pose of hands and feet,[2] these
two and thirty dancing-girls, — they tread their mazy rounds, their steps
keeping time with the music.[3] In thy court is seen the "Staff-dance."[4] 11
With their shoulders and heads even,[5] with their arms and hands even,
other maidens, each with clean-cut pose,[6] and ranged in two rows each
facing the other, are rendering the *challi*-dance [7] and regulating its tempo
by the beaten measure.[8] 12
Still others, quitting the jewelled cups, throw [direct] from the
showering-machine the jets of water.[9] These — fair as Cupid's arrows,
though consisting only of water [10] — fall on the person of friends [stand-
ing by]. 13
Here, coquettish girls, their bodies anointed with blackest collyrium,[11]

[1] **The Saṁgīta-Ratnākara, Ānanda-āçrama edition, in its nartana-chapter** (vii.), **explains** many of the technical terms that **here** follow. I am unable to go into the matter in detail, but give a few references to the **book**, whose title I cite as SR.

[2] I take **bandha** as pose in the nautch.

[3] 'Possessing steps (**pada**) that have followed the beats' (**tāla**), that is, 'the time *or* measure,' which was marked by clapping of hands, and perhaps also (as in iv. 17[a]) by the rhythm of the song.

[4] The **rāsa** is a rustic dance like that of Krishṇa with the herdswomen. See Vishṇupurāṇa, v. 13. 23, or Hall's Wilson, vol. iv., p. 324 f. — From SR. I cite **daṇḍa-pakṣa**, vii. 642; **daṇḍa-recita**, vii. 651; **daṇḍa-pāda**, vii. 711, 965, 1015, 1186.

What the "staff-dance" is I know not. Perhaps a dance in which the dancers were arranged in "columns" (cp. iv. 12, and **daṇḍa** as used at ii. 9[a])? — I recently witnessed, as part of a light entertainment, a "cane-dance," in which a negro performer held a staff, and struck the floor rhythmically with it, in time with his feet. — Has it aught to do with the "staff-dancer" of the Çatapatha-brāhmaṇa? see Eggeling, Sacred Books of the East, 44. 417.

[5] **Sama** seems to be a technical term for 'in a natural position.' **Svabhāvena sthito bhūmāu samaḥ pādo 'bhidhīyate**, SR. vii. 316. Konow cites **Nāṭya-çāstra**, x. 13.

[6] OB. defines **rekhā** as 'correct pose of all the limbs in dancing.' "Pose-clear," "with clean-cut poses," may be an **avyayībhāva**, or else an adjective with **callim**.

[7] SR., vii. 1215, enumerates ten rustic dances. The first is **cāli**: it is "not too fast nor too slow" (in the **madhya-laya**); and is characterized by the "simultaneity" (**yāugapadya**) of the movement of the feet, thighs, waist, and arms. The same dance, performed quickly and with the dancers facing each other, is called **cālivaḍa**.

[8] 'The calli, possessing a connection of **tāla** and tempo': that is, 'whose tempo is regulated by the **tāla**' (see above). The layas or tempi are fast, middling, and slow.

[9] 'Others throw jet-water by means of the **jantas**.' They don't use the cups, just mentioned at iv. 10; but perhaps they put their fingers partly over the orifices of the **jantas** so as to make the water squirt directly on their playmates. See **muc**.

[10] 'These (**tāo** — sc. **dhārāo**, 'jets'), having a beauty [as] of water-arrows of Cupid.' Konow cites Viddh. iii. 25[b].

[11] 'Possessing lampblack-collyrium-black-bodies.'

holding triple[1] bows, and adorned with tail-feathers of peacocks, are parading about as savage mountaineers,[2] [and so] making sport for the people. **14**

Yet others, bearing in their hands offerings of human flesh, and terrible with their groans and shrieks and cries, and wearing the masks of night-wandering ogresses, are enacting a cemetery-scene. **15**

And one fawn-eyed girl, sounding the drum that makes you shudder,[3] and with the pleasant noise of a tambour, with her creeper-like arms alternately[4] swaying, has started to execute the performance of the *challi.* **16**

Others are performing, as might a fay, a graceful dance in tempo,[5] with a jingling made by their bells, with the measure regulated by the tempo of vocal music,[6] and with the clear tinkle of anklets. **17**

Still others, their garments a-flutter by reason of their eagerness, intently playing the flutes, and setting the people a-laughing by their dark dress, recede, bow, and laugh. **18**

[*Enters Sārañgikā.*]

SĀRAÑGIKĀ. [*Looking before her.*] Here is the King, who has come from the Emerald Seat[7] into the Plantain Arbor. — Well, I'll go to him and announce the Queen's message. [4] [*Approaches.*] Victory, victory to my lord! The Queen's message is: "This evening I will bring it about that you shall lead a new bride around[8] the nuptial fire." [7]

JESTER. But Lady! what means this shower of watermelons[9] from a clear sky?

KING. Sārañgikā, explain it all in full. [9]

SĀRAÑGIKĀ. You shall hear. On the fourteenth day,[10] just past, the

1 "Triple": made in three pieces?

2 Πουλῖνδαι ἀγριοφάγοι, Ptolemy, vii. 1. 64.

3 SR. treats **huḍukkā** at vi. 1072. Molesworth defines it as a small drum, shaped like an hourglass. It is held in the hand and rattled. — Is not this the drum formed of the tops of two human skulls cut in bowl-shape and with skin stretched across the bowls, and set crown to crown? Clappers are fastened to it by thongs a few inches long, so that if you grasp the constricted part and twist the wrist, the clappers thump the membranes. — See root **vad**.

4 Contradicts **yāugapadya**, p. 280, note 7.

5 'Perform tempo-dance-grace.'

6 For **jantia**, see under **yantra-**. — Cp. note to iv. 11^{b}.

7 See page 254, note 1.

8 See root **nī-pari**.

9 Properly, 'white gourds,' the Benincasa cerifera of iii. 24 — see note. Cp. p. 205 end.

10 Of the bright fortnight of **Jyāiṣṭha**; see p. 216. Cp. Kādambarī, p. 128^{6}, where the Queen goes to pay homage to Çiva "on the fourteenth day" of the month. Gāurī is Çiva's consort.

Queen had Bhāiravānanda make an image of Gāurī bejewelled with rubies and set it up. [11] And he, the master Magician, was consulted by the Queen, after she had begun the observances for its consecration, with regard to the matter of a reward for [him, as] her preceptor. And he replied: "If you absolutely must give a reward, then I suggest the following."[1] To which the Queen said, "As your Reverence directs." [16] And he continued and said: "There, in the Lāṭa country,[2] is a King named Chaṇḍasena. He has a daughter named Ghanasāra-mañjarī.[3] She has been pointed out by the astrologers as destined to become the consort of an Emperor. [20] So the King must marry her, in order not only that the preceptor may not fail of his reward, but also that your husband may become an Emperor." [22] Then the Queen laughed and said, "As your Reverence directs." And I was sent to make the announcement. And the reward to the preceptor has been given. [25]

JESTER. [*Laughing.*] Here's an instance of that old saw, "Snake on your head — and the doctor away" (*or* in some other country).[4] The wedding is [set for] today and here, while Ghanasāra-mañjarī is in the country of Lāṭa. [28]

KING. Have you never seen Bhāiravānanda show his magic power?[5]

SĀRAÑGIKĀ. [Continuing her message.] The Queen has had a sanctuary to Chāmuṇḍā[6] built at the foot of the banyan that stands in the middle of the pleasure-garden. [30] And Bhāiravānanda is going to meet the Queen there. And in the hall of state which is there situated and has just been put in readiness for it, the wedding is to take place. [*So saying, she steps about and exit.*] [33]

KING. Man, I have a notion that this is all a blooming job of Bhāiravānanda. [34]

JESTER. That's a fact. Nobody but the moon — you'd better believe — can make the moonstone statue to ooze[7] or the [night-blooming] çephālikā to blossom profusely.[8] [36]

[1] 'Then let this [reward] be given.'

[2] For Lāṭa, see p. 214.

[3] See iv. 20^{16} and note.

[4] The proverb is discussed elaborately and interestingly by Pischel, Festgruss an Roth, p. 115. Cp. Böhtlingk, Berichte der sächsischen Gesellschaft, 1894, xlvi. 7.

[5] For if you (the Jester) have, you know he can bring the bride here in a trice.

[6] Çiva's consort, in a terrible form.

[7] The moonstone is a fabulous gem, supposed to ooze or deliquesce under the moon's rays: cp., for example, Kādambarī, p. 395^{8}.

The "Thirty-two tales of the throne" are related by 32 heavenly nymphs who have been transformed into statues (puttalikās) of moonstone: see Indische Studien, xv. 442, 294.

[8] None but the Magician could bring all

[*Enters the Magician.*] **[37]**

BHĀIRAVĀNANDA. Here is the Chāmuṇḍā idol serving to screen the [new] entrance which has been opened from the root of this banyan to the subterranean passage.[1] [*He stretches out his hand to it in worship,*] [saying to Chāmuṇḍā, or rather, saying of her:]

A dissolution of the universe[2] is her pleasure-house; the blood of the demons is her fiery draught; victorious is Kālī[3] as she quaffs it, in presence of Kāla,[4] from a goblet made of the skull of Parameshṭhin.[5] **19**

[*Enters* (the sanctuary) *and sits down.*] Not even yet is Karpūra-mañjarī [to be seen] coming out by the exit from the subterranean passage!

[*Karpūra-mañjarī, in pantomime, makes an opening in the mouth of the passage, and enters.*]

KARPŪRA-MAÑJARĪ. Reverend Sir, I salute thee. **[4]**

BHĀIRAVĀNANDA. Mayst thou get a suitable husband. Sit down right here.

[*Karpūra-mañjarī sits down.*] **[7]**

BHĀIRAVĀNANDA. [*To himself.*] Not even yet does the Queen seem to be coming![6]

[*Enters the Queen.*] **[10]**

QUEEN. [*Stepping about, and looking in front of her.*] Here is the exalted Chāmuṇḍā. [*Pays homage to it. Then looking about, she says:*] Karpūra-mañjarī *here!*[7] Well, what *does* this mean? [*To Bhāiravānanda.*] I have this to tell you: I have made ready, before coming to you, all things needful for the wedding; but they are in my own apartments of the palace. So I will get them and return to you. **[18]**

BHĀIRAVĀNANDA. Do so, my darling.

[*The Queen takes a few steps about the stage,* (as if she were) *departing.*[8]] **[20]**

---

this about, just as the moon is the only one able to make the çephālikā bloom. Konow cites Viddh., p. 63[4], 65[1]. Cp. ii. 50, note 7.

The stage-directions ought here to add, **iti niṣkrāntāu**, 'Exeunt' [King and Jester]. Cp. p. 221.

[1] 'Here at the banyan-tree-root is the Chāmuṇḍā-idol, a cover of the [newly] opened-out entrance to the subterranean passage.'

[2] That is, the scene of the dissolution etc.; the expression is a little loose.— For a classification and description of the various dissolutions of the universe, see Vishṇu-purāṇa, book vi., chapters 3, 4, 5.

[3] Or Chāmuṇḍā, Çiva's consort, in a terrible form.

[4] Death or Time, the Death-god or All-destroyer.

[5] 'From a goblet made of the skull of Brahmán,' whom Çiva slew for his pride on the occasion of an "incidental" dissolution of the universe (**kalpa-kṣaye**) as narrated in Kathā-sarit-sāgara, ii. 13.

[6] 'Not even yet does the Queen come.'

[7] See p. 286, note 4.

[8] The Queen does not actually leave the stage. The stage continues to represent the shrine of Chāmuṇḍā; but the audience is re-

BHĀIRAVĀNANDA. [*To himself, laughing.*] She's gone to search Karpūra-mañjarī's apartment! [*Aloud.*] Karpūra-mañjarī, my daughter, by way of the subterranean passage, not otherwise, and at a quick pace, do you go to your own apartment and stay there. — When the Queen comes back, you're to come back. **[25]**

[*Karpūra-mañjarī does so.*]

QUEEN. Here is the prison-room. **[27]** [*Enters and looks around. — To herself.*] Well, I *am* surprised![1] Karpūra-mañjarī *here!* It's somebody that looks very much like her! [*Aloud.*] Karpūra-mañjarī, my darling, how are you feeling? [*Pretends to listen and repeats the imaginary reply.*][2] What's that you say, that you've just got a headache? [*To herself.*] Well then, I'll go back there [to my own apartments]. [*Enters*[3] *and looks to one side and another.*] Hallo, friends, be quick and take the things for the wedding and return [with me]. **[39]** [*With these words, she steps about.*[4]]

[*Karpūra-mañjarī enters and sits just as before.*[5]] **[41]**

QUEEN. [*Looking before her.*] Karpūra-mañjarī *here!*[6]

BHĀIRAVĀNANDA. Vibhrama-lekhā, my darling, the things for the wedding have been brought? **[44]**

QUEEN. Certainly. But some ornaments which would be suitable for Ghanasāra-mañjarī have been forgotten. So I'll go back.

BHĀIRAVĀNANDA. Very well. **[48]**

[*The Queen acts a little pantomime as if she were making an exit.*] **[49]**

quired to imagine that it represents also at the same time, for a few minutes, as the action requires, first the shrine and the prison, and then the shrine and the Queen's apartments; and that it does so for two occasions, the first being for the action of iv. 19^{27-39}, and the second being for the action of iv. 19^{52-57}. See the Synoptic Analysis, p. 221-2.

[1] This phrase renders ae.

[2] Literally, 'in the air.' This is a "dramatic phrase" (nāṭya-ukti) used to designate an imaginary reply which the actor is supposed to hear and to repeat for the benefit of the audience. The device is familiar to English readers from Douglas Jerrold's "Curtain Lectures." There the unhappy Mr. Caudle's replies are regularly "in the air." See Sāhitya-darpaṇa, no. 425, or Monier Williams, Çak., p. 96.

[3] That is, the audience has to imagine that she enters her own palace-apartments.

[4] In order to indicate to the spectators that she is returning with her attendants from her private apartments to the shrine of Chāmuṇḍā.

[5] That is, while the Queen is delaying to get the things, the Heroine hastens back by the secret passage, arrives before the Queen, and so is discovered seated in the sanctuary, just as she was when the Queen (supposedly) left her at iv. 19^{20}.

[6] In the sanctuary, to which the Queen is now supposed to have returned.

BHĀIRAVĀNANDA. Karpūra-mañjarī, my daughter, do just as you did before.[1] [50]

[*Exit Karpūra-mañjarī.*] [51]

QUEEN. [*Pretending in pantomime to enter the prison-room, and seeing Karpūra-mañjarī.*] Well, well, I *am* nonplussed[2] by the resemblance! [*To herself.*] It's the magic car of the master Magician, which moves about through the air or through walls,[3] that brought her here! [55] [*Aloud.*][4] Friends, take each of you what I told you to take and come along back with me. [57] [*She enacts a little pantomime as if she had* (come back and) *entered the sanctuary of Chāmuṇḍā and espied her* (Karpūra-mañjarī).] Oh, what a resemblanee! [59]

BHĀIRAVĀNANDA. Sit down, O Queen. The King also has just arrived. [60]

[*Then enters the King, with the Jester, and Kurañgikā.*]

BHĀIRAVĀNANDA. Place, place for the King! [62]

[*All sit down in due order.*]

KING. She is, in embodied form, a paragon of the Dolphin-bannered God; she is a transformed bow-staff of the wild mountaineer "Passion"; she is the light of the full moon, abroad by day.[5] [64]

And again:

She is the casket for the rubies of a host of excellences; a jewelled doll. Likewise, as she wanders about, she is the flowery beauty of spring. [66]

Moreover:

If[6] the beauty[7] of this maiden's form, which is the ensign of her conquest of the world, comes — in whatever way[8] — within range of a man's eyes, then there takes up his abode in that man's bewildered[9] heart the

1 Namely, as at iv. 19^{24-41}.

2 Molesworth gives this very meaning for the Marāṭhī naḍaṇeṁ, Prākrit ṇaḍ.

3 'Without hindrance *or* obstruction' — from gravity, walls, or the like. Cp. note to i. 34^{27}.

4 Between iv. 19^{53} and iv. 19^{56} the Queen is supposed to go from the prison-room to her own apartments.

5 See additional note, p. 289.

6 'To the range of whose eyes beauty goes, in the heart of that [man] Cupid dwells.'

7 I would assign to **rehā** here and at ii. 41^{c} the meaning 'beauty.' The verb **reh** means 'is lovely, rājate,' in Hāla, no. 308; cp. H. 4. 100. — Molesworth defines Marāṭhī **rekhalā** (from **rekhaṇeṁ**, from Skt. **rekhā**, 'line') as 'neat, comely, pretty.' — But it may be that two words of quite diverse origin have flowed together in the Prākrit **rehā**. See additional note, p. 289.

8 **Jaha taha**, as a phrase.

9 I take **vicitte** as = Skt. **vi-citte**, 'besinnungslos,' not **vicitre**. Cp. note to ii. 40^{b}.

Dolphin-bannered God, his bow-staff bent almost double with the arrows on the string.[1] 20

JESTER. [*Aside, to the King.*[2]] You *have* made the old saw come true, "Can't trust a boat even when it's touched the shore."[3] Now just cork up! [4]

QUEEN. [*To Kurañgikā.*] Kurañgikā, do you arrange the wedding costume for the King; and let Sārañgikā arrange it for Ghanasāra-mañjarī.[4] [6]

[*Thereupon both busy themselves in pantomime about the wedding of the two.*] [7]

BHĀIRAVĀNANDA. We must summon a preceptor.[5]

QUEEN. Here stands the crest-jewel of all learned Brahmans, my husband's Preceptor, the worthy Kapiñjala. So let him start the sacred fire. [10]

JESTER. Here I am and ready! Say, man, now I'll tie a knot in your upper garment.[6] With your hand take the hand of — Karpūra-mañjarī! [13]

[*The Queen utters an exclamation of surprise and looks on with a touch of despondency.*]

BHĀIRAVĀNANDA. [Well, O King], you *have* lost your head![7] for Ghanasāra-mañjarī is only another name for Karpūra-mañjarī.[8] [16]

KING. [*Taking her hand.*]

The prickles that are on the lovely fruits of the gourd-melon,[9] and on

[1] Valaia, 'bent almost into a circle' — cp. ii. 6^d. — For puñkhia, see ii. 3^d note.

[2] For the "dramatic phrase," see Sāhitya-darpaṇa, no. 425.

[3] Here you are, in plain sight of the goal of your wishes, like a boat that has crossed the water and reached the farther shore. And yet you persist in this sentimental gush (iv. 19^{64}–iv. 20). I can't trust you. — Root çvas, passive, impersonal, with locative.

[4] The Queen, on entering, iv. 19^{10}, expects to find the "Ghanasāra-mañjarī," whom (at iv. 18^7) she had promised as a new consort for the King. Instead, she finds the Heroine, iv. 19^{14}. Hurrying to the prison, she finds (iv. 19^{29}) there also the Heroine. Or is it the Heroine's double, so like her (iv. 19^{30}) as to deceive the Queen's eyes? She will rather trust her ears, and so elicits a reply from the prisoner (iv. 19^{34}) and recognizes by her voice that she is certainly the Heroine. On her return to the sanctuary, she finds (iv. 19^{43}, for the third time) again the Heroine. Her second visit to the prison (and fourth finding of the Heroine) suggests the suspicion, iv. 19^{55}, of supernatural means of communication between the two places. And yet, on her second return, iv. 19^{69}, it may be, after all, a resemblance! — Her perplexities are still unsolved when she bids Sārañgikā, at iv. 20^6, to array the bride; they reach their climax at iv. 20^7; and give place to unpleasant certainty upon the utterance of the Jester's last word at iv. 20^{13}.

[5] To conduct the nuptial ceremony.

[6] The symbolical wedding-knot, p. 289.

[7] 'You are forgetting yourself extremely.' Cp. Molesworth, s.v. bhulaṇeṁ, 'become infatuated, lose one's understanding (by drinking, through riches, honors, love, etc.).' Even the King is still in the dark about the identity of the new bride!

[8] See p. 251, n. 5: ghaṇasāra = karpūra.

[9] The whole stanza is simply a variation

the rows of leaf-petals that contain the ketaka-bloom,[1] — the touch of thee, fair maid, assuredly hath transferred these to my limbs as a thick-set mass of bristling down.[2] **21**

JESTER. Come, man, let the circumambulations[3] be performed and the parched grain be thrown into the fire.

[*The King acts as if he were doing all this. The Heroine stands abashed. The King, having brought the wedding ceremony to an end, in happy mood,*[4] *saluting all in fitting manner, takes his seat as an Emperor.*] [4]

[*Behind the stage.*]

A BARD. May the wedding feast bring delight to the King!

The lovely gourd-melon,[5] the fresh young bread-fruit,[6] the coral trees,[7] the stalks of the lotus-blossoms,[8] the bloom of the ketaka besides, — I fancy that thy person must have taken to itself by force the qualities [of these plants, because] over all thy limbs appear such horripilations, like unto prickles that one could see and touch.[9] **22**

of a theme which we have heard — see iii. 24 and the notes, and iv. 22[a]. For the gourd-melon in particular, see note to iii. 24[a]. — As to horripilation, see note to ii. 46[d].

[1] Concerning odor etc. of the ketaka or screw-pine, see note to ii. 6[21]. The leaves, says Roxburgh, p. 707, are closely imbricated in three spiral rows, very smooth and glossy, margins and back armed with very fine spines. . . . The female flowers have no other calyx than the termination of the three rows of leaves. The text is in good accord with this fact. — Kālidāsa speaks of "ketakī-needles," Ṛtu-saṁhāra, ii. 23.

[2] 'As a thick-set horripilation-shoot-range.' — It may be that **aṅkura** is to be taken as 'hair' rather than as 'shoot,' although both amount to the same thing here. As for **ālī**, I despair of finding a fit English word for it; see my note to iii. 26[d]. Perhaps the word *range*, considering its scope, is as good as any.

[3] The groom leads the bride thrice sunwise around the nuptial fire. See my Sanskrit Reader, p. 400.

[4] Molesworth gives 'joy, delight, gratification' for **utsāha**: cp. BR. v. 1168.

[5] Already mentioned twice: iii. 24[a] (see note) and iv. 21[a].

[6] The Artocarpus integrifolia or jack-fruit: see Roxburgh, p. 633. For pictures, see Century Dic'y, s.v. bread-fruit; or H. W. Cave's Picturesque Ceylon, volume "Colombo," p. 52, and plate xxx, a beautiful one. In Ceylon, Cave has counted as many as 80 fruits on one tree, some weighing 40–50 pounds each. They are pale green with *granulated* surfaces. Other species of Artocarpus, the hirsuta and the echinata, have, as their names imply, very spinous fruits.

[7] The Erythrina indica: see Roxburgh (p. 541), who mentions other spinous species. The bark of its younger branches is armed with small black sharp prickles. The tree or shrub is used for hedges and is largely employed to support the black pepper vine. See Century Dic'y, under Erythrina.

[8] The **kamala** is the blossom of the Nelumbium speciosum. "Flowers large, and beautiful beyond description," says Roxburgh, p. 450. There are two varieties, one with rose-colored flowers, and one with perfectly white flowers. **Daṇḍa** here evidently means the peduncles. These "are armed with small inoffensive prickles." Cp. Sprüche, 2988, 6432, 2250. — Beautiful pictures of lotuses, Griffiths, figs. 61–63.

[9] 'I suspect in thy body [this] collection

BHĀIRAVĀNANDA. Is there anything else that you would wish done?

KING. Is there anything I could wish better even than this? For

The Queen, although she now has a rival in my affections,[1] is not angry; I have obtained a maiden who has a face like the full moon's orb and who awakens my passion to new life; and I have attained to the rank of Emperor![2] What else could one ask for? By thy favor I have gained all that men think worth the having.[3] 23

Yet for this would I pray:

[*Words of Bharata.*[4]]

May the forest-fire of Poverty, which day after day gleams far and wide, which brings to naught all the excellences of men of learning,[5] be quenched by the rain of the sidelong glances of Fortune! 24

[*Thereupon, exeunt omnes.*]

[*End of the Fourth Act.*]

of qualities [to have been] attained by force; such horripilations, under the semblance of evident and touched prickles, are coming out, continually appearing.' —

Phuḍa, 'open, manifest, clear to the senses, palpable.' I take it as coördinate with puṭṭha. — Mellanti, 'are let loose, shoot out,' equivalent to mucyante. — Perhaps ṇiccullasā is 'uninterruptedly arising.'

The whole verse repeats the substance of iii. 24 and iv. 21 — see the notes.

[1] 'The Queen, in the position of rival wife, is not angry.'

[2] 'The rank of Emperor has come to pass.'

[3] 'All that which is obtained among mankind.'

[4] The author of the famous Nāṭya-çāstra: see Lévi, Théâtre, p. 297 etc. Cp. the close of the Çakuntalā, of the Mālavikā (2d ed. Pandit, p. 162[12]), of the Urvaçī (ed. Kale, 1898, p. 146[9]), and of the Ratnāvalī (ed. Cappeller, p. 329[5]).

[5] Sanskrit books make frequent allusion to the poverty of men of learning. Fortuna has no fondness for them — Sprüche, 2570. See also 6432, 2081. The enmity (vāira, virodha) between the Goddess of Fortune (Çrī) and the Goddess of Learning (Sarasvatī) is proverbial: Sprüche, 4086, 3941.

Additional Notes.

ii. 6^{23}. — **Swing** festival of Gāurī: see **Hemādri** (1260 A.D.), ed. Bibl. Ind., ii. 2, p. 453, quoting Devī-purāṇa, **āndole dolayet** (**Devīm**); Nirṇaya-sindhu, Benares, 1875, ii., folio 2a, 6 (ibidem, 5a, 1, swinging of Lakshmī); Vratārka, Benares, 1875, folio 15a, 11; Dharma-sindhu, Bombay, 1888, p. 31 end (the festival lasts to the end of the month, **māsa-paryanta**). For **āndolana-vidhi**, Hemādri, l.c., p. 745 f.

ii. 41^9, 50^2. — The "appointment" here mentioned would seem to have been arranged by Vichakshaṇā with the Jester during or before the scene between King and Porteress, ii. 0^1. The interval is "long" to the King, ii. 6^2: cp. ii. 6^{15}. To this arrangement, perhaps, the **saccaṁ edaṁ** of ii. 6^4 refers. At ii. 41^2 the Jester gives the King to understand, if only in the vaguest way, that he is to meet the Heroine. I think the clandestine meeting which results from this appointment must take place in the night of the evening with which act ii. closes, since the meeting was then "at hand." It cannot be the meeting of act iii., which is some 40 days later. And the açoka scene involves no "meeting." — In this clandestine meeting, finally, we may see the occasion of the culmination of the Queen's jealousy and of her imprisoning the Heroine.

iii. 26. — Dr. Konow writes me that he now renders this stanza as follows: Als ein Schmuck für die Weltgegendfrauen, ohne (d.h. verschieden von) Safran und ohne Sandel, als eine Zierde für den Erdenrund, ohne Arm- und Ohren-ringe, als eine Waffe des Liebesgottes, die von Sosana und Mohana verschieden ist (die nicht versiegt und nicht bethört), werden die Mondstrahlen angehäuft. — That is, he takes the three nouns substantive at the end of a, b, c. as in apposition with **-āvali**.

iii. 27. — "Some reference should be made to the profusion of jewelled ornaments of goldsmiths' work everywhere displayed. Strings of pearls and precious stones are hung on houses, doorways, and canopy-pillars, and worn by men and women. Hindu poetry constantly speaks of them as festive decorations of towns and houses, till it is not surprising that conventionalized jewelry should come to be a regular element of painted and carved architectural ornament (plates 6, 10, and 13)." — Griffiths, i., p. 16 a.

iv. $19^{64, 66}$. — Konow writes me that these two passages seem to have been originally metrical [such was my own opinion], but that he has not been able to restore the verses.

iv. 20. — Since my note on **rehā** was written, I find that Dr. Konow has altered the electroplate of p. 158 and set up two articles **rehā**. — He doubts my interpretation of **vicitte**.

iv. 20^{12}. — A symbolical tying together of the ends of the sari-like garments of bride and groom is doubtless here intended. Dr. Konow refers me to Winternitz, das altindische Hochzeits-rituell, Vienna, 1892, where similar customs are cited: see pages 60, 64, 49. The like still obtain in Southern India: see J. F. Kearns, Marriage Ceremonies, etc., Madras, 1868, p. 40, 57. Cp. also G. A. Grierson, Bihar Peasant Life, § 1331, 1337.